Manufacturing
and Machine
Tool Operations

MANUFACTURING AND MACHINE TOOL OPERATIONS

Second Edition

Herman W. Pollack

Chairman, Physical Sciences Division
Orange County Community College

PRENTICE-HALL, INC., ENGLEWOOD CLIFFS, NEW JERSEY 07632

Library of Congress Cataloging in Publication Data

POLLACK, HERMAN W.
    Manufacturing and machine tool operations.

    Includes index.
    1. Metal-work. 2. Machine-tools. I. Title.
TS205.P57 1979   671   78-8250
ISBN 0-13-555771-2

10   9   8   7   6   5   4   3   2   1

Printed in the United States of America

PRENTICE-HALL INTERNATIONAL, INC., *London*
PRENTICE-HALL OF AUSTRALIA PTY. LIMITED, *Sydney*
PRENTICE-HALL OF CANADA, LTD., *Toronto*
PRENTICE-HALL OF INDIA PRIVATE LIMITED, *New Delhi*
PRENTICE-HALL OF JAPAN, INC., *Tokyo*
PRENTICE-HALL OF SOUTHEAST ASIA PTE. LTD., *Singapore*
WHITEHALL BOOKS LIMITED, *Wellington, New Zealand*

To my uncle, Dr. JOSEPH COHNE

Contents

8　Dies: Bending and Drawing　182

9　Measuring Instruments　204

10　Cutting Tools　228

11　The Shaper and the Planer　260

12　The Drill Press　288

Preface to the Second Edition

The revision of this text resulted from a radical change in the concepts of machining that developed since the publication of the first edition in 1968. During the interim period, numerical control and computer numerical control emerged as the major development in the machining industry. The shift in emphasis to tape and computer controlled machine tools changes the entire approach and philosophy to machining processes. The changes that have taken place over the past five years are staggering. These changes are continuing at the same pace!

The fact remains that the fundamental principles of fabricating materials become more important than ever before. A thorough knowledge of cutting tool materials, clearances, rakes, cutting speeds and feeds, and so on, are essential to successful NC and CNC machining.

Programming has emerged as a major requirement for the designer. The approach to tolerances, jig and fixture design has changed radically. In the near future the machine tool companies will standardize the language of these machines, and once again the designer will need to update his knowledge.

With the above in mind, the author has rearranged the material in the first edition, updated other information, deleted obsolete materials, and expanded NC.

Once again, I wish to acknowledge those people who have had a constructive effect upon this, the revised edition: people such as William C. Hammen, John P. Corbin, and Russell F. Jerd. To my wife, Ruth, who in spite of everything, continues to give the impression that the many hours that I spend in isolation in my study is tolerable. If it has had a negative effect on her, I have not noticed it. In addition, Mrs. Regina Westeris, my secretary, has expended her usual effort in the preparation of this revision. Finally, I wish to thank Mike Melody (Prentice Hall) for his effort and faith, and Arthur Lizza, Jr. (Prentice Hall) for his dedication to excellence.

Herman W. Pollack

Preface to the First Edition

This book is intended as a text to be used by students in technical institutes, junior colleges and similar institutions which offer a course in manufacturing processes or machine tool operations. Almost the entire first half of this text is largely descriptive in nature and may be used by high school graduates who have completed one year of algebra. The second half of the text is more heavily mathematical. It correlates theory with practice supported with many mathematical examples.

It is intended that this text be used in a freshman course in manufacturing processes of a two-year curriculum. A concurrent college level mathematics course is recommended. The value of using this text in the freshman year is that the materials included are intended to give the student a strong background for such second year courses as Machine Design, Kinematics, Mechanisms, Tool and Fixture Design, etc.

If used in the second year in a course in Manufacturing Processes, the text material is presented so that whole blocks of chapters may be dovetailed with other second year courses.

The general purpose machine tools are discussed in some detail in an attempt to present the fundamental principles inherent in all machine tool operations. It is hoped that many of the mechanisms which make up a machine tool will be studied since they are fundamental to the design of mechanisms and machines used in automated processes. Thus the theory of gears applies to the machining of gear teeth, as well as to their use in gear trains in automated machinery. It is important that the student understand the limitations and capabilities of machine tools. New designs must be capable of being built. It is not enough to merely design mechanisms.

Many of the latest machining processes are included in this text. In many instances enough material is presented to whet the student's appetite. It should be obvious that almost every topic in this text may be expanded into a full text in its own right. The author uses the technique of requiring each student to select a topic for further library study and to expand and report on this topic to the class. However, the processes are included in this text in sufficient depth to make them meaningful.

The author owes much to his family for their patience throughout the preparation of the manuscript. Special recognition and thanks are extended to Professor Charles Toole for his review and criticism. The author also wishes to thank Irving J. Levinson (Dean of Instruction, Oakland Community College) and Stanley Brodsky (Chairman, Physical Sciences Division, N.Y.C. Community College) for their review of the final draft of the manuscript. I also wish to thank and give credit to my former secretary, Miss Gertrude Ruby, for her beyond-the-call-of-duty efforts during the early preparation of the manuscript and to my present secretary, Mrs. Regina Westeris, who continued the effort so effectively. Finally the author wishes to thank Mr. Anthony Caruso (Prentice-Hall) for an excellent job in the preparation of this text and to Mr. Matthew I. Fox (Prentice-Hall) for his guidance throughout the entire project.

Herman W. Pollack

The Manufacture of Iron and Steel

1

1.1. Production of Iron and Steel

The production of iron and steel starts with the mining of iron ore and the processing of those substances and chemicals used in their manufacture. The flow chart, Fig. 1.1, is a pictorial representation of the processing of the iron ore into iron and steel. It is to be noted that the end product of the blast furnace, if followed through the purification processes, eventually becomes steel; or the end product may find its way into one of the casting processes.

Essentially the mined iron is in the form of oxygen compounds. Coke is the fuel in the blast furnace. When this mixture is burned at high temperature, the oxygen is removed from the compounds and is replaced by carbon from the coke, and cast iron is formed. Secondary processes remove the carbon to form steel.

1.2. The Blast Furnace

Dating back to about the 14th century, the blast furnace, Fig. 1.2, is a large steel shell about 30 ft in diameter set on top of a brick foundation. The steel shell is lined with heat-resistant brick. The lining is replaced when it wears out.

The blast furnace has four major regions: the top, the stack, the bosh, and the hearth.

The *hearth* is a storage region for the molten metal and the molten slag. Since the specific gravity of molten slag is less than the specific gravity of molten metal, the slag will float on top of the metal. When it is time to remove the slag, the *slag door* is opened and the molten slag runs off into slag cars.

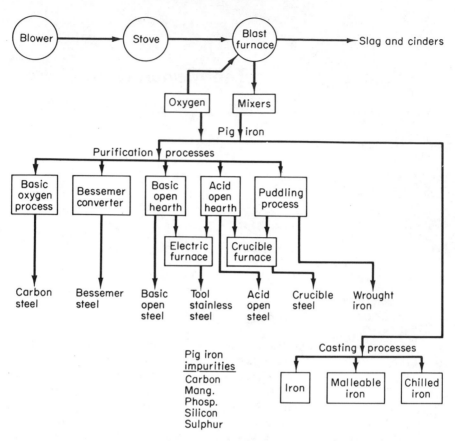

Figure 1.1 Flow chart. (Blast furnace charge: iron ore; coke; limestone; scrap.)

The slag cars carry the slag away for disposal. The *tap hole* at the lower part of the hearth is then opened and the metal allowed to run off into large *ladles*. The ladles transport the molten metal to large storage tanks, called *mixers*, or to the *molds* where the metal is poured and allowed to solidify into *pigs*.

Above the hearth are the combustion zone and the fusion zone. These two zones comprise a region called the *bosh*. The bosh is the region where melting takes place. The temperature is about 3000°F as a result of combustion, aided by a continuous hot-air blast, which furnishes the oxygen necessary to support combustion. The air enters the furnace from bustle pipes (at about 30 psi) through twenty openings in the side of the furnace. These openings are called tuyeres (see Fig. 1.2). During this process the iron picks up carbon from the coke and silicon from the slag.

On top of the bosh zone is the *stack*. This region is made up of the heat absorption zone and the reduction zone. The temperatures range from about 2200°F at the bottom of the heat absorption zone to 400°F at the top of the reduction zone. The temperatures are continuous, and there are no distinct

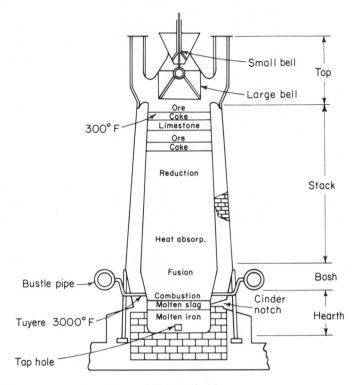

Figure 1.2 The blast furnace.

dividing lines between the various zones. The function of the heat absorption zone is to preheat the charge so that the melting process will be continuous once the charge reaches the fusion zone. The reduction zone also preheats the charge, but its main function is to burn out oxygen. The *top* of the blast furnace houses two inverted cone-shaped bells. These bells ensure an even distribution of the charge. The gaseous products of combustion are carried off through four ducts spaced around the top of the furnace.

The *charge*, made up of successive layers of *iron ore*, *scrap steel*, *coke*, and *limestone*, is dumped into the top of the furnace. As the coke burns, aided by the air forced into the furnace, the ore melts and collects in the hearth. As the melting process proceeds, the entire mass settles and thus makes room for the addition of charges at the top. While the melting takes place, the limestone forms a slag with the impurities.

1.3. The Charge

The *charge* in the blast furnace is made up of four materials: *iron ore*, *scrap steel*, *coke*, and *limestone*.

Iron ore exists as an aggregate of iron-bearing minerals. These aggregates are oxides of iron called *hematite, limonite,* and *magnetite.* Hematite contains about 70% iron, 60% limonite and 72% magnetite. It takes approximately 1.6 tons of iron ore, 0.65 ton of coke, 0.2 ton of limestone, 0.05 ton of scrap iron and steel, and about 4 tons of air to produce one ton of pig iron.

The impurities in the *ore* are determined by analysis. These impurities may be silicon, sulfur, phosphorus, manganese, calcium, titanium, aluminum and magnesium. After analysis the ore is graded and mixed to achieve the desired balance. The amounts of silicon, phosphorus, and sulfur present will determine the purification process to be used when steel is manufactured.

Coke, the second component of the charge, is made from coal. The coke supplies the heat that reduces the ore and melts the iron. The iron picks up carbon from the coke and impurities from the ore. The amount of carbon picked up by the iron is more than is needed in the production of steel. Nevertheless, the carbon becomes part of the pig iron used in the making of steel. The control of this carbon during the subsequent processes determines the properties of the steel.

The manufacture of coke from bituminous coal is a distillation process. The impurities are driven off, leaving coke. Coke must be dust proof, not overly combustible, and strong, since it must support the charge. There are two methods for making coke: the *beehive process* and the *recuperative process.*

The *beehive* oven is started after it is loaded with coal. The gases are ignited and burned until the fuel assumes a semifused state. A spray of water over the hot mass causes contraction, which breaks the fused mass into irregular pieces.

The *recuperative* process heats the coal until the gases are released. These gases are piped away, the ingredients extracted, and the gas piped back into the oven for heating purposes. The process is completed when the coal fuses and develops a large crack. The mass is pushed into cars, taken to the quenching house, sprayed, sifted, and stored.

The third ingredient in the charge is limestone (calcium carbonate). It takes about 800 lb of limestone to produce 1 ton of pig iron. Since most of the impurities in the charge will not melt at the operating temperature of a blast furnace, it becomes necessary to fuse them with a material which can be removed. This material is limestone. It combines with the impurities to form slag which can easily be removed.

The fourth component of the charge is scrap steel. Two types of scrap steel are used: scrap produced in the steel mills is called *home scrap*; steel purchased from the outside is called *purchased scrap*. All scrap is graded according to the furnace in which it is to be used. The blast furnace uses about 8% scrap in its charges. The purpose of the addition of scrap iron is to control the grade of cast iron produced.

The end product of the blast furnace is pig iron. The pig iron may be stored in large tanks in the molten state; or it may be poured into molds, allowed to solidify into pigs, and then stored. Pig iron is about 90% iron and contains the following impurities: about 4% carbon, 1.25% silicon, 1 to 2.5% manganese, 0.04% sulfur, 0.06 to 3% phosphorus.

The secondary refining processes produce steel. It is only after further refining of the pig iron has taken place that impurities may be added in desired amounts to produce steels which will possess the characteristics needed for a wide range of applications.

There have been attempts, which have not yet gone beyond the pilot plant stage, to replace the blast furnace with direct reduction processes. These processes attempt to reduce iron ore to sponge iron, which is then processed directly into steel. This eliminates the need for melting the ore before steel production begins.

There are, in general, three types of direct reduction processes: (1) the kiln process; (2) the retort, or batch process; (3) the fluidized bed process.

The *kiln process* utilizes a long, rotating circular kiln lined with refractory brick. The charge of high-grade ore pellets moves through the cylindrical kiln as a result of a 2° slope and the rotation of the kiln. It is fired with natural gas. The material drops through chutes into a rotating cooling kiln which cools the iron to about 150°F. The charge is then ready for subsequent processing.

The *retort process* uses parallel retorts which contain fixed beds of high-grade ore. The fuel, processed natural gas, passes into the retorts and reduces the iron ore to the desired purity.

The *fluidized bed process* uses the partial combustion of air and natural gas (one process uses hydrogen) to reduce the iron ore. The material is pressed into briquettes for further processing.

1.4. The Cupola

The *cupola*, Fig. 1.3, is essentially a smaller version of the blast furnace. Its purpose is to melt the pig iron so that it may be poured into controlled cavity shapes. It provides molten iron for the casting processes shown on the right side of the flow chart in Fig. 1.1. The end product may be cast iron, chilled iron, or malleable iron.

The bottom of the cupola is formed by two semicircular hinged doors. A prop supports both doors and a sand bottom. This sand bottom is made so that it slopes toward an opening in front of the cupola. The opening is called the *breast-hole*. After igniting the bed charge (coke), the breast is made up by mixing one part fire clay with two parts of fire sand. An opening of approximately 2.5 in. is left as a taphole. This is plugged with a cone-shaped mixture of fire clay and molding sand called a *bott*. The bott is inserted to permit molten iron to collect. Once the iron is collected, the bott is knocked out, and the molten metal flows out the taphole, down the spout and into the ladle.

Encircling the lower part of the cupola are the *tuyeres*. These are openings in the side of the furnace through which air passes into the combustion zone. Each tuyere has a sight window in it so that the condition of the molten iron

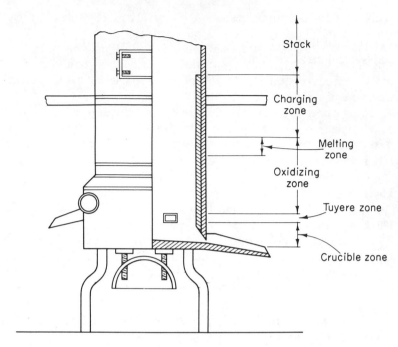

Figure 1.3   The cupola.

may be watched. At the back of the cupola and below the tuyeres is the *slag hole*. The slag hole is also plugged with a bott.

A bed charge of coke is placed in the bottom of the cupola. The larger pieces of coke are placed at the bottom of the bed charge, after which the bed charge is completed to a depth of approximately 60 in. above the tuyeres. This bed charge is ignited with a torch through the breast-hole.

Charges of iron and coke are placed on top of the bed charge. Cupolas have different melting ratios. A 10 : 1-ratio cupola dictates a charge of 700 lb of iron to 70 lb of coke. The cupola should be filled to the charging door with successive charges of iron and coke.

After an hour and a half has passed, the blast is turned on and the air from the tuyeres causes the temperature within the cupola to melt the iron so that after about 10 minutes iron appears at the taphole. The bott is inserted, and the molten iron is allowed to collect for about five minutes. The bott is knocked out, and the molten metal is permitted to run into a ladle. A new bott is inserted, and the process is repeated.

1.5.   Charge Calculations

If a cupola is examined after a heat, it will be noted that a groove exists in the lining. This groove locates the high-temperature zone. The bed charge should reach this zone.

EXAMPLE 1

It is assumed that a groove exists 60 in. above the sand bottom in a 36-in. diameter cupola. Calculate the weight of the bed charge. Coke weighs 30 lb/ft^3.

Solution:

The weight of the bed charge

$$w_b = \frac{\pi d^2}{4}(h_b)(W) = \frac{\pi(3)^2}{4}(5)(30)$$

$$= 1060 \text{ lb}$$

$W = 30 \text{ lb/ft}^3$
$d = \text{dia cupola}$
$\quad = 36 \text{ in.} = 3 \text{ ft}$
$h_b = \text{ht bed charge}$
$\quad = 60 \text{ in.} = 5 \text{ ft}$
$w_b = ?$

EXAMPLE 2

Assume that not more than 8 in. of coke is burned at a time in Example 1 and that this layer of coke is covered by a layer of iron that weighs 10 times as much as the coke. Calculate: (1) The weight of the regular charge of coke; (2) the weight of the iron in this charge.

Solution:

1. The regular charge of coke

$$w_c = \frac{\pi d^2}{4}(h_c)(W) = \frac{\pi(3)^2}{4}\left(\frac{8}{12}\right)(30)$$

$$= 141.3 \text{ lb}$$

$W = 30 \text{ lb/ft}^3$
$d = 3 \text{ ft}$
$h_c = \dfrac{8}{12} \text{ ft}$
$w_c = ?$

2. The weight of the iron charge is

$$w_i = w_c \times 10 = 141.3 \times 10$$

$$= 1413 \text{ lb}$$

$\text{ratio} = 10:1$

1.6. The Melting Rate

The melting rate of a cupola is generally 10 lb of iron per hour per sq in. of cross-sectional area. Cupolas may have melting rates of $10:1$, $8:1$, etc.

EXAMPLE 3

Assume the melting ratio of $10:1$ and a melting rate of 4 lb per hr per sq in. (1) How much iron is melted in an hour in the cupola in Example 2? (2) How many charges are needed to produce iron for one 8-hour day?

Solution:

1. The iron melted per hour, assuming no losses

$$I_h = \frac{\pi d^2}{4}(M_r) = \frac{\pi(36)^2}{4}(4)$$

$$= 4070 \text{ lb/hr}$$

$d = 36 \text{ in.}$
$M_r = 4 \text{ lb/hr/in.}^2$
$I_h = ?$
$\text{ratio} = 10:1$

2. The charges needed for an 8-hour run

$$N = \frac{8(I_h)}{w_i} = \frac{8(4070)}{1413}$$

N = number of charges
w_i = 1413 lb

$$= 23 \text{ charges}$$

1.7. The Volume of Air

In order to determine the quantity of air needed to melt the charge, it is necessary to calculate volume of air needed to burn a pound of carbon.

To burn 1 lb of carbon requires 2.67 lb of oxygen. Since air contains 23% oxygen by weight, the weight of air required to produce the 2.67 lb of oxygen is

$$\frac{2.67}{0.23} = 11.6 \text{ lb of air}$$

If air weighs 0.08 lb/ft^3, the volume of air required for every pound of carbon is

$$\frac{11.6}{0.08} = 145 \text{ ft}^3 \text{ of air}$$

EXAMPLE 4

Using the ratio 10 : 1 calculate: (1) the air needed for complete combustion; (2) the air needed to melt 1000 lb of iron at this ratio; (3) the coke needed to melt 1000 lb of iron at ratios of 8 : 1 and 6 : 1, (4) the air needed to melt 1000 lb of iron at ratios of 8 : 1 and 6 : 1.

Solution:

1. At 10 : 1, 70 lb of coke melts

$$70 \times 10 = 700 \text{ lb of iron}$$

The volume of air needed is

$$70 \times 145 = 10,150 \text{ ft}^3$$

But coke is 88% carbon, therefore, the volume of air needed to burn 70 lb of coke and melt 700 lb of iron is

$$10,150 \times 0.88 = 8932 \text{ ft}^3 \text{ (use 9000 ft}^3\text{)}$$

Note: Only the carbon burns.

2. The air needed is

$$\frac{1000}{700} \times 9000 = 12,857 \text{ ft}^3$$

3. The coke needed to melt 1000 lb of iron at 10 : 1

$$\frac{1000}{10} = 100 \text{ lb of coke}$$

at 8 : 1

$$\frac{1000}{8} = 125 \text{ lb of coke}$$

at 6 : 1

$$\frac{1000}{6} = 167 \text{ lb of coke}$$

4. The air needed to melt 1000 lb of iron at 8 : 1

$$\frac{12,857 \times 125}{100} = 16,071 \text{ ft}^3$$

at 6 : 1

$$\frac{12,857 \times 167}{100} = 21,471 \text{ ft}^3$$

1.8. The Manufacture of Steel

The purification processes shown in Fig. 1.1 produce as an end product one of the classes of steel by controlling the lining of the furnace and either removing or adding ingredients. Acid-lined furnaces have linings of silica, sand, and brick. Chemically, silica is acid. Basic linings are made from magnesite.

The union of iron and carbon produces plain steel. In order to achieve special characteristics in steel, other elements are added. The special characteristics desired may be deep hardening, strength, corrosion resistance, high-heat resistance, resistance to abrasion, impact, etc. The elements that may be added to produce these characteristics (not in the order listed above) are molybdenum, manganese, chromium, nickel, tungsten, etc. These alloying elements will be discussed at greater length later in this text.

It seems that the easiest way to control the percentage of a desirable alloy is to eliminate that alloying element and then add the desired amount to the melt. To accomplish this the following purification furnaces are used.

1.9. The Open-Hearth Furnace

In the *open-hearth furnace*, Fig. 1.4, air and fuel are passed through a honeycomb of hot firebrick, called checkers. This preheats the air and fuel so that they are ready for combustion when they enter the hearth. At the same time, the products of combustion pass through the checkers at the other end of the furnace. These hot gases heat the checkers. The process then reverses itself, and the newly heated checkers now are used to heat the air and the fuel. This is referred to as a regenerative process. The products of combustion, after giving up their heat to the checkers, pass up through the stack. The burning of the fuel heats the charge. Part of the heat necessary results from radiation from the low hot roof of the chamber.

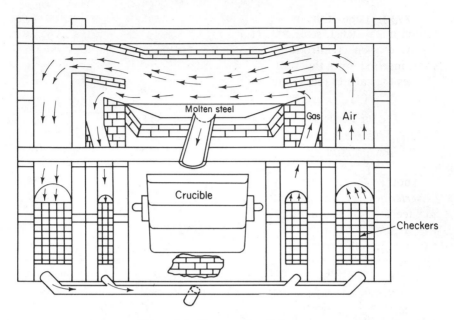

Figure 1.4 The open-hearth furnace.

The furnace is raised on a stiltlike structure (bricked in) with the charging platform, at the rear, also raised so that the charge may be put into the furnace. The melt is tapped off the front into large ladles.

The chemical composition of the end product depends upon the lining, the charge, and the control impurities added during the melt or after the melt has been tapped off into the ladle.

In the *basic* (magnesite) *lined furnace*, the charge consists of pig iron, limestone, and scrap iron. As before, the limestone forms a slag which combines with the oxygen in the air to remove impurities. The slag reacts with the sulfur and the phosphorus in the metal, while the bubbling air causes oxidation of the carbon and silicon. If too much carbon is present in the melt, iron ore is added. The oxygen from the ore (iron oxide) burns out the excess carbon. If the carbon content is too low, pig iron is added to replenish the carbon. Other elements are added as needed. Spiegeleisen may be added to the melt before tapping, or ferromanganese may be added to the crucible after tapping.

The lining plays a major role in the control of impurities. An acid lining (almost obsolete today) cannot reduce phosphorus or sulfur. Thus, if the lining is silica brick, the charge should be scrap iron and low-phosphorus pig iron. Limestone is needed to keep the slag fluid. As described above, the basic lining "burns" phosphorus, silicon, and carbon. The slag is tapped off by allowing the molten metal to overflow the sides of the crucible into a slag pot.

Oxygen is one of the most important elements used in the reduction of the molten metal. Rust, scale, slag, and limestone are some sources of oxygen. Today, oxygen is introduced into the furnace through a hollow oxygen lance inserted into the roof of the furnace. Doubling the oxygen input doubles the carbon reduction. This increases the steel production of the furnace.

1.10. The Bessemer and Basic Oxygen Processes .

Another method used in the making of steel is called the *Bessemer converter process*. The Bessemer converter, Fig. 1.5, is a pear-shaped cylindrical, steel structure supported by trunnions. One of the trunnions is equipped with a power gear to permit tilting the furnace. The hollow center of the trunnion acts as a passageway for air under pressure to be conducted to the bottom of the furnace when the furnace is in an upright position.

The bottom of the furnace is a windbox. The air enters the inside of the furnace through holes (tuyeres) in a large removable plate at the base of the furnace. These tuyeres are made of some refractory material; for instance, in the acid furnace they are silica.

The converter is tilted on its side and hot molten steel from the mixers is poured into the open end. As the converter is righted, the air is turned on; 30,000 cfm of air at 25 psi is forced through the tuyeres. This pressure supports the molten metal and keeps it from flowing back through the tuyeres.

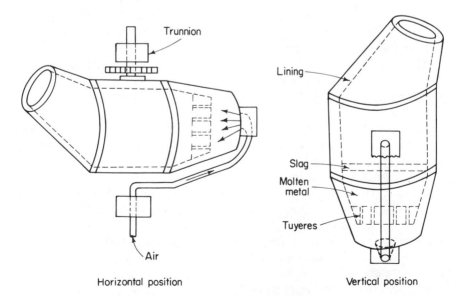

Horizontal position   Vertical position

Figure 1.5 The Bessemer converter.

The air burns out the silicon and the manganese with a yellow flame and a high increase in temperature results. Scrap steel is added to control this temperature. As soon as the silicon is burned out, the carbon begins to burn rapidly. If the temperature is too high, the carbon will begin to burn before all the silicon has burned out and will stop the silicon burn.

Once the silicon has burned out, and once the carbon starts to burn, the flame changes from yellow to a brilliant white flame accompanied by a deep roar caused by the rapid generation of gases. Suddenly this flame dies down, a signal that the converter must be tilted on its side and the air turned off. If this were not done, the iron would oxidize. Iron is the next element that will combine with oxygen and burn off. The contents of the converter consist of molten "blown" iron covered with a slag. The metal contains much iron oxide. The addition of "spiegel" or ferromanganese causes an oxide of manganese to form. This is removed when the slag is removed. However, the addition of these metals adds manganese and carbon to the blown metal. Spiegel is used to make high-carbon steels and ferromanganese is used to make low-carbon steels, since their carbon content is high and low, respectively.

At the end of the blow the converter is tilted on its side, and the melt is permitted to flow into ladles. The slag forms a solidified covering over the top of the melt in the ladle. After pouring off the melt, the ladle is turned upside down and the slag is permitted to fall onto cinder cars for disposal.

If the phosphorus and the sulfur inherent in the Bessemer process are objectionable, a *duplexing process* may be used. In the straight duplexing process the basic open-hearth furnace uses the end product of the Bessemer converter and reduces the phosphorus and sulfur. This is a time-saving device, since all the impurities except phosphorus and sulfur have already been removed in the Bessemer process. Thus the basic open hearth completes the operation left undone by the Bessemer converter.

The *oxygen furnace*, shown in Fig. 1.6, utilizes an oxygen lance to inject oxygen downward into a bath of molten pig iron and scrap. Steels of any carbon content may be produced with this method with somewhat lower percentages of nitrogen, sulfur, and phosphorus contents than can be produced by the open-hearth method. The main advantage of this process is the tap-to-tap cycle. It takes about 45 minutes as contrasted with 10 hours for the open-hearth furnace.

This vessel is shaped somewhat like the Bessemer converter. It is mounted so that it may be tilted through 180° from charging floor to pouring position. It has a basic lining. The iron used is of the low-manganese basic variety. It is transported molten and at high temperatures from the blast furnaces. The temperature is controlled by the addition of cooler scrap before it is charged into the furnace. The furnace is righted, and the oxygen lance is lowered into the furnace above the molten pool and turned on.

Shortly after the oxygen ignites, the blow starts and limestone and scale are added. The blow proceeds until there is a visible drop in the flame. Control of the oxygen input will yield low- or high-carbon steels.

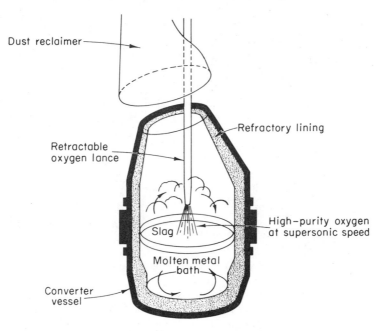

Figure 1.6   Basic oxygen furnace.
(*Courtesy American Iron and Steel Institute.*)

At this point the oxygen is turned off, and the lance is retracted. The furnace is rotated in the direction of the charging platform so that the temperature and carbon content may be checked. The furnace is then rotated to allow the molten metal to flow into the ladle. The slag is retained in the furnace and disposed of subsequently. Alloys are added immediately to the molten metal in the ladle. A different oxygen process uses a rotating furnace with one or two oxygen lances.

1.11.   The Electric Furnace Process

The *electric furnace*, Fig. 1.7, is made of a circular steel shell with some mechanical method for tilting. In the basic furnace the lining to the slag line is magnesite brick. Above the slag line the lining is silica brick. Acid furnaces have a lining made completely of silica brick. The taphole is in the front of the furnace and the charging door in the back. A slag hole is placed directly under the charging door so that the slag may be poured off by tilting the furnace backward.

Large carbon or graphite rods are inserted through holes in the roof to within an inch of the slag. The current jumps this gap to the slag, passes into the molten steel, back to the slag, and then back to the other electrode. The gap between the slag and the rod creates an arc which generates the heat necessary for combustion. The amount of heat generated is controlled automatically by raising or lowering the electrodes.

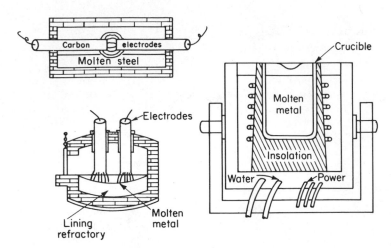

Figure 1.7 The electric furnace.

Some of the finest steels are produced by this method because the atmosphere inside the furnace may be more closely controlled and losses by oxidation thereby eliminated. Temperatures, as indicated, are closely and quickly controlled. Because of the ease of adding alloys without fear of loss through oxidation it is possible to manufacture stainless steel as well as tool steel by this method. The use of the electric furnace in the making of high quality steel has replaced the old crucible method.

1.12.   From Ingot to Steel Sections

After the molten metal is produced it is poured into molds. As soon as solidification has occurred, the molds are stripped off the ingots. While still hot, these ingots are lowered into *soaking pits*. Soaking pits are oil- or gas-heated furnaces designed to bring the temperature of the ingots to a uniform 2200°F throughout.

Once the temperature is uniform throughout, the hot ingots pass through the blooming mill. The two-roll mill passes the hot bloom between its grooved rolls and thus reduces its size. The ingot is manipulated as it is worked, and the direction of rotation of the rolls is reversed at the end of each pass. The three-roll mill does not need reversing. Instead, the steel is passed through the bottom and middle rolls, the table is reversed, and the steel is returned through the upper and middle rolls. At this time the rear table is raised, receives the steel, returns it through the rolls for further reduction, and the process continues. The steel is then cut to length by a shear.

Blooms, billets, or slabs may then be worked into smaller shapes as desired. The rolling process consists of passing the steel between two rolls. If the opening between the rolls is less than the material being rolled, the steel will be reduced in size and become the desired shape.

For each set of rolls through which the steel is drawn, its length must be increased as its cross-sectional area is decreased. Thus if the same volume of steel must pass in the same length of time through the entire series of rolls, each successive set must have a greater surface speed than the previous one. In a continuous bar mill the steel may be traveling at about 2600 ft/min when it leaves the last set of rolls. After leaving the rolls, it runs out onto a cooling

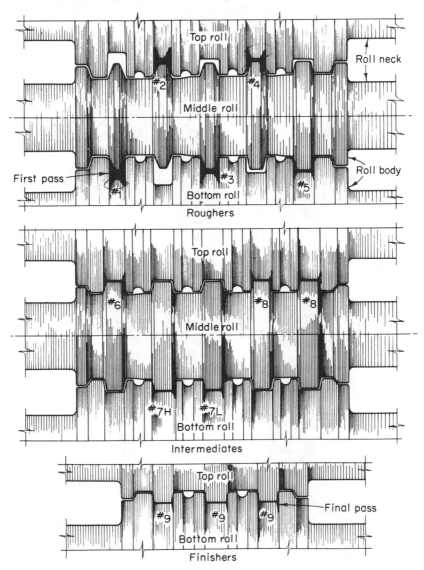

Figure 1.8 I-beams.
(*Courtesy American Iron and Steel Institute; THE MAKING OF STEEL, 1945, page 47.*)

bed. From the cooling bed it goes to the shears where it is cut into desired lengths (about 15 ft).

Figure 1.8 shows roughing, intermediate rolls and at the bottom the finishing rolls. These rolls are used to form I beams. Notice that the first pass is through the lower-middle rolls and the second pass is through the upper-middle rolls, etc. Figure 1.9 shows the stages for rolling steel rails.

Figure 1.10 is a flow chart showing the entire process discussed in this chapter.

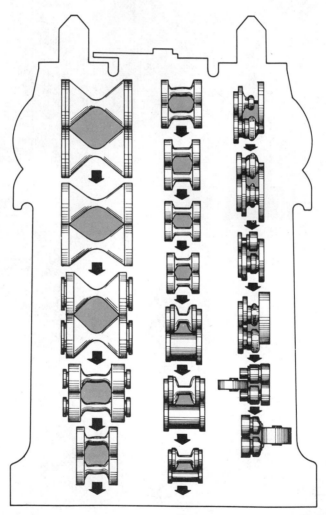

Figure 1.9   Steel rails.
(*Courtesy American Iron and Steel Institute; THE MAKING OF STEEL, 1945, page 53.*)

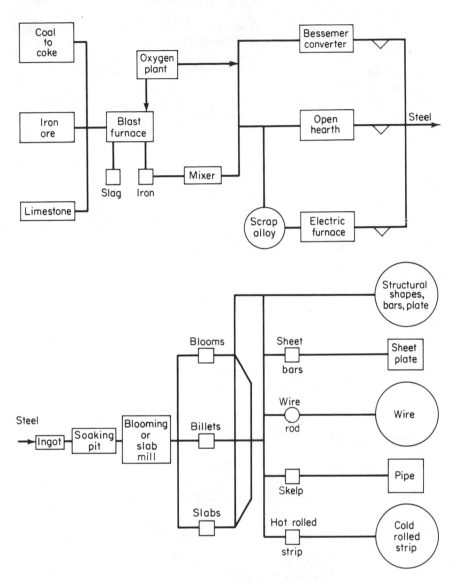

Figure 1.10 Flow chart.
(*Courtesy American Iron and Steel Institute.*)

1.13. Supplementary Mathematics

The cross-sectional area, Fig. 1.11, is

$$A = \pi r^2 = \pi \left(\frac{d}{2}\right)^2 = \frac{\pi d^2}{4}$$

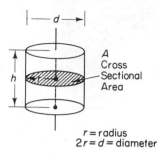

Figure 1.11

$r = $ radius
$2r = d = $ diameter

The sum of these cross-sectional areas is the volume of the cylinder. It is represented as

$$V = A(h) = \frac{\pi d^2}{4}(h)$$

The weight of a volume of material may be obtained by multiplying the volume by the weight per unit volume of that material. The weight per unit volume (W) is defined as the *specific weight.* Thus the weight of one cubic foot of coke weighs 30 lb, designated as 30 lb/ft³. The weight of two cubic feet of coke will be twice as much, or 60 lb. That is

$$w_c = VW = 2\cancel{ft^3} \times \frac{30\ lb}{\cancel{ft^3}} = 60\ lb$$

EXAMPLE 5

If a cylinder 4 ft in diameter by 10 ft high is filled with water, specific weight 62.4 lb/ft³, the weight of the water will be

Solution:

The weight of the water

$$w = VW = \frac{\pi d^2}{4}(h)(w) = \frac{\pi 4^2}{4}(10)(62.4)$$

$$= 7837\ lb$$

$d = 4\ ft$
$h = 10\ ft$
$W = 62.4\ lb/ft^3$

Assume that an equation reads

$$V = \frac{\pi d^2}{4}(h)$$

and that it is to be solved for h. The process is as follows:

1. Multiply both sides of the equation by 4. Thus

$$4V = (4)\frac{\pi d^2}{4}(h)$$

2. Divide both sides by πd^2. Thus

$$\frac{4V}{\pi d^2} = h$$

EXAMPLE 6

Assume the volume of a cylinder is 64 in.³ and its diameter is 9 in. Calculate the height of the cylinder.

$$V = \frac{\pi d^2}{4}(h)$$

$V = 64\ in.^3$
$d = 9\ in.$

Solve for h.

$$h = \frac{4V}{\pi d^2} = \frac{4(64)}{\pi(9)^2} = 1 \text{ in.}$$

QUESTIONS AND PROBLEMS

1.1 The end product of the blast furnace is used in the manufacturing of iron and steel. Trace both uses through the flow chart, Fig. 1.1, and identify the end product.

1.2 What are the four major regions of the blast furnace? Identify each in Fig. 1.2.

1.3 Identify the zones in each of the four regions of a blast furnace. Explain the function of each zone and its contribution to the melting process.

1.4 (a) List the four ingredients which make up the charge in a blast furnace. (b) What is the purpose of each ingredient?

1.5 Name and describe the two processes discussed in this chapter for making coke.

1.6 Describe the direct reduction processes used in the manufacture of steel.

1.7 (a) What is a cupola? (b) What is the end product of the cupola process? (c) Compare the end product of the cupola process with that of the blast furnace. Include the composition of both.

1.8 Explain the process for making cast iron in the cupola.

1.9 (a) What is the meaning of the cupola ratio of 10 : 1? (b) What is the meaning of the term "melting ratio"? (c) Is there any relationship between the two? Explain.

1.10 What is the difference between a bed charge and a regular charge in a cupola? Discuss the purposes of each.

1.11 You are asked to design a 32-in. diameter cupola. The high-temperature zone is to be 36 in. above the sand bottom. The regular coke charge is to be 9 in. deep when the ratio is 8 : 1. Calculate: (a) the weight of the bed charge; (b) the weight of the regular charge; (c) the weight of the iron charge.

1.12 Assume a 4-ft diameter cupola operating at a 6 : 1 ratio. This cupola uses a bed charge of 1570 lb of coke. (a) What is the depth of this bed charge? (b) If the weight of the regular coke charge is to be 20% of the weight of the bed charge, what is the depth of the regular charge of coke? (c) What is the weight of the charge of iron?

1.13 The cupola in Problem 1.11 has a melting ratio of 6 lb/hr/in.^{2} (a) How much iron is melted in 8 hours? (b) Calculate the number of charges needed.

1.14 What is the melting rate in Problem 1.12 if the cupola produces 160 tons of iron in a 36-hr week?

1.15 You are to design a 24-in. diameter cupola. You assume the high-temperature zone to be 40 in. above the sand bottom. The regular coke charge is to be 5 in. deep in a 6 : 1-ratio cupola. (a) What is the weight of the bed charge? (b) What is the weight of the regular bed charge of coke? (c) What is the weight of the iron charge?

1.16   Explain the control of the special characteristics desired when manufacturing steel.

1.17   The open-hearth furnace process for making steel is the most widely used. (a) Explain the process. (b) What is regenerative process?

1.18   What is the role of the two types of lining in the manufacture of steel? Explain each type of lining.

1.19   Explain operation of the Bessemer converter.

1.20   (a) How do the Bessemer converter operation and the basic oxygen process differ? (b) What is the lining in the basic oxygen processes? (c) What is the purpose of the oxygen lance when used in the basic oxygen at the open-hearth processes?

1.21   Describe the duplexing process for making steel.

1.22   (a) How are the high temperatures achieved in the electric furnaces? (b) What are the end products?

1.23   What are soaking pits?

1.24   Trace the process for making steel sections from the soaking pits to the completely formed bar.

1.25   What is the difference between an ingot, a billet, a bloom, and a slab?

Mechanical Properties
and Metallurgy

2

2.1. The Structure of Metals

Metals are crystalline substances. The basic building blocks are the atoms that arrange themselves into orderly structural patterns which we call *cubic lattices*. The fundamental cubic structure, the unit cell, Fig. 2.1, has an atom in each corner of the cube. When several unit cubes join, as shown in Fig. 2.1 (dotted lines), each atom is shared by eight such cubes. The nature of the relationship of these atomic configurations and of the forces involved is left for study in a course in metallurgy.

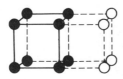

| Figure 2.1 | Figure 2.2 |

Figures 2.2, 2.3, and 2.4 show three lattice structures found in metals.

Figure 2.2 shows a *body-centered cubic* (BCC) structure with an atom in each corner of the unit cube and one atom at the center of the cube.

Figure 2.3 shows a *face-centered cubic* (FCC) structure with an atom in each corner of the cube and one at the intersection of the diagonals of each of the six faces of the cube.

Figure 2.4(a) shows a *hexagonal close-pack* (HCP) structure. This structure is made up of three configurations of the kind shown in Fig. 2.4(b). The unit cell is a rhombus with a 120° base. In addition to the atoms in each

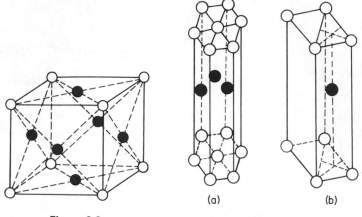

(a)   (b)

Figure 2.3   **Figure 2.4**

corner of the hexagon, each rhombus has an atom at the center of a line connecting the perpendiculars, as shown in Fig. 2.4(b).

It is important to note that in all configurations the atoms "touch" each other. The small spheres, which represent atoms, are drawn small for convenience.

A combination of lattice structures bound together in a regular pattern form a *crystal*, as shown in Fig. 2.5(a). Several crystals oriented in different directions, Fig. 2.5(b), form a *grain boundary* and taken as a whole form the *material*.

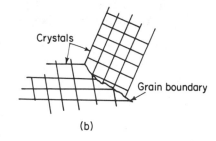

Crystals

Grain boundary

(a)   (b)

Figure 2.5

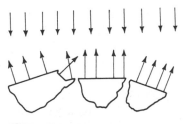

Figure 2.6

The directional aspect of a structure makes possible the preparation of a sample for microscopic investigation by polishing and chemically etching the material. This etching is directional. It is dependent upon the grain orientation, which it exposes by removing such imperfections as grain boundaries.

Light bounced off these surfaces will be reflected in varying intensity and will appear as either black or white with all of the intermediate shades of gray in photographs taken of them (see Fig. 2.6). Grain boundaries, grains, and different types of grains all react differently to the etching fluids.

2.2. Observation and Testing of Materials

The metallurgical microscope.   This instrument is used to investigate the microstructure of metals (Fig. 2.7). A knowledge of the microstructure is the basis for an analysis of the past history of the metal and the prediction of the physical properties which may be anticipated.

The specimens which are examined are opaque and, as already stated, the instrument must operate on the principle of reflected light. It is possible to equip this instrument with a camera so that photographs of the structure may be made.

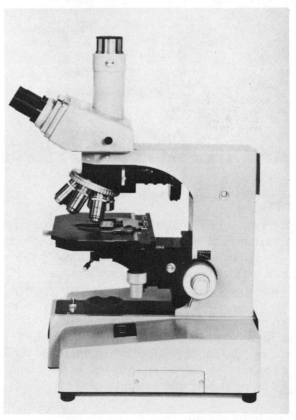

Figure 2.7 Metallurgical microscope.
(*Courtesy of Nikon Mfg. Co.*)

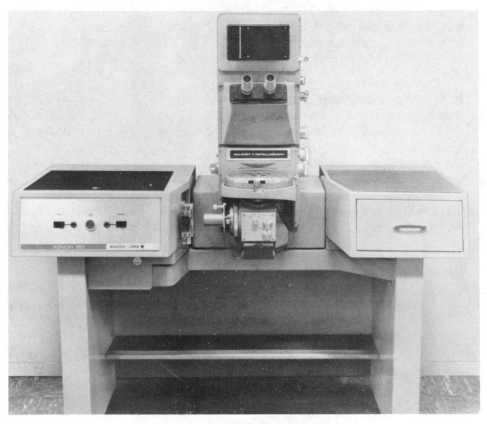

Figure 2.8 Balphot Metallograph.
(*Courtesy of Buehler Mfg. Co.*)

The metallograph.   This sophisticated metallurgical microscope, Fig. 2.8, permits visual examination of the polished and etched specimen as well as the permanent recording of the structure in the form of photomicrographs.

The specimen for both of these instruments is prepared in four steps. The first step is sampling, the selection of a representative piece of the material to be investigated. The second step is the mounting and grinding of the specimen so that it is optically flat. The third step is the polishing of the specimen so that a smooth surface, free from scratches, is obtained. This is necessary for uniform etching, the last step before inspection of the surface.

The etching process is a differential corrosion of the ground and polished surface. The following etching solutions may be used:

Low-carbon steel and welds
   Nital: 2% HNO_3 in ethyl alcohol
Medium- and high-carbon steel, pearlitic steel, and cast iron
   Picral: 5% picric acid and ethyl alcohol

Aluminum
   Hydrofluoric acid: 1% HF in water
Copper
   50% NH_4OH and 50% water

The Rockwell tester.   One of the several instruments which may be used to determine the hardness of steel, the Rockwell tester consists of a penetrator, an anvil, an indicator, and a loading device [Fig. 2.9(a)].

The Rockwell scale is related to the depth to which the penetrator pierces

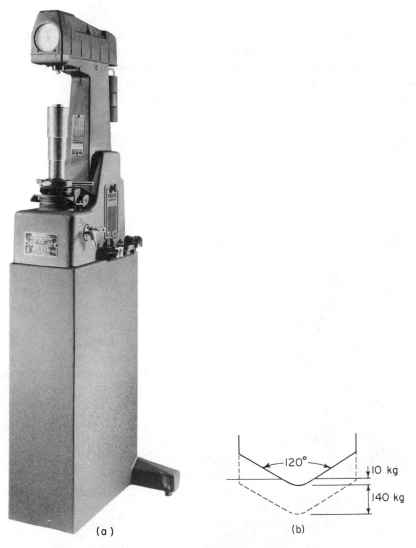

(a)   (b)

Figure 2.9 Rockwell hardness tester.
(*Photo courtesy of Rockwell Mfg. Co.*)

the material being tested. Eighty millionths (0.000080) of an inch of penetration represents one Rockwell number.

The specimen is placed on the anvil and the penetrator is brought into contact with the specimen. A minor load is applied (the dial indicator needle reads zero) to equalize the errors due to small surface imperfections, faulty contact, and deflection in the machine itself. The major load is then applied slowly and removed. The Rockwell reading is now taken with the minor load still applied: this eliminates the error due to the recovery in the material which occurs after the major load is removed. Thus the Rockwell reading is a measure of the penetration caused by the major load alone.

There are many combinations of major load and type of penetrator available for checking different ranges of hardness. The Rockwell "C" scale (R_c) is the most frequently used scale. It uses a 120° diamond penetrator with a 150 kg load. The minor increment is 10 kg, and the major increment is 140 kg [see Fig. 2.9(b)]. Readings of 60 and 65 R_c mean that the 60 R_c (softer spot) penetration is $5 \times 0.00008 = 0.0004$ in. deeper than the 65 R_c penetration. The dial recorder, however, reads hardness rather than depth of penetration.

Irregular surfaces, scale, and imperfect flatness will give false readings. Very thin pieces will also give false readings and will reflect the hardness of the anvil as well as of the piece of material. Several readings should be taken and averaged and these should not be taken at the same place on the specimen.

For checking the hardness of thin pieces, a *superficial Rockwell* may be used. This machine uses a 3-kg minor load and 15-, 30-, and 45-kg major loads. It is calibrated for a depth of penetration of 0.000040 in. for each Rockwell increment. The symbol is R_N.

The Brinell tester.   This instrument forces a 10-mm hardened steel ball into the surface of the material. A constant load of 3000 kg, or 500 kg for soft materials, is applied and then released. The diameter of the impression is measured with a 20-power microscope which has a millimeter scale etched on its lens. This diameter is referred to a table, and the Brinell hardness number (BHN) read. The softer the material, the longer the diameter of the indentation; the harder the material, the shorter the diameter. The BHN is a function of the ratio of the applied load to the area of the impression. The Brinell machine is shown in Fig. 2.10.

Figure 2.10 Brinell hardness tester.
(*Courtesy of Riehle Testing Machines.*)

The Shore scleroscope.   This instrument works on the principle of recovery (see Fig. 2.11). A diamond-tipped hammer is allowed to drop and strike the specimen. The rebound is read on a graduated scale (0 to 140) in back of the vertical glass tube through which the hammer drops. The rebound of the hammer is related to the recovery: the greater the recovery, the greater the Shore number.

Care must be taken that the drop of the hammer is vertical, that the material is clean and smooth, and that the specimen is moved after each reading is taken.

There are other methods for testing hardness of materials. The *Vickers* and *Knoop* tests, for example, are classified as microhardness tests because of the small impression which they make in the specimen.

The universal impact testing machine.   This machine performs another type of test important to manufacturing processes. This machine may perform a series of tests: Charpy, Izod, and tensile impact tests (see Fig. 2.12).

With the specimen held in a vise, a hammer is raised to a fixed height and released. On impact, the specimen absorbs some of the energy of the swinging hammer. The loss of energy by the hammer means that it will not return to

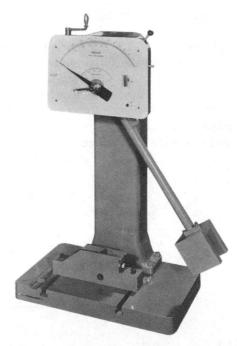

Figure 2.11 Shore scleroscope. (*Courtesy of Shore Instrument Co.*)

Figure 2.12 Riehle universal impact tester. (*Courtesy of Riehle Testing Machines.*)

its original height. The more energy absorbed by the specimen, the shorter is the return swing of the hammer. This loss of energy is recorded by the machine as foot-pounds of energy absorbed.

The *Charpy* test requires that the prepared specimen, Fig. 2.13(a), be held at the ends and loaded as a simple beam. In the *Izod test*, the specimen, Fig. 2.13(b), is held at one end, as a cantilever. The *tensile impact test*, Fig. 2.13(c), loads the specimen in tension.

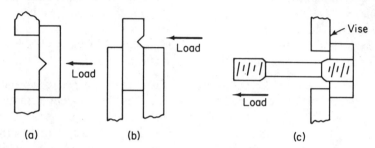

(a)   (b)   (c)

Figure 2.13

2.3. Equilibrium Diagrams*

A piece of ice at 20°F is heated to the freezing point at 32°F. For every half Btu put into the ice, the temperature of the system increases 1F° (assuming no losses). In Fig. 2.14 the temperature is plotted as the ordinate, and the Btu input is plotted as the abscissa. If more heat is pumped into the system, the ice at 32°F will change to water at 32°F. This creates the first plateau in the heating (or cooling) curve.

Once all the ice has changed to water, the curve will once again continue to rise until it reaches 212°F, at which time another plateau appears. These

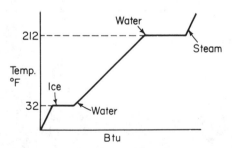

Figure 2.14

---

*A complete set of equilibrium diagrams belongs in a text on metallurgy. However, in order that the student may understand the heat-treating processes, some knowledge of equilibrium diagrams is necessary.

plateaus appear because a phase change is taking place, that is, a change in the physical state of the hydrogen and oxygen alignment. There has been no chemical change. If reversed, the same phenomena, or cooling curve, occurs, and this is characteristic of metals as well as water.

Assume a piece of metal X contains 100% X and 0% Y [Fig. 2.15(a)]. The metal is heated to the liquid state and then cooled very slowly. A temperature T_1 is reached at which the metal X will continue to precipitate out as a solid without any change in temperature until all the metal has solidified.

Suppose now a small percentage by weight of metal Y is alloyed with metal X (assume 10% Y alloyed with 90% X). This alloy is again heated to the liquid state and permitted to cool very slowly. Upon reaching T_2 [Fig. 2.15(b)] metal X starts to precipitate out. At T_3 the mixture consists of the solid metal X and the liquid X and Y of a fixed percentage. The percentage of 40% X and 60% Y, as seen in Fig. 2.15(e), cools as though it were a pure metal, and this solidification creates a plateau in the curve. The cooling curve for the entire process is shown in Fig. 2.15(b). Figures 2.15(c and d) exhibit the same kind of cooling curves except that the upper critical temperatures T_4 and T_5 occur at different places. Figures 2.15(f and h) give the same type of cooking curve except that metal Y precipitates out first. Note the percentages of the alloy.

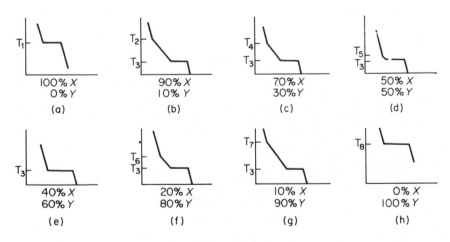

Figure 2.15

Figure 2.15(e) is a special case. A combination of this percentage of X and Y (40% X and 60% Y) precipitates from the liquid state to the solid state at one temperature, namely T_3. Above T_3 the alloy is all liquid and the metals X and Y cannot be distinguished one from the other; below T_3 the metal is all solid. Metal X and metal Y are easily identifiable. Above T_3 we say the state is single phase. Below T_3 we say the state is two phase.

These phenomena may take place in several different ways and are important enough to be given special names. The transformation just described and shown in Fig. 2.15(e) is called a *eutectic change*, that is, the transformation of metal, on cooling, from a single-phase liquid to a two-phase solid. When an alloy of two metals changes from a single-phase solid to a two-phase solid, it is said to be *eutectoid*. The transformation of two alloyed metals from a two-phase liquid-solid combination to a single-phase solid is said to be *peritectic*. If a two-phase solid combination changes to a single-phase solid, the transformation is said to be *peritectoid*. The eutectoid transformation is very important and will be referred to again.

In Fig. 2.16(a) a graph is plotted with the temperature as the ordinate and the percentages of metal X and metal Y as the abscissa. The various cooling curves in Fig. 2.15 are shown connected in Fig. 2.16(a). The resultant equilibrium diagram is shown in Fig. 2.16(b). If the cooling is very slow, the transformations are said to take place under equilibrium conditions. Thus a line drawn parallel to the ordinate in Fig. 2.16(b) will yield valuable information concerning a given alloy of metal X and metal Y as it appears on the abscissa.

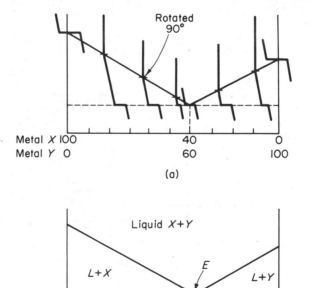

Figure 2.16

2.4. Iron-Iron Carbide Equilibrium Diagrams

Figure 2.17 is the equilibrium diagram for combinations of *iron* (Fe) and *carbon* (C) alloyed in various percentages. The ordinate at the left of the diagram is pure iron. The ordinate at the right of the diagram is 6.67% carbon composition and represents 100% *cementite* (Fe₃C), designated Cm. Three additional single phases exist: *delta* (δ) iron; *gamma* (γ) iron, also called *austenite*; and *alpha* (α) iron, also called *ferrite*. Given these five single-phase regions, all additional regions may be determined by using the 1-2-1 rule. In this procedure, a horizontal line is drawn so that it starts in a single-phase region, passes through a two-phase region, and terminates in a single-phase region. Consider line *AB*, Fig. 2.17. The left end of the line terminates in the single-phase gamma region (γ); the right end of the line in the single-phase liquid region (L). The intermediate region is a two-phase gamma-liquid region (γ + L). The student is charged with checking the other two-phase regions, using this 1-2-1 rule.

Also included in the diagram, Fig. 2.17, are four transformation lines: A_1, A_2, A_3, and A_{cm}. The A_3 line is the temperature at which the gamma transformation takes place. The A_{cm} line is the temperature at which the cementite (Cm) transformation takes place. The eutectoid transformation

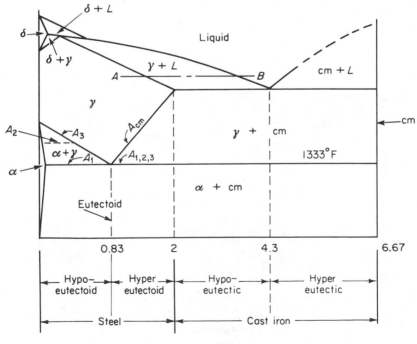

Figure 2.17

takes place at the A_1 line. A 0.83* of 1% carbon steel alloyed with ferrite is called a *eutectoid steel*, or *pearlite*.

Now let us consider the left ordinate of Fig. 2.17. Steel at room temperature and up to a temperature at the A_2 line is magnetic. At temperatures above the A_2 line steel is nonmagnetic.

At temperatures below the A_3 line steel has a BCC lattice structure. At temperatures between the A_3 line and the delta region, steel has an FCC lattice structure. Whereas, when steel is at a temperature in the delta region, the structure returns to a BCC lattice.

Now consider the abscissa of Fig. 2.17. Iron alloyed with from 0 to 2% carbon as shown on the equilibrium diagram is called *steel*. When iron is alloyed with carbon in percentages greater than 2%, the alloy is called *cast iron*.

Steels that have a carbon content of 0.83 are said to have a eutectoid structure and are called *pearlitic steels*. *Pearlite* has constituents of 88 parts of ferrite in combination with 12 parts of cementite (Fe + Fe$_3$C). An alloy that lies to the left of 0.83 carbon is said to have a *hypo-eutectoid* structure. An alloy that is more than 0.83 carbon and up to 2% carbon is called *hyper-eutectoid* steel. Pearlite makes up the entire structure of the eutectoid steels. Hypo-eutectoid steels have phases of ferrite and pearlite, while hyper-eutectoid steels have phases of cementite and pearlite. Figure 2.18 shows the microstructure of the various phases under equilibrium conditions.

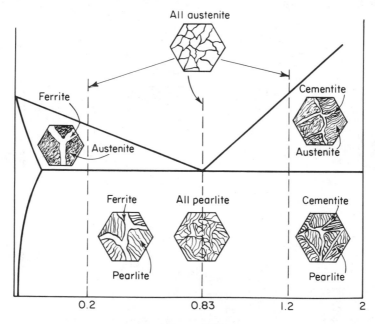

Figure 2.18

*Sometimes referred to as "83 points of carbon."

2.5. The Time-Temperature-Transformation (TTT) Curves

Sections 2.1 through 2.4 dealt with equilibrium cooling conditions. Thus in Fig. 2.17, if a piece of steel is heated into the austenite (γ) range and cooled very slowly, the structure will have time to change into its original state. If cooling is accelerated, other structural changes will take place. In such cases the equilibrium diagram no longer applies by itself, but must be studied in conjunction with cooling curves which interpret the structural changes that take place under conditions of nonequilibrium cooling. These curves are called *time-temperature-transformation* (TTT) curves.

TTT curves are developed when a fixed temperature curve is drawn which is related to the time required for a transformation of structure. A large number of curves are drawn for various temperatures, as shown in Fig. 2.19(a). The ordinate axis becomes the temperature and the related points

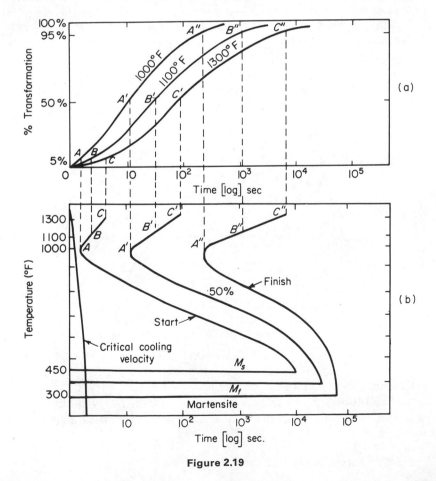

Figure 2.19

from Fig. 2.19(a) are plotted as shown in Fig. 2.19(b).* With these time-temperature-transformation curves plotted, it is now possible to superimpose cooling curves on them. This in turn permits the prediction of the structure of a material at various temperatures.

If the specimen is heated into the austenite range and quenched very rapidly, the austenite transforms into a hard structure called *martensite*. At the austenite temperature the carbon atoms are diffused in the FCC lattice structure. On slow cooling, these atoms can diffuse out of solution and the structure has time to transform to its original BCC lattice structure, but on rapid cooling, neither process can take place. The resulting structure, martensite, is hard, having an elongated, body-centered tetragonal structure resulting from the trapped carbon. The three horizontal lines at the lower part of the diagram, Fig. 2.19(b), are the three martensite transformation lines.

Figure 2.20 shows a series of cooling curves which result from different rates of cooling when superimposed on the TTT curves. Assume a cooling rate *a* (Fig. 2.20). Since this curve does not "cut the nose" of the TTT curve, the pearlite transformation does not take place. However, since this cooling curve does cut the horizontal martensite transformation curves, the resulting structure at room temperature is martensite. Cooling curve *b* is quenched into a bath at 600°F and held for 100 seconds before it is quenched in a bath at room temperature. Again the resulting structure is martensite.

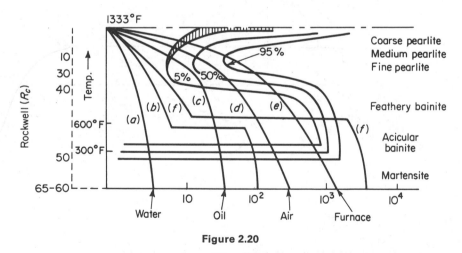

Figure 2.20

Cooling curves *c* and *d* do cut the nose of the TTT curves. Parts of the austenite transform to fine and coarse pearlite, respectively, while the remaining austenite transforms to martensite. This is referred to as a split transformation.

*The TTT diagram shown is idealized.

Cooling curve *e* crosses all three TTT curves. Almost all of the austenite transforms to pearlite with a coarse crystal structure.

If pearlitic steel, quenched into a bath at 600°F so that the cooling curve *f* misses the nose of the TTT curves, is then held at 600°F until the cooling curve cuts the three transformation curves, as shown in Fig. 2.20, and then is quenched to room temperature, an intermediate structure between pearlite and martensite, called *bainite*, results.

When bainite results from low temperatures, it is called *acicular* (needles) bainite. When quenched at upper temperatures, it is called *feathery* bainite. As the quenching temperature increases, the hardness of the specimen decreases and its structure becomes coarser and coarser, as shown in Fig. 2.20. If one specimen is quenched into an 800°F bath and another into a 600°F bath and held, the former will result in a coarser structure than the latter.

Various quenching rates are obtained by quenching in different media. Quenches in decreasing order of severity are shown in Fig. 2.20. Brine water (not shown) is a very severe quench. A water quench results in martensite; oil, in fine pearlite; air, in intermediate pearlite; and furnace cooling, in coarse pearlite.

2.6. Hardenability Curves

The Jominy test. This is a test for determining the hardenability of a piece of steel (Fig. 2.21). Hardenability is defined as the depth of penetration of the martensite structure from the point of most severe quenching. The Jominy test uses the specimen shown in Fig. 2.21.

Without the specimen in the fixture and with the baffle plate swung out of the way, the height of the column of water in a $\frac{1}{2}$-in. inside diameter pipe is preset so that the top of the column is approximately 0.5 in. below the holding fixture. This establishes the rate of water flow and consequently the rate of quench.

The baffle is swung into position with the water still flowing. The specimen is heated to the desired temperature (austenite range), rapidly removed from the furnace, and placed in the Jominy fixture. With the specimen in the fixture the baffle plate is swung free, and the quench is permitted to impinge on the bottom of the specimen. Obviously the most severe quench takes place at the end

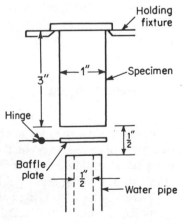

Figure 2.21

of the specimen close to the jet. The farther away from the quenched end, the less severe is the quench. Once the specimen has cooled sufficiently so that it may be handled, it is removed from the fixture and two flats of 0.015 in. are ground opposite each other for the full length of the specimen. An attachment for the Rockwell machine permits movement of the specimen in increments of $\frac{1}{16}$ in. at which Rockwell readings are taken and plotted against distance from the quenched end. A few typical curves are shown in Fig. 2.22(a).

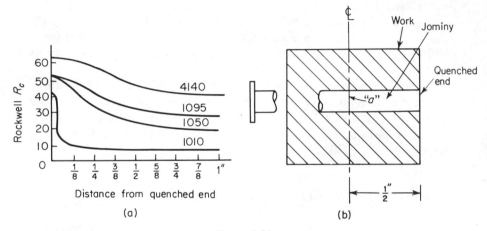

Figure 2.22

If the distance from the quenched end is related to half the thickness of a workpiece, Fig. 2.22(b), the center of the workpiece will have the same hardness as the Jominy test bar. The workpiece should have about the same Rockwell reading because the cooling rates at this point are about the same for both the specimen and the workpiece.

The hardness, as related to the distance from the quenched end, may be designated as a J number. A 50 R_c reading at $\frac{3}{16}$ in. from the quenched end is designated as

$$J_{50} = 3$$

A reading of 22 R_c at $\frac{7}{8}$ in. ($\frac{14}{16}$) from the quenched end may be designated as

$$J_{22} = 14$$

There are many types of informative curves that are useful in the heat treatment of steels. As pointed out previously, large cross sections of a workpiece transform differently throughout the section owing to the temperature gradient, or cooling rate. Full hardness takes place only in very thin pieces.

These effects of varying hardness with thickness may be plotted against diameter, as shown in Fig. 2.23. Various diameter bars are quenched from a given temperature in a given quenching medium. Curve a is a 4-in. diameter

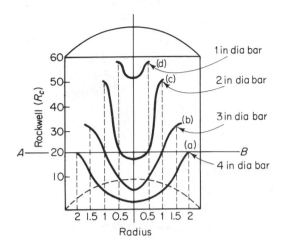

Figure 2.23

(2 in. radius) bar; b is a 3-in. diameter ($1\frac{1}{2}$ in. radius) bar; c is a 2-in. diameter (1 in. radius) bar; d is a 1-in. diameter ($\frac{1}{2}$ in. radius) bar. Line AB cuts three curves, bar diameters 4, 3, and 2 inches. The 1-in. diameter is not cut by the AB line. This AB line represents a reading of 20 R_c. Thus, the surface of the 4-in. diameter (curve a) bar should read Rockwell 20 on the "C" scale. Curve b represents the 3-in. diameter bar. At the intersection of line AB and curve b—approximately $\frac{1}{2}$ in. below the surface—the specimen Rockwell is 20 on the "C" scale. Curve c is intersected by line AB at the 1-in. diameter, or $\frac{1}{2}$ in. below the surface of the 2-in. diameter bar. The AB line does not intersect the 1-in. diameter bar because even the center of this bar never "Rockwells" less than 50 R_c. That cooling rate is the important factor is evidenced by the fact that the curves represent different diameters of the same material.

2.7. Tempering

A piece of pearlite steel is heated into the austenite range and quenched. The cooling curve when superimposed on the TTT curves indicates a martensitic structure that will not take impact loading because it is brittle. A secondary heat-treating process is required to make the steel usable. As the martensite is reheated, its structure again undergoes change. As a result of this *tempering process*, the hardness and strength of the structure are reduced, while the toughness and ductility are greatly increased. Figure 2.24 shows the three tempered states of martensite: troosite, sorbite, and spherodite.

Martensite is achieved by quenching austenite. If the martensite sample is heated into the 400 to 700°F range, a fine carbide dispersion takes place. We call this structure *troosite*. If the piece is heated into the 700 to 1200°F range, spherical carbides start to form. We call the structure *sorbite*. At still higher

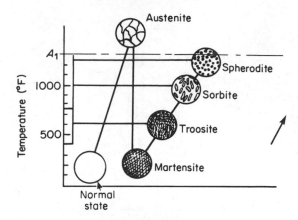

Figure 2.24

temperatures, 1200 to 1300°F, and given time, the carbide spheres become coarse. This structure is called *spherodite*.

It is important to note that tempering is a one-way, irreversible process. If a hardened sample is heated into the sorbite range when a troosite structure is desired, the procedure requires that the original structure be restored to destroy the sorbite structure. This is accomplished by heating the piece into the austenite range and cooling to room temperature very slowly. Once the original structure has been obtained, the entire process of hardening and tempering is repeated.

The student is alerted to two phenomena which could occur during the tempering process: (1) Certain alloy steels when cooled slowly from the tempering temperature do not increase in toughness and ductility. This is called *temper brittleness* and may be corrected by fast cooling from the tempering range. (2) There are some alloys that retain some austenite when quenched to the martensite temperature range. This retained austenite could transform to martensite during the tempering process. If this should happen it would be necessary to repeat the tempering process to eliminate this newly formed martensite. This is referred to as *secondary tempering*.

2.8. Non-Martensitic Secondary Heat-Treating Processes

Figure 2.25 shows shaded areas, or bands, which represent temperatures that must be reached in order to carry out certain heat-treating processes. Throughout this section the *upper-* and *lower-critical temperatures* will be mentioned. The lower-critical temperature is shown as the A_1 and $A_{1,3}$ lines, and the upper-critical temperature by the A_3 and A_{cm} lines.

Full annealing. To perform this process on hypo-eutectoid steels, they are heated to just above the A_3 line and cooled very slowly in a furnace. The

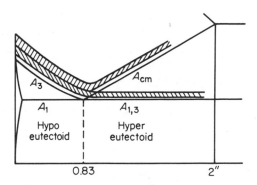

Figure 2.25

destruction of the existing structure is the main purpose of full annealing, and this is accomplished by heating into the austenite range. Slow cooling causes grain refinement, softening, toughening, and relatively low-tensile strength steel. The ideal full-annealing temperature is just above the A_3 line in the equilibrium diagram. In practice, the process is carried out at about 50 to 75°F above the A_3 line.

Hyper-eutectoid steels may also be *full annealed*. The specimen is heated to just above the $A_{1,3}$ line and allowed to cool very slowly. If the steel had been heated to above the A_{cm} line and allowed to cool slowly, cementite "jackets" would have formed around the soft pearlite. It is to avoid this that the hyper-eutectoid steels are heated to temperatures which are just above the $A_{1,3}$ line (lower-critical range). On slow cooling from this range, the original structures of pearlite and cementite result.

Normalizing.   The specimen is heated to above the upper-critical temperature (A_3 for hypo-eutectoid steel and A_{cm} for hyper-eutectoid steel) and cooled in air instead of in the furnace. This increased rate of cooling results in a slight hardening of the steel and less ductility than in annealed steel. The pearlite formed has a finer structure than the pearlite formed during annealing. Normalizing is used to remove stresses, strains, and undesirable crystal structures and to improve strength and machinability.

Process annealing.   Accomplished by heating the specimen to temperatures below the A_1 line, process annealing makes steels ductile so that they may be cold worked.* The process is quite different from full annealing.

Stress relieving.   This is similar to process annealing. Stress relieving requires the specimen be heated to below the lower-critical temperature (A_1 for hypo-eutectoid steels and $A_{1,3}$ for hyper-eutectoid steels) and then cooled slowly. Whereas process annealing softens the material through a process of cold working and recrystallization, stress relieving removes internal stresses

---

*Cold working is discussed in Chapter 7. Recrystallization refers to the regrouping of the crystal structure within the material.

without visibly changing the microstructure. The elevated temperature allows the atoms to move about a little more freely. They rearrange themselves and in the process remove internal stresses.

If hyper-eutectoid steels are heated for long periods of time at a temperature just below the A_1 line, cementite forms as spheres in a matrix of ferrite. The steel has maximum ductility and low tensile strength and becomes soft. Since the carbide forms spheres instead of jackets, the structure achieved is the softest possible structure for hyper-eutectoid steels and yields the best possible machining conditions.

2.9. Carburizing and Case Hardening

It should be remembered that the nose of the TTT curves shifts far to the left for low-carbon steels. This makes it difficult, if not impossible, to quench fast enough so that the cooling curve misses the nose of the curves. The case-hardening process may involve increasing the carbon content of the surface of the steel or relying upon alloys within the structure to aid hardenability. The former is accomplished by the *carburization process.*

Carburizing consists of packing a specimen into a sealed container in the presence of a carbon material or carbon gas. The carbonizing agent may be charcoal, cyanide, propane, or other hydrocarbon gases. The pack is heated well above the upper-critical temperature (1600 to 1750°F) and held from 4 to 10 hours to produce a desired depth of carbon penetration. The best results may be obtained if the pack is furnace cooled after the required soaking period.

The austenite structure of a piece of steel will absorb enough carbon to place the structure of the case well into the hyper-eutectoid range (well above 0.83% carbon). The core is not affected. Figure 2.26 shows the duplex structure of a segment of a piece of low-carbon steel which has been carburized. The carbon will penetrate to a maximum depth of slightly over $\frac{1}{4}$ in. Since the carbon content of this $\frac{1}{4}$-in. case ranges from approximately 1% carbon

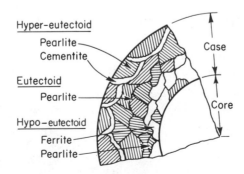

Figure 2.26

at the outer surface to the original carbon content (usually 0.2% C) at the inner surface of the case, penetration of appreciable hardness may be attained up to about $\frac{1}{16}$-in. depth with a secondary heat-treating process.

Once the high-carbon case has been formed, a secondary heat treatment is used to harden this case. The process used depends upon the original structure of the steel and the results desired. The following discussion should be related very carefully to the equilibrium diagram for grain-size control and to the TTT curves for martensite formation, Fig. 2.27(a).

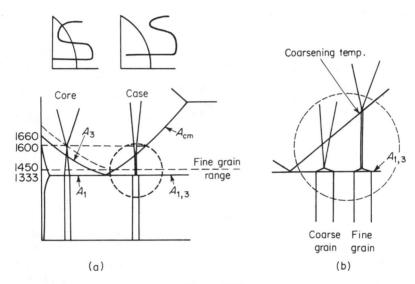

(a)   (b)

Figure 2.27

It should be noted in the insert, Fig. 2.27(b), that in both a coarse-grain and a fine-grain hyper-eutectoid case the grain size is refined at A_1. However, inherently coarse-grain materials start to grow as soon as the temperature is increased beyond the $A_{1,3}$ line; whereas in an inherently fine-grain structure, the grain growth is delayed until an elevated temperature is reached, at which the grain growth takes place rapidly.

If the original grain size is fine, the material may be reheated after carburizing to 1450°F and quenched. This is shown at the right of Fig. 2.28. At 1450°F the core has a fine-grain structure which is soft. Since the noses of the TTT curves are close to the ordinate, Fig. 2.27(a), the cooling curve will cut the noses of these curves and the core will therefore not harden.

The cooling curve for the high-carbon case misses the nose of the TTT curves, Fig. 2.27(a), and permits the martensite transformation to take place. The case will therefore harden, having a fine-grain structure because its original structure was fine grain and because the quenching temperature did not destroy this fine grain, Fig. 2.27(b).

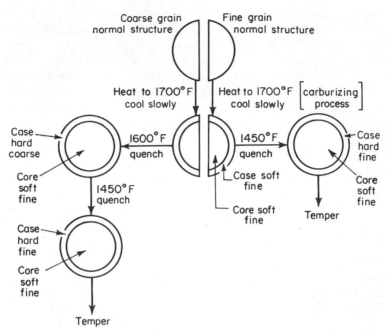

Figure 2.28

If the original grain size is coarse, as shown at the left of Fig. 2.28, an additional heat-treating step must be included. The carburized specimen is heated to 1600°F: the grain size of the case at this temperature is coarse and the grain size of the core is refined. If quenched at this temperature, these grain sizes are trapped. The case is hard and coarse, the core is soft and fine.

If this specimen is reheated to 1450°F, the grain size in the case is refined and the grain in the core, although some growth takes place, remains much finer than it was in its original state. Therefore the resulting structure is a hard-fine case and a soft-fine core. These heat-treating processes may be followed with a tempering process if desired.

If the above sophistication is not required, the secondary heat-treating, or hardening, process may be carried out by quenching directly from the carburizing temperature. That is, instead of permitting the pack to cool, the carburized specimens are removed from the pack and quenched to room temperature in water or oil. A hard case results which is usually acceptable. Since carburizing is carried out at high temperatures, the student should note the effect of these high-temperature quenches on the grain size.

Cyanide hardening. This is another case-hardening process. It is applied to medium-carbon steels and results from the absorption of carbon and nitrogen. If the steel is heated in the presence of sodium cyanide at about 1600°F, hard nitrides are formed. Quenching forms carbides. These two produce high hardness case to a depth of about 0.010 in.

The nitriding process. This requires an alloy steel which has been previously hardened and tempered to the sorbite structure. The steel is machined to the desired shape, then placed in a container, sealed in the presence of ammonia gas, and heated to 900°F for a long period of time, usually from 8 to 24 hours. A complex layer of nitrides is formed to a depth of 0.005 to 0.020 in. This layer is very hard and will retain its hardness at temperatures of 750 to 1000°F, which makes the steel suitable for operations requiring resistance to severe stress and wear. Steels containing alloys of chromium, molybdenum, vanadium, or aluminum may be nitrided.

Carbonitriding. Carbon in the gaseous form is added to nitrogen and thus permits the carburizing and the nitriding processes to be carried out simultaneously. Various degrees of carburizing and nitriding may be obtained by controlled heat treating and cooling.

Flame hardening and induction hardening. These are two processes which do not require the addition of materials to carry out the hardening process. Flame hardening requires a 0.30 to 0.60% carbon structure. An acetylene torch is used to heat the material to about 1500°F when it is immediately quenched. Cast iron may also be flame hardened with this process. It should be noted that coarse-grain steels have a strong tendency to crack when subjected to this heat treatment.

In the *induction hardening* process localized heating of a specimen is accomplished with high-frequency induction coils which set up magnetic fields. Using a rapidly oscillating electric field, the resulting oscillating magnetic fields pass through the specimen, causing it to be heated. The heating is rapid and deep, hence warping is held to a minimum. The hardening is completed by quenching.

2.10. Alloy Tool Steels

Plain carbon steels lack certain necessary characteristics for use in high-speed production cutting tools, particularly red hardness, abrasive resistance, and hot strength. It is true that plain carbon steels have their place in history as cutting tools. The alloying of fundamental elements in steel is a great advantage in yielding tool steels which overcome many of the shortcomings of plain carbon steels.

Carbon is a most important alloy and determines many of the mechanical properties which may be utilized in steel. As the carbon content increases, the hardness, strength, wear resistance, and red hardness increase; the toughness and impact strength decrease.

In general, compared with alloy tool steels, carbon steel high-temperature strength and hardness are poor. They deform during hardening so that cracking and distortion take place. Also, unlike alloy steels, they do not "deep" harden.

The low-carbon steels (up to 0.35%) are used for structural steels, bars, sheet steels, etc. Medium-carbon steels (up to 0.50%) are used for forgings and high-strength steel castings. High-carbon steels are used for forgings, high-strength wire, high-strength tools, and cutting tools.

The following elements when *alloyed in tool steels* have the effects indicated:

Chromium

1. Increases hardenability, wear and abrasion resistance, and toughness.
2. Is in the medium range as a carbide former.
3. Raises the critical temperature.
4. Resists tempering.
5. Increases corrrosion and oxidation resistance.

Manganese

1. Increases the hardenability of steel cheaply because manganese is low in cost.
2. Lowers the critical temperature range so that 1% carbon and 1.5% manganese make the steel oil harden.
3. Carbide-forming tendency is greater than Fe and less than chrome.
4. Counteracts sulfur brittleness.
5. Effect upon tempering is practically nonexistent.

Molybdenum

1. Greatly increases the hardenability of steel. Its effect is greater than chrome and creates a deep-hardening steel.
2. Promotes skin decarburization if the heat treating is not carefully controlled.
3. Carbide-forming tendency is strong and it opposes softening during tempering by promoting secondary hardening.
4. Raises the grain-coarsening temperature of the austenite phase.
5. When used with chrome and vanadium, it raises the hot strength and red hardness of the steel.
6. When used with chrome, silicon, and manganese, the strength, toughness, and hardness of the steel are increased.

Silicon

1. Increases hardenability, but not as much as manganese.
2. Carbide-forming effect is less than Fe.
3. Sustains hardness during tempering.
4. Between 0.25 and 2.0% it intensifies the effects of molybdenum, manganese, and chrome.
5. Acts as a deoxidizer and increases the resistance to oxidation in steel.
6. May be alloyed for use in electrical and magnetic steels.

Nickel

1. Has some effect on hardenability, but retains some austenite in high-carbon steels, especially when the steel has a high chrome-iron content.
2. Is a weak carbide former.
3. Has no effect during tempering.
4. Increases, the toughness and strength of the core (carburizing) and permits lower hardening temperatures.

Phosphorus

1. Increases hardenability to about the same degree as manganese.
2. Increases the strength of the low-carbon steels.
3. Increases the machinability such as in the free cutting steels.
4. Has no effect on the carbide-forming tendencies, nor does it have any effect on the tempering process.
5. Increases the corrosion resistance.

Cobalt

1. Decreases hardenability when alloyed with other elements.
2. When used with tungsten, vanadium, or chrome, its red hardness increases greatly.
3. Carbide-forming tendency is about the same as Fe.
4. During tempering it sustains hardness.
5. Impairs impact strength slightly.
6. Promotes skin decarburization if not handled properly.

Tungsten

1. In low- and medium-carbon steels, hardenability is increased slightly.
2. In high-carbon steels, 4% imparts hardness and wear resistance; 18% imparts red hardness and hot strength to the steel.
3. Forms abrasive-resistant particles in tool steel.
4. Carbide-forming tendency is very strong.
5. Opposes softening during tempering by secondary hardness.

Titanium

1. Increases the austenitic hardenability.
2. Carbide-forming effect is very marked.
3. Reduces the martensitic hardness in medium-chrome steel.

Vanadium

1. Increases the hardenability of steel.
2. Very strong carbide-forming tendency.
3. Produces fine-grain steel by elevating the grain-coarsening temperature.

4. Resists tempering and increases secondary hardening in steel.

Aluminum

1. A deoxidizer when used as an alloy in steel.
2. Restricts grain growth.
3. In nitriding steels, when alloyed with chrome, it aids in the formation of complex nitrides.

2.11. Heat Treatment of High-Speed Steels

Certain steels when alloyed with tungsten, molybdenum, and approximately 0.83% carbon are classified as high-speed steels. They need a special heat-treating procedure.

After machining, the specimen is placed in a sealed pack in the presence of carbon (coke) and heated to 1600°F, soaked, and then furnace cooled. This process is called *pack annealing*. The pack-annealed specimen is then placed in an atmosphere-controlled furnace or salt bath and heated to 1400°F. From this preheat temperature the specimen is transferred into another atmosphere-controlled furnace which maintains a temperature of about 2500°F. After a time the specimen is quenched in a bath at 1100°F. Sufficient time is allowed so that the specimen will reach an equilibrium temperature throughout its structure of 1100°F. It is then removed from the 1100°F bath and cooled to room temperature in the atmosphere.

The tool is then given a secondary tempering treatment by heating it to 1100°F and cooling it in air. At times tempering is carried out in stages to take advantage of secondary hardness which may take place.

QUESTIONS AND PROBLEMS

2.1 Draw the lattice structure for each of the following: (a) BCC; (b) HCP; (c) FCC.

2.2 Explain the formation of a grain boundary when a metal solidifies from the liquid state.

2.3 Why do some regions on a photomicrograph appear white or dark? Use the light ray process to explain your answer.

2.4 Explain the 4-step procedure for preparing a specimen for metallurgical inspection with a microscope.

2.5 Why is it important to study the microstructure of a metal?

2.6 What are the components of each of the following etchants: (a) picral; (b) nital; (c) hydrofluoric acid?

2.7 Which of the etchant solutions is used to etch: (a) carbon steel; (b) cast iron; (c) aluminum; (d) medium or high-carbon steel; (e) copper?

2.8 Describe the operation of a Rockwell tester when using the "C" scale.

2.9 Why is a minor load used prior to applying the major load during the Rockwell test?

2.10 How much deeper is the indentation for two Rockwell "C" readings when they are respectively 40 R_c and 72 R_c?

2.11 List the shortcomings of the Rockwell test. Explain.

2.12 (a) If the Rockwell machine is to be used to test very thin specimens, which scale should be used? (b) Explain the characteristics of this test.

2.13 (a) What does the symbol R_c mean? (b) R_N?

2.14 Describe the operation of a Brinell tester.

2.15 Describe the operation of a Shore scleroscope.

2.16 Explain the basis used to calibrate: (a) a Rockwell tester; (b) a Brinell tester; (c) a Shore scleroscope.

2.17 Explain the use of the Universal impact tester as: (a) an Izod; (b) a tensile; (c) a Charpy tester.

2.18 Explain the development of an equilibrium diagram similar to Fig. 2.16(b). Start with the cooling curves and assume the eutectic is at 45% X and 55% Y.

2.19 Define the terms (a) eutectic; (b) eutectoid; (c) peritectic; (d) peritectoid. (e) Locate the eutectic, eutectoid, and peritectic phase changes in Fig. 2.17.

2.20 Draw the iron-iron carbide equilibrium diagram (Fig. 2.17), label the regions α, γ, δ, cm, L only. Close your book. Use the 1-2-1 rule and label all unidentified regions on the diagram.

2.21 (a) Identify the A_1, A_3, A_{cm} lines on the diagram. (b) What are their significance?

2.22 What is the carbon content of a pearlitic steel?

2.23 Define each of the following terms: (a) hypo-eutectoid; (b) hyper-eutectoid; (c) eutectoid steels.

2.24 Distinguish between the purposes of equilibrium diagrams and TTT curves.

2.25 The lattice structure of steel when heated into the austenite range is FCC. On slow cooling below 1333°F the structure is BCC. What happens to carbon atoms (a) when slow cooling takes place? (b) When fast cooling takes place?

2.26 Explain the room temperature structure of each of the cooling curves *a*, *b*, *c*, *d*, *e*, and *f* in Fig. 2.20.

2.27 How are various quenching rates achieved? Explain.

2.28 Explain the procedure followed during the Jominy end quench test. Include an explanation of the curves in Fig. 2.23.

2.29   Examine Fig. 2.22(a). What are the hardness values for the four specimens $\frac{1}{4}$ inch from the quenched ends?

2.30   Write the J numbers for Prob. 2.29.

2.31   Write the J numbers for the following readings: (a) 25 R_c at $\frac{5}{8}$ in.; (b) 50 R_c at $\frac{3}{4}$ in.; (c) 15 R_c at $1\frac{1}{2}$ in. from the quenched end.

2.32   Given the following Jominy numbers, indicate the Rockwell reading and its location: (a) $J_{20} = 5$; (b) $J_{55} = 2$; (c) $J_{25} = 28$; (d) $J_{15} = 22$.

2.33   In Fig. 2.23, a line is drawn parallel to AB through 30 R_c. Note the diameters of the bars for these readings in the four curves.

2.34   (a) Why is it impractical to use a martensitic as quenched structure? (b) What process is used to make the steel usable? (c) What does this process do to the physical properties of the steel?

2.35   (a) Explain the three tempering states. (b) Are any of the processes reversible? Explain.

2.36   (a) What is retained austenite? (b) How is it eliminated?

2.37   Distinguish between the upper- and lower-critical temperatures.

2.38   Describe the full annealing process for (a) hypo-eutectoid and (b) hypereutectoid steel. (c) What does this process accomplish?

2.39   Describe the normalizing process for (a) hypo-eutectoid and (b) hypereutectoid steel. (c) What does this process accomplish?

2.40   What does process annealing accomplish?

2.41   (a) Explain the stress relieving process. (b) What does it accomplish? (c) How does it differ from process annealing?

2.42   (a) Describe the carburizing process. (b) Why is it necessary to carburize some steels? (c) What kind of carbon penetration can be achieved? How is this accomplished?

2.43   Explain the grain growth in Fig. 2.27(a) and (b) for (a) hyper- and (b) hypoeutectoid steels.

2.44   Explain the process and importance of the diagram in Fig. 2.28.

2.45   Using the iron-iron carbide diagram in conjunction with the hypo- and the hyper-eutectoid TTT curves, analyze the heat-treating process of a carburized sample of steel. Include a discussion of grain growth in your explanation.

2.46   Describe (a) cyanide hardening; (b) carbonitriding; (c) nitride hardening. Make certain you indicate the purpose of each process.

2.47   Describe (a) flame and (b) induction hardening.

2.48   (a) Indicate the effect on the physical properties of steel when the carbon content is increased. (b) List the uses of low-, medium-, and high-carbon steels.

2.49 How do the properties of carbon steels compare with alloy steels? Explain.

2.50 What effect does the addition of each of the elements listed in Section 2.10 have on hardenability?

2.51 What is the effect of adding each of the elements listed in Section 2.10 on the formation of carbides?

2.52 What effects do the following elements have when used as alloys in tool steel? (a) molybdenum; (b) chromium; (c) tungsten; (d) vanadium; (e) manganese.

2.53 Repeat Question 2.52 for (a) silicon; (b) nickel; (c) cobalt; (d) titanium; (e) phosphorus; (f) aluminum.

2.54 (a) What is high-speed steel? (b) Explain the heat-treating process.

Patterns and Sand Molds

3

3.1. The Mechanism of Metal Solidification

One of the oldest methods of reproducing *metal objects* is the sand casting process. A cavity which has the shape of the desired object is made in sand; molten metal is poured into it and permitted to solidify. The casting thus forms the desired part and is now ready for further processing.

We must now examine the mechanism of metal freezing. Molten metal possesses a great deal of energy in the form of heat. On cooling, the greatest initial heat loss occurs at the mold wall, and this is where crystal formation begins, as the metal proceeds to a lower state of energy. This takes place wherever there are impurities which may act as nuclei for crystal growth.

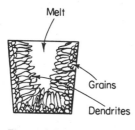

Figure 3.1

Crystal growth forms long cones in a direction perpendicular to the mold wall as shown in Fig. 3.1. The growth progresses at the liquid-solid interface. The release of heat at this interface sets up an energy balance which causes the crystal to stop growing. Other nuclei take up the process until a solid layer of metal forms at the mold walls. These crystal "fingers" are called *dendrites*. As the liquid metal loses more heat, more dendrites form, and the process continues until the entire melt is solid.

While the process is continuing, the dendrites already formed are shrinking into compact crystals, called *grains*. Slow cooling permits the dendrites to grow long, which results in a large-grain structure material. Fast cooling shrinks the dendrites into small grains and ultimately into a fine-grain structure in the solid material.

Fortunately, through the use of controlled cooling methods, the grain size can be controlled. The mold sides may be tapered so that the metal first solidifies at the bottom of the mold. Under severe cooling conditions it sometimes becomes necessary to place pieces of steel in strategic places in the mold. These steel "chills" remove heat from predetermined areas of the mold.

3.2. The Pattern

The shape of the mold cavity is produced with a pattern. Since there are many variables which are built into the pattern, it must be planned very carefully. The pattern size and shape are determined from the finished parts drawing, making allowances for finish, shrinkage, draft, warpage, etc. Other considerations are: the type of material to be cast, the casting method, and the numbers of castings to be made. These allowances and considerations all determine the type of material to be used in the pattern and its design.

As will be seen in Sect. 3.4, the mold is housed in a two-part container called a flask, Fig. 3.5(a), which separates in the center. Where the two halves of the mold separate, a seam called a *parting line*, Fig. 3.2, is created. The position of this parting line determines the orientation of the pattern in the mold. Figures 3.2(a, b, c) show three orientations of a pattern relative to the parting line. The parting line also determines the direction of the tapered side of the pattern. This taper is called *the draft* and without it, the pattern could not be removed from the mold. Figure 3.2(d) shows a pattern with incorrect draft applied; it cannot be removed from the sand mold.

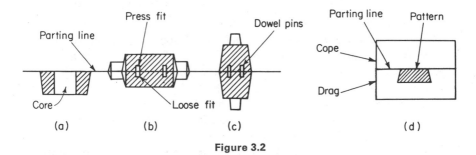

Figure 3.2

There are many types of patterns. A discussion of the various types of patterns follows:

One-piece patterns. The simplest types of patterns, these are made from one piece, as the name indicates. See Fig. 3.2(a). They usually are the same shape and size as the cast part, except for the allowances which must be provided.

They are inexpensive and used only when the required production is limited, either small runs which require reorder, or first runs which require changes.

This kind of pattern is usually made from wood. When the pattern is to be saved for a long period of time for rerun, it is usually made from metal.

Split patterns. These are two-piece patterns, Fig. 3.2(b and c), constructed so that the upper part of the pattern makes a cavity in the cope and the lower part of the pattern makes the matching cavity in the drag portion of the mold. The two parts of the pattern are aligned with dowel pins press-fitted into the cope part of the pattern. These dowel pins fit into carefully drilled holes in the drag part of the pattern. The parting line is common with the split in the pattern.

This type of pattern is used when the contour of the pattern makes it difficult or impossible to remove a one-piece pattern from the cope. It is the most widely used of all types of patterns.

Follow-board patterns. Shown in Fig. 3.3(a), these are boards made to support thin patterns while the drag is being filled with sand and rammed, a procedure which might collapse the pattern. Once the drag is rammed, the follow board is removed, the drag is inverted, and the cope is mounted on the drag, filled with sand and rammed with the pattern in position. The sand in the drag will support the pattern.

Cope and drag patterns. A type of split pattern, each part is mounted on separate metal plates which fit the respective halves of the flask. Thus both halves of the mold may be worked by two people. The gates, risers, etc. are included on the respective plates so that the entire operation is completed as one. When the two halves of the mold are closed, a complete cavity results. This method is used when the molds are so large that they cannot be handled easily.

Match-plate patterns. These are made by fastening each half of a split pattern to the opposite sides of one plate. See Fig. 3.3(b). The gates and runners are also attached to the plate. The plate is equipped with locator holes which fit the pins on the drag portion of the flask.

Once the mold is completed, the two halves of the flask are separated and the match plate removed. When the cope and drag are assembled, a mold results with gates and runners in position.

It is also possible to mount several patterns on the same plate. It is important to note that the patterns need not produce the same shape or size cavities if several patterns are mounted on the same plate.

If the two halves of the patterns are symmetrical, they may be mounted on one side of the match plate. In this instance the plate may be used twice. First, the cavity is made in the drag, inverted, and used to make the cavity in the cope. When the two halves of the flask are assembled, the cavity is complete. If the cavity needs to be made in the drag only, the plate forms the parting line of the mold.

Match plates, patterns, gates, runners, etc., are made from metal, usually cast aluminum. When making the match-plate assembly, the components are

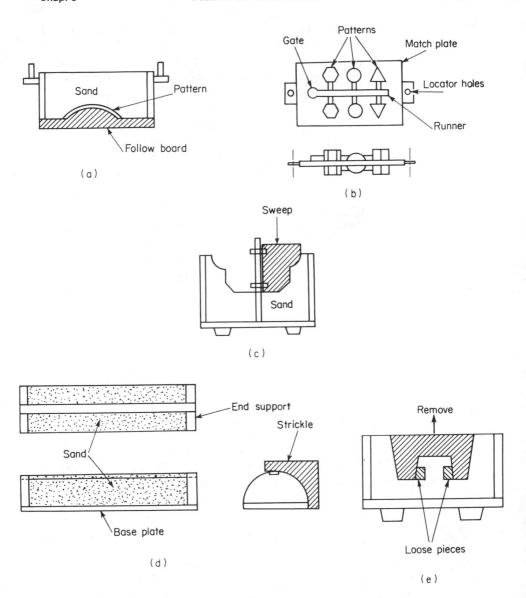

Figure 3.3

either screwed to a flat plate or made from wood integral with a wooden match plate. The entire assembly is used as a pattern to make a mold. Aluminum is poured into this mold, cleaned, and used as a match plate in the operations just described.

　　Sweep patterns.　　Forms used to sweep the desired shape into the sand mold [Fig. 3.3(c)], these eliminate the need for costly three-dimensional patterns. They may be used on green or dry sand.

Skeleton patterns. These are made as a skeleton of the desired shape and then this frame structure is mounted on a metal base. After the frame is packed with sand and shaped, the entire assembly of base plate, wood frame, and packed sand is used in the same manner as a regular one-piece pattern. Two halves may also be made. In this case the pattern may be used as a split pattern.

A skeleton pattern is made from strips of wood, as shown in Fig. 3.3(d), supported by end pieces for rigidity. The sand is packed and shaped to the desired form with a strickle. Complicated forms may be made this way for economy and lightness. Supports should be used freely to ensure that the pattern will not buckle or twist out of shape when in use. This type of pattern is only one or two large molds.

Loose-piece patterns. These are used when the pattern cannot be drawn from the mold, Fig. 3.3(e). Loose pieces are provided which can be removed separately after the main pattern has been removed. The main body of the pattern and the loose pieces form the cavity. The pattern is removed, leaving the loose pieces in the cavity. The mold is complete once the loose pieces have been removed.

3.3. Sand Technology

The factors to be controlled in the preparation of sand for making molds are clay content, moisture content, grain size, permeability, and strength of the sand and mold.

Sand used in molding is silica, the oxide of silicon. Quartz is the most commonly used of the silicas. It changes its structure as the temperature is increased. The structure which will withstand temperatures over approximately 2600°F is called *cristobalite*. This structure can be artificially produced, or it may exist at room temperature in its natural state as quartz. It is this type of quartz which is used as molding sand in the foundry.

Green sand. Molds and cores may be made from green sand, which contains about 5% moisture, and both may be baked to drive out the moisture. However, the most commonly used molds are of green sand that is not dried. They are called *green-sand molds*. They must be used soon after they are made so that their moisture content does not change. The moisture content and permeability (ability of the gases and steam to escape through the mold) may be closely controlled to prevent the trapping of gases which could cause voids in the casting.

Dry sand. The moisture having been driven out by heating or by letting the mold stand for a long period of time, this sand is completely dry. If baked, it is heated at about 350°F. Once dried, the mold is closed and the molten metal poured into the mold. This kind of mold gives a smoother cast surface and a stronger mold may be used for heavy castings.

Sometimes only the surface in contact with the molten metal is dried. This skin drying is done with a torch or may sometimes be accomplished by applying special quick-drying materials to the cavity surface. In localized heating, the surface dries rapidly but leaves the body of the mold green.

Synthetic sands are mixtures of washed and graded silica sands. They are economical because of the easy control of sand grain size and mixture. They possess high permeability and may be rammed harder than natural sands. Cereals such as ground corn, rye, or wheat are added and tend to diffuse the moisture throughout the sand, increase the ease with which a mold may be collapsed after the casting has solidified, and decrease the tendency of the sand to cling to the casting.

Synthetic sand molds also have the advantage of not having the organic matter content which natural sands possess. One of the effects of the lack of organic matter is that the synthetic molds have high refractory properties and give better surface finish to the casting.

Parting sand and parting compounds are of two general varieties: dry and liquid. Parting refers to the separation of the mold at the contact surface of the cope and drag and in some instances the cheek. To ensure good parting, the mold surface should be treated with a sand or compound. These sands or compounds are also used to permit easy withdrawal of the pattern from the mold.

Dry parting may be accomplished by dusting fine dried sand over the surfaces. Charcoal, ground bone, and limestone may also be used, but lycopodium, a yellow vegetable matter, and tripolite, a silicate rock, are the most widely used of the parting compounds. Other parting compounds are ground nutshells (walnut), chalk (a magnesium silicate), and the so-called "nonsilicate" (calcium phosphate) parting compounds.

Wet parting compounds, not used with wooden patterns, are used mostly in machine molding with metal patterns. They are wax-based preparations. Petroleum jelly mixed with oil, paraffin, and stearic acid may be used as a wet parting preparation.

Sands may be graded according to their clay content or grain size, distribution, or shape. Clay content is determined by first shaking a 50g sample of dried sand mixed with water and sodium hydroxide. A predetermined amount of water is added, allowed to settle, and the top water siphoned off. This is repeated until the water is clear. The sand is heated to drive off the remaining water and weighed. The weight difference from the original sand sample is the clay content. If the retained sample weighs 44.8g the

$$clay\ content = 100 - 2(44.8) = 10.4\%$$

Grain sizes are classified using a set of screens standardized by the U.S. Bureau of Standards (No. 6, 12, 20, 30, 40, 50, 70, 100, 140, 200, 270, and pan).

These sieves are stacked with the number 6 sieve at the top. A 50g sample is placed in the top sieve and shaken for a predetermined period of time. The last sieve through which the grains pass determines the grain size. Thus grains which pass through a 50 sieve but not through a 70 sieve have a 50-mesh grain size.

The sand retained in each sieve is weighed and calculated as a percentage of 50g, which when multiplied by a factor yields a distribution number. The sum of the distribution numbers divided by the sand remaining is the grain fineness number. From Table 3.1

$$\text{the grain fineness number} = \frac{\text{distribution number}}{\text{sum of the retained sample, }\%}$$

$$= \frac{7831.6}{89.8} = 87.2$$

TABLE 3.1

Screen no.	Opening, in.	Retained sample		Multiplier	Distribution no.
		Wt, g	% of 50		
6	0.1320	0.10	0.2	3	0.6
12	0.0661	0.30	0.6	5	3.0
20	0.0331	1.60	3.2	10	32.0
30	0.0232	3.60	7.2	20	144.0
40	0.0165	5.40	10.8	30	324.0
50	0.0117	7.80	15.6	40	624.0
70	0.0083	9.20	15.8	50	790.0
100	0.0059	6.10	12.2	70	854.0
140	0.0041	3.80	7.6	100	760.0
200	0.0029	1.50	3.0	140	420.0
270	0.0021	1.00	2.0	200	400.0
Pan		5.80	11.6	300	3480.0
Totals		46.20	89.8		7831.6

It is a number which defines the average grain size retained in a sample.

The *grain distribution* number defines the distribution of the grains. Thus it is possible to have the same grain sizes distributed in different percentages of concentration. It is read from a graph of U.S. Sieve Number as the abscissa plotted against the percentage of retained sand as the ordinate as shown in the graph, Fig. 3.4(a). *Grain shapes* are also classified by the American Foundrymen's Association as angular, subangular, round, and compound.

Strength and permeability.   These are related to the moisture content of a sand sample which should be about 7%. Once the moisture content is determined to be correct, the permeability and the strength of the sand may be controlled by adding clay or new molding sand. The strength is defined as the ability of the sand to hold together. Permeability is the ability of the sand to allow gases to pass through its structure.

As the sample of sand is rammed, its hardness increases, its strength

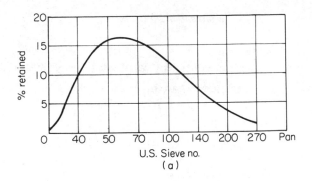

(a)

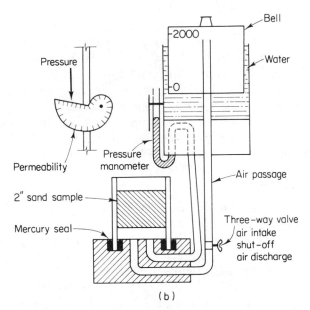

(b)

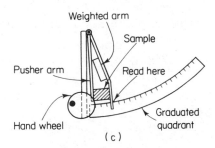

(c)

(d)

Figure 3.4

increases, and its permeability decreases. Ideally, a compromise must be reached for optimum strength consistent with optimum permeability.

Hardness. This is tested with an instrument which records depth of penetration of a needle into the mold. It is graduated from 0 to 100, and a reading of 50 is average hardness.

Moisture content. This may be determined through the use of the conductivity of electricity through wet sand, by blowing air through a standard sample which has been heated, or by weighing a 100g sample of sand, heating it, and determining the loss of weight.

The better method for determining the moisture content is to ram up a standard sample (163g) of sand in a 2-in.-diameter tube. If the moisture content is correct, the height of the sand slug will be 2 in. If the moisture content is high, the sample will ram up to less than 2 in. If the moisture content is too low, the sample will ram up more than 2 in.

The ramming must be controlled. The rammer weighs 14 lb and is dropped three times from a fixed height. Before ramming an indicator is set at zero to designate a 2-in. height. The permissible variation from 2 in. is ± 0.010 in. and sand with a moisture content outside these limits may not be used in a mold. The advantage of this test is that the 2-in. sample of rammed sand may be used to test the permeability and strength of the sand.

Permeability. Using the rammed sample just discussed and the Dietert permeability machine, Fig. 3.4(b), permeability is determined by passing a given volume of air through an orifice and then through the sample. Once the passage of air stabilizes, the pressure in the manometer stabilizes. The spiral calibrated scale yields the permeability number.

If an orifice is not used the 0–2000 cm³ bell may be used. Once it stabilizes the pressure is read from the vertical scale. As the 0 mark passes the top of the tank a stop watch is started. The time it takes the bell to pass the 2000 cm³ mark is recorded. The values of pressure and time are inserted into the permeability equation

$$P = \frac{Vh}{Apt} = \frac{2000(5.08)}{20.268\,pt}$$
$$= \frac{501.2}{pt}$$

P = permeability
V = volume of air
   = 2000 cm³ = 122 in.³
h = height of sample
   = 5.08 cm = 2 in.
A = area
   = 20.268 cm²
   = 3.1416 in.²
p = pressure, g/cm²; lb/in.²
t = time, min

EXAMPLE 1

The pressure on a manometer gage is 5.15 g/cm² and the time on a stop watch is 1 minute, 25 seconds when the 2000 cm³ mark is passed. Calculate the permeability of the sand.

Solution:

The permeability is

$$P = \frac{501.2}{pt} = \frac{501.2}{5.15 \times 1.42}$$

$$= 68.5$$

$p = 5.15 \text{ g/cm}^2$
$t = 1'25'' = 1.42 \text{ min}$

The same rammed sample may also be used to test compressive strength, Fig. 3.4(c), and shear strength, Fig. 3.4(d).

3.4.　The Molding Tools

The mold is housed in a *flask*, Fig. 3.5(a), which consists of two parts. The upper part of the flask is called the *cope*. The lower part is called the *drag*. If the pattern is too high, an intermediate section, called the *cheek* (not shown) may be inserted between the cope and the drag. In the normal position the flask is placed so that the drag rests on a *bottom board*.

The face board.　This is a flat, rectangular board [Fig. 3.5(b)] used when the molding operation is begun. When using a split pattern, the drag half of the pattern is placed face down on the face board to permit ramming the molding sand into the drag.

The bottom board.　When made from wood, the bottom board is similar in appearance to the face board except that its surface is rough. If made from metal, its surface is perforated. The purpose of the roughness or perforations is to prevent the sand mold from slipping during the molding operation.

The riddle.　This is a round sieve made from wood with a wire-mesh bottom. See Fig. 3.5(c). As the sand is being sifted into the flask, lumps of sand, metal, and other foreign materials are trapped by the riddle.

The trowel.　Shown in Fig. 3.5(d), the trowel is a long, flat metal plate fitted with an offset handle. It is usually 6 in. long by 2 in. wide and is used to flatten and smooth the sand during the molding operation.

The slick.　Used to make or repair corners in a mold, it is made in various shapes and sizes each to suit some particular need. The most common shape is that of a spoon which has been flattened. See Fig. 3.5(e).

The lifter.　This is a flat bar about 1 in. wide by 15 in. long, Fig. 3.5(f). About 2 in. from the end the bar is bent into a 90° angle. It is used to scoop sand from deep in the mold.

The bellows.　The common fireplace variety of bellows, Fig. 3.5(g), is used to blow excess sand or dusting compound from the mold. The gentle action of the air stream keeps the mold from being damaged.

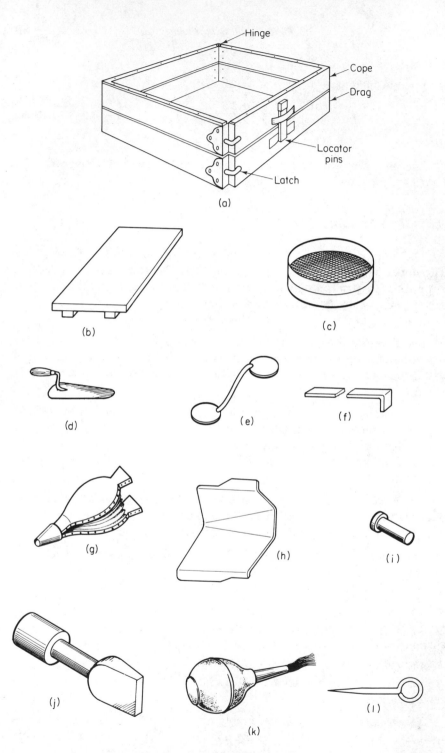

Figure 3.5

The gate cutter.   Used to cut gates into the mold, it is usually made from flat copper or brass bent into a 120° angle and tapered toward the end. See Fig. 3.5(h). It may also be used to shape the gate basin.

The gate pin.   This cylindrical wooden pin has a head at one end, Fig. 3.5(i). The pin is placed in the desired location in a vertical position before the cope is rammed with sand to form the downgate, or sprue.

Rammers.   These are wooden handles fitted with large cylindrical wooden heads at one end and blunt chisel-shaped sections at the other end, Fig. 3.5(j). They are used for tamping the sand around the pattern and over the mold.

Swabs.   These are rubber bulbs with strands of camel hair inserted into the bulb opening, Fig. 3.5(k). The soft hair is used to swab the edges of the mold cavity with small amounts of water before the pattern is drawn. This prevents the edges from breaking off during the drawing operation. Swabs are also made from hemp in the form of long, soft brushes.

Draw spikes and screws.   Shown in Fig. 3.5(l), these are used to lift the pattern out of the mold cavity. The draw spike is driven into the cavity with care. The spike is fitted with an "eye" to permit gripping. Lifting screws are screwed into the surface to provide a means of drawing the pattern.

Vent wires.   Wires $\frac{1}{16}$ of an inch in diameter are used to punch holes into the mold to facilitate the escape of gases during the pouring operation.

3.5. The Mold and the Molding Operation

When the metal is poured into the *pouring basin*, Fig. 3.6(d), it will flow into the cavity formed by the pattern. Once the metal has solidified, the resulting casting will take the shape of the mold cavity. If the casting is to have a hole, a *core* is placed into the cavity as shown in Fig. 3.6(d). The casting is then said to have a *cored hole.*

The molten metal flows from the upper basin into a round hole called the *sprue*. It enters a lower basin and flows over a *gate* into the mold cavity. The purpose of the gate is to reduce turbulence. At times a riser is provided to permit gases to escape and to ensure fluidity until the mold cavity is full of molten metal before solidification takes place.

The following is a step-by-step analysis for making a sand mold with the split pattern, Fig. 3.6(a).

1. Place the molding board on the sand floor so that its surface is level. Place the drag half of the flask on the molding board, pins down, as shown in Fig. 3.6(b). Place the drag half of the pattern (without the locator pins) flat side down on the molding board. The pattern should be offset about 3 in. from the side of the drag walls.

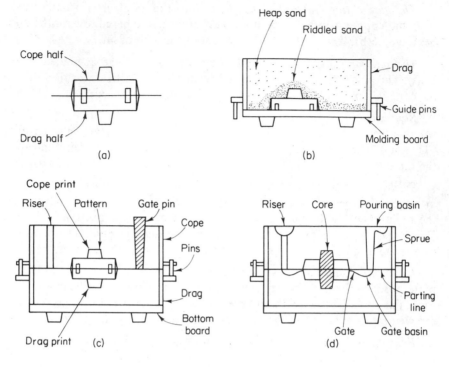

Figure 3.6

2. Using the riddle, sift about 1 in. of sand over the pattern and the molding board. Fill the drag with heap sand, and ram the sand around the edge of the mold. Ramming over or too close to the pattern may damage it. It should also be remembered that the sand must "breath" during the pouring operation. The sand should not be packed too hard.

Refill the drag with heap sand, ram, and strike off the excess sand using a flat bar and the top edges of the drag as guides. The striking operation should make the top of the sand mold even with the top of the drag. It should be noted that after the first ramming the sand may be rammed over the pattern. With a vent wire poke vent holes into the sand mold. These vent holes may be made anywhere in the mold, especially over the pattern and to the full depth of the drag.

3. Push the bottom board firmly into the sand floor making certain it is level. Roll the flask over, pins up, and place it upon the bottom board with the pattern exposed. Slick the sand edges toward the pattern. Place the cope half of the pattern so that the pins line up with the exposed drag half of the pattern. Place the cope half of the flask on the drag so that the pins are in the position shown in Fig. 3.6(c).

4. Dusting compound or parting sand is dusted over the drag surface. The gate pin is placed in position about 2 in. away from the pattern.

One inch of sand is riddled over the pattern and mold surface. The cope is filled with heap sand, rammed, refilled, rammed again, and the excess sand struck off level with the top of the cope. Vent all over.

5. Remove the gate pin, and cut the riser with a thin-wall, 1-in. diameter piece of brass tubing. Then cut the pouring basin and the opening (head) for the riser [see Fig. 3.6(d)]. Cut the pouring basin in the cope for the sprue.

6. Remove the cope, and blow the excess sand from the face of the drag. Draw the pattern in the cope and the drag. Cut the gate and basin for the sprue and the riser. Press the sand down in the gate basin so that it is firm to prevent loose sand from getting into the mold when the metal stream strikes the gate basin. Using the bellows and the lifters, blow and remove all excess sand from the mold cavity. Dust blacking compound (plumbago) on the mold gate and cavity. This gives the cast surface a smoother finish. Place the core in position.

7. Put the cope on the drag in the original position, and set the flask and mold on the foundry floor. It should be level. Cover the pouring basin with a canvas, remove the flask, and put a pouring jacket on the mold. This will support the sidewalls of the mold during the pouring operation. The covering may now be removed. Place a weight on top of the mold to counteract the buoyant force in the mold when the liquid metal is poured into the mold cavity. The weights have openings through which the molten metal may be poured.

8. Pour the metal into the mold. Allow it to solidify. Remove the jacket. Break up the mold. Cut the risers, sprues, and gates off the casting. Sandblast.

3.6. Gates, Sprues, Risers

The purpose of the *gate*, Fig. 3.6(d), is to feed the casting at a rate consistent with the rate of solidification. If the casting solidifies slowly, the gates must be made small. The possibility of a small gate freezing and choking off the flow of molten metal becomes greater as the gate becomes smaller. If the feeding is to be increased because of a faster solidification rate, the gate should be made larger. For the cross section of a gate, see Fig. 3.7(a). If one gate is insufficient to feed a fast-freezing casting, several gates may be introduced, feeding off one sprue.

All edges of the gate should be rounded to prevent pieces of sand from breaking off and being carried into the mold cavity. Sharp edges may also cause localized delay in freezing, which may result in the formation of inclusions or voids in the casting.

The gate basin acts as a reservoir for molten metal. It prevents turbulent molten metal from entering the gate and traps loose sand and other particles which are undesirable.

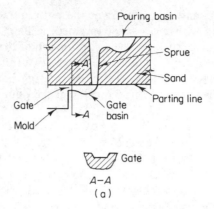

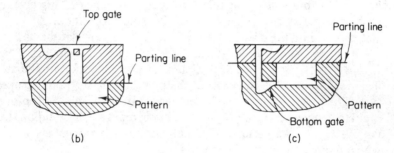

Figure 3.7

Gates may be built into the pattern or cut, as indicated in Section 3.5 with a gate cutter. They may be cut at the parting line, Fig. 3.6(a), into the top of the mold, Fig. 3.7(b), or into the bottom of the mold, Fig. 3.7(c). Gates cut at the parting line are the most desirable.

Top gates and bottom gates may have very serious effects on the quality of the casting produced unless designed very carefully. Pouring directly into the mold cavity can be controlled by restricting the metal flow at the top to prevent too much metal from entering the cavity at once, which creates high turbulence in the mold. Bottom gates permit the melt to enter the mold cavity at the bottom. If freezing takes place at the bottom, it could choke off the metal flow before the mold is full. Risers inserted between the gate and the mold with large openings into the side of the mold cavity may help feed the casting.

Sprues.   Usually made round in cross section [Fig. 3.6(d)], these should also be as small in cross section as is consistent with easy filling of the mold cavity. They should permit enough metal to flow so as not to starve the feeding process. They should also be vertical, without any change in direction, so that the gate section is fed directly.

Risers.   These should be round in cross section and about equal in depth to the largest diameter, as shown in Fig. 3.6(d). Thus the riser basin should hold enough metal to feed the casting with the metal not supplied by the sprue. Since metal freezes at the mold walls first, the center of large castings may still be liquid when the flow of molten metal is cut off at the sprue gate. This trapped melt contracts as it solidifies. If molten metal is not added as the inner solidification progresses, a void will be left and an imperfect casting will result. Thus the molten metal in the riser helps feed the casting until all solidification takes place. Metal melt may be poured into the riser and "pumped" with a rod to keep the melt in motion. Turbulent metal or flowing metal takes longer to solidify than nonturbulent melt.

3.7. Cores

As indicated earlier, *cores* serve the purpose of creating planned obstructions in a mold cavity. Recesses are built into the mold which hold sand bars, called cores, in position. The recesses are made by additions to the pattern. These additions are called *core prints*, Fig. 3.8(a). They do not appear in the casting which results from the molding operation.

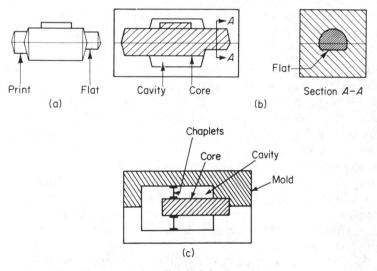

Figure 3.8

Cope and drag prints.   Used as shown in Fig. 3.6(c), the drag print is integral with or fastened to the pattern so that it is removed with the pattern. It needs very little draft and should be long enough to support the core. The length should be equal to the diameter of the print up to 1 in. of diameter. Its length should not exceed 1 in. for diameters over 1 in.

Parting line prints.   These are made integral with the pattern, being inserted into the mold in a horizontal position. If orientation is important, some means for ensuring that the core can be placed into the mold in one position must be taken. Figure 3.8(a and b) show the prints, core, and orientation of the core.

The cope print.   This is made to fit loosely in the pattern so that it will remain in the cope half of the flask when the flask is opened. When the cope half of the flask is placed upon the drag, the core cavity in the cope must pick up the core easily. For this reason the cope print usually has about a 15° draft angle. Up to about $1\frac{1}{4}$ in. in diameter, the length of the body of the print equals the diameter. For diameters greater than $1\frac{1}{4}$ in., the length should be $1\frac{1}{2}$ in.

Overhanging core prints.   These are made on one side of the pattern to make an impression which will support a core that must extend into the mold cavity. If the casting requires a blind hole, an overhanging core may be used. If the core overhang is not too long, it may be supported by the sand itself. If the core overhang is too long, it may be supported by the mold at one end and by small metal chaplets at the other end. This is shown in Fig. 3.8(c).

Cores may be made from green sand or from dry sand. When the core is made by the pattern from the molding sand, as shown in Fig. 3.2(a), the core is said to be a *green-sand* core. Since green sand is not very strong, the core made this way has limitations as to length and thickness. It also needs more draft than the main body of the pattern to aid in the drawing of the pattern.

Dry-sand cores.   Shaped in a separate box, they must be strong enough to withstand the pressures set up by turbulent molten metal but weak enough to collapse as the melt solidifies and shrinks. It is also necessary that they break up easily after the casting has been removed from the mold. They must be porous enough to permit gases to pass through them but they must not generate their own gases.

The process for making a dry-sand core requires that the sand be free from clay. The sand is mixed with a binder such as linseed oil, rosin, core oil, or gums and packed into the preshaped core box. The box is opened and the core removed and baked in an oven at about 350 to 550°F. The baking temperature is important as there is an optimum temperature at which maximum strength is developed.

It should be noted that a commercial binder of silicate of soda is rapidly replacing the binders described above, even though it is more expensive. Its one advantage is that there is no need to bake the core. In this process the sand is mixed with about 5% silicate of soda and rammed into the core box. Carbon dioxide is then blown under pressure into the core. This hardens it. The core is removed and used in the intended manner.

Dry-sand core boxes are made from wood or metal. All requirements of draft and shrinkage are applied to the box in the same manner as in pattern making. It should be remembered that dry-sand cores before baking are soft and must be supported until the drying process is complete. Thus the size and shape of the core dictates the design, type, and construction of the core box.

If the core is capable of supporting itself while drying and on end, a simple box is used, as shown in Fig. 3.9(a). The two halves of the box are fitted with locator dowels. A variation of this kind of core box is the rectangular box shown in Fig. 3.9(b). It separates at the two opposite corners.

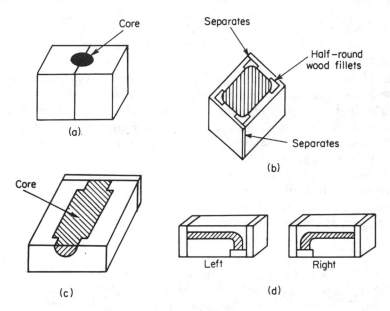

Figure 3.9

Cores which will sag during the drying process may be made in a half core box, Fig. 3.9(c). This provides a flat surface upon which the core may rest while being baked. This type of core box may be used when the core is symmetrical about a center plane. After drying has been completed, the two halves are fastened together with glue or wires to form the whole core. Sometimes wires are used internally to strengthen the core before and after drying, and also for support during drying.

If the core is not symmetrical about the parting plane, a right- and left-hand core box may be made, as shown in Fig. 3.9(d). Each half is made in its own core box. After baking they are fastened together.

Other types of core boxes employ strickles to form the intricate shapes in the core sand, loose pieces, or frames. The making of a core may be much more complicated than the making of the pattern itself. A complete pattern includes the pattern and all the necessary core boxes and loose pieces.

Sometimes a core blowing machine is used to blow core sand into the core box. Uniform cross section cores may be extruded by a core extruding machine. These machines may extrude cores with a center hole used for venting.

3.8. Mold Pressures

There are many forces operating in a mold during the molding process. The weight of the molten liquid metal, which eventually solidifies and becomes the casting, exerts a force on the drag. The turbulence of the hot metal and the column of liquid in the sprue exert forces on the core and mold.

When an object is placed in a liquid, an upward buoyant force is exerted upon the object by the liquid. This force is transmitted equally in all directions. If a core is placed in the mold, this buoyant force is exerted on the core as well as on the sides, top, and bottom of the mold.

The drag must be strong enough to withstand all these forces. The cope must be strong and weigh enough to prevent the cope from being "floated." If there is any doubt that the mold will stay together, a weight must be placed on top of it.

It should also be remembered that when hot molten metal comes in contact with moisture, steam is generated. This steam creates forces which must be released by venting. The following illustrated example will demonstrate the magnitude of these forces.

EXAMPLE 2

Assume a flask 14 by 14 by 12 in. deep, shown in Fig. 3.10(a). The depth of the cope and drag are each 6 in. A cast iron bar, 3 by 4 by 5 in. long is to be cast. The weight of cast iron is 0.28 lb/in.^{3}, and the weight of sand is 0.06 lb/in.^{3} Calculate the following: (1) the magnitude of force of the casting on the drag; (2) the buoyant force on the cope; (3) the weight of the sand in the cope; (4) the net force at the liquid-sand interface; (5) the force at the bottom of the mold.

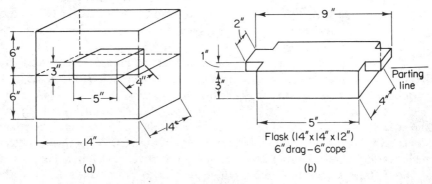

(a)   (b)

Figure 3.10

Solution:

1. The force of the casting on the drag

$$W_c = V w_m = (4 \times 5 \times 3)(0.28)$$
$$= 16.8 \text{ lb} \downarrow$$

2. The lifting force on the cope results from the longitudinal area of the mold cavity, the head pressure at the gate of the column of liquid in the sprue, and the weight of the metal.

$$F_c = A h_1 w_m = (4 \times 5)(6)(0.28)$$
$$= 33.6 \text{ lb} \uparrow$$

W_c = weight of the casting
W_{sc} = weight sand in cope
W_m = sp. wt. of metal
     = 0.28 lb/in.^{3}
W_s = sp. wt. of sand
     = 0.06 lb/in.^{3}
F_c = force on cope
F_d = force on drag
h_1 = head pressure—sprue
     = 6 in.
h_2 = head pressure at bottom of drag
     = (6 + 3) = 9 in.

3. The weight of the sand in the core is

$$W_{sc} = V w_s = (14 \times 14 \times 6)(0.06)$$
$$= 70.6 \downarrow$$

4. The net force at the liquid-cope interface is

$$W_{sc} - F_c = 70.6 - 33.6 = 37 \text{ lb} \downarrow$$

5. The force at the bottom of the mold cavity is

$$F_d = A h_2 w_m = (4 \times 5)(6 + 3)(0.28)$$
$$= 50.4 \text{ lb} \downarrow$$

EXAMPLE 3

Assume the same conditions as in Example 2, except that a core 9 in. long by 2 in. wide by 1 in. thick is inserted in the cavity as shown in Fig. 3.10(b). Calculate: (1) The net force on the core and (2) the net force on the cope. (3) Is a weight needed?

Solution:

1. The net force on the core is calculated as follows:
   a. The weight of the core is

   $$W_k = V w_s = (2 \times 1 \times 9)(0.06)$$
   $$= 1.1 \text{ lb} \downarrow$$

   W_k = weight of the core
   F_k = force on the core
   h_3 = head pressure on the core

   b. The upward force on the core is

   $$F_k = A_c h_3 w_m = (5 \times 2)(7)(0.28)$$
   $$= 19.6 \text{ lb} \uparrow$$

   h_3 = 6 + 1 = 7 in.

   c. The net force on the core is

   $$F_k - W_k = 19.6 - 1.1$$
   $$= 18.5 \text{ lb} \uparrow$$

2. The net force on the cope is obtained as follows:
   a. The upward force on the cope area segment is

   $$F_c = 2Ah_1w_m = 2(1 \times 5)(6)(0.28)$$
   $$= 16.8 \text{ lb} \uparrow$$

   b. The total lifting force is

   $$F_c + (F_k - W_k) = 16.8 + (19.5 - 1.1)$$
   $$= 35.3 \text{ lb} \uparrow$$

   c. The weight of the sand in the cope is the same as in Example 1.

   $$W_{sc} = 70.6 \text{ lb} \downarrow$$

   d. The net force is in favor of the weight of the cope.

   $$\text{Net } F_c = 70.6 - 35.3$$
   $$= 35.3 \text{ lb} \downarrow$$

3. No weight is needed since the weight of the sand in the cope exceeds the sum of the upward forces acting on the cope and the core.

3.9. Estimated Weight of the Casting

In many instances the weight of a casting needs to be known when only the pattern is available. Two methods may be used to find the weight of the casting.

One method is to find the volume (in cubic inches) of the pattern and then multiply this volume by the specific weight of the casting material as shown in Table 3.2.

TABLE 3.2

Casting Material Factors

Pattern mat.	Cast iron	Aluminum	Brass	Zinc
White pine*	16.5	5.8	19.0	15.0
Yellow pine	14.0	4.2	16.0	12.0
Cherry	10.4	3.8	13.0	10.0
Mahogany	12.5	4.5	14.0	12.0
Aluminum	2.8	1.0	3.3	2.7
Cast iron	1.0	0.4	1.2	0.9
Dry core sand	4.0	1.4	4.8	3.6
Sp. wt., lb/in.^{3}	0.2778	0.09375	0.3112	0.2532

*Sp. wt. of white pine = 0.017 lb/in.^{3}

EXAMPLE 4

Assume that the pattern in Fig. 3.11(b) is a pattern to be used to make a cast iron part, Fig. 3.11(a). Calculate the weight of the casting using the volume method.

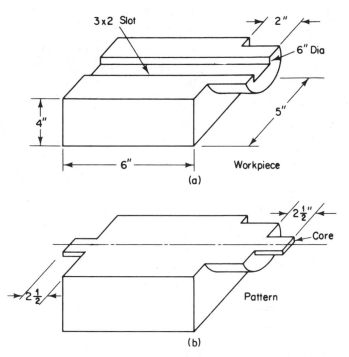

Figure 3.11

Solution:

1. The volume of the body of the pattern is

$$W \times H \times L = 5 \times 4 \times 6 = 120 \text{ in.}^3$$

$D = $ dia.—in.
$V_n = $ net volume—in.^{3}
$w = $ sp. wt.—lb/in.^{3}
$W_c = $ weight of casting—lb

2. The volume of the semi-circular boss is

$$V = \frac{\pi D^2 L}{4} = \frac{\pi 6^2}{4}(2) = 56.5 \text{ in.}^3$$

3. The volume of the keyway is

$$W \times H \times L = 3 \times 2 \times 8 = 48 \text{ in.}^3$$

4. The net volume is

$$V_n = 120.0 + 56.5 - 48.0 = 128.5 \text{ in.}^3$$

5. The weight of the casting is

$$W_c = V_m w = 128.5(0.2778)$$
$$= 35.7 \text{ lb}$$

The weight of a casting may also be found by multiplying the weight of the wood pattern by a constant. These constants are shown in Table 3.1. Thus

$$W_c = K_p W_p$$

W_c = weight of casting—lb
W_p = weight of pattern—lb
K_p = constant

EXAMPLE 5

Calculate the weight of an aluminum casting if a cherry wood pattern from which the casting is made weighs 18 lb.

Solution:

The weight of the casting is

$$W_c = K_p W_p = 3.8(18)$$
$$= 68.4 \, \text{lb}$$

W_p = 18 lb
K_p = 3.8 (Table 3.2)

EXAMPLE 6

Calculate the weight of the casting in Example 5 if the casting is cored and the sand core weighs 3 lb.

Solution:

The weight of the cored casting is

$$W_c = K_p W_p - K_s W_s$$
$$= (3.8 \times 18) - (1.4 \times 3)$$
$$= 64.2 \, \text{lb}$$

W_s = 3 lb
W_p = 18 lb
K_s = 1.4
K_p = 3.8 (Table 3.2)

3.10. Finish Allowances

Casting surfaces which are to be machined must have metal added. The amount to be added is a function of the size and shape of the casting, the type of metal used, the machining operation, the number of cuts to be taken, and the casting conditions.

Obviously, if several cuts are to be taken, more material must be added to the casting. If the casting is to be made from iron or steel, it will have a scale, and this must be taken into consideration. If the casting is to be nonferrous, allowance for scale need not be considered. In the cases where warping is expected, more material must be allowed to ensure that the casting can be cleaned up.

The finishing allowance may be $\frac{1}{8}$ in. for most medium-size cast iron castings. For larger castings the allowance can range up to $\frac{3}{4}$ in. Brass and aluminum have allowances which vary from $\frac{1}{32}$ to $\frac{1}{8}$ in. It is to be noted that diameters will have double allowance because opposite sides of a diameter must be cleaned up.

EXAMPLE 7

In Fig. 3.12(a), note the surfaces to be machined. They are marked with a finishing (f) mark. Add the allowances to the dimension.

Solution:

The finishing allowance for cast iron is $\frac{1}{8}$ in. See Fig. 3.10(b).

1. The 6 in. nominal diameter becomes

$$6 + 2(\tfrac{1}{8}) = 6\tfrac{1}{4} \text{ in.}$$

2. The 4 in. nominal diameter becomes

$$4 + 2(\tfrac{1}{8}) = 4\tfrac{1}{4} \text{ in.}$$

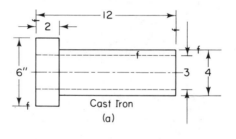

Cast Iron
(a)

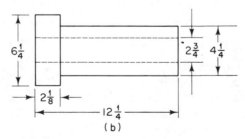

(b)

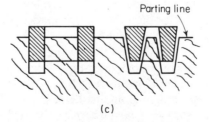

Parting line

(c)

Figure 3.12

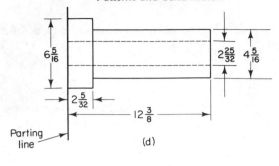

Parting
line

(d)

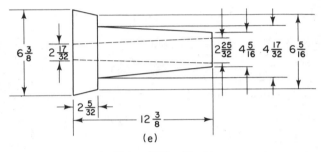

(e)

Figure 3.12   (Cont.)

3. The 3 in. hole becomes

$$3 - 2(\tfrac{1}{8}) = 2\tfrac{3}{4} \text{ in.}$$

4. The 12 in. overall length becomes

$$12 + 2(\tfrac{1}{8}) = 12\tfrac{1}{4} \text{ in.}$$

5. The 2 in. shoulder needs to be finished on one face. It becomes

$$2 + \tfrac{1}{8} \times 2\tfrac{1}{8} \text{ in.}$$

3.11. Shrinkage Allowances

Shrinkage of metal on cooling is related to the material in the casting, the design and size of the casting, the temperature of the melt, and to some extent the molding conditions.

Brass will shrink more than cast iron but less than steel. The softer grades of cast iron will shrink less than the harder grades. Cast iron poured *cold* will shrink less than cast iron poured *hot*.

Confined castings will shrink less than those which are restrained by the mold or core. Thus a cast bushing which has a cored hole will be restrained by the core but unrestrained along its length centerline. More allowance will be needed along its length than along its diameter.

Wood patterns used to cast *metal patterns* need double allowances for shrinkage. One allowance is needed to take care of the shrinkage in the cast metal pattern; the other allowance is needed to take care of the shrinkage in the casting to be made from the metal pattern.

Because of the variations mentioned above, shrinkage allowances are usually given as a range. In general the shrinkages listed in Table 3.3 may be used and the appropriate metal added to the dimension. The dimension used

TABLE 3.3

Materials	*Shrinkage allow. in./ft*
Cast iron	1/8
Steel	1/4
Aluminum	5/32
Brass	3/16
Magnesium	5/32

should not be in increments smaller than $\frac{1}{32}$ in. The theoretical dimension when corrected to the nearest $\frac{1}{32}$ in. should be *added* in the direction of more metal. Thus shrinkage allowances should be made by adding to the dimension for outside dimensions and subtracted from internal dimensions.

It is possible to buy shrinkage rules which are longer than standard rules. The allowance is built into the rule. A shrinkage 12-in. rule for layout of a pattern to be used to cast an iron casting is $\frac{1}{8}$ in. longer than a standard rule.

EXAMPLE 8

Using Fig. 3.12(b), allow $\frac{3}{32}$ in./ft (0.0078 in./in.) for confined shrinkage in the cored hole. The allowance for cast iron, in Table 3.3, is $\frac{1}{8}$ in./ft (0.0104 in./in.) of length. Calculate the corrected dimensions. They are shown in Fig. 3.12(c).

Solution:

1. The 6 in. nominal diameter becomes
$$6\tfrac{1}{4} + (\tfrac{6.250}{12} \times \tfrac{1}{8}) \simeq 6\tfrac{5}{16}$$

2. The 4 in. nominal diameter becomes
$$4\tfrac{1}{4} + (\tfrac{4.250}{12} \times \tfrac{1}{8}) \simeq 4\tfrac{5}{16}$$

3. The 3 in. hole becomes
$$2\tfrac{3}{4} + (\tfrac{2.750}{12} \times \tfrac{3}{32}) \simeq 2\tfrac{25}{32}$$

4. The 12 in. nominal overall length becomes
$$12\tfrac{1}{4} + (\tfrac{12.250}{12} \times \tfrac{1}{8}) \simeq 12\tfrac{3}{8}$$

5. The 2 in. nominal shoulder becomes
$$2\tfrac{1}{8} + (\tfrac{2.125}{12} \times \tfrac{1}{8}) = 2\tfrac{5}{32}$$

3.12. Draft Allowances

Draft allowance refers to the taper applied to the pattern to facilitate drawing the pattern out of the mold without damage to the mold. The largest cross section of the pattern is applied at the parting line. See Fig. 3.12(d). Internally the reverse is true.

If no draft were applied, as in Fig. 3.12(c), the pattern would be in contact with the sand mold all the time that it is being withdrawn from the mold. This could damage the mold. In Fig. 3.12(d), the instant the pattern is moved, it comes free from contact with the sand mold. Note that when dealing with tapers applied to outside surfaces, the smallest dimension should not be less than the finished casting dimension.

In general $\frac{1}{8}$ in./ft of surface to be drawn is applied to *each side* of the pattern. The taper may be less than $\frac{1}{8}$ in./ft for small castings. As a general rule the amount of draft is a function of the length of the contact surface to be withdrawn from the mold. Also, if the pattern is complicated, it might require more draft, possibly as much as $\frac{1}{4}$ in./ft. Internal draft may range to as much as $\frac{3}{4}$ in./ft.

EXAMPLE 9

Using the dimensions in Fig. 3.12(c), calculate the dimensions for draft. Allow $\frac{1}{8}$ in./ft for external dimensions and $\frac{1}{4}$ in./ft for internal dimensions. The dimensions are shown in Fig. 3.12(e).

Solution:

From Fig. 3.12(c)

1. The 6 in. nominal diameter becomes

$$6\tfrac{5}{16} + 2(\tfrac{0.125}{12} \times 2\tfrac{5}{32}) \simeq 6\tfrac{3}{8} \text{ in.}$$

2. The 4 in. nominal shoulder becomes

$$4\tfrac{5}{16} + 2[\tfrac{0.125}{12}(12\tfrac{3}{8} - 2\tfrac{5}{32})] \simeq 4\tfrac{17}{32} \text{ in.}$$

3. The hole diameter becomes

$$2\tfrac{25}{32} - 2(\tfrac{0.125}{12} \times 12\tfrac{3}{8}) = 2\tfrac{17}{32} \text{ in.}$$

3.13. Distortion, Shake, and Machining Bosses

Distortion. This takes place in irregular-shaped castings, usually when part of the casting shrinks while the other part (end) is restricted, such as "V" and "U" shapes. Long, flat castings will also distort. The amount and type of distortion and the allowance for the distortion should be taken care of by the foundry. The reasons for and the place where distortions can take place are best known to the experienced foundryman.

Shake. This is a result of rapping patterns to loosen them in the mold so that they may be easily removed. The rapping operation enlarges the cavity. In large castings this may be considerable and therefore should be provided for. In small castings it may usually be ignored.

The amount of rapping may usually be reduced by increasing the draft. Shake allowances should be subtracted from the pattern dimensions. Since

rapping is done in the foundry and since every foundry has its own characteristics, the amount of rapping allowance should be left to the foundryman.
At the very least the foundry which will make the castings should be consulted.

Machining bosses.   Additions which usually do not appear in the
finished parts print, these may be in the form of bosses, lugs, or recesses which
aid in the handling of the casting. Locator bosses for banking in a fixture may
help and make for better machining practices. Lugs may be added to aid in
clamping. Sometimes clearances and reliefs may be added to the pattern when
such are difficult to machine into the casting.

3.14. Pattern Materials

The selection of the materials to be used in a pattern depends upon the
use the pattern is to receive and the number of castings to be made. Pattern
material must withstand moisture, rough handling, wear, ramming, and
rapping. Because sand is abrasive, wood patterns are coated to resist this type
of damage. The coating must also be moisture resistant, otherwise warping,
shrinkage, or swelling may occur. Rapping and ramming are shock type load-
ings which could damage or change the shape of a pattern. Materials which
are used in pattern making are wood, metal, and plaster.

Wood.   One of the most widely used pattern material is wood, primarily
because it is cheap, plentiful, and easy to work. If the pattern is constructed
properly, its strength is quite good. It should be kiln or air dried, have
straight grain, and be free from knots, cracks, and sap. It is available as white
pine, mahogany, maple, birch, cherry, etc. It is measured by the *board foot*.
The board foot is obtained from the equation

$$B = N(Lwt)$$

L = length, ft
w = width, ft
t = thickness, in.
N = number of boards
B = board ft

EXAMPLE 10

Calculate the board feet of 35 boards, 2 in. by 6 in. by 12 ft long.

Solution:

The number of board feet is

$$B = N(Lwt) = 35(12 \times \tfrac{6}{12} \times 2)$$
$$= 420 \text{ board ft}$$

$N = 35$
$L = 12$ ft
$w = 6$ in.
$t = 2$ in.

White pine is the most widely used wood in patternmaking because of its
straight grain and light weight and because it is soft, easy to work, and

unlikely to warp. Mahogany is a harder and more durable wood than white pine. It is less likely to warp than some of the other woods and can be worked easily if straight grained.

Maple, birch, and cherry are harder and heavier than white pine. They tend to warp in large sections and therefore should be used for small patterns only. They should be carefully treated because they pick up moisture readily.

Wood in general has a cellular structure called fibers. The cells are tubular and hollow and contain mostly air and water. Gums, resins, and other matter are sometimes found in the tubes. The collection of many fibers forms a porous material.

The annual rings formed give rise to different concentrations of cells. The center, or heartwood, is dense and usually has deposits of gums and resins, but the cells are dead. The sapwood makes up most of the trunk. The cells are alive and are less concentrated and lighter in color than the heartwood. As growth proceeds, sapwood changes to heartwood. Because of its close structure heartwood is preferred to sapwood.

Swelling and shrinkage result from the absorption and evaporation of moisture. Warping, on drying, is affected by the orientation of the annual rings to the sides of the board. Quartersawing produces a board with the rings as shown in Fig. 3.13(a). Plain-sawing is shown in Fig. 3.13(b). Quarter-sawed lumber shrinks, twists, and warps less than plain-sawed wood and is subject to uniformly distributed drying rates. Plain-sawed lumber is cheaper than quartersawed lumber and will dry more quickly, but not as uniformly.

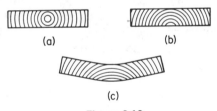

(a)   (b)

(c)

Figure 3.13

Since wood has a cellular structure it shrinks unevenly. A quartersawed piece of lumber will not warp as readily as plain-sawed lumber, because the rings in plain-sawed lumber change orientation to the side of the board as the distance from the center of the board increases. See Fig. 3.13(c).

Uneven shrinkage also results in check (cracks) along the grain while drying, because the outside dries before the inside. This uneven shrinkage of the fibers sets up stresses and strains as the wood dries which will also cause warping.

The total shrinkage from green to oven-dried lumber varies with the type of board and the method used to cut the board. Volume changes may vary as much as 10 to 20%. Length shrinkage along the axis of the board is less than across the width of the board. Cross-grain board shrinks more in length than does straight-grain board. Shrinkage in quartersawed lumber is greater through the thickness of the board than across its width, but in plain-sawed lumber this shrinkage is the reverse. Radial shrinkage occurs in quartersawed wood and is about 6% greater through the thickness of the board than across its width. In plain-sawed wood the shrinkage is tangential and is about 10% greater across the board width than through its thickness. The percentages will vary according to the type of wood.

Moisture in wood is contained in the cell cavities and in the cell walls. The moisture in the cavities dries before the moisture in the cell walls. Wood does not begin to shrink until the cell walls start to dry.

A method for calculating the percentage of moisture in the wood is to weigh a piece of lumber before and after drying. The cut should be well away from the end of the board. The board is heated in an oven at about 212°F until the dry weight stabilizes. The percentage of moisture is then calculated from:

$$M = \frac{(W_g - W_d)100}{W_d}$$

W_g = green weight
W_d = dry weight
M = % moisture

EXAMPLE 11

The weight of a section of wood before drying is 365g. The weight after drying is 305g. What is the percentage of moisture content?

Solution:

The percentage of moisture is

$$M = \frac{(W_g - W_d)100}{W_d} = \frac{(365 - 305)100}{305}$$

$W_g = 365\text{g}$
$W_d = 305\text{g}$

$$= 19.7\%$$

Since wood is considered dry when its moisture content is below 15%, the sample is classified as green.

When boards are laminated (built up), they should be glued in such a way that the tendency to warp in one direction is counteracted by the tendency to warp in the opposite direction.

3.15.　Metal Pattern Materials

When metal is used as a pattern material, the pattern may be machined to size with all the necessary allowances. If the contours of the workpiece are complicated, it is generally cheaper to make a wood pattern first. This pattern is then used to cast the desired metal pattern which is then used to cast the workpieces. Note that a double set of allowances must be calculated and included in the wood pattern. The metal pattern will contain one set of allowances.

Cast iron with a fine grain may be used as a metal pattern. It has the disadvantages of low corrosion resistance unless protected, great weight, and being difficult to work. However, it is cheaper and more durable than other metals.

Brass as a pattern material may be easily worked and built up by solder or braze, and it has a smooth, closed pore structure. It is expensive and therefore generally used for small cast parts.

Aluminum is the best pattern material because it is easily worked, light in weight, and corrosion resistant. It is, however, subject to shrinkage and wear by abrasive action, especially when used in a sand mold.

White metal (tin base) alloys have low shrinkage, cast very easily, have low melting points, are light in weight, and may be built up by soldering. They are subject to wear by the abrasive action of sand. Since their shrinkage is low, additional patterns may be made from the white metal pattern itself. Double shrinkage allowance need not be included.

Plastic has several advantages which make it a good pattern material. It is durable, does not change size or shape appreciably, has a smooth surface, does not absorb moisture, and may be quickly finished when the pattern is removed from the mold. It may be molded in a plaster of paris or metal mold.

3.16. Accessory Materials

Pure shellac varnish in white or orange is the most commonly used protective material for wood patterns. Orange shellac is preferred, but both dry with hard, smooth, and moisture- and abrasion-protective coatings. Shellac is cheap and can be applied easily. Lacquer may also be used as a coating material. It is more expensive than shellac but offers more protection against moisture.

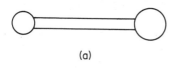

(a)

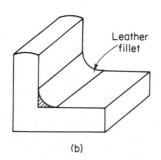

Leather fillet

(b)

Figure 3.14

Several thin coats of shellac or lacquer should be applied and each coat should be permitted to dry thoroughly before sandpapering to smooth the surface. Sanding should be done after every coat.

Fillets are radii machined or applied to the pattern to eliminate sharp corners in the casting. They may be made from beeswax, leather, or wood. Machining the fillets into the pattern gives the strongest construction, but when this is not possible, one of the fillet materials should be used. Beeswax, the most commonly used material, is purchased in strips and shaped into the corner with a warm fillet iron, Fig. 3.14(a). It should be applied after the first protective coating is applied. The disadvantage of wax is that it is not very durable.

Leather fillets, Fig. 3.14(b) are expensive but give long life. After being cut to size the angle sides are treated with glue and pressed into the corner.

Wood fillets are not easily bent and therefore should be used on long straight work. They are glued or nailed into position. If nailed, the nails must be "set" beneath the surface and the holes filled before shellacking.

Glues are of two varieties, hot and cold. Hot glues are stronger: these are animal glues made in flake or sheet form and soaked at a suitable temperature until they become liquid. They may be thinned with water.

Since the strength of a glued joint depends upon the glue's entering and filling the pores, open-grain wood needs a thicker coating of liquid glue than close-grain wood (mahogany). When gluing two pieces of wood, both faces should be cleaned and given a prime coating of glue. The two faces are rubbed together, clamped, and allowed to dry. Nails or screws may be used to reinforce the joint. About 3 hours is required for drying hot glue, 8 to 10 hours for cold glues.

End grain pieces should be given a prime coating of thin glue to fill the pores before applying the regular glue for joining. This type of joint is weak.

Fish glue is another adhesive material sometimes used. It may be used hot or cold. Water-resistant glues may also be purchased. One class of water-resistant glue is made from milk and is classified as casein glue. Still other commercial glues are made from proteins.

Nails or brads are used extensively in pattern making. Brads are made with small heads, which permits driving the head below the surface of the wood. Nails have larger heads and therefore cannot be set below the surface. Brads are classified according to their length and a steel-wire gage number. Thus a brad 2 in. long by 14 gage is 2 in. long by 0.080 in. in diameter. Common nails are classified according to penny weight. Thus a nail is of such weight that 1000 nails will give the penny weight. Approximately 1000 six-penny (6d) nails weigh 6 lb.

Wood screws are classified according to the American screw wire-gage number and their length. They are better than nails because of their greater holding power. However, to exert maximum holding power, the first piece through which the screw passes must have a clearance hole drilled into it about $\frac{1}{32}$ in. larger than the screw gage size. The holding force should come from the thread contact in the second piece.

In some instances the upper piece is counterbored to allow sinking the head of the screw below the surface of the wood. The counterbore is then plugged by gluing a dowel into it.

Dowels are made from dowel wood, metal plates, or specially made dowel screws. The screws come in pairs. One screw has a dowel end, the other a cavity for locating the dowel end. Dowels should be offset so that the pattern can go together in only one way.

Dowels are always pressed into the cope half of the pattern with their mating locating holes drilled into the drag half of the pattern. Dowel ends should be tapered to permit easy assembly or separation but must be tight enough to prevent side motion between both halves of the pattern when assembled.

Dowel plates are sunk into the wood or metal surface and fastened with flat head screws. One plate is made with a projecting dowel which alone extends above the surface of the pattern and inserts into the dowel hole in the mating plate. Drawing plates and lifting screws may be fastened to the pattern to facilitate drawing the pattern from the sand mold or rapping when necessary.

Letters and numbers may also be purchased. Used for identification purposes, they are made from soft metal so they will bend around the contours of the patterns to which they are glued or nailed.

QUESTIONS AND PROBLEMS

3.1 Describe the mechanism by which metal solidifies in a mold.

3.2 List the allowances and considerations which determine the type of material to be used in a pattern.

3.3 Discuss and illustrate the importance of the parting line to the design of a pattern.

3.4 What is draft? Why is it necessary?

3.5 List the types of patterns discussed in this chapter. Make a statement about each which describes its characteristic and sets it apart from the others.

3.6 (a) What is a flask? (b) Draw it and label all parts.

3.7 Describe the differences between the face and bottom board.

3.8 Make a sketch of any simple object, select a parting line, apply draft, and describe the making of the related mold.

3.9 (a) Describe three ways in which gates may be applied to a mold. (b) What are the disadvantages encountered when two of the three types are used?

3.10 Explain the need for gates in a mold.

3.11 Four types of molding sand are discussed in this chapter. List them and explain their composition and uses.

3.12 How many ways are there for grading sand? Make a statement about the purpose for each.

3.13 Discuss the relationship between moisture content, permeability, and strength in sands. Define each term as it relates to sand.

3.14 Describe the Dietert method for checking permeability.

3.15 What is the percentage of moisture content in a 100g sample of sand if the final weight of the sample is 87.8g?

3.16 Calculate the permeability number of a 2-in. sample of sand if the pressure reading is 4.2 g/cm^2 and the time required to pass 2000 cm^3 of air is 1 minute 15 seconds.

3.17 How high did a sand sample ram up if the permeability number is 64, the pressure reads 5.2 g/cm² and the time required to pass 2000 cm³ of air is 1 minute 40 seconds? Was the moisture content high or low?

3.18 Describe the uses and differences between sprues and the risers.

3.19 (a) What are cores? (b) What are core prints? (c) What purposes do each serve?

3.20 List and describe four types of core prints.

3.21 (a) Make a sketch showing the use of a green-sand core. (b) What are several of its disadvantages?

3.22 List the characteristics of a dry-sand core which contribute to its effectiveness.

3.23 Itemize the steps used in the making of a dry-sand core.

3.24 Discuss the making of core boxes. Support your explanations with sketches.

3.25 Describe the forces operating in a mold. Assume the mold is fitted with a core.

3.26 What is the purpose of venting?

3.27 Given a flask 14 × 14 × 12 in. deep shown in Fig. 3.15(a). The cope depth is 6 in. and the drag depth is 6 in. A cast iron bar 2 × 4 × 8 in. is to be poured. The weight of cast iron is 0.28 lb/in.³ and sand 0.06 lb/in.³ Calculate: (a) the force of the casting on the drag; (b) the buoyant force on the cope; (c) the weight of the sand in the cope; (d) the net force at the liquid-sand interface; (e) the force at the bottom of the mold.

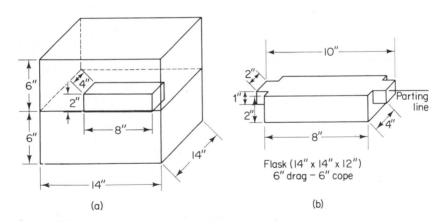

Figure 3.15

3.28 Assume the same conditions as in Problem 3.27 except that a core 10 in. long by 2 in. wide by 1 in. thick is inserted into the cavity as shown in Fig. 3.15(b). Calculate: (a) the weight of the core; (b) the upward force on the core; (c) the net force on the core; (d) the upward force on the cope area sequent; (e) the total lifting force; (f) the weight of the sand in the cope; (g) the net force on the cope. (h) Is a weight needed?

3.29 Given the mold in Fig. 3.16 when the core is omitted, calculate: (a) the buoyant force on the cope; (b) the weight of the sand in the cope; (c) the force of the casting on the drag; (d) the force at the bottom of the mold; (e) the force at the liquid-solid interface. (f) Will the cope float?

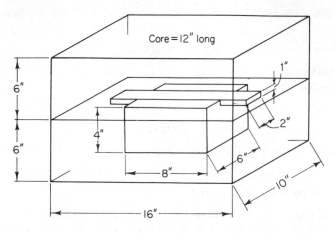

Figure 3.16

3.30 Assume the core is added as shown in Fig. 3.16. Calculate: (a) the buoyant force on the two segments of the cope; (b) the buoyant force on the core; (c) the weight of the core; (d) the net upward force on the cope; (e) the weight of the sand in the cope; (f) the buoyant force on the cope. Will it float?

3.31 Consider the split pattern, Fig. 3.17; calculate: (a) the force at the bottom of the mold cavity; (b) the force at the top of the mold cavity; (c) the weight of the sand in the cope; (d) the net force on the cope. Will the cope float?

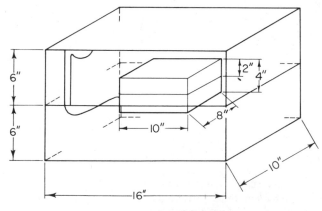

Figure 3.17

3.32 Consider Fig. 3.18. Calculate: (a) the upward force on the cope; (b) the weight of the cope; (c) the net force on the cope. Will the cope float?

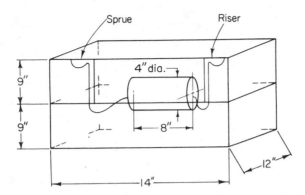

Figure 3.18

3.33 If a 2 1/2 in.-diameter core 10 inches long is added to the mold in Fig. 3.18, calculate the weight needed to hold the cope in position.

3.34 Discuss the two methods which may be used to calculate the weight of a casting from the pattern.

3.35 Assume the pattern in Fig. 3.19 is to be used to cast brass. Calculate the weight of the casting from the volume.

3.36 Assume the pattern is made from yellow pine. Calculate the weight of the brass casting, Fig. 3.19.

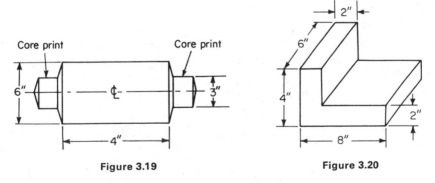

Figure 3.19   **Figure 3.20**

3.37 Calculate the weight of the casting in Fig. 3.20 if the part is cast iron.

3.38 Calculate the weight in Fig. 3.20 if the casting is to be aluminum.

3.39 Assume that Fig. 3.20 is a pattern made from cherry wood which weighs 3 lb. (a) What will be the weight of a zinc casting? (b) Check this value using the method of volume.

3.40 (a) Calculate the weight of the casting using the method of volumes in Fig. 3.21. The casting is cast iron. (b) Calculate the weight of the yellow pine pattern needed to make this casting.

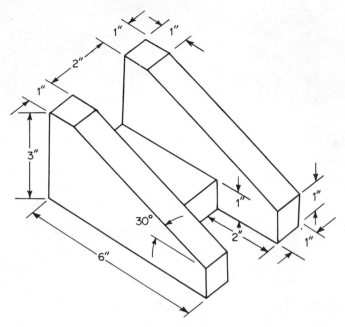

Figure 3.21

3.41 If the pattern in Fig. 3.21 is made from white pine, calculate the weight of the brass casting using the weight of the pattern.

3.42 A cherry pattern weighs 22 lb. Calculate the weight of the aluminum casting made with this pattern.

3.43 A solid core weighs 8 lb and an aluminum pattern weighs 26 lb. What is the weight of a cast-iron casting which is made with this pattern?

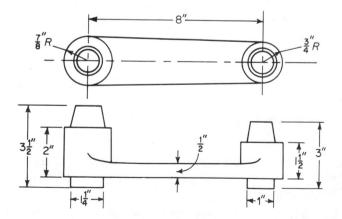

Figure 3.22

3.44 Calculate the approximate weight of a brass casting made with the pattern in Fig. 3.22. The pattern is mahogany.

3.45 List the conditions which affect the amount of metal added to a casting as finish allowance.

3.46 List the factors affecting the amount of shrinkage that takes place when a metal cools.

3.47 Why is draft on a pattern necessary?

3.48 (a) Describe the direction for applying draft to a pattern. (b) How should it be applied to a finished surface if the surface is external? (c) internal?

3.49 Explain each of the following terms and state the purpose of each: (a) machining bosses; (b) distortion; (c) shake.

3.50 Wood patterns must resist moisture, shock, rough handling, wear, ramming, or rapping. Explain how each of these may be overcome.

3.51 Discuss the use of wood as a pattern material.

3.52 (a) How does mahogany differ from white pine as a pattern material? (b) from cherry wood?

3.53 (a) Sketch the annual ring structure for a piece of plain sawed wood. (b) Quartersawed wood.

3.54 What is heartwood? Sapwood?

3.55 Which shrinks more, straight-grain wood or cross-grain wood?

3.56 When does moisture-saturated wood start to shrink upon drying?

3.57 Assume the pattern in Fig. 3.20 is to be cast as a one-piece pattern. The parting line is above the 4 × 6 in. plane. (a) Assuming all surfaces are to be finish machined, add the finish allowance. The material is cast iron. (b) Using the values from part (a) calculate and add the allowances for shrinkages. (c) Using the values from part (b) calculate and add the allowances for draft.

3.58 Assume that the parting line is taken at the base of the casting in Fig. 3.21. The casting is aluminum. If only the base is to be machined, calculate: (a) the dimensions allowing for shrinkage; (b) the allowances for draft.

3.59 Explain the effect of the method of sawing a log into lumber on the warpage.

3.60 At what percentage of moisture is wood considered dry?

3.61 Describe the process used to calculate the percentage of moisture in wood.

3.62 How does lamination counteract warpage?

3.63 Calculate the board feet of wood received when 60 boards, 2 × 6 × 14, are ordered.

3.64 You order 1600 board ft of 2 × 8 lumber. How many boards are delivered?

3.65 The weight of a piece of wood before drying is 430g. The weight after drying is 395. Calculate the percentage of moisture content.

3.66 The moisture content of a sample of wood is 16%. It weighs 180g after drying. Calculate its weight before drying.

3.67 Discuss the five materials, other than wood, which may be used as a pattern material. Include their advantages and disadvantages as materials.

3.68 How are fillets made on patterns?

3.69 Describe the process for gluing wood.

3.70 Describe the method for fitting patterns with wood dowels.

Other Casting Processes

4

4.1. Shell Molding

In this process fine grades of washed sand and a thermosetting plastic powder, which acts as a binder, are thoroughly mixed. A metal pattern in the bottom of the flask is heated to approximately 350 to 450°F and sprayed with a parting grease. The mixture of sand and binder is heaped on the pattern. The temperature of the pattern is high enough to partially cure the plastic and causes a thin layer of sand to cling to the pattern. [See Fig. 4.1(a and b).]

At this point the pattern is inverted to remove all loose sand. The pattern and partially cured sand shell are then heated to about 600°F for 1 minute in a furnace to complete the curing process. Once cured, the shell is stripped off the pattern. The shell wall is about $\frac{1}{8}$ to $\frac{1}{4}$ in. thick. See Fig. 4.1(c).

The usual practice is to make many shells, which are then glued or clamped together to form a thin-wall mold. The mold may be fitted with shell cores, gates, runners, pouring basins, or sprues as needed. The entire mold is then placed in a container, supported with coarse sand, metal shot, or gravel, and the casting material poured. [See Fig. 4.1(d).] Small molds (shells) may be filled without support. The finished workpiece is shown in Fig. 4.1(e).

This process lends itself to mass production because the accuracies which can be achieved are from 0.003 to about 0.005 in./in. Since shrinkage and draft requirements are much less than in ordinary sand-casting processes, the physical shape of the mold may be controlled. Except for the metal pattern, this process is fast and inexpensive, especially when production requirements are high.

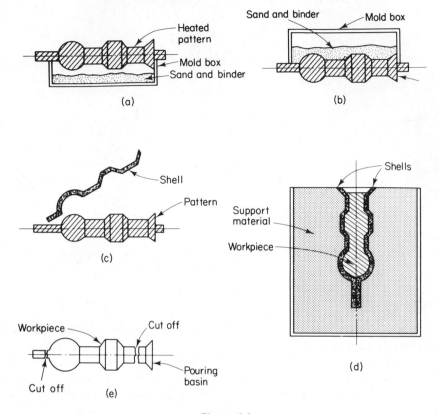

Figure 4.1

4.2. The Lost-Wax, or Investment, Casting Process

This process requires a master pattern which is then used to make a die. Any complicated cavities that are required may be machined or engraved directly into the die cavity. Once the die is made, wax is poured or forced into the die cavity under pressure and permitted to solidify. A cluster of wax patterns may then be assembled to wax runners and a wax sprue to form a "tree" using a heated spatula to make the connections. See Fig. 4.2(a and b). It is to be noted that very complicated shapes may be built up at this stage of the process.

Repeated dipping into a fine refractory material builds a thin layer on the surface of the tree. The coated tree is next placed in a fine refractory material such as plaster after which a coarser investment (refractory material) is poured into the container until it is filled. The container is vibrated to remove all air bubbles and cause the investment to fill the entire cavity.

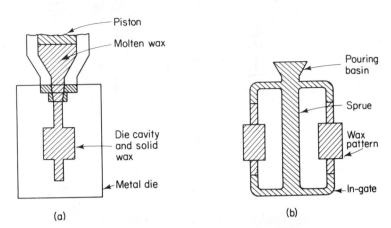

Figure 4.2

Once the investment has hardened, the container is placed in a furnace and heated. This serves to harden the mold further and melt the wax. The wax continues to run off as the process continues, leaving the desired cavity in the hardened mold.

The mold is then heated to between 1000 and 1800°F and the molten metal is poured into the mold. The heated mold ensures that the molten metal will fill the entire cavity. The molten metal may also be forced into the mold under pressure or by vacuum.

Castings made by this process may have high surface finish, close dimensional accuracy, complicated shapes, and thin cross sections. Shapes can be made by this process that may be impossible to make by other processes. Because of the close dimensional accuracy that is possible, very little machining allowance need be provided. This is very important when hard materials are cast or when machining is difficult because of the shape of the end product.

Variations of this process use plastics, frozen mercury, or low-melting-point materials which either melt and run off or vaporize and leave the desired cavity.

Shells are now produced by dipping the wax pattern into a ceramic slurry. The wax removed, a thin-walled ceramic shell results and is then filled with the casting material which solidifies as the desired casting.

4.3. Plaster Molds

A plaster of paris slurry is prepared by adding gypsum to water. This slurry is then poured over a pattern made of metal or some other moisture-resistant material and allowed to preset. [See Fig. 4.3(a).] The pattern is withdrawn, and the preset mold is heated in an oven at about 600°F for several hours to drive off the moisture.

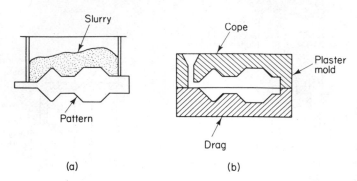

Figure 4.3

The cope and drag method used in sand casting, Fig. 4.3(b), may be used in this process. Once dried, the mold is assembled and pouring may take place.

Surface finish and dimensional accuracy in this process are very good. However, this process should be used only for casting nonferrous materials. The molds are fragile and should be handled with care. Nevertheless, since plaster of paris has a low thermal conductivity, the metal remains liquid longer and therefore thinner cross sections can be cast than by other methods.

Sometimes permeability is a problem. A special process, known as the *Antioch process*, has been developed to create a porous mold for better permeability. The slurry is poured over a match plate into a cope and drag flask. The mold presets after several hours. The pattern is drawn and the mold is placed in a steam autoclave at 2-atmosphere pressure. It is at this point in the process that the porosity develops. The mold is removed from the autoclave and air-dried for 12 hours. The final step is to oven-dry the mold at 450°F for approximately 15 hours after which the mold is ready for pouring.

4.4. Centrifugal Casting

In this process the mold is fitted to a revolving disc and rotated at about 1500 rpm. The centrifugal force causes the metal to be distributed to all parts of the mold. The casting that results has a high degree of detail and superior density. Impurities collect at the inner wall of the casting because the mass of the impurities is lower than the mass of the molten metal. This tends to localize the impurities and, to some extent, purify the metal melt.

True centrifugal casting. Used to cast symmetrical objects such as pipe, the metal is forced against the mold wall by the centrifugal force until it solidifies. [See Fig. 4.4(a).] No core is needed to form the hole in the casting. Molten metal distributed by this process may be forced into molds where rapid solidification takes place before the freezing process starts.

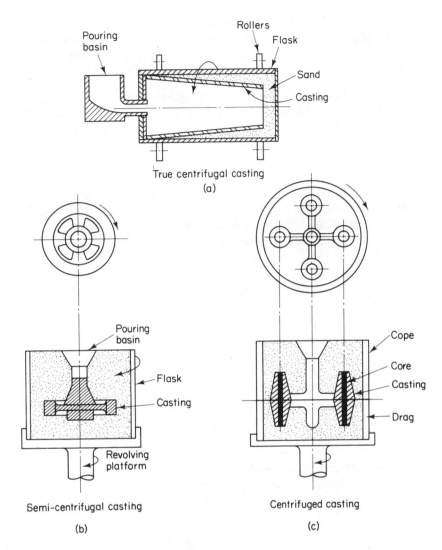

Figure 4.4

Centrifugal castings may be rotated about a vertical or horizontal axis. At low speeds the vertical-axis rotation leaves the inner hole parabolic, but at high speeds this effect disappears.

Semicentrifugal casting. This process, Fig. 4.4(b), is used to ensure purity and density at the extremities of a casting such as a cast wheel. The sand mold (cope, drag, and center core) is rotated at a lower speed (350 rpm) than in the centrifugal casting process. Since the poorer structure collects at the center of the casting, it may be necessary to machine the center if this structure is objectionable.

Several molds may be stacked one on top of the other and rotated, and molten metal fed through a center pouring basin. Rotation takes place about a central axis. The number of molds which may be rotated at one time depends upon the conditions prevailing at the time and the size of the mold.

The centrifuge. This method of casting takes advantage of the fact that the mechanical properties of the casting about the periphery of rotation increase as the distance from the center of rotation increases. [See Fig. 4.4(c).] Thus if several molds are grouped about a central down gate, the molten metal will be forced through the runners into the mold and yield high density and pure castings.

Other centrifugal casting methods are: the Watertown method which uses a heavy cast-iron mold to act as a chill; the DeLavaud method which uses a thin-wall metal mold fitted with a water jacket; the sand-spun method which uses a steel shell into which is rammed a sand lining.

4.5. Permanent-Mold Casting

Permanent-mold casting refers to the process of die casting in which the molten metal is fed into the cavity by gravity. The head pressure of the molten metal forces the metal into the mold.

The molds are coated with a refractory material and lampblack. The dies are closed, and the metal is poured into the dies and allowed to solidify. The dies are opened, and the casting is ejected. The dies are then cleaned and the process repeated.

Cores may be positioned in the dies before they are closed and removed as soon as solidification starts. Or sand cores may be used and knocked out of the casting after solidification has taken place. The latter method is referred to as *semipermanent die casting*. This process is used for making steel and cast-iron castings as well as alloy castings having a copper, aluminum, or magnesium base.

The slush process. In this variation of the permanent-mold process, the melt is poured into the die cavity. At a predetermined time the mold is inverted to permit the part of the metal still in the molten state to flow out of the cavity. The hollow shell casting which has solidified is then removed. Ornaments, toys, etc., may be cast by this process. The inside wall of the casting is usually rough and irregular.

The Corthias process. Still another variation of the permanent-mold process, the cavity is filled with a precalculated quantity of metal. A core or plunger is inserted under low pressure to force the melt into the cavity. As the metal sets, the core or plunger is withdrawn. A hollow casting is the result.

4.6. Die Casting

The die casting processes are permanent-mold casting methods which force the metal into the mold under high pressure. The pressures vary from 20,000 to 75,000 psi for the *cold chamber method* to about 500 psi for the *hot chamber method*.

The hot chamber method. Using the gooseneck machine shown in Fig. 4.5(a), the gooseneck either remains totally immersed in the melt or is lowered into the melt to be filled. The metal is then forced out of the small end of the gooseneck by a pressure cylinder or by air pressure applied at the large end. The molten metal leaves the small end of the gooseneck, enters the die, and is maintained under pressure in the die until it solidifies. Once solidified, the die is forced open and the casting is forced out of the die.

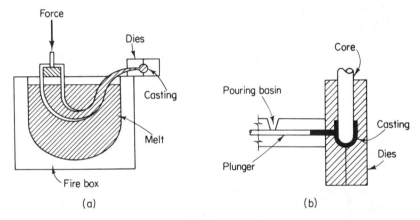

Figure 4.5

Since the gooseneck and the crucible pot are made of iron and since most metals react with iron at elevated temperatures, only the low-melting-point metals such as alloys of lead, tin, and zinc may be cast with this process.

For casting metals such as aluminum, magnesium, and brass, which have higher melting temperatures, a melting pot may be used, but higher pressures are necessary. This requires that the cold chamber method be used.

The cold chamber method. A ladle is used to transfer the molten metal by hand from a melting pot to the cold chamber of the die machine and is then forced under high pressure into the die cavity. [See Fig. 4.5(b).] With the die closed, the core in position, and the plunger retracted beyond the pouring basin, the molten metal is poured into the basin. The plunger is forced forward filling the mold cavity. Once the metal has solidified, the core is retracted, the mold is opened, and the ejector pins free the casting from the cavity.

95

4.7. Continuous Casting

Continuous casting is accomplished by pouring molten metal into the mold and by keeping the mold filled at all times. The metal at the lower end of the mold is cooled so that it solidifies. Rollers grip the solid metal and pull it out from the end of the mold at a controlled speed. As the metal is withdrawn, a cutting torch or saw is used to cut the continuously moving metal to length.

It is important that the mold sides be smooth. Lubricants help reduce the friction between the mold walls and the metal. Sometimes graphite molds are used because of their self-lubricating properties. The metal should move freely through the mold. It should not adhere to the sides of the mold. The rate at which heat is removed from the melt must be synchronized with the molten-metal input and the rate of removal of the solid material. The turbulence of pouring and the quantity of impurities permitted in the melt must be kept to a minimum.

Materials such as brass, zinc, copper and its alloys, aluminum and its alloys, and carbon and alloy steels may be cast by one of the several continuous-casting processes. When steel is cast, a brass or thin-steel-wall mold is used. The outside of these molds must be cooled. Circles, tubes, squares, and other geometric shapes may be continuously cast as well as ingots, slabs, and sheet metal.

4.8. Electroforming*

Electroforming requires that a negative mold be made of the part to be reproduced. This mold may be made from plaster, or it may be machined from solid stock. A fusible low-melting alloy, wax, rubber, or chemically soluble substance is then poured into the negative mold. A pattern results which is then coated with a metallic electricity-conducting material, such as graphite or silver.

Once coated, it is placed in an electrolytic solution and, by electrolysis, plated. When the plating is thick enough (about 0.5 in.), the pattern is removed either by withdrawing it so that it may be used again or by melting or chemically dissolving it and leaving the part.

The shell which remains has excellent internal detail, good internal finish, and practically no shrinkage, and it may be held to close tolerances. It is also possible to plate several different kinds of metals, one on top of the other, to create laminations which might be difficult by some of the other methods of lamination. This is especially true if a high degree of detail is required. It is also possible to make very thin wall parts, either laminated or not laminated,

---

*It should be noted that electroforming is not a casting process.

96

by this process. Heat treating of parts produced by this method may also be accomplished if the metals used are capable of being heat treated. Any material capable of being electroplated may be electroformed.

4.9. Powder Metallurgy

The method of making objects from pressed powders is not one of the casting processes. It is however an important process in manufacturing because of its use in making carbide tools. These will be studied in Chapter 10.

Powders are selected, mixed, and pressed into the desired shape under high pressures to form a compact. The compact is then heated at high temperatures in a controlled atmosphere to produce a metal part of desired mass and mechanical properties. The process consists of very carefully producing, grading, and mixing the metal powders, pressing them into a compact, and then sintering the compact.

The powders may be produced by the following methods: electrolysis and mill grinding (iron, copper, and tantalum); the reduction of compounds at elevated temperatures with hydrogen or carbon monoxide (iron, copper, cobalt, etc.); the formation of pellets by pouring molten metal through a sieve and the subsequent milling of the pellets by grinding them into powders. Other methods used are atomizing, precipitation, condensation, and machining.

These powders are then graded and blended wet or dry. In wet mixing a lubricant is used to aid in the press operation during compacting.

The mixed powders are then placed in a die and compacted into a briquette at pressures of up to 75,000 psi and in some instances even higher depending upon the material being pressed. It is necessary to use enough pressure to compress the powder into a self-supporting briquette. When compacting ductile materials, no binder is necessary because the pressure creates cold welds between the powder particles. When compacting briquettes from hard materials, most of the holding force between the powder particles results from an interlocking effect which takes place between the irregular surfaces of the powder particles. A binder is usually needed to make the compact self-supporting.

During the sintering process the briquette is heated to some desirable temperature below the melting temperature of the principal powder for about 30 minutes. A controlled atmosphere is used to keep the surfaces of the powder particles free from oxide films. The elimination of the oxide films permits the interatomic forces between the particles to exhibit greater holding forces. Sometimes one of the phases becomes liquid during sintering and permits diffusion of the primary constituent throughout its structure. Surface tension aids in the compacting of the solid mass.

When necessary, sintered parts may be further processed by coining for higher strength and better sizing. Shrinkage during sintering is sometimes a problem and results in the need for coining or further machining.

With this process it is possible to produce parts of high hardness and forms which could not otherwise be made. Since powder does not exhibit the same characteristics of plastic flow which metals exhibit under pressure, it is important that dies be carefully designed. Allowing for this disadvantage and the shrinkage which takes place, parts can be made so that no machining, or very limited machining, is required.

The production of cutting tools under the general heading of cemented carbides is of special interest to us. The earliest carbide material was made by mixing tungsten carbide and cobalt powders. A presintering operation at 1800°F resulted in a compact which was then shaped to the desired form and dimensions. The final sintering operation which took place at about 2500°F in a controlled-atmosphere furnace resulted in a superior cutting tool. This tool material was far superior to that of the tools existing at the time.

Other experiments with carbides resulted in the mixing of tungsten and titanium carbide with cobalt; or the combination of tungsten, titanium, and tantalum carbide with cobalt. The cobalt served as a binder during and after the sintering operation. The use of these tools will be further discussed in Chapter 10.

QUESTIONS AND PROBLEMS

4.1 Describe the shell molding process.

4.2 What accuracies can be expected from the shell molding process?

4.3 Describe the investment casting process.

4.4 What are some of the advantages of investment casting?

4.5 Describe the plaster mold process of casting.

4.6 Why is the plaster mold process restricted to nonferrous materials?

4.7 How can the problem of permeability be overcome in plaster molds?

4.8 (a) Describe the three centrifugal casting processes. (b) How does the semi-centrifugal process differ from the centrifuge method of casting?

4.9 What is the chief difficulty encountered in centrifugal casting? What must be done to overcome this difficulty?

4.10 Describe at least one of the permanent-mold casting processes.

4.11 How does the hot chamber method of permanent-mold casting differ from the cold chamber permanent-mold casting?

4.12 Check your library and draw a sketch of the mechanism used in continuous casting. Explain the process which you have selected.

4.13 What is the chief difficulty when continuously casting steel? How may it be overcome?

4.14 Describe the electroforming of metals.

4.15 Describe the production of the powders used in the powder metallurgy process.

4.16 What is sintering?

4.17 Describe and explain the forces operating in the end product of the powder metallurgy process.

4.18 Describe the process for making a carbide slug which is to be used in a carbide tool.

Joining Processes

5

5.1. The Metallurgy of Welding

Welding in its broadest aspect may be divided into four categories. They are (1) processes requiring pressure, (2) processes requiring no pressure, (3) low-temperature alloying, and (4) processes requiring chiefly adhesion. Although there may be some overlapping in the above categories, for the purpose of presentation they will be referred to as (1) pressure welding; (2) fusion welding; (3) brazing; and (4) soldering.

In the first two categories and to some extent in the third process alloying takes place between the filler metal and the base metal. The first two processes require melting of the base metal.

The principles of metallurgy set forth in the preceding chapters apply and affect the end results. Important considerations are melting temperature, heating and cooling rate, grain growth, etc.

Ideally, the two pieces to be joined and the filler rod should be of the same composition. If all three are heated into the melt and allowed to cool very slowly (cooled under equilibrium conditions), the weld should be homogeneous. However, actual cooling of a consummated weld is rarely, if ever, under equilibrium conditions. Cooling takes place under less than equilibrium conditions and follows the cooling rates shown in Fig. 2.20. To keep the martensite structure to a minimum, the maximum safe cooling rate is that which touches or is greater than the 95% transformation curve. Since martensite is hard and has a greater volume than austenite, cracking may occur during or after the weld is completed.

If the presence of martensite is suspected, tempering will help. If the metal develops stresses which could cause cracking, then preheating and in some instances postheating will help.

Grain size developed as a result of temperature increases as the weld centerline is approached. This is shown in Fig. 5.1. As a result volume changes occur which stress the metal. Uneven heating and shrinkage during cooling may also stress the metals and cause distortion. These stresses place the metal under tension at the weld and under compression along a line perpendicular to the direction of the weld. (See Fig. 5.1.) They become locked into the weld and must be removed.

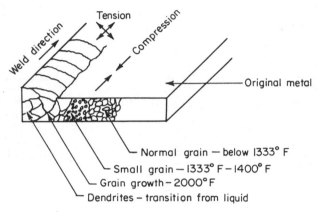

Figure 5.1

5.2. Weld Joints

If many pieces are to be "built up" or fabricated by welding, it is important to remember that a welded joint is a permanent joint. If for any reason the pieces to be joined are to be taken apart, other methods of fastening should be investigated and used.

Accessibility is also important because blind welding rarely gives satisfactory results. If many pieces are to be joined, the advisability of using a jig should be investigated. It is always more economical to weld all pieces into position in one setup than to do half the job and then set up for the second half. The possibility of completing all beads in one setup is cheaper than "tacking" all pieces into position and then running all beads. However, tacking all pieces in a fixture is always more economical than multiple setups. The tacked assembly is then removed from the fixture and the completed beads run. Multiple setups should be avoided and used only as a last resort.

Freedom from distortion, etc., should be built into the design. Pressures used in forge welding processes should not be relied upon to hold pieces in alignment or to straighten them during or after the welding process.

Since electrical resistance at the joint in many cases is relied upon to generate the heat needed during the welding operation, it is important to clean the surfaces of the pieces thoroughly. Foreign substances coating the surfaces of the metals act as insulators and can affect the welded joint. Oxides, dirt, grease, etc. also affect the amount and distribution of the heat generated.

The type of joint used is a matter of need. Figure 5.2(a through t) shows the various joints which may be used.

The three considerations which dictate the type of joint to be used are (1) the type of load to be carried by the weld (tension or compression); (2) the nature of the load (steady, impact, etc.); and (3) the cost of preparation prior to or after welding.

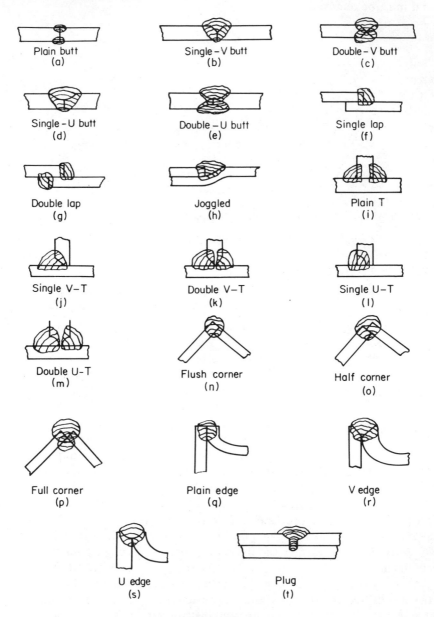

Figure 5.2

The "V-" and "U-butt" welds [Fig. 5.2(a through e)] are used where usual loads are to be carried. The double "V-" and "U-butt" welds will carry greater loads than the "single-V' or "-U" welds. The "V" and "U" welds will usually require more than one bead. The "single-V' and "-U" welds, in addition to the multiple passes in the "V" and "U," will also require a single pass on the opposite side from the "V" or "U." The plain- and single-butt welds may be used on materials up to approximately 1 in. thick. The double-butt welds are used where thicker materials are welded.

The single-lap joint may be used where light loading is required. The double-lap will withstand heavy loads, both static and dynamic. Since the preparation of the ends of the pieces to be welded is negligible, the cost is low. These joints are shown in Fig. 5.2(f and g). Figure 5.2(h) shows another kind of lap weld which will take severe loading. The preparation is costly, but it may be used where the upper surfaces of both pieces must be in the same plane.

Figure 5.2(i through m) shows "T" joints where longitudinal shear is present. The plain "T" and the single "V-T" joints are used where normal loading is to be overcome. The single "V-T" joint is used where only one side of the pieces to be welded is accessible. These joints should be used on plates approximately $\frac{1}{2}$ in. thick. The "U" joints will withstand more severe loading than the "V" joints. "Double-V's" and "-U's" should be used on plates thicker than 1 in. and where welding can be accomplished on both sides.

Figure 5.2(n through p) shows the corner joints. The flush-corner joint will withstand usual loads and is used on plates up to approximately $\frac{1}{8}$ in. thick or less. The full-corner joint is used for plates of any thickness and where loading is severe. It requires multiple beads in the top and possibly one bead at the inside corner. Where the inside corner is not accessible, the half-open corner is used. It is used on plates over $\frac{1}{8}$ in. thick.

Figure 5.2(q through s) shows the edge welds that may be used on thin plates. If a "V-" or "U-edge" weld is used, the plates must be thick enough to permit making the "V" or "U." The plain-edge weld is used for joining metals $\frac{1}{4}$ in. thick or less. A bead may also be applied at the inner surface.

Figure 5.2(t) is a plug-weld joint and is used to join two pieces of metal in the same manner as rivets join metals. This is sometimes referred to as a rivet-butt joint.

5.3. *Forge Welding*

In pressure welding, two metals are heated to the plastic state, and pressure is applied before, during, and after this state is reached. The pressure required to complete the weld may be mechanical, hydraulic, or pneumatic, and it should be continuously applied after the current is turned off to allow time for solidification.

The heat is usually supplied by the resistance to electric flow. The air gap at the joint creates the increased resistance to electric flow which generates heat. If alternating current is supplied to the welding machine, a transformer reduces the voltage to about 10 volts with a corresponding amperage output increase. Since the heat generated ($H = I^2Rt$) is a result of current I, resistance R, and time t, all three factors must be considered when planning the welding operation.

Hammer welding. The most primitive method of applying pressure is the hammer blow. The process consists of preparing the ends to be welded, the addition of a flux and iron oxide, heating, and the application of an impact blow. The slag, when in the liquid form, is squeezed out under the pressure, and the weld is completed. It is slow, costly, and not suitable for welding structural shapes.

It should be noted that the blows need not come from a blacksmith's hammer. Hot forging with a gravity drop hammer may be used to join two metals. Although more sophisticated, it is nonetheless the same process.

Spot welding. The two pieces to be joined are overlapped and placed between two electrodes—one stationary and the other movable. (See Fig. 5.3.)

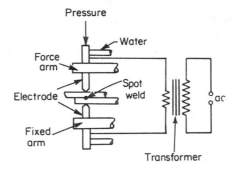

Figure 5.3

The movable electrode places a load on the work, which holds it in position. After the force is applied, the low-voltage, high-amperage current is caused to flow through the water-cooled electrodes. Resistance causes the temperature to be raised very rapidly at the point of contact between the two metal pieces. As the metal becomes plastic, pressure forces the two metals together to complete the weld. The current is shut off, but the pressure remains until the weld cools. If desired, the process is repeated at another point on the same two pieces. This process is very rapid since the cycle time for the entire operation may not be more than a minute (60 cycles). Cycle times are usually preset so that current and pressure are applied and released automatically.

The two metals must be free from scale or other surface impurities and should be of the same thickness. Because the position of the "spot" between the two pieces of metal is related to the size of the electrodes, two sheets of the same material but of different thicknesses or two sheets of different materials but of the same thickness may be welded by changing the size of one electrode. This will cause the spot to appear at the interface of the two metals. Almost any kind of metal can be spot welded. The upper thickness limit is about $\frac{1}{2}$ inch. The lower thickness limit is very thin foil. These limits are not the result of amperage requirements but of the pressures needed.

Seam welding. In this continuous spot welding process, Fig. 5.4, pressure is applied by two powered rollers which act as electrodes. Current is intermittent and regulated by a timer and the on-off cycles may be spaced so that they cause overlapped spots or spaced spots. It is possible to form pressure-tight joints with overlapped spots.

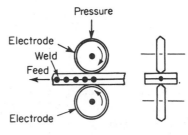

Figure 5.4

If two sheets are overlapped slightly and large-faced rollers are used, the metal may be squeezed together while it is in its plastic state. The multiple spots are hidden at the joint so that a relatively flat surface results. The completed weld is shown in Fig. 5.4. The process is referred to as *finish seam welding* or *mash seam welding*.

Seam welding is used for drawn and rolled products or sheet welding of metal containers, stove pipe, gas tanks, etc. Where necessary, machines are designed with multiple rows of electrodes and movable tables to feed the materials.

Projection welding. Projections are used to concentrate the current, Fig. 5.5. Localized current and the multiple projections create a multiple spot-weld effect. The pieces to be welded are held in position under pressure supplied by the electrodes. The current consummates the weld.

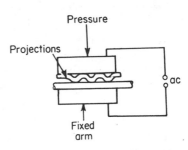

Figure 5.5

The projections at the point of contact should be approximately equal to the thickness of the metal and increase in cross section. The height of the projection should be 10 to 80% of the thickness of the material welded. If pieces of unequal thickness are to be welded, the thicker piece should have the projections. The number of spots desired determines the number of projections pressed into the sheet.

Cross-wire welding. A variation of projection welding, crossed wires touching at a point give the same effect as projections. Large surface-area electrodes apply pressure to the pattern. As the pressure and current are applied, the wires are welded at the points of contact to form the desired mesh. Wire baskets, lampshades, etc., may be joined by this process.

Flash butt welding and upset butt welding.   Butt welding, in general, requires a controlled pressure and amperage (See Fig. 5.6). Two pieces are brought into contact with the proper pressure and proper alignment. Once the current is turned on, the air gap creates the resistance needed to generate heat. The ends of the pieces become plastic and are forced together to form the weld. Materials to be welded must not become too soft, otherwise the metal will collapse and at best give a very uneven weld. If the pressure and heat are correct, a uniform weld is achieved. The joining of unlike materials or materials of different sizes needs special control of pressure and current.

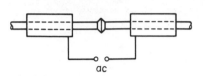

Figure 5.6

If two pieces are to be *flash butt* welded, they are first clamped into electrode holders. Current is applied, and, as they contact, arcing takes place and generates the necessary heat to burn away the ends of each piece. The forward motion of the electrodes is increased to maintain the arc and eventually complete the weld. The rate of movement of the electrodes and the pressure forge the welded joint. The flash* which results is small and may be removed by grinding.

In the *upset butt* welding process the pieces are clamped in the same manner as in the flash butt weld process. Pressure is applied, and then the current is turned on, heat being generated as a result of gap resistance instead of arcing. The pressure is increased as the pieces become plastic which causes an upset as the weld proceeds.

Percussion welding.   This method relies upon arcing to generate the heat needed to complete the weld. The pieces are clamped and held apart. Electrical energy is stored in a capacitor or results from a rapid breakdown of a magnetic field. In both instances the pieces are caused to move rapidly toward each other. At the proper instant the discharge from the capacitor causes an arcing which makes the ends of the materials plastic. Impact extinguishes the arc and completes the weld. The short arc time (0.1 to 0.2 second) practically eliminates the need to anneal the adjacent sections of the material and permits the welding of dissimilar metals. This process is limited to comparatively small pieces because of the impact required.

5.4. Fusion Welding

Fusion welding relies on the creation of a pool of molten metal. The pool is generated by the heat source and may be supplemented with additional

---

*"Flash" refers to the metal raised above the surfaces of the workpieces as a result of the pressure of one piece against the other.

molten metal from forge welding because no pressure is required to complete the weld. On cooling, the solidification of the melt completes the weld.

The addition of filler rod makes it necessary to choose rods which have the same material composition as the base metal. Since this is not always possible, care must be exercised in the choice of filler rod to insure that the expected performance is achieved from the weld.

5.5. Arc-Welding Machines

Arc-welding machines may be either ac or dc. Figure 5.7 shows the basic principle. One end of a *ground* cable is attached to the work, the other end to the machine. One end of a *power* cable is attached to an electrode holder. This cable gets its power from the machine. If the electrode is allowed to touch the work and is quickly removed to create a gap, an arc is formed which may generate a temperature up to 10,000°F. The heat forms a pool of molten metal which upon solidification becomes the weld.

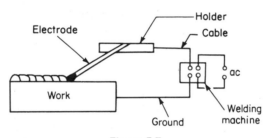

Figure 5.7

Alternating- and direct-current welding equipment is rated according to the output at the electrodes. The ac welder receives current from the source. A transformer reduces the voltage, which increases the amperage output at the electrode. This output current may be controlled either by placing a plug in an appropriately rated tap or by control dials. The taps take the current from several points on the secondary windings. The dial control uses a core which changes the magnetic coupling in the transformer.

Because the current is reversing rapidly, the polarity at the electrode is changing rapidly so that the polarity may be discounted. However, appropriately coated electrodes must be used. A coated electrode has high efficiency and low splatter, uses less input current, and has low leakage loss. Alternating-current welders are rated from 150 to 1000 amp.

Direct-current welding machines get their power from an ac motor or gasoline engine which is connected to a dc generator. The generator supplies current to the electrode. Since the current flows in one direction, the polarity of the hookup is important. If the electrode holder is connected to the negative terminal of the welding machine and the work connected to the positive terminal of the machine, the operation is called *straight polarity welding*. If the holder is positive and the work negative, the operation is called *reverse polarity welding*. The appropriate welding rod must be used. Unless the appropriate connections are made, poor results are obtained. The polarity may be checked by striking an arc, maintaining an arc length of about 4 in. for about 5 minutes. If black smears are observed, the polarity is reversed.

5.6. Carbon Arc Welding

In this process a carbon arc created by straight polarity current acts as the electrode and supplies the dc current. A filler rod, uncoated, is used (as shown in Fig. 5.8) with or without flux. The filler rod is consumed and mixes with the base metal. Since only dc is used in this method, splatter may occur because of the magnetic fields created. This is called *magnetic arc blow*. The arc tends to wander and very careful controls must be instituted. Edge welding is almost impossible because of the high concentration of magnetic fields at the edge of the work.

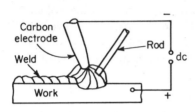

Figure 5.8

5.7. Welding Rods and Their Uses

Several factors must be taken into account when selecting the proper welding rod. They are (1) the coating; (2) the core composition; and (3) the diameter of the core. The requirements for these are related to the position and preparation of the workpieces, the current requirements, the thickness of the workpieces, the depth of penetration of the finished weld, and the physical properties desired. There are three basic kinds of electrodes: bare, fluxed, and coated.

Bare electrodes, Fig. 5.9, may be used to weld wrought iron or low-carbon steels but must be used only with straight polarity. A coating of flux and slagging materials may be added to yield better welding conditions. Flux prevents oxides from forming and removes oxides already formed.

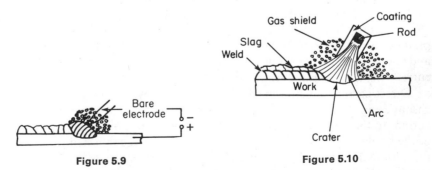

Figure 5.9　　　　　　　　　　**Figure 5.10**

The greatest amount of welding is done with coated rods. Figure 5.10 shows a coated electrode in operation. The rod is coated with the composition material. As the arc is struck, a pool of molten metal forms. The intense heat also melts the electrode, which mixes with the molten pool of base metal. The coating, which melts at a higher temperature than the rod, forms a slag with the impurities which solidifies over the bead to form a protective coating over the completed weld. Gases also form which shield the molten pool from the nitrogen and oxygen in the atmosphere.

In Fig. 5.10 it can be seen that the coating melts *after* the rod and thus forms a recess in the end of the electrode. This also protects the end of the rod from the atmosphere.

Coatings are also used to produce gas shields to protect the weld itself from the atmosphere. Stabilizers are added to the coatings to prevent splattering. Titanium oxide or potassium compounds are added to increase the melting rate of the metal being welded for better penetration. Titanium oxide or calcium fluoride are added as slag formers. Ferromanganese is added as a deoxidizer. In addition, alloying and hardening elements may be added to the coating.

The American Welding Society has classified welding rods by number. In general a number such as E6015 may be read as follows: The letter E refers to an electrode. The next two or three digits refer to the minimum tensile strength after stress relieving. Thus 60 means 60,000 psi. The next to the last digit represents the position of the welding process. Thus 1 denotes an all-position rod for flat, vertical, overhead, or horizontal positions; 2 denotes horizontal and flat positions only; and 3 denotes a flat position only. The last digit may be obtained from Table 5.1. It denotes the type of coating

TABLE 5.1

Fourth digit	Type of coating	Welding current
0	*	*
1	Cellulose potassium	ac or dc reverse or straight
2	Titania sodium	ac or dc straight
3	Titania potassium	ac or dc straight or reverse
4	Iron powder titania	ac or dc straight or reverse
5	Low hydrogen sodium	dc reverse
6	Low hydrogen potassium	ac or dc reverse
7	Iron powder iron oxide	ac or dc
8	Iron powder low hydrogen	ac or dc reverse or straight

*When the fourth digit is 0, the type of coating and current to use are determined by the third digit. For example, E6010 indicates a cellulose sodium coating and operates on dc reverse, while both E6020 and E6030 have iron oxide coatings and operate on ac or dc current.

(Courtesy of Hobart Brothers Co.)

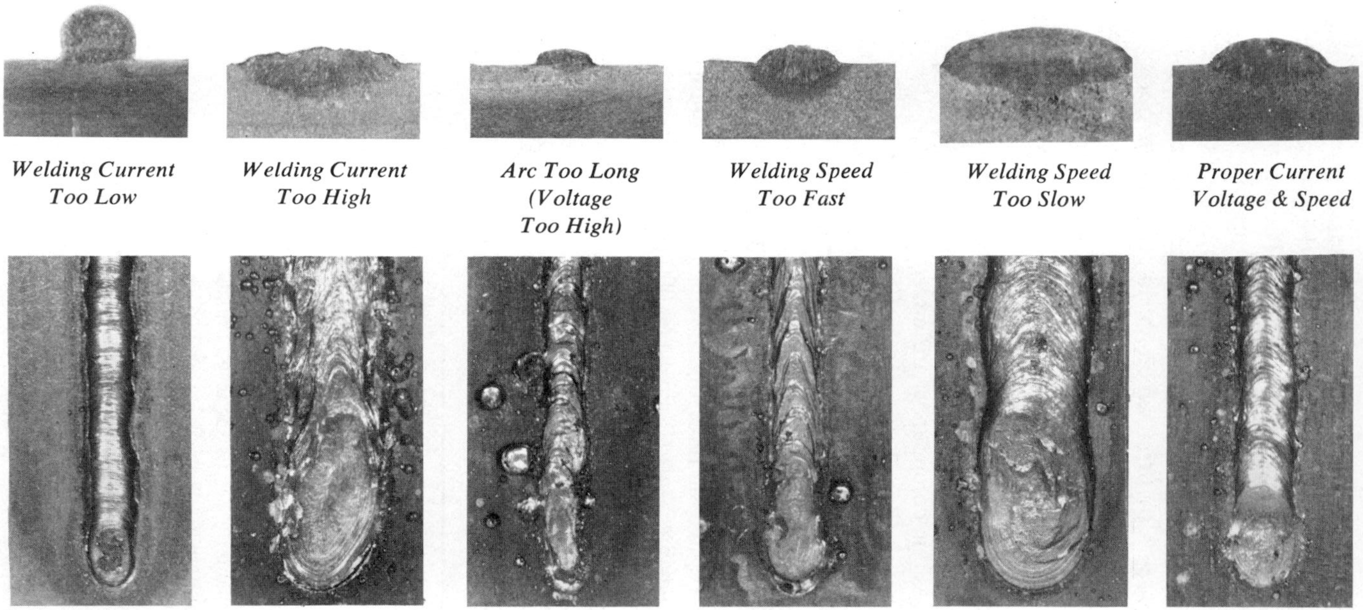

Welding Current Too Low

Excessive piling up of weld metal.

Overlapping bead has poor penetration.

Slow up progress.

Wasted electrodes and productive time.

Welding Current Too High

Excessive spatter to be cleaned off.

Undercutting along edges weakens joint.

Irregular deposit.

Wasted electrodes and productive time.

Arc Too Long (Voltage Too High)

Bead very irregular with poor penetration.

Weld metal not properly shielded.

An inefficient weld.

Wasted electrodes and productive time.

Welding Speed Too Fast

Bead too small, with contour irregular.

Not enough weld metal in the cross section.

Weld not strong enough.

Wasted electrodes and productive time.

Welding Speed Too Slow

Excessive piling up of weld metal.

Overlapping without penetration of edges.

Too much time consumed.

Wasted electrodes and productive time.

Proper Current Voltage & Speed

A smooth regular, well formed bead.

No undercutting over-lapping or piling up.

Uniform in cross section.

Excellent weld at minimum material and labor cost.

Figure 5.11   (Courtesy of Hobart Bros. Co.)

and the current to be used. When the fourth digit is 0, the current and the type of coating is determined by the next to the last digit in the rod number.

The amperage to be used is determined by the rod thickness. Thus, if a rod wire measures $\frac{1}{8}$ in., the amperage to be used is the decimal equivalent of the diameter of the rod, in this case 125 amp.

In general the arc length should be equal to the rod diameter. If the arc is too long, the metal forms large globules in an irregular pattern because the arc wanders. Poor fusion with the base metal also results. If the arc is too short, the electrode sticks to the base metal. Also, if the arc is not hot enough or is too short, not enough of the base metal melts and the bead rests on top of the work. The results are poor fusion and gas and slag holes.

Figure 5.11 shows some of the welds achieved with too low and too high currents, long and short arcs, and fast and slow speeds. The last photograph shows a proper weld.

After the rod has been selected, the polarity checked, and the current set, the procedure for electric arc welding is as follows:

1. Place the rod in the electrode holder.
2. Pull the shield over your eyes and strike an arc by striking the work and quickly opening up the gap to the right distance. The arc may be generated by striking the work directly, Fig. 5.12(a), or by scraping the work, Fig. 5.12(b). A $\frac{1}{8}$ inch gap will generate the necessary arc.

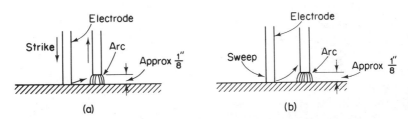

Figure 5.12

3. Several motions are available for running good beads. A side to side motion may be used to produce an acceptable bead. The motion should move uniformly while it advances. There should be a momentary pause at the reversing point to ensure uniform heating where the direction of the weave changes. This will eliminate undercuts at the sides of the weld. A fast forward motion should be used for lap welds.

   Still another motion is the figure-eight weave. In this weave a figure-eight pattern is formed as the rod moves forward. A half-moon weave may also be used when welding with a coated rod. If a bare rod is used, the best results may be achieved with the half-moon weave. A combination of half moon and straight stroke may be used for mul-

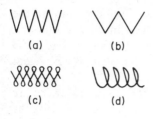

(a)   (b)

(c)   (d)

Figure 5.13

tiple beads which overlap each other, as in the case of second and third passes for built-up welds. These weaves are shown in Fig. 5.13.

4. Craters at the end of the welds may be eliminated with several backward and forward short passes and then, instead of pulling the rod free with a vertical motion, let the rod sweep in an arc away from the weld but over the completed weld.

5.8. Causes and Cures of Common Welding Troubles*

Porous welds [Fig. 5.14(a)]
   Why?
  1. Short arc, with the exception of low hydrogen and stainless.
  2. Insufficient puddling time.
  3. Impaired base metal.
  4. Poor electrodes.
   What to do?
  1. Check impurities in base metal.
  2. Allow sufficient puddling time for gases to escape.
  3. Use proper current.
  4. Weave your weld to eliminate pinholes.
  5. Use proper electrodes for job.
  6. Hold longer arc.
Poor penetration [Fig. 5.14(b)]
   Why?
  1. Speed too fast.
  2. Electrodes too large.
  3. Current too low.
  4. Faulty preparation.
   What to do?
  1. Use enough current to get desired penetration-weld slowly.
  2. Calculate electrode penetration properly.
  3. Select electrode according to welding groove size.
  4. Leave proper free space at bottom of weld.
Warping [Fig. 5.14(c)]
   Why?
  1. Shrinkage of weld metal.
  2. Faulty clamping of parts.

*Reprinted from Hobart Brothers, *Vest Pocket Guide*, Hobart Brothers, Troy, Ohio, 1964.

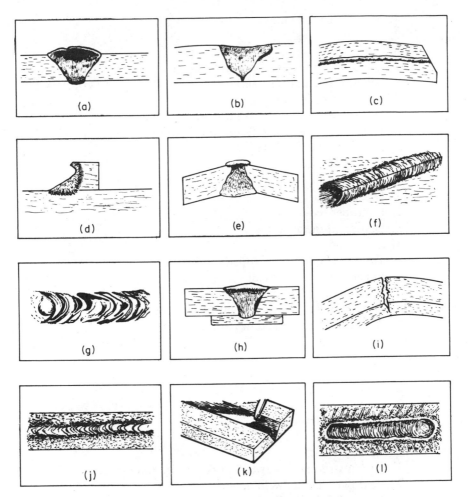

Figure 5.14 *(Courtesy of Hobart Bros. Co.)*

3. Faulty preparation.
4. Overheating at joint.

What to do?

1. Peen joint edges before welding.
2. Weld rapidly.
3. Avoid excessive space between parts.
4. Clamp parts properly; back up to cool.
5. Adopt a welding procedure.
6. Use high-speed, moderate penetration electrodes.

Undercutting [Fig. 5.14(d)]

Why?

1. Faulty electrode manipulation.

2. Faulty electrode usage.
3. Current too high.

What to do?

1. Use a uniform weave in butt welding.
2. Avoid using an overly large electrode.
3. Avoid excessive weaving.
4. Use moderate current; weld slowly.
5. Hold electrode at a safe distance from vertical plane in making horizontal fillet welds.

Distortion [Fig. 5.14(e)]

Why?

1. Uneven heat.
2. Improper sequence.
3. Deposited metal shrinks.

What to do?

1. Tack or clamp parts properly.
2. Form parts before welding.
3. Dispose of rolling or forming strains before welding.
4. Distribute welding to prevent uneven heating.
5. Examine structure and develop a sequence.

Cracked welds [Fig. 5.14(f)]

Why?

1. Wrong electrode.
2. Weld and parts sizes unbalanced.
3. Faulty welds.
4. Faulty preparation.
5. Rigid joints.

What to do?

1. Design structure and welding procedure to eliminate rigid joints.
2. Heat parts before welding.
3. Avoid welds in string beads.
4. Keep ends free to move as long as possible.
5. Make sound welds of good fusion.
6. Adjust weld size to parts size.
7. Allow joints a proper and uniform free space.
8. Work with as low an amperage as possible.

Poor appearance [Fig. 5.14(g)]

Why?

1. Faulty electrodes.
2. Overhang.
3. Improper use of electrodes.
4. Wrong arc and current voltage.

What to do?

1. Use a proper welding technique.

2. Avoid overheating.

3. Use a uniform weave.

4. Avoid overly high current.

Poor fusion [Fig. 5.14(h)]

Why?

1. Wrong speed.

2. Current improperly adjusted.

3. Faulty preparation.

4. Improper electrode size.

What to do?

1. Adjust electrode and V size.

2. Weave must be sufficient to melt sides of joints.

3. Proper current will allow deposition and penetration.

4. Keep weld metal from curling away from plates.

Brittle welds [Fig. 5.14(i)]

Why?

1. Wrong electrode.

2. Faulty preheating.

3. Metal hardened by air.

What to do?

1. Preheat at 300 to 500°F if welding on medium-carbon steel or certain alloy steels.

2. Make multiple-layer welds.

3. Anneal after welding.

4. Use stainless or low-hydrogen electrodes for increasing weld ductility.

Spatter [Fig. 5.14(j)]

Why?

1. Arc blow.

2. Current too high.

3. Arc too long.

4. Faulty electrodes.

What to do?

1. Whitewash parts in weld area.

2. Adjust current to needs.

3. Adjust to proper arc length.

4. Lighten arc blow.

5. Pick suitable electrodes.

Magnetic blow [Fig. 5.14(k)]

Why?

1. Magnetic fields cause the arc to deviate from its intended course.

What to do?

1. Use steel blocks to alter magnetic path around arc.

2. Divide the ground into parts.

3. Weld in same direction the arc blows.
4. Use a short arc.
5. Locate the ground properly on the work.
6. Use ac welding.

Weld stresses [Fig. 5.14(l)]

Why?

1. Faulty welds.
2. Faulty sequence.
3. Rigid joints.

What to do?

1. Allow parts to move freely as long as practical.
2. Make as few passes as possible.
3. Peen deposits.
4. Anneal according to thickness of weld.
5. Move parts slightly in welding to reduce stresses.

5.9. Additional Electric Welding Processes

Inert-gas arc welding.   Figure 5.15(a) shows the torch and filler rod used in the process known as *Gas Tungsten Arc Welding* (*TIG*). Figure 5.15(b) shows the *Gas Metal Arc Welding* (*MIA*) process. In the latter process the filler rod is fed through the center of the torch. Helium, argon, or carbon dioxide is introduced into the chamber which houses either a tungsten or carbon electrode. Gas emitted through an opening circumscribes the electrode and forms a protective cloud about the arc when aluminum or magnesium are being welded. Both metals oxidize rapidly and need this protection during the welding process. Arcing takes place between the electrode and the work.

In the case of magnesium a noncombustible electrode is used in combination with helium and dc current. In the case of aluminum a combustible electrode and argon are used in combination with ac current. Straight-polarity dc current may be used to weld steel, stainless steel, copper, or cast iron.

It is also possible to use a consumable wire electrode and reverse-polarity dc current with either argon or helium gas to weld aluminum, magnesium, or other metals. Straight-polarity and ac current are not suited to this method because they cause excess splatter.

Carbon dioxide gas, because of excellent penetration and high speed, is at times used to weld carbon steels.

Atomic hydrogen welding.   Two tungsten electrodes are housed in a multiple chamber that transports molecular hydrogen past them. An ac arc is generated between the two electrodes. The heat disassociates the hydrogen molecules, which absorb large amounts of heat and separate into atoms. This

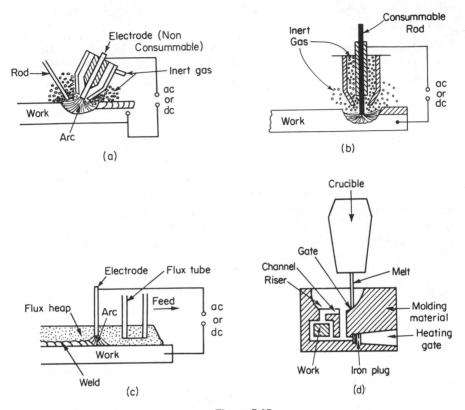

Figure 5.15

heat is released when the hydrogen atoms contact the metal to be welded. The heat and temperature attained this way are very high.

If desired, a filler rod may be used to supply additional metal during the fusion process. The gas acts as a shield for both the weld and the electrode while the process is taking place. Materials not usually able to be joined by other processes may be welded in this manner, such as alloy tools, dies, punches, etc. Especially good results are obtained if a filler rod of the same material as the base metal is used. With this method it is also possible to weld thin sections, monel, stainless steel, etc.

Submerged arc welding. In this process a consumable bare rod is used in combination with a flux feeder tube. The flux is used freely and an arc is maintained under a blanket of flux. The feed of the electrode and tube is automatic. The flux melts and forms a protective coating of slag over the weld. The use of high current permits higher welding speeds than in other processes. Since the melt is composed mostly of base metal, the finished weld resembles the base metal and makes for homogeneous structure. [Fig. 5.15(c).]

This process may be used to weld low-carbon steels, nickel, bronze, and other nonferrous metals.

Thermite welding. A mixture of iron oxide and granular aluminum is ignited. [See Fig. 5.15(d).] The rapid reaction that follows converts aluminum and iron oxide to steel and aluminum oxide. If desired, other alloys may be added to the mixture before ignition.

Heat is generated by the current passing through the electrically conducive slag. Slag is added continuously.

A specially prepared mold is made around the section of the part to be welded. Wax is poured around the pieces to be joined and supported by a refractory sand mold. Risers and a pouring gate are cut into the sand. The wax is then burned out and the entire mold preheated through the heating gate. The mixture of aluminum flake and iron oxide is ignited by a special ignition powder or a magnesium strip in the crucible. The melt is then tapped off into the pouring gate and permitted to flow around the joint to be welded. The aluminum oxide slag flows off.

The electroslag process. Used to join large plates, the weld is accomplished by maintaining a hot molten metal pool between plates. A welding wire is fed into the melt to maintain the pool. Water-cooled jackets cool and solidify the metal, moving with the weld at a predetermined speed to produce a continuous weld.

The electron-beam process. The electron-beam is started in a highly evacuated chamber and directed at the surfaces to be joined. The temperature achieved by this process is very high and localized to such a degree that the parent metal structure remains unaffected. Penetration and feed rate are much better than those obtained with any of the other processes. Thus, metals may be joined that cannot be joined by other methods.

Friction welding. One member of the two pieces to be joined is rotated at high speed while the other member is pressed against it with a high axial pressure. The weld is completed when the friction heats the contact surfaces to the plastic state.

Ultrasonic welding. High frequency vibrations are directed parallel to the welded surfaces. Clamping force and preset timing are important. The clamped pieces are brought near the vibrating machine and the vibrations increased until the weld is completed.

Several *gas metal-arc* welding processes have been developed. One process uses carbon dioxide (CO_2), or a mixture of CO_2 and one of the inert gases, as a shield. These processes may use an electrode and a separate filler rod, or a consumable flux cored filler rod. The latter deposits a slag.

Another method is the *micro-wire* gas metal-arc process. A small diameter filler rod (0.030 to 0.045 in.) and CO_2 are used. This produces a smooth weld and may be used to weld very thin metal (0.025 to 0.250 in.). The *self shielding electrode wire* process uses a tubular electrode wire which contains a core of gas and a deoxidizing flux.

Advantages of these processes are: (1) high welding speeds and metal deposit; (2) good wire size-to-penetration ratio; (3) minimum splatter, and a wide work thickness range.

5.10. Gas Welding

In these processes the combustion is obtained by mixing oxygen with a fuel to support combustion at high temperatures. Hydrogen, natural, or producers gas may be used, but acetylene is by far the most popular because the equipment and gas are comparatively inexpensive and portable. The flame produces a temperature of about 6300°F.

The oxygen (O_2) combines with the acetylene (C_2H_2) which burns at temperatures well above the melting point of the metal to be welded. This process may be used to fuse metals with or without adding filler rod. No pressure is needed to consummate the weld.*

The equipment consists of an oxygen cylinder and an acetylene cylinder and auxiliary equipment. The oxygen cylinder contains about 250 ft³ of gas at about 2200 psi at 70°F and measures about 9 in. in diameter by 4 ft high. The acetylene cylinder is filled with a material saturated with acetone. Acetone absorbs the acetylene when under pressure and acts as a quieter. The tank contains about 275 ft³ of gas at 250 psi and is about 12 in. in diameter and $3\frac{1}{2}$ ft high.

Oxygen is produced by a fractional distillation process. Pure oxygen is highly combustible. It will burn rapidly when in contact with oil or other foreign substances. Acetylene is produced from calcium carbide and when combined with oxygen, it burns very rapidly. Both tanks are equipped with shutoff valves and regulators. The valve on the oxygen tank is constructed with a double seat because of the high pressure in the tank. Turning the hand-wheel counterclockwise until the upper seat on the stem registers, seals off any leakage around the stem. A safety disc is also provided in case the tank is subjected to excessive heat.

The acetylene tank is equipped with a valve and a special wrench. When opening, the valve is cracked open about one-fourth of a turn. The bottom of this tank is supplied with fusible plugs which melt at elevated temperatures.

The regulators generally used are of the diaphragm type, as shown in Fig. 5.16. When the adjusting screw is turned out (counterclockwise), a rubber diaphragm pulls the valve shut and the gas flow is cut off. The pressure against the valve holds it shut, especially if the line is "bled off." If the diaphragm is compressed, the valve opens and permits the gas (oxygen or

---

*Processes are being developed that use special torches to heat the contact ends of the metals to be joined. As the ends become plastic, pressure is used to force them together.

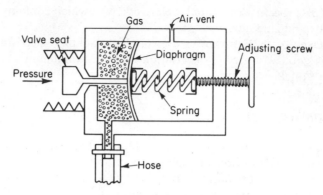

Figure 5.16

acetylene) to flow into the hose. If the gas is not being drained off the hose, the pressure from the tank balances the spring pressure. The valve closes and cuts off the gas flow. As the gas is used, the hose pressure drops, opening the valve and supplying gas as needed. These valves are also equipped with safety devices. On each tank are two Bourdon gages, one to register the pressure in the tank, the other to monitor the pressure in the hose.

Twin hoses are used. The red hose indicates acetylene; the dark green or black hose, oxygen. The oxygen hose has right-hand connections, and the acetylene hose has left-hand connections. The acetylene connection has a groove machined on its outside. Special wrenches should be used when making the connections. One end of the hose is connected to the tank, the other end to the torch. Figure 5.17 shows the construction of the torch. This type of torch delivers oxygen and acetylene at equal pressures. Another type, called the *injection torch*, utilizes the oxygen pressure to carry low-pressure acetylene to the tip.

Welding tips are provided in various sizes to control the quantity of heat delivered. The student should realize that a large tip opening delivers more

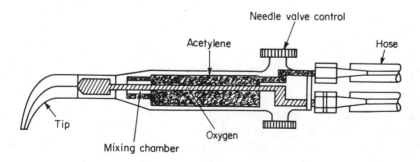

Figure 5.17

heat than a small tip. The temperature in both instances, nonetheless, is 6300°F.

Tips are classified by number, and the orifice sizes are according to numbered drill sizes. Plate thickness to be welded is related to the pressure at the tip and orifice opening. Generally, the larger the tip number, the larger is the orifice opening. The manufacturer should be consulted for proper tip rating, and the rod size and composition.

Valves and needle controls regulate the ratio of the mixtures at the tip. There are three flames that may be obtained by regulating the ratio of oxygen to acetylene: (1) the carburizing flame, Fig. 5.18(a); (2) the neutral flame, Fig. 5.18(b); and (3) the oxidizing flame, Fig. 5.18(c).

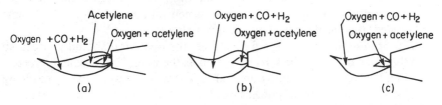

Figure 5.18

If the oxygen to acetylene ratio is 1 : 1 in the inner cone, a neutral flame, Fig. 5.18(b), is said to exist. The temperature at the inner cone is about 6000°F and has a light-blue appearance. The outer envelope forms a shield from the atmosphere and burns with a dark-blue color. This flame is used to weld steel and, assuming control of other variables, a sound weld results.

The oxidizing flame, Fig. 5.18(c), results from a mixture of oxygen with acetylene in a ratio of about 1.5 : 1. The inner cone is shorter, necked down to a point much more, and has a darker bluish color than the inner cone for neutral flame. The outer cone is shorter and broader than that of the neutral flame. The inner cone is hotter than the neutral inner cone and will cause splatter and burning of the steel. It also oxidizes most metals on contact and causes them to be brittle. Metals such as copper and brass may be welded with this flame because the oxide film protects the metal from hydrogen.

The carburizing flame, Fig. 5.18(a), mixes the oxygen and acetylene in the ratio of about 0.9 : 1. This flame is characterized by three cones, or envelopes. The outer envelope will be longer than the neutral envelope and brighter. The inner cone will be as distinct in shape as the neutral cone. Between the outer envelope and the inner cone will be another cone caused by the excess acetylene being delivered at the tip. Its length will depend upon the overbalance of acetylene to oxygen. Its color approaches white. This flame may be used to weld aluminum, stainless steel, zinc die castings, nickel, monel, etc. Excess carbon content will form carbides in steel that are hard and brittle and may be objectionable.

5.11. Gas Welding—The Operation

Assume all connections are made and that the proper tip has been selected and attached to the torch. Before opening the valves on the tanks, unscrew the regulator controls until they turn freely. A sudden pressure on the regulator may damage the diaphragm in the regulator. Close the needle valve on the torch. Cover your eyes with welding goggles.

The oxygen valve should be opened all the way and the acetylene valve cracked open about a quarter turn. The acetylene needle valve on the torch should be opened about one full turn and ignited with a spark lighter. The flame should burn about $\frac{1}{4}$ in. from the tip after adjustment of the regulator control. Open the oygen needle valve one full turn and adjust the regulator until the center cone disappears. This is a neutral flame. If fine adjustments are needed, the needle valves on the torch should be used.

If a bead is to be run on a flat surface, the operation should proceed so that the flame moves in the same direction as the weld. This is called *forehand* welding. The torch should make an angle of 45° with the weld, the flame facing away from the weld so that preheating of the metal not yet welded takes place. The flame is held stationary until a molten pool develops. The weave and travel proceed. Penetration and appearance are important.

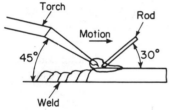

Figure 5.19

A small clockwise circular weave perpendicular to the plate may be used as the movement proceeds in the direction of the incompleted weld. If a welding rod is used, the angle between the rod and the work should be 30°. The included angle between the torch tip and the rod should be about 100°. (See Fig. 5.19.)

When welding heavy plate, a half-moon weave may be used to give greater weld width. If a welding rod is to be used, the motion of the torch and the rod is circular and parallel to the surface of the plate to be welded. The rod is manipulated so that it is always at the opposite side of the pool from the torch.

In *backhand* welding the torch and the rod in Fig. 5.19 are interchanged so that the flame faces the completed weld. Flux may be used to reduce oxides already formed or which might form during the welding operation.

5.12. The Cutting Operation

Oxyacetylene cutting tips are constructed with a center hole for delivering oxygen at high pressures (30 to 60 psi). Circumscribed around this hole are other orifices which deliver oxygen and acetylene at low pressures (3 to 5 psi) and temperatures (about 1700°F). This is called the ignition temperature.

The oxyacetylene flame is directed over the edge of the plate to be cut to bring the steel to the oxidizing temperature. Once this is achieved, the pure oxygen pressure stream is turned on with a lever or button on the torch. The stream of oxygen causes very rapid oxidation (burning) of the metal. This releases additional heat which causes further oxidizing of the metal. The melt is blown away by the pressure stream, and the cut is completed with a slow steady speed.

Cutting operations may be done by hand or machine. Special machines (pantographs) for cutting shapes have been developed by which a pointer traces the desired shape from a template. The cutting torch (or torches) is actuated (manually, electrically, or electronically) by the motion of the tracing head.

Flame machining.   This is used for rough-machining surfaces rapidly. The torch is set to remove metal rather than to cut through the metal.

Hard facing and flame hardening.   In *hard facing*, a rod or powder alloy possessing hardness is melted with the oxyacetylene flame to a suitable base metal. *Flame hardening* consists of heating hardenable steel above the critical temperature with the torch, followed by spraying with water, which quenches and surface hardens the preheated piece.

5.13.   The Brazing Process

The brazing of two parts in most instances requires the use of a nonferrous filler rod. The parts to be joined and the filler rod are brought to a temperature which is *below* the melting point of the parts to be joined but *above* the melting point of the brazing material. The brazing material must wet the surfaces to be joined and through capillary action draw the melt into the space between the two parts. Therefore, space should be provided between the parts to be brazed so that the capillary action can take place.

Capillary action takes place when the attracting forces between the braze (or solder) material and the material being brazed is greater than the attractive forces within the braze material itself. This causes the braze material to spread over the surface being brazed. The phenomenon is called *wetting*.

If the space between the two pieces to be brazed is *too large*, the strength of the brazed joint is a function of the attraction forces between the molecules of the brazing material, rather than the attraction forces between the brazing material and the base metal. If the space between the two pieces being brazed is *too small*, neither capillarity nor wetting can take place. At best, the braze is discontinuous and the joint is weak.

The optimum strength which can be achieved with brazing occurs when adhesion is present between the molecules of the braze material and the molecules of the base metal. Under these conditions, some alloying takes place between the base metal and the braze material. As a result, the strength of a brazed joint is *greater* than the strength of the braze material alone but *less* than the strength of the base material alone. To achieve this condition the separation between the parts to be brazed should be from a minimum of 0.001 in. to a maximum of $\frac{1}{32}$ in.

The temperature at which brazing material melts should be above 1000°F. This temperature should be well below the melting point of the parts joined. It is interesting to note that the welding processes require that both the base material and the filler material melt so that upon solidification they form a single solid. The brazing (or soldering) processes rely upon close molecular contact, so that the magnitude of the forces between the two materials establishes the effectiveness of the brazed joint.

To consummate a good brazed joint, cleanliness is of the utmost importance. The use of fluxes insures clean surfaces and promotes filler-material flow. That is, the cleaner the surface of the workpiece and the shorter the interface distance between the work and the braze molecules, the greater are the attraction forces between the two. Overheating causes zinc oxides to form, and a green flame results. Of course, this should be avoided.

It is also important that the parts being brazed are held stationary until the liquid phases of the braze solidify. Any movement of the workpieces during solidification will cause a weak joint to form.

Blind holes must be vented; otherwise the braze will not flow into the joint, or pressure may be built up behind the liquid braze and cause holes in the solid braze upon cooling.

The three basic joints used are: the butt joint, Fig. 5.20(a); the lap joint, Fig. 5.20(b); and the scarf joint, Fig. 5.20(c). All other joints are variations of these three.

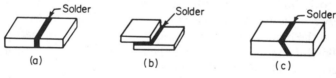

Figure 5.20

The brazing operation may be done as described in Section 5.15 of this chapter. It may also be done by using formed strips of brazing material. These strips are made to fit the shape of the joint to be brazed. Heat is applied to melt the braze and cause it to flow. When using formed strips, foils, or formed wires, a furnace should be used to melt the braze material uniformly.

The methods for generating the necessary heat are limitless. The economy of the operation usually dictates the type of heating operation to be used. Two of the considerations for furnace selection are the need for uniform heating of both members and the need for, and type of, controlled atmosphere.

Torch brazing.   In this most common brazing method a neutral flarne is directed at both parts so as to get uniform heating of both pieces before the braze melts. The fuels used may be oxyacetylene, oxyhydrogen, or natural gas. Oxidization and distortion may be factors in this type of operation which must be dealt with if the operator is not skilled.

Resistance brazing.   An electric current is passed through the parts being brazed. The resistance to the passage of the current generates heat and melts the braze material and the flux. Any of the resistance machines discussed earlier may be used for this type of brazing. Special machines using water-cooled carbon electrodes have been designed for use in resistance brazing. These machines are equipped with accurate time-controlling devices. The size of the work is one of the limitations of this type of machine. Because heating is rapid and localized, distortion may occur in the work.

Induction furnaces.   Workpieces are heated with a high-frequency alternating current which generates a rapidly oscillating magnetic field. The parts to be brazed are placed in a specially designed water-cooled coil made to fit the shape of the workpiece. The parts, Fig. 5.21, are assembled with the brazing material and flux in position. The coil is fitted to the part, the current is turned on for a predetermined length of time, and the braze is consummated.

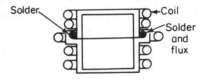

Figure 5.21

Because the heating cycle is short and because the heating takes place within the parts to be joined, localized heating can be achieved without heating the rest of the workpiece. Since localized heating may warp the workpiece, strict control must be exercised.

Furnace brazing.   An electric furnace and a controlled atmosphere will give the best results. Any of the inert gases may be used to prevent copper braze from oxidizing. If oxide formation is no problem, a controlled atmosphere is not necessary.

With this method many parts may be assembled with the brazing material and flux (if used) in position. The entire assembly is then placed in the furnace and brazed in one operation. The heating is uniform and relatively free from distortion. Good control of temperature and atmosphere gives good surface conditions. Localized heating, which was possible with the induction process, cannot be achieved with this method.

Dip brazing.   When accomplished by dipping the assembled parts into a molten bath of the filler material, this method is called *metal bath brazing.* In *chemical bath brazing* the assembly is dipped into a neutral salt bath with the filler rod in position on the work. Oxidization is negligible because the parts do not come into contact with the atmosphere. In both processes accurate temperature control is possible. In the chemical bath process no flux is needed.

5.14. Brazing Materials and Fluxes

Silver brazing.   Commonly called *silver soldering*, this is a low-temperature brazing process. A copper-silver-phosphorus alloy filler is the most common type used for brazing copper or brass, with the phosphorus acting as a flux. The temperature range for copper-silver-phosphorus brazing material to flow freely is from 1150 to 1500°F. Materials such as steel, stainless steel, and nickel alloys may be brazed with silver alloys containing silver, copper, cadmium, and zinc but containing no phosphorus. Phosphorus alloys might form, causing brittle joints.

Copper.   Used in its pure state, copper has the highest melting point (1982°F) of all the brazing materials and because of this should be used on workpieces which are high-melting-point alloys such as high-speed steel and carbide. The brazing process is accomplished in a hydrogen atmosphere with the parts to be brazed in direct contact (press fitted) with each other. At this high temperature an alloy of the base material and the copper forms and causes a very strong joint.

Copper alloys.   Tobin bronze and phos-copper are the two most commonly used brazing materials in this class. Tobin bronze is an alloy of copper-zinc-tin and melts at about 1625°F. It is used to braze cast iron, steel, or copper. Phos-copper alloys are used for brazing copper, tungsten, or molybdenum. Its temperature range is from 1300 to 1700°F depending upon the ratio of the two alloys. They are not to be used with ferrous materials and materials having more than 10% nickel content. When used on copper, the phosphorus acts as a flux.

Aluminum alloys.   The alloy is usually formed with silicon and has a temperature range of 1050 to 1180°F. These brazing materials may be used only on aluminum or aluminum alloys. Since the melting point of the aluminum brazing material is close to the melting point of the base material, a very careful control of the temperature must be maintained. A flux is always needed to reduce the oxides which form. Sheets coated with a brazing material may be purchased to facilitate the brazing process.

Nickel-chrome.   Nickel-chrome braze (called *heat-resistant braze*) is used to join alloys high in nickel, stainless, alloy, and carbon steels. The temperature range for using this material is above 2000°F. The brazing operation may be achieved in a hydrogen atmosphere furnace without flux. If used in other atmosphere-controlled furnaces, a flux is needed. Corrosion resistance, as well as high-heat resistance, is obtained by using this process.

Silver manganese.　　Another of the high-heat-resistant brazes, it is used to join stainless steel and alloys having a high nickel content. Its brazing temperature range is about 1780 to 2100°F. But its operational strength at temperatures over 900°F once the braze is completed, decreases. A reducing controlled-atmosphere furnace is required.

Fluxes.　　Chemicals are used to dissolve surface oxide coatings which have formed prior to brazing; to prevent oxides from forming during the brazing operation on both the base metal and the brazing material; and to facilitate the wetting process by reducing the viscosity of the melt. Parts must be cleaned to remove foreign substances such as oils and greases because brazing fluxes will not remove these.

On brass, copper, bronze, and low-carbon steels a mixture of boric acid, borax, and a wetting agent may be used. The mixture will not dissolve molybdenum, silver, chrome, or tungsten oxides. They can only be used with the high-melting-point brazing materials, because of the high temperature (1400°F) at which they become fluid. The student is reminded that, in order to be effective, fluxes must melt before the brazing material melts.

For cast iron a wetting agent is used with boric acid, borax, or a fluoride. It can be used as either a powder or a paste. The flux "floats" the oxide, which is removed. The appearance of white specks in the molten flux indicates that more flux is needed.

For brazing aluminum and magnesium a flux of chlorides and fluorides mixed with water to form a paste may be used in a temperature range of 700 to 1200°F. If a wetting agent is added, the paste may be used to braze titanium. Aluminum alloys containing bronze or brass need a borate and a wetting agent to give better flow and oxide-dissolving properties. The temperature range of the flux increases by about 300°F.

In general the materials which may be found in flux compounds are the borates, fused borax, boric acid, fluoborates or fluorides, chlorides, and to some extent potassium and sodium hydroxide, wetting agents, and water.

Of all the chemicals, only borax need not be removed after brazing unless the surface is to be treated further. Residue from the others has all the characteristics of glass and should be removed since corrosion sets in immediately. The removal of the flux may be accomplished with a water or an acid bath, as flux is water soluble. Sometimes a hot water spray or hot water bath will dissolve the flux. A wet cloth applied while the part is still hot will also remove the flux. Chemical dips may be used when the above is ineffective. Sand blasting, emery cloth, wire brushing, or steam jets may also be used.

Fluxes may be applied in the form of powder, paste, or liquid. Powder flux in its dry form may be sprinkled on the joint to be brazed. Care must be taken not to lose the powder, which does not have good adhesive qualities. Some success has been achieved in brazing by mixing powdered filler rod and powdered flux.

Paste fluxes may be brushed or sprayed on the joint with good adhesive qualities. This method of applying flux is the most widely used. Unlike the powdered fluxes, the paste will cling to vertical surfaces. Liquid fluxes, such as the basic acid-borate-fluoride variety can be made when the chemical ingredients will dissolve in water. Liquid fluxes of the borax-boric acid-borate variety may be used in the spray process in which the gas passes through the liquid flux picking up small particles of flux and delivering them to the joint as the brazing proceeds.

When brazing copper or iron in a hydrogen-atmosphere furnace, the atmosphere acts as a flux by reducing the oxides. In some instances, especially when the atmosphere fails to reduce the oxides, one of the above fluxes must be used. The salt bath also acts as a flux.

5.15. The Brazing Operation

When two pieces of steel are to be brazed with a bronze rod, the work should be placed in such a manner that the surfaces upon which the work rests should not absorb the heat needed during the brazing operation. The pieces to be brazed should be chemically clean, free from scale and iron oxide.

Butt the two pieces together in the joining position. Any of the joints referred to in the preceding chapters may be used here. Adjust the flame, heat the brazing rod, and dip it into the flux. The flux will cling to the rod. Heat the work and the flux-coated rod until a drop of braze appears on the work. Withdraw the rod. Heat the work and the drop of braze until the drop of braze melts and runs.

Once the drop runs, the rod should be inserted into the flame, and with a circular motion the brazing operation may be completed. The angle between the rod and the work and between the torch tip and the work should be about 75°. As the operation proceeds, the flux will run ahead of the brazing deposit and be consumed. Once the flux is consumed, the rod should again be dipped into the flux and the operation continued.

When brazing cast iron, the joint must be preheated to a dull red. Flux is sprinkled on the work or applied to the rod. Since the surfaces to be brazed are usually prepared in a "V," it is important to tin both sides of the "V" before the bead is run. In most instances several beads must be run, one on top of the other.

At times it is necessary to braze carbide tool tips to a steel shank. Since carbide is an expensive material and because it is brittle in large cross sections, it is usually brazed to a low-alloy carbon-steel shank. This usually requires that the shank be prepared with a recess [Fig. 5.22(a)] into which the carbide blank is set, as shown in Fig. 5.22(b).

The recess must be chemically clean. The brazing material may be copper, Tobin bronze, or silver solder. A flux brazing foil is placed in the recess and the carbide slug is then placed on the foil. Heating may be done in a furnace

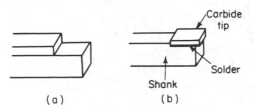

Figure 5.22

or with an oxyacetylene flame. The underside of the shank, directly under the carbide slug, is heated until the braze material is liquid. The slug is pressed down and held until the braze solidifies.

If desired, the recess in the shank may be coated with a flux, or, if a rod is used, the rod may be coated with a flux. The recess is then tinned or coated with the brazing material, the tool inserted, and the brazing process continued as above.

Because of the high temperatures and the danger of cracking the carbide, slow cooling is very important. The finished tool should not be permitted to cool in air. Covering with powdered coal, asbestos, mica, or lime may be used to slow down the cooling process.

5.16. Solder Technology

Solder may be purchased in almost any desired form (bar, wire, slab, foil, or powder). It has essentially a tin-lead base and melts below 800°F. Other alloys such as bismuth and cadmium may be added to reduce the melting point. Antimony raises the melting point slightly.

The formation of an intermetallic solution at low temperature is the mechanism of the soldering process. The solder acts as a metal solvent by melting small amounts of the base metal, and these form a chemical bond with one of the solder constituents. Since a new alloy is formed in a good solder joint, the strength of the joint is a function of the alloy rather than of the solder used to form the joint. Thus a thickness of about 0.005 in. of solder is maximum for maximum strength. Fillets add little to the strength of the joint.

Figure 5.23 shows the tin-lead equilibrium diagram. An alloy of 63% tin and 37% lead has a melting point of 361°F. Both constituents must melt before the temperature begins to rise. This transformation is a eutectic transformation, as discussed previously. A eutectic solder is ideal because both phases melt at the same time. Thus, once the solder begins to melt, the operator is certain that both phases are melting.

Assume a 50 : 50% lead-tin composition. If the solder is heated to 361°F, it will absorb heat at that temperature until the entire eutectic phase has melted. Once the eutectic phase has melted, the lead-rich solid melts and

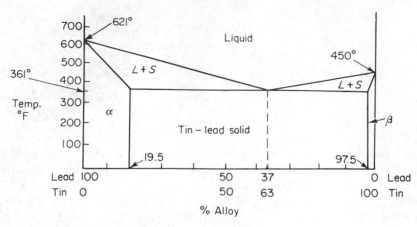

Figure 5.23

becomes increasingly liquid as the temperature increases. At the upper transformation line the entire solder structure is liquid.

If a 70% tin to 30% lead alloy is used, the tin-rich solid starts to liquefy after the eutectic phase has turned liquid. The significance of this mechanism is that in the $L + S$ region the solder is not completely melted. For a good solder joint, the heating must proceed until both constituents are liquid.

During the above processes, at least one of the molten constituents must be soluble in the base metal. Adhesion between the solder and the base metal is far more important than cohesion between the solder-to-solder particles. As a matter of fact, if little balls of solder form on the work surface, the cohesion forces are greater than the adhesion forces and a poor solder joint results. Adhesion forces are greater between the solder and the base metal only if the solder wets the surface of the base metal.

Solder may be classified as corrosive and noncorrosive. The term corrosive refers to the reaction which takes place after the soldering operation is consummated.

A corrosive flux may be made by mixing three parts of zinc chloride and one part of sal ammoniac with water. Copper, brass, aluminum, carbon steel, or nickel may be soldered with this flux. It has a low melting point and may be used with eutectic solders and is very effective in removing oxides. Dilute solutions of phosphoric acid or hydrochloric acid may be used as a flux when soldering stainless steel. For soldering aluminum an effective flux may be made by adding hydrofluoric acid to hydrochloric or phosphoric acid. A paste flux may be made by mixing zinc chloride, sal ammoniac, water, and petroleum jelly.

To render the solder joint noncorrosive, a solution of 5 oz hydrochloric acid to 1 gal water may be used as a wash. After washing with this solution, water must be used to dilute it and then the part must be thoroughly dried.

Rosin is used as a noncorrosive, nonconducting fluxing agent. The surface to be soldered must be cleaned before the flux is applied since the rosin will not remove heavy coats of oxide.

One of the noncorrosive fluxes may be made by dissolving one part of rosin in two parts of wood alcohol or naphtha. Rosin may be removed with naphtha or alcohol. If the flux is a water solution, hot flowing water may be used to remove it.

The heat generated for the soldering processes may come from a soldering iron, an induction furnace, or by any one of the electric resistance methods discussed in the preceding chapter.

Tinning, or wetting, is an important part of the soldering operation. After the surface of the pieces to be soldered are cleaned and after the flux has been applied, both pieces should be tinned. Molten solder will flow by capillary action along the surfaces which have been treated with flux, primarily because these are chemically cleaner than the base metal which has not been chemically cleaned with flux. A solder bath (pot) may also be used to tin, or it may be used to solder small assemblies.

5.17. The Soldering Process

Copper, steel, and other materials.   Soldering may be accomplished if the surfaces are flat and clean. The pieces are heated to a temperature which will melt the solder when it contacts the work and are tinned after the flux has been applied. If an iron is used, it must be tinned. The flat of the iron is placed in contact with the work with the solder held at the joint but at the side of the iron. The solder should not be in contact with the top of the iron during the operation. A slow uniform motion of the iron and the solder wire will complete the tinning; the two surfaces are then placed in contact with each other and the hot iron run over the joint.

Stainless steel.   Because of a stubborn corrosive film and low heat conductivity some problems may be encountered in soldering; cleaning with an abrasive or acid pickling solution is essential. Muriatic acid and zinc may be used as a flux. It must be washed off with soap and water after the operation is complete.

Aluminum.   Soldering is difficult because of its oxide coat and its high heat conductivity. A suitable flux which will dissolve the aluminum oxide film may be used. Since the oxide film forms very rapidly, the flux must melt at the soldering temperature so that the solder replaces the flux before the oxides can form. Or, as the soldering process proceeds, a wire brush or some other abrasive is used to remove the oxide, which is immediately replaced by the molten solder. This protects the aluminum from the atmosphere during the soldering operation.

Solders of pure aluminum or wrought aluminum may be used to solder aluminum alloys. A noncorrosive paste flux of analine phosphate may be used. A corrosive flux that may be used is zinc chloride, sal ammoniac, and water in liquid form. Soldering of cast or forged aluminum should be avoided.

Magnesium. Soldering is restricted to filling imperfections in the material. The part to be corrected is cleaned thoroughly by the brush method described for aluminum. A solder of cadmium-zinc-tin is used without a flux.

QUESTIONS AND PROBLEMS

5.1 List the four categories of welding. Explain each category and illustrate with at least one example.

5.2 Referring to the earlier chapters, list the metallurgical principles which apply to (a) the melt; (b) the structure as the metal cools at various temperatures; and (c) the structure and mechanical properties after the metal has cooled to room temperature.

5.3 Referring to the TTT curves (Fig. 2.20), explain the effects of several cooling rates upon the structure of the completed weld.

5.4 Assume a weld has cooled too rapidly and the metal develops stresses, martensite, and grain growth. How may each of these be corrected after the weld has been completed?

5.5 Discuss the economics of fabricating a fixture which consists of multiple pieces of varying cross sections.

5.6 Discuss the advantages and disadvantages of the following welding procedures: (1) welding all pieces into position; (2) tack welding all pieces before welding them permanently into position; (3) tacking pieces into position in a fixture, removing the assembly from the fixture, and then completing the weld.

5.7 Why is it important to clean the surfaces to be welded?

5.8 Explain the following welding joints: butt, lap, "T," corner, plug, and edge.

5.9 What are the three considerations which dictate the kind of weld joint to be used?

5.10 Discuss the reasons for using several of the joints referred to in this chapter.

5.11 (a) List and explain the components of *pressure welding*. (b) How does this differ from fusion welding?

5.12 Explain the source of heat and how it is generated in electric resistance welding.

5.13 Explain the necessity of considering the components of the equation $H = I^2 Rt$ when planning the welding operation.

5.14 How many ways may pressures be applied in pressure welding? Why is it necessary that the material be plastic instead of molten during pressure welding?

5.15 Describe the four steps needed to complete a hammer weld.

5.16 Explain the spot weld process. What are the metal thickness limits?

5.17 What must be done to join different thicknesses of the same metals by spot welding? What must be done to join the same thicknesses of different metals?

5.18 Explain seam welding. What is one of the purposes of overlapping the spots in seam welding?

5.19 What is mash seam welding? Explain the process.

5.20 Explain projection welding.

5.21 Describe the cross section of the "dimple" in the projection welding process.

5.22 What is cross-wire welding?

5.23 Explain both butt welding processes discussed in this text, and explain their differences.

5.24 What is percussion welding? Describe it.

5.25 Define or explain fusion welding.

5.26 Explain the ac welding machine.

5.27 Is the polarity important in using an ac machine? A dc welding machine? Why?

5.28 Why is it necessary to use a coated rod in the ac welding operation?

5.29 Draw a diagram of the hookup for straight-polarity welding. Do the same for reverse-polarity welding. Mark all terminals.

5.30 How may the polarity of a dc welder be checked if the poles on the machine are not marked?

5.31 What is magnetic arc blow? What effect does it have on the welding process?

5.32 What are the three factors which must be considered when selecting a coated welding rod? What are the related considerations listed in the text?

5.33 List some of the reasons for using a coated welding rod.

5.34 Why is it necessary that the coating have a higher melting point than the rod?

5.35 Interpret the coated electrode numbers: (a) E5026; (b) E8017; (c) E7532.

5.36 Interpret the following coated electrode numbers: (a) E6013; (b) E6010; (c) E6027; (d) E7010; (e) E6028.

5.37 What amperage should be used with the following rod diameters: (a) $\frac{1}{16}$ in.; (b) $\frac{5}{32}$ in.; (c) $\frac{3}{16}$ in.; (d) $\frac{1}{4}$ in.; (e) $\frac{7}{32}$ in.?

5.38 How is the length of the arc determined in electric arc welding?

5.39   What results are obtained if the arc is too long? Too short?

5.40   What are the results if the arc is too hot? Too cold?

5.41   Discuss the weaves available, and discuss their uses.

5.42   Discuss the causes and cures for each of the following: (a) porosity; (b) penetration; (c) warpage; (d) distortion; (e) poor fusion; (f) cracking; (g) undercutting.

5.43   Describe the essentials of MIG welding.

5.44   Describe the essentials of TIG welding.

5.45   Explain the inert-gas welding operation and the relationship between the types of current, electrode, and gas used.

5.46   How is the intense heat generated in the hydrogen (atomic) welding process?

5.47   Describe the submerged melt process of welding.

5.48   Describe the thermite welding process.

5.49   Check your library and expand on the following processes: (a) electroslag welding; (b) electron-beam welding; (c) fusion welding; (d) ultrasonic welding.

5.50   Discuss: (a) gas metal arc (CO_2); (b) micro-wire; (c) self-shielding electrode wire welding processes. You should check your library and expand on the discussion in this text.

5.51   What are some of the factors which make acetylene welding desirable?

5.52   Describe the oxyacetylene equipment.

5.53   Describe the operation of the regulator.

5.54   Discuss the uses of the neutral, carburizing, and oxidizing flames.

5.55   Discuss the three envelopes of the carburizing flame.

5.56   What precautions does the manufacturer take to ensure proper hose connection?

5.57   State the ratios of oxygen to acetylene for each of the three flames discussed in this text.

5.58   Explain the lighting of the oxyacetylene torch.

5.59   Explain the oxyacetylene welding process after the torch has been ignited.

5.60   Describe forehand and backhand welding.

5.61   Describe oxyacetylene cutting.

5.62   Check your library and expand on flame machining with a gas torch, hard facing, and flame hardening.

5.63   What is the temperature requirement of a good brazing rod? Why?

5.64   What is the function of capillary attraction in the brazing operation?

5.65   Why is the clearance between two pieces to be brazed important?

5.66 Discuss the strength of a brazed joint.

5.67 Why must all foreign matter such as oils, etc., be removed before flux is applied?

5.68 Why is distortion a factor in torch brazing?

5.69 Name five brazing methods, and describe two.

5.70 What is the principle of induction brazing?

5.71 Describe the two dip-brazing processes.

5.72 Why is silver brazing classified as a brazing process rather than a soldering process?

5.73 Describe copper as a brazing material.

5.74 Which material may be brazed with Tobin-bronze brazing rod?

5.75 What precaution must be taken when brazing with an aluminum brazing material?

5.76 What is the chief characteristic of heat-resistant brazing?

5.77 What are the three functions of flux?

5.78 What is the composition of the flux used for brazing copper, brass, bronze, low-carbon steel?

5.79 What is the composition of the flux needed to braze cast iron?

5.80 What is the composition of the flux needed to braze aluminum?

5.81 How may the flux be removed after the brazing operation is completed?

5.82 What are the three physical forms of flux? What is the advantage of a paste flux over the others?

5.83 Describe the brazing operation used to braze two pieces of steel.

5.84 Describe the brazing operation used to braze cast iron.

5.85 Describe the process of brazing a carbide tip to a steel shank.

5.86 What is the advantage of a eutectic solder? What is its composition?

5.87 Assume a 40% tin to 60% lead solder composition. What are the phases as the solder is heated from room temperature to 550°F?

5.88 Assume an 80% tin to 20% lead composition. Describe the phases as the solder is heated from room temperature to 550°F.

5.89 Why is it important that both phases become liquid during the soldering operation?

5.90 What is the significance of the formation of small solder balls during the soldering operation?

5.91 What does the term *corrosive* refer to in the soldering operation?

5.92 Describe the constituents of a corrosive flux.

5.93 Describe the composition of a noncorrosive flux used to solder copper.

5.94 What is the composition of the flux used to solder aluminum?

5.95 What is the prime difficulty encountered in the soldering of stainless steel and aluminum?

5.96 What wash may be used to remove a corrosive flux after the soldering operation?

5.97 How may a noncorrosive flux be removed?

5.98 Describe the soldering process for soldering two pieces of copper.

5.99 Describe the soldering process for soldering two pieces of aluminum.

5.100 How are magnesium castings brazed? What type of filler material is used?

Hot and Cold Working
of Metals

6

6.1. The Mechanism of Hot and Cold Working

A discussion of the iron-iron carbon equilibrium diagram appeared in Chapter 2. This discussion also included the mechanism of recrystallization and grain growth in which it was pointed out that the structure of the grains is altered as a piece of steel is cooled below the A_3 and A_1 lines. This change of structure due to the loss of heat is called *allotropic recrystallization*.

The recrystallization temperature may be lowered by increasing the deformation during the cold working to which a piece of steel is subjected. This kind of recrystallization is called *strain recrystallization*. Other methods of lowering the recrystallization temperature are grain refinement, purification of the metal, and working the metal at low temperatures. The mechanisms of hot and cold working are discussed at this point so that the student may see the relationship between the two processes.

The significance of the above statements is that the recrystallization temperature of a material is the dividing line between cold and hot working. Technically, cold working takes place at temperatures below the recrystallization temperature, whereas hot working takes place at temperatures well above the recrystallization temperature.

Since cold-worked materials are usually strained, the metal must be annealed after cold working. However, since hot working takes place above the annealing temperatures, the material is being annealed as it is being hot worked and therefore needs no secondary heat treatment to relieve the stresses. Metals can be hot-worked as long as their temperature is above the recrystallization temperature. Once the temperature drops below the recrystallization temperature, the workpiece must be reheated.

A simultaneous mechanism which takes place when a workpiece is hot-worked at elevated temperatures is grain growth. During hot working the grains are elongated in the direction of the hot working. Impurities may also be elongated or broken up. These grains break up and reform as smaller grains (recrystallize). They then proceed to grow in proportion to sizes characteristic of the temperature of the workpiece. Thus, if hot working could stop at the recrystallization temperature, grain growth would be impossible and a fine-grain structure would result.

The ideal stopping temperature range for hot working is about 100 to 300°F above the recrystallization temperature. In steels containing sulfur high temperatures may cause brittleness (hot shortness) because of the deposits of sulfides in the grain boundaries of the steel.

The binding forces of the atoms—attraction and repulsion—impart elastic and inelastic properties to the metal. *Elastic deformation* takes place if the atoms return to their original positions in the structure once the deforming force is removed. *Plastic deformation* is said to take place if the atoms fail to return to their original position once the deforming force is removed.

During cold working the deformation of the metal takes place by mechanisms called *slip* or *twinning*. The mechanism of slip requires that a force be applied to the lattice structure of the metal. [See Fig. 6.1(a).] As the energy wave reaches a lattice plane, it causes a shift of one full plane. As the energy wave proceeds from lattice plane to lattice plane, each successive plane moves one full lattice space. Thus a complete dislocation may take place such that the defect becomes microscopically visible only at the surface of the exposed metal. This is possible only if the crystal structure and orientation are preserved.

Slip will continue in one direction until forces build up which oppose slip in that direction. When this occurs, the forces start operating on the planes which offer less resistance to dislocation and slip proceeds along the new planes. If the forces should build high enough, fracture will take place. The reaction forces which cause this slip appear to result from dislocated atoms or rows of atoms which create *keying effects* and disoriented or distorted lattice planes. Slip appears to be easier along planes in which the grains are approximately aligned with each other.

Sometimes deformation will take place by a mechanism known as *twinning* [See Fig. 6.1(b)]: the movement of a plane of atoms that forms a mirror image of the original layer of atoms. It is a mechanism by which an entire segment of the material has moved as a result of a shearing force. The movement need not be one full lattice-plane spacing but rather some proportion of a lattice-plane spacing. Thus the twinning plane may come to rest in a direction perpendicular to the original plane direction and be dislodged $\frac{1}{3}$ of a lattice-plane spacing; the next plane, $\frac{2}{3}$ of a plane spacing; etc. Thus twins can be microscopically detected under the surface of the metal, for instance, if the surface is removed by polishing and then repolished. This is possible since the

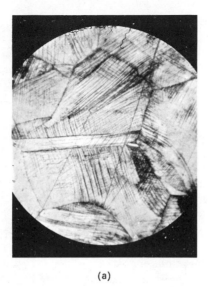

(a)

(b)

Figure 6.1

atom spacing and the orientation of the atom planes have been disturbed by more than, or less than, one full plane spacing.

Since relatively few atomic planes are dislodged when slip finally comes to rest, the microscopic picture of a slip line is very thin. However, since many atoms are involved in the twinning mechanism, a board band is observed.

6.2.   Advantages and Disadvantages of Hot and Cold Working

Some of the advantages and disadvantages of hot and cold working will be stated at this time. The student should keep these in mind as he studies this part of the text.

The advantages of hot-working metals are:
1. The danger that worked metal will crack is much less because of the increase in the plasticity of the metal as its temperature increases. Also because of the increased plasticity larger sections can be worked than during cold working. Metals such as zinc, molybdenum, magnesium, and tungsten must be hot-worked because they are brittle at low temperatures.
2. Grain refinement is possible. Active grain growth occurs within the hot-working temperatures. Grain growth is proportional to the temperature. Normal grain growth is slow compared with recrystallization grain growth. Thus, if hot working is fast enough, the effect of normal grain growth will be negligible. The resulting grain sizes may be controlled by recrystallization.
3. Intermediate annealing is not necessary since strain hardening is nonexistent. This eliminates the need for expensive intermediate annealing operations.
4. The hot-working power requirements are less than for cold working since the metal at elevated temperatures is plastic and strain hardening is removed as it occurs.

The disadvantages of hot-working metals are:
1. Some metals cannot be hot worked. These metals have the characteristic of hot shortness referred to in Section 6.1, which makes the metal brittle.
2. In operations such as deep drawing (Chapter 7) strain hardening is important and, if eliminated, becomes a disadvantage. It will be seen that, in order to draw a shell, there must be resistance to the drawing operation. If this resistance is eliminated, the bottom of the shell will be punched out. It should be noted that in most instances the elimination of strain hardening is an advantage.
3. In hot working, because of the oxide coating which is formed, surface finish is usually poor.
4. Dimensional control is difficult owing to metal contraction on cooling and loss of metal due to scaling.
5. Maintaining high temperatures is expensive and difficult. Handling of heated metals is also dangerous and expensive. In some instances the input energy which takes place from the working also contributes to the temperature and may actually increase the final temperature of the piece beyond the desired temperature. This may make accurate temperature control difficult.

The advantages of cold working are:
1. Cold working increases the strength, elasticity, and hardness of the metal parts worked.
2. Dimensional tolerances and surface finish are usually good enough

so that additional finishing or finish machining operations are unnecessary.
3. Small parts may be shaped rapidly and at a lower cost per part than by most other methods.
4. It is easier and cheaper to handle cold parts than hot parts.

The disadvantages of cold working are:
1. Some parts cannot be worked cold because they are too brittle. In some instances cold working produces hardness and stresses, which make subsequent operations prohibitive.
2. Large sections of most metals and extensive cold working of the high-strength metal alloys require too much energy to be practical and may even be beyond the range of most presses.
3. The effect on corrosion resistance, electrical resistance, and magnetic properties is marked. The effect is to reduce corrosion resistance, increase the electrical resistance, and change the magnetic properties of the metal worked. A full discussion of these effects is beyond the scope of this text.

6.3. Hot Rolling of Metal

Figure 6.2 shows a few of the methods used to roll hot billets, blooms, or slabs into desired shapes. The material is processed hot and usually reprocessed to desired shapes by cold working.

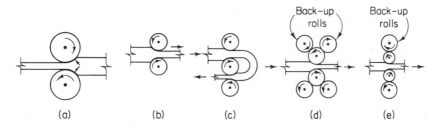

Figure 6.2

Hot ingots are soaked in pits to achieve uniform temperatures (2000 to 2200°F) throughout their structure. From the soaking pits they are transferred to the rolling mills where they are worked into blooms, billets, or slabs. Blooms have square cross sections of 6 in. or greater. Billets have square cross sections of from $1\frac{1}{2}$ to 6 in. Slabs range up to about $1\frac{1}{2}$ in. in thickness and have widths which are about three times the thickness or more.

The *volume* of the entering billet and the emerging slab are equal. If the *width* of the entering billet and the emerging slab change slightly, the major change in the dimension takes place along the *length* of the slab when compared to the length of *original* billet. The emerging slab will, therefore, travel much faster than the entering billet from which it was made. End rolling-operation speeds may be as high as 60 to 80 mph. Thus roll-speed control is of utmost importance.

In Fig. 6.2(a) the rolling operation reduces the thickness and to some extent the width of the emerging material. The arrows indicate the approximate point at which the speed of the material is the same as the surface speed of the rollers. The friction at the contact arc draws the material through the rollers and reduces its size.

In Fig. 6.2(b) a two-high rolling mill shows the material being processed. If reversing two-high rolls are used, many passes are made by reversing the rolls until the material reaches the desired thickness or shape. If the continuous two-high rolling mill is used, many sets of rolls are used, so that each set of rolls reduces the material as it passes through the mill. Very high speeds are attained with this method.

In Fig. 6.2(c) is shown a three-high rolling mill. In this process the material is passed through the middle and upper rollers and then passed back through the middle and lower roller for further reduction. Roller speeds are very difficult to control as the thickness decreases. As the thickness decreases, the speeds must increase. Yet this process produces shapes faster than the reversing processes because in the reversing processes inertia must be overcome with each reversal.

In Fig. 6.2(d and e), back-up rollers are used for support when wide sections are to be produced. Deflection of the rollers would produce uneven material thickness.

The following hot-rolling operations are used for tubing.

Piercing operations. Figure 6.3(a) shows the Mannesmann process for making seamless tubing. A small hole is punched, pierced, or drilled into the end of a round billet. The heated billet is forced between the two tapered rollers so that the mandrel picks up the hole in the end of the stock. The roller shafts, mandrel, and work are in a parallel plane. The shaft axes are at an angle of about 6° to each other.

It is to be noted that the mandrel does not actually pierce the center of the stock to create the hole in the tubing. Compressive forces (created by the rollers) applied at opposite sides of a round bar set up tensile forces at 90° to the compressive forces at the center of the bar. A defect (the pierced hole at the end of the bar) at the center of the bar will tear open. The mandrel assists this action. The action of the rollers causes the bar to revolve and feed in the direction of the mandrel. As the bar revolves and feeds toward the mandrel, the tearing action is propagated along the length of the bar and compressed between the mandrel and the rollers. A seamless tube is produced.

Plug rolling. This is used to reduce wall thickness and increase diameter of tubes already made. This process cannot be used to make seamless tubing from solid billets.

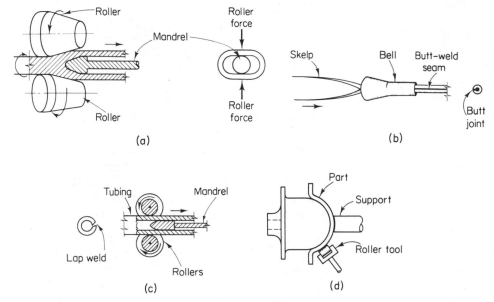

Figure 6.3

A reeling mill.   The tube is rolled between another set of rollers creating tubes of reduced wall thicknesses. In this process the tubes are processed for better size, roundness, and finish.

Welded steel tubing processes.   Seamed tubing is made by rolling a flat sheet or strip of steel into a tube so that the edges of the stock either butt against each other or overlap. Butted or overlapped stock is then welded to form the tubing. Steel used in these processes, called *skelp*, is passed through a bell die, Fig. 6.3(b), which rolls it into a tube. The welding may be completed at the time of rolling or after the material has passed through the bell die.

The edges of the skelp may also be prepared so that they overlap when rolled in the bell die. The tube is then passed over a mandrel between grooved rollers and electric resistance welded as shown in Fig. 6.3(c).

Hot spinning.   This is another process which uses pressure and plastic flow to shape material. [See Fig. 6.3(d).] The metal is forced to flow over a rotating shape by pressure of a blunt tool or rollers. The pressure of the tool against the disc generates heat. Hot spinning is restricted to thick wall forming. The temperature is maintained by the heat generated by the spinning operation.

Cold spinning.   Essentially the same as hot spinning, the difference is the temperature of the material in the two processes. The use of heat requires heat-resistance forms and tools. In cold spinning smaller thicknesses of metal may be worked, and the forms may be made from wood or metal.

6.4. The Forging Processes

Forging operations are of two varieties, those in which the metal is not confined and those in which the metal is confined. The former processes include operations such as bending, upsetting, punching, drawing, etc. The confined metal processes require that the volume of the metal be precalculated so that it will flow under pressure to all parts of the die cavity. An extra amount of metal is usually added to the volume needed to ensure a completed part. The *flash* which results is trimmed off.

Low-carbon steel and many of the alloy tool steels and stainless steels can be forged. Aluminum, magnesium, and copper alloys lend themselves to the forging operations. The forging temperatures required for the nonferrous materials are much lower than for the ferrous materials. However, many of the high-alloy nonferrous materials present problems of die wear.

Smith forging.   One of the oldest of the types of forging processes, the blacksmith type of smith forging requires hand tools to shape desired parts. This process is used when low production is required. Complicated shapes and close tolerances are uneconomical with this process. The process is carried out by striking the heated part repeatedly until it takes on the desired shape and size.

The modern version of the blacksmith process is the substitution of a power-actuated hammer for the hand hammer. These tools are large flat-face hammers of the single- or double-housing kind. They are also made with open frames.

The forces generated by the hammer may result from gravitational attraction that results from free fall; or the free fall may be aided by steam pressure. In another type of hammer the impact is cushioned with a steam cylinder.

The ram may be raised by a steam or air cylinder, an electric motor, or rollers which engage two boards (called *board hammer*) fastened to the ram. In the last method, once the ram reaches a desired height, clamps engage the ram and the rollers retract. Hammer energy is generated by gravity.

The point at which the impact blow strikes the workpiece may be controlled by the operator as he rotates the workpiece. Blows shape the workpiece to the form which the operator is trying to achieve. Limited types of forms may be made with attachments when using open-face dies.

Drop forging.   Forms are machined into two halves of a closed die set. Metal is heated and under impact it becomes plastic. Under repeated blows the metal fills the die cavity. Excess metal (flash) is trimmed off.

Most drop-forging dies have several cavities machined into their surface. This makes it possible to preshape a forging before it is hammered into its final form. Bending, upsetting, and drawing may be incorporated in a set of drop-forging dies. Thus the part may go through several successive operations incorporated in one die set before it is completed.

Because the size and shape of the finished parts are controlled by the die cavity, parts may be duplicated readily. The grain structure obtained produces a workpiece of high tensile strength. It is important that the parting line and the cavity be designed so that there is a uniform distribution of metal flow and impact force.

Fillets should be $\frac{1}{8}$ in. or larger. Draft should be between 5 and 8° to aid in the removal of the parts from the die cavity. Tolerances that can be achieved are related to the weight of the forging. The heavier the forging, the more open are the tolerances that are permitted. The tolerances always favor the *plus* side of the dimension. Thus a typical dimension would be $2.000^{+0.030}_{-0.010}$.

Another type of forging operation is accomplished in a horizontal machine that uses two opposing rams. Each carries half the die set, and both rams retract and impact the part as they come together. This type of operation eliminates energy loss to the frame of the machine.

Hot press forging.   This causes a steadily applied pressure instead of an impact force. Under impact the energy is transmitted through the surface of the workpiece, whereas under a steady high pressure the entire workpiece is subjected to the deforming pressure. Multiple die cavities may be machined into one die set, and usually only one stroke is needed to complete a particular forging operation. As the pressure is applied, the metal flows into and fills the die cavity.

Upset forging.   Used to force the end of a heated bar into a desired shape, the bar is heated, clamped, and upset into the die opening. The pressure builds rapidly and becomes a maximum at the end of the stroke. Figure 6.4(a through c) show the limitations of die design for the upsetting operation.

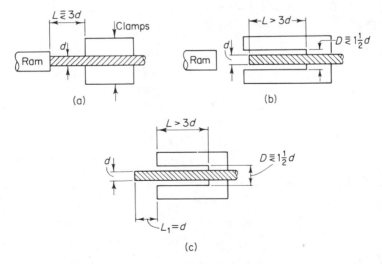

Figure 6.4

In Fig. 6.4(a) the length L of the unsupported bar should not exceed *three* times the diameter d of the bar before upsetting takes place. The unsupported end should collapse evenly without buckling. Thus

$$L = 3d$$

EXAMPLE 1

Assume the diameter of a bar is $\frac{1}{2}$ in. before upsetting takes place [Fig. 6.4(a)]. What is the permissible unsupported maximum length of the bar?

Solution:

$$L = 3(d) = 3(\tfrac{1}{2}) \qquad\qquad d = \tfrac{1}{2} \text{ in.}$$
$$= 1.500 \text{ in.} \qquad\qquad\qquad L = ?$$

If it becomes necessary to upset lengths greater than three inches, the cavity diameter D into which the stock is to be upset should not exceed $1\frac{1}{2}\,d$.

$$D = 1.5d \qquad\qquad\qquad d = \text{dia of material}$$
$$D = \text{dia of cavity}$$

EXAMPLE 2

In Fig. 6.4(b), the length L of the bar to be upset is 4 in., and the diameter d of the bar before upsetting is $\frac{1}{2}$. What is the permissible maximum diameter after upsetting?

Solution:

$$D = 1.5(\tfrac{1}{2}) \qquad\qquad d = \tfrac{1}{2} \text{ in.}$$
$$L = 4 \text{ in.}$$
$$= 0.750 \text{ in.} \qquad\qquad D = ?$$

When the cavity is $1\frac{1}{2}d$ and L is greater than $3d$, the stock must *not* protrude L_1 beyond the face of the die cavity by more than one d as shown in Fig. 6.4(c). If D is reduced to $1\frac{1}{4}d$, then L_1 may be increased to $1\frac{1}{2}d$.

EXAMPLE 3

Assume in Fig. 6.4(c) a diameter before upsetting of $\frac{1}{2}$ in. and a length of 4 in. The die cavity diameter is $\frac{3}{4}$ in. (a) How much stock may safely protrude beyond the die face? (b) What is the total unsupported length of stock? (c) Assume that the upset diameter D of the stock is to be $\frac{5}{8}$ in. instead of $\frac{3}{4}$ in.; calculate the maximum values for part (a) and (b).

Solution:

1. The maximum length of the protruding stock is

$$L_1 = d = \tfrac{1}{2} \text{ in.} \qquad\qquad d = \tfrac{1}{2} \text{ in.}$$
$$L = 4 \text{ in.}$$

2. The total unsupported stock is $\qquad\qquad D = \tfrac{3}{4} \text{ in.}$

$$L_1 + L = \tfrac{1}{2} + 4 = 4\tfrac{1}{2} \text{ in.}$$

3. Since the new upset diameter is equal to or less than

$$1\tfrac{1}{4}d = 1\tfrac{1}{4} \times \tfrac{1}{2} = \tfrac{5}{8} \text{ in.}$$

the new amount of protruding is

$$L_1 = 1.5(\tfrac{1}{2}) = \tfrac{3}{4} \text{ in.}$$

and the new unsupported length may be increased to

$$L_1 + L = \tfrac{3}{4} + 4 = 4\tfrac{3}{4} \text{ in.}$$

Swaging. Two halves of a rotating die open and close rapidly while impacting the end of the heated tube or shell. The forging operation may reduce the diameter of the tube or taper the end of the tube as the tube is fed between the dies.

Roll forging. This forging method reduces the diameter of a bar and in the process makes it longer. Semicircular rollers, grooved, receive the heated round workpiece and reduce its diameter. The piece is then inserted into successive grooves and rolled. Each pass reduces the diameter of the rod. The process is continued until the desired diameter is reached.

6.5. Extrusion

In the extrusion process a heated billet is placed in a die and under pressure forced to flow through shaped dies. The emerging formed bar takes on the shape of the dies to tolerances of $\pm$ 0.003 in. Lengths of 24 ft are easily produced. It should be noted that the density of the resulting material is very good but that the extruded shapes have marked directional properties.

Two basic methods for forcing hot metal through a die opening are: (1) the direct pressure method, Fig. 6.5(a); (2) the indirect pressure method, Fig. 6.5(b).

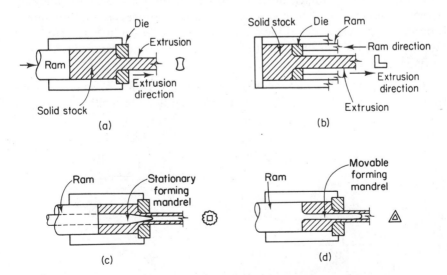

Figure 6.5

Figure 6.5(c) shows the method of direct extrusion with a forming mandrel affixed to the ram. The forming mandrel may have almost any desired shape. This mandrel may be stationary, as in Fig. 6.5(c), or move with the ram, as in Fig. 6.5(d). If the ram and mandrel are one piece, the billet must be pre-drilled or pierced. Soft material may be pierced by the mandrel before the ram starts to apply the extruding pressure to the billet. Once the mandrel has pierced the workpiece, its forward motion stops.

Aluminum alloys, magnesium alloys, copper, lead, brass, and steel are extruded by this process. Special lubricants must be used when extruding steel. The process requires that these metals be heated to just below the melting point so that the yield strength of the metal is low. The metal is under hydrostatic pressure and thus will flow readily through almost any opening of predetermined shape.

Indirect pressure extrusion, Fig. 6.5(b), forces the molten metal back through the ram. This is accomplished by closing one end of the container. One of the chief advantages of indirect extrusion over direct extrusion is that there is very little friction developed between the walls of the container and the billet during indirect extrusion. However, the ram used during indirect extrusion is hollow and therefore weaker than the solid ram used during direct extrusion. Since the material is forced back through the ram, it is difficult to support long extruded shapes.

Impact extrusion. Shown in Fig. 6.6(a), this is another method of hot extrusion. In this process the metal "squits" up along the sides of the punch when subjected to an impact blow. The resulting tube takes on the shape of the punch. The wall thickness of the resulting tube is controlled by the clearance between the punch and the die. Materials such as aluminum, zinc, lead, tin, and some copper alloys are being impact extruded. The tubes are stripped from the punch by an air jet. The Hooker process is another impact process. The cross section of the die assembly is as shown in Fig. 6.5(d). The Hooker process causes the metal to flow through the opening as the result of an impact force (as shown in the figure).

Hot drawing. Another method used in hot working for shaping materials, a heated blank is placed over a die opening. See Fig. 6.6(b). The punch

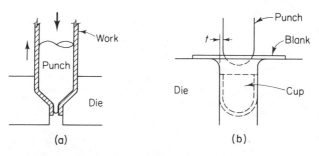

(a)   (b)

Figure 6.6

forces the blank through the die opening to form a cup or shell. Further reduction of the shell diameter and wall thickness may be accomplished by successive drawing operations. The use of multiple dies may sometimes be used to draw the finished cup in one stroke. Hot drawing is restricted to the drawing of thick-wall cylinders or shells.

6.6. The Mechanism of Cold Working

The mechanism, advantages, and disadvantages of cold working were discussed in Sections 6.1 and 6.2 and should be reviewed at this time. Almost all the operations discussed under hot working apply to cold working if the material is suitable for cold working.

The relationship of yield strength (YS), yield point (YP), and tensile strength (TS) is important in cold working. Figure 6.7 shows a typical stress-strain diagram of a specimen of low-carbon steel. The height of the "dome" of the curve represents the amount of work hardening which takes place as the force is applied to the sample. This work hardening causes problems of what is known as *spring-back* after the load is removed. Of course, if the applied load is below the elastic limit, the piece returns to its original length or shape when the load

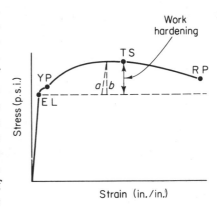

Figure 6.7

is removed. If the applied force elongates the sample to point *b*, the sample will not return to its original length but will return to point *a* because of the residual elastic properties, or springback, which still remain in the work sample.

6.7. Cold Rolling

Sheets, strips, bars, and wires may be rolled cold. The material is cleaned by pickling in a dilute sulfuric acid solution and washed with a hot limewater solution. The material is then rolled in the same kind of rolling mill as the one used in hot rolling, Fig. 6.2.

The rolling process gives directional properties to the material, Fig. 6.8(a), and imparts a surface skin which has been work hardened. Excessive working of the material causes embrittlement. Therefore, cold working of metals may require annealing after which the material is sized with additional passes through a finishing mill.

Roll forming machines use a series of matched rollers which progressively

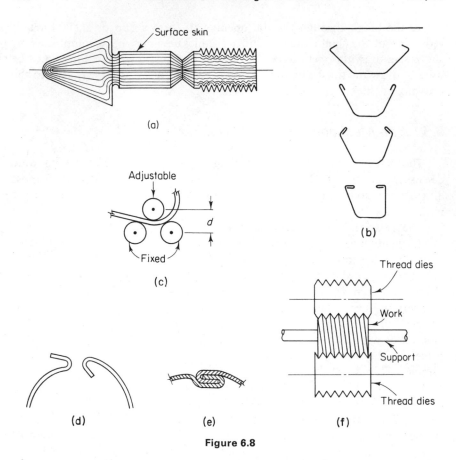

Figure 6.8

roll the material into the desired shape. Rollers placed at the sides of the form will shape the sides of the tube. If needed, the forms may be seam welded with rollers acting as electrodes. Straightening rollers complete the operation.

The number of pairs of rollers needed depends upon the shape and ductility of the material. The radius of corner bends should not be less than the thickness of the material. A series of bends which have been rolled to form a drain gutter are shown in Fig. 6.8(b). Materials up to 0.156 in. may be rolled successfully with standard equipment. Thicker materials need specially designed equipment.

Plate may be rolled into tubes or rings if passed through three rollers. Two of the rollers are fixed, and a third adjustable roller forms the piece, as shown in Fig. 6.8(c). As the distance d is reduced, the radius of the bend is reduced.

Seaming. This is accomplished with rollers so that the bends lap the material back on itself to close the form. See Fig. 6.8(d and e). This type of seam may be made in various types. They may be single or multiple seam laps.

Thread rolling.   Threads may be rolled into cylindrical surfaces by either flat-face dies or rollers. See Fig. 6.8(f). In either case the barstock diameter before rolling is equal to the pitch diameter of the finished thread. Under pressure, the metal between the pitch diameter and the root diameter is forced to flow above the pitch diameter to form the addendum of the thread.

Rollers have the thread form, pitch, and lead machined into their surfaces. As the bar stock is fed between sets of two or three form rollers under pressure, the material displaces to form the thread. Flat-face dies have the desired form and pitch machined into their surface with the longitudinal thread form machined at an angle to form the thread. Figure 6.8(f) shows the top view of two rollers forming the thread.

6.8. Cold Forging

Swaging.   Tubes and round bars are swaged with a rotary type head, as shown in Fig. 6.9(a). The rollers cause the dies to impact and squeeze the work thus forming it into tapers, points, or reduced diameters. The dies are rotated so that the work is struck many blows in a short time. The number of blows struck is a function of the kind of material used and the type of job. Thus 10 rollers rotating at 250 rpm means that 2500 blows per minute will be struck.

The interform system uses a shaped mandrel over which the inside of the work may be formed. If the external rotating dies are round and the mandrel is formed, the resulting part will have a shaped inside and a round outside. Other forms, or combination of forms, are possible.

Work hardening during the swaging operation is rapid, and annealing operations are required.

Several stations may be required before the final operation in order to preform the part. Shearing dies may be used to cut the blank to size before cold heading takes place. The cut piece may be preformed in a double-action machine. A preform may take the shape of a cone during the first stroke, and the final shape be formed by the second stroke.

Formed diameters 2.5 times the original diameter must be formed in a double-action press to prevent buckling or imperfections. All or any part of the form may be machined in the die or punch used.

Cold heading.   The metal is confined in all directions even though the impact forces are longitudinal. The metal under impact flows into all parts of the punch cavity, Fig. 6.9(b). Large sections of work are heated to aid the operation. Bolts, screws, rivets, nails, etc., may be cold headed and formed with this process.

Riveting.   Used to fasten two parts together, the upsetting or cold heading is applied to both ends of a precalculated length of material. See Fig. 6.9(c). The slug of metal is placed in aligned holes in the parts to be fastened.

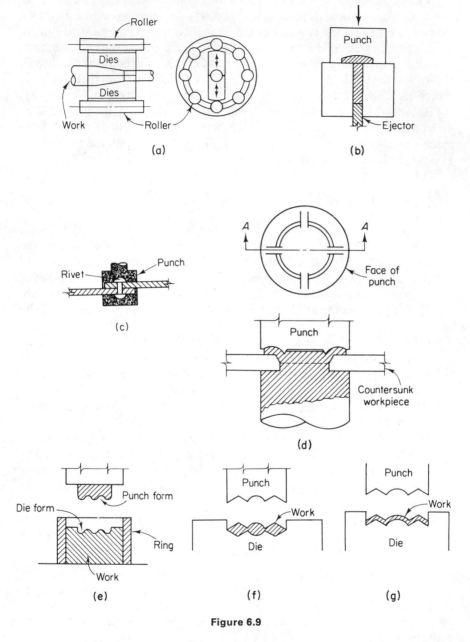

Figure 6.9

The forms are machined into the punch and die. Both ends of the slug are struck to form the heads of the rivet. Punching the holes in the pieces to be fastened, inserting the rivet, and cold heading may all be accomplished in one operation in specially designed machines.

Staking. This may also be used to fasten two pieces by forming the metal against the sides of punched or drilled holes or into grooves in the upper piece. The pressures required are small in comparison with the pressures required in riveting. See Fig. 6.9(d).

Hobbing. Also called *hubbing*, Fig. 6.9(e), this operation is used to form impressions, or patterns, in annealed steel. The desired pattern is machined into the punch, which is then hardened. The punch is next forced into the annealed steel. The annealed steel block is reinforced with a steel retainer ring while the hobbing is being done. Any excess metal resulting from the plastic flow of the metal is machined away. Since the pressures are high (up to 10,000 tons) and the working severe, several operations may be required with the necessary annealing operations in between.

Complicated forms may be successfully hobbed with high finish. Duplicate cavities are easily made by this process. The cavities, because of the finish required, may be used as molds for plastic molding or die casting.

Coining. The work is confined while the impression is forced into the surface or surfaces. See Fig. 6.9(f). The thickness of the metal is being changed as the process progresses. The coining operation requires high pressures. Since the length of the stroke is fixed, the volume of the metal must be accurately calculated. There is no way in which the metal can escape. Small amounts of metal flow are involved. The materials must have good ductile qualities. This process may be used to force impressions into metal for coins, medals, jewelry, etc.

Embossing. This operation employs a matching punch and die with the impression machined into both surfaces. See Fig. 6.9(g). However, it differs from the coining process in that the material thickness remains constant. It is actually a shallow drawing process rather than a squeezing process and the forces required are much less than in coining. The metal flow in the coining process is lateral, whereas the metal flow in embossing is in the direction of the applied force.

Shot peening. Large quantities of steel shot are fired at the surface of a workpiece. The size of the shot determines the finish achieved. The fibers in the surface of the workpiece stretch and place the subsurface fibers in tension. These subsurface tensile forces place the outer fibers in compression. The compression forces counteract failures which might occur owing to tensile forces applied to the workpiece, such as fatigue failures. The surface of the workpiece is work hardened by the process.

Cold extrusion. Similar to the hot extrusion processes discussed in Section 6.5, the material in cold working must possess the necessary ductility without the application of heat. The processes may require that the material be forced through an opening in the die as in the Hooker process, Fig. 6.5(d), or the impact method, Fig. 6.6(a).

6.9. Cold Drawing

Cold drawing of bars. Hot-rolled bars which are first cleaned by pickling and then washed are then drawn through dies which reduce the diameter and elongate the outer grain fibers. The surface is smooth and sized to a tolerance of a few thousandths of an inch. The working is severe enough to work harden the surface.

Wire drawing. This is accomplished by pulling a wire through a hardened die, usually carbide. See Fig. 6.10(a). Small-diameter wires are drawn through a diamond die.

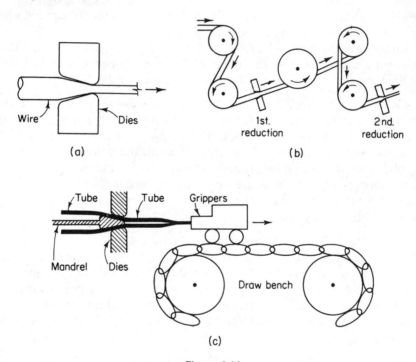

Figure 6.10

The wire is cleaned by pickling and then washed. A pointed or reduced cylindrical diameter at the end of the wire is pushed through the die, gripped with a pair of tongs, and pulled through until it can be attached to a power driven reel. The reel continues to pull the wire through the die as it is being rolled onto the reel.

The material is lubricated to aid in the drawing operation and to impart a good surface finish to the wire. The dies themselves are usually water cooled because of the heat generated by the severe cold working. Annealing in a controlled-atmosphere furnace is required to restore the ductility lost during the cold working.

Reductions in each pass through a die range from about 10% for steel to 40% for more ductile materials. If greater reductions are required, the wire may be drawn through several dies, Fig. 6.10(b), until the required diameter is obtained. Strength control is possible by controlling the drawing and annealing operations.

The cold drawing of tubes, seamless or welded, is accomplished by drawing the tube over a mandrel and through a reduced die opening, as shown in Fig. 6.10(c). The tube is pickled, washed, and lubricated. The end diameter is reduced so that it may be attached to grippers. The tube is then pulled through the die on a drawing bench. Forces of up to 150 tons may be employed on benches 100 ft long. The reductions range from 15% for steel to 50% for nonferrous metals.

Dimensional accuracy in the outside or inside diameter of the drawn tube, smoothness, increased strength, and hardness may be achieved by cold drawing. It is also possible to draw shapes other than round sections by this method.

Spinning.   This was discussed in Section 6.3 under hot working. The same principles are used in cold spinning. The differences in treatment arise from the differences in the ductility of the metal.

Shear forming.   In this variation of the spinning process, the mechanism of shear causes the metal to be displaced. The *reverse shear* spinning operation is shown in Fig. 6.11(a). The roller pressure is at the left against the flange of

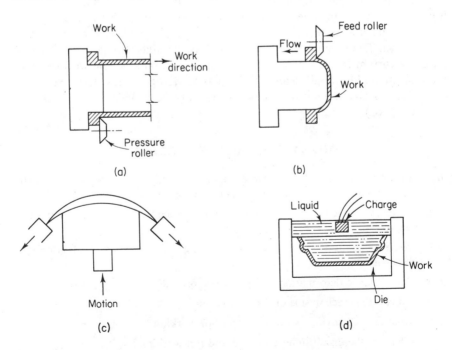

Figure 6.11

the fixture. The metal elongates and flows toward the right. In Fig. 6.11(b) the *direct method* is shown. The reduction takes place over the mandrel.

In conventional spinning the wall thickness remains constant. In shear spinning the wall thickness is reduced, sometimes up to 80%. Since the process is one of severe cold working, annealing must be employed if successive operations are to be used.

Stretch forming.   This process of cold working employs the principle of stretching and wrapping a metal sheet around a form. A form mounted on a ram is forced up, as shown in Fig. 6.11(c), as the grippers move out and down. The metal is stretched above its elastic limit and wrapped at the same time. Multiple curvatures may be achieved with this method since there is practically no springback.

High-energy forming.   The detonation of a high explosive such as dynamite or gases produces very high energy shock waves which fan out in all directions and force the metal into a preformed die cavity. Because of the high energies employed, very high strength materials may be formed by this method. High strength materials, when deformed, will spring back excessively. However, as a result of the high energies employed, very little springback takes place.

Besides the powder explosives and the high-velocity expanding gases employed, shock waves generated from a capacitor discharge across a gap have also been employed. The shock waves fan out through a nonconducting liquid in all directions and impact the workpiece causing it to deform.

Forces have also been developed by charging capacitors through a preformed coil. The magnetic fields generated as the high voltage is discharged induce a current in the workpiece. The forces generated in the workpiece as the current builds rapidly cause the metal to deform. This deformation is controlled to give the desired shape to the workpiece. This process is shown in Fig. 6.11(d).

QUESTIONS AND PROBLEMS

6.1   (a) Define the terms allotropic recrystallization and strain recrystallization. (b) How may the recrystallization temperature be lowered?

6.2   Explain the mechanisms of hot and cold working of metals, and discuss the relationships of one to the other.

6.3   Discuss the effect of hot and cold working on grain growth. Relate your discussion to the iron-iron carbon diagram.

6.4   Define elastic deformation and plastic deformation.

6.5   Explain the mechanisms of slip and twinning.

6.6   What are the advantages of cold and hot working?

6.7   What are the disadvantages of cold and hot working?

6.8 "The volume of the entering billet and the emerging slab are equal. Assume the width of the entering and emerging slab is uniform but the thickness decreases." What must happen to the length of the emerging slab? Explain.

6.9 Describe the two-, three-, etc., roller methods of hot rolling.

6.10 Describe the various methods of hot-rolling tubing.

6.11 What is spinning? How does hot spinning differ from cold spinning?

6.12 Describe the forging process when (a) the metal is *not* confined; (b) when the metal is confined.

6.13 Describe (a) the drop forging process; (b) hot press forging.

6.14 What is upset forging? Discuss the process.

6.15 Discuss the theory of upset forging related to the length of the unconfined metal, Fig. 6.4(a through c). Use *actual dimensions* for the stock diameter, length, etc. Support your results.

6.16 Assume the unsupported length of a bar to be $2\frac{1}{4}$ inches during the upsetting operation, Fig. 6.4(a). What is the minimum allowable diameter of this bar?

6.17 If the length of the bar in Problem 6.16 is $4\frac{1}{2}$ inches, calculate the maximum diameter of the cavity.

6.18 Assume a diameter of a cavity before upsetting of $\frac{3}{4}$ in. and a length of protruding stock of $2\frac{1}{4}$ in. as shown in Fig. 6.4(c). (a) How much stock may protrude beyond the face of the die? (b) What is the total unsupported length of stock? (c) Calculate the new upset diameter and length.

6.19 Explain direct-pressure extrusion.

6.20 Explain indirect-pressure extrusion.

6.21 What is the main advantage of direct over indirect extrusion?

6.22 Define yield point, yield strength, and tensile strength.

6.23 Interpret and explain the significance of the dome in the stress-strain diagram, Fig. 6.7.

6.24 Explain how points *a* and *b* in Fig. 6.7 show springback in cold working.

6.25 How is annealing accomplished for hypo- and hypereutectoid steel?

6.26 Why must cold-worked metals be annealed?

6.27 Select some arbitrary cross-sectional shape, and show how sets of rollers can form this shape. Your may have to go to the library for reference material.

6.28 Figures 6.8 (d and e) show a lock seam. There are many other varieties of lock seams. Draw the sequences for producing other types of lock seams. (Library assignment.)

6.29 Describe thread rolling.

6.30 Discuss the operation of swaging. What is the interform swaging process?

6.31 Make a sketch of the cold heading process for making the head of a hexagon bolt.

6.32 How does the riveting process differ from the staking process?

6.33 What is hobbing? Explain the need for annealing.

6.34 How does coining differ from embossing?

6.35 Explain the forces generated in the surface of a piece of steel which has been subjected to shot peening.

6.36 How does cold extrusion differ from hot extrusion?

6.37 Explain the process for cold-drawing wire.

6.38 What is shear forming? How does it differ from cold spinning?

6.39 What is reverse shear spinning? Direct shear spinning?

6.40 Explain the stretch forming process of a sheet of aluminum.

6.41 Explain high-energy forming.

Dies: Shearing and Blanking

7

7.1. Selection of Materials

Punch and die processes for manufacturing sheet metal parts are probably the most widely used of the cold or hot working processes. Almost any quantity or quality of material may be ordered from the steel mill if the customer is willing to pay the price. In addition to the material cost there may be extra charge for cutting to special sizes, for special percentages of carbon, for the inclusion of special alloying materials, for special surface or heat treatment, or for straightening materials to other than the standard straight or flatness tolerances. The standard for the latter is approximately $\frac{1}{4}$ in. variation from true flatness over 8 ft.

Material thicknesses are listed in the table of wire sizes in Appendix I at the end of this text. It is important to note that although rod and sheet material is designated with gage sizes, the practice of ordering material using the exact decimal equivalent of the gage sizes desired is becoming more accepted. The use of decimal equivalents when describing thickness of material is descriptive whereas gage numbers are not. Because gage sizes are still widely used, they are included in Appendix I.

The Manufacturers' Standard Gage Sizes are used for carbon and alloy sheet steels. The table has been standardized at 41.82 lb/ft² for 1 in. of thickness. The United States Standard Gage, although still used for cold-rolled strip, nickel alloy steel, and stainless steel tubing, has been superseded by the Manufacturers' Standard Gage Sizes.

Steel tubing and hot-rolled carbon and alloy strip has been standardized according to the Birmingham Wire Gage Sizes. Copper, brass and bronze strip; brass, bronze, aluminum and magnesium sheet have been standardized according to the American Wire Gage or Brown and Sharpe Wire Gage Sizes. Stainless steel has been listed according to the American Standard ASA numbers.

The next phase in selecting the appropriate material is to test for mechanical properties. Material hardness is important and has been discussed in Chapter 2. Hardness together with ductility are used to determine the desirability of a particular material. The student should realize that ductility is important for at least two reasons. First, the ductility of a material establishes whether it can be deformed and how easily this can be done. Second, to shear, bend, or draw a material successfully, it must offer resistance to the operation being performed. For example, deep-drawing lead presents some rather insurmountable barriers, because the lead offers little resistance to the drawing operation and as a result the bottom of the shell is usually punched out before the drawing operation is completed.

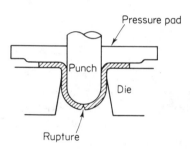

Ductility may be tested by drawing a standard sample with a standard tool, Fig. 7.1. A reading is taken at the beginning of the test and at the moment of rupture. One of the tests (the Ericksen ductility test) measures the *depth* of draw by using a micrometer reading as a standard. Another test (the Olsen ductility test) measures the *pressure* necessary to draw a shell to rupture. Rupture is indicated by a sudden drop in pressure.

Figure 7.1

7.2. Die Components

The components generally incorporated in a blanking or piecing die are shown in Fig. 7.2(a). The cutting tool assembly is shown in the conventional closed position. The die set is made up of the punch holder, which fastens directly to the ram of the punch press, and a die shoe, which fastens to the bolster plate of the punch press. Guideposts may be used to better align the punch holder with the die shoe. The die set may be purchased with two guideposts located at the rear of the die set (called back posts), diagonally, one in the rear and one in the front of the die set, or with four posts, one in each corner.

In the conventional position the punch holder is press fitted with bushings. The guideposts and the bushings have a slip fit so that the guideposts may move freely in the bushings. The opposite ends of the guideposts are press fitted into the die shoe.

The punch is fastened to the punch holder and aligned with the opening in the die block which is fastened to the die shoe. Since the punch and die block are the cutting tools, they are both hardened.

Once the cutting action has taken place, the punch starts to retract. Because of the nature of the material the hole in the scrap strip contracts and the strip clings to the punch, whereas the blank (workpiece) expands and clings to the die opening. A stripping action is needed to free the scrap strip from the punch. The stripper shown in Fig. 7.2(a) is the simplest of such. Its purpose is to align the blank and strip the scrap off the punch on the upstroke. Other types of strippers used are spring pads or plates; some are hydraulically operated.

Besides the clinging of the scrap to the punch and the clinging of the blank to the die opening, a third set of forces is operating. The blank also adheres to the face of the punch. If the forces holding the blank to the face of the

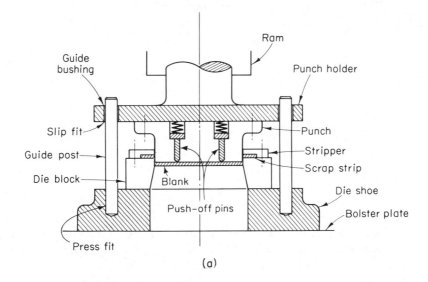

(a)

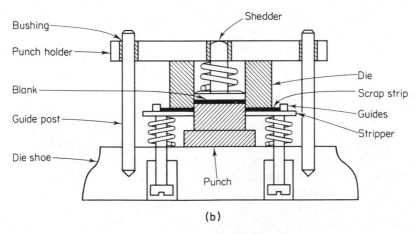

(b)

Figure 7.2

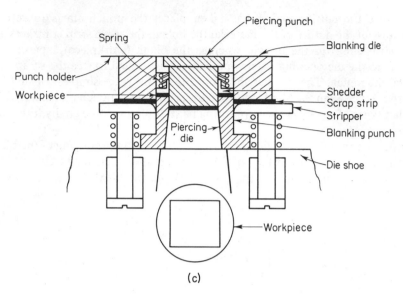

(c)

Figure 7.2 (Cont.)

punch are greater than the forces holding the blank in the die opening, push-off pins are necessary to help the blank free itself from the punch face. This is usually necessary for thin blanks or blanks which have been treated with a lubricant.

The shut height position of the die assembly is shown in Fig. 7.2(a) with the various components crosshatched to avoid hidden lines and confusion. Sometimes it is advisable to show the assembly with the right half in the closed position and the left of the assembly in the open position. Other drawing conventions will be noted as this presentation develops.

Once the die assembly is in position in the machine, the material may be fed into the die by the operator. This may be done by hand, off a strip, or off a reel. In instances when individual parts are fed into the die, this may be accomplished with a chute or conveyor belt. The finished blank may be removed by the operator, may drop out the bottom of the machine, may drop or be blown out the rear of the machine, etc. The method selected depends upon the operation being performed.

Sometimes it becomes necessary to invert the positions of the punch and the die. Such an inverted die is shown in Fig. 7.2(b). This may become necessary when the opening in the bolster plate is too small to permit the finished product to pass through the bolster opening. It may also happen when drawing large shells or punching large blanks.

Inverted dies are designed with the die block fastened to the punch holder and the punch fastened to the die shoe. As the ram descends, the blank is sheared from the strip. The blank and shedder are forced into the die opening, which loads a compression spring in the die opening. At the same time that the punch is forced through the strip stock, a compression spring attached to the stripper is compressed and loaded. On the upstroke of the ram, the shedder pushes the blank out of the die opening and the stripper forces the scrap strip off the punch. The finished blank falls or is blown out the rear of the press. Usually the press is inclined to aid the discharge operation.

Combination die assemblies, called *compound dies*, which incorporate the principles of conventional dies and inverted dies in one station may be used, as shown in Fig. 7.2(c). This type of die assembly produces a workpiece which is blanked out and pierced in one station and one operation. The piercing punch is mounted in the conventional position and fastened to the punch holder of the die set. The matching die opening for piercing is machined into the blanking punch. The blanking punch and the blanking die opening are mounted in an inverted position, the blanking punch being fastened to the die shoe and the blanking die opening being fastened to the punch holder.

7.3. Progressive Dies

Progressive dies, Fig. 7.3(f), are made with two or more stations. Each station performs an operation on the workpiece so that the workpiece is completed when the last operation has been accomplished. Thus a four-station die produces a finished piece after the fourth stroke and a finished piece with each successive stroke. Operations which may be included are piercing, blanking, forming, drawing, cutoff, etc. The list is long. The number and types of operations which may be performed in a progressive die depend upon the ingenuity of the designer.

Figure 7.3(f) shows a progressive die with four stations. The die block is machined out of four pieces and fastened to the die shoe. Thus, if one of the die openings wears or is damaged, it can be replaced economically. The stock is fed from the right; it registers against a finger stop (not shown). The first stroke, Fig. 7.3(a), of the press produces the square hole and two notches. These notches form the left end of the first piece.

The press ram retracts, and the stock moves to a finger stop (not shown) which positions it in preparation for the second press stroke. The second station, Fig. 7.3(b), is an idle station. On the second ram stroke the right end of the first piece, the left end of the second piece, and the square hole in the second piece (first station) are pierced.

The ram retracts, and the stock moves to the third station. At this point an automatic stop, Fig. 7.3(c), comes into use. This stop picks up the "V" pierced in the first station. The third stroke of the ram pierces the four holes, Fig. 7.3(c). The fourth stroke, Fig. 7.3(d), cuts off and forms the radii at the ends of the finished part. Thereafter every stroke will produce a finished part, as shown in Fig. 7.3(e).

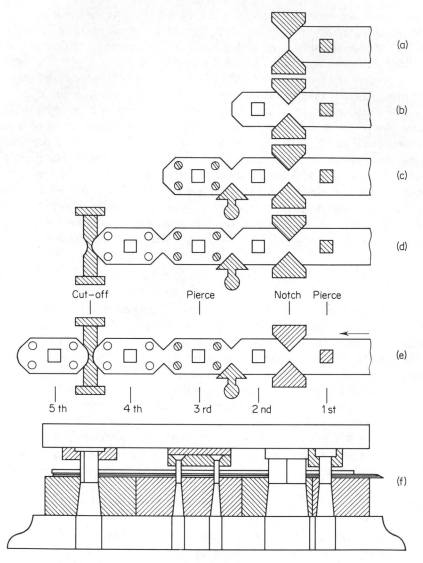

Cut–off   Pierce   Notch   Pierce

5 th   4 th   3 rd   2 nd   1 st

Figure 7.3

7.4. Scrap Strip Layout

The scrap strip is the waste material which remains after the press operations have been completed. Since the workpiece, size, and position were cut from the strip stock, the holes which remain in the scrap strip are very important in determining the subsequent position of the various die components.

The first thing which must be determined after the press has been selected is the position of the parts in the strip and their orientation, one to the other. Figure 7.4(a) shows a *single-row, single-pass* scrap strip; Fig. 7.4(b), a *double-*

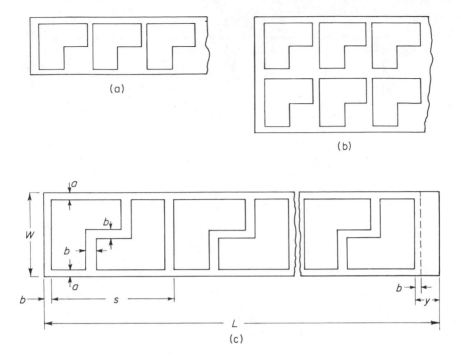

Figure 7.4

row, *double-pass* scrap strip; and Fig. 7.4(c), *a single-row*, *double-pass* scrap strip. It should be obvious that Fig. 7.4(c) produces less scrap material and is more economical than either of the other two methods.

Both Figs. 7.4(b and c) require the strip (usually 8 ft long) to be passed through the dies once, turned over, and passed through the dies a second time. In Fig. 7.4(c) y is the scrap material remaining at the end of the run when there is not enough material left to complete another part. Figure 7.5(a) shows a scrap strip of the part shown in Fig. 7.5(b).

Before the material requirements can be calculated, the values a and b, Fig. 7.5(a), must be determined. The material allowances for a and b should be strong enough so that the strip does not tear when being pulled through the dies. If there is insufficient material between the blanks, it is also possible that the sheared workpiece may buckle under the shearing pressure. These allowances are a function of the thickness of the material.

The equation for determining the material between the edge of the strip and blank is

$$a = t + 0.015d$$

a = edge of blank to side of the strip
t = material thickness
d = width of the blank

The allowances between successive blanks, b, is a function of the material thickness and is shown in Table 7.1.

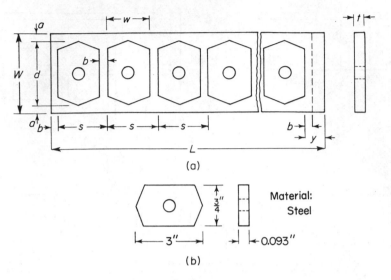

(a)

(b)

Figure 7.5

TABLE 7.1

Material thickness, in.	b
0.03125	0.03125
0.03125 to 0.1875	t
over 0.125	0.125

EXAMPLE 1, Fig. 7.5

1. Find the value for *a*.
2. Find the value for *b*.
3. Given the value of *a*, find the theoretical and actual width of the strip.
4. Find the length of one piece of stock needed to produce one part.

Solution:

1. The value of *a* is

$$a = t + 0.015d = 0.093 + (0.015)3.000$$

$$= 0.138 \text{ in.}$$

2. The value of *b* is

$$b = 0.093 \text{ in. (from Table 7.1)}$$

3. The theoretical width of the strip is

$$W_t = d + 2a = 3.000 + 2(0.138)$$

$$= 3.276 \text{ in.}$$

$t = 0.093$ in.
$d = 3.000$ in.
$a =$ edge of blank to edge of strip
$b =$ distance between blanks
$W_t =$ theor. strip width
$W =$ actual strip width
$s =$ length of one piece of stock
$w =$ width of one part

The actual width is W, *rounded up* to the nearest 1/32 in.

$$W = 3.281 \text{ in.}$$

4. The length of one piece of stock needed to produce one blank is

$$s = w + b = 0.750 + 0.093$$
$$= 0.843 \text{ in.}$$

The number of blanks which can be made from one length of stock is given by the formula

$$N = \frac{L - b}{s}$$

N = no. blanks
L = length of stock
b = allow. between blanks

EXAMPLE 2

Assume a strip 8 ft long. Find: (1) the number of parts which can be punched from the strip (Example 1); (2) the scrap remaining at the end of the 8-ft strip.

Solution:

1. The number of blanks which can be punched from an 8-ft strip are

$$N = \frac{L - b}{s} = \frac{96 - 0.093}{0.843} = 113.77$$

L = 8 ft = 96 in.
b = 0.093 in.
s = 0.843 in.

$$\simeq 113 \text{ blanks}$$

2. The scrap remaining at the end of the 8-ft strip may be calculated from

$$y = L - (Ns + b) = 96 - [113(0.843) + 0.093]$$
$$= 0.648 \text{ in.}$$

A much more general method would be to select the centerline of the strip and calculate s from a point on the centerline to the same point on the next blank having the same orientation. If the distance s is as shown in Fig. 7.4(c), the number of blanks should be doubled.

In Fig. 7.6 the number of blanks produced in one pass is given by the equation

$$N = \frac{L - (2b + w) + s}{s} \qquad \text{where } w = u + v$$

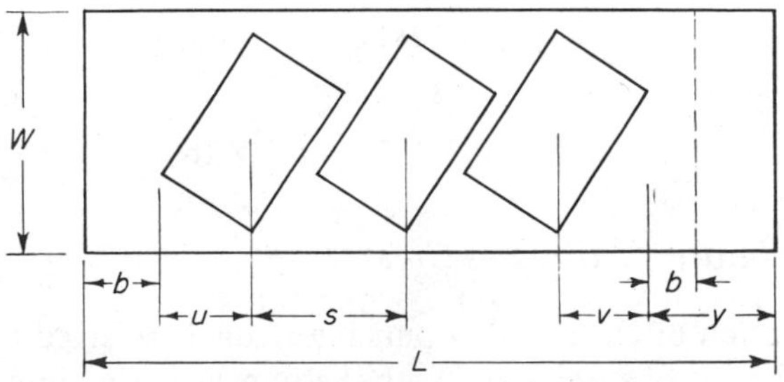

Figure 7.6

The scrap remaining may be calculated the same way as in Example 2, part 2.

The weight of a blank may be found by multiplying the volume of the material needed to produce one blank by the weight of a cubic inch of material shown in Table 7.2.

TABLE 7.2

Material	Weight lb/in.^{3}	K
Steel	0.2833	3.40
Brass	0.3042	3.65
Copper	0.3217	3.86
Aluminum	0.0967	1.16

EXAMPLE 3

Find the weight of the material needed to produce one blank in Fig. 7.5(a).

Solution:

$$\text{Weight} = Wst(0.2833)$$
$$= 3.281 \times 0.843 \times 0.093 \times 0.2833$$
$$= 0.073 \text{ lb/blank}$$

The weight of the material needed to produce all the parts, including allowances, may be calculated by multiplying the linear material requirements by the weight per linear foot for a given thickness by the constant K in Table 7.2 for a particular material. The constant to be used as a multiplier, the weight per linear foot, may be found by using the equation

$$\text{weight/linear ft} = tWK$$

EXAMPLE 4

(1) What is the weight per linear foot of the strip in Fig. 7.5(a) if the material is steel? (2) What is the weight of an 8-ft strip?

Solution:

1. The weight per linear foot in Fig. 7.5(a) is
$$tWK = 0.093(3.281)3.4 = 1.037 \text{ lb/linear ft}$$

2. The weight of an 8-ft strip is
$$8(1.037) = 8.296 \text{ lb}$$

7.5.   The Theory of Shear—Clearance

The separation of metal with a punch and die is referred to as a *shearing action*. The process of shear starts with the punch sinking into the metal and stressing the metal to its elastic limit. As the punch penetrates further into the metal, the elastic limit of the material is exceeded and a rupture appears at the cutting edge of the punch. There is rupture at the cutting edge of the die also. As the punch penetration continues, the fractures meet and a clean break results. This is shown in Fig. 7.7(a).

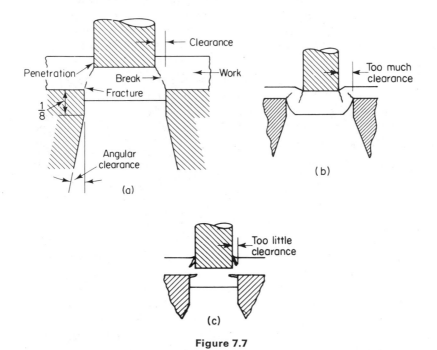

Figure 7.7

*Clearance** is the space between the punch and die. For a *round* punch and die opening it is the difference of the two *radii*. If the clearance is correct, based on the type and thickness of the material, the two fractures will meet as stated above and a blank having good clean edges will result. The edge of the blank will appear burnished for about one-third of its edge length. This is the depth to which the punch penetrated before complete fracture took place.

Angular clearance, Fig. 7.7(a) may be applied to the die opening and at times to the punches. The amount of angular clearance ranges from 1 to 4 degrees. Dies which are to produce a small number of blanks are generally machined with 4 degrees angular clearance. When large production runs are scheduled, the die opening is usually machined with 1-to-2 degrees of clearance.

It is also good practice to leave about $\frac{1}{8}$ in. width as shown in Fig. 7.7(a). This practice makes it possible to grind the die block face without changing

---

*In this text the word "clearance" refers to the *cutting clearance*. Angular punch clearance and angular die clearance will be designated as such.

the die opening diameter. In cases where production runs are small, or where the material is soft, the die clearance may extend to the face of the die block opening.

If this clearance is *too great*, the punch and die action will act like a drawing die and force material into the die opening. The fracture will take place at the punch after some of the material has been forced to flow under pressure into the excess clearance. Thus the fractures will not meet and a burr will appear on the blank edge and at the edge of the pierced hole. This is shown in Fig. 7.7(b).

If the clearance between the punch and die is *too little*, the force on the material is transmitted from the punch through the material to the die block in an almost vertical direction. That is, if there is no clearance, the punch will be exerting a force on the die block as though there were no die opening. Thus, where the clearance is too little, a great deal of pressure is required to cause penetration, rupture, and the final break. The edge of the blank will have poor finish because the ruptures will have started before the punch has penetrated the material very far. The ruptures start too early and do not meet as they should. This is shown in Fig. 7.7(c).

One of the conditions needed for any shearing action to take place is sufficient resistance to shear. Since hard materials offer more resistance to shear than soft materials, it would appear that more clearance should be allowed for the harder materials. This is the current practice. Indications from actual tests are that the clearance allowance should decrease in proportion to the hardness of the material.

In any case the clearance allowance applied to one side of a punch and die is shown in Fig. 7.7(a) and in Table 7.3. The range of percentages is from 3 to 10% of the thickness of the material to be sheared. The percentages are approximate. The amount of clearance is a function of the type of material and its thickness. There are other considerations which should be taken into account, such as the condition of the press, off-center spring loads, etc.

The general rule for the application of clearances is as follows: *The size of the punch determines the size of the pierced hole. The size of the die opening determines the size of the blanked part.* The application of the rule can best be explained with an illustration.

TABLE 7.3

Material	Clear. allow., %
Aluminum	6.0
Brass	3.0
Copper	3.0
Soft steel	3.0
Med. steel	3.5
Hard steel	4.0

In addition to the above clearance, the condition of "recovery" that takes place within the structure of the material must be considered. It has been pointed out that the material being worked will cling to the piercing punch. Once this material is stripped off the punch, the material recovers and the hole size decreases so that the hole is actually *smaller* than the punch which produced it. The same thing happens when a part is blanked in a press. The blanked part is *larger* than the die opening which produced it.

The next question is: "How much smaller is a pierced hole than the punch which produced it, or how much larger is the blanked part than the die opening which produced it?" The answer depends upon many variables. Usually 0.002 in. is arbitrarily taken as an allowance for a *round punch and die.* If the punch is not round, 0.001 in. may be used. Thus, to produce a 1-in. round hole, the punch must be made 1.002 in. in diameter. To produce a 1-in. round blank, the die opening should be 0.998 in. in diameter.

EXAMPLE 5

The washer in Fig. 7.8(a) has a $\frac{1}{2}$-in. hole and an outside diameter of 1 in. It is 0.050 in. thick and is made from SAE 1020 steel. Find: (1) the clearance,

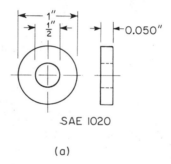

SAE 1020

(a)

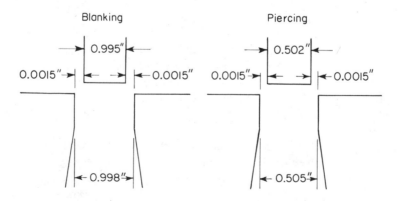

(b)

Figure 7.8

(2) the piercing punch size, (3) the piercing die-opening size, (4) the blanking die-opening size, and (5) the blanking punch size.

Solution:

1. The clearance is

$$c = at = 0.03(0.050)$$
$$= 0.0015 \text{ in.}$$

c = clearance (one side)
t = thickness = 0.050 in.
a = allowance = 3%

2. The material to be removed from the $\frac{1}{2}$-in. hole is scrap. Since we are interested in maintaining the nominal $\frac{1}{2}$-in. hole size and since our rule states that the punch size determines the size of the hole produced, the punch will be

$$P_p = 0.500 + 0.002 = 0.502 \text{ in.}$$

P_p = punch (piercing)
D_p = die (piercing)

3. Since the piercing punch size and the clearance between the punch and the die are to be preserved, the clearance must be *added* to the piercing punch size to find the *die size*. Thus

$$D_p = P_p + 2c = 0.502 + 2(0.0015) = 0.505 \text{ in.}$$

4. The 1-in. nominal dimension is determined by the blanking die opening. The die opening should be made smaller to allow for the expansion of the blank. The blanking die opening will be

$$D_b = 1.000 - 0.002 = 0.998 \text{ in.}$$

D_b = die (blanking)
P_b = punch (blanking)

5. Again, if the blanking die opening and the clearance are to be preserved, the clearance must be subtracted from the blanking die opening. This will establish the punch size. It will be

$$P_b = D_b - 2c = 0.998 - 2(0.0015) = 0.995 \text{ in.}$$

7.6. Blanking and Stripping Forces

The forces required to punch materials are related to the type and thickness of the material, the length of the cut edge, and the *shear strength* of that material. Table 7.4 shows the values for the ultimate shear strength of some common materials. Slightly higher values will be obtained if tensile strength instead of shear strength tables are used. In some instances this may be desirable.

The equation for determining the force required to pierce a hole or shear a blank out of a given thickness of material is

$$F = \frac{LtS_s}{2000}$$

L = length of cut edge, in.
t = thickness of material, in.
S_s = ultimate shear strength, psi
F = force, tons
F_s = force of sheared punch, tons

TABLE 7.4

Material	Ultimate shear strength, S_s 1000 psi
Steel	
Hot-rolled	42–60
Carbon, low	40
medium	65
high	80
Nickel	70–80
Stainless	60
Iron	
Grey	20
Malleable	40
Wrought	36
Brass	
Bronze	30–40*
Bronze as cast	56
Brass	32–45*
Brass as cast	36
Copper	
Drawn	36
Aluminum	
Annealed	9–20
Heat-treated	13–40
As cast	15
Zinc	10
Tin	5
Lead	5

*Lower figure is the annealed state; higher figure is the hard state.

If shear is applied to either the punch or the die, then the force necessary to cut through the stock is reduced according to the penetration before the breakthrough. See Fig. 7.7(a). The ratio of the penetration-to-shear applied to the face of the punch (or die) yields the reduction factor, K. The equation, when shear is applied, becomes

$$F_s = KF \qquad \text{where } K = \frac{tp}{s_1}$$

K = constant
p = penetration, %
s_1 = shear, in.
t = thickness, in.

The value of p can be obtained from any materials handbook.* It should be noted that s_1 should always be greater than tp, otherwise F_s will be greater than F. There would be no purpose in applying the shear to the cutting members if F_s is greater than F.

*For mild steel these percentages range from 25% for 1 in. to 87% penetration for $\frac{1}{32}$ in. thickness.

Figure 7.9 shows a die with shear applied to the punch.
The stripping force is given by the equation

$$f_s = 850Lt \qquad\qquad f_s = \text{stripping force, lb}$$

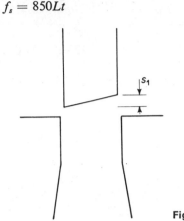

Figure 7.9

EXAMPLE 6

The washer in Fig. 7.8(a) is to be made. The ultimate shearing strength
of the SAE 1020 material is taken as 40,000 psi. (1) Find the force needed to
do the job if both punches act at the same time and *no* shear is applied to
either the punch or the die. (2) What is the force needed in part 1 if the punches
are staggered so that only one punch acts at a time? (3) Assume 60% penetration for SAE 1020 steel and shear on the punch of 0.040 in.; what is the force
needed if both punches act together? (4) What stripping force is needed to
strip both punches?

Solution:

1. The force if both punches act at the same time, no shear applied, is

$$F = \frac{LtS_s}{2000} = \frac{\pi(D + d)tS_s}{2000}$$

$$= \frac{\pi(1 + 0.500)(0.050)40,000}{2000}$$

$\qquad t = 0.050$ in.
$\qquad S_s = 40,000$ psi
$\qquad L = $ length cut, in.
$\qquad D = $ large dia, in.
$\qquad d = $ small dia, in.

$$= 4.71 \text{ tons}$$

2. If the punches are staggered, the punch taking the largest cut will
require the greatest force. Thus the force required to cut the 1-in. hole
will be

$$F = \frac{\pi DtS_s}{2000} = \frac{\pi 1(0.050)40,000}{2000}$$

$$= 3.14 \text{ tons}$$

Since the force required to operate the smaller punch is less than 3.14
tons and since the smaller punch will not operate until the larger

punch has cut through the material, the 3.14 tons will be more than enough to take care of the smaller punch.

3. If 0.040 in. of shear is applied, then

$$F_s = KF = \frac{tp}{s_1} F \qquad \qquad p = 60\%$$
$$s_1 = 0.040 \text{ in.}$$

$$= \left(\frac{0.050 \times 0.60}{0.040}\right) 3.14$$

$$= 2.36 \text{ tons}$$

4. The stripping force is

$$f_s = 850[\pi(1 + 0.500)]0.050$$

$$= 200 \text{ lb}$$

It should be noted that for materials under $\frac{1}{32}$ in. thick the ultimate strength used in the force equation should be one-half the value shown in Table 7.4. This will give a better approximation for the force required to blank or pierce a hole in a strip. It is also important to note that all force equations give approximate values.

7.7. The Machining of a Die

It was pointed out earlier that the first step before machining a die is to design and lay out the position of the blanks in the scrap strip for the most economical production. The layout may save material by the way in which the blanks are positioned in a single-row, single-pass design; by using a multiple-row, multiple-pass design; or by using a multiple-row, single-pass arrangement; etc.

Figure 7.10(a) shows a part which is to be produced in a single-row, single-pass two-station die. The first step is the making of the die block.* The die block is machined, in its soft state, square and oversize so that all surfaces may be ground after heat treating. The dimensions shown in Fig. 7.10(b) are finished dimensions. Thus, if 0.010 in. is allowed for grinding, the dimensions of the block before heat treating will be as shown in Fig. 7.10(c). The block, Fig. 7.10(c), is then coated with a blue layout dye, copper sulfate, or is heat treated until it turns blue.

With a height gage the various dimensions are determined and scribed on the surface of the block. These dimensions may be referenced to two sides of the block, to two centerlines, or to any point in space if numerical control is to be used.

The $\frac{1}{4}$-in. and the two $\frac{3}{8}$-in. holes (with allowance for grinding) will become the die openings for the piercing punches. All additional holes to be

---

*It would be better to make this die block out of two pieces. For purposes of illustration the author has elected to machine both stations into one block.

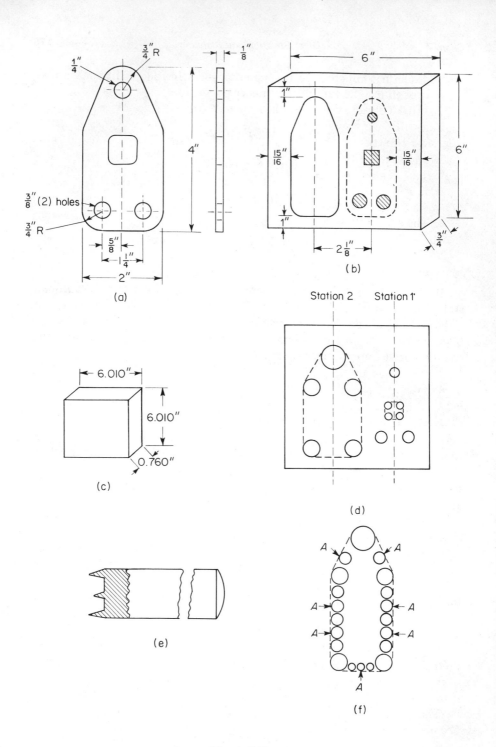

Figure 7.10

machined into the block form the four peripheral radii in the square die opening, station 1, and the five peripheral radii in station 2. These are shown in Fig. 7.10(d).

Lines are then drawn tangent to these layout circles to outline the center square and the peripheries of the part. A hollow center punch may then be used to locate the center of the hole when the circle is tangent to the sides of the part. The center punch is shown in Fig. 7.10(e).

If desired, a template may be made of the finished part and used to form the outline of a particular station in the die block. The template is positioned and clamped. With a sharp scriber, the outline of the opening in the die block is scored into the surface of the die block.

Various methods for machining away the excess metal are available. With the use of a bandsaw blade the center slug of material may be removed. Many models of bandsaws have attachments for welding and grinding a broken blade. The blade can be broken, inserted into a predrilled hole in the die block, and welded. The contour of the opening in the die block is cut away very close to, but not crossing, the layout lines.

Since the die opening must have angular clearance, the degree requirements are set on the bandsaw table. Once completed, the blade is broken again and removed from the block.

A vertical milling machine may also be used to machine the die block opening. The disadvantage of this method is that the part must be continually repositioned. If a tracer contouring miller is available, the cutter may be used to follow any contour which the follower traces on the template. In addition the movement of an end mill may be programmed into a tape and used in a numerically controlled vertical milling machine.

A common method is to drill a series of holes and break away the scrap slug of metal. These holes may be center punched with a hollow punch, as shown in Fig. 7.10(f). All the A holes are drilled first, and then the remaining holes are drilled.

The finishing of the sides of the die openings may be done in a shaper, die slotter, or miller. Filing to the desired dimension by hand or machine is still the best method available for finishing the side walls of a die opening. The accuracy of filing may be greatly aided by fastening hardened parallels or discs to the desired contour of the die block. The accuracy to which the parallels or the discs are made depends upon the accuracy desired in the die block.

It is important that the student keep in mind the necessity of providing angular clearance, grinding allowances, and in some instances allowances for warpage or change in dimensions due to heat treating.

It should be noted that any holes (screw or dowel holes), slots, dovetails, etc., must be machined into the block before heat treating. Once heat-treated, the block is ground and the die openings are ground or lapped to size. The die block is then ready for positioning on the die shoe.

Punches to be used are also blued, scribed, machined, heat-treated, and ground to size. Allowance must be made for fastening to the punch holder.

The die block is positioned and clamped to the die shoe. With a drill, the holes in the die shoe are *spotted* through the existing holes in the hardened die block. (NOTE: If the die block is to be fastened from underneath, the hardened die block will be threaded. If the hardened die block has clearance holes for the fastening screws, the die shoe will be threaded.)

Once the block is fastened to the die shoe, the punches are inserted with shim stock as spacers to ensure uniform clearance between the punches and the die openings. The punch holder is brought into contact with the punch heads and clamped. It is then spotted, drilled, etc. The punches are fastened to the punch holder.

Since some shifting will take place, the punches are realigned with the die openings and securely fastened with screws. Once the diemaker is satisfied with the alignment, the punch holder and the punches are retracted from the die shoe. The dowel holes are drilled and reamed. The dowels are inserted. The additional accessories are machined and fastened to the die set, which is now ready to be used.

QUESTIONS AND PROBLEMS

7.1 Which of the gage-size tables is used for sheet steel? Cold-rolled strip? Steel tubing?

7.2 The Brown and Sharpe Wire Gage Sizes have been standardized for which materials?

7.3 Using illustrations, discuss the advantages of the use of decimal equivalents instead of gage numbers when designating material thicknesses.

7.4 Discuss the importance of resistance to deformation as related to the drawing operation.

7.5 As a library assignment, report fully on either the Ericksen or the Olsen ductility test.

7.6 Draw a die set with all its components in the conventional position. Label all parts.

7.7 Why is a stripping action necessary in the press operation?

7.8 State the function of push-off pins.

7.9 What are some of the methods for feeding materials into a press?

7.10 Draw a sketch of an inverted die, and label all parts.

7.11 Starting with a punch and die in the open position, trace the action of an inverted die through one cycle.

7.12 Draw a sketch of a compound die, and label all parts.

7.13 Trace one cycle of the operation of a compound die.

7.14 Write a report on a progressive die operation other than the one described in this text.

7.15 Show how a U section may be positioned in a scrap strip for (a) single-row, single-pass operation; (b) single-row, double-pass operation; and (c) double-row, double-pass operation. Which is the most economical method? Why?

7.16 In Fig. 7.11 assume dimension $D = 2$ in., $d = 2\frac{3}{4}$ in., and $w = 3$ in. Calculate: (a) the value of a; (b) the value of b; (c) the theoretical and actual width of the scrap strip; and (d) the length of one piece of stock needed to produce one blank. The material thickness is 0.090 in.

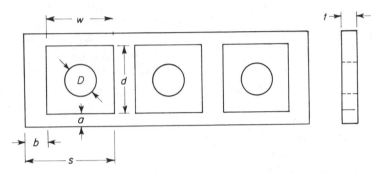

Figure 7.11

7.17 You are to make a 2-in. square washer as shown in Fig. 7.11. The value of d and w are 2 in., D is $1\frac{1}{4}$ in., and t is 0.060 in. Calculate: (a) the value of a; (b) the value of b; (c) the theoretical and actual width of the scrap strip; and (d) the length of one piece of stock needed to produce one blank.

7.18 If the stock in Fig. 7.6 is 0.040 in. thick and the rectangle is 2 by 4 in. and inclined at 60° to the longitudinal centerline, find: (a) the value of a; (b) the value of b; (c) the theoretical and actual width of the strip; and (d) the length s.

7.19 Given an equilateral triangle 2 in. on each side, Fig. 7.12, find: (a) the value of a; (b) the value of b. (c) What is the theoretical and actual width of the scrap strip? (d) What is the length of the stock s needed to make two adjacent pieces?

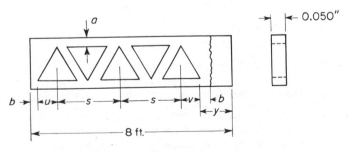

Figure 7.12

7.20 (a) Calculate the number of parts which can be punched from an 8-ft length of stock in Problem 7.16. (b) How much scrap remains at the end of the strip?

7.21 (a) Find the number of parts in Problem 7.17 which can be punched from an 8-ft length of stock. (b) How much scrap remains at the end of the strip?

7.22 (a) In Fig. 7.6 find the number of blanks which can be made from an 8-ft strip. (b) How much material remains as scrap?

7.23 (a) In Fig. 7.12 find the number of blanks which can be made from an 8-ft strip. (b) How much material remains at the end of the strip?

7.24 Assume the parts in Problem 7.16 are made from copper. (a) What is the weight of the material needed to make one part? (b) Using the K factor from Table 7.2 calculate the weight of an 8-ft strip of this material.

7.25 Assume the parts in Problem 7.17 are made from steel. (a) What is the weight of the material needed to make one part? (b) Using the K factor from Table 7.2, find the weight of an 8-ft strip of this material.

7.26 (a) What is the weight of the material needed to make one piece in problem 7.18 if the material is aluminum? (b) What is the weight of an 8-ft strip of material?

7.27 (a) Calculate the weight of copper needed to make one piece in Problem 7.19. (b) What is the weight of an 8-ft strip of the material?

7.28 Explain the effect of clearance on the shearing action in the punch and die process.

7.29 (a) How is clearance defined in this text? (b) Angular clearance?

7.30 State and explain the general rule for the application of clearance for piercing and for blanking.

7.31 How much is allowed for recovery when a hole is pierced into a piece of sheet metal? Is this allowance added or subtracted from the nominal size? Is this new dimension applied to the punch or the die?

7.32 If the operation were a blanking operation, how would you answer Question 7.31?

7.33 What determines the force required to shear a blank from a strip of stock?

7.34 What effect does shear, when applied to a punch, have on the forces needed to operate a punch and die?

7.35 What effect does the constant K have on the forces operating when shear is applied to a punch or die?

7.36 Refer to Problem 7.16; assuming the material to be copper (a), calculate the force needed to punch the blank and pierce the hole. Both punches act together and no shear is applied. (b) What is the stripping pressure?

7.37 (a) What force is needed to punch the blank and pierce the 1.25-in. hole in Problem 7.17. Assume the material is medium-carbon steel, no shear is applied to the punch or die, and both punches act together. (b) What is the stripping pressure?

7.38 Refer to Problem 7.36 and calculate the force needed to complete the part if the punches are staggered and shear is applied to both punches. The percentage penetration is 55% and the shear is 0.060 in.

7.39 Refer to problem 7.37, and find the force needed to complete the part if the punches are staggered and shear is applied to both punches. The percent of penetration is 75%, and the shear is 0.055 in.

7.40 (a) What force is needed to blank the equilateral triangle in Fig. 7.12? Assume the material to be brass; ultimate strength, 40,000 psi; penetration, 40%; and shear applied to the punch, 0.040 in. (b) What is the stripping pressure?

7.41 In Problem 7.17 find the sizes of the punches and dies if the material is medium steel. Make a sketch similar to Fig. 7.8, and show all dimensions.

7.42 Repeat Problem 7.41 with reference to Problem 7.16.

7.43 List the procedures followed for machining the die block discussed in Section 7.7 of this text.

7.44 Describe the various methods of machining away the scrap material after the die block has been scribed.

Dies: Bending and Drawing

8

8.1. The Theory of Metal Flow

The mechanism of metal displacement during the bending operation is quite different from the mechanism for drawing a shell. Since this chapter deals with both bending and drawing, the theory of metal flow is discussed here.

Figure 8.1(a) shows the bending operation. The material is clamped, as shown, so that it cannot escape the clamping device. The unsupported end of the material is forced down over the radius. The only movement of the grains in the material is at the point where the bend takes place. The outer fibers in the external radius are stretched because they are under tension. The fibers at the inner radius are under compression. At some point within the thickness of the material the forces are neither compressive nor tensile. This plane of the material is called the *neutral bending line*.

It should be noted that bending should take place at right angles to the grain direction, as shown in Fig. 8.1(b). If the bending operation takes place parallel to the grain direction, as shown in Fig. 8.1(c), a separation will occur and cracking will develop. Stock may be bent safely at angles up to 45° with the grain direction. If there is any doubt whether a piece will bend without cracking, a test should be run on the material to be used.

Usually quarter-hard cold-rolled sheet can be bent with the grain if a small radius is permissible in the inner corner of the bend. Half-hard steel should not be bent at angles greater than 45° with the grain direction. Hard steel should be bent only across the grain.

The drawing operation, Fig. 8.2, on the other hand, results in a radical displacement of the grains throughout the structure of the material. As the

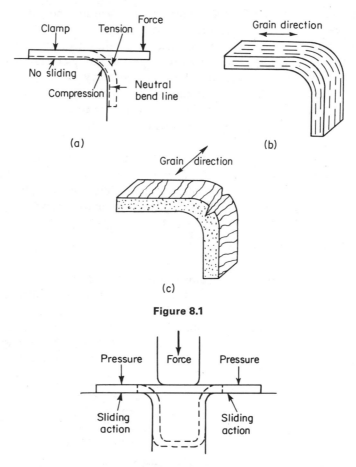

Figure 8.1

Figure 8.2

material is pulled and caused to slide over the radius of the die ring from underneath the pressure pad, every crystal in the material is displaced. At the radius the crystal displacement is analogous to water flowing over a dam.

The bottom of the shell is not affected by any of the forces operating during the drawing operation. The sidewalls of the shell are under tension. The larger-diameter blank being pulled and forced into a smaller-diameter die opening places the material under compression at the lip of the die-ring opening. The material under the pressure pad is under tension.

It should be pointed out that at the beginning, when the bottom of the punch first touches the unsupported material, the operation is a bending or forming operation.

If the wall thickness of the shell is to be the same thickness as the original material from which it is to be drawn, the area of the original blank will be approximately the same as the area of the final shell. However, it should be emphasized that, except for the bottom of the shell and possibly the lower radius, every crystal will have been rearranged.

If the crystal structure is short (cast iron), the metal crystals will not stretch or slide easily and the metal may separate. Long-crystal planes (lead and copper) permit easy bending. Some metals may prove poor risks for drawing because they do not offer enough resistance to the tensile forces in the sidewalls of the shell. The materials may stretch too much and rupture. Other materials such as brass or hearth steels may be drawn or bent rather freely without rupturing.

Many materials require heat treating between successive drawing operations to make them more plastic (remove work hardening, stresses, slip planes, etc.). Given enough time, enough operations, and enough heat treatment, almost any metal can be bent or drawn—even cast iron.

8.2. Developed Lengths

Blueprints show the finished dimensions applied to the finished product. The material before bending is flat stock. The question arises as to how long the flat stock is to be cut so that, once the stock is bent, the finished part will meet the print requirements. It should be noted very carefully in Fig. 8.3(a), that a piece of material which is cut $4.500 + 3.000 = 7.500$ in. long will be too long once bent. If the internal dimension is taken and the strip cut to

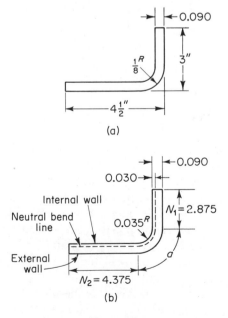

(a)

(b)

Figure 8.3

$(4.500 - 0.090) + (3.000 - 0.090) = 7.320$ in., the legs will be too short once the bend is completed. The length of the *neutral bending line*, shown in Fig. 8.3(b), will give the true length of the piece after it has been bent, because this line remains unchanged. Its length is the same after bending as before bending.

All bending equations in this text are based on the length of the neutral bending line and *internal* dimensions. Figure 8.3(a) with *external* dimensions applied has been converted to Fig. 8.3(b) showing *internal* dimensions. It is good practice to make a sketch and to convert all external dimensions to internal dimensions before applying the equations which follow.

The length of the neutral bending line, Fig. 8.3(b), is

$$L = N_1 + N_2 + a$$

L = developed length
N = length of leg at neutral bending line
a = length of arc at neutral bending line

The neutral bending line is sometimes taken as one-fourth the thickness of the material, applied from the inside of the bend. In this text it will be taken as *one-third the thickness* of the material, applied from the *inside* of the bend.

The general equation for the length of the neutral bending line at a radius corner for any angular bend is

$$a = \frac{\theta\pi}{180}\left(r + \frac{t}{3}\right)$$

θ = angle through which stock is bent—degrees
r = internal radius
t = thickness of material
a = length of arc at neutral bending line

$$= 0.017450\theta\left(r + \frac{t}{3}\right)$$

If $\theta = 90°$, then the value of $(\theta\pi)/180 = 1.5708$ and the equation for a 90° bend becomes

$$a_{90} = 1.5708\left(r + \frac{t}{3}\right)$$

EXAMPLE 1

What is the developed length of the part shown in Fig. 8.3(a)?

Solution: [Fig. 8.3(b)]

The internal radius is

$$r = 0.125 - 0.090 = 0.035 \text{ in.}$$

The length of the short leg is

$$N_1 = 3.000 - (0.090 + 0.035) = 2.875 \text{ in.}$$

The length of the long leg is

$$N_2 = 4.500 - (0.090 + 0.035) = 4.375 \text{ in.}$$

The length of the arc at the neutral bending line is

$$a = 1.5708\left(r + \frac{t}{3}\right) = 1.5708\left(0.035 + \frac{0.090}{3}\right)$$
$$= 0.102 \text{ in.}$$

The developed length is

$$L = N_1 + N_2 + a = 2.875 + 4.375 + 0.102$$
$$= 7.352 \text{ in.}$$

EXAMPLE 2

Find: (1) the lengths N_1, N_2, N_3, a, and b in Fig. 8.4(b); and (2) the developed length of Fig. 8.4(a).

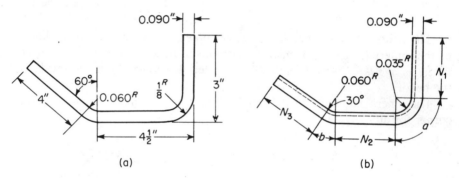

(a)   (b)

Figure 8.4

Solution: [Fig. 8.4(b)]

1. The internal dimensions are

$$N_1 = 3.000 - (0.090 + 0.035)$$
$$= 2.875 \text{ in.}$$

$$N_2 = 4.500 - (0.090 + 0.035)$$
$$= 4.375 \text{ in.}$$

$$N_3 = 4.000 \text{ in.}$$

$$a = 1.5708\left(r + \frac{t}{3}\right) = 1.5708\left(0.035 + \frac{0.090}{3}\right)$$
$$= 0.102 \text{ in.}$$

$$b = 0.01745\theta\left(r + \frac{t}{3}\right) = 0.01745(30)\left(0.060 + \frac{0.090}{3}\right)$$
$$= 0.047 \text{ in.}$$

2. The developed length is

$$L = N_1 + N_2 + N_3 + a + b$$
$$= 2.875 + 4.375 + 4.000 + 0.102 + 0.047$$
$$= 11.400 \text{ in.}$$

Figure 8.5(a) shows a part which has been bent so that front, rear, left side, and bottom are mutually perpendicular to each other. The rear wall is notched out (dotted lines), and the right wall is bent 30° to the base.

The developed length L_1 results from tracing the length of the left wall, base, and inclined wall. The developed length L_2 is a trace of the length of the cross section AA. The developed length L_3 is a trace through the cross section BB. The three developed lengths are part of the drawing shown in Fig. 8.5(b).

EXAMPLE 3

Find the developed length in Fig. 8.5(b) of (1) L_1; (2) L_2; and (3) L_3.

Solution:

1. The length L_1 is the sum of all the segments, Fig. 8.5(c). (Sect.C-C)

$$N_1 = 3.000 - (0.090 + 0.180)$$
$$= 2.730 \text{ in.}$$
$$N_2 = 4.500 - (0.090 + 0.180)$$
$$= 4.230 \text{ in.}$$
$$N_3 = 5.000 \text{ in.}$$
$$a = 1.5708\left(r + \frac{t}{3}\right) = 1.5708\left(0.180 + \frac{0.090}{3}\right)$$
$$= 0.330 \text{ in.}$$
$$b = 0.017450\left(r + \frac{t}{3}\right) = 0.01745(30)\left(0.180 + \frac{0.090}{3}\right)$$
$$= 0.110 \text{ in.}$$
$$L_1 = N_1 + N_2 + N_3 + a + b$$
$$= 2.730 + 4.230 + 5.000 + 0.330 + 0.110$$
$$= 12.400 \text{ in.}$$

2. The length L_2 is taken through section AA, Fig. 8.5(a), and is shown in Fig. 8.5(d).

$$N_4 = 3.000 - (0.180 + 0.090)$$
$$= 2.730 \text{ in.}$$

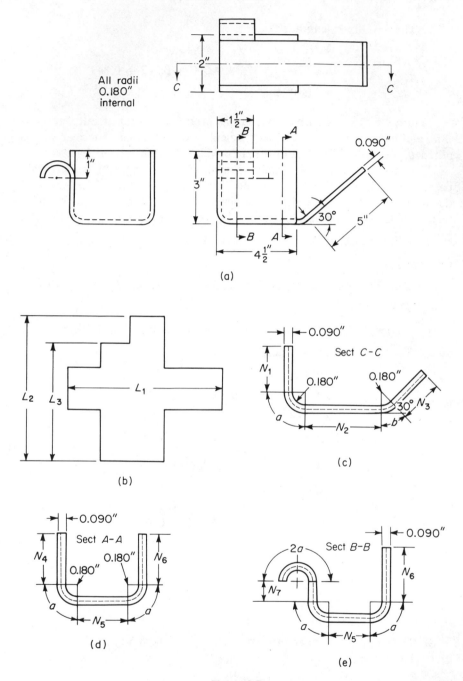

All radii
0.180"
internal

(a)

(b)

Sect C-C

(c)

Sect A-A

(d)

Sect B-B

(e)

Figure 8.5

$$N_5 = 2 - 2(0.180 + 0.090)$$
$$= 1.460 \text{ in.}$$
$$N_6 = 2.730 \text{ in. (Same as } N_4)$$
$$a = 1.5708\left(r + \frac{t}{3}\right) = 1.5708\left(0.180 + \frac{0.090}{3}\right)$$
$$= 0.330 \text{ in.}$$
$$L_2 = N_4 + N_5 + N_6 + 2a$$
$$= 2.730 + 1.460 + 2.730 + 2(0.330)$$
$$= 7.580 \text{ in.}$$

3. The length L_3 is a summation of all its parts and is taken through section *BB*, Fig. 8.5(a), and shown in Fig. 8.5(e).

$$N_6 = 2.730 \text{ in. (Same as } N_4)$$
$$N_5 = 1.460 \text{ in.}$$
$$N_7 = 3.000 - (1.000 + 0.180 + 0.090)$$
$$= 1.730 \text{ in.}$$

The developed length L_3 is

$$L_3 = N_6 + N_5 + N_7 + 4a$$
$$= 2.730 + 1.460 + 1.730 + 4(0.330)$$
$$= 7.240 \text{ in.}$$

8.3. Bending and Forming—Springback

The fundamental principle for bending or forming is that the material will take the shape of the punch with the material bending where the greater pressures are applied first.

One of the problems encountered is that of springback. That is, in order to make a 90° bend in a piece of stock, it may be necessary to overbend the material so that, when it springs back, it will come to rest at 90°. The question of how much overbend is needed is difficult to answer. The best method of determining the amount of overbend is to try a sample, make the necessary adjustments, and try again.

Many other devices are used to cause the metal to "take a set." Some of the other methods are (1) undercutting the punch so that the material is free to overbend, (2) pinching the inside corner of the bend, (3) hollow concave punches, etc. As a matter of fact, when making a bending or forming tool, the procedure is one of trial and error, especially if there is no case history of the operation to be performed or of the material to be deformed.

The toolmaker makes a complete die for bending the final part. Three developed blanks are made as nearly alike as possible. One of the blanks is then bent in the die. Corrections are made in blanks 2 and 3. After the corrections have been made, blank 2 is bent in the die. If the finished bend is correct, blank 3 is used as a template to make the blanking die for punching or bending the developed length.

It is to be noted that the same procedure may be followed for making an accurate forming or drawing die. In this instance the shape and size of the developed blank are made accurately, and the punch and die openings are corrected until the end product meets the print requirements.

8.4. The Theory of Drawing

The forces necessary in drawing a shell were discussed in Section 8.1. The area of the developed blank before drawing should be the same as the surface area of the shell after drawing, providing the thickness of the material remains unchanged.

As the metal is pushed through the die opening over a radius, the drawing action causes the shell to hug the punch. This requires a stripping action. One of these devices is shown in Fig. 8.6, but there are many more. The student is referred to his library for a further discussion of strippers for drawing dies.

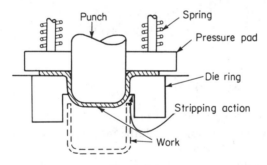

Figure 8.6

The pressure pad, Fig. 8.6, exerts a force on the "lip" of the partially drawn shell. This force holds the lip down with a pressure just strong enough to permit the material to slide out from underneath once the punch starts to descend. Under this kind of action, the metal must flow over the die radius without flapping up.

If the metal lips on the partially drawn shell were permitted to flap up, a larger circumference of material would try to crowd into the smaller die opening circumference. Folding would take place at the die radius. As the punch continued down, these folds would be too thick to pass through the punch and die clearance. The folds would be "ironed" out and appear on the finished product as wrinkles.

If the metal lips are held too tightly, the punch would either tear the bottom out of the shell, or stretch the material in the walls of the shell.

Based upon the statements just made, large die radii or unconfined metal will cause wrinkles to form in the finished shell. These may be ironed out so they are not visible. However, the weakness created is always there no matter how much ironing the shell has undergone. Certainly, if there are to be several drawing operations, any defects such as wrinkles, cracks, thinning, etc., should be corrected when they occur. If the radii are too small, breaks will occur near the punch radius or soon after the material enters the die opening. As a general rule for sheet metal the radius over the die ring should be about four times the thickness of the material. The punch radius should be at least the same size as or larger than the radius in the die ring.

Since the material is pulled over the die-ring radius, friction is a factor which must be considered. The die-ring radius must be highly polished and lapped. This will reduce the tensile forces on the shell and will eliminate the possibility of the radius picking up metal from the shell walls, which will cause scratches in the sides of the shell.

It is also possible to reduce the wall thickness of shells by controlling the clearance between the punch and the die. As a general rule wall thickness for ductile materials may be reduced by 10% of the original thickness of the material. Other factors such as the type of material, the ductility, and the work hardness which takes place during the operation must be considered. When the operation reduces the wall thickness of the material, the developed blank will be different from a drawn shell, which has the same material thickness as the operation described just above.

8.5. Drawing Dies

Single-action dies. Figure 8.6 is an illustration of a single-action die representing a simple operation of forcing a blank workpiece through an opening. The punch is attached to the punch holder and the ram of the machine. It operates through the drawing ring which is attached to the die

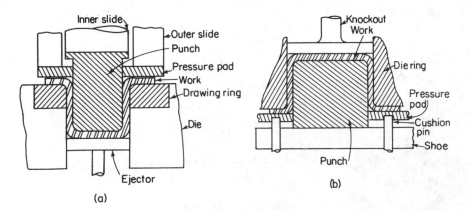

Figure 8.7

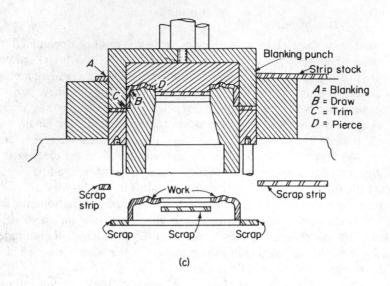

A = Blanking
B = Draw
C = Trim
D = Pierce

(c)

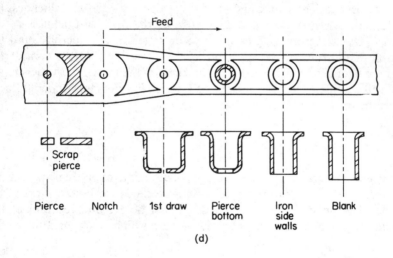

(d)

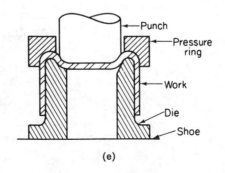

(e)

Figure 8.7 (Cont.)

shoe and the press platten. The pressure pad may be spring or hydraulically operated.

Double-action dies. Figure 8.7(a) shows a conventional drawing die set. The difference between this configuration and Fig. 8.6 is the action of the pressure pad. In this instance the pressure pad is attached to an outer ram, placing a constant pressure on the workpiece blank as it is being drawn.

Inverted dies. These dies, Fig. 8.7(b), permit the use of "double-action" without the need of a double-action press. The die ring is mounted on the punch holder whereas the punch is mounted on the die shoe. The knock-out rod ejects the shell at, or near, the top of the stroke.

Compound dies. These dies are intended to accomplish several operations with each stroke of the ram. The die shown in Fig. 8.7(c) blanks, draws, pieces, and trims in one operation. The blank is cut at A. The drawing operation then takes place at B, trimming at C, and piercing at D.

Progressive and transfer dies. These are not drawing dies: they are multiple station dies which may have drawing operations included in one or more stations. Figure 8.7(d) shows a scrap strip, the design of which is the initial step in designing a progressive die. Transfer dies use a mechanical mechanism to move the workpiece instead of a scrap strip.

Reverse drawing dies. Figure 8.7(e) shows a pre-drawn shell inverted and drawn in a reverse manner. The shell in effect is turned inside-out by changing compressive forces (first draw) into tensile forces (reverse drawing).

8.6. Shell-Blank Calculations

Before a shell can be drawn, the diameter of the developed blank must be known. The calculations which follow are approximate. They yield accurate results when the operation is performed under ideal conditions. If the wall thickness of the material remains the same after drawing as it was before drawing, the surface area of the blank and the subsequent surface area of the drawn shell should remain the same.

If the shell has no corner radius and is plain, as shown in Fig. 8.8(a), the formula for the developed-blank diameter can be derived as follows. See Fig. 8.8(b).

1. Lay out the diameter d of the base of the shell and twice the height $2h$ of the shell on d extended.
2. With 0 as the center and a radius $d + 2h$ scribe the arc AB.
3. Erect a perpendicular from e to the arc AB.
4. D is the diameter of the required blank.
5. From the triangle shown

$$R^2 = D^2 + (2h)^2$$

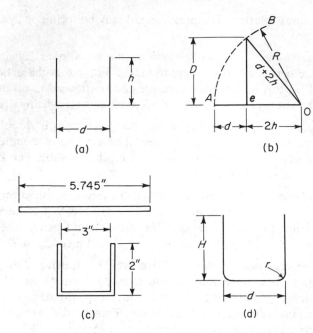

Figure 8.8

6. Solve for D^2

$$D^2 = R^2 - (2h)^2$$

7. Substitute $d + 2h$ for R

$$D^2 = (d + 2h)^2 - (2h)^2$$

8. Solve for D

$$D = \sqrt{d^2 + 4dh + (2h)^2 - (2h)^2} = \sqrt{d^2 + 4dh}$$

EXAMPLE 4

Find the blank diameter in Fig. 8.8(c). Use the method of areas.

Solution:

$$D = \sqrt{d^2 + 4dh} = \sqrt{3^2 + 4(3)2} = \sqrt{33} \qquad \begin{array}{l} d = 3 \text{ in.} \\ h = 2 \text{ in.} \end{array}$$
$$= 5.745 \text{ in.}$$

If the shell is plain but has an internal radius r, see Fig. 8.8(d), the equation for converting this shell to a square shell is

$$h = H - 0.43r$$

EXAMPLE 5

Assume the same dimensions as in Fig. 8.8(c) except that the shell has a $\frac{1}{2}$-in. radius, as shown in Fig. 8.8(d). Find the developed blank for drawing this shell.

Solution:

To convert the shell to a square-corner shell

$$h = H - 0.43r = 2 - 0.43(0.500) = 2 - 0.215$$

$$= 1.785 \text{ in.}$$

$H = 2$ in.
$r = 0.500$ in.

The developed blank diameter is

$$D = \sqrt{d^2 + 4dh} = \sqrt{3^2 + 4(3)(1.785)} = \sqrt{30.420}$$

$$= 5.515 \text{ in.}$$

The formulas for calculating many kinds of developed blank diameters are shown in Appendix II.

If the shell walls are to be reduced, the equation for the mean height is a function of the ratio of the shell wall thickness after ironing to the shell wall thickness before ironing. This equation gives a good approximation of the mean height to be used in the general equation for determining shell diameters which have been ironed.

$$h = \frac{h_i t_i}{t}$$

$h = $ mean height
$h_i = $ ironed height
$t = $ original thickness
$t_i = $ ironed thickness
$R_e = \%$ reduction

The percent of reduction of a shell may be calculated from

$$R_e = \frac{(t - t_i)100}{t}$$

EXAMPLE 6

A shell is to have its wall thickness reduced from 0.064 in. by 12.5%. The new shell will have a new height of 3.430 in. and a new diameter of 2.000 in. (1) What is the mean height of the shell? (2) What is the shell diameter needed to draw the ironed shell?

Solution:

1. The new wall thickness will be

$$t_i = 0.064 - [0.064(0.125)]$$

$$= 0.056 \text{ in.}$$

$t = 0.064$ in.
$h_i = 3.430$ in.
$R_e = 12.5\%$
$d = 2.000$ in.

The mean height of the shell is

$$h = \frac{h_i t_i}{t} = \frac{3.430(0.056)}{0.064}$$

$$= 3.000 \text{ in.*}$$

*NOTE: A reduction of the diameter of 3.430 in. by 12.5% also equals 3.000 in.

2. The shell diameter required to draw the ironed shell is

$$D = \sqrt{d^2 + 4dh} = \sqrt{2^2 + 4(2)3}$$
$$= 5.290 \text{ in.}$$

The blank diameter may also be found by using the sum of the areas of segments of the shell. The table of area parts in the appendix gives various areas so that a shell may be broken down into matching components and the area of each component calculated. The sum of the area components is inserted into the equation below. The result is the developed blank.

The area of a circular blank is

$$A = \frac{\pi D^2}{4} \qquad\qquad \begin{array}{l} A = \text{sum of the areas} \\ D = \text{dia of developed blank} \end{array}$$

The diameter of the developed blank is

$$D = \sqrt{\frac{4A}{\pi}} = 1.128\sqrt{A}$$

The area of a segment is based upon the radius from the center of the shell part to the center of gravity of the configuration. Thus for an exterior radius r, as shown in Fig. 8.9(a),* the radius R to the center of gravity of the external radius will sweep out an area A which may then be used in the equation above.

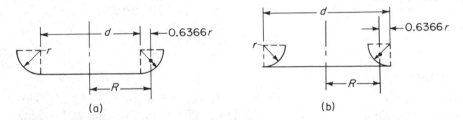

(a)   (b)

Figure 8.9

The distance to the center of gravity on the radius r lies on the radius bisector $0.6366r$ from the center of the radius r. The radius R is given by

Exterior radius, Fig. 8.9(a)

$$R = \frac{d}{2} + 0.6366r \qquad\qquad \begin{array}{l} r = \text{radius of arc} \\ R = \text{radius to c.g. of } r \\ d = \text{dia to center of genera-} \end{array}$$

Interior radius, Fig. 8.9(b)

$$R = \frac{d}{2} - 0.6366r \qquad\qquad \begin{array}{l} \text{tion of radius } r \\ A = \text{area of segment} \\ L = \text{length of arc} \end{array}$$

The area in both instances is

$$A = 6.283RL$$

*This is also shown in Appendix III.

When the thickness of the stock is given, the distance L should be obtained from the equation

$$L = 1.5708 \left(\frac{t}{3} + r \right)$$

EXAMPLE 7

Figure 8.10(a) shows a shell to be drawn from a circular blank. Using the methods of area segments, find the diameter of the blank needed to draw the shell. Neglect the thickness of the material.

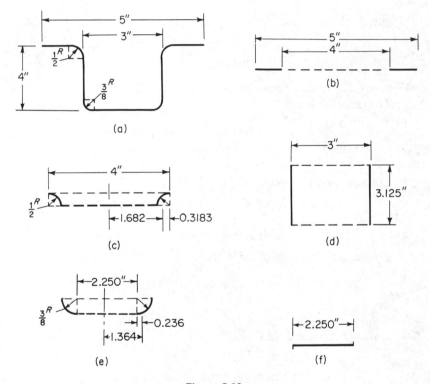

Figure 8.10

Solution:

The blank may be divided into five areas. These are shown in Fig. 8.10(b), the ring; Fig. 8.10(c), the interior arc; Fig. 8.10(d), the cylinder; Fig. 8.10(e), the exterior arc; and Fig. 8.10(f), the disc.

Figure 8.10(b), the area of the ring, is

$$A_b = \frac{\pi}{4}(5^2 - 4^2)$$

$$= 7.069 \text{ in.}^2$$

Figure 8.10(c), the interior arc:
The radius R is

$$R = \frac{d}{2} - 0.6366r = \frac{4}{2} - 0.6366(0.500)$$

$$= 1.682 \text{ in.}$$

The area of the segment is

$$A_c = 6.283RL = 6.283(1.682)\frac{2\pi 0.500}{4}$$

$$= 8.300 \text{ in.}^2$$

Figure 8.10(d), the area of the cylinder, is

$$A_d = \pi dh = \pi(3.000)(3.125)$$

$$= 29.452 \text{ in.}^2$$

Figure 8.10(e), the exterior arc, is:
The radius R is

$$R = \frac{d}{2} + 0.6366r = \frac{2.250}{2} + 0.6366(0.375)$$

$$= 1.364 \text{ in.}$$

The area of the segment is

$$A_e = 6.283 \, RL = 6.283(1.364)\frac{2\pi 0.375}{4}$$

$$= 5.048 \text{ in.}^2$$

Figure 8.10(f), the area of the disc, is

$$A_f = \frac{\pi d^2}{4} = \frac{\pi(2.250)^2}{4}$$

$$= 3.976 \text{ in.}^2$$

The sum of the areas is

$$A = A_b + A_c + A_d + A_e + A_f$$

$$= 7.069 + 8.300 + 29.452 + 5.048 + 3.976$$

$$= 53.845 \text{ in.}^2$$

The developed blank diameter is

$$D = 1.128\sqrt{A} = 1.128\sqrt{53.845}$$

$$= 8.277 \text{ in.}$$

In many instances it is necessary to draw a shell several times if the final diameter after drawing is more than a 50% reduction of the diameter before drawing. Reductions of the diameter for the first draw, from the first developed blank to the first shell, may be as much as 50%. If the shell is annealed before the second shell is drawn (first redraw), the reduction of the diameter may be as much as took place during the first drawing. If there is no annealing operation intervening, the percent of reduction of the diameter must be 40% or less. The percent of reduction of the shell diameter must be decreased if there is no intervening annealing operation.

The percent of reduction in Example 4 is very slightly over 50% and is probably acceptable.

$$5.745 - [(5.745)\ 50\%] = 2.873 \text{ in.}$$

The required shell diameter is 3.000 in. The shell in Example 7 would require several drawing operations.

EXAMPLE 8

Assume a shell to be drawn to a diameter of 3.000 in. and a height of 8.000 in. How many drawing operations would be necessary if there were no annealing operations intervening? Assume reductions of 50, 40, 30%, etc., for each draw without annealing.

Solution:

The blank diameter needed is

$$D = \sqrt{d^2 + 4dh} = \sqrt{3^2 + 4(3)8} = 10.247 \text{ in.} \qquad \begin{aligned} d &= 3 \text{ in.}\\ h &= 8 \text{ in.} \end{aligned}$$

A developed blank, 10.247 in. in diameter, drawn to a shell of 50% reduction, would give a diameter after the first draw of

$$D_1 = 10.247 - [(10.247)50\%] = 5.124 \text{ in.}$$

A second draw with a reduction of 40% would give a shell diameter of

$$D_2 = 5.124 - [(5.124)40\%] = 3.074 \text{ in.}$$

A third draw may be necessary to bring the shell diameter to 3.000 in.

The height of the shells may be found by considering the vertical height only. That is, if the shell has radii, flanges, or a bottom, the area of these segments should be taken and subtracted from the area of the developed blank. The area remaining is the area of the vertical wall (cylinder). Since the area of a cylinder is the circumference times the height, the height may be found by dividing the net area by the circumference. Thus in Example 8
The area of the blank is found to be

$$\text{Area of the blank} = \frac{\pi D^2}{4} = \frac{\pi 10.247^2}{4} = 82.467 \text{ in.}^2$$

$$\text{Area of the base} = \frac{\pi 5.124^2}{4} = 20.620 \text{ in.}^2$$

$$\text{Area of the vertical cylinder} = 82.467 - 20.620 = 61.847 \text{ in.}^2$$

The height of the *first* draw is

$$h_1 = \frac{61.847}{\pi D} = \frac{61.847}{\pi 5.124} = 3.844 \text{ in.}$$

The height of the *second* draw may be found in the same way:

$$\text{Area of the base} = \frac{\pi 3.074^2}{4} = 7.422 \text{ in.}^2$$

$$\text{Area of the cylinder} = 82.467 - 7.422 = 75.045 \text{ in.}^2$$

The height of the second draw is

$$h_2 = \frac{75.045}{\pi 3.074} = 7.776 \text{ in.}$$

The height of the *third* draw is

$$\text{Area of the base} = \frac{\pi 3^2}{4} = 7.069 \text{ in.}^2$$

$$\text{Area of the cylinder} = 82.467 - 7.069 = 75.398 \text{ in.}^2$$

The height of the third draw is

$$h_3 = \frac{75.398}{\pi 3} = 8.000 \text{ in.}$$

Therefore three drawing operations are required to draw an 8.000 in. height shell.

QUESTIONS AND PROBLEMS

8.1 Why is it necessary to have a neutral bending line when calculating developed lengths?

8.2 Explain the differences between the bending and drawing operations which prevail within the structure of a material.

8.3 Should a metal be bent with or against the grain? Why? Relate your answer to the hardness of the material.

8.4 Describe the forces operating during the bending operation.

8.5 Describe the forces operating during the drawing operation.

8.6 Why is it possible to bend copper and not cast iron?

8.7 Why is it difficult to draw lead?

8.8 Calculate the developed length of the part in Fig. 8.11.

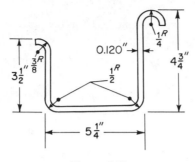

Figure 8.11

8.9 Calculate the developed length of the part in Fig. 8.12.

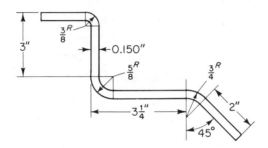

Figure 8.12

8.10 Calculate the developed length of the part in Fig. 8.13.

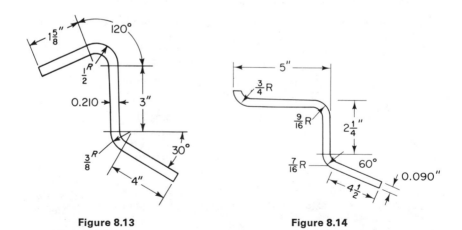

Figure 8.13   **Figure 8.14**

8.11 Calculate the developed length in Fig. 8.14.

8.12 In the bending operation does the metal take the shape of the punch or the die?

8.13 What is the most practical method for taking care of springback during bending?

8.14 Describe the "cut and try" method for determining the developed length of a blank.

8.15 How does the area of a developed blank compare with the area of the finished shell if the wall thicknesses are the same before and after drawing?

8.16 What is ironing when referred to drawing a shell?

8.17 What role does a pressure pad play during the drawing operation?

8.18 Describe the formation of wrinkles in a shell.

8.19 What effect does unconfined metal have on the finished product during the drawing operation?

8.20 As a general rule what should the radius be on a drawing punch? A drawing die?

8.21 How much may the wall thickness of a shell be reduced?

8.22 Compare the operations of single- and double-action dies.

8.23 Make a sketch of an inverted die and label all parts.

8.24 (a) Make a sketch of a compound die. Label all parts. (b) Explain its operation.

8.25 How does a progressive die differ from a transfer die?

8.26 Check the literature in your library. Find a progressive or a transfer die *scrap strip*. Make a sketch of the scrap strip and explain the sequence of operations.

8.27 What is the reverse drawing? Why is it used when drawing shells?

8.28 Using Appendix II, find the diameter of the developed blank in Fig. 8.15.

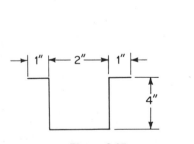
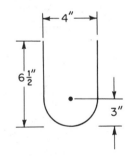

Figure 8.15   **Figure 8.16**

8.29 Using the method of areas from Appendix II, find the diameter of the developed blank in Fig. 8.16.

8.30 Using Appendix II calculate the developed length of the shell shown in Fig. 8.17.

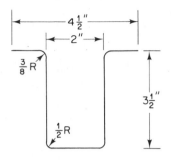

Figure 8.17

8.31 Find the diameter of the developed blank, Fig. 8.8(d), if the dimensions are $H = 4\frac{3}{8}$ in.; $d = 2$ in.; $r = \frac{1}{4}$ in. Use the equation $h = H - 0.43r$.

8.32 A shell wall is reduced from 0.120 to 0.108 in. What is the per cent of reduction of the shell thickness?

8.33 A shell has a wall thickness after ironing of 0.060 in. This represents a 15% reduction of wall thickness. The height of the shell after ironing is 4.750 in. and the diameter is 1.500 in. (a) What was the original wall thickness? (b) What should the blank diameter be to draw the ironed shell? (c) What should the diameter of the blank be if there had been no ironing? (d) What would the height of the blank be if there had been no ironing?

8.34 Using the method of segments, find the diameter of the developed blank for the shell shown in Fig. 8.18. Neglect the material thickness.

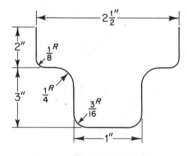

Figure 8.18

8.35 Given a shell 2.000 in. diameter and $6\frac{1}{2}$ in. deep, assume possible successive reductions of 50, $33\frac{1}{3}$, 20, and 15% when the shell is redrawn without annealing. How many drawing operations are needed?

8.36 Find the height of all the shells drawn in problem 8.35. Check the last draw.

Measuring Instruments

9

9.1. Steel Scales and Calipers

Steel scales, Fig. 9.1, are the most common of all the measuring instruments in a machine shop. Scales are made from flat tempered-spring steel. Although they can be bought from 1 up to 144 in. long, the popular range is from 6 to 12 in. long and from $\frac{3}{16}$ to $1\frac{1}{2}$ in. wide.

Usually the four edges of the scale are machine engraved to give very accurate divisions. The inch divisions are the longest engraved lines; the half-inch lines, slightly shorter; etc. Each edge has its own set of graduations. One edge may be graduated in 64ths of an inch and in 16ths of an inch on the reverse side. The other edge may be engraved in 32nds of an inch with its reverse side graduated in 8ths of an inch. Such a combination is classified as a number 4 scale. Scales may also be graduated along one or both ends.

Hook scales, Fig. 9.1(a), are made with a hardened and ground hook screwed to one end of the scale. The beveled edge of the hook is in line with the zero reading on the scale. These scales are used to take measurements with the assurance that the zero reference end of the scale is in line with the edge of the work from which the reading is being taken. Blind shoulders may also be measured with hook scales. Still another use for the hook scale is the setting of inside calipers. One leg is set against the hook edge, and the other leg is adjusted to the desired reading.

Figure 9.1(b) shows a set of five small rules suitable for measurements to be taken in hard-to-reach places, such as keyways, grooves, etc. The rules are furnished in lengths of $\frac{1}{4}$, $\frac{3}{8}$, $\frac{1}{2}$, $\frac{3}{4}$, and 1 in.

Although the ends of steel scales are made very accurately, the end of the scale should not be used as a starting point for measuring. If the length of

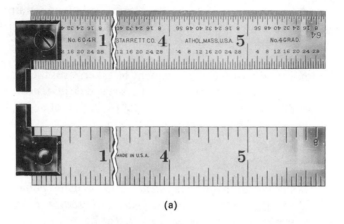

(a)

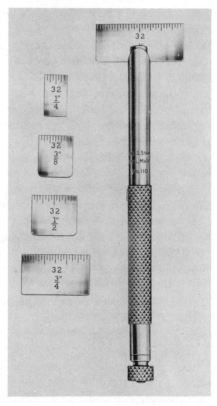

(b)

Figure 9.1 *(Courtesy of The L.S. Starrett Company.)*

a piece of work is to be measured, the 1-in. line should be lined up with one edge of the work and a reading taken at the other end of the work. When 1 in. is subtracted from the reading, the true length of the work has been measured. This practice will eliminate error due to wear at the end of the scale.

It is also important that the measurement be taken with the scale perpendicular to the user's line of sight. Since the scale has thickness, error will result if the scale is held at an angle with the user's line of sight. This error may be considerable if the scale is thick.

Although the long edge of a scale is manufactured straight, it should not be used against a piece of work to "sight" flatness. If it is desired to check the flatness of a piece of work, a straightedge should be used.

Calipers are designated as *outside, inside,* and *hermaphrodite.* They may also be referred to as *spring, firm-joint, lock-joint,* or *transfer calipers.* Figure 9.2(a) shows a spring outside caliper, Fig. 9.2(b) shows a firm-joint inside caliper, Fig. 9.2(c) shows a lock-joint hermaphrodite caliper, and Fig. 9.2(d) shows a transfer outside caliper.

In the spring-joint caliper, the spring holds the legs apart while adjustments are made with the adjusting nut. The firm-joint caliper is set by tapping the outside of one leg when closing or the inside of the "V" formed by the two legs when opening the calipers. The lock joint permits adjustment by turning the small knurled nut after the locknut is secured. The transfer-joint caliper permits setting the caliper to size, destroying the setting, and resetting by opening the legs until the grooved nut enters the slot of the transfer arm.

Calipers are used to pick off diameters or distances from a piece of work. This setting is then measured with a scale or micrometer. There is no provision for reading the calipers directly, but they may be used in the reverse order. The dimension may be set with a scale or micrometer and then checked against the workpiece.

The technique of measuring with calipers depends upon the skill of the user. When using an outside caliper to measure a workpiece, the caliper is set larger than the work. One leg is anchored against the work; the other leg is rocked back and forth while the adjustment is made. As soon as the operator feels contact, he removes the calipers, transfers the setting to a scale, and takes the reading.

If a micrometer reading is desired, the setting of the outside calipers may be accomplished by adjusting the jaws of a vernier caliper, Fig. 9.5(a), until contact is made with the caliper jaws. The vernier caliper reading is then taken. If a micrometer is to be used, the setting of the outside caliper is transferred to an inside caliper. The micrometer reading is taken over the jaws of the inside calipers.

When using inside calipers, the contact points of the calipers are set smaller than the hole to be measured. One leg is anchored, and the other leg is rocked until a feel is obtained. The transfer is made to a scale or micrometer and a reading taken. Lock-joint calipers are provided with adjustment nuts for fine settings.

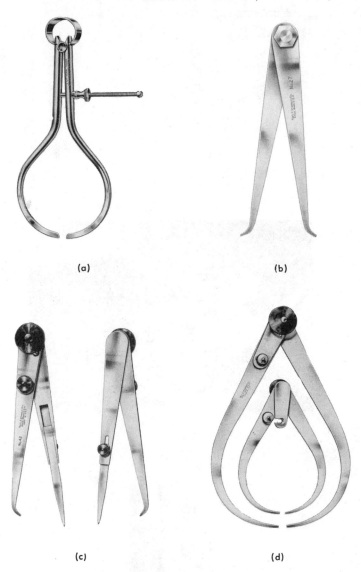

(a)　　　　　　　　　　　(b)

(c)　　　　　　　　　　　(d)

Figure 9.2　*(Courtesy of The L.S. Starrett Company.)*

Hermaphrodite calipers have one bent leg and one leg equipped with a scriber. Distances from the edge of a workpiece may be scribed or measured with this instrument.

Dividers are used for taking accurate measurements or scribing arcs. They are used mainly for the layout of a workpiece. They are equipped with two scribers.

Telescoping gages, shown in Fig. 9.3(a), are made with an adjustable crossbeam fastened to a handle with a locking device at the end of the handle.

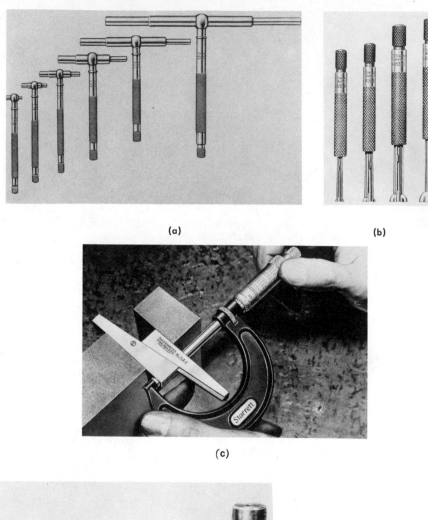

(a)

(b)

(c)

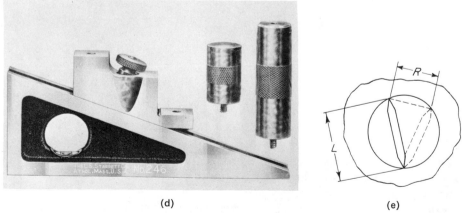

(d)

(e)

Figure 9.3 (*Photo courtesy of The L.S. Starrett Company.*)

The crossbeam is compressed, inserted into the hole to be measured, and released so that the crossbeam contacts the largest diameter of the hole and the knurled knob at the end of the handle is locked. The gage is withdrawn and the crossbeam measured with a micrometer. Telescoping gages are available from $\frac{5}{16}$ to 6 in. Small hole gages, Fig. 9.3(b), are used in the same manner as telescoping gages. They range from $\frac{1}{8}$ to $\frac{1}{2}$ in.

Adjustable parallels are two ground pieces of stock fitted with dovetails machined into the tapered section. They may be inserted into a slot, expanded, and measured with a micrometer, as shown in Fig. 9.3(c). They may also be used to set up cutters, wheel heights in grinding, and tool heights for shaping, planing, etc. They range from about $\frac{3}{8}$ to $2\frac{1}{4}$ in.

Planer gages are another version of adjustable parallels. A planer gage is shown in use in Fig. 9.3(d).

A convenient method for measuring large-diameter holes is to insert a rod and rock it, as shown in Fig. 9.3(e). Since the length of the rod is known and the amount of rock may be measured, the diameter of the hole may be calculated from

$$D = L + \frac{0.128R^2}{L}$$

$R =$ rock, in.
$L =$ length of rod, in.
$D =$ dia of hole, in.

EXAMPLE 1

A 6-in. rod has a $\frac{1}{2}$-in. rock when inserted into a bored hole. Calculate the diameter of the hole.

Solution:

The diameter of the hole is

$$D = L + \frac{0.128R^2}{L}$$

$R = \frac{1}{2} = 0.500$ in.
$L = 6.000$ in.

$$= 6.000 + \frac{0.128(0.500)^2}{6.000}$$

$$= 6.005 \text{ in.}$$

9.2. Vernier Scales and Measuring Instruments

Most measuring operations in a machine shop are made to the thousandth of an inch. Since it is impractical to engrave a scale to 0.001-in. increments, another method had to be developed so that a movement of 0.001 could be "amplified" and read easily. The vernier was developed to make this possible.

A main scale is graduated into a convenient number of divisions, Fig. 9.4(a). A movable vernier scale is graduated to one more or one less division than the length of a division on the main scale. Thus, if the smallest main

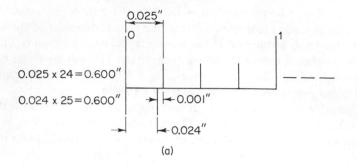

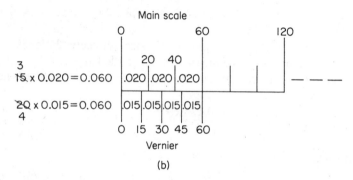

Figure 9.4

scale division is 0.025 in., the *vernier scale* may be divided into increments of 0.024 in. Each division on the vernier scale is 0.001 in. shorter than each division on the main scale. It should be noted that each division on the vernier scale could have been made 0.001 in. longer than each division on the main scale.

If the zero on the vernier scale coincides with the zero on the main scale, the next line on the main scale will be out of alignment with the next line on the vernier scale by exactly 0.001 in. Thus, when the zeros coincide, the jaws (or anvils) are closed. When the vernier scale is moved so that the next two lines coincide, the jaws will separate by 0.001 in.

The following illustrated examples will show how a vernier may be constructed.

EXAMPLE 2

Construct a vernier having 40 divisions/in. on the main scale to read in increments of 0.001 in. (1) How many divisions will the main scale have? (2) What is the length of each division on the vernier scale? (3) What is the minimum length of the vernier scale? What are the matching numbers of divisions on both scales? (4) Make a partial drawing showing your results.

Solution:

1. The main scale division is

$$D_m = \tfrac{1}{40} = 0.025 \text{ in./division}$$

2. The length of a vernier division is

$$D_v = 0.025 - 0.001 = 0.024 \text{ in./division} \qquad \begin{array}{l} D_m = \text{main scale division} \\ D_v = \text{vernier scale division} \end{array}$$

3. The minimum vernier length is

Main scale matching length $= 0.025(24) = 0.600$ in.

Vernier scale matching length $= 0.024(25) = 0.600$ in.

The matching number of divisions is 24 divisions on the main scale matching 25 divisions on the vernier scale.

4. The partial construction is shown in Fig. 9.4(a).

EXAMPLE 3

Calculate and construct a vernier having 50 divisions/in. which is to read in increments of 0.005 in.

Solution:

1. The main scale will be

$$D_m = \frac{1.000}{50} = 0.020 \text{ in./division [see Fig. 9.4(b)]}$$

2. The length of one division on the vernier scale may be 0.005 in./division more or 0.005 in./division less than each main scale division. We will use 0.005 in./division less to illustrate.

$$D_v = 0.020 - 0.005 = 0.015 \text{ in./division}$$

3. The number of divisions on the main scale which match the number of divisions on the vernier scale is found as follows: The main scale is constructed with 50 divisions/in., each division to be 0.020 in. long. The vernier scale is constructed 0.015 in./division long. Thus, if the zeros coincide, the number 60 on the main scale and the vernier scale will coincide. The minimum length of the vernier scale is 0.060 in. This may be arrived at in the following manner:

Length of main scale $=$ length of the vernier scale

$$0.020 \text{ in.} \times \overset{3}{\cancel{15}} = 0.015 \text{ in.} \times \overset{4}{\cancel{20}}$$

$$0.060 \text{ in.} = 0.060 \text{ in.}$$

Thus the minimum length of the vernier scale is 0.060 in. The above calculation also shows that three divisions on the main scale correspond to four divisions on the vernier scale.

Illustrated in Example 2 is the scale used on micrometers, vernier calipers, vernier height gages, vernier depth gages, etc. Figure 9.5(a) shows a 25-division vernier caliper. The inside flats are used for external measurements. The outside ends of the jaws are circularly ground for measuring internal dimensions. The reverse side of the beam is graduated to read "inside" by compensating for the thickness of the jaws. This type of vernier caliper is available in beam lengths from 6 to 48 in. long.

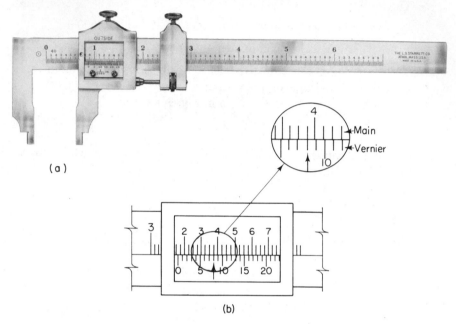

(a)

(b)

Figure 9.5   (*Photo courtesy of The L.S. Starrett Company.*)

Figure 9.5(b) reads 3.158 in. The method for finding the reading is as follows:

1. Start at the left of the *main scale*. The first major division is 3 in.
2. Find the 0 on the *vernier scale*. It is positioned between 3.150 in. and 3.175 in. Thus the vernier reading is greater than 3.150 in. and less than 3.175 in.
3. After the position of the 0 on the vernier scale has been located, the position of the *vernier line* which matches an engraved line on the main scale is found. Note that an 8 on the vernier scale matches a line on the main scale. It should be noted that the seventh division on the vernier scale is slightly to the right of a division on the main scale and that the ninth division on the vernier scale is slightly to the left of a division on the main scale. The eighth division on the vernier scale matches a division on the main scale exactly.
4. The reading is

$$3.000 + 0.150 + 0.008 = 3.158 \text{ in.}$$

It is very important that the student realize that the vernier caliper must be held perpendicular to the line of vision when attempting a reading.

Figure 9.6(a) shows the parts of a micrometer caliper. The micrometer is a vernier measuring instrument with the main scale graduated along the sleeve and the vernier wrapped around the thimble. The spindle has 40 threads/in. accurately ground on it. Thus one revolution of the spindle will move it $\frac{1}{40}$ or 0.025 in.

Figure 9.6(b) shows a *micrometer* graduated to read in thousandths of an inch. The reading is taken as follows: The thimble exposes two major and two minor divisions on the sleeve. Each major division equals 0.100 in. and each minor division equals 0.025 in. The matching line on the sleeve is the number 13 which is read thirteen thousands (0.013 in.). Thus the reading is

$$0.200 + 2(0.025) + 0.013 = 0.263 \text{ in.}$$

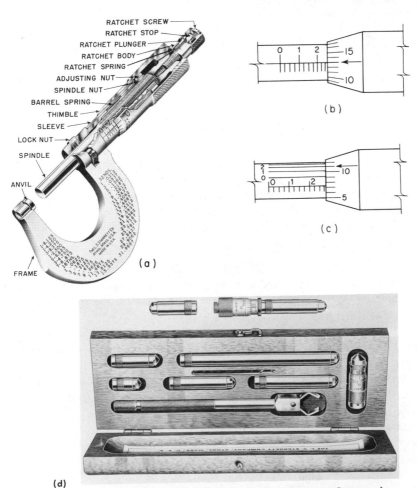

(a)

(b)

(c)

(d)

Figure 9.6 (*Photos courtesy of The L.S. Starrett Company.*)

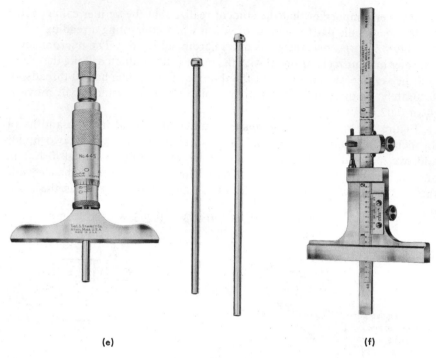

(e)   (f)

Figure 9.6 (Cont.)

Figure 9.6(c) shows the main scale on the sleeve and its matching vernier on the thimble. Also, the main scale graduations on the thimble operate as a main scale for the vernier (long numbered lines) engraved on the sleeve. Each of these lines divides 0.001 in. on the thimble into 10 parts. Thus it is possible to read this micrometer to four decimal places.

The reading in Fig. 9.6(c) is

$$0.2000 + 3(0.0250) + 0.0070 + 0.0002 = 0.2822 \text{ in.}$$

Micrometers can be purchased to read up to 60 in. These differ from the 1-in. micrometers only in the size of the frames: the spindle travel in the larger micrometers is still 1 in.

Inside micrometers, Fig. 9.6(d), may be used for measuring the diameter of holes. When extension rods are used, they range from 2 to 40 in. The micrometer heads read from 0 to $\frac{1}{2}$ in. or 0 to 1 in.

Depth micrometers, Fig. 9.6(e), with the use of extension rods are available from 0 to 9 in. Depth verniers, Fig. 9.6(f), are available with a vernier scale of 6, 12, or 18 in.

The height gage also operates using a vernier scale. This instrument is an important measuring device used by toolmakers, and it will be discussed in Chapter 21.

Figure 9.7(a) shows a *universal bevel protractor*. The main scale is circular and graduated in degrees. The vernier scale is graduated in increments of

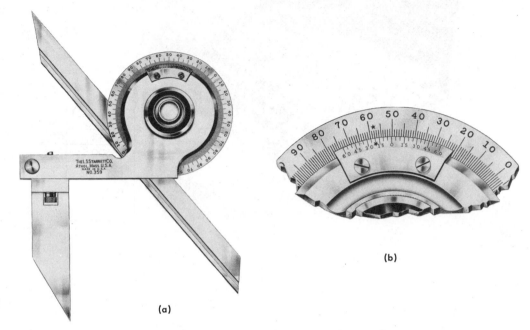

Figure 9.7 (*Courtesy of The L.S. Starrett Company.*)

5 minutes of a degree (5′). The graduations are read to the right and left on both scales. When the main scale is read to the left of the main scale zero, the vernier is read to the left of the vernier zero. The reading shown in Fig. 9.7(b) is

$$50° + 20′ = 50°20′$$

9.3. Gage Blocks and the Sin Bar

Gage blocks are used for setting up dimensions by stacking. They are made to high accuracy in size, parallelism, and flatness. Two blocks can be rubbed (wrung) together, and because of their accuracy they will adhere. Many blocks can be wrung together to make up many sizes.

Gage blocks are designated as A, A +, AA, and master. Table 9.1 shows the accuracy of each class of blocks. Values are to the millionth of an inch.

TABLE 9.1

In Inches

	A	*A+*	*AA*	*Master*
Length	+0.000006	+0.000004	+0.000002	+0.000001
	−0.000002	−0.000002	−0.000002	−0.000001
Flatness	0.000004	0.000003	0.000003	0.000002
Parallel	0.000004	0.000003	0.000002	0.000001

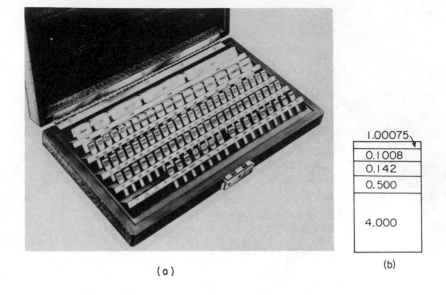

(a)

1.00075
| 0.1008 |
| 0.142 |
| 0.500 |
| 4.000 |

(b)

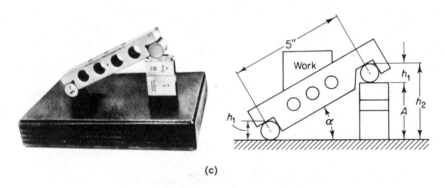

(c)

Figure 9.8 (*Courtesy of Brown & Sharpe Manufacturing Company.*)

TABLE 9.2

British Blocks (88)

No. of blocks	Range, in.	Increments, in.
9	0.1001–0.1009	0.0001
49	0.101–0.149	0.001
19	0.050–0.950	0.050
4	1.000–4.000	1.000
3	1.00025–1.00075	0.00025
4	$\frac{1}{16}, \frac{5}{64}, \frac{3}{32}, \frac{7}{64}$	

The set of 88 blocks shown in Fig. 9.8(a) is composed of the blocks shown in Table 9.2.

When stacking a dimension, the procedure is to eliminate the right digit first.

EXAMPLE 4

Stack a dimension of 5.74355 in. using the blocks from Table 9.2. The stack is shown in Fig. 9.8(b).

Solution:

$$
\begin{array}{ll}
\begin{array}{r}
5.74355 \\
-1.00075 \\
\hline
\end{array} & \text{block 1} \\
\begin{array}{r}
4.74280 \\
-0.1008 \\
\hline
\end{array} & \text{block 2} \\
\begin{array}{r}
4.6420 \\
-0.142 \\
\hline
\end{array} & \text{block 3} \\
\begin{array}{r}
4.500 \\
-0.500 \\
\hline
\end{array} & \text{block 4} \\
\begin{array}{r}
4.000 \\
-4.000 \\
\hline
\end{array} & \text{block 5} \\
\begin{array}{r}
0.000 \\
\end{array} &
\end{array}
$$

The use of gage blocks will be illustrated more fully in Chapter 21, "Toolmaking".

The sine bar, Fig. 9.8(c), is used to set up or measure angles. The sine bar is the hypotenuse of a triangle having an angle alpha (α). The diameter of the buttons and the distance between them may be accurate to 50-millionths in. over 5 in.

If side A is desired, the sine of the angle is found in a table of sine functions and multiplied by 5 to get the height A in Fig. 9.8(c).

$$\sin \alpha = \frac{A}{5}$$

or

$$A = 5 \sin \alpha$$

This equation may also be used to find the angle α.

When using the sine bar, the difference between the two readings h_2 and h_1, Fig. 9.8(c), is taken to give A

$$A = h_2 - h_1$$

9.4. Optical Flats

Another very accurate method used to measure work is the method of *optical flats*. These flats are very accurately ground for parallelism. Bands created by wave interference are shown in Fig. 9.9(a). Optical flats have sur-

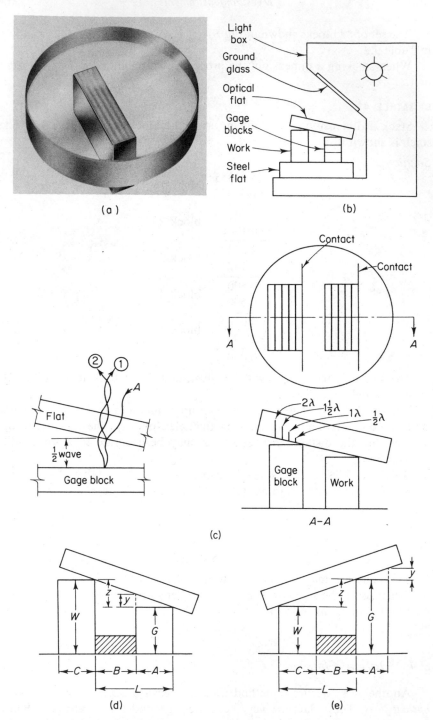

Figure 9.9 (*Photo courtesy of The L.S. Starrett Company.*)

faces which are accurate from 0.000001 to 0.000004 in. They are available in sizes from 1 by $1\frac{1}{2}$ in. to 12 by $2\frac{3}{4}$.

Figure 9.9(b) shows an optical box being used to supply monochromatic (single wavelength) light. Helium light is usually used: its wavelength is 23.2-millionths in.

In Fig. 9.9(c) the incoming light divides at the lower surface of the optical flat and the upper surface of the work. These energy waves may either reinforce or destroy each other after reflection from both surfaces. Figure 9.9(c) shows destruction. This is so, even though the distance (air gap) at the point indicated is one-half wavelength long. Wave 1 traverses the air gap and travels one-half wavelength down and one-half wavelength back. Wave 2 rebounds off the lower surface of the optical flat one-half wavelength out of phase with the other reflected wave. On reflection wave 1 will destroy wave 2, and a dark band will appear.

Thus in Fig. 9.9(c), when helium light with a wavelength of 23.2-millionths in. is used, four dark bands are shown. Considering the contact point of the optical flat and the workpiece as the zero point, the first dark band will indicate an air wedge of one-half a wavelength or an air gap of 0.0000116 in. (11.6-millionths in.); the second dark band will be 0.0000232 in.; the third dark band will be 0.0000348 in.; and the fourth dark band will be 0.0000464 in. It is therefore possible to find the height of the air wedge at the place where the last dark band appears. The process is simply to count the number of dark bands from the contact point and multiply by the wavelength of the light used.

$$y = N11.6(10^{-6})$$

y = height of air wedge
N = number of bands

Figure 9.9(d) shows the relationship between the air gap y and the difference in height z between the gage block G and the work W. The equation for finding z is

$$z = (11.6)10^{-6}N\frac{L}{A}$$

Since W is greater than G, the correction factor is added to the height of the gage block to find the height of the work.

y = air gap at gage block
z = correction factor work
A = width of gage block
B = length of spacer
C = width of work
L = distance between contact points = $A + B$
N = number of bands

$$W = G + z$$

If the work W is shorter than the height of the gage block, as shown in Fig. 9.9(e), then z is subtracted from G to get W.

$$z = (11.6)10^{-6}N\frac{L}{A}$$

L = distance between contact points = $C + B$

The height W is

$$W = G - z$$

It is important to notice that L is the distance between the contact points.

EXAMPLE 5

When a workpiece is measured with a micrometer, it measures 3.0000 in. Assume 8 bands appear when the setup is the same as in Fig. 9.9(e). The width of the gage block is $\frac{7}{8}$ in., the width of the spacer is $1\frac{1}{2}$ in., and the width of the work is $\frac{3}{4}$ in. (1) Find the length of the work when helium light is used. (2) How many bands would appear if G had been taken as 2.9998 in. and W remains constant?

Solution:

Since in Fig. 9.9(e) the gage-block stack is to be taken as longer than the workpiece, the gage-block stack should be 0.0002 in. longer than 3.0000 or 3.0002 in. Let us assume that eight bands appear at G when a 3.0002-in. gage-block stack is used.

1. The length of the work will be

$$z = (11.6)10^{-6}N\frac{L}{A} = (11.6)10^{-6}N\frac{C+B}{A}$$

$$= (11.6)10^{-6}(8)\frac{0.750 + 1.500}{0.875}$$

$$= 0.000239 \text{ in.}$$

$$W = G - z = 3.0002 - 0.000239$$

$$= 2.999961 \text{ in.}$$

$A = 0.875$ in.	
$B = 1.500$ in.	
$C = 0.750$ in.	
$N = 8$ bands	
$G = 3.0002$ in.	

2. If we assume the answer in Example 5, part 1, to be correct and the gage-block stack to be taken 0.0002 in. less than the nominal 3.000-in. dimension, the number of bands appearing would be

$$N = \frac{A(W - G)}{(11.6)10^{-6}(A + B)} = \frac{0.875(2.999961 - 2.9998)}{(11.6)10^{-6}(0.875 + 1.500)}$$

$$= 5 \text{ bands}$$

The flatness of a surface may be checked with an optical flat which is placed on the work surface to create a wedge. If the bands appear regularly

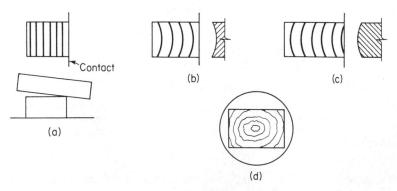

(a)

Contact

(b)

(c)

(d)

Figure 9.10

spaced, as shown in Fig. 9.10(a), the surface is flat. If the bands curve toward the contact edge, the surface is concave, as shown in Fig. 9.10(b). If the bands curve away from the contact edge, the surface is convex, as shown in Fig. 9.10(c). Bands which take the shape shown in Fig. 9.10(d) indicate high spots. This happens when the optical flat is pressed against the surface.

9.5. Metric Systems and Instruments

The vernier system of amplifying measurements may be applied to metric measuring instruments. Figure 9.11(a) shows a metric vernier *main scale*. It

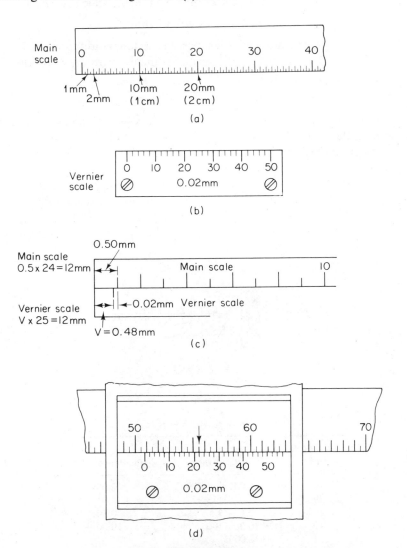

Figure 9.11

is numbered 10, 20, 30, . . . , each division representing 10 mm, or 1 cm. This major division is divided into ten parts, each line representing 1 mm. The smallest division on the main scale is 0.5 mm.

The *vernier scale*, Fig. 9.11(b), is numbered 10, 20, 30, 40, 50 and is divided into 25 equal parts matching 24 on the main scale. The 24 main scale divisions represent 12 mm (each division is 0.5 mm long). Since the matching segments are 12 mm long, the length of each vernier scale division in Fig. 9.11(c) is

$$V(25) = 0.5 \times 24$$
$$V = \tfrac{12}{25} = 0.48 \text{ mm}$$

Each vernier scale division is *shorter* than each main scale division by

$$0.50 - 0.48 = 0.02 \text{ mm}$$

In Fig. 9.11(d), the vernier 0 is just past the 50 mm graduation on the main scale and the 0.22 mm line on the vernier coincides with a line on the main scale. The vernier reading is

$$50 + 0.22 = 50.22 \text{ mm}$$

This system may be used with vernier calipers, height gages. Micrometer or micrometer, Spindles move 25 mm for 50 turns of the spindle. Thus for one revolution the Spindle moves 0.5 mm. In Fig. 9.12 the sleeve is graduated in 0.5 mm.

The 5 and the 0.5 mm lines on the sleeve are exposed by the thimble. In addition the horizontal line on the sleeve matches the 32 line on the thimble: thus the reading in Fig. 9.12 is

$$5 + 0.5 + 0.32 = 5.82 \text{ mm}$$

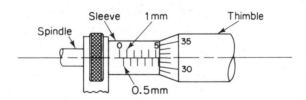

Figure 9.12

TABLE 9.3

Metric Blocks (88)

No. of blocks	Ranges, mm	Increments, mm
9	1.001 — 1.009	0.001
49	1.01 — 1.49	0.01
19	0.5 — 9.5	0.50
10	10.0 — 100	10.00
1	1.0005	

Metric gage blocks are also available in various sets containing different combinations. A metric set of 88 blocks, comparable to the British set (Table 9.2), is shown in Table 9.3. Stacking is accomplished in the same manner as shown in Example 4.

QUESTIONS AND PROBLEMS

9.1 How are a number 5 and a number 9 scale graduated?

9.2 Draw a sketch showing how you would set an inside caliper to $4\frac{1}{2}$ in. using a hook scale.

9.3 Using a steel scale, measure a piece of work several times. Take an arithmetic average of your readings. Then measure the same piece of work with a micrometer. How much error did you get with the scale?

9.4 Describe the following: (a) firm-joint calipers; (b) spring-joint calipers; (c) lock-joint calipers; (d) transfer calipers.

9.5 Show how to use each of the calipers listed in question 9.4.

9.6 Measure the outside diameter of a piece of work with an outside caliper. Transfer this setting to an inside caliper. Transfer the inside caliper reading to a micrometer. Measure the same piece with the micrometer. How much error did you get?

9.7 Using an inside caliper, measure the inside diameter of a hole. Measure the hole with a vernier caliper. How much error did you get?

9.8 What are hermaphrodite calipers? How are they used?

9.9 Practice setting telescoping gages in a known inside diameter bore. How accurate is your reading?

9.10 What is an adjustable parallel? A planer gage?

9.11 An 8-in. rod has a $\frac{5}{8}$-in. rock when inserted into a bored hole. What is the diameter of the hole?

9.12 What is the diameter of a hole when measured with a $4\frac{1}{2}$-in. rod and the rock is $1\frac{1}{2}$ in?

9.13 Assume a 9-in. rod and a hole of 9.0568 in. How much rock will the rod have when measuring the hole?

9.14 Define (a) a vernier scale; (b) a main scale.

9.15 A vernier beam is to have 20 divisions per in. and is to read in increments of 0.004 in. (a) What is the length of each division on the main scale? (b) What is the length of each vernier division? (c) What is the minimum length of the vernier scale? (d) What are the matching divisions on both scales? (e) Make a drawing of the vernier.

9.16 Repeat problem 9.15 for 10 divisions/in. and increments of 0.005 in.

9.17 List the parts of a micrometer. Why does the micrometer have 40 threads/in.?

9.18 If each division of the thimble of a 0.0001-in. micrometer equals 0.001 in. and each division on the vernier equals 0.0001 in. smaller than each division on the main scale, how many divisions on the vernier match how many divisions on the main scale?

9.19   What are the vernier readings in Fig. 9.13?

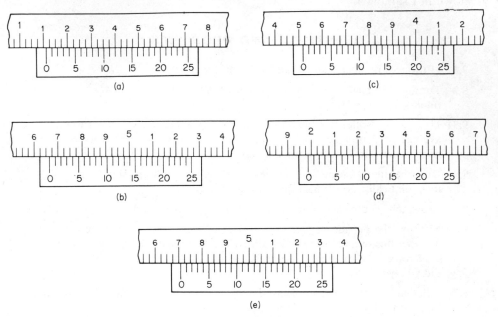

Figure 9.13

9.20   What are the micrometer readings shown in Fig. 9.14?

9.21   What are the readings on the one ten-thousandth-in. micrometer in Fig. 9.15?

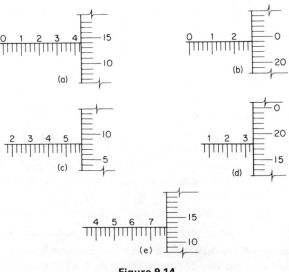

Figure 9.14

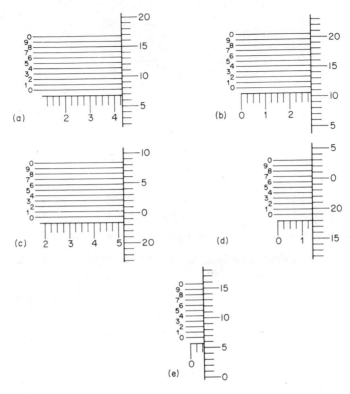

Figure 9.15

9.22 Measure a tapered piece of work with a bevel protractor, and check your reading with a sine bar.

9.23 What are the bevel protractor readings in Fig. 9.16?

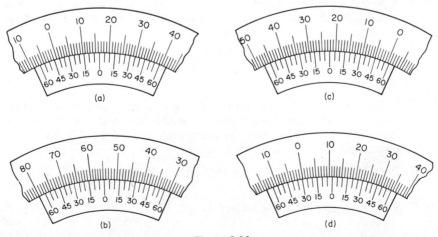

Figure 9.16

(e)

Figure 9.16 (Cont.)

9.24 State the accuracies of length, flatness, and parallelism of an *AA* set of gage blocks.

9.25 (a) Describe the principle of a 5-in. sine bar. (b) What advantages does a 10-in. sine bar have over a 5-in. sine bar?

9.26 Stack a 4.68485-in. dimension using the blocks in Table 9.2.

9.27 Stack the following dimensions, using the 88-gage set, Table 9.2: (a) 1.74835 in.; (b) 2.3254 in.; (c) 5.4537 in.; (d) 4.9654 in.; (e) 1.11325 in.

9.28 What is the difference between h_2 and h_1, Fig. 9.8(c), when a sine bar is used to measure an angle of 34°35′?

9.29 In Fig. 9.8(c) the gage blocks measure 2.3061 in. What is the angle measured by a sine bar?

9.30 Height h_1 measures 1.0000 in., and h_2 measures 2.6897 in. What is the angle when measured with a sine bar, Fig. 9.8(c)?

9.31 Discuss the principle of destructive interference of light waves.

9.32 What type of surface is indicated when optical bands curve (a) toward the contact edge and (b) away from the contact edge? (c) What type of surface is indicated when the patterns are irregular and circular?

9.33 A workpiece measured with a micrometer reads 1.7650 in. In Fig. 9.9(d), $A = 1\frac{3}{16}$ in., $B = 1\frac{3}{8}$ in., and $C = 1\frac{1}{2}$ in. What is the actual size of the workpiece if six bands are counted?

9.34 How many bands are visible if all the conditions and the answer in problem 9.33 prevail? Assume the gage blocks to be taken 0.0002 in. greater than the work.

9.35 In Fig. 9.9(e), $A = 0.950$ in., $B = 2.000$ in., and $C = 1.000$ in. If the work measures 2.6255 in. with a micrometer, what is the actual size of W if G is taken 0.0002 in. larger than the micrometer reading of W? The bands counted are 15.

9.36 Describe the divisions on the metric main and vernier scales in Fig. 9.11 (a and b).

9.37 What is the reading on the vernier, Fig. 9.17?

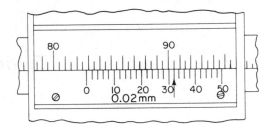

Figure 9.17

9.38 Explain the divisions on the micrometer, Fig. 9.12.

9.39 What is the reading on the micrometer, Fig. 9.18.

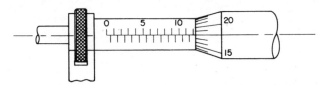

Figure 9.18

Cutting Tools

10

10.1. The Theory of Cutting

The operation of a cutting tool, whether it is on a lathe, milling machine, or any other machine tool, is based upon theory which is the same for all processes. The purpose of any cutting operation is to achieve good surface finish at high speeds and feeds with the least effort and at the lowest cost.

The desirability of getting the maximum use from a tool before it needs regrinding is one of the objectives of tool technology. Assuming that a tool has been properly designed and made, failure may result from the wearing away of the tool's cutting edge, which changes the geometry of the tool. This geometric change may be in the nature of a dull edge, roughness, or a shift in the clearance angles. Any of the changes will generate heat, which may cause the tool to lose hardness. This does not mean that the tool is soft. It simply means that the tool has softened to the point where the movement of the tool in relation to the work makes the tool too soft for efficient cutting. If the relative motion of the tool to the work is too great, the tool material will be "rubbed" off the cutting edge, and the conditions which prevail after the rubbing away has taken place create even higher temperatures so that larger sections of the tool's cutting edge are rubbed away. The process of softening and rubbing away continues until the tool breaks down completely.

Thus, proper lubrication or cooling, sharp tools, proper angles, careful selection of tool materials, proper feeds and speeds, and the proper setting-up of the tool relative to the work all help in cutting down the heat generated and prolong the tool's life. Tool life is defined as the length of time a tool will operate before failure occurs.

Another cause of tool failure results from the high stresses set up by the tool within the workpiece and within the resulting chip. The metal is said to work-harden, and as a result greater forces are needed to separate the chip from the parent metal. Some materials (stainless steel, 18-8) work-harden severely which becomes an important factor in the cutting process.

Work-hardening can be circumvented by taking cuts deep enough so that the previously hardened surface of the work is removed farther up the cutting edge where the tool is stronger and creates a "chipping" effect. The same technique may be used for removing scale from hot-rolled material. Still another method is to remove the work-hardened surface by preheating the work.

Chip formation is a function of the tool bit and the nature of the material being cut. It may be classified as continuous, discontinuous, or built-up edge and is always the result of shear.

The planer tool will be used to illustrate chip formation because the tool is set perpendicular to the work and operates along the length of the work.

A continuous chip, Fig. 10.1(a), is obtained when cutting ductile materials.

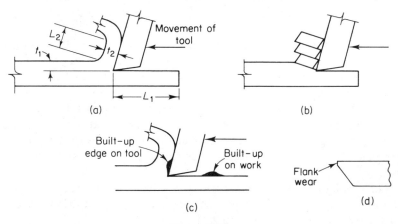

Figure 10.1

The chip is severely deformed and either comes off in the form of a long string, or curls into a tight roll. Metal prior to being cut is much longer than the chip which is removed. Since the volume of the material before cutting and after cutting is the same and, during the planer operation, the width of the cut remains unchanged, the thickness of the chip after cutting must be greater than before cutting. See Fig. 10.1(a). Thus

$$r = \frac{t_1}{t_2} = \frac{L_2}{L_1}$$

r = ratio
t_1 = chip thickness before cutting
t_2 = chip thickness after cutting
L_1 = length of chip before cutting
L_2 = length of chip after cutting

If the ratio *r* is large, the cutting action is good. Thus a ratio of 1 : 2 should yield good results.

A discontinuous chip, such as results when cutting cast iron, is shown in Fig. 10.1(b). Assume that the cutting action is just starting. The material starts to slide up the face of the tool. Since the shearing forces are high, a crack develops early as the cut proceeds. This cut fractures small pieces of material off the work. The results are discontinuous. In gray cast iron the structure of the material—long graphite stringers—means that the forces need only break through the material which separates one graphite stringer from the next.

Another action which takes place in continuous cutting results in what is called a *built-up* edge, Fig. 10.1(c). In this action, the high heat generated welds a small chip to the tool. As the weld builds up, the welded chip grows and finally breaks away from the tool. Figure 10.1(c) shows part of the weld remaining with the work and the rest of the weld moving up the face of the tool. Neither of these is desirable because one leaves a rough work surface and the other, while welded to the tool, interferes with the cutting action of the tool.

Another result of welded chips is *cratering* in the face of the tool. Each time the chip breaks away from the face of the tool, it takes a very small amount of material off the face of the tool. The accumulated effect of many such actions is a crater in the face of the tool.

Flank wear, Fig. 10.1(d), is a continuing process that takes place below the cutting edge in the face of the flank. As the wear flat widens, it destroys the clearance below the cutting edge, which in turn causes rubbing, increased heat generation, increased cutting forces against the tool, and greater plant wear.

The cutting action of a tool bit may be divided into three zones: Z_f, the friction zone; Z_d, the deformation zone; and Z_w, the work-surface zone. These zones are shown in Fig. 10.2(a).

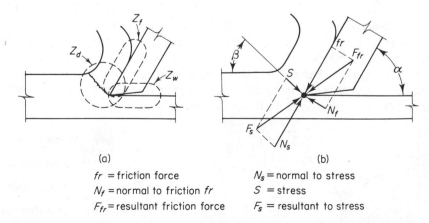

(a)

(b)

fr = friction force
N_f = normal to friction *fr*
F_{fr} = resultant friction force

N_s = normal to stress
S = stress
F_s = resultant to stress

Figure 10.2

The forces shown in Fig. 10.2(b) are fr, the friction force along the face of the tool and the normal force N_f. The resultant of these two forces, F_{fr}, is the force exerted by the tool on the work.

The work exerts an equal but opposite force F_s to F_{fr}. This resultant force F_s has two components, a normal force N to the shearing action and the shearing force S.

It should be pointed out that, if the angle alpha(α) gets larger, the angle beta(β), Fig. 10.2(b), gets smaller and the force required to cut the material becomes greater.

There are additional forces operating at the cutting edge, which are very small and have not been considered here.

From the above discussion it can be seen that the friction must be kept as low as possible to reduce the heat generated. This can be done by using lubricants which form an oily film on the surface of the metal and thus make the shearing of the metal easier. This is the primary purpose of a lubricant. It may be a fatty oil, mineral oil, or sulfurized mineral or fatty oil.

Its secondary effect is to remove heat generated during the cutting operation both from the energy converted to heat during the shearing process and from the friction of the chip against the tool face.

Where the cutting operation is severe and the lubricant cannot remove the heat rapidly enough, water-soluble oils may be used. When mixed with a high concentration of water, the cooling effect is greatly increased with some lubricating properties retained. These mixtures do not corrode the steel parts with which they come into contact.

Thus, lubricating oils are used chiefly to reduce friction and water-soluble oils are used chiefly as coolants. In general, recommended coolants and lubricants are: for steels and wrought iron, water-soluble oils or sulfur-based and mineral oils; for aluminum, mineral and fatty oils or soluble oils; for brass, copper, bronze, monel metal, and malleable iron, soluble oils. Cast iron is machined dry.

10.2. Tool Bit Materials

The materials used for tool bits must possess certain qualities to be effective. They must possess hardness, strength, and toughness, and they must be heat resistant. Tool materials that have been developed with these qualities will now be considered.

High-carbon steel. Tools made from high-carbon steels, 0.80 to 1.30%, are used for small-quantity production of wood parts or machining soft materials such as free cutting steels and brass. It is important that the operational temperatures be kept below 400°F because the material loses its hardness above this temperature. For this reason coolants should be used freely. Sometimes vanadium and chromium are added to give better hardenability. However, any temperature increase will affect the hardness and effectiveness of the tool.

High-speed steel. These tool materials are of several varieties. The most common type is the 18-4-1 high-speed steel. This tool material has approximately 18% tungsten, 4% chromium, and 1% vanadium as its alloying elements. Another type has about the same percentage of tungsten but from 5 to 12% cobalt added as one of the principal alloying elements. This improves the red hardness of the material. This type of tool material, although able to operate at higher temperatures than 18-4-1 steel, is more expensive. To reduce the amount of tungsten required, another high-speed steel has been developed, which has a high molybdenum content. About 9% molybdenum permits the reduction of the tungsten content to about 2%. The chromium and vanadium content remains about the same. The carbon content of these materials ranges from about 0.6 to 0.8%.

High-speed steel will operate up to about 1100°F and retain its effectiveness. This ability to operate at these higher temperatures makes it possible to increase the cutting speed or depth of cut. However, a coolant should be used freely to increase maximum tool life.

See Chapter 2, Section 11, for the heat treatment of high-speed steels.

Nonferrous cast tool steel. There are several varieties of cast tool steels. In general, they contain about 2% carbon; 15 to 20% tungsten; 30 to 35% chromium; and 40 to 50% cobalt. This material cannot be effectively or economically shaped by cold or hot working and is therefore cast to the desired shape. It operates best at elevated temperatures (approximately 1500°F), losing efficiency if operated at "cold" temperatures. Therefore, the cutting speeds may be increased without damage to the cutting edge of the tool: deeper cuts are taken at higher cutting speeds and reduced feeds.

Carbides. These are sintered materials. There are three elements usually "cemented" with cobalt as a binder: tungsten, titanium, and tantalum. The titanium and tantalum are added to the tungsten to achieve various desirable properties which tungsten alone might not have.

Powdered cobalt is mixed with tungsten, tungsten-titanium, and tungsten-tantalum carbide powders. The mixture is then cold compressed into a briquette in a mold under about 10 tons of pressure and then presintered in a nonoxidizing-atmosphere furnace. The temperature of the furnace should be about 1500°F. The briquettes are then reheated to 2500°F. At this temperature the cobalt melts but the other components remain solid. On cooling the cobalt solidifies, and the compact becomes a very hard material which can be shaped only with difficulty. Rockwell hardness depends upon the pressures used during the process. Rockwell hardness of the finished material ranges from 70 to 95 R_c.

Tungsten carbides are used primarily to machine cast iron, nonferrous metals, plastics, rubber, etc. Tungsten-titanium and tantalum-titanium carbides may be used to machine steels, tough materials, and most materials which may be machined with tungsten carbides. In general, the deeper the cut or the tougher the material being cut, the lower should be the Rockwell hardness of the tool material to be used. Higher Rockwell-hardness materials may be used for taking light cuts. Carbides in general may be used at cutting speeds which are about three times that used with high-speed steels.

Ceramic tool material.   Ceramic tool materials, namely aluminum oxide or silicon carbide, may be mixed with a glass binder. Sometimes the material is compacted without a binder. Under pressures of about 25 tons and a temperature of 2000°F, sintering takes place and the material becomes hard and brittle. It will withstand operational temperatures of about 2000°F without losing hardness or strength. Because of its high compressive strength and low coefficient of resistance, the cutting speeds used may be about two times higher than for carbides.

The limitations of ceramic tools primarily are within the bonding material itself and the present-day machine tools. The bonding materials develop microscopic structural cracks which set up areas of high stress concentration under loading. The tools are brittle and need machine and setup rigidity for maximum efficiency. The spindle speeds and rigidity needed are not sufficient in most machine tools manufactured today.

Industrial diamonds.   These have limited use in present-day machining of metals. They may be used to machine aluminum, plastics, hard rubber, and, if used with very fine feeds and high spindle speeds, for fine finishing of bored holes in steel. They are expensive and difficult to shape into desired forms.

10.3. Terminology, Clearance, Rakes, Chip Breakers

The principles which apply to single-point tool bits also apply to other types of cutting tools. Probably the most important single aspect of any type of cutting tool is the fact that the cutting edge must be free to cut without interference from either the tool itself or from the work. The question of how much support is needed for the cutting edge depends upon the type of material in the cutting tool, the type of material being cut, the feed, the cutting speed, rigidity, etc. The full implication of this paragraph will become more evident as this presentation unfolds.

There are several types of single-point tools available. They are solid tools which fit directly into the holder, Fig. 10.3(a); solid tools which fit directly into a tool post, Fig. 10.3(b); tool inserts which are clamped to a solid piece of material, Fig. 10.3(c); or tool inserts which are brazed to a tool shank, Fig. 10.3(d). Figure 10.4 shows several configurations of inserts which are available commercially.

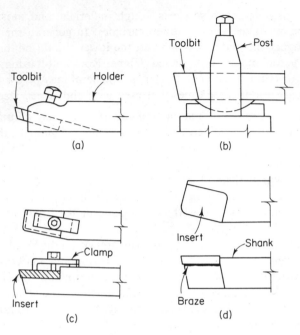

Figure 10.3

Figure 10.5(a) shows the tool bit in Fig. 10.5(b) in operation. Figure 10.5(b) shows three views of a tool bit. The following notations indicate the terminology of the various parts of the tool bit:

$a =$ the back rake angle $f =$ the side cutting-edge angle

$b =$ the side rake angle $g =$ the cutting angle

$c =$ the front relief angle $h =$ the lip angle

$d =$ the side relief angle $i =$ the nose angle

$e =$ the end cutting-edge angle $j =$ the nose radius

In Fig. 10.5(b) the tool is ground with a *front relief angle c* and an *end cutting-edge angle e* so that only the tip of the tool touches the work. Since the feed is from left to right in the front view, section $A - A$ Fig. 10.5(a), the tool must be ground with a *side relief angle d* so that the tool material below the cutting edge does not interfere with the cutting action.

The *back rake angle a*, the *side rake angle b*, and the *side cutting-edge angle f* are ground to produce the desired effect in cutting. These effects will be presented later in this section. All remaining angles (h, g, i) result from the manner in which the former angles are applied to the tool bit. The method of grinding a tool bit will be presented in Chapter 13.

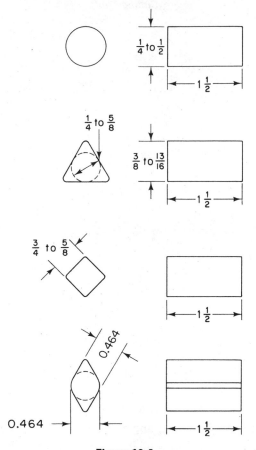

Figure 10.4

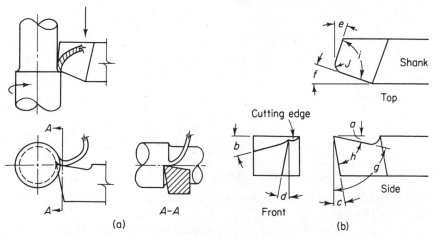

Figure 10.5

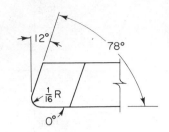

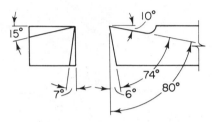

Figure 10.6

In general the following clearance and rake angles, those shown in Fig. 10.6, are recommended:

$$
\begin{aligned}
\text{Front relief angle} &= 6° \\
\text{Side relief angle} &= 7° \\
\text{Back rake angle} &= 10° \\
\text{Side rake angle} &= 15° \\
\text{Nose radius} &= \tfrac{1}{16} \text{ in.} \\
\text{End cutting-edge angle} &= 12° \\
\text{Side cutting-edge angle} &= 0°
\end{aligned}
$$

The relief angles will form the following angles:

The lip angle of

$$90° - (10° + 6°) = 74°$$

A cutting angle of

$$90° - 10° = 80°$$

A nose angle of

$$90° - (12° + 0°) = 78°$$

Table 10.1 shows some recommended relief and rake angles for high-speed steel tools.

Angles and rakes for carbide tools should be carefully controlled. These are shown in the solid carbide toolbit, Fig. 10.7. Inserts are also used. They have been standardized and are shown in Fig. 10.8.

TABLE 10.1

Relief and Rake Angles,
in Degrees

Material	Front relief angle	Side relief angle	Back rake	Side rake
Steel				
SAE	8	10–12	10–15	10–20
Stainless	8	10	10	15
Tool	8	10	10	10
Cast iron				
Gray	8	10	5	10
Aluminum	8	12	30	15
Brass & bronze	8	10	0	0 to −15
Copper				
Soft	10	15	15	20
Hard	10	8	0	0 to −5

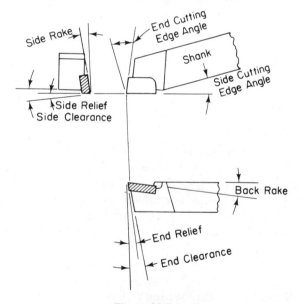

Figure 10.7

Side relief angles should be ground consistent with the feed used and the material cut. In general, the side relief angle and the front relief angle should be kept as small as possible. It should be remembered that carbide is brittle and the more support the tip has from the body of the tool, the less likely it is that the tip will break or chip. Front relief angles and side relief angles are ground to between 3 and 10°, with most tools being ground to 5°. The softer

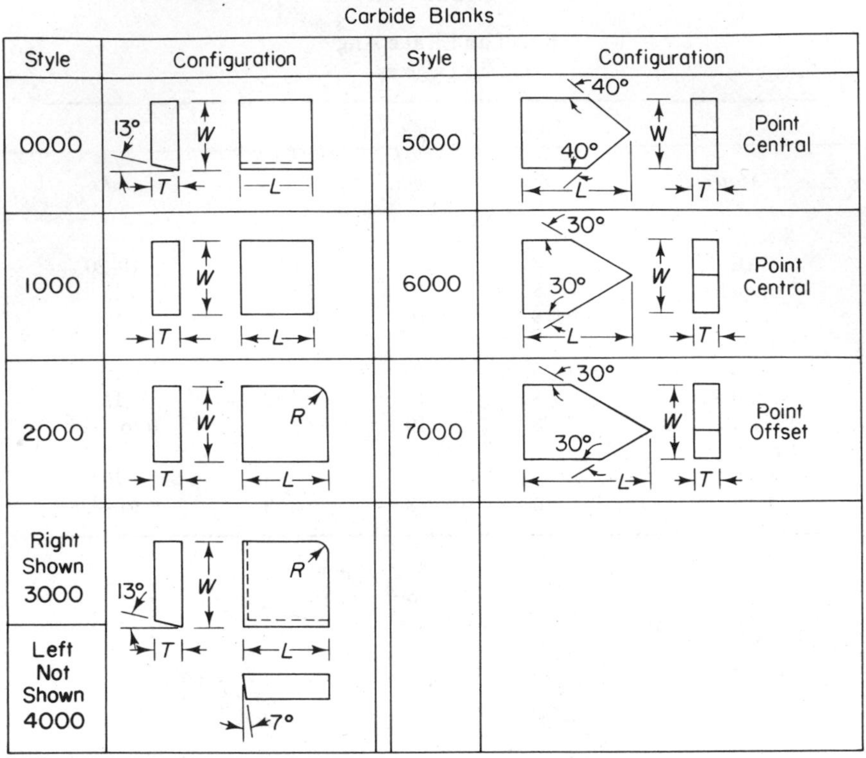

Carbide Blanks

Style	Configuration	Style	Configuration
0000	13° W T L	5000	40° 40° W L T — Point Central
1000	W T L	6000	30° 30° L W T — Point Central
2000	W R T L	7000	30° 30° L W T — Point Offset
Right Shown 3000 / Left Not Shown 4000	13° W R T L 7°		

Figure 10.8

the material, the greater the angle. The shank side relief angle should be about 2° greater than the tip side relief angle.

The side cutting-edge angle of 15° and an end edge-cutting angle will be satisfactory for most turning operations. This produces a shearing action as the tool feeds along the work and provides a 70° nose angle. Another important effect of the side cutting-edge angle is that the solid part of the cutting edge contacts the work first. This heavier cross section of tool bit is better able to take the first shock of the cutting action than the tip of the tool is.

Rakes are used to aid the shearing action of the tool as the work revolves onto the tool surface. However, it is important to recognize that sometimes this shearing action must be sacrificed in the interest of tool strength. When this is necessary, negative rake angles are used.

Figure 10.9(a) shows a tool with a 0° back rake; Fig. 10.9(b) one with a positive back rake; and Fig. 10.9(c) one with a negative back rake. A zero rake will project a line from the top of the tool through the center of the work, as shown. Positive rake sets up a "scooping" action. Negative rake sets up

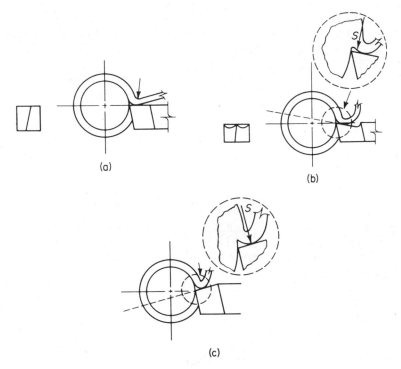

(a)

(b)

(c)

Figure 10.9

a "bulldozer" action. Tools may also have negative side rake or combinations of positive and negative back and side rakes.

Figure 10.9(b) shows the shearing force of the material acting on the tip of the tool. In Fig. 10.9(c) the shearing force is greater but acts back of the tip where the strength of the tool is greater.

Chip breakers, Fig. 10.10, are used to control the directional flow of chips. This may not be necessary for ordinary lathe work, but it becomes important in semi-automatic or automatic boring or any place where chip production could interfere with the cutting operation. Therefore, chip breakers are used to curl and break off chips into small pieces so that they may be removed easily by the coolant or air or simply allowed to fall into the chip pan of the machine.

There are several varieties of chip breakers which may be used on any type of tool. In general the groove needs to be slightly longer than the depth of cut. The width of the groove, the depth of the groove, and the width of the land (or area) between the cutting edge and the groove depend upon the feed. Some typical chip-breaker dimensions are shown in Fig. 10.10(a).

Figure 10.10(a) has a ground-in groove. The land on this type of chip breaker may have up to a 5° negative rake. Figure 10.10(b) and (c) shows the

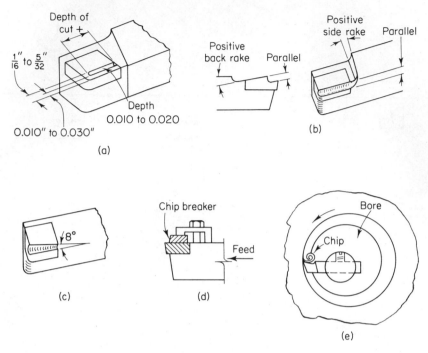

Figure 10.10

step type of chip breakers. They may be parallel to the cutting edge or at an angle to the cutting edge for better control of chip flow. The flat section at the bottom of the step type of chip breaker may itself create positive, zero, or negative rake with the top of the tool. This is shown in Fig. 10.10(b) inset, where the chip breaker has a positive rake ground parallel to the face of the tool.

Figure 10.10(d) shows a mechanical chip breaker which can be set at any desired distance from the end of the tool edge. Figure 10.10(e) shows the advantage of having a chip breaker on a boring tool. The chip curls into a tight roll, breaks off, and falls out of the hole.

10.4. Milling Cutters

Figure 10.11(a) shows a high-speed steel milling cutter. Other types of milling cutters are shown in Chapter 15. Relief and rake angles are applied to milling cutters in the same manner in which they were applied to tool bits. The milling cutter is actually a multiple tool bit arrangement.

Figure 10.11(b) shows the relief and rake angles for a single-side milling cutter. This cutter has both axial and radial rakes. The axial rake angle is the angle made by the peripheral cutting edge and a line parallel to the axis

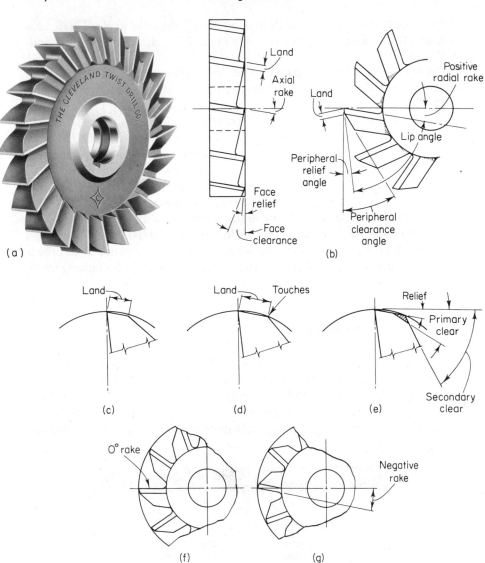

Figure 10.11   *(Photo courtesy of the Cleveland Twist Drill Company.)*

of the cutter. The radial rake angle is the angle made between the side cutting edge and the radius of the cutter. Rake angles of about 10 to 15° are used.

The "flat" created by the relief angle is called the *land*. The land is usually about $\frac{1}{32}$ to $\frac{1}{16}$ in. wide, depending on the size of the cutter. This is shown in Fig. 10.11(c). If the land becomes too large, the heel of the land will touch the work and interfere with the cutting action, as shown in Fig. 10.11(d). This is avoided by grinding a relief angle and then getting the additional clearance by grinding a clearance angle. This operation is shown in Fig. 10.11(e). The primary clearance angle is usually ground double the relief angle. This avoids the need for grinding the larger—usually about 35°—clearance angle (secondary clearance).

Relief angles are necessary to free the cutting edge. The relief angle depends upon the diameter of the cutter. In general the relief angle is about 3 to 5° and the clearance angle, as stated above, about 35°. The larger the diameter of the cutter, the smaller a relief angle is needed. The relief and clearance angles should be kept as small as is consistent with the diameter of the cutter and the nature of the operation. Initially the land should be small enough to achieve the desired results and still allow for several grindings of the cutter before the primary clearance is ground.

A milling tooth may have positive rake, as shown in Fig. 10.11(b), zero rake, as shown in Fig. 10.11(f), or negative rake, as shown in Fig. 10.11(g). Negative rake is used primarily on carbide milling cutters. A negative radial rake of −5 to −10° in combination with +5 and +10° positive axial rake is used for severe cutting conditions such as interrupted cuts or for cutting tough steel.

10.5. Drills and Reamers

Figure 10.12(a) shows a high-speed drill and the drill nomenclature is shown in Fig. 10.12(b). The relief angle for drills ranges from 8 to 12°. The chisel-edge angle is usually 135°. A standard ground drill has a point angle of 118°. This angle is increased for harder materials and decreased for softer materials. Thus for hard or tough steels the point angle could be as much as

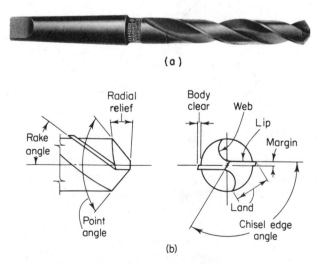

(a)

(b)

Figure 10.12 *(Photo courtesy of the Cleveland Twist Drill Company.)*

150°; for aluminum and cast iron, 90 to 130°; and for plastics and wood, 60 to 118°.

The rake angle is created by the helix of the flute. This is shown in Fig. 10.12(b). This angle may vary from 0 to 45°. The greater the helix angle, the less torque is required for the drilling operation. With the steeper angles the shearing effect is increased and so is the chip removal. Gun drills, Chapter 24, have 0° rake. The flute is parallel to the centerline of the body of the drill.

Reamers are designed to take small amounts of material out of a pre-drilled hole. They are used for sizing the hole and for high finish usually not possible with a drill. Figure 10.13(a) shows a chucking reamer with

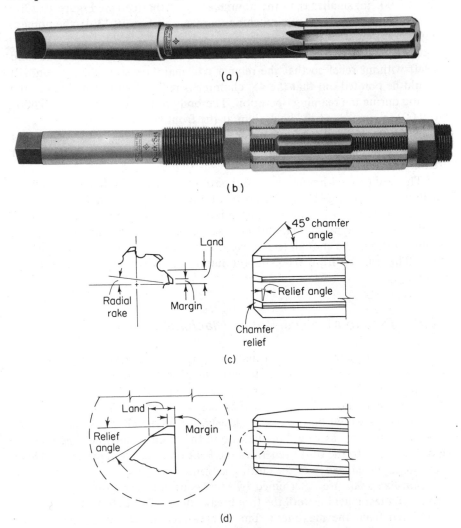

(a)

(b)

(c)

(d)

Figure 10.13 (*Photos courtesy of the Cleveland Twist Drill Company.*)

straight flutes and a tapered shank. This may also be purchased with either straight or helical flutes. Other types are shell, tapered, and hand reamers.

Straight and tapered reamers may also be of the solid or expansion variety. The expansion reamers may be expanded as much as 0.010 in. beyond the nominal size.

Hand reamers may also be of the solid or expansion type. A hand expansion reamer is shown in Fig. 10.13(b). The taper at the end of the hand reamer is usually about 0.015 in./in. of the length with a 45° chamfer at the starting edge. If the flutes have a helix, it is usually left handed to create an axial rake which will create a back pressure against the feed. The shank is about 0.005 in. smaller than the nominal size of the reamer. Figure 10.13(c) shows the nomenclature of a machine reamer, and Fig. 10.13(d), the nomenclature of a hand reamer.

Radial relief is provided for the land. But a small segment of the land is left without relief so that the reamer can maintain size when ground. It should be pointed out that the 45° chamfer is relieved and actually does the cutting during the reaming operation. The body of the reamer is from 0.0005 to 0.001 in. smaller at the back than at the front to prevent drag.

Rose reamers have a land which is not relieved. This is to ensure that only the lead 45° does the cutting. The body of the reamer guides it as it reams the hole.

The feed used with reamers should be about three times that employed for drilling. The cutting speeds should be about 75% greater than for drilling. The amount of stock removed depends upon many factors such as feeds, cutting speeds, type of material cut, setup, etc. The amount of material removed should be enough to remove the feed helix from the former operation. This can be from 0.003 in. for hand reamers to $\frac{1}{64}$ in. for machine reaming.

10.6. Time to Machine-Rotary Machines

The relationship of the tool material and the material being machined is the same whether it takes place between the tool bit and the work, a milling machine cutter and the work, or any other type of cutter and the work. Also, it makes no difference whether the work moves and the cutter is stationary, as would be the case with a lathe; or the cutter moves and the work is stationary, as would be the case in the milling machine. The relative motion of one to the other generates the heat or creates the pressures which determine the efficiency of the cutting action.

Cutting speeds are determined by increasing the revolutions per minute (rpm) of a test machine until the tool breaks down. The cutting speed is then calculated from the maximum rpm at breakdown. Of course the various

TABLE 10.2

Cutting Speeds,*
ft/min

| *Work* | | *Cutter material* | | |
material	*Carbon*	*HSS†*	*Cast steel*	*Carbide*
Aluminum	300	700	900	1000
Brass	50	200	500	700
Bronze	40	120	200	300
Copper	40	120	250	300
Magnesium	250	700	1000	1200
Steel				
Soft	40	90	250	400
Medium	30	70	200	250
Hard	...	40	100	150
Stainless	30	70	150	250
Iron				
Gray	30	50	125	150
Malleable	50	100	175	250

*Values are approximate.
†High-speed steel.

angles, feed, tool setting, etc., must be kept constant and many tests made before a table of cutting speeds, Table 10.2, is established.

The cutting speed is the distance a tool cuts in 1 minute, or the length of the cut in 1 minute. This distance is usually given in feet per minute.

The *feed* of a tool is the displacement of the tool for each revolution or stroke of the machine. Thus on a lathe, if the tool moves a distance of 0.004 in. parallel to the center line of the work as the work rotates, the feed is 0.004 in./revolution. Feeds may also be given as inches per minute instead of inches per revolution.

Depth of cut affects the life of a cutting tool less than the feed, and much less than the cutting speed. For this reason the depth of cut should be set to a maximum consistent with the cutting conditions such as rigidity of the work, power available, rigidity of the set-up, and the metallurgical conditions.

The following equations are based upon the fact that by far the greatest amount of heat is generated by the cutting speed. Thus, increasing the feed or depth of cut slightly or increasing both slightly, will remove more metal without appreciably increasing the temperature at the tool. If the student needs more accuracy, he is referred to the tables of cutting speeds, feed, and depth of cut in any standard handbook.

Some handbooks are using a correction factor to adjust the cutting speeds whenever the feed and/or depth of cut are changed for a lathe turning operation. Table 10.3 shows a table of correction factors. Example 2 illustrates

TABLE 10.3

Cutting Speed Correction Factors*
Turning Only

Feed in./min	Factor Z_f	Depth of cut, in.	Factor Z_d
0.003	2.00	0.005	1.80
0.005	1.69	0.010	1.50
0.008	1.27	0.020	1.40
0.010	1.12	0.031	1.30
0.012	1.00	0.062	1.15
0.018	0.78	0.125	1.00
0.020	0.74	0.150	0.96
0.022	0.70	0.200	0.91
0.025	0.64	0.250	0.87
0.028	0.61	0.302	0.83
0.030	0.58	0.375	0.80
0.036	0.52	0.500	0.76
0.040	0.48	0.625	0.72
0.050	0.42	0.750	0.70
0.060	0.38	1.000	0.66

*Based on a feed of 0.012 in/rev and a depth cut of $\frac{1}{8}$ in. (*From Oberg, Jones, and Horton: MACHINERY'S HANDBOOK, 20th Edition. Copyrighted © 1975 by Industrial Press Inc. Reprinted with permission.*)

the use of such a correction factor. These factors are to be used with the understanding that they are included to demonstrate one method of adjusting for changes of cutting conditions.

The correction factor to adjust the cutting speed for turning is

$$C_z = C_s Z_f Z_d$$

C_z = corrected cutting speed
C_s = normal cutting speed
Z_f = feed correction factor
Z_d = depth of cut correction factor

On the lathe the largest diameter turned is taken as D. When boring a piece of work, D is also the largest diameter being cut. The length of the cut L is the linear distance the tool travels, as shown in Fig. 10.14(a); L is the distance ab in Fig. 10.14(a).

From the definition of cutting speed the length of cut for one revolution is πD. If the work revolves N number of revolutions every minute, the length of the cut taken every minute will be πDN. However, since the diameter is given in inches, it is necessary to convert this product into feet per minute by dividing by 12.

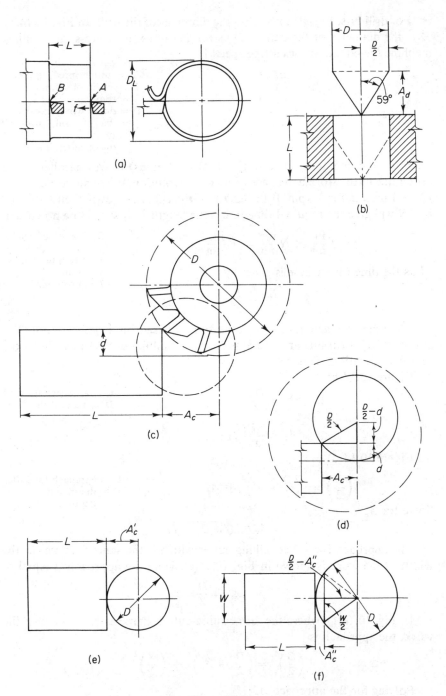

Figure 10.14

For drill bits, Fig. 10.14(b), D is the diameter of the drill. In Fig. 10.14(c), D is the diameter of the cutter. Thus for the lathe, drill press, and milling machine the equation for cutting speed is

$$C_s = \frac{\pi D N}{12}$$

C_s = cutting speed, ft/min
L = length of cut, in.
N = rpm
D = dia of work, in.—lathe
   = dia of drill, in.—drill press
   = dia of cutter, in.—miller

From the definition of feed, if a tool (no radius) moves parallel to the center line of the work a distance f for each revolution, it will move a distance fN in 1 minute for N rpm. If the length of the cut L is known, then L divided by fN will give the required time to cut the length L. It should be noted that

$$f \frac{\text{in.}}{\text{rev}} \times N \frac{\text{rev}}{\text{min}} = F \frac{\text{in.}}{\text{min}}$$

L = length of cut, in.
f = feed, in./rev
F = feed, in./min
N = rpm
T = time, min

Thus the time to machine is given by

$$T = \frac{L}{fN} = \frac{L}{F}$$

The time to machine for the lathe tool is based on a pointed tool. The approach A_d (drill bit) and the approach A_c (milling cutter) must be taken into consideration. Thus in

Figure 10.14(b)

$$\tan 59° = \frac{D/2}{A_d}$$

A_d = approach for drill
D = dia of drill

$$A_d = \frac{D/2}{\tan 59°}$$

Figure 10.14(d)

$$\left(\frac{D}{2}\right)^2 = \left(\frac{D}{2} - d\right)^2 + A_c$$

A_c = approach for cutter
D = dia of cutter
d = depth of cut

Solve for A_c

$$A_c = \sqrt{d(D - d)}$$

The approach for a face milling cutter which is the same diameter as the width of the work is shown in Fig. 10.14(e). Here the approach is equal to

$$A'_c = \frac{D}{2}$$

In Fig. 10.14(f), where the face-milling-cutter diameter is larger than the work, the approach is

$$\left(\frac{D}{2}\right)^2 = \left(\frac{D}{2} - A''_c\right)^2 + \left(\frac{W}{2}\right)^2$$

Solving for the approach A''_c

$$A''_c = \tfrac{1}{2}(D - \sqrt{D^2 - W^2})$$

EXAMPLE 1

Figure 10.14(a) shows a 3-in. diameter soft steel shaft. The length of cut is 8 in. If the feed is 0.012 in./rev, calculate: (1) the rpm; (2) the time to machine the length with a high speed tool bit.

Solution:

(1) The rpm is

$$N = \frac{12C_s}{\pi D} = \frac{12(90)}{\pi(3)}$$

$$= 115 \text{ rpm}$$

$D = 3 \text{ in.}$
$C_s = 90 \text{ ft/min}$
(from Table 10.2)
$L = 8 \text{ in.}$
$f = 0.012 \text{ in./rev}$

(2) The time to take one cut is

$$G = \frac{L}{fN} = \frac{8}{0.012(115)}$$

$$= 5.8 \text{ min}$$

EXAMPLE 2

Assume a depth of cut of $\frac{1}{8}$ in. in Example 1. If the depth of cut is changed to 0.200 in. and the feed is changed to 0.020 in./rev, calculate: (1) the new cutting speed; (2) rpm; (3) time to machine.

Solution:

(1) The new cutting speed is

$$C_z = C_s Z_f Z_d = 90(0.74)(0.91)$$

$$= 60.6 \text{ ft/min}$$

$C_s = 90 \text{ ft/min}$
(from Table 10.2)
$f = 0.020 \text{ in./rev}$
$d = 0.200 \text{ in.}$
$Z_f = 0.74$ (from
$Z_d = 0.91$ Table 10.3)

(2) The rpm is

$$N = \frac{12C_z}{\pi D} = \frac{12 \times 60.6}{\pi 3}$$

$$= 77.2 \text{ rpm}$$

(3) The time to machine is

$$T = \frac{L}{fN} = \frac{8}{0.020 \times 77.2}$$

$$= 5.2 \text{ min}$$

EXAMPLE 3

A $\frac{3}{4}$-in. hole is to be drilled into a cast-iron block with a feed of 0.015 in./rev. The thickness of the block is $2\frac{3}{8}$ in., and the drill is high-speed steel. Find: (1) the rpm; (2) the approach; (3) the time to machine.

Solution:

1. The rpm is

$$N = \frac{12C_s}{\pi D} = \frac{12(50)}{\pi 0.750}$$

$$= 255 \text{ rpm}$$

$D = 0.750 \text{ in.}$
$L = 2.375 \text{ in.}$
$f = 0.015 \text{ in./rev}$
$C_s = 50 \text{ ft/min}$
(Table 10.2)

2. The approach is

$$A_d = \frac{D/2}{\tan 59°} = \frac{0.750/2}{1.664}$$

$$= 0.225 \text{ in.}$$

3. The time to machine is

$$T = \frac{L + A_d}{fN} = \frac{2.375 + 0.225}{(0.015)255}$$

$$= 0.68 \text{ min}$$

EXAMPLE 4

A 6-in. diameter carbide, inserted milling cutter is to be used to cut medium-hardness steel, as shown in Fig. 10.14(c), with a feed of 0.008 in./rev. If the depth of the cut is to be 0.050 in. and the length of the work is 8 in., find: (1) the rpm; (2) the approach; (3) the time to take one cut.

Solution:

1. The rpm is

$$N = \frac{12C_s}{\pi D} = \frac{12(250)}{\pi 6}$$

$$= 159 \text{ rpm}$$

$D = 6$ in.
$f = 0.008$ in./rev
$d = 0.050$ in.
$L = 8$ in.
$C_s = 250$ ft/min
(Table 10.2)

2. The approach is

$$A_c = \sqrt{d(D - d)} = \sqrt{0.050(6 - 0.050)}$$

$$= 0.545 \text{ in.}$$

3. The time to take one cut is

$$T = \frac{L + A_c}{fN} = \frac{8 + 0.545}{(0.008)159}$$

$$= 6.72 \text{ min}$$

EXAMPLE 5

Assume the same conditions as in Example 4 except that the cutter is a face mill, as shown in Fig. 10.14(e). Find: (1) the rpm; (2) the approach; (3) the time to take one cut.

Solution:

1. The rpm is the same as in Example 4

$$N = 159 \text{ rpm}$$

2. The approach is

$$A'_c = \frac{D}{2} = \frac{6}{2}$$

$$= 3 \text{ in.}$$

3. The time to take one cut is

$$T = \frac{L + A'_c}{fN} = \frac{8 + 3}{(0.008)159}$$

$$= 8.65 \text{ min}$$

EXAMPLE 6

Assume the same conditions as in Example 4 except that the work is 5 in. wide and the cutter is a face mill. Find: (1) the rpm; (2) the approach; (3) the time to take one cut.

Solution:

1. The rpm is the same as in Example 4

$$N = 159 \text{ rpm}$$

2. The approach is

$$A''_c = \tfrac{1}{2}(D - \sqrt{D^2 - W^2}) = \tfrac{1}{2}(6 - \sqrt{6^2 - 5^2})$$

$$= 1.342 \text{ in.}$$

3. The time to take one cut is

$$T = \frac{L + A''_c}{fN} = \frac{8 + 1.342}{(0.008)159}$$

$$= 7.344 \text{ min}$$

10.7. Time to Machine-Reciprocating Machines

Shapers, planers, hacksaws, surface grinders, etc., are reciprocating machines. In this chapter the shaper and the planer will be discussed. The construction of these machines will be presented in Chapter 11.

Shapers may be either the crank or hydraulic type. The cutting speed of the crank shaper is based on the crank effect obtained when a crank pin revolves about a bull wheel, as shown in Fig. 10.15. The crank pin is fastened to the bull wheel so that it reverses the direction of the ram after it has revolved three-fifths of the circumference of its path on the forward stroke and two-fifths of the circumference of its path on the reverse stroke. The

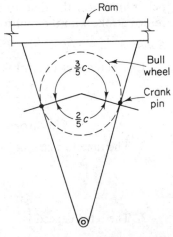

Figure 10.15

length of the stroke may be adjusted by offsetting the crank pin. The ratio of $\frac{3}{5}$ to $\frac{2}{5}$ remains the same. See Fig. 11.3(b). Since the distance traveled by the ram is the same on the forward stroke as on the return stroke, the cutting speed of the forward stroke is less than the return speed. The ratio of forward to return stroke for the hydraulic shaper is $1:2$.

The cutting speed equation for the crank shaper is

$$C_s = \frac{L}{12} N \frac{5}{3}$$

$N =$ strokes/min
$L =$ length of stroke, in.
$C_s =$ cutting speed, ft/min

The time to machine a workpiece is a function of the width W of the work and the feed f. The equation is

$$T = \frac{W}{fN}$$

$W =$ width of work, in.
$f =$ feed in./stroke
$R_s =$ return speed, ft/min

The return speed may be found from

$$\tfrac{3}{5}C_s = \tfrac{2}{5}R_s$$

Solving this equation for R_s

$$R_s = 1\tfrac{1}{2}C_s$$

The return speed may also be found using the equation

$$R_s = \frac{L}{12} N \frac{5}{2}$$

EXAMPLE 7

A medium-steel block is to be machined with a high-speed steel tool bit on a crank shaper at a feed of 0.010 in./stroke. The width of the block is 4 in., and the length of stroke is $5\frac{1}{2}$ in. Find: (1) the number of strokes per minute; (2) the time to machine; (3) the return stroke. (4) Check the return stroke with the return speed equation.

Solution:

1. The number of strokes per minute is

$$N = \frac{12 \times 3 \times C_s}{L \times 5} = \frac{12 \times 3 \times 70}{5\frac{1}{2} \times 5}$$

$C_s = 70$ ft/min (Table 10.2)
$f = 0.010$ in.
$L = 5\frac{1}{2}$ in.
$W = 4$ in.

$$= 91.6 \text{ strokes/min}$$

2. The time to machine is

$$T = \frac{W}{fN} = \frac{4}{(0.010)91.6}$$

$$= 4.37 \text{ min}$$

3. The return speed is

$$R_s = 1.5(70)$$

$$= 105 \text{ ft/min}$$

4. The return speed using the speed equation is

$$R_s = \frac{L}{12}N\frac{5}{2} = \frac{5\frac{1}{2}}{12}(91.6)\frac{5}{2}$$

$$= 105 \text{ ft/min (check)}$$

The planer has a ratio of cutting to return speed built into its drive mechanism. Thus, if the *time* required to complete the cutting stroke is three times the return stroke, the ratio R of the planer is said to be 3. The total *time* for the planer to cut a length L in feet is therefore the sum of the cutting and return stroke. This is shown in Fig. 10.16

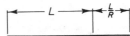

$$L + \frac{L}{R}$$

Figure 10.16

If this total length traveled is equal to one complete stroke, then the equation for cutting speed is

$$C_s = N\left(L + \frac{L}{R}\right)$$

The time to machine is

$$T = \frac{W}{fN}$$

The return speed is

$$R_s = RC_s$$

N = strokes/min.
L = length of stroke, ft
R = planer ratio
C_s = cutting speed, ft/min
R_s = return speed, ft/min
W = width of work, in.
f = feed, in./stroke

EXAMPLE 8

A cast-iron (gray) block, 8 in. wide, is to be planed with a stroke of 5 ft by using a feed of 0.030 in./stroke. The tool bit is cast steel, and the ratio of the planer is 2. Find: (1) the strokes per minute; (2) the return speed; (3) the time to machine the surface.

Solution:

1. The strokes per minute are

$$N = \frac{C_s}{L + L/R} = \frac{125}{5 + \frac{5}{2}}$$

$$= 16.67 \text{ strokes/min}$$

C_s = 125 ft/min (Table 10.2)
L = 5 ft
R = 2
W = 8 in.
f = 0.030 in./stroke

2. The return speed is

$$R_s = RC_s = 2(125)$$

$$= 250 \text{ ft/min}$$

3. The time to machine the surface is

$$T = \frac{W}{fN} = \frac{8}{0.030(16.67)}$$

$$= 16 \text{ min}$$

10.8. Horsepower Requirements

The horsepower requirements for a *lathe* may be calculated as follows:

1. The cross-sectional area of a chip is the product of the depth of cut and the feed in inches per revolution. Thus

$$A = df$$

d = depth of cut, in.
f = feed, in./rev
A = area of chip, in.^{2}
F = force against the tool
k = constant for material
K = hp constant
C_s = cutting speed

2. The force of the chip on the tool is the product of the area of the chip and the constant k, Table 10.4. The constant is related to the material being cut. Thus

$$F = kA$$

3. The horsepower at the cutting edge is related to the force on the tool and the cutting speed. Thus

$$\text{hp} = \frac{FC_s}{33,000} = \frac{kAC_s}{33,000}$$
$$= KAC_s$$

4. Thus the horsepower at the cutting edge of the tool bit for a lathe may be written

$$\text{hp} = KdfC_s$$

K is a conversion constant which may be found in Table 10.4.

This equation may be used to get a close approximation for single-point tools.

TABLE 10.4

K Constants (Lathe)

Material	K
Aluminum	4
Brass (med.)	6
Bronze (med.)	6
Iron	
Cast	4
Wrought	6
Malleable	4
Steel	
Low-carbon	6
Mild	8
High C and alloy	10

EXAMPLE 9

Find the horsepower at the cutting edge if the material being cut on a lathe is mild steel. The depth of the cut is $\frac{1}{16}$ in., the feed is 0.012 in./rev, and the cutting speed is 70 ft/min.

Solution:

$$\text{hp} = KdfC_s = 8(0.0625)(0.012)70$$
$$= 0.42 \text{ hp}$$

$$K = 8$$
$$d = 0.0625 \text{ in.}$$
$$f = 0.012 \text{ in./rev}$$
$$C_s = 70 \text{ ft/min}$$

The efficiency of machines ranges from 60% for 3-hp motors to about 80% for large motors. The losses result from friction which develops when machine parts are moved. The horsepower requirements are based on the volume of metal removed per minute.

The horsepower requirements for *one milling cutter tooth* is

$$\text{hp}_t = \frac{V}{K'} = \frac{dWF}{K'}$$

The horsepower at the cutter is

$$\text{hp}_c = \frac{ndWf'N}{K'}$$

The horsepower of the machine is

$$\text{hp}_m = \frac{\text{hp}_c}{EFF}$$

W = width of cut, in
d = depth of cut, in.
F = feed, in./min
f' = feed, in./tooth
N = rev/min
K' = milling constant
n = number of teeth
hp_t = horsepower=one tooth
hp_c = horsepower = cutter
hp_m = horsepower = machine

The values of K' for a milling cutter are shown in Table 10.5

TABLE 10.5

K' Constants (Milling)

Material	K'
Aluminum	2.25
Brass	1.75
Cast iron	
Soft	1.25
Medium	1.00
Hard	0.75
Malleable	1.00
Steel	
Soft	0.80
Medium	0.60
Hard	0.50

EXAMPLE 10

A 6-in. milling cutter which has 12 teeth is to machine a soft steel surface by removing a chip 1 in. wide and $\frac{1}{4}$ in. deep with a feed of 0.005 in./tooth. Find the horsepower requirements of the operation if the machine is 60% efficient.

Solution:

The rpm of the cutter is

$$N = \frac{12C_s}{\pi D} = \frac{12(90)}{\pi 6}$$

$$= 57.3 \text{ rpm}$$

The horsepower requiremenets at the cutter are

$$\text{hp}_c = \frac{ndWf'N}{K'}$$

$$= \frac{12(\frac{1}{4})1(0.005)57.3}{0.80}$$

$$= 1.1 \text{ hp}$$

$D = 6$ in.
$n = 12$ teeth
$d = \frac{1}{4}$ in.
$W = 1$ in.
$f' = 0.005$ in./tooth
$K' = 0.80$
$C_s = 90$ ft/min
$e = 60\%$
$\text{hp}_c = $ horsepower at cutter
$\text{hp}_m = $ horsepower of machine

The horsepower requirements of the motor are

$$\text{hp}_m = \frac{1.1}{0.60}$$

$$= 1.8 \text{ hp}$$

The horsepower for a drill is given by the equation

$$\text{hp} = K''C_s D^{0.8} f^{0.7}$$

$K'' = $ drill constant
$f = $ feed, in./rev
$D = $ dia, in.
$C_s = $ cutting speed, ft/min

The horsepower of a drill bit is based on the ratio of the drill diameter to the length of the chisel edge. The values for K'' are given in Table 10.6.

TABLE 10.6

K'' Constants (Drill Press)

Material	K''
Cast iron	0.54
Carbon steel	
Low	1.2
Medium	1.4
High	1.7

EXAMPLE 11

A 1-in.-diameter drill is used with a cutting speed of 50 ft/min and a feed of 0.012 in./rev. The material is cast iron. What is the horsepower required at the drill point?

Solution:

The horsepower at the drill point is

$$\text{hp} = K'' C_s D^{0.8} f^{0.7}$$

$$= 0.54(50)1^{0.8}(0.012^{0.7})$$

$$= 1.22 \text{ hp}$$

$K'' = 0.54$
$f = 0.012 \text{ in.}$
$D = 1 \text{ in.}$
$C_s = 50 \text{ ft/min}$

QUESTIONS AND PROBLEMS

10.1   Describe the mechanism by which a tool dulls.

10.2   Define tool life. Describe the effect of heat, feed, and speed on tool life.

10.3   Describe the formation of (a) a continuous chip and (b) a discontinuous chip.

10.4   What is the significance of the cutting ratio r as related to the cutting action of a tool?

10.5   What effect does a built-up edge have on (a) the cutting action of a tool and (b) the surface finish on the workpiece?

10.6   What is cratering?

10.7   Make a vector diagram of the forces acting on a planer tool.

10.8   What effect does friction have on the operation of a tool bit? Discuss your answer.

10.9   Discuss the three cutting zones in Fig. 10.2(a).

10.10   Define each of the vectors in Fig. 10.2(b). What is the significance of each?

10.11   State the primary purpose of (a) a lubricant and (b) a coolant.

10.12   List the recommended lubricants for; (a) steel and wrought iron; (b) brass and bronze; (c) cast iron.

10.13   (a) What is flank wear? (b) What is its effect on the cutting operation?

10.14   List the six types of tool materials used in industry today. State the major advantages and disadvantages of each material.

10.15   State the optimum operating temperature of each of the six tool materials used in industry today.

10.16   Describe the heat treating of high-speed steel.

10.17   What is sintering? How are carbide tools made? Describe the process.

10.18   Make a drawing of a tool bit, and label all angles.

10.19 Define the terms relief angle, clearance angle, and rake angle as used in this text.

10.20 Draw tool bits having a 0° rake angle, a negative rake angle, a positive rake angle. Discuss the effect of each on chip formation.

10.21 A lathe takes a depth of cut of 0.030 in. at 50 rpm. The thickness of the chip removed is 0.060 in. (a) What is the ratio *r* for this operation? (b) If the work diameter is 2 in. before the cut is taken, what is the approximate length of the chip removed in 1 minute? Assume a continuous chip.

10.22 A tool bit has the following angles: front relief, 8°; side relief, 8°; negative back rake, 4°; negative side rake, 7°; end cutting-edge angle, 10°; side cutting-edge angle, 6°. Find: (a) the lip angle; (b) the nose angle; (c) the cutting angle.

10.23 The diameter of a soft steel shaft is 4 in. The length of the cut is 7 in. If the feed is 0.020 in./rev, calculate: (a) the corrected cutting speed; (b) the rpm; (c) the time to machine the length with a high speed tool bit.

10.24 An aluminum shaft $2\frac{1}{2}$ in. in diameter is to be machined with a high-speed tool bit with a feed of 0.030 in./rev. The length of the cut is 10 in. Calculate the time required for one cut on a lathe.

10.25 Assume the tool bit in Problem 10.23 is capable of taking a maximum of $\frac{3}{8}$ of an inch off the diameter of the shaft. If the shaft diameter is to be machined to $1\frac{3}{4}$ in., how long will it take to machine the shaft, allowing 5% of the total time for positioning? Consider all correction factors.

10.26 A cast-iron shaft is machined on a lathe in 1 minute with one cut. The shaft is 4 in. long and 3 in. in diameter. If the feed used is 0.012 in./rev, what cutting speed is used?

10.27 Make a drawing of a ground-in chip breaker. What are the dimensional parameters of this type of chip breaker?

10.28 Make a drawing of a milling cutter tooth, and label all parts.

10.29 Make three drawings of a milling tooth showing 0° rake angle and positive and negative rake angles.

10.30 A $1\frac{1}{4}$-in.-diameter high-speed steel drill is used to drill 16 holes into a medium-hardness steel drill plate. The drill plate is $1\frac{1}{2}$ in. thick, and the feed used is 0.008 in./rev. How long will it take to drill the 16 holes. Neglect positioning time.

10.31 Make a drawing of a drill bit, and label all parts.

10.32 Why is the margin on a reamer ground without relief?

10.33 How does a rose reamer differ from a machine reamer?

10.34 How does a hand reamer differ from a machine reamer?

10.35 How much material should a reamer remove from a pre-drilled hole?

10.36 Define cutting speed and feed.

10.37 Describe the ratio of cutting speed to return speed for a crank shaper.

10.38 A 9-in. high-speed steel milling cutter is used to cut a groove into a piece of brass with one cut. The groove is $\frac{3}{4}$ in. deep and 10 in. long. How long will it take to mill the groove if a feed of 0.018 in./rev is used?

10.39 If the cutter in problem 10.38 has 24 teeth: (a) How many chips per minute are cut? (b) What is the thickness of each chip?

10.40 An 8-in. inserted-tooth carbide-face milling cutter is used to surface a soft steel block. The cutter is the same width as the surface to be machined. The feed used is 0.032 in./rev, and the length of the block is 14 in. Find the time to take one cut.

10.41 Find the time to take one cut in problem 10.40 if the work is 5 in. wide.

10.42 A malleable iron block, $5\frac{1}{2}$ in. wide, is to be machined on a crank shaper with a feed of 0.005 in./stroke, using a high-speed steel tool bit. The length of the stroke is 9 in. Calculate: (a) the time to machine the surface and (b) the return speed.

10.43 A medium-steel block is machined with a high-speed steel toolbit on a planer of ratio 3 and a feed of $\frac{1}{32}$ in./stroke. The block is 29 in. long and 15 in. wide. Calculate the time to take one cut.

10.44 (a) Find the horsepower at the cutting edge on a lathe using the conditions in problem 10.26. The depth of cut is $\frac{1}{8}$ in. (b) What is the cross-sectional area of the chip? (c) What force does the chip exert on the tool?

10.45 A $1\frac{1}{2}$-in.-wide chip is removed by an 8-in.-diameter high-speed steel milling cutter which has 18 teeth. The depth of cut is $\frac{3}{8}$ in., and the feed is 0.002 in./ tooth. The material machined is soft steel. The operation is 52% efficient. What is the horsepower requirement of the machine?

10.46 A $\frac{3}{4}$-in.-diameter high-speed steel drill is used to drill a hole into a medium-hardness steel block with a feed of 0.015 in./rev. What is the horsepower required at the drill?

The Shaper and the Planer

11

11.1. Construction of the Shaper

Shapers are made either with a bull wheel which oscillates a vibrating arm or with a hydraulic drive (See Fig. 11.1.). In either case the forward stroke is usually the cutting stroke. A ram pushes a tool bit forward while it is in contact with the work and thereby removes metal. The stroke may be as short as 6 in. or as long as 40 in. Shapers which cut on the return stroke are usually large and not very common. The reverse stroke of the shaper is used to return the tool bit to its initial position in preparation for the next forward stroke and since it does no work, it is usually faster than the forward stroke.

During the return stroke the work also moves in a direction perpendicular to that of the tool; this is called feed. Unlike the continuous feed of the lathe or milling machine, this type of feed has an interrupted motion. The work should never feed during the forward stroke since cutting takes place on the forward stroke.

Figure 11.2(a) shows the toolslide head which houses the down feed, vertical slide, graduated swivel plate, clapper box, and tool post.

Since the tool bit climbs the work on the return stroke, some method must be provided for allowing the tool post and tool bit to swivel. This is accomplished with either a clapper box or some mechanical means for swinging the tool away from the work. The clapper box in Fig. 11.2(a) is shown in the open position on the return stroke. As soon as the tool loses contact with the work at the extreme back position, the clapper box closes. The cutting force of the forward stroke holds the clapper box in position.

It is very important that the apron be set so that the clapper box is always operating to rotate the tool bit away from the work. If the top of the apron is rotated in a circular path away from the raised part of the work, this will be accomplished. Several illustrations are shown in Fig. 11.2(b).

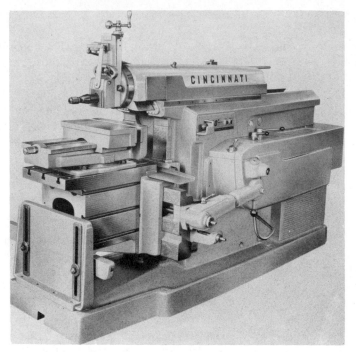

Figure 11.1 *(Courtesy of the Cincinnati Shaper Company.)*

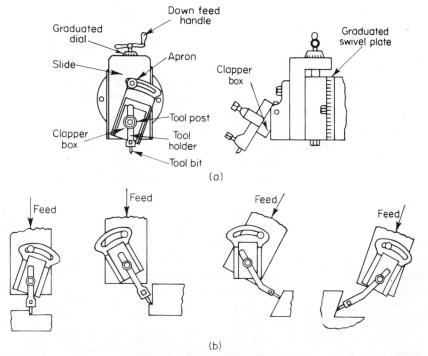

(a)

(b)

Figure 11.2

The toolslide may also be swiveled for angle cutting. The angle is set on the graduated swivel plate. Figure 11.2(b) shows the swivel head rotated and clamped so that angular cuts may be taken.

It is also important to note that the bottom of the toolslide should get as much support from the ram as is possible and that the tool bit should be kept as short as is consistent with the cutting operation. Excess overhang of the slide and tool bit causes severe stresses in both the toolslide and the tool bit.

The table is fastened to the apron, which is fastened to the crossrails with gibs and then to the column. The end of the table is supported by an adjustable table-support brace. An elevating screw permits raising or lowering the crossrails, apron, and table to set the desired distance between the work and the tool bit. Once set, it is clamped and the table support is released and clamped so that the end of the table is supported under the load of cutting.

Some shapers are provided with universal tables which may be swiveled parallel to the crossrails, which permits angular cuts. In combination with a swivel vise, compound angles may also be cut.

The crossrails house the feed screw, at the end of which is the feed mechanism. The feeds are set with a knob which actuates cams or with a ratchet and pawl. The ratchet and pawl arrangement is constructed so that a pushrod operating off an adjustable eccentric causes the pawl to engage the ratchet wheel on the forward stroke and slide over the ratchet teeth on the return stroke. The eccentric adjustment determines the number of teeth engaged on the forward stroke of the pushrod. A knob attached to the pawl also permits feeding the table to the right, stopping the feed, or feeding to the left. This setting and the eccentric feed adjustment must be set so that the feed occurs during the return stroke.

Whereas a crank-shaper feed can only be set for feeds which are in multiples of the feed achieved from one tooth, the hydraulic-shaper feed possibilities are continuous from zero to maximum.

Some machines are equipped with rapid feed mechanisms for rapid positioning of the table with the cross feed. Large machines are provided with both rapid and regular vertical feeds. The vertical feed of the table may be used for vertical cutting instead of having to use the vertical hand feed or the vertical slide on the head.

The top of the main housing is machined to take the ram. The ram is fastened to this housing with gibs. The front of the ram carries the toolslide head and is equipped with a lead screw, ram-positioning shaft, and clamp, as shown in Fig. 11.3(a). This permits positioning the ram without changing the length of the stroke. The ram is moved to the extreme back position, the ram-positioning clamp is loosened, the ram-positioning screw is turned to position the tool bit approximately $\frac{1}{4}$ to $\frac{3}{8}$ in. from the work, and the clamp is locked. The length of the stroke is then set.

The vibrating arm, shown in Fig. 11.3(a), is equipped with a slot which guides the crankpin block. This crankpin can revolve in the block as the block

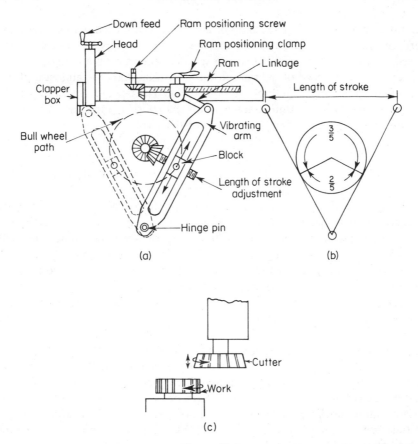

Figure 11.3

revolves with the bull wheel. The length of stroke may be adjusted by shortening the radius of the circle which the block follows around the bull wheel. This is accomplished through a pair of bevel gears. The crankpin and sliding block are caused to revolve by the bull wheel, which also causes the block to slide in the vibrating arm slot. The action causes the vibrating arm to move and drive the ram through a linkage, as shown in Fig. 11.3(a). The vibrating arm is hinged at the bottom.

Figure 11.3(b) shows the relative motion of the block (cutting speed-to-return speed) as it revolves with the bull wheel. Since it is desirable that the speed of the cutting stroke should be slower than the return stroke, the block causes the ram to change direction after having traversed three-fifths of the circumference of its path for the cutting stroke to two-fifths of the circumference of its path for the return stroke. Assume that the ram makes a complete cycle for a 10-in. stroke in 1 second. It therefore takes the ram $\frac{3}{5}$ second to move 10 in. while cutting and only $\frac{2}{5}$ second to move the same 10 in. on the return stroke. The ratio is therefore 1.6 : 1. The hydraulic shaper usually operates on a 2 : 1 ratio. The length of the stroke is adjusted with a lever from zero to maximum. The cutting speed may also be adjusted to any desired speed with its own lever. Whereas the speed of the ram on a crank shaper is not uniform, the speed of the ram on the hydraulic shaper is almost uniform throughout the entire length of the ram stroke. The use of a hydraulic piston makes it possible to transmit greater power than with a crank shaper and also permits easier control of the end points of the stroke.

The vertical shaper or slotter has its ram in a vertical position so that it works up and down. Some shapers are manufactured so that the ram may be swung out for angular cuts. The table may be moved longitudinally as well as laterally. This type of shaper may be equipped with a rotary table.

Shapers for doing special kinds of work are also available. The keyseater is used to cut keyways. The gear shaper is used to generate gear teeth. The cutter oscillates up and down and rotates very slowly at the same time. The workpiece is geared through the table to the cutter so that it rotates at the same surface speed as the cutter. Slightly more than one revolution of the cutter is required to generate one gear. See Fig. 11.3(c).

Planetary gear shapers will machine several gears at one time. The gear cutter cuts on both sides of the cutter. The blanks are mounted about the periphery of the gear cutter. The omission of teeth on alternate sides of the cutter permits the mounting of gear blanks and the removal of finished gears.

The shaping of helical gears requires that the cutter oscillate up and down as it also oscillates in a rotary direction. Thus on the downward stroke, the cutter may rotate clockwise. On the return, or upward stroke, the cutter may rotate counterclockwise. The combination of these two reciprocating motions of the cutter produces the helix in the gear blank. The gear blank must match the rotating oscillations of the cutter.

11.2. Accessories for the Shaper

The shaper tool bit. The type of tool used is determined by the type of machining operation, the finish required, the kind of material in the work-piece and the tool bit, and the feed and speed used. Clearance angles must be ground into the tool bit because the shaper tool rest does not have a rocker as does a lathe. Side clearances of about 4° for surface machining and 2° for slotting are required. A front clearance of from 2 to 4° is adequate. Side rake angles may be from 3 to 15°. Back rakes are usually 3° for surface machining tools or have a $\frac{1}{2}$- to 4-in. radius. Several tools are shown in Figs. 11.4(a through c). They may be rectangular cross-section or forged tools.

Shaper tools may be mounted directly in the tool post or in a toolholder. The toolholder slot must be parallel to the base of the toolholder so that the longitudinal axis of the tool bit is perpendicular to the work surface. This prevents the tool from digging into the work as a result of the torque placed on the tool.

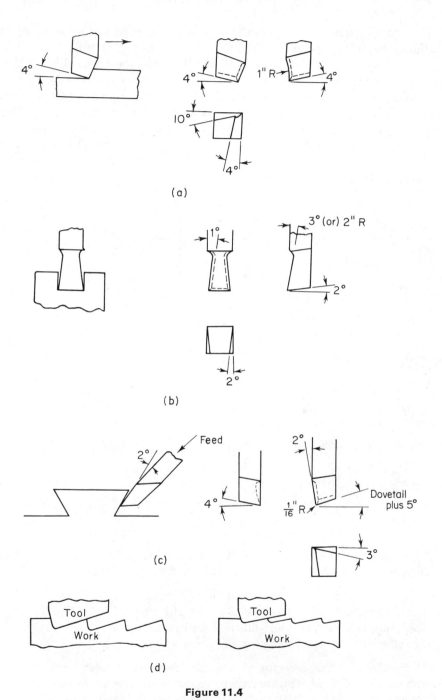

(a)

(b)

(c)

(d)

Figure 11.4

Smooth surfaces are achieved by keeping the edge cutting angle small during the cutting operation. This effect is shown in Fig. 11.4(d).

Two types of toolholders are available. The solid toolholder, Fig. 10.3(a), is similar to the lathe toolholder except that the slot is parallel to the base.

The Armstrong toolholder, Fig. 11.5(a), permits various positions of the tool. Figure 11.5(b) shows a slotting toolholder for internal shaping. This toolholder may also be used for external cutting. There are many instances when the motion of the clapper box is objectionable. This may be the case when the slotting holder is used. If this is true, the clapper box must be clamped into position.

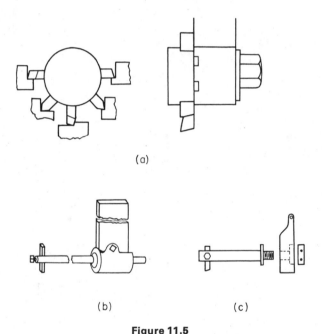

(a)

(b)   (c)

Figure 11.5

Figure 11.5(c) shows a heavy-duty slotting bar which is fastened to the clapper box. The clapper box should be locked when this tool is used.

The vise.   Similar to the vise used on a milling machine, this is usually constructed with allowance for a larger jaw opening [See Fig. 11.6(a).]. They may also be equipped with two lead screws or a swivel movable jaw for self-alignment when clamping angular work.

Parallels.   Precision-ground and hardened rectangular steel or cast-iron parallels, Fig. 11.6(b), are used to support and raise the work so that the surface to be machined clears the hardened-steel vise jaws as shown in Fig. 11.6(a). Angular parallels, Fig. 11.6(c), are used to hold angular work. The angle is determined by the angle to be machined.

Angle plates.   These slots cast into their surfaces may also be used to support work. The work is clamped to the angle plate with C clamps, straps, or any other method which will hold the work firmly against the surface of the angle plate. The angle plate may then be bolted to the T slots in the surface of the worktable of the shaper.

Hold downs.   These beveled wedges have one edge machined to an angle of about 92°. The width of the parallel tapers to an edge such as is shown in the inset of Fig. 11.6(d). When the vise is tightened, the 92° face of the parallel slips on the face of the vise jaw causes the parallel to rise. This action forces the work against the supporting parallel. This is shown in the inset of Fig. 11.6(d). This type of holding devise is particularly helpful for holding thin workpieces.

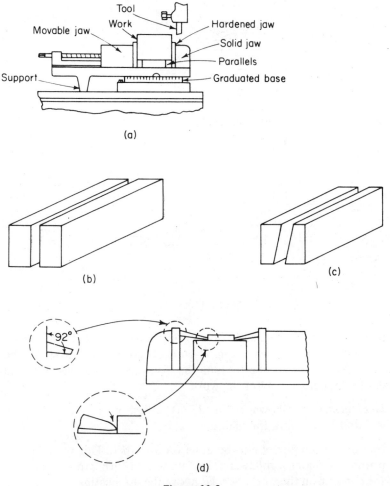

(a)

(b)

(c)

(d)

Figure 11.6

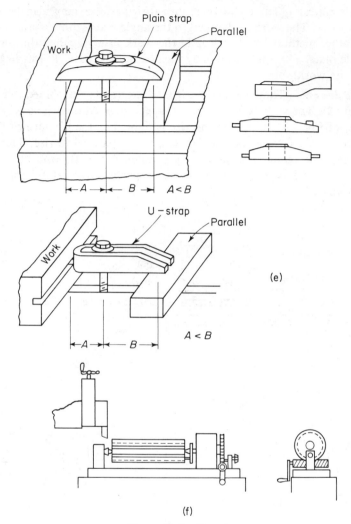

Figure 11.6 (Cont.)

Straps. Work may also be held in position on the table with plain or U straps, such as those shown in Fig. 11.6(e). This type of clamp should be used so that the distance *A* is shorter than the distance *B*; otherwise the strap will fasten the support instead of the work.

Index centers. Shown in Fig. 11.6(f), these may be used on a shaper to hold and index work for spaced cuts.

Contour shaping may also be done on a shaper. This requires a master form which actuates a follower. The follower in turn causes the tool bit to cut the contour on the work. Special hydraulic duplicating equipment is also available. The duplicating head follows the template, which controls the depth to which the tool bit cuts.

11.3. Aligning a Vise

After mounting the vise on the worktable, it is necessary to check the work seat of the vise to make sure it is flat with the table of the machine. It is also necessary to check the squareness of the solid jaw of the vise, since the solid jaw determines how the work is held. The movable jaw has some play for limited self-alignment.

Before any machining is attempted on a shaper using a vise either parallel or at right angles to the stroke, the operator must check these conditions. The graduations at the base of the vise should not be relied upon for accurate alignment. The following explains the method used for aligning the vise jaws parallel to the ram stroke. The procedure is similar when it is desired to align the vise jaws perpendicular to the ram stroke. The student need only remember which hand feed to use—the motion of the ram or the motion of the cross feed.

To check the vise for flatness after clamping, the vise is rotated until the vise jaws are parallel to the direction of the ram stroke. The jaws are opened, and two accurately ground parallels are placed on the machined surface of the vise. A dial indicator is clamped into the tool post. The spindle of the indicator is brought into contact with point A, Fig. 11.7(a), set at 0, and moved to the other three points, B, C, and D. For flatness, the needle should read 0-0 at all points. If the needle does not read 0-0 at all four points, the vise must be unclamped and *shimmed* until the readings are 0-0 when the vise is clamped.

To check the squareness of the solid jaw, a precision square may be clamped gently against the jaw, as shown in Fig. 11.7(b). The hand feed is used to move the table under the indicator. The needle must once again read 0-0 at both ends of the square. If it does not, the hardened insert of the solid jaw must be shimmed.

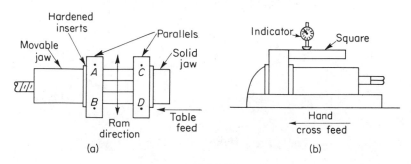

Figure 11.7

The third check which must be made is for parallelism of the face of the jaw to the ram direction. In this instance the indicator button is caused to register against the solid vise jaw. The stroke is set for the length of the jaw and then the ram is moved, preferably by hand. The indicator must read 0-0. If it does not read 0-0, the appropriate radial adjustment must be made.

11.4. Cutting an Internal Keyway

The calculations for determining the depth of a keyway will be given in Chapter 15. The essential dimensions are shown in Fig. 11.8(a). It will also state in Chapter 15 that the depth of the keyway *in the bore* will be calculated from the instant the corners of the tool touched the sides of the bore at A and B. Let us use the slotting bar, Fig. 11.5(c), because of the size of the rough-

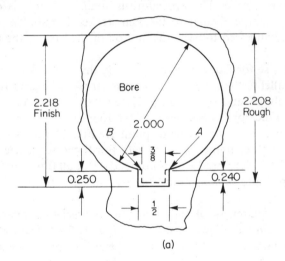

(a)

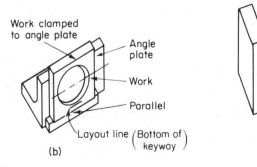

(b)   (c)

Figure 11.8

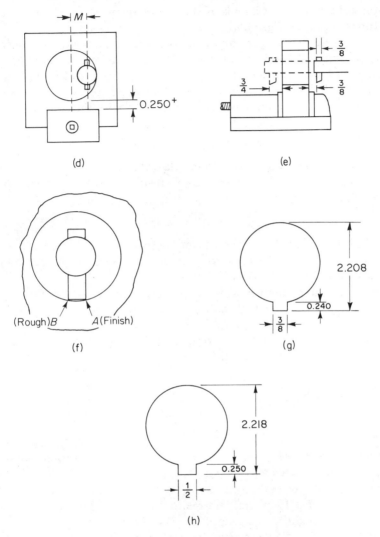

0.250⁺

(d)

(e)

(Rough)*B*   *A*(Finish)

(f)

2.208

0.240

(g)

2.218

0.250

(h)

Figure 11.8   (Cont.)

ing tool, $\frac{3}{8}$ in., and the size of the finishing tool, $\frac{1}{2}$ in. This keyway will be cut in two operations as follows.

Laying out the keyway.   The first step that should be taken is to lay out the keyway on the face of the work. It is assumed that the bore is finished and that the faces of the work have been machined square to the bore. The face of the work is painted with layout blue or in the case of a ferrous material with copper sulfate. The work is supported on a parallel and rests against the face of a precision angle plate. The angle plate, parallel, and work are placed on a precision surface plate. A clamp is used to fasten the work to the angle plate. The setup is shown in Fig. 11.8(b).

With a vernier height gage and a scriber, the vernier slide is moved so that the bottom of the scriber *coincides with the center of the bore.* Assume the reading of the height gage at this point to be 3.475 in. In Fig. 11.8(a) the distance from the bottom of the keyway to the opposite side of the bore is 2.218 in. Thus, to scribe the layout line in Fig. 11.8(b), the scriber must be dropped 2.218 in. minus the radius of the bore. Thus

$$2.218 - 1.000 = 1.218 \text{ in.}$$

If the height-gage reading is 3.475 in. when the *bottom of the scriber coincides with the center line of the bore*, the new reading of the height gage at the bottom of the *keyway* [the scribed line in Fig. 11.8(b)] will be

$$3.475 - 1.218 = 2.257 \text{ in.}$$

The scribed line is drawn into the face of the work.

The angle plate with the workpiece clamped to its surface is then rotated 90°, as shown in Fig. 11.8(c).

The center line of the work in Fig. 11.8(c) is picked up by the height-gage scriber again. Assume this reading to be 2.888 in. Half the width of the keyway is 0.250 in. This is added to the height-gage reading to give the upper line of the keyway and subtracted from the height-gage reading to give the lower line of the keyway. Thus the *upper line* is

$$2.888 + 0.250 = 3.138 \text{ in.}$$

and the *lower line* is

$$2.888 - 0.250 = 2.638 \text{ in.}$$

The scribed lines are shown in Fig. 11.8(c).

Setting the work and the slotting bar. The work is removed from the angle plate and mounted in the vise. The work must then be checked for parallelism, as described in the preceding section. It will be assumed that the diameter of the bar is $1\frac{1}{4}$ in. and that the tool protrudes $\frac{3}{8}$ in. below the bar.

The bar is brought to the side of the 2-in. bore until it just touches. A *feeler* gage of known thickness may be used between the bar and the bore wall for greater accuracy. The setting of the bar is shown in Fig. 11.8(d). Since the table is moved to the left to register the bar against the bore wall, the *backlash* must be taken out of the feed screw before the table can be moved to the right in Fig. 11.8(d).

The calculation for moving the table to the right is

$$M = \frac{D - d}{2} = \frac{2.000 - 1.250}{2} = 0.375 \text{ in.} \qquad \begin{array}{l} D = \text{dia of bore-2 in.} \\ d = \text{dia of bar-}1\frac{1}{4} \text{ in.} \\ M = \text{movement of table} \end{array}$$

If the table is moved 0.375 in. to the right, the center line of the boring bar and the center line of the bore should coincide. This may be checked by measuring the distances between the bar and the bore wall on both sides of the bar. They should be the same.

Setting the length of the stroke, the feed of the table, and the speed of the ram.   To set the length of the stroke, the shaper ram is moved to the extreme back position. The positioning clamp nut is loosened and the positioning screw turned, as shown in Fig. 11.3(a and b). The tool is set about $\frac{3}{8}$ in. from the work and the ram positioning screw locked.

The length of the stroke is then set so that the tool overshoots the bore length by approximately $\frac{3}{4}$ in. It is advisable to move the ram manually to avoid accidents. If the ram is power driven, the operator must be sure that the tool and bar clear the work. Both extremes of the stroke are shown in Fig. 11.8(e).

The longitudinal feed is not used for cutting a keyway. The toolslide head down-feed is used and the clapper box is fastened in a vertical position. The cutting speed is calculated by using the method in Section 10.7 and set on the machine.

Roughing and finishing the keyway.   The bottom of the toolslide is set even with the bottom of the ram. The table clamps are loosened, and the table raised until the tool *almost* touches the work. The table is clamped, and the table support adjusted and locked. The longitudinal feed is set at neutral and locked if a locking mechanism is available.

The ram is set in motion, and the points of the tool, A (finishing) or B (roughing) in Fig. 11.8(f), are caused to touch the bore by using the down-feed handle on the toolslide. *A tool should never be set to touch the work with the ram stationary. A high spot in the work may cause damage to the work, tool, and machine.*

At this point the ram is stopped and the graduated collar on the down-feed screw is set at zero. The depth of the cut will be a function of the incompleted arc for the *roughing tool*, which is $\frac{3}{8}$ in. wide.

$$I = \tfrac{1}{2}(D - \sqrt{D^2 - w^2}) = \tfrac{1}{2}(2.000 - \sqrt{2.000^2 - 0.375^2})$$
$$= 0.018 \text{ in.}$$

The measurement from the bottom of the *rough* keyway to the opposite side of the bore should be 0.010 in. less than the finish depth. Therefore, from Fig. 11.8(a), the dimension should be 2.208 in. It should be noted that the incompleted arc for the $\frac{1}{2}$-in. finishing tool is 0.032 in. and the incompleted arc for the roughing tool is 0.018 in. Thus, when the roughing tool touches the bore, it has already consumed

$$0.032 - 0.018 = 0.014 \text{ in.}$$

This is 0.014 in. of the $\frac{1}{4}$-in. depth required for finishing. The down feed of the $\frac{3}{8}$-in. roughing tool should reflect the 0.010 in. for finishing and the 0.014 in. for the difference of the roughing and finishing incompleted arc. The down feed should be

$$0.250 - (0.010 + 0.014) = 0.226 \text{ in.}$$

The distance from the bottom of the rough keyway to the opposite side of the bore should be

$$2.218 - 0.010 = 2.208 \text{ in.}$$

Note that this measurement needs only to reflect the 0.010 in. left in the bottom of the keyway for finishing.

The ram is started and with each return stroke of the ram the down feed is lowered approximately 0.002 in. This is continued until the graduated dial reads 0.216 in.

A measurement is taken with vernier calipers, inside micrometer, or some other suitable measuring instrument. The additional amount is removed in small increments of feed until the 2.208-in. dimension is achieved. The dimensions are shown in Fig. 11.8(g).

The toolslide is retracted to the zero reading on the graduated dial. The $\frac{3}{8}$-in. tool is replaced with the $\frac{1}{2}$-in. tool. The tips of the tool are caused to touch the bore, and the procedure of down-feeding the tool is continued for a depth of 0.240 in. on the graduated dial. A measurement is taken and the difference between this measurement and the desired 2.218 in. shown in Fig. 11.8(h) is carefully cut from the bottom of the keyway.

11.5. Cutting a Dovetail

The following is the procedure for cutting an internal dovetail shown in Fig. 11.9(a). The procedure is very much the same if an external dovetail is to be cut.

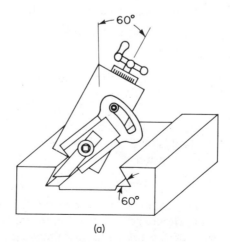

(a)

Figure 11.9

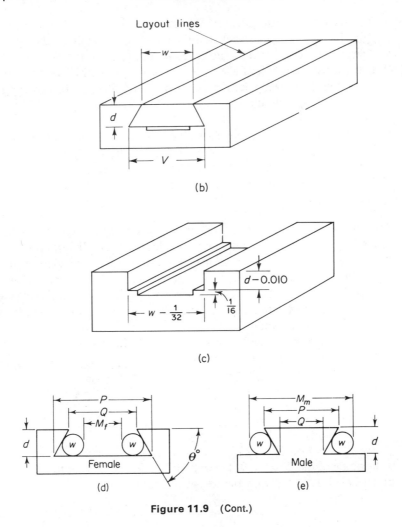

Figure 11.9 (Cont.)

1. The two faces and the ends of the piece are blued and scribed to the finished dimensions. The two lines across the top of the workpiece are also scribed. This is done with the use of a height gage and a surface plate. The scribed block will appear as shown in Fig. 11.9(b). It is assumed that the block is machined on all sides and that all sides are mutually perpendicular. If the workpiece is a casting or irregular shaped metal, appropriate means must be used to ensure 90° rotation for the scribing of square layout lines.

2. The workpiece is then clamped to the table of the shaper or held in a vise. A slot is cut into the block to within about 0.010 in. of the required depth near the dovetails and $\frac{1}{16}$ in. less than the finished depth at the center, as a recess. The width of the slot is cut approximately $w - \frac{1}{32}$. The block will now appear as shown in Fig. 11.9(c).

3. The swivel toolhead is set at the desired angle, in this instance 60°. The clapper box is swiveled, as shown in Fig. 11.4(c).
4. The sides of one dovetail and its base (not the $\frac{1}{16}$-in. relief) are rough cut, with the down feed at the desired angle, to within about $\frac{1}{32}$ in. of the layout line. The piece may be turned end for end for roughing the second side but should not be turned end for end when finishing cuts are taken.
5. Finally the face of the angle and the base of the dovetail are finished. Without moving the workpiece, the swivel head is set at 60° to the vertical on the opposite side of the vertical center line, an opposite hand tool is inserted, and the second side of the dovetail is finished to the desired dimensions.

Since it is important that measurements be taken at all stages of the above procedure, the student must know how to calculate these dimensions.

The angle is measured with a vernier bevel protractor. The various depths are measured with a depth vernier, and the various widths may be measured with a vernier caliper. The dovetail is measured with wires. Figure 11.9(d) shows the use of wires with a female dovetail, and Fig. 11.9(e) shows the use of wires with a male dovetail.

The best wire size is found with the use of the following equation:

$$w = \frac{d}{1 + \cos \theta}$$

M = measurement over wires
P = large measurement over sharp corners
Q = small measurement over sharp corners
d = depth
θ = dovetail angle
w = dia of wires

If the angle of the dovetail θ, the dimension Q, and the depth d are given, the dimension P is found with the use of the equation

$$P = Q + Kd$$

where $K = \dfrac{2}{\tan \theta}$

The measurement over the wires for a female dovetail M_f is given by the equation

$$M_f = P - G$$

where $G = w\left(\cot \dfrac{\theta}{2} + 1\right)$

The measurement over wires for a male dovetail M_m is

$$M_m = Q + G$$

EXAMPLE 1

Assume a 60° female dovetail with a 3-in. dimension across the corners at the small width and a depth of $\frac{3}{4}$ in. Find: (1) the dimension across the corners at the bottom of the dovetail, (2) the best wire size, and (3) the measurement over the wires.

Solution:

1. The constant K is

$$K = \frac{2}{\tan \theta} = \frac{2}{\tan 60°}$$

$$= 1.155$$

$Q = 3.000$ in.
$d = 0.750$ in.
$\theta = 60°$

The dimension P is

$$P = Q + Kd = 3.000 + 1.155(0.750)$$

$$= 3.866 \text{ in.}$$

2. The best wire size is

$$w = \frac{d}{1 + \cos \theta} = \frac{0.750}{1 + \cos 60°}$$

$$= 0.500 \text{ in.} = \tfrac{1}{2}\text{-in. wire}$$

3. The constant G is

$$G = w\left(\cot \frac{\theta}{2} + 1\right) = \tfrac{1}{2}(\cot \tfrac{60°}{2} + 1) = \tfrac{1}{2}(1.7321 + 1)$$

$$= 1.366$$

The measurement over the wires for a female dovetail is

$$M = P - G = 3.866 - 1.366 = 2.500 \text{ in.}$$

EXAMPLE 2

Assume a 60° male dovetail with a dimension of 3.500 in. across the sharp corners at the large end of the dovetail tapers. The depth of the dovetail is $\frac{5}{8}$ in. Find: (1) the dimension Q, (2) the best wire size, and (3) the measurement over the wires.

Solution:

1. The constant K is

$$K = \frac{2}{\tan \theta} = \frac{2}{\tan 60°}$$

$$= 1.155$$

$Q = 60°$
$P = 3.500$ in.
$d = 5/8 = 0.625$ in.

The dimension Q is

$$Q = P - Kd = 3.500 - 1.155(0.625)$$

$$= 2.778 \text{ in.}$$

2. The best wire size is

$$w = \frac{d}{1 + \cos \theta} = \frac{0.625}{1 + \cos 60°} = \frac{0.625}{1.5}$$

$$= 0.417 \text{ in. (use } \tfrac{7}{16} \text{ in.-dia wire)}$$

3. The constant G is

$$G = w\left(\cot\frac{\theta}{2} + 1\right) = \tfrac{7}{16}(\cot\tfrac{60°}{2} + 1) = \tfrac{7}{16}(1.7321 + 1)$$
$$= 1.195$$

The measurement over the wires is

$$M = Q + G = 2.778 + 1.195$$
$$= 3.973 \text{ in.}$$

11.6. Types and Construction of Planers

The principle of planing is very similar to that of shaping in that both are reciprocating. On the shaper the tool oscillates over the work and the table hitch-feeds at 90° to the oscillating motion. On the planer the platen (table) oscillates under the tool and the tool hitch-feeds at 90° to the oscillating motion.

Planers may have mechanical as well as hydraulic drives. The mechanical planer uses gear arrangements for both the platen drive and the feed. The gears are powered with electric motors. The hydraulic planer platen is actuated with a cylinder (or cylinders). The piston rod is attached directly to the platen. It should be noted that the down feed of the head in both types of planers may be either by hand or by power. This may be vertical or at an angle with the work.

Planers also may be fitted with a tool-block lifting mechanism for raising the tool at the end of the cutting stroke in preparation for the return stroke. Tools have been developed which will cut on both the forward cutting and return strokes. In this case, the return stroke is used for roughing, whereas the forward stroke is used for finishing. The forward stroke may also be used for roughing and finishing combination cut. The apron and tool block must be securely fastened to prevent lifting during the cutting operation.

Multiple heads for surface cutting and heads mounted to cut the sides of large workpieces are also used. Such an arrangement is shown in Fig. 11.10(a).

The most common types of planers are the double-housing planer, Fig. 11.10(a), and the open-side planer, Fig. 11.10(b), which has one rigid column to support the crossrail and heads. Work which cannot pass between two columns may be machined on this type of machine. The work may overhang the platen with the overhanging work being supported with a mechanism which moves on its own bed. Still another adaptation of a planer is the milling planer, which makes it possible to plane and mill at the same time.

Pit planers are special machines wherein double columns are mounted on separate beds. The planer table is stationary, but the column straddles the platen. The columns move the length of the bed while the work remains stationary.

There are also many attachments, some of which make possible large radii cutting, contour cutting, tracing of irregular shapes, and helical cutting. Multiple heads are used, which are fed independently of each other so that

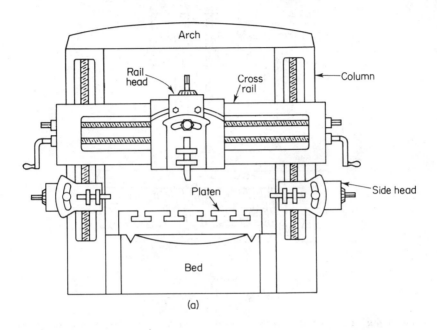

(a)

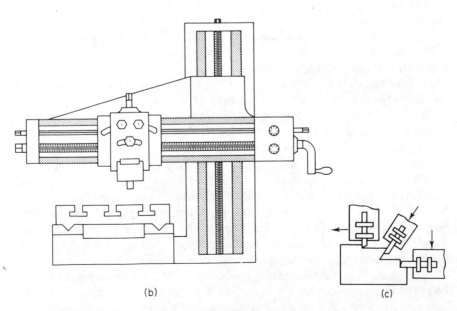

(b)   (c)

Figure 11.10

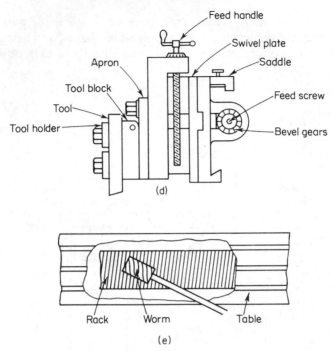

Figure 11.10 (Cont.)

one head may cut parallel to the platen while another head is cutting perpendicular to the platen and still a third head is cutting at an angle to the platen. See Fig. 11.10(c).

The crossrail mounts the head (or heads) and therefore must carry the feed and rapid traverse for feeding the head horizontally or vertically. The crossrail can also be moved along the column for up or down adjustment. Once positioned, it is clamped so that the toolslide will have the minimum amount of overhang for maximum support.

The toolhead, Fig. 11.10(d), has a construction somewhat similar to that of the toolhead on the shaper. It may be swiveled for angle cutting, and it is also equipped with a tool block which is pinned at the top so that it can swivel on the return stroke. Two straps hold the tool rigidly against the tool block.

One of the features of the toolhead is that it has its mechanism arranged so that one of the feed screws, through a system of bevel gears, will cause it to feed along the center line of the head at whatever angle the head happens to be set. The tool block apron should be set in the same manner as described for setting the toolhead apron on the shaper. Planers equipped with side heads may be fed by hand or power from a feed screw in the column.

The platen is a massive casting mounted on "V" ways machined into the bed. The bed may have one "V" and one flat, two "V" 's, or one center "V" and two flat ways. The platen on a mechanical planer carries the adjustable trip dogs for reversing the direction of motion of the platen. It is fitted with "T" slots for clamping work, and it also has accurately machined holes in its surface for receiving stops for banking work in position.

On the underside of the platen is a rack which is driven by a bull-spur, helical, or herringbone gear. One such mechanism is shown in Fig. 11.10(e).

The hydraulic planer uses the pull stroke of a hydraulic piston to power the platen. Its action is smooth during the acceleration and deceleration portion of the stroke. The cutting and return strokes are adjustable through a valve with a handwheel. It has a rapid traverse and a means for inching the table short distances.

11.7. Accessories

A good deal of the work mounted on a platen of the planer does not require a fixture for holding the work. The reason usually is that it is faster and cheaper to fasten the work directly to the platen than it is to design and build an expensive fixture. However, the work must be positioned and held. Therefore, in most instances the platen becomes the base of a fixture, and the fixture components are used directly on the platen. Such fixture components as clamps, straps, stops, jacks, angle plates, "V" blocks, parallel strips, and vises are used. When using these components, the student must always keep in mind that they must be kept out of the path of the tool. These components are shown in Fig. 11.11.

Parallels, Fig. 11.6(b); hold downs, Fig. 11.6(d); and straps, Fig. 11.6(e); may all be used on a planer. In addition, toe dogs, Fig. 11.11, may be used for holding thin pieces. Figure 11.12(a) shows the use of a toe dog, a poppet, and

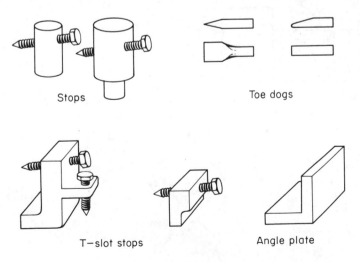

Stops   Toe dogs

T−slot stops   Angle plate

Figure 11.11

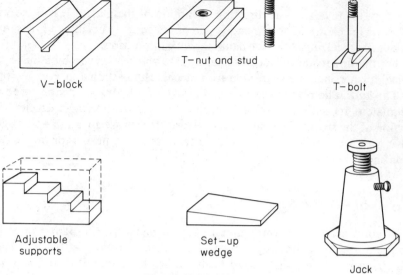

V-block

T-nut and stud

T-bolt

Adjustable supports

Set-up wedge

Jack

Figure 11.11 (Cont.)

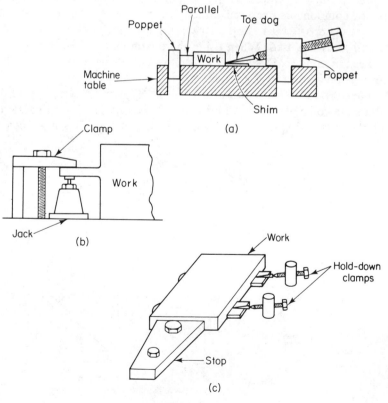

Poppet

Parallel

Toe dog

Machine table

Work

Poppet

Shim

(a)

Clamp

Work

Jack

(b)

Work

Hold-down clamps

Stop

(c)

Figure 11.12

a parallel strip. Note that the toe dog is kept off the table with a spacer called a *shim*.

Supporting the work where the clamp could bend or distort the workpiece requires a supporting jack directly under the point where the clamp puts pressure on the work. This is shown in Fig. 11.12(b).

It is also very important that stops should be placed at the end of the work to "take up" the forces put on the work by the tool during the cutting operation. Figure 11.12(c) shows such a support opposing the cutting action. Generally, stops should be used wherever possible to eliminate the need for additional clamps. It is always better to take up cutting thrust with stops than to rely upon clamps for absorbing such forces.

Fixtures are used wherever clamps are not practical. When planing multiple pieces, a fixture is more convenient than clamps and stops. This ensures that a workpiece can be quickly placed in position and clamped.

The *surface gage*, Fig. 11.13(a), is an instrument which is used to level work quickly during the setup. The scriber is set to the desired height and slid along the work with the base resting on the platen. If the scriber contacts all points on the piece, the work is said to be level. Usually it is only necessary to average the alignment so that all necessary surfaces will "clean up" before the desired dimension is reached.

The surface gage may also be used to scribe lines into chalked or blued surfaces. These scribed lines are used as guidelines as the cutting operation proceeds. If it appears that the workpiece may not clean up, the workpiece may have to be shimmed (raised) to average out the misalignment or warpage.

The *planer gage*, Fig. 11.13(b), may be set with a micrometer, a height

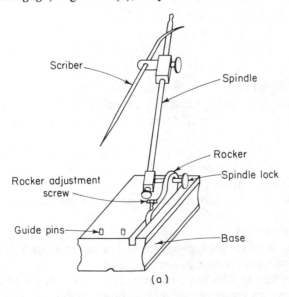

(a)

Figure 11.13

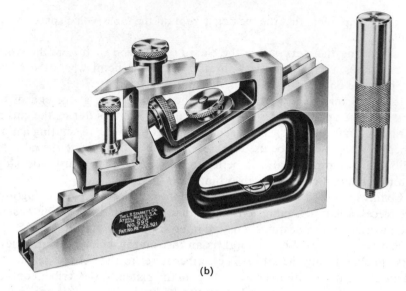

(b)

Figure 11.13 (Cont.) (*Photo courtesy of The L.S. Starrett Company.*)

gage, or gage blocks. The planer gage shown has the scribers which may be used for checking or scribing lines on work. This gage may also be used to set the height of the toolbit above the table of the planer.

The *depth micrometer*, Fig. 9.6(e), the *depth vernier*, Fig. 9.6(f), and the *bevel protractor*, Fig. 9.7(a), are all measuring instruments which can be used on a planer. The student should realize that any of the measuring instruments available may be used on the planer when appropriate.

11.8. Planer Tools

The planer toolholder shown in Fig. 11.14(a) may be used with solid or inserted tool bits. The cutting tools used on the planer differ very little from those described for the shaper. If there is a difference, it is one of size, the planer tool being larger.

Finishing tools and roughing tools are shown in Fig. 11.14(b). When a finishing tool is set on a planer, it must be positioned so that the full width of the tool cuts. Depths of from 0.001 to 0.005 in. with coarse feeds are taken for cutting cast iron. For finishing steel the flat broad point is usually not used.

Inserts are also used when clamping tools in position on a toolholder. These insets may be of forged high-speed steel or have clamped tips or button tips. The last two types are usually carbide inserts.

The "T"-slot tool usually has a lift mechanism to raise the tool so that it will clear the work on the return stroke, as shown in Fig. 11.14(c). This lifter

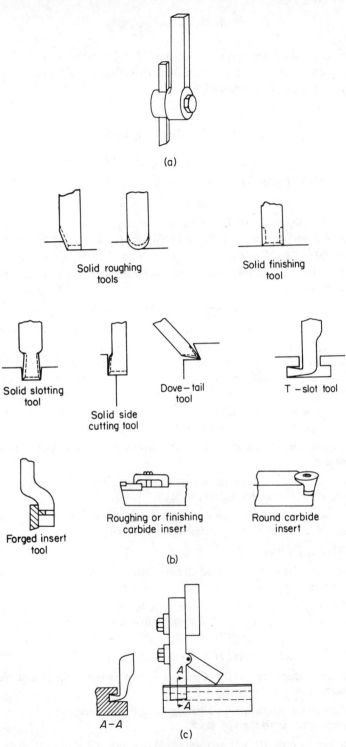

(a)

Solid roughing
tools

Solid finishing
tool

Solid slotting
tool

Solid side
cutting tool

Dove-tail
tool

T-slot tool

Forged insert
tool

Roughing or finishing
carbide insert

Round carbide
insert

(b)

A-A

(c)

Figure 11.14

prevents the tool from jamming in the "T" slot being cut. Jamming may damage the tool or the work. Sometimes this lifter is used to raise the tool to prevent damage to finished surfaces.

QUESTIONS AND PROBLEMS

11.1 Describe the differences in the operations of a shaper and a planer.

11.2 Why is it important to feed the work on the return stroke of the ram?

11.3 Make a drawing of a shaper toolslide head and label all parts.

11.4 Explain the action of the clapper box and its relationship to the action of the tool bit on the return stroke in Fig. 11.2(b). What is the rule for setting the apron?

11.5 Examine your shaper and explain the mechanism which allows either an angular or a vertical cut.

11.6 The tool slide may be used to make angle cuts. Explain.

11.7 Why is it necessary to keep the toolbit overhang as short as possible?

11.8 (a) What determines the feed on a crank shaper? (b) How is the feed set on a crank shaper? Assume the table to be feeding during the cutting stroke; how may the setting be changed so that the table will feed during the return stroke?

11.9 The position of the ram can be changed without changing the length of the ram stroke. Explain how this may be accomplished.

11.10 Explain the transmission of power from the bull wheel to the ram in a crank shaper.

11.11 Explain and illustrate the method by which the return stroke is caused to move faster than the cutting stroke.

11.12 Explain the generating of a spur gear on a gear shaper. How do the relative motions of gear blank to cutter differ when cutting a helical gear?

11.13 What is a keyseater?

11.14 Why is it important to grind all rakes and clearances on the toolbit which is to be used in a shaper?

11.15 (a) Why is it desirable that the tool bit in a shaper should be mounted perpendicular to the work? (b) What affect does this have on the construction of a shaper tool holder?

11.16 What are hold downs? How do they operate?

11.17 Explain the procedure for aligning a vise on a shaper when the stroke is to be parallel to the vise jaws.

11.18 Explain the procedure for aligning a vise on a shaper when the stroke is to be perpendicular to the vise jaws.

11.19 In Fig. 11.6(e) why is it necessary that distance A is shorter than distance B?

11.20 Describe the procedure for roughing and finishing a $\frac{5}{16}$-in. keyway in a 1-in. hole. Your description should include the *layout* of the blank, all *calculations*, and the *setup* as well as the *cutting operations*. Assume an initial height gage reading.

11.21 Answer Problem 11.20 for a $\frac{5}{8}$-in. keyway in a $2\frac{1}{2}$-in. bore.

11.22 Describe the process used to cut an internal dovetail on a shaper.

11.23 Repeat Problem 11.22 for an external dovetail.

11.24 Given a 60° female dovetail with a 5-in. dimension across the corners at the small width and a depth of 1 in., find: (a) the dimension across the corners at the bottom of the dovetail; (b) the best wire size; (c) the measurement over the wires.

11.25 Do the calculations in problem 11.24 for a male dovetail.

11.26 Given a 55° female dovetail with a 4-in. dimension over the sharp corners at the greatest width and a depth of $\frac{1}{2}$ in., find: (a) the dimensions across the corners at the small width of the dovetail; (b) the best wire size; (c) the measurement over the wires for the female dovetail; (d) the measurement over the wires for the male dovetail.

11.27 How does the relationship of the movement of the tool to the work differ on a planer from that on a shaper?

11.28 What are the advantages of a hydraulic-drive planer over a mechanical drive planer?

11.29 Why is a tool-life mechanism important on a planer? Explain.

11.30 Describe the essential differences between a double-housing planer and an open-side planer. What are the advantages of one over the other?

11.31 Describe the feed mechanism of a planer head.

11.32 What is the purpose of the "T" slot in a planer platen? What is the purpose of the reamed holes in the platen of a planer?

11.33 What are poppets? Toe dogs? Illustrate how each may be used to hold work.

11.34 Explain how a planer gage is used to level work on a planer. Do the same for a surface gage.

11.35 How should a tool bit on a planer be oriented to the top of the workpiece for taking a finishing cut on cast iron? On steel?

The Drill Press

12

12.1. Types of Drill Presses

Drill presses may be classified according to one of their construction characteristics. The vertical drill press may be the sensitive type, Fig. 12.1(a), or the power feed type, Fig. 12.1(b). In both instances the spindles are mounted in a vertical position. The essential difference is that the sensitive drill press is hand fed so that the hand is sensitive to the action of the drill. In the power feed type of drill press, once the power is engaged, the sensitivity at the drill handle is lost. Some drill presses are equipped with sensing devices, but these are rare, except in the very large units. Both types of drill presses may be purchased in bench or floor models and in a wide range of sizes.

Gang drill presses may be several sensitive or power drill heads mounted over one table. One such is shown in Fig. 12.1(c). This type of drill press should not be confused with the drill press called the multiple-spindle drill press, shown in Fig. 12.1(d). In the case of the gang drill press each spindle has its own power unit. In the case of the multiple-spindle drill press, a power unit may drive several spindles. There may be several power units driving banks of drills.

Transfer drill units are banks of drill spindles between which the work passes on a conveyor belt.

Radial drill presses, Fig. 12.1(e), have a radial arm mounted on a column. The drill head is mounted on this radial arm. With this arrangement, the radial arm may be rotated about the column or raised and lowered along the column, and the drill head may also be moved along the radial arm. The combination of these three motions provides a great deal of flexibility for

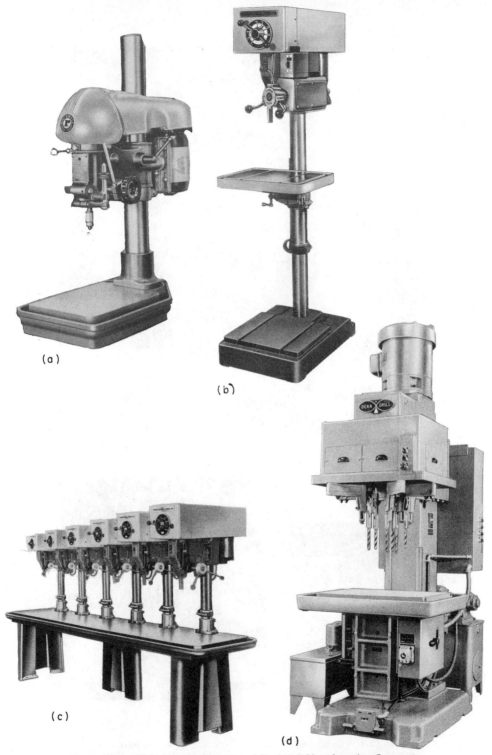

Figure 12.1 [(a), (b), (c) Courtesy of Rockwell Manufacturing Company, Power Tool Division; (d) courtesy of South Bend Lathe, Cicero Plant.]

(e)

(f)

Figure 12.1 (Cont.) [(*e*) *Courtesy of Giddings & Lewis-Bickford Machine Company;* (*f*) *courtesy of Pratt and Whitney Company, Inc.*]

positioning the drill bit over the work. Also provided is a positioning and power feed unit for the drill-head spindle.

Deep hole drills, Fig. 12.1(f), are production machines on which either the work or the drill is stationary and only one rotates and feeds. Deep hole drills use a special drill bit, known as a *gun* drill and shown in Fig. 12.4(d and e). Multiple pieces may be drilled with repetitive accuracies in hole size and straightness. They may be of the horizontal or vertical type.

More recently hydraulically or pneumatically controlled and operated drill presses have been developed for high production. These machines, although highly specialized, may be converted from one job to another by changing the fixtures and the drills.

Other recent developments which are not truly drilling operations but which may be used to "drill" holes in very hard or difficult-to-work materials are ultrasonic machining and electron drilling. Also yet to be developed is the laser beam as a machining tool.

The ultrasonic method uses vibrational energy and an abrasive suspended in a liquid, such as water. The drill bit is usually made from cold-rolled steel, unhardened, or tungsten carbide. The unhardened tool wears very rapidly but yields desired results because of the high impact force involved. The abrasive acting under the high-frequency vibrations and impact of the tool removes metal from the workpiece. It is possible with this method to shape regular or irregular contours or holes in such materials as carbide, ceramics, glass, jewels, and a host of other materials which could not ordinarily be machined.

The electron discharge method of drilling very hard or tough materials uses a dielectric material and an electrode as a tool. The work is the other electrode. An electric arc breaks up the workpiece material into minute particles which are washed away. The drill is usually a hollow tube made from a good conducting material. At all times the electrode (cutting tool) must be kept separated from the work to create an arc. Grinding, tapping, lapping, etc., have been accomplished with this process on ferrous or nonferrous materials.

Laser beams (light amplification by stimulated emission of radiation) may be used to melt holes in any material known in a matter of seconds. The principle is one of putting energy into a crystal and thereby causing electrons to jump into higher orbits. Since the electrons are unstable in these high-energy orbits, they jump back into their neutral orbits with a release of energy The energy released is characteristic of a particular jump from one orbit to another since the wavelengths are characteristic for that same jump. Thus, even though multiple wavelengths are introduced, the electrons absorb the needed energy to jump into higher orbits and release the energy in a highly concentrated beam having that frequency and energy. The energy obtained in this manner is very high and can be focused to melt materials.

The laser material (chromium or *rare-earth* material) acts as an amplifier in that it accumulates wavelengths of all magnitudes of energy (intense light) and releases it as selected concentrated energy. It appears to be a collection process rather than a selection or sifting process.

Under proper control, welding and machining have already been accomplished with the laser beam. This source of energy has yet to be developed to its full potential. Laser beams may become the tool bit of the future.

12.2. Construction and Accessories

The standard drill press, Fig. 12.2(a), has a base which may be used as a table for mounting work when the maximum distance between the spindle and the table is desired. This *base table* is different from the *regular work table* in that it acts as the support for the column and is in a fixed position relative to the spindle. The regular work table is clamped to the column so that it can be positioned vertically along the column or radially about the column. Some of the more complex drill presses have provisions for moving this table laterally and longitudinally as well as vertically along the column.

The drill head and power unit are mounted at the top of the column. The classification of *bench* versus *floor* drill press is essentially related to the length of the column.

The drill head construction varies from the single-cone pulley type to the completely geared and powered head with automatic feed controlled through numerical tapes. The sleeve has a rack attached to it which is engaged by a pinion gear for vertical movement by hand or power. Inside this sleeve is the spindle which drives through a spline engaged with a mating spline inside a drive pulley or gear. This enables the spindle to move vertically without losing its power source. This is shown in Fig. 12.2(b). A variable speed drive is shown in Fig. 12.2(c).

These are the essential parts of a drill press and apply to all drill presses. The differences that exist are those of size, precision, or flexibility. The flexibility ranges from a plain drill press through the universal drill press whose head may be swiveled through almost any angle with the vertical axis.

Small drill presses usually have their spindles equipped with drill chucks for holding straight shank drills. Larger drill presses have their spindles tapered to receive sockets, such as shown in Fig. 12.3(a). Cutting tools which have tapered shanks may also be used with this type of spindle. A drill chuck with a tapered shank is shown in Fig. 12.3(b). Some drill chucks provide methods for changing drills while the spindle is revolving.

Also available are floating holders which provide parallel floating as well as angular floating motion. This type of holder is generally used for the self-aligning of reamers without loss of power.

Tapping attachments range from those requiring a spindle-reverse drill press to those which will reverse the rotation of the tap when the spindle is

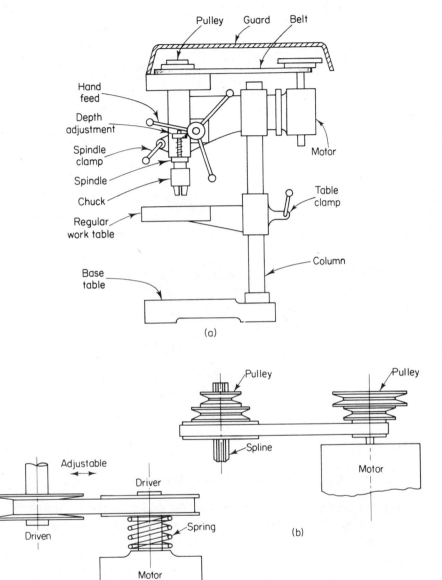

Figure 12.2

retracted. Tapping may be done with a regular drill chuck if there is no danger of the tap binding in the work. If the tap should bind while the power is engaged, either the tap will break or, if the tap slips in the chuck, it may damage the chuck jaws.

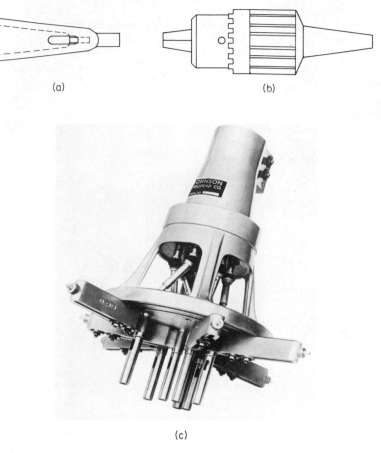

(a)   (b)

(c)

Figure 12.3 *(Photo courtesy of Johnson Drill Head Co.)*

Another attachment used for production drilling is the multiple-spindle drill head, Fig. 12.3(c). These drill heads distribute the power from the machine spindle to many spindles built into the head. The multiple spindle head shown in Fig. 12.3(c) is made with adjustable center-to center drill spindles. In others the center-to-center distances may be designed with fixed centerline distances. The adjustable spindle drill head need not be discarded once a job for which the head was designed is completed.

Devices for holding work on the drill-press table are the vise, fixtures, or straps. If a vise is used, it should be registered against a stop unless it is bolted to the table. If a vise is not bolted to the drill table, it has the advantage of aligning itself when the drill touches the work. However, if the vise is not bolted, care must be taken not to let the drill action raise the work and the vise above the stop or tip them over. In either case the drill may be damaged or the operator injured.

12.3. Drill Bits

The nomenclature for the standard drill bit was given in Fig. 10.12(b). These drill bits may be used, or adapted for use, on the rotary type of power tools. They are manufactured with straight, tapered, or special kinds of shanks for quick locking. The shank is usually soft to facilitate holding. The cutting portion of the drill is made from hardened high-carbon high-speed or cobalt-alloy steels. The drill bit may also be made from carbide or fitted with carbide inserts, as shown in Fig. 12.4(a). The flutes may be straight or have long leads or short leads. The helixes of most manufactured drills

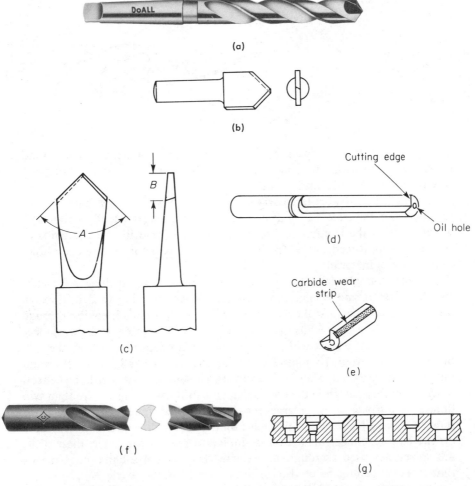

(a)

(b)

Cutting edge

B

A

Oil hole

(d)

Carbide wear strip

(c)

(e)

(f)

(g)

Figure 12.4 [(*a*) *Courtesy of DoAll Company;* (*f*) & (*g*) *courtesy of Cleveland Twist Drill Company.*]

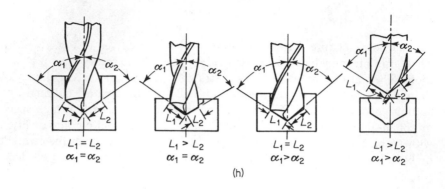

$$L_1 = L_2 \qquad L_1 > L_2 \qquad L_1 = L_2 \qquad L_1 > L_2$$
$$\alpha_1 = \alpha_2 \qquad \alpha_1 = \alpha_2 \qquad \alpha_1 > \alpha_2 \qquad \alpha_1 > \alpha_2$$

(h)

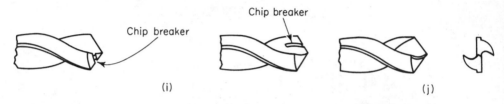

(i)   (j)

Figure 12.4   (Cont.)

are right-hand. When viewed from the cutting edge, the helix winds around the drill in a clockwise direction. Thus the drill must rotate counterclockwise when viewed from the cutting end.

The high-helix (short-lead) drill is used when it is necessary to clear chips rapidly from the hole being drilled. The helix angle is usually about 45°, which reduces the friction between the flutes of the drill and the chips as they are being forced out of the hole. They are used for cutting deep holes in nonferrous materials.

Low-helix-angle drills (long lead) drills are used for drilling nonmetals such as plastics and nonferrous materials. Anyone trying to drill through thin sheet metal has had the experience of the drill point's breaking through the bottom of the sheet while the lip of the drill is still cutting. If the workpiece is not clamped, the helix will catch the undrilled portion and climb the drill bit while it is rotating. To minimize this danger, low lead helix angle or straight flute drill bits are used. They are manufactured with right- or left-hand helixes.

Still another design is the core drill. This drill usually has more than two flutes. Its purpose is to enlarge previously drilled holes, cored holes, or punched holes. There is no chisel edge on the core drill. The chamfered edges do the cutting. Since this action is similar to that of a reamer, these drills are sometimes used as roughing reamers. The lack of a chisel edge means that this drill cannot be used to drill into solid stock.

Another function of the core drill is to correct the location of predrilled holes. In this instance no chamfer is used on the lips, and the drill-point angle is ground flat (180°).

Sometimes the tip of a core drill is a separate piece which may be changed when the size of the desired hole changes. These core drills are usually large and require that a pilot be used.

Flat drills, Fig. 12.4(b), may be made from drill rod. The end is forged flat, turned to the appropriate diameter and drill-point angle, heat treated, and ground with the proper lip clearance. This drill may be used when the appropriate drill size is not readily available.

Microdrills, Fig. 12.4(c), are flat drills mounted in an alloy holder. These drills are made from carbide. They range from 0.001 to approximately 0.125 in. in diameter. They may be purchased in increments of 0.0001 in. in diameter. Since they break very easily, they must be cleared frequently.

The operating rpm of these drills should be about 2000 with feeds determined by trial and error. As the diameter of the drill decreases below 0.020 in., the rpm and feed should be decreased. Web thickness, rake angles, point angles, and pressure all affect the hole size which is produced. Regular point angles A equal to $135°$ are used to drill very small holes and to drill hard materials. Drill-point angles of $118°$ are used to drill steel. Drill points of $90°$ are used for drilling plastics and other soft materials. The clearance angle B may range from 8 to $12°$. The harder or tougher the material to be drilled, the smaller is the angle B.

Gun drills, Fig. 12.4(d), are used for drilling deep holes. They have one flute, usually parallel to the center line of the drill. One of the lips extends beyond the end of the flute and has lip clearance which makes it possible for the drill to cut. Some method of creating a flow of water under pressure is provided. This is usually done through a long hole through the body of the drill. Thus the water flows through the drill to the cutting edge, keeps the drill cool, and washes the chips back through the flute. The V flute is usually $110°$, with the cutting edge having a radial clearance of $15°$. These drills may have carbide inserts at the cutting edge as well as carbide wear strips on the outside of the drill, as shown in Fig. 12.4(e).

It should be remembered that the drill cuts only at the end. Once started, the body of the drill acts as a guide for further drilling. Thus the drill is usually started through a bushing. If the drill is long, it is usually also supported with a steady rest. The wear strips prolong the life of the drill.

Where the hole to be drilled is large, an operation known as *trepanning* may be used. Trepanning does not remove all the material from the hole being drilled. It cuts a circular groove and leaves a core in the center of the hole. Since the core must enter the head, the head is made hollow and fastened to a drive tube. If the hole is long, the core must also be capable of entering the head holder. Under oil pressure, the chips are driven out through the hollow drive tube.

Step drills are specially ground drills which are capable of drilling more than one diameter in one operation. A step drill is shown in Fig. 12.4(f) and some of the possible combinations are shown in Fig. 12.4(g).

Conventional twist drills may be purchased in fractional, letter, number, or metric sizes. The fractional drills range from $\frac{1}{64}$ to $3\frac{1}{2}$ in. in diameter. The letter drill sizes are from A to Z, with the A drill equal to 0.234 in. in diameter to the Z drill equal to 0.413 in. in diameter. The number drills start with the number 1 drill, equal to 0.228 in. in diameter, and go to the number 80 drill, equal to 0.0135 in. in diameter. Since the letter drills pick up where the number drill sizes end and since the number and letter drill sizes fill many of the gaps between the fractional sizes, a wide variety of holes may be drilled between 0.0135 and 0.500 in. in diameter. Between $\frac{1}{2}$ and $1\frac{1}{4}$ in. the drill diameters increase in increments of $\frac{1}{64}$ in.; between $1\frac{1}{4}$ and $1\frac{1}{2}$ in. the diameters increase in increments of $\frac{1}{32}$ in.; between $1\frac{1}{2}$ and $3\frac{1}{2}$ in. the diameters increase in increments of $\frac{1}{16}$ in.

Metric twist drills have been standardized for tapered as well as for those which have straight shanks. Morse tapered shanks drills start at 3.00 mm and increase in size up to 100 mm in diameter. Jobbers parallel shank drills start at 0.20 mm and increase to 16.00 mm in diameter. Whereas the parallel shank long series has been standardized to start at 2 mm and increase to 13.80 mm.

It is important to note that the number and letter drill sizes are not used in the metric standards. They have been replaced with metric sizes. The number 80 drill has been replaced with a 0.35 mm size. As the numbers decrease from 80 to 1, the metric sizes increase from 0.35 to 5.80 mm. The A through Z sizes are replaced with 5.95 to 10.5 mm.

It is very important that drills are properly ground. The drill point must be in the center of rotation of the drill. Figure 12.4(h) shows a drill point centered so that angle $\alpha_1 = \alpha_2$. Also $L_1 = L_2$. If there is any variation of either the angle or the length of one side, a side thrust will be developed and the drilled hole will be larger than the drill diameter itself. The effect is shown in Fig. 12.4(h).

It should also be mentioned that chip breakers, Fig. 12.4(i), and web thinning, Fig. 12.4(j), are possible. Chip breakers are used to aid in chip removal by breaking up the chip. Web thinning is used to restore the original web thickness after grinding and may also be used to alter chip formation.

12.4. Reamers

Operations such as reaming, countersinking, counterboring, spot facing, boring, or tapping are some of the auxiliary operations possible on a drill press.

Reamers and their nomenclature are shown in Fig. 10.13 and discussed in Section 10.5. Reamers have right-hand cutting. They may have left-hand, Fig. 12.5(a), straight, or right-hand, Fig. 12.5(b), helixes. They may also have positive, negative, or zero radial rake, shown in the end views of Fig. 12.5(a) and (b).

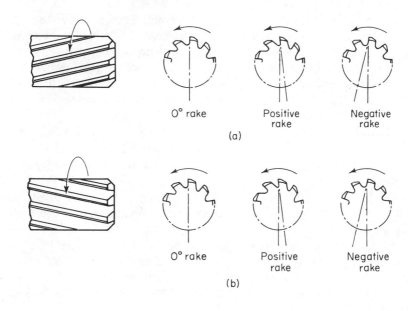

(a)

(b)

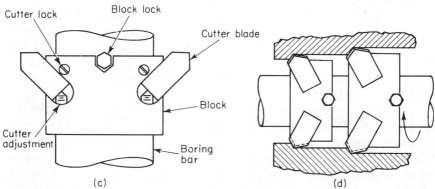

(c)   (d)

Figure 12.5

Viewed from the end, these reamers cut when rotating counterclockwise. The right-hand helix twists in a clockwise direction when viewed from the end, as seen in Fig. 12.5(b). The left-hand helix twists in a counterclockwise direction when viewed from the end, as shown in Fig. 12.5(a). Thus the right-hand helix creates a positive axial rake and tends to pull the reamer into the work. This pulling action may be objectionable if there is any "play" in the machine spindle. This can be overcome by using a left-hand helix-angle cutter which creates a negative axial rake, as shown in Fig. 12.5(a).

The theory of radial rake, although shown in the end view of Fig. 12.5(a) and (b), will be discussed more fully in Chapter 23.

Reamers may be either solid or expansion type. They may be purchased for machining one-diameter holes or tapered holes. They may be the rose type of reamer, with no margin relief, or the fluted type in which the margin is relieved. If they are to be used for roughing, their flutes may be notched to break up the chip formation and thus permit greater stock removal.

Stock removal should not exceed $\frac{1}{32}$ in. for roughing and 0.005 to 0.010 in. for finishing. The removal of too much stock will result in oversize and rough holes. It may also cause damage to the reamer as well.

Combination, or step, reamers may also be specially purchased, and one is available with multiple diameters for line reaming.

It should be noted that reamers may be carbide tipped for longer life. Solid carbide is usually reserved for reamers having diameters of less than $\frac{1}{4}$ in. All-carbide reamers need very careful handling. When used properly, they have the advantage of picking up less metal because they have high hardness and finish.

For reaming or boring large holes, inserted tooth blocks, Fig. 12.5(c), are used. The body of the block is made from a fine alloy steel and heat treated. The block-locking device positions the block so that the reamer blades will be equidistant from the center line of the boring bar when locked in position.

When grinding blades, the adjustments are turned to push the blades out the required amount. The block is then inserted into a short bar and fitted with hardened, ground, and lapped centers. The block is locked into this fixture in the same manner in which it is locked into the boring bar when it is being used. The fixture is placed into a grinding machine and the blades are cylindrically ground to size.

The fixture may also be equipped with eccentric centers which enable circular relief to be ground on the blades. Once the desired diameter across the blades is ground and the relief ground, the block is removed from the fixture and mounted in the boring bar with which it is to be used. If all conditions of grinding are correct, no additional adjustment of the blades is needed.

It should be noted that these blocks may be used for both rough and finish boring if the appropriate clearances and rakes are ground on the cutting blades. A multiple boring operation is shown in Fig. 12.5(d).

12.5. Auxiliary Operations

Countersink.   There are many kinds of countersinking tools. However, in almost all cases the operation is one of forming a chamfer of less than 90° with the center line of a previously drilled hole. A countersinking tool and a countersunk hole is shown in Fig. 12.6(a). Countersinks may be purchased with included angles of 45°, 53°, 60°, 78°, or 90°. They usually have three flutes. Six-flute countersinks are chatterless because of the uneven spacing of the flutes about the periphery.

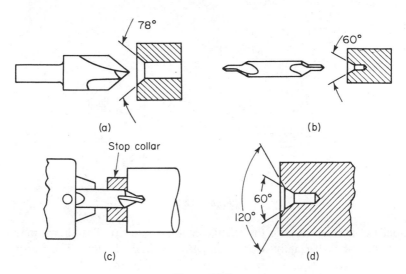

(a)   (b)

(c)   (d)

Figure 12.6

Figure 12.6(b) shows the combination drill and countersink used for centering work which is to be placed between centers of a lathe for turning or between the centers of a grinder when the work is to be ground. The included angle of the countersink is 60°.

Sometimes it becomes necessary to control the depth of the countersunk hole. Such an instance occurs in production grinding when a length dimension is to be maintained in grinding to a shoulder. In such cases some kind of a stop ring must be affixed to the countersink to control the depth of the countersunk hole. A simple collar is shown affixed to the countersink in Fig. 12.6(c). Countersinks fitted with micrometer stops may also be purchased.

In some instances, it is desirable to use a drill and countersink combination which has a 60° included angle and a secondary included angle of 120°. This serves the purpose of preserving the edge of the countersunk hole. This is shown in Fig. 12.6(d).

Spotfacing.   This is an operation in which a circular flat surface is machined perpendicular to a previously drilled hole. Slot-facing tools have pilots to ensure concentricity of the spot facing with the hole. Figure 12.7(a) shows a cast angle plate with a spot facing at the surface of a bolt hole. This ensures a flat bearing surface for a washer or bolt at 90° with the hole.

Back spot-facing tools are also available. The holder usually has an eccentric or cam locking device. The holder is inserted into the hole to be back spot-faced. The spotfacer is placed on this holder in a reverse position. The rotation of the spotfacer holds it on the holder. This is shown in Fig. 12.7(b).

Spot-facing tools may be of the shell type with an inserted blade, a solid

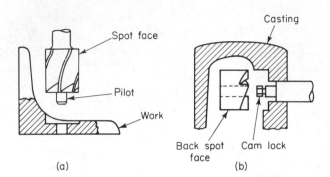

(a)   (b)

Figure 12.7

blade that is integral with the shank, or a carbide tip. The shank may be a straight, tapered (usually Morse tapered), or pinlock type. The pilots may be integral with the spot-facing tool or interchangeable.

Counterboring. This operation differs from the spot-facing operation in two essential ways: (1) The counterbore is deeper, and (2) its purpose is to enlarge a previously drilled hole for a given depth, terminating in a shoulder. The counterbored portion of the hole must be concentric to, and the shoulder is usually perpendicular to, the predrilled hole.

The counterboring tool is usually the same tool as that used for spot facing. It must also be piloted unless used through a guide bushing in a fixture. Counterbores may be fitted with a stop collar to ensure proper depth, or they may be stepped to give multiple diameters.

They may be made from high-speed steel or have carbide tips or inserted blades. The clearance at the cutting edge is about 5° and the helix angle is 0 to 15°.

Boring. Boring may also be done on a drill press. The purpose of boring on a drill press is usually to correct any runout created by the drilling operation before reaming. It is also possible that a hole may have to be bored on a drill press when an appropriate sized drill or reamer is not available. In this instance a rigid boring bar with an inserted tool bit is used. A hole is drilled and then enlarged with the boring operation and, if necessary, then reamed. All the principles of clearance, rake, feed, and speed must be adhered to.

Tapping. This is another operation which may be done on a drill press. The tapping head was described in Section 12.2. Tapping is a difficult operation under any conditions. The problems all relate to the amount of material to be removed with the first pass of the tap. This creates problems of torque, chip clearance, feeds, and speeds (the feed is fixed by the lead of the tap).

To ensure starting the tap straight, especially when hand tapping is done, three types of taps are manufactured. A set of taps includes the starting tap (tapered), plug, and bottoming taps. The starting tap is tapered from the end for about six to eight threads, the plug tap is tapered for about three threads from the end, and the bottoming tap is merely "backed off." The pitch diameter of all three taps is the same. The bottoming tap is used in blind holes.

Serial taps are different from the set of three taps just described. Serial taps come in a sequence of 1, 2, 3 and must be used in that order to achieve a full depth of thread. Each tap cuts more material than the previous tap. The number 1 tap can therefore be considered a roughing tap, and the number 3 tap, a finishing tap.

Taps are manufactured in fractional ($\frac{1}{2}$-13) and numbered taps (10 to 32) sizes. Tapered taps, such as pipe taps and acme taps, are also available as standard stock.

Gun taps have their cutting faces (in the flutes) cut back to give an axial rake, shown in Fig. 12.8(a). This gives a shearing action to the cutting but, more important, causes the chips to move ahead of the tapping action. It should be obvious that such an action will clear the chips by forcing them deeper into the drilled hole. Gun taps should therefore be used only on through holes. This type of tap is also suitable for machine tapping.

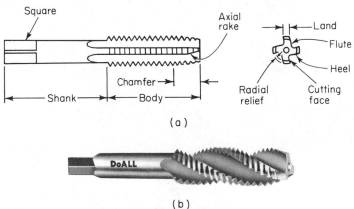

Figure 12.8 *(Photo courtesy of DoAll Company.)*

Spiral fluted taps, Fig. 12.8(b), differ from gun taps in that the flutes have a helix about the same as a twist drill's. A tap of this type which cuts a right-hand lead should have a right-hand helix. This tap is excellent for cutting tough or soft materials such as stainless steel, copper, aluminum, and plastics.

Collapsible taps are manufactured so that they will collapse when the desired length of thread is cut. They may be collapsed by hand, in which case they must be reset, or they may be fitted with a trip ring which causes the chasers to retract when the plate is tripped. They may be made for turret lathes or other automatic equipment where the tap does not revolve, or for machines such as a drill press where the tap revolves. The chasers may be removed for sharpening, replaced, and adjusted rather easily. Collapsible die heads for cutting external threads are also available for use on drill presses, turret lathes, automatic machines, etc.

12.6. The Use of the Drill Press

Figure 12.9(a) shows two blocks with the operations of center drilling, drilling, reaming, counterboring, and tapping being performed. The combination drilling and reaming operation is also shown. The student is warned

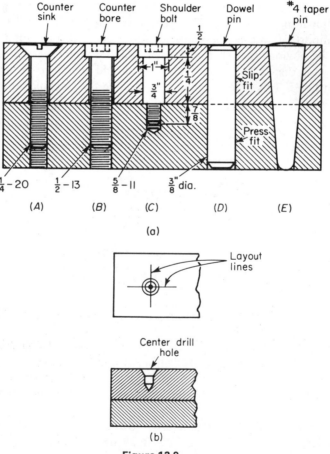

Figure 12.9

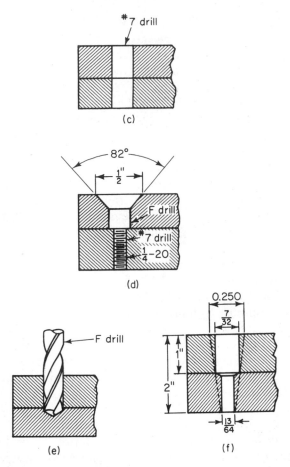

Figure 12.9   (Cont.)

that Fig. 12.9(a) is an exercise and that only one of the methods shown is needed to fasten two pieces together.

It is assumed that the upper plate has been blued and the location of all the holes have been scribed accurately on the upper plate. The two plates are clamped together so that all the locations on the upper plate can be transferred to the lower plate during the drilling operation.

Hole A.   This is a countersunk hole with clearance for the flathead screw in the upper plate and a $\frac{1}{4}$-20 thread in the lower plate. As the screw is tightened, the forces acting between the thread and the countersink draw the two plates together. Since the screw slips in the clearance hole, the two plates are pulled together. The procedure for machining A is as follows:

The smallest drill used for this operation has the minor diameter of the thread. For a $\frac{1}{4}$-20 thread the tap drill size is a number 7 drill (0.201 in.). This may be calculated by using the method in Section 14.5; or it can be taken from a tap drill size table. The spot where the layout lines cross is picked up with a center punch and punched lightly. Correction may be made by inclining the punch in the direction of any correction needed. Once the correction is made, the center punch is held vertical to the surface of the work and punched with a sharp blow.

The combination centerdrill-countersink is placed in a drill chuck, the center punch mark is picked up and the center is drilled, as shown in Fig. 12.9(b).

The countersink formed by this combination drill and countersink tool is not to be confused with the countersink used for a flathead screw. The countersink used for flathead screws is usually 82°. This countersink is 60°. Since a drill will follow a previously drilled hole, the combination countersink-center drill acts as a guide for the number 7 drill. (The student should note that, if a guide bushing mounted in a fixture is used, this operation is not needed.)

The pieces are then clamped to the drill-press table or in a drill vise and moved about until the number 7 drill is in exact alignment with the countersunk hole. The table or vise is clamped, the feed and speed set, and a number 7 hole drilled through both pieces, Fig. 12.9(c).

The two pieces may now be separated and the upper plate drilled with an F (0.257 in.) drill for clearance for the body of the screw. This hole is then countersunk with an 82° countersink to a diameter of $\frac{1}{2}$ in. (two times the major diameter). The lower plate is tapped with a tapping head in the spindle of the drill press. The operation is shown in Fig. 12.9(d).

It should be noted that, if the tapping is to be done by hand, a better procedure is to drill the upper plate (when both plates are fastened together) with the F drill to a depth such that the point of the drill spots the lower plate, as shown in Fig. 12.9(e). With the plates still clamped together, the number 7 drill is used to drill the tap drill hole into the lower plate. Tapping the number 7 drilled hole is then accomplished by using the F drilled hole as a guide for aligning the tap. It may be advisable to use a starting drill followed by a plug tap.

Hole B.   The initial procedure of center punching and using a combination centerdrill-countersink is followed. In this instance the smallest drill is the tap drill size for a $\frac{1}{2}$-13 thread. The tap drill is $\frac{27}{64}$ in. (0.422 in.). With both plates clamped together, the hole is drilled through both plates. The plates are separated and the lower plate is tapped with the $\frac{1}{2}$-13 tap with a tapping head.

The upper plate is opened up to $\frac{1}{2}$ in., or, if this accuracy is not needed, a $\frac{33}{64}$-in. drill may be used. A $\frac{3}{4}$-in. counterbore with a $\frac{1}{2}$-in. diameter pilot is used to counterbore to a depth of $\frac{1}{2}$ in. as shown in Figure 12.9(a).

Hole C.   The same procedure of layout, etc., may be followed for this operation. This hole is to be used for a $\frac{3}{4}$-in. shoulder screw. The $\frac{3}{4}$ in. refers to the ground diameter, not the thread diameter. This is shown in Fig. 12.9(a) The smallest diameter to be drilled is the tap drill size for the $\frac{5}{8}$-11 thread. The tap drill size is $\frac{17}{32}$ in. This is drilled to a depth of approximately $1\frac{3}{4}$ in. ($1 + \frac{1}{4} + \frac{1}{2}$ in.) to allow for the back-off of the bottoming tap.

The plates are separated. The hole is machine tapped with a plug tap and finally with a bottoming tap to ensure full thread for $\frac{7}{8}$-in. depth in the lower plate.

The hole in the upper plate is then opened up to $\frac{47}{64}$ in. and reamed to $\frac{3}{4}$ in. A 1-in. counterbore with a $\frac{3}{4}$-in. pilot is used to counterbore the 1-in. diameter by $\frac{1}{2}$-in.-deep counterbored hole.

Hole D.   This hole is for the purpose of aligning the two plates so that, if they ever need to be separated and put together again, they will be aligned by the dowel pin. Thus the dowel pin is used as a locator. It must therefore be hardened and ground, be pressed into the lower plate, and have a slip fit in the upper plate, Fig. 12.9(a).

Both plates are clamped together and an undersize drill is used to drill a hole through both plates. In this instance a U (0.368 in.) drill may be used.

Since the dowel pin is 0.0002 in. oversize, a 0.3750-in. reamer may be used to ream both plates while they are clamped together. This will ensure a press fit between the dowel pin and the lower plate.

The fit between the upper plate and the dowel pin must be a slip fit. A machine-expansion or a hand-expansion reamer may be used in the lower plate to ensure a slip fit.

Hole E.   This hole needs to accommodate a number 4 taper pin. A number 4 taper pin has a large diameter of 0.250 in., a taper of $\frac{1}{4}$ in./ft, and a small diameter of 0.2083 in. if the length of the pin is 2 in. Thus a through drill of $\frac{13}{64}$ in. (0.203 in.) may be used. A number 4 taper reamer is used to ensure that the pin will fit and the radius of the pin protrudes above the hole, as shown in Fig. 12.9(a).

Sometimes it is recommended that the hole be step drilled, Fig. 12.9(f), to make it easier for the reamer. In this case another drill of $\frac{7}{32}$ in. (0.219 in.) may be used for a depth of 1 in.

QUESTIONS AND PROBLEMS

12.1   Explain why a sensitive drill press is called sensitive.

12.2   What is the difference between a gang drill press and a transfer drill press?

12.3   Explain the three motions which make the radial drill press more flexible than the standard drill press.

12.4   What is ultrasonic drilling? Explain.

12.5   What is electron discharge drilling? How does it operate?

12.6 What is the fundamental principle employed to concentrate energy in the formation of a laser beam?

12.7 Make a block drawing of a pedestal drill press. Label all parts.

12.8 Describe the variable drive mechanism shown in Fig. 12.2(c).

12.9 What mechanisms are used to drive the spindle of a drill press without loss of vertical motion?

12.10 Check your drill press. What kind of taper does the spindle have?

12.11 Check the drill press attachments which you have in your manufacturing laboratory, and describe how at least two of them are used.

12.12 What precautions must be taken when using a vise which is not bolted to the table of the drill press?

12.13 Review the drill-bit nomenclature in Chapter 10. Make a sketch of a twist drill, and label all the essential parts of the bit.

12.14 Explain the action of a drill bit. What effect does a right-hand, straight, or left-hand helix have on the cutting action as a drill bit revolves?

12.15 What advantages does a short-lead twist drill have over a long-lead twist drill?

12.16 What is a core drill? When is it advisable to use a core drill?

12.17 When should a pilot be used with a core drill?

12.18 If a piece of drill rod is available, make a flat drill in your shop. Describe the procedure which you followed in making and heat treating the drill. Try it on your drill press, and report your results to your instructor.

12.19 (a) What is a microdrill? (b) In what sizes are they available? (c) What are the operating speeds of these drills? (d) What point angles should be used on small holes in hard materials? For steel? For soft materials?

12.20 (a) Describe the action of a gun drill. (b) What is the characteristic of a gun drill which makes it possible to drill a straight hole?

12.21 What is trepanning?

12.22 Make several drawings of step drills which you have found in a text other than this text.

12.23 (a) What is the range of diameters of letter drills? (b) Of number drills?

12.24 Explain why imperfect holes are drilled (a) when the length of the cutting edge, L_1, is less than L_2; (b) when the lip angle α_1 is less than the lip angle α_2; (c) when both L_1 and α_1 vary from L_2 and α_2. The notations refer to Fig. 12.4(h).

12.25 Is it possible to use chip breakers on a drill bit? How?

12.26 When is web thinning used on a drill? Why is it important?

12.27 Review the standardized English drill sizes, fractional, letter, and number.

12.28 Compare the metric standard drill sizes with those in Problem 12.27. What has happened to the letter and number drill sizes?

12.29 When are left-hand helixes used on reamers? Why is their use important?

12.30 What is a block reamer?

12.31 When finish reaming, how much material should be removed from a predrilled hole?

12.32 List the standard included angles of countersinks.

12.33 What is the advantage of a six-flute over a three-flute countersink?

12.34 What is the purpose of a double-angle drill-countersink combination?

12.35 (a) What is a combination drill and countersink? Make a sketch of this tool. (b) How can the depth to which this drill combination operates be controlled? (c) Why is it important to control this depth on a cylindrical grinder? Explain.

12.36 What is back spot facing?

12.37 How does the counterbore operation differ from the spot-facing operation?

12.38 How is boring done on a drill press?

12.39 Describe the lead threads on a starting tap, a plug tap, and a bottoming tap.

12.40 How do serial taps differ from a set of starting-plug-bottoming taps?

12.41 What is a gun tap? A spiral tap? When is it appropriate to use each?

12.42 Describe the procedure for fastening two plates together with a $\frac{3}{4}$-10 flathead screw.

12.43 Describe the procedure for fastening two plates with a 10–32 socket head screw.

12.44 Describe the machining procedure for achieving a slip and press fit for a $\frac{1}{2}$-in. dowel pin.

12.45 Check the tables in a handbook and describe the procedure for fitting a hub and shaft with a number 6 taper pin.

The Lathe—Construction and Operation

13

13.1. Types and Construction of Lathes

Essentially, a lathe is a power tool which causes work to revolve so that a tool in contact with the work moves laterally and removes metal. The control of the speed with which the workpiece revolves may be obtained with belts or through a gear arrangement. The power from a motor is transmitted to the spindle of the headstock through the belts or gears. This power also controls the lateral movement of the tool. This movement is the feed. The lathe is also equipped with a handwheel for hand feeding the tool.

Lathes are classified according to the largest diameter which can be rotated over the ways of the machine. The *swing* of a lathe is twice the distance from the headstock center to the ways of the machine. Thus a 16-in. lathe measures 8 in. from the ways to the center of the spindle of the machine. Actually a small allowance, approximately $\frac{1}{4}$ in., is allowed beyond the designated swing. There are many types of lathes in use today. The major classes are those described below.

The bench lathe. This may be a simple *jeweler's lathe* that is totally manual except for the power which drives the work. The cross feed and the longitudinal feed may or may not have graduated dials. Its purpose is to achieve high degrees of machining precision on small parts, but precision depends on the ability of the operator. The bench lathe may also be more sophisticated and have power feeds and power speeds built into its construction. It is small so that it may be mounted on a bench. All attachments which are available for the larger types of lathes are available for this type of lathe.

The engine lathe. This fully-powered lathe is the most widely used in machine shops today. See Fig. 13.1(a). The spindle speed may be changed

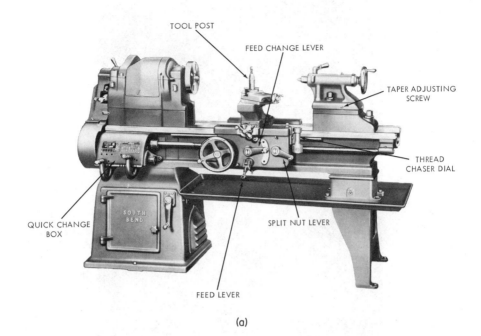

(a)

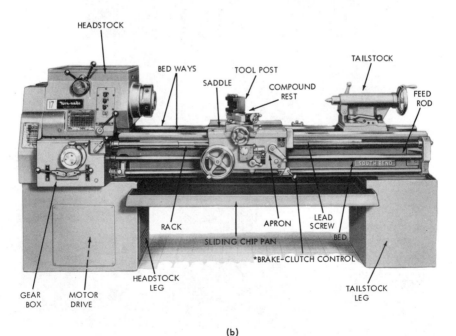

(b)

Figure 13.1 (*Photos courtesy of South Bend Lathe, Inc.*)

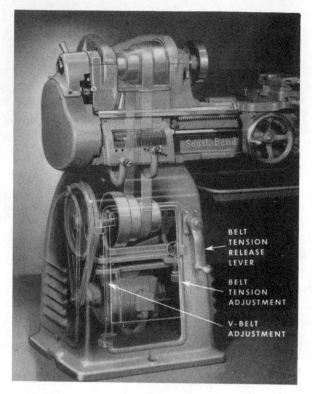

(c)

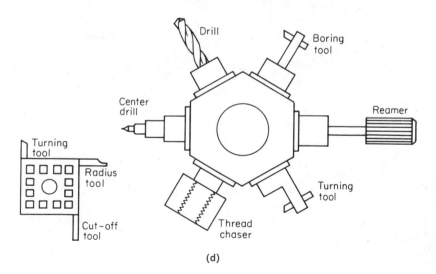

(d)

Figure 13.1 (Cont.)

through the use of belts or speed selectors. Many lathes are equipped with rheostats for a wider selection of spindle speeds. The longitudinal and cross feeds may be engaged to feed automatically. The swing of these lathes ranges approximately from 8 to 40 in. The components are shown in Figs. 13.1(b and c).

Turret lathes.   Whether it is the hand-screw machine, the power feed (common turret lathe), semiautomatic, fully automatic, or vertical type, the distinguishing characteristic of the turret lathe is the hexagon turret, Fig. 13.1(d). This turret is fed longitudinally on the bed of the machine, whereas the square turret is mounted on the cross slide and fed at 90° to the hexagonal turret.

The hand-screw machine requires the turret to be hand fed into the work. In the common variety of turret lathe, the indexing of the turret is done by hand. Once indexing has been accomplished, the tool may be fed into the work automatically. The semiautomatic turret lathes are automatic except for the loading and unloading of the work. In this type of turret lathe the operator loads the work and then pushes a button to start the cycle. The machine automatically goes through its cycle, changing spindle speeds, feeds, indexing, etc., according to the way in which it has been set up. Once the cycle is completed, the machine shuts itself off. The operation is repeated. The fully automatic turret lathe operates off long bars. It continues to produce parts until the bars are used up. It may be of the multispindle or single-spindle variety. The vertical turret lathe has its hexagon turret set vertically with the table rotating horizontally. It may be a single or multi-spindle automatic or semiautomatic machine.

13.2. Lathe Components

The major components of a lathe are the headstock, the tailstock, the bed, the saddle, the apron, and the quick-change box [Fig. 13.1(b)].

The headstock is mounted at the left end of the machine and houses the spindle which goes through a cone pulley (for belt-driven machines) or gears (for gear-driven machines). The power is transmitted from the motor through belts to the cone pulley, Fig 13.1(c); or through belts through a pulley to drive the gears in the headstock. The spindle is hollow and tapered to receive a 60° live center or other attachments. The outside of the spindle may be threaded or tapered to receive a drive plate or other attachments. A spindle gear is mounted on the rear of the spindle to transmit power through the change gears to the quick-change box. The gear box distributes the power to the lead screw for threading or to the feed screw for turning. The cone-pulley headstock also houses the back gear lever for slower spindle speeds and high-torque turning. This is accomplished on gear-head machines through a speed-selector dial or levers.

(a)

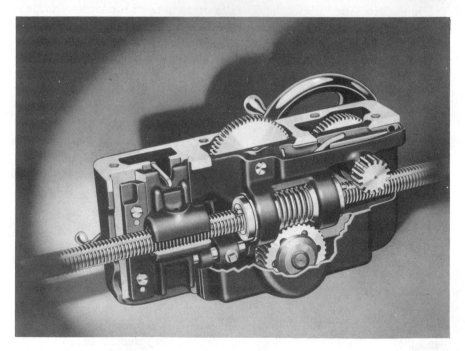

(b)

Figure 13.2 (*Photos courtesy of South Bend Lathe, Inc.*)

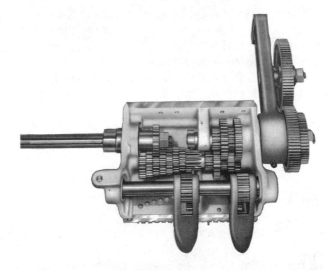

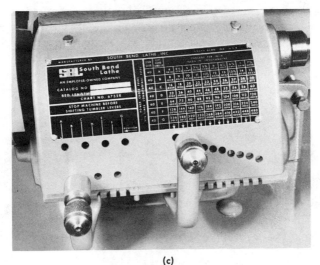

(c)

Figure 13.2   (Cont.)

The tailstock is mounted on the bed at the right end of the machine. It may be slid along the bed to hold different length workpieces between centers. To ensure alignment, one of the ways has a raised "V" which matches a "V" machined into the bottom of the tailstock. It houses the tailstock spindle and the 60° dead center. It is also constructed so that it may be offset, see Chapter 14, for taper turning.

The saddle, Fig. 13.2(a), is mounted on the ways and houses the cross-feed spindle and compound rest. It makes possible longitudinal, cross, and angular feeding of the tool bit.

The assembly of the saddle, apron, and compound is called the *carriage*. The apron, Fig. 13.2(b), is mounted on, and below, the saddle. The view shown is the rear of the apron. It shows the pinion gear which engages the rack for longitudinal feed, the feed clutch, and the split nut used for threading. Figure 13.1(a) shows the front of the apron and the split-nut lever, the feed lever, and the feed-change lever. The thread chaser dial is also shown in Fig. 13.1(a).

Figure 13.1(a) shows as well the quick-change box used for setting feeds for turning or leads for threading. The inside of the box is shown in Fig. 13.2(c).

13.3. Lathe Accessories

Standard accessories are shown in the photographs in Fig. 13.3.

The drive plate is shown in Fig. 13.3(a) for driving work with a lathe dog shown in Fig. 13.3(h). Work is mounted on the faceplate, Fig. 13.3(b). The workpiece may be a casting clamped directly to the plate, or it may be mounted on an angle plate which is then mounted on the faceplate. This plate may also be used to drive a dog. However, in many instances the tail of the dog will not match the slots provided. These plates may be made from cast steel or cast iron. They may have threads machined into them to fit the

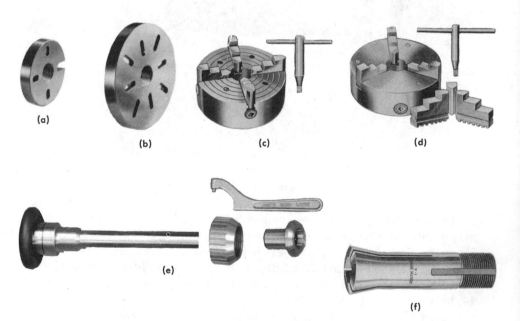

(a)

(b)   (c)   (d)

(e)

(f)

Figure 13.3   *(Photos courtesy of South Bend Lathe, Inc.)*

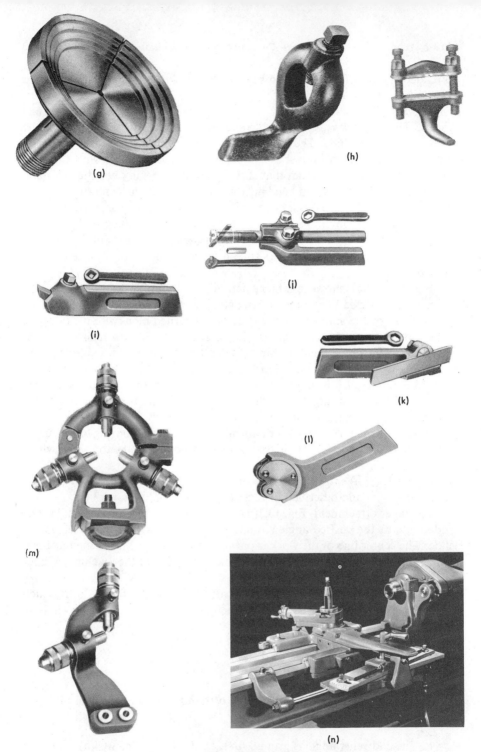

(g)

(h)

(i)

(j)

(k)

(l)

(m)

(n)

Figure 13.3 (Cont.)

threaded spindle. They may also be tapered and keyed or tapered and fitted with prongs to fit the spindle.

Figures 13.3(c and d) show an indepedendent chuck and a universal chuck. These chucks are threaded, tapered, or fitted with prongs to fit the spindle of the machine. The independent chuck shown has four jaws which may be used in the position shown or turned around and used with the steps in the opposite position from that shown. These jaws may be adjusted independently so that work can be aligned to rotate about the center of rotation of the spindle. The universal chuck, Fig. 13.3(d), is constructed so that the three jaws move simultaneously. If operated properly, they will align the work about the center of rotation of the spindle. They cannot be adjusted independently. The alternate jaws shown may also be used in place of those shown mounted.

Figure 13.3(e) shows another method for gripping work. The collet drawbar is inserted at the rear of the spindle, and the collets, Fig. 13.3(f), in the front of the spindle. As the drawbar is turned clockwise it draws the collet into the spindle. This causes the taper on the collet to register against the taper in the collet adapter. Since the collet is split, it will close down on a piece of work which has previously been inserted. The step collet shown in Fig. 13.3(g) may also be used with the drawbar. Since the steps are soft, they may be machined to any desired diameter up to the limit of the flange. This provides a quick method for gripping thin rings.

Figures 13.3(i through l) show a turning-tool holder, a boring bar, a cut off tool, and a knurling tool. These tools may be mounted in the tool post which is shown in Fig. 13.1(a).

Figure 13.3(m) shows two types of support for long work. Both of these rests are shown and described in Figs. 13.6(a and b), Section 13.6.

The taper attachment, Fig. 13.3(n), mounts on the rear of the saddle. The slide is set at the desired angle so that the tool follows the angle set on the slide. The center line of the work is parallel to the center line of the machine. Since the tool is traveling at an angle to the center line of the machine, a taper is cut.

There are other specialized attachments available for a lathe, such as backing-off attachments, tracer attachments, and grinding and milling attachments.

13.4. Grinding a Tool Bit

Figure 13.4 shows the procedure for offhand grinding of a tool bit, such as the tool shown in Fig. 10.4(b).

1. The end relief angle is ground first, as shown in Fig. 13.4(a). The tool is placed flat on the tool rest. The back of the tool is rotated clockwise to give the end cutting angle and down to give the end relief angle.

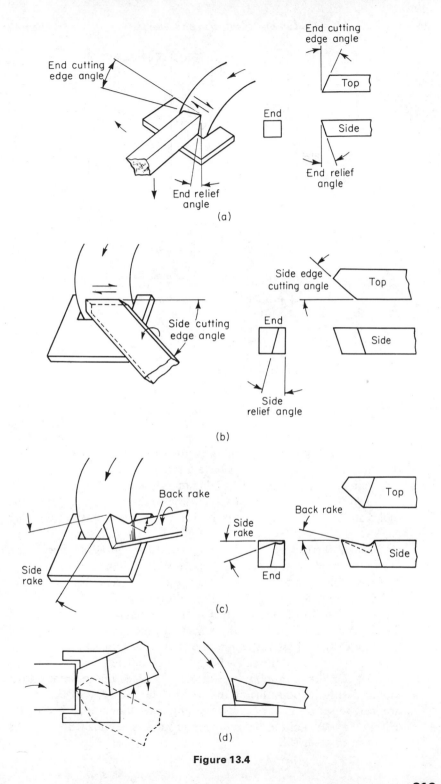

Figure 13.4

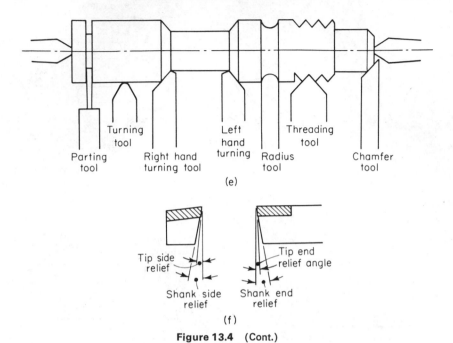

Figure 13.4   (Cont.)

The tool is pushed gently into the grinding wheel. The top and side
view of the tool are shown after they have been ground. Good grinding
practice dictates that the tool be moved across the face of the grinding
wheel. If the tool is held in one position, a groove will be worn into
the wheel and the tool will not have a straight edge.

2. The next step is to grind the side relief and the side cutting-edge angles,
   as shown in Fig. 13.4(b). Once again the tool is placed flat upon the
   tool rest. The rear of the shank is rotated to establish the side relief
   angle and the side cutting-edge angle. With this compound angle
   established, the tool is pushed gently against the grinding wheel. The
   same motion of the tool across the face of the grinding wheel is used.

3. Next the compound rake angle is ground by placing the tool on the
   tool rest, as shown in Fig. 13.4(c). The tool is placed flat on the tool
   rest with the top of the tool facing the grinding wheel. The end of
   the shank is rotated toward the wheel and then rotated as shown in
   Fig. 13.4(c) to establish the compound angle. The tool is pushed against
   the wheel gently until the rakes have been completed.

4. The last step in the grinding operation is to place the tool flat on the
   tool rest with the point facing the wheel. The back end of the tool is
   dropped to set up the end clearance angle, as shown in Fig. 13.4(d).
   With a circular motion, the radius is ground. The finished tool bit is
   shown in Fig. 10.5(b).

Various tool bits are shown in Fig. 13.4(e). Note that a right-hand turning tool operates from right to left and that a left-hand turning tool operates from left to right.

When grinding a tool bit, the student should ask himself which part of the tool bit must be removed by grinding. If the bottom of the shank must be ground away, it should be evident that the portion to be ground away must touch the grinding wheel first. Too often students think in terms of which part of the tool is to remain. The student is further cautioned that he must think carefully about what is to be done. Once the material has been ground away, it cannot be put back.

Several precautions should be taken when grinding a tool bit:

1. As mentioned, the tool bit should be moved to avoid grinding a groove into the wheel and an irregular surface into the tool bit.
2. Never force the tool against the wheel. Grinding requires a gentle pressure. A feel should be developed to avoid overheating the tool.
3. Water should be kept available and used freely. This means that the tool should be dipped frequently. It also means that there must be a facility for placing the tool back into its original position with reference to the grinding wheel before grinding started. If the tool is not replaced in its original position, facets will be ground into the tool. The ground surface must be continuous.
4. Overheating should be avoided at all cost. It softens the cutting edge.
5. Do not grind on the side of the wheel. The wheel is constructed to take radial pressures only. Grinding on the side of the wheel is dangerous. Grinding goggles should be used to avoid grinding dust getting in the student's eyes.

When grinding carbide or ceramic tools, special grinding wheels must be used which will be discussed in Chapter 21 on grinding. Since the tips are brazed into a soft shank, the soft portion below the carbide tip is ground away first on a "regular" grinding wheel. The appropriate reliefs and clearances are then ground into the carbide insert, as shown in Fig. 13.3(f).

13.5. Turning a Cylinder

One of the fundamental uses of a lathe is the turning of cylinders between centers. The ends of the bar must be prepared for centering. They are scribed with a hermaphrodite caliper, Fig. 9.2(c), or a centering head, shown in Fig. 13.5(a). The result of scribing with hermaphrodite calipers is shown in Fig. 13.5(b), and the result of scribing with a centering head is shown in Fig. 13.5(c).

A punch is used to punch the center of the scribed lines. The indentation

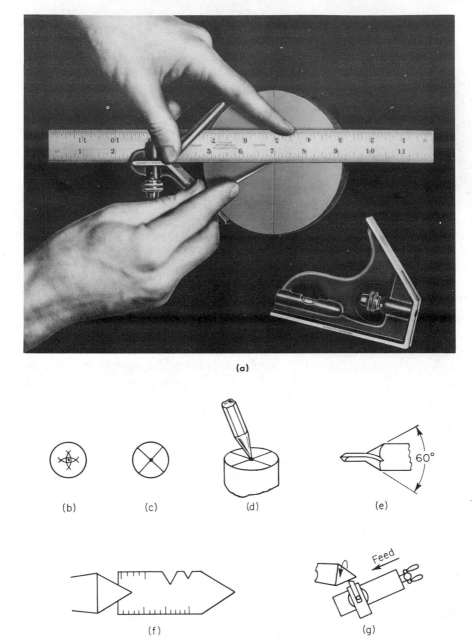

(a)

(b)   (c)   (d)   (e)

(f)   (g)

Figure 13.5   *(Photo courtesy of The L.S. Starrett Company.)*

is examined. If it is not in the center of the scribed lines, the punch is angled and struck again lightly. See Fig. 13.5(d). Once the punch mark is in the desired position, the punch is placed in an upright position and struck sharply. The process is repeated at the opposite end of the work.

Both ends of the workpiece are then drilled with a combination center drill-countersink tool in a drill press. The combination tool is shown in Fig. 13.5(e).

The entire operation may be accomplished by mounting the workpiece in a collet or chuck so that its center of rotation is established and may therefore be picked up easily with the center drill-countersink tool from the tailstock. The need for layout, centerpunching, etc., is eliminated.

The headstock of the lathe has the center mounted in the spindle. This center is called a *live* center because it rotates with the work. The tailstock spindle is fitted with the *dead* center, which is so named because it does not rotate with the work. Since the live center must rotate true and since it rotates with the work, it is not hardened. Thus, if the 60° included angle of this center needs correcting or if it should not run true when mounted in the spindle, its soft state ensures that both or either of these conditions can be corrected. The 60° angle may be tested with the 60° center gage shown in Fig. 13.5(f).

If the 60° angle is found to be incorrect or if the center "runs out," these conditions may be corrected as follows: The compound rest is set at the desired angle, as shown in Fig. 13.5(g). A tool bit is put into the tool post and set on the centerline of the live center. The carriage longitudinal direction is then secured by clamping. By using the compound feed knob, the tool is moved to cut the desired 60°.

Since the dead center in the tailstock does not revolve with the work, it must be hardened because it acts like a bearing surface for the center in the workpiece. For this reason also it must be lubricated. White lead is often used.

Sometimes this dead center becomes scored from friction. To machine this hardened center, a grinding attachment is mounted in place of the tool bit in Fig. 13.5(g). The procedure for grinding the dead center is the same as for turning the live center.

Dead centers are hardened, or they may have carbide inserts for better service. Ball-bearing centers may also be used in the tailstock. These last centers rotate with the work and eliminate the friction and resulting heat which develops with stationary centers.

Once the centers have been trued, it becomes necessary to check their alignment when mounted in the machine. A test bar is fitted with a dog and mounted between centers, as shown in Fig. 13.6. Since the tool feeds parallel to the center line of the ways, the line generated by the tool must always be parallel to an imaginary line between the centers of the lathe. If this is true, the tool will turn a true cylinder. A cut is taken at the tailstock end of the testbar and then at the headstock end of the testbar, as shown in Fig. 13.6. Both diameters are measured with a micrometer. If they are the same size, the centers are aligned. If diameter *A* is smaller than diameter *B*, the tailstock must be adjusted toward the rear of the machine with the taper adjusting screw, Fig. 13.1(a). If diameter *A* is greater than *B*, the adjustment is made toward the operator. These adjustments are shown in Fig. 13.6.

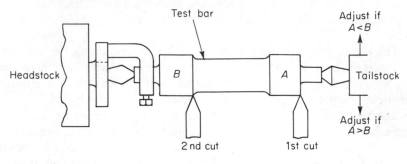

Figure 13.6

Two precautions should be taken when mounting the work between centers:

1. The center holes in the work must be clean and smooth and have an angle of 60° bearing surface, large enough to be consistent with the diameter of the work.
2. The drilled hole created by the combination center drill-countersink must be deep enough so that the 60° points of the live and dead centers do not rest at the bottom of the drilled hole. Bearing must take place on the 60° countersunk surface.

The testbar is removed. The work is mounted between centers. The tool bit is mounted in the tool post so that the point of the tool is on the center line of the work, as shown in Fig. 13.7(b).

Figures 13.7(c and d) are exaggerated. In Fig. 13.7(c) the tool is set too high and will be destroyed because of the friction generated. In Fig. 13.7(d) the tool is set too low and will dull rapidly. In both instances all the care taken in grinding relief and clearance angles, rake angles, etc., will have been canceled out.

The following illustrated examples will serve to show the effect of setting a tool above or below the center line of the work.

The angular change θ, Fig. 13.7(a), may be calculated with the equation

$$\sin \theta = \frac{O_f}{r}$$

θ = angular change
O_f = offset
r = radius of work

EXAMPLE 1

Assume a work diameter of 1.000 in., a positive back rake angle of 12°, and a front relief angle of 7°. These conditions are shown in Fig. 13.7(b). What is the effect on these angles when the tool is raised 0.030in. above the center line of the work, as shown in Fig. 13.7(c)?

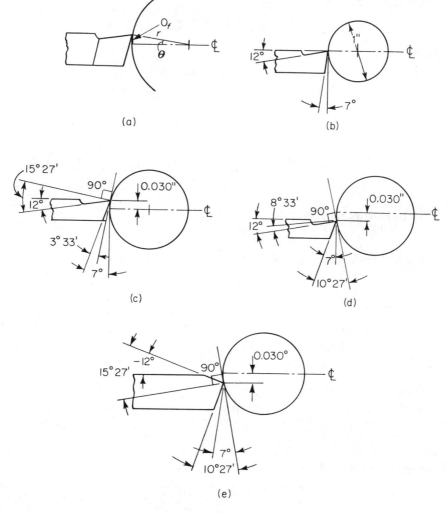

(a)

(b)

(c)

(d)

(e)

Figure 13.7

Solution:

The angular change is

$$\sin \theta = \frac{O_f}{r} = \frac{0.030}{0.5}$$

$$\theta = 3°27'$$

$O_f = 0.030$ in.
$r = 0.500$ in.

The actual front relief angle is

$$7° - 3°27' = 3°33'$$

The actual back rake angle is

$$12° + 3°27' = 15°27'$$

EXAMPLE 2

Assume the tool in Example 1 is set below the center line of the work, as shown in Fig. 13.7(d). What is the effect on the relief and the rake angles?

Solution:

The angular change will be

$$\sin \theta = \frac{-0.030}{0.500}$$

$$\theta = -3°27'$$

$O_f = -0.030$ in.
$r = 0.500$ in.

The actual front relief is

$$7° - (-3°27') = 10°27'$$

The actual back rake angle is

$$12° + (-3°27') = 8°33'$$

EXAMPLE 3

Assume all the conditions in Example 2 except that the back rake is negative. What is the effect on the relief and rake angles in Fig. 13.7(e)?

Solution:

The angular change is

$$\sin \theta = \frac{-0.030}{0.500}$$

$$\theta = -3°27'$$

$O_f = -0.030$ in.
$r = 0.500$ in.

The actual relief angle is

$$7° - (-3°27') = 10°27'$$

The actual back rake angle is

$$-12° + (-3°27') = -15°27'$$

The solution when the negative rake tool is set 0.030 in. above center is left to the student.

After the tool bit is properly positioned, the work is caused to revolve. Very carefully the work is touched with the tool bit. The carriage is moved to the right until the tool clears the work. Once the tool is free from the work, it is moved in approximately 0.010 in. on the dial. This depends upon how much material is to be removed from the diameter of the work. A light trial cut is taken. The carriage is once again moved toward the tailstock *without destroying the dial setting. This dial setting becomes the reference reading for further cutting.*

A micrometer reading is then taken. The remaining material which is to be removed is set on the dial by adding to the reference reading. The machining is completed.

It is good practice to work the diameter down to within 0.010 or 0.020 in. of the finished size. This 0.010 in. or 0.020 in. is then removed as a final finishing cut.

The student is cautioned to test the graduations on the cross-feed graduated dial before he starts to machine the workpiece. A lathe cut of 0.010-in. depth means a reduction of the diameter of 0.020 in. Since the work revolves, 0.010 in. is removed from both sides of the diameter. Some lathe dials are graduated to show a reduction of the work diameter. Others are graduated to show a reduction of the work radius. It is necessary to take a test cut, measure the resulting diameter, take another test cut noting the dial reading, and measure again. The difference in dial readings should be correlated with the difference in micrometer readings.

13.6. Chuck and Faceplate Operations

Chucks, Figs. 13.3(c and d), are convenient devices for holding irregularly shaped workpieces. This is especially true of the independent chuck, Fig. 13.3(c).

The universal chuck, Fig. 13.3(d), is shown in Fig. 13.8(a) holding a piece of work that is being drilled. The workpiece in this position may be drilled, bored, tapped, etc.

If the workpiece is a casting which is to have an offset boss machined, an independent chuck may be used. Figure 13.8(b) shows a cored-hole casting being bored. If desired, a turning tool may be mounted in the tool post in place of the boring bar and the outside of the boss machined. It should be noted that on an engine lathe there is no provision for mounting two tools which may operate together. Both tools may be mounted in a square turret and the desired results obtained by indexing the desired tool into position. The square turret is shown in Fig. 13.8(c).

Another method of mounting nonsymmetrical workpieces is shown in Fig. 13.8(d). An angle plate is bolted to a faceplate. Since this creates an unbalanced condition, a weight must be positioned, as shown in Fig. 13.8(d), to balance the eccentric loading of the faceplate. The hole in the casting is positioned to rotate about the center of rotation of the spindle.

The use of a steady rest for supporting long work was mentioned in Section 13.3. Figure 13.9(a) shows a steady rest mounted on the bed of a lathe supporting the work. The other end of the work should be gripped with a chuck or collet, or both ends may be supported by the lathe centers. Figure

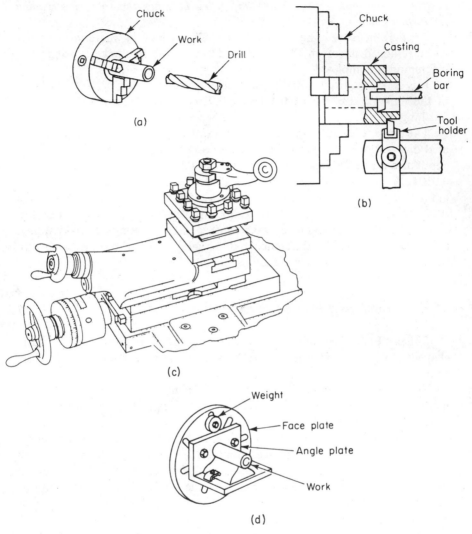

Figure 13.8

13.9(b) shows a follower rest bolted to the saddle of the lathe. This operation requires that both ends of the work be supported. The tool acts as the third support.

Figure 13.9(c) shows a micrometer carriage stop mounted on the lathe bed. It is mounted to the left of the carriage and is used to control the longitudinal stop position of the carriage. This attachment may be used to duplicate a length dimension on workpieces or to prevent overtravel of the longitudinal feed. It should be remembered that the automatic longitudinal feed must be disengaged before the carriage stop is reached and the feed finished by hand. This type of stop will not disengage the automatic lon-

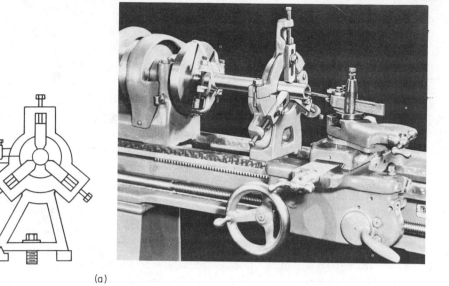

(a)

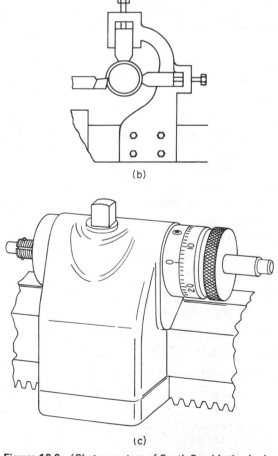

(b)

(c)

Figure 13.9 (*Photo courtesy of South Bend Lathe, Inc.*)

gitudinal feed. There are lathes manufactured which have trip dogs which automatically disengage the feed.

QUESTIONS AND PROBLEMS

13.1 Describe the basic principle of a lathe when used as a machine tool.

13.2 What is meant by "the swing of a lathe"?

13.3 How does a jeweler's lathe differ from a standard bench lathe?

13.4 Describe the three major lathe classifications as described in this text.

13.5 Trace the distribution of power from the motor to the work and to the tool for turning.

13.6 Trace the distribution of power from the motor to the work and to the tool for threading.

13.7 Make a sketch of a cone pulley headstock. Include the back gears.

13.8 What is the function of the back gears?

13.9 What is the purpose of the feed screw? The lead screw? What is the essential difference between the two in the manner in which they drive the tool? Explain.

13.10 What is a live center? Is it hardened? Why?

13.11 What is a dead center? Is it hardened? Why?

13.12 What is the purpose of the saddle? What components are mounted on the saddle? Describe the purpose of each component.

13.13 What is the carriage? What are the components which make up the carriage? What is the purpose of each of the components?

13.14 What is the quick-change box? What is its function? Check one of your lathes, and explain how it is used to drive the tool for turning and threading.

13.15 Describe a universal chuck and an independent chuck. How are they used? How do they differ?

13.16 Describe the use of a split collet. What is a step collet? Check your catalogs. How many types of split collets can you find?

13.17 How many kinds of turning tools can you find in your catalogs?

13.18 How many kinds of turning-tool holders can you find in your catalogs?

13.19 How many boring-tool holders can you find in your catalogs?

13.20 What is a knurling tool?

13.21 How does a backing-off attachment work?

13.22 Describe the grinding of a turning tool which has both back rake and side rake.

13.23 Do the same as in problem 13.22 for grinding a tool which has negative back rake and negative side rake.

13.24 Describe the preparation of both ends of a piece of work for centering.

13.25 Describe the procedure for testing a lathe to ensure that it will turn a true cylinder.

13.26 What are the precautions which must be taken when mounting a cylinder between lathe centers to ensure true cylindrical turning?

13.27 What is the effect on the rake and relief angles of setting a turning tool too high above the center line of the work? Too low?

13.28 Given a work diameter of 4 in., a positive back rake of 12°, a front relief angle of 8°, and an offset of 0.060 in. above center. Calculate the effects of this offset on the various angles of the toolbit.

13.29 Calculate the effects on the tool bit in problem 13.28 if the tool is set 0.060 in. below center.

13.30 Calculate the effect on the tool bit in problem 13.28 if the back rake has a negative angle of 15°.

13.31 Calculate the effect on the toolbit in problem 13.30 if the tool is set 0.060 in. below center.

13.32 Given a work diameter of $2\frac{1}{4}$ in. and a positive back rake angle of 18° and a front relief angle of 10°; what is the effect on these angles if the tool is set 0.040 in. above center?

13.33 Assume the tool in problem 13.32 to be set 0.040 in. below the center line of the work. What is the effect on the positive back rake and front relief angles?

13.34 In problem 13.32 assume the tool has a negative back rake of 18°. What is the effect on the front relief angle and the negative back rake?

13.35 In problem 13.33, if the back rake is negative, what is the effect on the front relief angle and the negative back rake?

13.36 In Example 1 in the body of the text assume the tool has a negative back rake. What is the effect on the relief angle and the rake angle?

13.37 What is the need of determining a reference cross-feed dial setting before starting a turning operation? Describe how you would use this reference reading.

13.38 Describe the use of a faceplate for machining castings.

13.39 What is a steady rest? A follower rest? How are they used?

13.40 Describe the use of a micrometer carriage stop.

13.41 Describe the use of a square turret on an engine lathe?

13.42 When using an angle plate mounted on a face plate, it is necessary to use weights. Why?

The Lathe Operations

14

14.1. Taper Calculations

Taper on a lathe is the difference between two diameters and may be expressed as taper per ft, T_f, or taper per in., T_t. In Fig. 14.1(a) taper per in is the difference in two diameters for a distance of 1 in. of length. If D is the large diameter and d is the small diameter and L is the length, or distance between the two diameters, then

$$T_t = \frac{D - d}{L_t}$$

EXAMPLE 1

Find the taper per in. in Fig. 14.1(a).

Solution:

Taper per in. is

$$T_t = \frac{D - d}{L_t} = \frac{1 - \frac{3}{4}}{1} = \frac{1}{4} \text{ in./in.}$$

$D = 1$ in.
$d = \frac{3}{4}$ in.
$L_t = 1$ in.

Taper per ft is equal to the taper per in. multiplied by 12.

EXAMPLE 2

Find the taper per ft in Fig. 14.1(a).

Solution:

Taper per ft is

$$T_f = \frac{12(D - d)}{L_t} = \frac{12(1 - \frac{3}{4})}{1}$$

$$= 3 \text{ in./ft.}$$

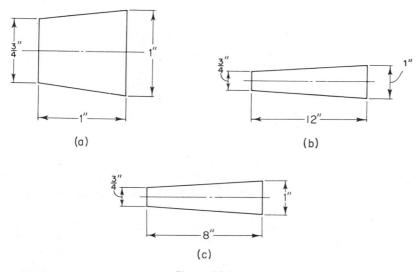

Figure 14.1

This means that taper per ft can be expressed as the difference between two diameters for a distance of 1 ft of length as shown in Fig. 14.1(b).

EXAMPLE 3

In Fig. 14.1(c) find: (1) the taper per in. and (2) the taper per ft.

Solution:

1. The taper per in. is

$$T_t = \frac{D - d}{L_t} = \frac{1 - \frac{3}{4}}{8}$$

$$= \tfrac{1}{32} \text{ in./in.}$$

$D = 1$ in.
$d = \frac{3}{4}$ in.
$L_t = 8$ in.

2. The taper per ft is

$$T_f = \frac{12(D - d)}{L_t} = \frac{12(1 - \frac{3}{4})}{8}$$

$$= \tfrac{3}{8} \text{ in./ft}$$

There are several methods for turning taper on a lathe: the form tool, compound rest, tailstock offset, taper attachment, and tracing. For the purpose of continuity let us study the offset method first.

As noted in the preceding chapter, the tailstock on a lathe may be adjusted to move at right angles to the center line of the bed of the machine. This is called *offset O_f.* Note that in offset the center line of the workpiece is offset and the tool bit traces a line parallel to the center line of the machine. See Fig. 14.2.

It should be noted that the tool cuts one-half of the material off one side of the round piece of work and removes the other half when the work rotates

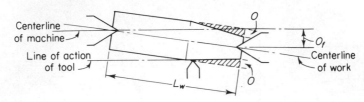

Figure 14.2

180°. Thus the offset O_f is the difference of the two radii, as shown in Fig. 14.2. It is very important to understand that the offset is a function of the angle made by the center line of the work and the center line of the lathe bed. This angle is also a function of the distance between the centers, or the length of the work, L_w.

This offset may be calculated by multiplying the taper per in. by the length of the work and then dividing by 2

$$O_f = \frac{\frac{1}{2}(D - d)L_w}{L_t}$$

O_f = offset
D = large dia.
d = small dia.
L_w = length of work
L_t = length of taper

EXAMPLE 4

Find the offset necessary to cut a taper in Fig. 14.1(c).

Solution:

The offset is

$$O_f = \frac{\frac{1}{2}(D - d)L_w}{L_t} = \frac{\frac{1}{2}(1 - \frac{3}{4})8}{8}$$

$$= \frac{1}{8} \text{ in.}$$

$D = 1$ in.
$d = \frac{3}{4}$ in.
$L_t = 8$ in.
$L_w = 8$ in.

EXAMPLE 5

Find the offset necessary to cut the taper in Fig. 14.3(a).

Solution:

The offset is

$$O_f = \frac{\frac{1}{2}(D - d)L_w}{L_t} = \frac{\frac{1}{2}(1 - \frac{3}{4})14}{8}$$

$$= \frac{7}{32} \text{ in.}$$

$D = 1$ in.
$d = \frac{3}{4}$ in.
$L_t = 8$ in.
$L_w = 14$ in.

EXAMPLE 6

In Fig. 14.3(b) find: (1) the taper per in.: (2) the taper per ft: (3) the offset: (4) the imaginary large diameter: (5) the imaginary small diameter. (6) Using parts (4) and (5), calculate the offset and compare with part (3).

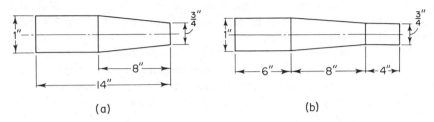

Figure 14.3

Solution:

1. The taper per in. is

$$T_i = \frac{D - d}{L_t} = \frac{1 - \frac{3}{4}}{8}$$

$$= \tfrac{1}{32} \text{ in./in}$$

$D = 1$ in.
$d = \frac{3}{4}$ in.
$L_t = 8$ in.
$L_w = 18$ in.

2. The taper per ft is

$$T_f = 12(\tfrac{1}{32})$$

$$= \tfrac{3}{8} \text{ in./ft}$$

3. The offset is

$$O_f = \frac{\frac{1}{2}(D - d)L_w}{L_t} = \frac{\frac{1}{2}(1 - \frac{3}{4})18}{8}$$

$$= \tfrac{9}{32} \text{ in.}$$

4. The imaginary large diameter D_i is

$$D_i = \tfrac{1}{32}(6 + 8) + \tfrac{3}{4}$$

$$= 1\tfrac{3}{16} \text{ in.}$$

5. The imaginary small diameter d_i is

$$d_i = 1 - \tfrac{1}{32}(8 + 4)$$

$$= \tfrac{5}{8} \text{ in.}$$

6. The offset is

$$O_f = \tfrac{1}{2}(D_i - d_i) = \tfrac{1}{2}(1\tfrac{3}{16} - \tfrac{5}{8})$$

$$= \tfrac{9}{32} \text{ in. (Check)}$$

14.2. Taper Turning

In all instances of taper turning the operation is started with the center line of the work and the center line of the machine parallel to each other. After the taper has been set, it is good practice to take a trial cut, check the taper, and then make the appropriate adjustment if needed.

In the *form-tool method* of taper turning, the centerline of the work remains parallel to the center line of the bed of the machine. The tool is fed into the work which causes the taper to be formed. See Fig. 14.4(a). It is obvious that this method can be used only for turning small tapers and is particularly appropriate for chamfering.

When the *compound rest* is used, the work center line remains parallel to the bed of the machine center line. The compound rest is offset the required amount, the carriage is locked into position, and the compound feed screw is used to feed the tool at the required angle, as shown in Fig. 14.4(b). The operation is usually manual.

The *tailstock method*, as has already been indicated, requires that the center line of the workpiece be offset from the center line of the machine bed. The tool traces a path parallel to the center line of the machine bed. The offset of the tailstock may be toward the rear of the machine, Fig. 14.4(c), in which case the large end of the taper will be at the tailstock end of the work. If the offset is toward the front of the machine, Fig. 14.4(d), the small end of the taper will be at the tailstock end of the machine.

The offset of the tailstock may be accomplished in several ways. If a master taper is available, it may be set into the machine. With a dial indicator needle touching the master, the carriage is moved longitudinally. If the needle reads 0-0, the offset has been achieved. The work may then be substituted for the master taper. The tool bit will trace the same path as the dial indicator needle and cut the desired taper.

Offset may also be accomplished by measuring the offset between the live and dead centers of the machine. A trial cut is taken, and the appropriate adjustment is made if needed.

The desired taper may also be set by using a dial indicator. With the center line of the work and the center line of the machine bed parallel to each other a dial indicator held in the tool post and touching the tailstock (usually the spindle in the tailstock) is set at zero. The cross feed is retracted (or fed in) the offset amount. Then the tailstock is offset toward the indicator needle. When the indicator needle once again reads zero, the offset has been accomplished. A trial cut must be used to verify the setting.

The taper attachment, Fig. 13.3(n), is operated with the center line of the work parallel to the center line of the machine bed. In this instance the tool is caused to move at an angle with the work. The tool holder is actuated by

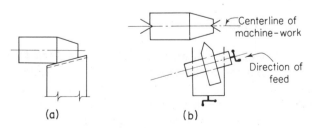

(a)   (b)

Figure 14.4

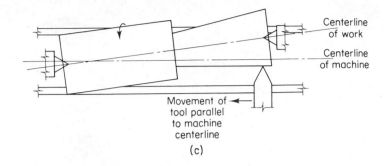

Centerline of work

Centerline of machine

Movement of tool parallel to machine centerline

(c)

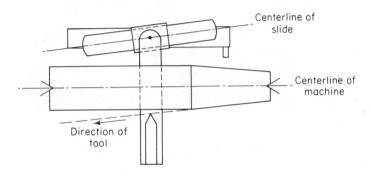

Centerline of slide

Centerline of machine

Direction of tool

(d)

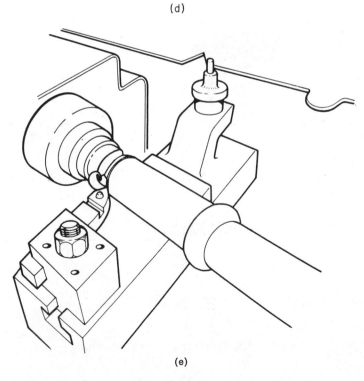

(e)

Figure 14.4 (Cont.)

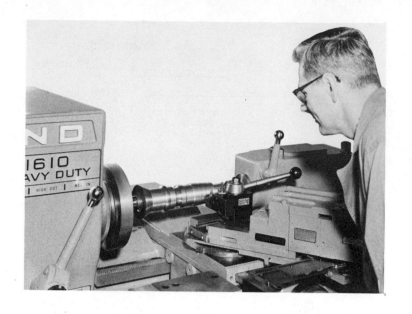

TOP VIEW

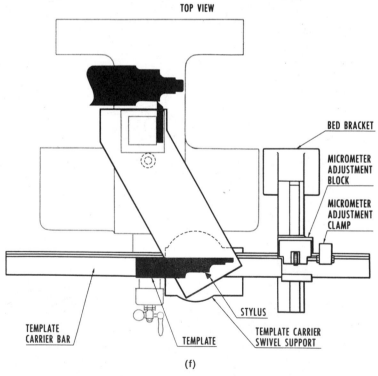

BED BRACKET

MICROMETER ADJUSTMENT BLOCK

MICROMETER ADJUSTMENT CLAMP

STYLUS

TEMPLATE CARRIER SWIVEL SUPPORT

TEMPLATE CARRIER BAR

TEMPLATE

(f)

Figure 14.4 (Cont.) [*Courtesy of LeBlond, Inc.*]

a dovetail slide which may be set at the desired taper per ft, or angle. See Fig. 14.4(d).

The tracer attachment is another device for contour turning. It operates off a template through a stylus transducer [See Fig. 14.4(e).]. The pressure against the stylus is amplified through a booster system. This amplified pressure actuates a piston which controls the cross-feed motion of the tool. The longitudinal motion of the lathe is set at a constant right to left feed. If the combined motion of the longitudinal feed and the controlled cross feed are set properly, the desired contour is cut.

To illustrate, if the longitudinal feed and the cross feed are moving with the same speed, the tool will cut a 45° angle. A taper is a special kind of contour. Thus, if the tool is caused to retract as it feeds from right to left, a taper will be cut. The tracing attachment is shown in Fig. 14.4(f).

Tapers may also be turned using numerically controlled lathes. These will be discussed in Chapter 20.

14.3. Types of Tapers

Tapers have been standardized. The most commonly used tapers are the Morse, Brown and Sharpe, milling machine quick-releasing, Jacobs, Jarno, and American Standard Self-holding tapers. The data for these tapers are shown in Appendix IV through VIII.

The *Morse taper*, used mostly on lathes and drill presses, has been standardized at $\frac{5}{8}$ in./ft and numbered from 0 to 7 with number 0 the smallest taper. See Appendix Table IV.

The *Brown and Sharpe tapers* range from 1 through 16. The taper is $\frac{1}{2}$in./ft (except for number 10, which is 0.5161 in./ft). This taper is used mostly on milling machines. See Appendix Table V.

The *quick-releasing taper* is used on milling machines and has been standardized at $3\frac{1}{2}$ in./ft. Since this is a rather steep taper, it must be locked into position. These tapers have been numbered from 10 to 60. See Appendix Table VI.

The *Jacobs tapers*, used for taper pins and drill chucks, have been standardized at $\frac{1}{4}$ in./ft. They have been assigned numbers from 0 to 13.

The *Jarno taper*, Appendix Table VII used on profilers and diesinking machines, has been standardized according to the following rules:

$$D = \frac{\text{no. of taper}}{8}$$

$$d = \frac{\text{no. of taper}}{10}$$

$$L_t = \frac{\text{no. of taper}}{2}$$

D = large dia
d = small dia
L_t = length of taper

The taper per ft is 0.600 in./ft.

EXAMPLE 7

Given a number 10 Jarno taper, find: (1) the large diameter; (2) the small diameter; (3) the length of the taper; (4) the taper per ft.

Solution:

1. The large diameter is

$$D = \frac{\text{no. of taper}}{8} = \frac{10}{8}$$

$$= 1\tfrac{1}{4} \text{ in.}$$

2. The small diameter is

$$d = \frac{\text{no. of taper}}{10} = \frac{10}{10}$$

$$= 1 \text{ in.}$$

3. The length of the taper is

$$L_t = \frac{\text{no. of taper}}{2} = \frac{10}{2}$$

$$= 5 \text{ in.}$$

4. The taper per ft is

$$T_f = \frac{12(D - d)}{L_t} = \frac{12(1\tfrac{1}{4} - 1)}{5}$$

$$= \tfrac{3}{5} \text{ in./ft} = 0.600 \text{ in./ft}$$

The American Standard self-holding taper series is made up from the three sizes taken from the Brown and Sharpe series, eight sizes taken from the Morse Taper series and eleven sizes taken from the $\tfrac{3}{4}$ in./ft taper series. It should be noted that the larger diameter size in this table refers to the gage line diameter.

14.4. Thread Standards

Threads have been standardized in several classifications, such as the American National Thread series, the Society of Automotive Engineers (SAE) Thread series, the Unified Thread series, the Acme Thread series and the American Pipe Thread series, etc. Much of the nomenclature which follows applies to all threads.

Figure 14.5(a) shows the thread parts for an external and internal thread. The major diameter D is the largest diameter of the thread. The minor diameter M is the smallest diameter of the thread. The tap drill size TD is the minor diameter of the internal thread and is used in selecting the appropriate drill size for machining (tapping) the thread. The pich diameter P is the diameter of an imaginary cylinder which passes through a thread so that the

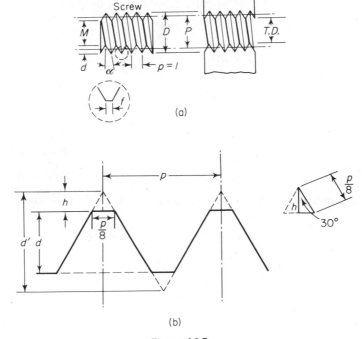

Figure 14.5

width of the space and the thickness of the tooth at the cutting plane are equal.

The depth d of a thread is the difference between one-half the major and minor diameters. The pitch p is the distance from a point on one thread to the same point on an adjacent thread. The lead l is the linear distance a thread moves in one turn when in contact with its mating thread. Thus for a single thread (one start) the pitch is equal to the lead; for a double thread, the lead is twice the pitch; etc.

The helix angle α is the angle between a plane perpendicular to the axis of a thread and the helix of the thread at the pitch diameter.

14.5. Thread Calculations

The symbol $\frac{1}{2}''$-20 is read "$\frac{1}{2}$-in. major diameter, 20 threads per in." See Appendix Chart IX for additional thread standards.

American National Standard Thread. If N is the number of threads to the in. then $1/N$ is the pitch p.

$$p = \frac{1}{N}$$

To find the constant for calculating the depth of a thread, the small h must be calculated. This is the truncation created by the definition

$$f = \frac{p}{8}$$

In the small triangle inset in Fig. 14.5(a) the altitude is

$$h = \frac{p}{8} \cos 30° = \frac{p}{8}(0.866)$$

$$= 0.10825p$$

Also the depth of the sharp V is

$$d' = p \cos 30°$$

$$= 0.866p$$

The depth of the American National Standard is

M = minor dia screw
D = major dia
N = no. threads per in.
P = pitch dia
p = pitch
h = altitude of incomplete triangle
d = depth
d' = depth of sharp V
TD = tap drill size
α = helix angle
f = width of flat

$$d = d' - 2h = 0.866p - 2(0.10825)p$$

$$= 0.6495p = \frac{0.6495}{N}$$

The minor diameter of the screw is

$$M = D - 2\left(\frac{0.6495}{N}\right)$$

The pitch diameter is

$$P = D - \left(\frac{0.6495}{N}\right)$$

The minor diameter of the nut (tap drill size) is

$$TD = D - 2\left(\frac{0.6495}{N}\right)75\%$$

The helix angle is

$$\tan \alpha = \frac{\text{lead}}{\pi P}$$

The minor diameter of the American National *internal* thread may be anywhere from 55 to 85% of the full depth of the thread. The most commonly used percentage is 75% of the full depth of the thread.

EXAMPLE 8

Given a $\frac{1}{4}$-20 thread to calculate: (1) the pitch-(2) the width of the flat; (3) the depth of the thread; (4) the minor diameter of the screw; (5) the pitch diameter; (6) the tap drill size; (7) the helix angle.

Solution:

1. The pitch is

$$p = \frac{1}{N} = \frac{1}{20}$$

N = 20 thds/in.
D = 0.250 in.

$$= 0.050 \text{ in.}$$

2. The width of the flat is

$$f = \frac{p}{8} = \frac{0.050}{8}$$

$$= 0.00625 \text{ in}$$

3. The depth of the thread is

$$d = \frac{0.6495}{N} = \frac{0.6495}{20}$$

$$= 0.0325 \text{ in.}$$

4. The minor diameter of the screw is

$$M = D - 2\left(\frac{0.6495}{N}\right) = D - 2d = 0.250 - 2(0.0325)$$

$$= 0.185 \text{ in.}$$

5. The pitch diameter is

$$P = D = \frac{0.6495}{N} = D - d = 0.2500 - 0.0325$$

$$= 0.2175 \text{ in.}$$

6. The tap drill size is

$$TD = D - 2d(75\%) = 0.250 - 2(0.0325)\,75\%$$

$$= 0.201 \simeq \#7 \text{ drill (See Appendix.)}$$

7. The helix angle is

$$\tan \alpha = \frac{\text{lead}}{\pi P} = \frac{0.050}{\pi(0.2175)} = 0.073$$

$$\alpha = 4.2°$$

Unified Thread.   In 1945 Canada, England, and the United States came to an agreement on standards which were to be applied to thread systems. The systems will best be demonstrated with an example referenced to Fig. 14.6(a and b).

EXAMPLE 9

Given a 1½-6 UNC (Unified National Coarse) thread, to calculate: (1) The depth of the sharp V thread; (2) the depth of the external thread; (3) the flat on the crest of the external thread; (4) the truncation of the crest (external); (5) the truncation of the root (external); (6) the addendum (external); (7) the depth of the thread (internal); (8) the flat across the crest (internal); (9) the flat across the root (internal); (10) the truncation of the crest (internal); (11) the truncation of the root (internal); (12) the pitch diameter; (13) the minor diameter (external); (14) the minor diameter (internal); (15) the helix angle.

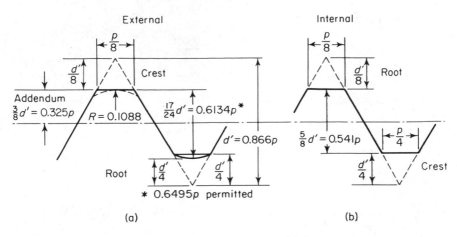

Figure 14.6

Solution:

1. The depth of the sharp V thread is

$$d' = \frac{0.866}{N} = \frac{0.866}{6}$$

$$= 0.1443 \text{ in.}$$

$N = 6$

2. The depth of the thread (external) is

$$d_e = \frac{0.6134}{N} = \frac{0.6134}{6}$$

$$= 0.1022 \text{ in.}$$

3. The width of the flat across the crest (external) is

$$f_e = \frac{p}{8} = \frac{1}{8N} = \frac{1}{8(6)}$$

$$= 0.0208 \text{ in.}$$

4. The truncation of the crest (external) is

$$h_{ec} = \frac{d'}{8} = \frac{0.1443}{8}$$

$$= 0.018 \text{ in.}$$

5. The truncation of the root (external) is

$$h_{er} = \frac{d'}{6} = \frac{0.1443}{6}$$

$$= 0.0241 \text{ in.}$$

6. The addendum (external) is

$$A_e = \frac{3}{8} d' = \frac{3}{8}(0.1443)$$

$$= 0.0541 \text{ in.}$$

7. The depth of the thread (internal) is

$$d_i = \frac{0.5413}{N} = \frac{0.5413}{6}$$

$$= 0.0902$$

8. The flat across the crest (internal) is

$$f_{ic} = \frac{p}{4} = \frac{1}{4N} = \frac{1}{4(6)}$$

$$= 0.0417 \text{ in.}$$

9. The flat across the root (internal) is

$$f_{ir} = \frac{p}{8} = \frac{1}{8N} = \frac{1}{8(6)}$$

$$= 0.0208 \text{ in.}$$

10. The truncation of the crest (internal) is

$$h_{ic} = \frac{d'}{4} = \frac{0.1443}{4}$$

$$= 0.0361 \text{ in.}$$

11. The truncation of the root (internal) is

$$h_{ir} = \frac{d'}{8} = \frac{0.1443}{8}$$

$$= 0.0180 \text{ in.}$$

12. The pitch diameter is

$$P = D - 2A = 1.500 - 2(0.0541)$$

$$= 1.3918 \text{ in.}$$

13. The minor diameter (external) is

$$M_e = D - 2\left(\frac{0.6134}{N}\right) = 1.500 - 2\left(\frac{0.6134}{6}\right)$$

$$= 1.2955 \text{ in.}$$

14. The minor diameter (internal) is

$$M_i = D - 2\left(\frac{0.5413}{N}\right) = 1.5000 - 2\left(\frac{0.5143}{6}\right)$$

$$= 1.3286 \text{ in.}$$

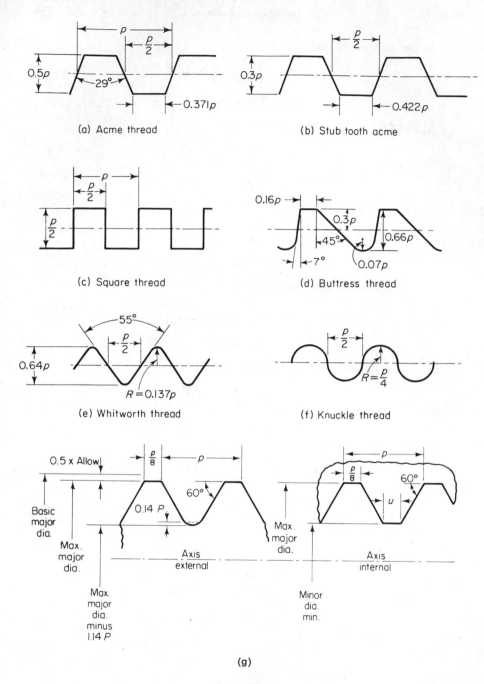

(a) Acme thread

(b) Stub tooth acme

(c) Square thread

(d) Buttress thread

(e) Whitworth thread

(f) Knuckle thread

(g)

Figure 14.7

15. The helix angle is

$$\tan \alpha = \frac{\text{lead}}{\pi P} = \frac{1/N}{\pi P} = \frac{1}{\pi NP} = \frac{1}{\pi(6)(1.3918)} = 0.0381$$

$$\alpha = 2.182°$$

Additional thread forms are shown in Fig. 14.7(a through f).

14.6. Metric Threads

At the time this text was written, the metric thread standards had not been totally established. Several committees had reviewed the possible standardization of metric thread series. The series which has been considered in the forefront for adoption is the IFI-500*. This series establishes two classes; the 6H/5g6g general application series which approximates the Unified class 2A/2B, and the 5H/4g6g close series which approximates the Unified class 3A/3B.

The contour is shown in Fig. 14.7(g). The width of the flat is $p/8$ and the depth of the thread is $p/2$. The included angle is 60°.

The symbol for metric thread may be 3P 0.5. The 3 indicates a nominal size of basic major diameter of 3 mm, P indicates that the thread is metric, and 0.5 mm designates the pitch. When the notation is followed by a C as in 3P 0.5C, it designates a close tolerance thread. No C means a general purpose thread. The letter A represents an external thread and letter B an internal thread. Thus 3P 0.5A is an external thread, whereas 3P 0.5B is an internal thread. Appendix X shows the proposed dimensions for this series of metric threads for external and internal gages.

14.7. Three-Wire Measurements

There are several methods for checking threads to different degrees of accuracy: thread micrometers, thread gages, etc. One of the most accurate methods for checking pitch diameter is the three-wire method, Fig. 14.8. If the proper size wire is used, the wire will be tangent to the side of the thread at the pitch line. This wire is called the *best wire* size, or

$$G = \frac{0.57735}{N}$$

The equation for the pitch diameter is

$$P = m + \frac{0.86603}{N} - 3G$$

G = best wire size
N = no. of threads/in.
m = measurement over wires
P = pitch dia
$\alpha = \frac{1}{2}$ included thread angle

*IFI Industrial Fasteners Institute

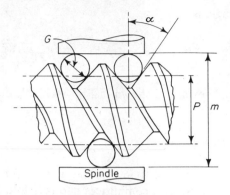

Figure 14.8

The best wire size for any thread is

$$G = \frac{\sec \alpha}{2N}.$$

Another form of the three-wire equation is used if the major diameter is known.

$$m = \left(D - \frac{0.6495}{N}\right) - \frac{0.86603}{N} + 3G$$

$$= D - \frac{1.51553}{N} + 3G$$

EXAMPLE 10

Calculate: (1) the best wire size for a National Standard thread 1″-8NC and (2) the measurement over the wires.

Solution:

1. The best wire size is

$$G = \frac{0.57735}{N} = \frac{0.57735}{8} \qquad\qquad N = 8 \text{ thds/in.}$$
$$ = 0.0722 \text{ in.} \qquad\qquad\qquad \alpha = 30°$$
$$\phantom{G = 0.0722 \text{ in.}} \qquad\qquad D = 1.000 \text{ in.}$$

2. The measurement over the wires is

$$m = P - \frac{0.86603}{N} + 3G$$

$$= \left(D - \frac{0.6495}{N}\right) - \frac{0.86603}{N} + 3G$$

$$= \left(1.000 - \frac{0.6495}{8}\right) - \frac{0.86603}{8} + 3(0.0722)$$

$$= 1.027 \text{ in.}$$

EXAMPLE 11

Check the measurement (m) over wires in Example 10 using the equation above.

Solution:

$$m = D - \frac{1.51553}{N} + 3G$$

$D = 1.000$ in.
$N = 8$ thds/in.

$$= 1.000 - \frac{1.51553}{8} + 3(0.0722)$$

$$= 1.027 \text{ in. (Check)}$$

14.8. Gear Trains for Cutting Threads

Assume a lathe is not equipped with a quick-change box for rapid selection of a gear ratio. It then becomes necessary to calculate this gear train.

The principle is to select a gear train such that the movement of the tool bears a relationship to the rotation of the work. Thus, if the work revolves 10 times for each inch of movement of the tool, the lathe will cut 10 threads/in. The number of threads cut on the work depends upon the number of revolutions the work makes with each inch of travel of the tool. This can be accomplished with the change gears shown in Fig. 14.9(a).

The change gears are the stud, screw, and intermediate. Since the power enters the stud gear first, that gear is the driving gear and must drive the small intermediate gear. The large intermediate gear is also a driving gear and is keyed to the small intermediate gear. The screw gear is a driven gear.

At this point something must be said about simple and compound gear trains. In Fig. 14.9(b) are shown two gears arranged in a *simple gear train*. Assume the 48T gear to be a driver gear, then the 24T gear is the driven gear. If the 48T gear moves one tooth, the 24T gear must move one tooth. If the 48T gear moves 48 teeth, then the 24T gear moves 48 teeth. But 48 teeth on the driver gear is 1 revolution and 48 teeth on the driven gear is 2 revolutions. The driver-driven ratio is 1 : 2.

In Fig. 14.9(c) 48 teeth on the driver gear moves 48 teeth on the idler, which in turn moves the driven gear 48 teeth. Again, as far as the driver and driven gears are concerned, the ratio is still 1 : 2. This intermediate gear, called the *idler*, has no effect on the driver-driven ratio. It should be noted that the direction of rotation of the driver and the driven gears *is* affected. In Fig. 14.9(b) the driver gear rotates clockwise and drives the driven gear counterclockwise. In Fig. 14.9(c) the driver again rotates clockwise, but the driven gear also rotates clockwise.

In Fig. 14.9(d) a driver-driven gear train is shown with a compound intermediate set of two gears keyed to the same shaft. In this arrangement, if the 48T driver gear moves 48 teeth, it will move the 32T gear 48 teeth. This represents $1\frac{1}{2}$ revolutions of the 32T gear. Since the 64T gear also turns $1\frac{1}{2}$ revolutions, it must move 96 teeth in $1\frac{1}{2}$ revolutions. This 64T gear becomes the driver gear for the 24T gear. If the 24T gear moves 96 teeth, it must rotate 4 revolutions. Therefore, 1 revolution of the 48T gear causes 4 revolutions of the 24T gear, or a ratio of 1 : 4.

Note that the compound, as a unit, affects the direction of rotation of the two end gears and acts like an idler.

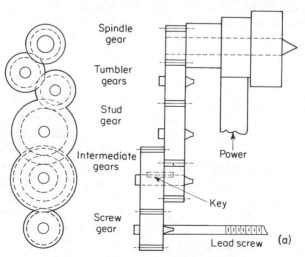

Figure 14.9 *(Photo courtesy of South Bend Lathe, Inc.)*

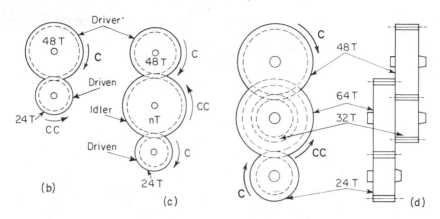

Figure 14.9   (Cont.)

In summation, an idler gear affects the direction of rotation of the two end gears but does not affect the ratio of one gear to the other. This is true no matter how many idlers are placed between the two end gears. In a compound arrangement, the direction of rotation of the two end gears is affected. The compound acts like an idler. In addition, the compound affects the ratio of the two end gears.

In order to calculate a gear train, the operator must first determine the constant. This is accomplished by selecting change gears having a 1:1 ratio. The gears are placed in the appropriate position on the lathe. If the number of threads cut is 8, the lathe constant is 8.

Each lathe is furnished with a set of change gears. Assume one of each of the following gears is furnished according to a gear progression. Thus a set of change gears having a progression of 4 will have gears with 24, 28, 32, . . . , 100 gear teeth. Therefore, if it is desirable to determine whether or not a gear belongs to an available train, it is only necessary to divide the number of teeth of the desired gear by the progression constant. If this constant divides into the number of teeth evenly, that gear is furnished with the set of gears.

The formula for calculating the gear train is

$$\frac{\text{Lathe constant}}{\text{Threads per inch required}} = \frac{\text{driver gear}}{\text{driven gear}}$$

EXAMPLE 12

Calculate the gears necessary to cut 16 threads/in. The lathe constant is 10, the gear progression is 4, and the gears available are 24, 28, 32, . . . 100.

Solution:

$$\frac{\text{Lathe Constant}}{\text{Threads per inch required}} = \frac{10}{16}$$

Since there are no 10 and 16 tooth gears, the numerator and the denomi-

nator must be multiplied by a constant which does not change the ratio of
10:16.

$$\frac{\text{Driver}}{\text{Driven}} = \frac{10}{16} \times \frac{4}{4} = \frac{40\text{T}}{64\text{T}}$$

The gear train appears as shown in Fig. 14.10.

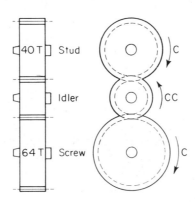

Figure 14.10

EXAMPLE 13

Find the gears needed to cut 30 threads/in. The lathe constant is 8, and the
gear progression is 5. The gears available are 25, 30, 35, . . . , 100.

Solution:

$$\frac{\text{Driver}}{\text{Driven}} = \frac{8}{30} = \frac{2 \times 15}{6 \times 15} \times \frac{4 \times 10}{5 \times 10} = \frac{30 \times 40}{90 \times 50}$$

It should be noted that there is no multiplier for 8 and 30 which will yield
gears to match those available. The factors of 8 and 30 do have multipliers
which will give the available gears. The product of all the driving gears and
the product of all the driven gears can be reduced to the original ratio. The
gear train arrangement has the four possibilities shown in Fig. 14.11.

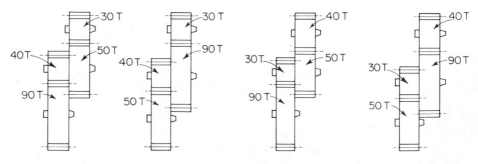

Figure 14.11

Metric-thread gear trains may be calculated as follows: There are 25.4 mm/in. Therefore,

$$\frac{\text{Lathe constant}}{25.4/\text{lead (mm)}} = \frac{\text{lathe constant} \times \text{lead(mm)} \times 5}{25.4 \times 5}$$

$$= \frac{\text{lathe constant} \times \text{lead(mm)} \times 5}{127}$$

This means that a special gear of 127 teeth is needed to cut a metric thread on an English lathe.

EXAMPLE 14

Calculate the gear train needed to cut a 3-mm thread on an English lathe. The lathe constant is 8, the gear progression is 4, and the gears available are 24, 28, 32, . . . , 100.

Solution:

$$\frac{\text{Driver}}{\text{Driven}} = \frac{\text{lathe constant} \times \text{lead(mm)} \times 5}{127}$$

$$= \frac{8 \times 3 \times 5}{127} = \frac{40 \times 3}{127 \times 1}$$

$$= \frac{40 \times 1}{127 \times 1} \times \frac{3 \times 24}{1 \times 24}$$

$$= \frac{40 \times 72}{127 \times 24}$$

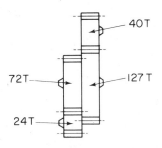

Figure 14.12

One possible gear train is shown in Fig. 14.12.

Figure 14.12

14.9. Cutting a Thread

After the appropriate gears are selected (or the quick-change box set) and installed on the machine, the threading tool is ground to a perfect 60° included angle using the center gage shown in Fig. 14.13(a). Appropriate front relief and side clearance are ground. The tool is then set on center, Fig. 14.13(b), and at 90° to the center line of the work, Fig. 14.13(a). Tapered threads are set at 90° to the center line of the work.

The compound rest is then set at 29° (especially for deep threads), as shown in Fig. 14.13(c). This permits feeding at 29° and causes the tool to cut on the left cutting edge only, Fig. 14.13(d). This permits rough cuts without too much tool surface being in contact with the work. If this method is used, several finishing cuts must be taken with the cross feed. This has the effect of using the tool as a 60° form tool and permits cleaning up the right side of the thread while the 60° angle is being corrected.

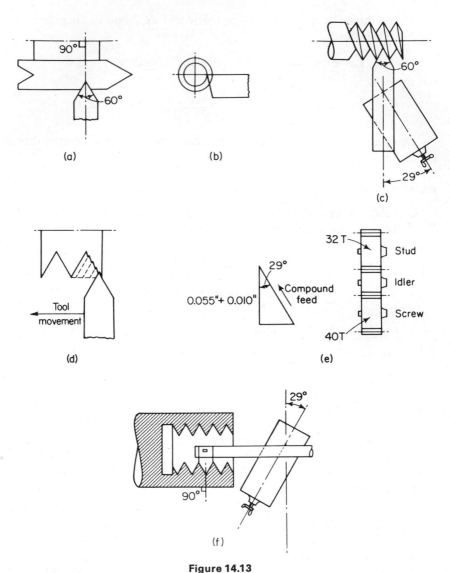

Figure 14.13

EXAMPLE 15

You are asked to cut a $\frac{3}{4}''$-10 NC (National Coarse) thread on a lathe having a lathe constant of 8, a progression of 4, and gears 24, 28, 32, . . . , 100. (1) Find the gear train and show each gear's position. (2) If the compound is to be set at 29° and roughing and finishing cuts are to be taken, how much is to be cut with the compound (roughing) rest if 0.010 in. is to remain for finishing?

Solution:

1. The gears are, Fig. 14.13(e).

$$\frac{\text{Driver}}{\text{Driven}} = \frac{8}{10} = \frac{8 \times 4}{10 \times 4} = \frac{32}{40}$$

2. The depth of the thread is

$$d = \frac{0.6495}{10} = 0.065 \text{ in.}$$

The rough cut should be

$$0.065 - 0.010 = 0.055 \text{ in.}$$

The equivalent feed at 29° is

$$d_{29°} = \frac{0.055}{\cos 29°} = \frac{0.055}{0.8746} = 0.063 \text{ in depth}$$

If each roughing cut removes approximately 0.010 in., approximately six cuts are needed for roughing. If 0.002 in. is removed for each finishing cut, five cuts are needed to finish the thread.

Internal threads are set as shown in Fig. 14.13(f) by using the same principle that is used for external thread cutting.

A thread chaser dial, Fig. 13.1(a), permits engaging the carriage so that the tool will pick up the lead of the thread after each cut is taken.

14.10. Multiple and Left-Hand Threads

It was pointed out earlier that a single thread has its pitch equal to its lead. For double threads the lead is twice the pitch, etc. Therefore, the gear train for multiple threads is related to the lead, and the depth of the thread is related to the pitch.

If it is desired to cut a 1″-8 double thread, the pitch is $\frac{1}{8}$ in. and the lead is $\frac{1}{4}$ in. The depth of the thread is calculated for 8 threads/in., and the gear train is calculated for 4 threads/in.

If it is desired to cut a double thread, the first lead is cut as shown in Fig. 14.14(a). The work is rotated 180°, and the second lead is cut as shown in Fig. 14.14(b).

For cutting multiple threads, the faceplate may be divided into 2, 3, 4, ... , parts and each lead cut separately. It is important that the dog and the carriage engagement is maintained until all the leads are cut.

Another method for cutting multiple threads is to rotate the compound rest through 90°. Thus the compound graduated dial may be used to move the tool one pitch. The movement of the compound rest is critical and should be done with great care.

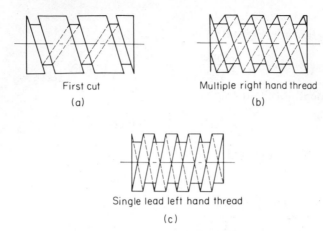

First cut

(a)

Multiple right hand thread

(b)

Single lead left hand thread

(c)

Figure 14.14

Still another method is to establish the ratio of the stud gear to the screw gear. The stud gear is rotated and then engaged with the idler gear. Thus the work has been rotated the desired amount without revolving the screw gear. In other words, the work has been revolved while the tool remains in a fixed position. This may be accomplished by counting the number of teeth on the stud gear.

A right-hand helix wraps the thread around the cylinder in a clockwise direction when looking at the work from the end. A left-hand helix wraps the thread around the cylinder in a counterclockwise direction.

A left-hand helix, Fig. 14.14(c), may be machined on a lathe in one of two ways. Either the tool, *in the conventional position*, may be caused to move from right-to-left (headstock-to-tailstock); or it may be placed in the tool-holder in an inverted position. In the latter case the rotation of the workpiece must be reversed. The tool (carriage) movement is conventional—from the tailstock to the headstock.

In either case, the clearance angles on the tool must be changed to avoid interference from the work during the cutting operation.

QUESTIONS AND PROBLEMS

14.1 Define taper as applied to the lathe.

14.2 Define taper per in. and taper per ft.

14.3 A tapered piece of work is 5 in. long. If the small diameter is 1.750 in. and the large diameter is 3.250 in. Calculate: (a) the taper per in. and (b) the taper per ft. It is tapered for the full 5 in.

14.4 A tapered piece of work is 3 in. long. If the large diameter is 2.700 in. and the small diameter is 2.375 in., find: (a) the taper per in. and (b) the taper per ft. It is to be tapered for its full length.

14.5 A tapered piece is 8 in. long and is to have a large diameter of 12 in. If the taper per ft is 0.960 in./ft: (a) What is the small diameter? (b) What is the taper per in.?

14.6 Describe the various methods used to turn a taper on a lathe.

14.7 A workpiece consists of a tapered cylinder and a constant diameter cylinder. (a) How is the taper per ft calculated? (b) What effect does the constant diameter have on the offset calculations?

14.8 A tapered reamer blank is to be turned. It has an overall length of $7\frac{1}{4}$ in. and a tapered section $4\frac{1}{4}$ in. long. The tapered section has a small diameter of 0.7748 in. and a large diameter of 0.9881 in. Find: (a) the taper per in.; (b) the taper per ft; (c) the setover.

14.9 Refer to the table of Morse taper standards at the end of this text. Find the small diameter of the socket for a No. 3 Morse taper.

14.10 The small end of a No. 1 Morse taper is 0.369 in. Using the data from the tables at the end of this text, verify the taper per ft.

14.11 From Appendix IV verify the small diameter of a No. 5 Morse taper using the other given data.

14.12 Find the large end of the socket for a No. 8 Brown and Sharpe taper using Appendix V at the end of this text.

14.13 Use the Brown and Sharpe table (Appendix V) verify the taper per ft for a No. 12 taper.

14.14 Refer to Fig. 14.15. (a) Find the diameter at the small end at *A* and *B*. (b) Find the imaginary small and large diameters at *A*. (c) Find the imaginary large diameter at *B*. (d) What are the setovers for *A* and *B*?

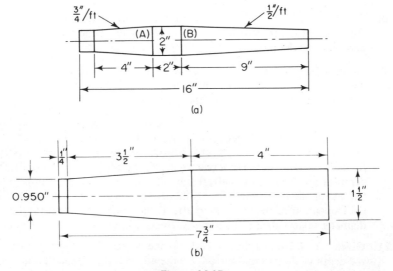

Figure 14.15

14.15 Using Fig. 14.15(b) calculate: (a) the taper per in.; (b) the taper per ft; (c) the imaginary small diameter; (d) the imaginary large diameter; (e) the set-over.

14.16 How do the American Standard self-holding tapers compare to the *B* and *S*, Morse, and the Steep Machine tapers. See Appendix VIII.

14.17 Given a No. 8 Jarno taper, find: (a) the large diameters; (b) the small diameter; (c) the length of the taper.

14.18 Why is it important to take a trial cut after setting a lathe for taper turning?

14.19 List the methods for turning a taper when the center line of the lathe bed and the center line of the work are parallel to each other. List the methods when the center line of the work is at an angle with the lathe bed.

14.20 List the instances where the tool bit traces a line parallel to the center line of the machine. When does a tool trace a line at an angle with the lathe bed in taper turning?

14.21 Explain fully the principle of the tracer lathe.

14.22 List the standard tapers discussed in theory and indicate the standards used to determine the various parts of a taper.

14.23 Define: major and minor diameter, pitch diameter, pitch, lead, helix, and helix angle.

14.24 Derive the depth equation for an American National thread.

14.25 Derive all the equations for an American National thread.

14.26 Derive the equations for a Unified thread.

14.27 How do the calculations for the tap drill size for an American National and a Unified thread differ?

14.28 Given a $\frac{1}{2}$-20NF thread, calculate: (a) the pitch; (b) the width of the flat; (c) the depth of the thread; (d) the minor diameter of the screw; (e) the pitch diameter; (f) the tap drill size; (g) the helix angle.

14.29 Given a $\frac{5}{8}$-11NC thread, find: (a) the pitch; (b) the width of the flat; (c) the depth of the thread; (d) the minor diameter of the screw; (e) the tap drill size; (f) the pitch diameter; (g) the helix angle.

14.30 Given a $2\frac{1}{8}''$-5 UNC (Unified National Coarse) thread, calculate: (a) The depth of the sharp V thread; (b) the depth of the external thread; (c) the flat on the crest of the external thread; (d) the truncation of the crest (external); (e) the truncation of the root (external); (f) the addendum (external); (g) the depth of the thread (internal); (h) the flat across the crest (internal); (i) the flat across the root (internal); (j) the truncation of the crest (internal); (k) the truncation of the root (internal); (l) the pitch diameter; (m) the minor diameter (external); (n) the minor diameter (internal); (o) the helix angle.

14.31 Given a $1''$-8 Unified thread, find: (a) the depth of the sharp V thread; (b) the depth of the external thread; (c) the addendum; (d) the flat on the crest (external); (e) the truncation of the crest (external); (f) the truncation of the root (external); (g) the depth of the thread (internal); (h) the flat on the crest (internal); (i) the flat on the root (internal); (j) the truncation of the crest (internal); (k) the truncation of the root (internal); (l) the pitch diameter; (m) the minor diameter (external); (n) the minor diameter (internal); (o) the helix angle.

14.32 What are the meanings of the notations 6H/5g6g and 5H/4g6g series?

14.33 Draw the contour for the proposed metric IFI-500 thread series. Label the pitch and depth.

14.34 Explain the meanings of the following symbols: (a) 3.5P 0.6A; (b) 16P 2B; (c) 16P 2C.

14.35 Given an Acme thread 2″-4, find: (a) the depth of the thread; (b) the width of the flat at the root; (c) the pitch diameter; (d) the minor diameter.

14.36 Derive the equation for three-wire measurement of threads.

14.37 Why is it necessary to use the best wire concept for threads?

14.38 Given a ¾-10NC thread, find: (a) the best wire size and (b) the measurement over wires.

14.39 Calculate the measurement over wires in Problem 14.28.

14.40 Calculate: (a) the best wire size and (b) the measurement over wires for Problem 14.29.

14.41 How is the lathe constant determined?

14.42 What is the effect of an idler or idlers on a gear train?

14.43 What effect does a compound gear arrangement have on a gear ratio?

14.44 Using the tooth to tooth concept, show the effect of an idler on a gear ratio. Do the same for a compound arrangement.

14.45 Find the gears necessary to cut 12 threads/in. The lathe constant is 10, the gear progression is 4, and the gears available are 24, 28, 32, . . . , 100.

14.46 Find the gears needed to cut 18 threads/in. The lathe constant is 6, the gear progression is 4, and the gears available are 24, 28, 32, . . . , 100.

14.47 Find the gears needed to cut 36 threads/in. The conditions are the same as in problem 14.46.

14.48 Find the gears needed to cut 36 threads/in. The lathe constant is 9, the gear progression is 5, and the gears available are 25, 30, 35, . . . , 80.

14.49 Find the gears needed to cut a 2-mm metric thread. The lathe constant is 8, the gear progression is 5, and the gears available are 25, 30, 35, . . . , 100.

14.50 The same as problem 14.49 except the thread to be cut is 2.5 mm.

14.51 You are asked to cut 14 threads/in. You set the compound at 29°. How much is to be cut at 29°?

14.52 Why is it good practice to set a threading tool (compound rest) at 29° in the threading operation?

14.53 What effect does the tool bit have on the thread form when the tool bit is ground to 60° but possesses a positive back rake?

14.54 Explain the function of a thread dial chaser.

14.55 Explain fully the process of setting a lathe for cutting threads.

14.56 Explain the relationship between pitch and leads for multiple threads.

14.57 Explain the process of rotating change gears in multiple threading.

14.58 Explain the processes used to cut a left-hand helix.

14.59 How would you distinguish between a right- and left-hand helix.

14.60 Describe the position of the tool bit, and the rotation of the work. Use a diagram and explain the clearances needed to cut a left-hand helix.

The Milling Machine

15

15.1. Types and Construction

Milling machines may be classified in three groups: The bed type, the column and knee type, and special milling machines.

The bed type milling machine is used for production manufacturing. The general characteristics of this type of machine are that the height of the table is fixed and the adjustments for height are made with the spindles. This height adjustment is made by moving the spindle head up or down. On some machines the transverse adjustment may be made with the table. On others, the spindles may be adjusted in or out.

In construction, these machines are very rigid, permitting greater metal removal. Since adjustments are rather time consuming, it takes longer to set them up than it takes to set up the knee and column type of machine. For this reason the production run must be substantial for the cost to warrant their use.

They are either fully automatic or semi-automatic, and most of them are capable of running through a complete cycle from start to finish. A machine may have one spindle mounted on the single column or two spindles mounted on both sides of the table on two columns. In the latter case the table feeds longitudinally between the two heads. This is shown in Fig. 15.1.

The planer type of milling machine is a bed type machine which is usually very large. The table moves under an arch very much as the table of a planer. The cutter heads are mounted above and at the sides of the table.

The column and knee type of milling machine is the most commonly used because of its flexibility. Because of the ease with which it can be set up and its versatility, it is more adaptable for quick single-piece setups. If more

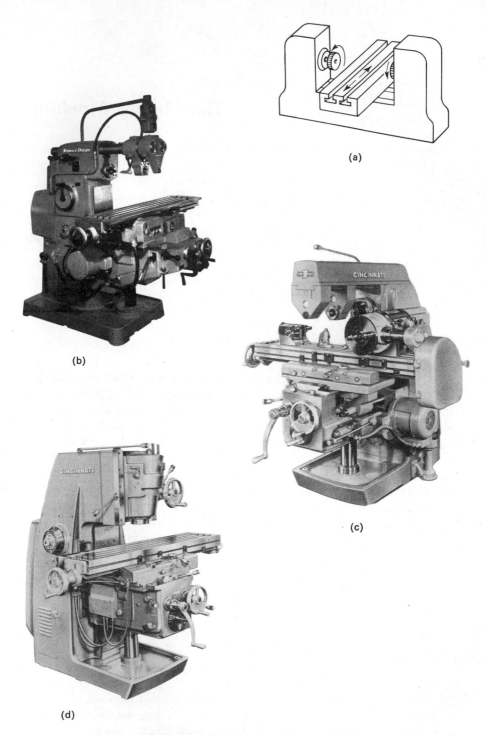

(a)

(b)

(c)

(d)

Figure 15.1 [(*b*) *Courtesy of Brown & Sharpe Manufacturing Company;* (*c*) & (*d*) *courtesy of Cincinnati Milacron, Inc.*]

complicated setups are desirable, this is also possible. These machines are not as rugged as the bed type of milling machine, and therefore for production purposes the machining times may be somewhat longer.

The knee carries the feed mechanism and mounts the saddle and the table. The column of the machine is the machined front of the main casting. The knee is mounted on this column and fastened by dovetail ways which permit movement of the knee in a vertical plane.

In general, there are two types of column and knee milling machines: the horizontal and the vertical milling machines. These may be either plain or universal.

The difference between the horizontal and vertical milling machine is the position of the spindle in relation to the machine table. The spindle is mounted vertically on the vertical miller and horizontally on the horizontal miller.

The difference between a universal and a plain milling machine is that on the horizontal universal milling machine the table may be swiveled and on the vertical universal the vertical head swivels, whereas on the plain millers the saddle and table must operate at right angles to each other.

The plain horizontal milling machine, Fig. 15.1(b), is made so that the table can be fed longitudinally, transversely, or vertically by hand or power. Its one distinguishing feature, as indicated, is that the table cannot be swiveled. Almost all attachments, which will be discussed later in this chapter, are available for the plain milling machine. The major exceptions are those attachments which require that the table be swiveled. Such is the case with the universal dividing head; see Fig. 15.5(a).

The universal horizontal milling machine, Fig. 15.1(c), has all the features of the plain milling machine plus the swivel table. The spindle operates in a plane parallel to the table. All the feeds, longitudinal (table), transverse (saddle), and vertical (knee), may be operated manually or with power.

The plain vertical milling machine, Fig. 15.1(d), has its spindle set to operate in a vertical plane. Longitudinal, transverse, and vertical feeds are possible. The vertical spindle may be moved up or down but cannot be swiveled.

The universal vertical milling machine operates in the same manner as the plain vertical milling machine. In addition to the three motions, the vertical head may be swiveled.

The vertical milling machines described above have their vertical heads clamped to the main housing. One type of milling machine has an adjustable upper section called the *ram*. The ram can be pulled out and clamped into position. A vertical head may be mounted on it, or it can be used to support an overarm so that the machine can be used as a horizontal machine.

There are also several special-purpose machines such as thread millers, tracer-controlled (profilers) milling machines, rotary millers, and many others each designed to do a very special job. The horizontal boring mill, Fig. 15.2(a), in contrast to the special purpose machines just listed, is a very general machine. This machine could be discussed here or in the chapter on

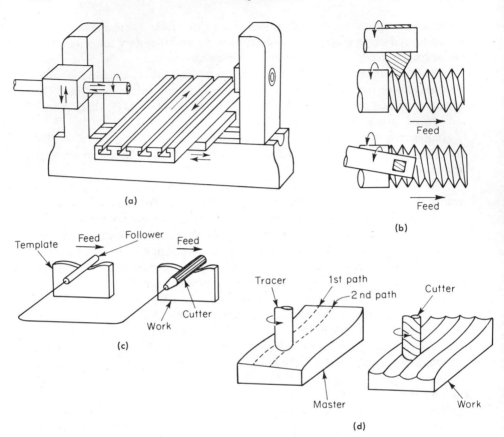

(a)

(b)

(c)

(d)

Figure 15.2

toolmaking. Its construction will be discussed here, and its use left for the subsequent chapter.

The horizontal boring mill is usually a large machine designed with a retractable spindle mounted in the headstock of the machine. The headstock can be moved in a vertical direction. A bushing mounted in a block in the tailstock is caused to move up and down, always in alignment with the headstock spindle. Thus a long boring bar, capable of mounting cutters, can be supported at both ends. The boring bar receives its power from the spindle. It should be noted that milling cutters, drills, etc., can be mounted directly in the spindle without using the boring bar or the tailstock.

The table is mounted on a saddle. The saddle moves longitudinally and the table transversely. All motions may be either hand operated or power fed. In addition all motions are equipped with rapid traverse for quick positioning. All motions may be controlled by using the graduated collars or long vernier scales.

Thread millers use a cutter called a *hob*. The cutter is made with a helix whose teeth are in the form of the desired thread. The hob sinks into the work while rotating. The work rotates at a peripheral speed equal to the lead of the hob at the same time that the work (or hob) is feeding along the central axis of the work.

Figure 15.2(b) illustrates the principle of hobbing. The single-point form tool revolves and forms the thread. The rotation and the lateral movement of the work form the helix.

If a cutter which has the thread form ground into its teeth were to replace the single-point tool and if the length of the cutter (hob) were to cover the length of the thread, the entire thread would be formed in one revolution of the *work*.

Tracer-control machines, such as profilers, are machines which use a stylus to trace the desired shape which has been previously machined into a template. This template may have two or three planes. It can be made from wood, plaster, or soft metal, or it may be one of the finished pieces which is to be reproduced.

In the two-plane machine the follower traces the path shown in Fig. 15.2(c). This causes the cutter, usually a radius end mill, to trace the same path on the work.

If the tracer is three-dimensional, the tracing is accomplished through two planes in very much the same manner as that shown in Fig. 15.2(c). The third plane is accomplished by moving the table. Thus the work will have a series of single-plane cuts, which, when taken together with the tracing planes, produce a three-dimensional object, as shown in Fig. 15.2(d). The surface is a series of two-dimensional grooves. Handwork is required to remove the grooves and give the desired smooth contour surface. The larger the radius of the tool or the closer the cuts taken, the better is the blending. The operation is slow and expensive but effective.

Numerical control may also be used for contour milling. Numerical control will be discussed in Chapter 20.

Special milling machines for continuous milling are also manufactured. The rotary miller, which uses a vertical spindle and a power-actuated rotary table, provides an opportunity for continuous milling. Many pieces of work may be mounted in a circle. The table feeds circularly under the cutter. Since the rotation of the table is slow, the operator has the chance to remove the finished workpiece and load an unfinished workpiece.

15.2. Accessories

Accessories for milling machines may be classified in two groups: (1) those which hold and power the cutter and (2) those which hold and move the work. The accessories, or attachments, which hold and power the cutter are discussed first.

Various types of arbors. Cutter arbors, Fig. 15.3(a), are equipped with spacers which permit locating the cutter with reference to the workpiece. Once spaced, a threaded nut is used to lock the cutter in position. A square key is used to transmit power from the arbor to the cutter. An oversize spacer is provided as a bushing which fits into the overarm for support. One end of the arbor has a 60° center hole so that it may be supported by a 60° center when the bushing is not used. The other end of the arbor is supported by either a milling-machine quick-releasing taper, Fig. 15.3(a), or a Brown and Sharpe taper or in some instances it is fastened directly to the front of the spindle.

Another method for holding cutters is shown in Fig. 15.3(b). This is

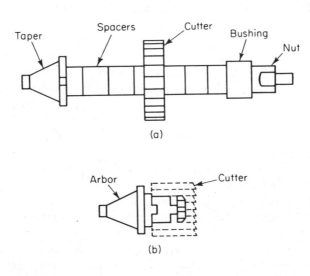

(a)

(b)

(c)

(d)

Figure 15.3 *(Courtesy of Brown & Sharpe Manufacturing Company.)*

(e)

(f)

Figure 15.3   (Cont.)

a shell end-mill arbor. Arbors for holding end mills, drills, taps, boring tools, etc., are available. Spring collets and tapered sleeves may also be used to hold cutters.

The Brown and Sharpe tapered arbor may or may not be locked into the spindle with a drawbar. An arbor with a steep milling taper must be locked into the spindle with a drawbar. Another method for holding arbors in the spindle is the cam lock mechanism. Some are made to be fastened to the spindle flange. All arbors drive cutters through keys or projections which fit the cutter. It is not safe to rely on friction alone to drive the arbor in the spindle or to drive the cutter on the arbor.

The vertical head.   The vertical head is shown in Fig. 15.3(c). It may be mounted in several ways. It may be clamped to the column, or it may be mounted on the overarm of the machine. No matter how it is mounted, it must pick up power from the spindle, which it then transmits through gears to the cutter. The vertical head attachment in Fig. 15.3(c) may be rotated for angular cuts.

A universal milling head is shown in Fig. 15.3(d). It can be set at a compound angle to the work. Rotary adjustments may be made about the machine spindle and about an axis perpendicular to the milling machine spindle. A support is usually needed at the end of the head.

The slotting attachment.   The tool is oscillated by the power from the spindle [See Fig. 15.3(e).] Various shaped tools may be used, depending upon the shape of the slot desired. The head may be swiveled 90° either side of the zero position.

High-speed milling attachment.   Used for small cutters, the increase in cutter speed is achieved through a gear train which gives speeds four to five times the speed of the machine spindle.

Rack milling attachment.   Shown in Fig. 15.3(f), this is used to mill spur racks or helical racks. A rack is a flat bar which has gear teeth milled into its surface perpendicular to or at an angle to the length of the rack.

The accessories which hold workpieces, other than specially designed fixtures, are described below.

The vise.   Vises may be plain, have a flange and a swivel base, or be universal. The function of a vise is always to hold the workpiece rigid in a desired position. The jaws are cast steel or cast iron fitted with hardened and ground steel inserts. Only one jaw is movable.

The plain vise has a counterbored hole in its base. When a bolt is inserted into this hole, the head of the bolt is below the top of the vise base so that it does not interfere with the movable jaw. This bolt can be screwed into a T nut in the milling-machine table and thus fasten the vise to the milling table.

The flanged vise, Fig. 15.4, is much more rigid than the plain vise. The flanges are integral with the main casting. They have machined slots on both sides and both ends, which make fastening the vise to the milling table much easier.

This flanged vise may be fitted to or mounted on a graduated base. This permits swiveling so that the vise may be set at an angle with the feed of the table.

The universal vise may be swiveled in a perpendicular and in a horizontal

Figure 15.4 *(Courtesy of Brown & Sharpe Manufacturing Company.)*

plane to the milling table. The base is graduated for horizontal setting. The vertical setting is obtained with a knee arrangement. This makes possible the milling of compound angles without destroying the setting when it is necessary to make additional pieces.

The dividing head. Plain or universal dividing heads provide an easy method of dividing a circle into almost any number of divisions. They are mounted on and bolted to the milling-machine table. A tailstock is provided, which is also mounted on the table. This provides an easy method of holding workpieces between centers. The workpiece is fitted with a dog which is driven by a slotted yoke. The workpiece may also be held in collets or chucks mounted on the dividing-head spindle.

The plain dividing head may be fitted with a slotted plate having equally spaced holes or some kind of ratchet arrangement for hand or direct indexing. If fitted with a slotted plate, the plate may be removed and others substituted as needed.

Dividing heads are also manufactured to operate through a worm and worm wheel arrangement. The worm is rotated by a handle fitted with a pin in its end. A carefully divided plate is mounted so that this pin may be slipped into one of the holes drilled into its face. Once a cut is taken, the pin is retracted, the handle rotated the required amount, and the pin slipped into another hole. The relationship between the rotation of the index handle, the worm and worm wheel, and the workpiece will be discussed in Chapter 18.

The universal dividing head, Fig. 15.5(a), is equipped with a worm and worm wheel. It has all the features of the plain index head, in addition to which the headstock may be swiveled. The universal dividing head is equipped with change gears for differential indexing, helical milling, cam milling and graduating a scale, Chapter 16.

If desired, the worm and worm wheel may be disengaged. This permits the work to be indexed by hand. A 24-hole plate straddles the headstock spindle and is used for direct indexing. This is shown in Fig. 15.5(b). If the index pin is pulled out, the index handle may be rotated. This rotates the worm shaft which is engaged with the worm wheel. The worm wheel straddles and is keyed to the headstock spindle which drives the work during the indexing operation.

With the index-plate lockpin disengaged and a gear train mounted at the rear of the headstock, either helical or differential indexing may be done.

Some dividing heads are equipped with three plates which have different hole circles accurately spaced and drilled into their faces. See Fig. 15.5(c). The Brown and Sharpe Company provides three plates. The hole circles are listed in the next chapter. The Cincinnati Milling Machine Company provides one plate with accurately spaced hole circles on both faces of the plate. These are also listed in the next chapter. Cincinnati Milling Machine Company also can provide three additional plates drilled on both sides.

The sector arms, Fig. 15.5(c), consist of two arms which can be rotated

(a)

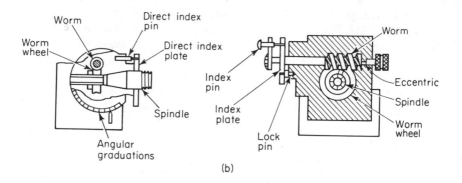

(b)

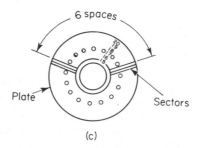

(c)

Figure 15.5 [(*a*) & (*d*) *Courtesy of Brown & Sharpe Manufacturing Company;* (*e*) *courtesy of Cincinnati Milacron, Inc.*]

(d)

(e)

Figure 15.5   (Cont.)

independently, set, and locked into the position desired relative to each other. A circular spring permits rotating both arms as a unit. The index pin is placed in one hole. The sector arms are rotated until one arm contacts the pin. The pin is retracted, the index handle rotated, and the pin inserted at the second sector arm. Then the sector is rotated until the first sector arm contacts the pin again. The operation is then repeated.

The rotary table.   Used for circular milling. It may be hand fed, Fig. 15.5(d), or power fed, Fig. 15.5(e). It is sometimes used to position work for milling angles. The table is graduated in $\frac{1}{2}°$ increments with the possibility of reading to increments of 2 minutes off the graduated worm-shaft dial.

Rotary index tables have an index plate and operate very much like the dividing head.

Tilting tables are also available for milling machines to permit the cutting of tapered work such as wedges or flat tapers. When used with an index head, they may be used to cut flutes in tapered reamers or taps.

There is a class of attachments used to provide accuracy for positioning work. The longitudinal and transverse position of the table is controlled entirely with inside micrometers, measuring rods, and dial indicators. These are shown in Fig. 15.6(a). The measuring rods provide even inches, the micrometer the 0.001 in. increments, and the dial indicator the 0.0001 in. increments.

Where greater accuracy is desired several optical systems may be used. Figure 15.6(b) shows an optical system. It provides for point-to-point movement of the table. The inserted reading shows that all direct readings may be read to 0.001 in.

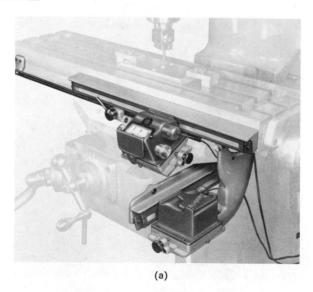

(a)

Figure 15.6   *(Courtesy of Bridgeport Machines, Division of Textron, Inc.)*

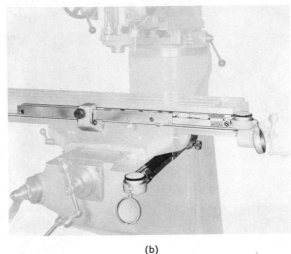

(b)

Figure 15.6　(Cont.)

15.3.　The Cutting Tool

Cutters are classified according to the manner in which they are used, such as gear cutters, slitting saws, radius cutters, etc. They may also be classified according to how they are mounted, such as arbor or shank types of cutters. In some instances they are classified according to some construction feature, such as carbide, face mill, etc.

The following will attempt to classify cutters according to some distinguishing characteristic of the cutter.

Figure 15.7(a) shows a plain milling cutter with straight teeth on the periphery and no cutting edge on the face of the cutter. A single-side milling cutter cuts on the periphery and one face. A double-side milling cutter, Fig. 15.7(b), cuts on the periphery and both faces.

Plain milling cutters may have helical teeth. If, when viewed from the end of the cutter, the helix rotates clockwise away from the viewer, the helix is said to be *right hand*. If the helix rotates counterclockwise away from the viewer, the helix is said to be *left hand*. Figure 15.7(c) shows a plain milling cutter with helical teeth. The helix angle of the cutter shown is 18° and is right handed. Other cutters have helix angles of 45° for heavy-duty cutting and 52° for fine finishing cuts. The high shear angle will produce fine surface finishes. Sometimes a pair of these cutters with opposite helix angles are mounted on one arbor. The alternate helix equalizes the thrust developed by the shearing action of the helical teeth.

Figure 15.7(d) shows a stagger-tooth side-milling cutter. In this instance adjacent teeth have alternate helix angle direction. Again the shearing action of the opposite helix-angle directions equalizes the thrust on the cutter.

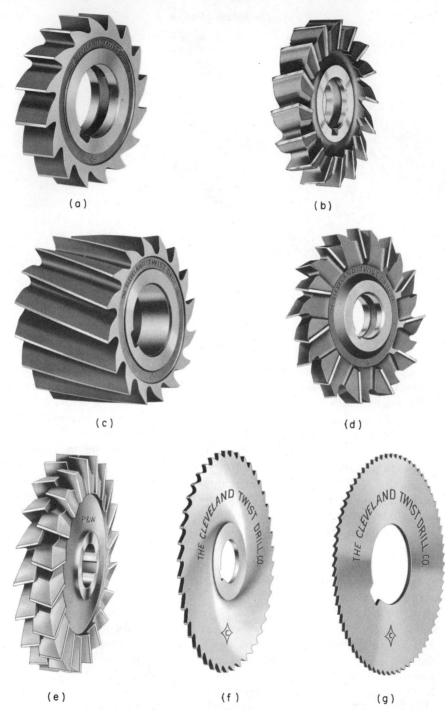

(a)

(b)

(c)

(d)

(e)

(f)

(g)

Figure 15.7 [(a), (c), (d), (f)–(m) Courtesy of Cleveland Twist Drill Company; (b), (e) courtesy of Pratt and Whitney Company, Inc.; (n) & (o) courtesy of DoAll Company.]

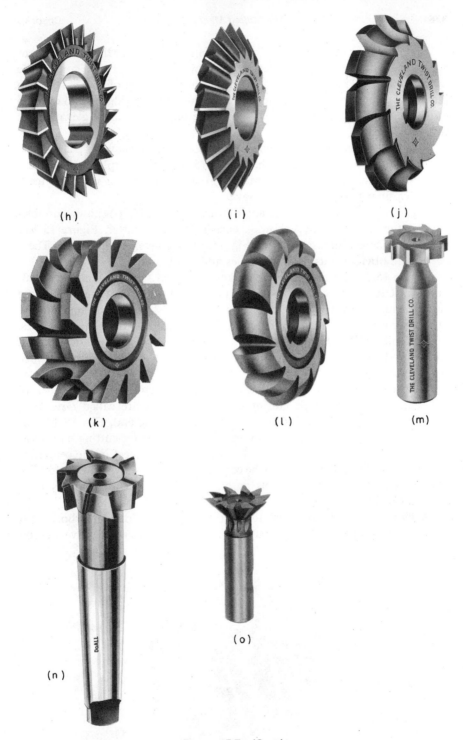

(h) (i) (j)

(k) (l) (m)

(n) (o)

Figure 15.7 (Cont.)

Figure 15.7(e) shows a pair of interlocking cutters. With this arrangement it is possible to insert spacers between the two cutters and thus control the width of a slot without developing a ridge in the center of the slot. If two plain milling cutters were to be separated at the center, a ridge would develop on the work at the point of separation. The opposite helix angles equalize the side thrust on the cutters.

Slitting saws may be ground concave on both sides, or have chip clearance. They may also have stagger teeth. Figure 15.7(f) shows a plain slitting saw for cutting steel, brass, etc. Figure 15.7(g) shows a slotting saw. The teeth are much finer than in the slitting saw.

Figure 15.7(h) shows a single-angle cutter and Fig. 15.7(i) shows a double-angle cutter. Figure 15.7(j) shows a corner-rounding cutter. Figure 15.7(k) shows a concave-radius cutter, and Fig. 15.7(l), a convex-radius cutter. These cutters are obviously used to cut angles and radii.

Figure 15.7(m) shows a Woodruff keyseat cutter. This is a small special-purpose plain milling cutter. The T-slot cutter, Fig. 15.7(n), of the side milling variety, usually has stagger teeth. It is used to cut T slots, as the name implies. Dovetail cutters, Fig. 15.7(o), are used to cut dovetail, as the name indicates.

Shell mills, Fig. 15.8(a), are mounted on the type of arbor shown in Fig. 15.3(b). When large, they usually have inserted teeth and are called *face* milling cutters.

Solid end mills may have two cutting edges, when they are called *two-flute* end mills, or multiple cutting edges, when they are called *three-flute*, *four-flute*, etc., end mills. End mills may also be single end, Fig. 15.8(b), or double end, Fig. 15.8(c). They may in addition be center-cutting end mills, in which case the cutting edges on the end of the mill meet in the center, as shown in Fig. 15.8(c), or they may be center relieved, as shown in Fig. 15.8(b). Other end mills may have radius or ball ends, and still others may have tapered ends.

A fly cutter is a single-point tool bit mounted in a disc or arbor. As it revolves and sweeps the work, it cuts the material. This is an effective method

(a)

Figure 15.8 (*Photos courtesy of Pratt and Whitney Company, Inc.*)

4 – Flute gashed end

(b)

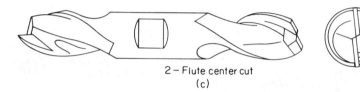

2 – Flute center cut

(c)

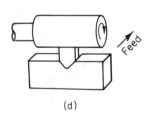

(d)

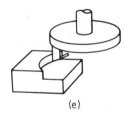

(e)

(f)

Figure 15.8 (Cont.)

377

(g)

Figure 15.8 (Cont.)

for cutting some types of contours or for surface milling at a very low cost. Figure 15.8(d) shows a fly cutter machining a small V slot. Figure 15.8(e) shows a fly cutter machining a flat surface. End mills may also be purchased with straight, standard tapered, or interlocking tapered shanks.

Most large cutters may be purchased with inserted blades, Fig. 15.8(f). Almost any type of cutter may be purchased with carbide inserts, Fig. 15.8(g).

Cutters for making gears, taps, reamers, etc., are special-purpose cutters. They will be shown in the succeeding chapters when their uses are discussed.

15.4. The Operation of a Milling Machine

Although it is not possible to describe all operations that can be done on a milling machine, some of the basic operations can be described. What follows will illustrate fundamental guidelines necessary to accomplish good machining practices.

To start, it is necessary to expand on how cutters operate. A cutter may operate clockwise or counterclockwise. The *direction* in which the cutter is cutting is termed *the hand of the cut*. Figure 15.9(a and d) are called right hand cutters. In these two illustrations the cut is progressing toward the right. Figure 15.9(b and c) are left hand cuts.

The *hand of the helix* is the direction that the helix wraps around the cutter. If the cutter is viewed from the end, and the helix wraps counter clockwise, it is a left hand helix. This is shown in Fig. 15.9(c and d). If it wraps clockwise, it is a right hand helix, Fig. 15.9(a and b).

Except when a machine has been preset for production, no milling operation should be attempted before a trial cut is taken. The procedure for taking a trial cut is as follows: The knee of the milling machine is raised until the revolving cutter touches the work. The work is moved free from the cutter by using the longitudinal hand feed. The knee is raised a small amount (or to a layout line), a short cut is taken, the table is retracted again, and a mea-

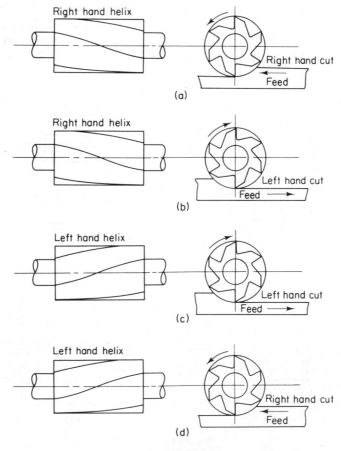

Figure 15.9

surement is taken. The vertical-feed graduated-collar lock screw is loosened, rotated, set at 0, and locked. From the measurement previously taken, the table is raised the required amount. The table is then advanced until the work touches the cutter. The automatic feed is engaged, and a cut is taken. At the end of the cut, the automatic feed is disengaged, the table is returned to its starting position, and the power turned off. If additional material must be removed, a measurement is taken, the knee is raised the required amount, and another cut is taken.

One of the most common methods for holding work, especially in single-piece operations or toolmaking operations, is the vise. The setting of the vise on the milling-machine table is therefore very important.

The alignment of a vise may be accomplished in several ways. The simplest method is to use a T square, as shown in Fig. 15.10(a). This enables setting the vise perpendicular to the milling arbor. When setting a vise parallel to the arbor, the vise may be aligned as shown in Fig. 15.10(b).

On a plain milling machine a dial indicator may be clamped between two of the collars on the arbor and rotated until the indicator picks up the *solid jaw* of the vise. The cross feed is used to set the needle of the dial indicator on zero. The longitudinal feed is operated by hand, and the position of the vise adjusted until the needle reads 0-0 at both ends of the solid jaw of the vise. This is shown in Fig. 15.10(c).

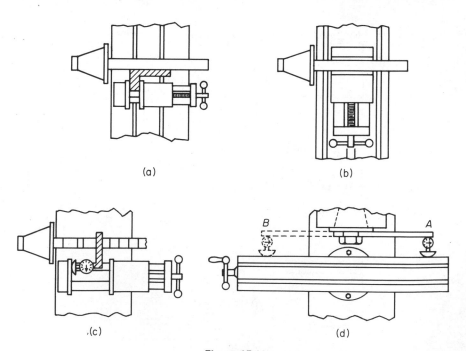

(a) (b)

(c) (d)

Figure 15.10

If it is desired to set the vise parallel to the arbor, the cross feed is operated by hand and the vise is adjusted until the needle reads 0-0.

The graduated base of a vise should not be relied upon for correct alignment. This is so, even though the vise base is fitted with keys which fit the T slots in the table.

On a universal milling machine, the swivel table itself must first be aligned before the vise can be set. Once the table is set, the methods above may be used to align the vise.

The table alignment for a universal milling machine is shown in Fig. 15.10(d). One end of a bar is fitted with a dial indicator. The other end is locked to the milling-machine spindle. The spindle is rotated until the indicator button contacts the machined surface of the table at *A*. The hand cross feed is operated until the needle reads 0. The spindle, bar, and indicator are rotated until the indicator button contacts the table at *B*. If the needle reads 0 at *B* and 0 at *A*, the table is aligned perpendicular to the spindle. The student should investigate why the longitudinal hand feed cannot be used to align a universal milling-machine table when the dial indicator is stationary but in contact with the machined surface of the table.

Next the desired cutter is mounted on the machine. The work is mounted in the vise on parallel bars (if needed) to elevate the work above the jaws of the vise. A trial cut is taken, the graduated collar adjusted, and the knee raised the required amount. The work is brought into contact with the cutter by *hand feed*. Once contact is made with the cutter, the automatic feed is set.

It should be noted that two kinds of milling operations are possible. *Conventional milling* in which the work is moving into the cutter is shown in Fig. 15.11(a). Figure 15.11(b) shows the work moving into the cutter with the cutter teeth trying to climb the work. This is called *climb milling*.

Conventional milling attempts to lift the work off the table. This can be overcome by rigidly clamping the work to the table or in some holding device. Notice that the feed is to the right in Fig. 15.11(a) with the cutting force acting as the reaction force to the feed. In climb milling the cutting force is

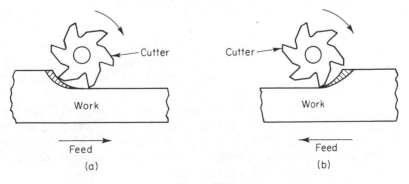

Figure 15.11

in the same direction as the feed, or "with the backlash" in the lead screw of the machine. Since the thick part of the workpiece is to the right of the cutter, Fig. 15.11(b), unless the operator is careful (rigid table, work clamped rigidly to the table, etc.), the cutter will climb the work and damage it, the cutter or both. If all precautions are taken, fine finish can be achieved with climb milling. Thin pieces may be cut by using climb milling because the cutter action tends to hold the work to the table instead of lifting it.

Squaring a block.   One of the seemingly easy operations which must be performed many times is the *squaring of a block*, or at least the squaring of two surfaces which are to act as reference surfaces for further operations. The following procedure may be used to machine the surfaces of a block to achieve squareness:

1. Machine surface 1, Fig. 15.12(a).

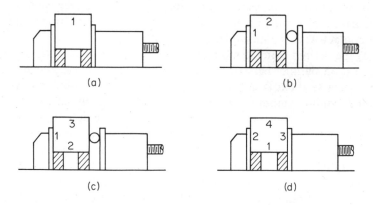

(a)   (b)

(c)   (d)

Figure 15.12

2. Place side 1 against the solid jaw and a round bar between the work and the movable jaw. Let the work find its equilibrium position. Cut surface 2, Fig. 15.12(b). Surfaces 1 and 2 should now be 90° to each other.
3. Rotate the work end for end so that surface 1 is against the solid jaw and surface 2 is against the parallels. Use the rod, but tap the block firmly against the parallels. Cut surface 3. This is shown in Fig. 15.12(c).
4. Place surface 2 against the solid jaw and surface 1 against the parallels. The round rod is not necessary. Cut surface 4. See Fig. 15.12(d). NOTE: The burrs should be removed with a fine file after each surface is finished. After removing the sharp edges, the squareness of the sides should be checked with a precision square.

Milling a cavity with an end mill

1. The workpiece face is painted with layout blue as shown in Fig. 15.13(a). The workpiece is placed in a vise and, if necessary, raised with parallels. Of course, the vise should be square with the table.

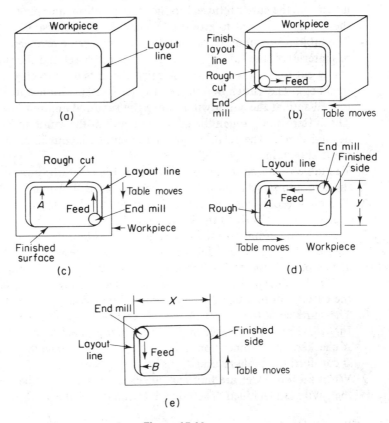

Figure 15.13

2. A two-lip end mill is inserted into the vertical head spindle. It is moved over the work. The table is raised until the end mill touches a shim placed between the work and the end of the cutter. The vertical feed dial is set at zero. The shim is removed. The table is raised so that the end mill sinks into the scrap portion of the work. The end mill should penetrate the work about 0.010 in. less than the finish depth. Once this depth is reached the scrap material in the cavity is removed. Care should be taken to stay about $\frac{1}{16}$th in. inside the layout line. Once finished the table is lowered, the end mill is removed and another end

383

mill inserted into the spindle to produce the appropriate corner radii. If the cavity does not have a bottom, the end mill should continue to remove the scrap material until it breaks through the bottom.

3. The end mill is again placed into the cavity so that it barely touches the bottom. The end mill is caused to touch the side. A light cut is taken off the bottom using the appropriate feed. The depth of the hole is measured, the cutter returned to the start position, and the table raised the required amount to give the finished depth dimension.

4. The table is now moved, causing the cutter to remove a small amount of material off the side of the cavity. The feed is set and the side of the cavity cut for a short distance. A micrometer is used to check the wall thickness. The cutter is returned to the start position and the table moved so that the cutter will remove the required amount of material. The cutter should touch the layout line and at the same time be at the desired depth. The relationship of the cutter, layout line, and rough cut is shown in Fig. 15.13(b).

5. The table is caused to move as shown in Fig. 15.13(b) until it touches the layout line at the bottom of the workpiece as shown in Fig. 15.13(c).

6. The crossfeed is engaged and a cut taken in the direction shown in Fig. 15.13(c), *almost* to the layout line, face A.

7. It now becomes important to take a test cut off face A. The longitudinal feed is set to cut face A for a short distance. The width of the cavity at this point is measured. The cutter is returned to the position shown in Fig. 15.13(d) and the hand crossfeed used to move the table so that the cutter will produce the appropriate dimension y.

8. The same condition exists at the left end of the workpiece at side B, Fig. 15.13(e) as had existed in (7). The cutter is again set and dimension X checked. Once dimension X is set, the crossfeed is engaged and face B cut until the table returns to its start position.

9. When all four sides are finished, the excess material in the bottom of the cavity is machined. The table is lowered and the work removed.

Milling a chamfer or an angle on a block. Figure 15.14 shows two ways in which a block may be held to mill a chamfer. A shallow chamfer may be milled if the workpiece is held between two tapered parallels as shown in Fig. 15.14(b).

Of course, angles may be milled on long workpieces if the work is set at the desired angle to the movement of the table as shown in Fig. 15.14(c).

Milling a square at the end of a round workpiece. Figure 15.15(a) shows a top view of a dividing heading with a round piece of stock which has just had two flats milled at its end. The work is then indexed 90° and two more flats milled. It should be noted that if the work is indexed through 60°, it will produce a hexagon.

Figure 15.15(b) shows the use of an end mill to machine a square or a

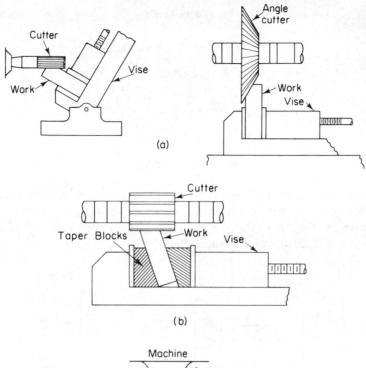

(a)

(b)

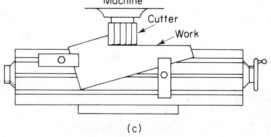

(c)

Figure 15.14

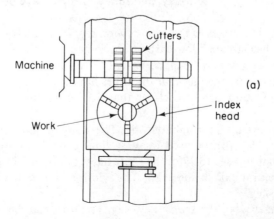

(a)

Figure 15.15

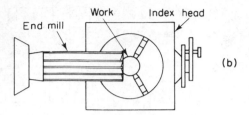

Figure 15.15   (Cont.)

hexagon. The procedure requires that appropriate indexing procedures be used. Many of these procedures are discussed in the next chapter.

Figure 15.16(a and b) shows a slot milled with an end mill and a keyway milled into a shaft using a keyway cutter.

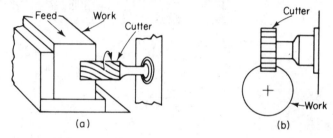

Figure 15.16

15.5.   Keys and Keyways

The purpose of any key is to act as a connecting link between the driving member of a mechanism and the driven member of the mechanism. There are many types of keys in use today, and many of them have been standardized.

The simplest kind of key is the *plain square* key, Fig. 15.17(a). These keys are made from heat-treated low-carbon stock and machined to size. The stock itself, although square, can be visually distinguished from standard SAE square steel bar by the fact that the edges have a very small radius. The tolerances for key stock are held closer than for the standard SAE square bar stock.

Plain flat keys are used for light driving. They may be sunk into the shaft, as shown in Fig. 15.17(b), or used for very light driving, as shown in Fig. 15.17(c). Note that in Fig. 15.17(c) the shaft has a flat milled into its surface parallel to the central axis of the shaft. The width of this flat is the same as the width of the key.

For very light driving the *saddle* key, Fig. 15.17(d), may be used. In this instance the key has the radius of the shaft milled into its surface.

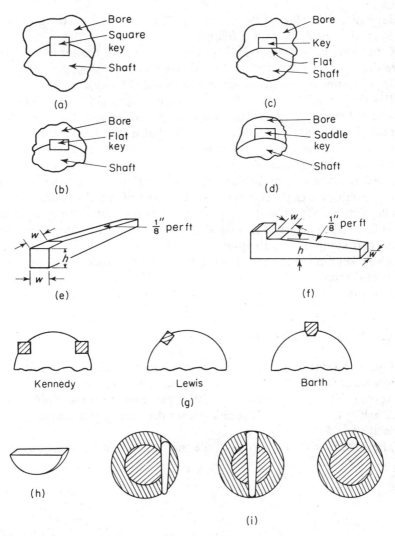

Figure 15.17

Keys which are tapered may be made from square or flat stock with a taper of $\frac{1}{8}$ in./ft of length. At a distance from the large end equal to the width w of the key, the dimensions of the keys are the same as those of parallel keys, whether they are flat or square tapered keys. This is shown in Fig. 15.17(e).

The *gib-head* key, shown in Fig. 15.17(f), is made from similarly tapered stock. The gib-head key is essentially a square key with a *head* machined at the large end. The head provides a method for releasing ("breaking") the taper to aid in removal of the key. If a gear or pulley is mounted at the end of a shaft, this key can be pried loose without too much effort and with practically no damage to either the key or the keyway. There are other methods of releasing keys when their removal is frequent.

Other keys called *tangential* keys are used to take the thrust of driving more directly. They are not as common as those just discussed. The cross sections of some of these keys are shown in Fig. 15.17(g).

Woodruff keys, Fig. 15.17(h), are circular keys made so that they are somewhat less than a semicircle. These keys will be discussed later in this chapter. The advantage of a circular key is that it may be rotated into position in crowded assemblies. It will also rotate if the keyway is not perfectly parallel to the center line of the shaft.

Feathered keys may be fastened to the keyseat in the hub of a clutch plate or in the hub of a gear. This permits movement of the clutch plate or gear parallel to the shaft without losing power from the shaft. Sometimes a long key is fastened to the keyseat in the shaft. This also permits movement of the driven part along the shaft without loss of power.

Round keys in the form of straight, tapered, or threaded pins are inserted in any of the three ways shown in Fig. 15.17(i). These pins are sometimes used as shear pins.

15.6. Keyway Calculations

Figure 15.18(a) shows a *square keyway* cut into a shaft and bore. It should be noted that the depth of the keyway in the shaft is figured from the side of the keyway. Thus half of the key width is machined into the shaft $T/2$. The other half of the key width is machined into the bore d_b. The calculations are made at the *side* of the keyway.

The dotted arc is that portion of the shaft which is machined away before

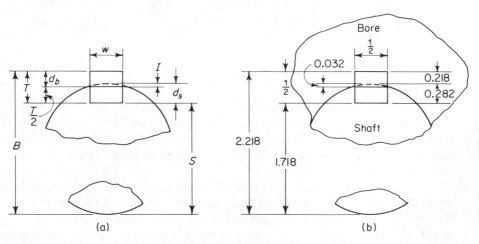

(a)   (b)

Figure 15.18

$T/2$ starts to operate. "T" is the thickness of the key in inches. The height of this arc, which is called the *incompleted* arc, is designated by I. It is given by the equation

$$I = \tfrac{1}{2}(D - \sqrt{D^2 - w^2})$$

D = dia of shaft, in.
w = width of keyway, in.
I = height of incompleted arc, in.

The keyway is machined into the shaft to a depth of

$$d_s = \frac{T}{2} + I$$

d_s = depth of keyway in shaft, in.

The depth of the keyway in the bore is

$$d_b = \frac{T}{2}$$

d_b = depth of keyway in the bore, in.

The distance S from the bottom of the keyway in the shaft to the opposite side of the shaft is

$$S = D - \left(\frac{T}{2} + I\right)$$

The distance B from the bottom of the keyway in the bore to the opposite side of the bore is

$$B = D + \left(\frac{T}{2} - I\right)$$

EXAMPLE 1

Given a shaft with a nominal size of 2 in., and a $\frac{1}{2}$-in. square key, calculate: (1) The height of the incompleted arc; (2) the depth of the keyway in the shaft; (3) the depth of the keyway in the bore; (4) the distance from the bottom of the keyway in the shaft to the opposite side of the shaft; and (5) the distance from the bottom of the keyway in the bore to the opposite side of the bore.

Solution:

1. The height of the incompleted arc

$$1 = \tfrac{1}{2}(D - \sqrt{D^2 - w^2})$$

$$= \tfrac{1}{2}(2.000 - \sqrt{2.000^2 - 0.500^2}) = 0.032 \text{ in}$$

$D = 2$ in.
$w = \frac{1}{2}$ in. = 0.500 in.
$T = \frac{1}{2}$ in. = 0.500 in.

2. The depth of the keyway in the shaft

$$d_s = \frac{T}{2} + I = \frac{0.500}{2} + 0.032$$

$$= 0.282 \text{ in.}$$

3. The depth of the keyway in the bore

$$d_b = \frac{T}{2} = \frac{0.500}{2}$$

$$= 0.250 \text{ in.}$$

4. The distance S in Fig. 15.18(a)

$$S = D - \left(\frac{T}{2} + I\right) = 2.000 - (0.250 + 0.032)$$

$$= 1.718 \text{ in.}$$

5. The distance B in Fig. 15.18(a)

$$B = D + \left(\frac{T}{2} - I\right) = 2.000 + (0.250 - 0.032)$$

$$= 2.218 \text{ in.}$$

The dimensions calculated above are shown in Fig. 15.18(b).

From the above calculations and from Fig. 15.18(b) it should be evident that $T/2$ is calculated from the flat once the incompleted arc has been removed from the *shaft*. Thus in Fig. 15.18(b) an empirical method can be used to cut the keyway. For example, if a $\frac{1}{2}$-in. milling cutter is used and a flat the exact width of the cutter is cut, the incompleted arc will have been cut off. Once this has been done, the graduated dial on the vertical feed may be set at zero. The table is raised $T/2$, in this case 0.250 in., and the cut taken.

When cutting the keyway in the bore, a $\frac{1}{4}$-in. tool bit may be used with the slotting attachment or a $\frac{1}{4}$-in. cutter on a keyseater. The graduated dial is set at zero the instant the tool bit or keyseat cutter touches the bore. The depth of the cut is 0.250 in.

When completed, a micrometer reading from the bottom of the keyway to the opposite side of the shaft should read 1.718 in. A vernier caliper reading from the bottom of the keyway in the bore to the opposite side of the bore should read 2.218 in.

The method just described for cutting a square key was an empirical method. Judgment on when a complete flat or when the tool bit just touches the bore is subject to error. A more accurate method is to use the calculations from Example 1. The graduated dial is set at zero once the outer surface of the shaft has been picked up. The full depth of the keyway, including the incompleted arc, is set on the graduated dial, and a cut taken. (This may require more than one cut.) Note that measurements may be taken from the bottom of the keyway to the opposite side of the diameter as the operation progresses.

Woodruff keys have been standardized so that the number of the key may be used to determine the thickness of the key or cutter and the diameter of the cutter. The first digit (or first two digits) of the Woodruff number in 32nds gives the width of the cutter. The last two digits in eighths give the diameter of the cutter. Thus a Woodruff key which has a 1210 American Standard number yields the following information:

The cutter width is

$$w = \tfrac{12}{32} = \tfrac{3}{8} \text{ in.}$$

w = width of cutter
c = dia of cutter

The cutter diameter is

$$c = \tfrac{10}{8} = 1\tfrac{1}{4} \text{ in.}$$

In Fig. 15.19(a) it can be seen that the height of the key is less than the radius of the cutter by an amount k. The values of k are shown in Table 15.1. Therefore the height of the key h is

$$h = \frac{c}{2} - k$$

h = height of key
c = dia of cutter
k = conversion factor

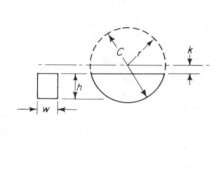

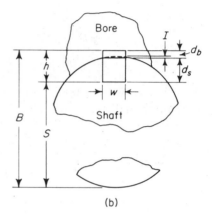

(a)   (b)

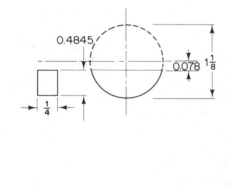

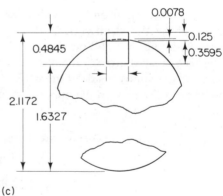

(c)

Figure 15.19

TABLE 15.1

Key no.	XX4	XX5–XX8	XX9–XX10	XX11	XX12
Conversion k	$\frac{3}{64}$	$\frac{1}{16}$	$\frac{5}{64}$	$\frac{3}{32}$	$\frac{7}{64}$

Another rule used is: The depth of the keyway in the shaft is such that one-half the width of the key protrudes above the shaft when inserted in the keyway. Thus

$$d_s = h - \tfrac{1}{2}w \qquad\qquad d_s = \text{depth of keyway in shaft}$$

Since one-half the width of the keyway will protrude above the shaft, the keyway in the bore must equal one-half the width of the key, neglecting clearance.

$$d_b = \tfrac{1}{2}w \qquad\qquad d_b = \text{depth of key in bore}$$

The incompleted-arc height I is the same as for a square key.

$$I = \tfrac{1}{2}(D - \sqrt{D^2 - w^2})$$

D = dia of shaft
w = width of key or cutter
I = height of incompleted arc

The distance S from the bottom of the keyway in the shaft to the opposite side of the shaft is

$$S = D - (d_s + I)$$

The distance B from the bottom of the keyway in the bore to the opposite side of the bore is

$$B = D + (d_b - I)$$

These dimensions are shown in Fig. 15.19(b).

EXAMPLE 2

Given a 2-in. shaft and a number 809 Woodruff key, find: (1) the dimensions of the Woodruff cutter; (2) the height of the key; (3) the depth of the keyway in the shaft; (4) the depth of the keyway in the bore; (5) the height of the incompleted arc; (6) the distance from the bottom of the keyway in the shaft to the opposite side of the shaft; (7) the distance from the bottom of the keyway in the bore to the opposite side of the bore.

Solution:

1. The cutter dimensions are

$$w = \tfrac{8}{32} = \tfrac{1}{4} \text{ in.} \qquad\qquad D = 2 \text{ in.}$$
$$c = \tfrac{9}{8} = 1\tfrac{1}{8} \text{ in.} \qquad\qquad \begin{array}{l} \text{Key no.} = 809 \\ k = \tfrac{5}{64} = 0.078 \text{ in.} \end{array}$$

2. The height of the key is

$$h = \frac{c}{2} - k = \frac{1.125}{2} - 0.078$$

$$= 0.4845 \text{ in.}$$

3. The depth of the keyway in the shaft is

$$d_s = h - \tfrac{1}{2}w = 0.4845 - \tfrac{1}{2}(0.250)$$

$$= 0.3595 \text{ in.}$$

4. The depth of the keyway in the bore is

$$d_b = \tfrac{1}{2}w = \tfrac{1}{2}(0.250)$$
$$= 0.125 \text{ in.}$$

5. The height of the incompleted arc is

$$I = \tfrac{1}{2}(D - \sqrt{D^2 - w^2}) = \tfrac{1}{2}(2.000 - \sqrt{2.000^2 - 0.250^2})$$
$$= 0.0078 \text{ in.}$$

6. The distance S is

$$S = D - (d_s + I) = 2.000 - (0.3595 + 0.0078)$$
$$= 1.6327 \text{ in.}$$

7. The distance B is

$$B = D + (d_b - I) = 2.000 + (0.125 - 0.0078)$$
$$= 2.1172 \text{ in.}$$

The dimensions are shown in Fig. 15.19(c). British metric standards for square and rectangular keys have been developed; some of these are shown in Table 15.2.

EXAMPLE 3

Given a 46 mm diameter shaft, find: (1) the key size; (2) the distance from the bottom of the keyway in the shaft to the top of the incompleted arc; (3) the distance from the incompleted arc to the bottom of the keyway in the bore; (4) the distance from the bottom of the keyway in the shaft to the opposite side of the shaft; (5) the distance from the bottom of the keyway in the bore to the opposite side of the bore.

Solution:

1. The key size from Table 15.2 is

$$w \times T = 14 \text{ mm wide} \times 9 \text{ mm thick} \qquad D = 46 \text{ mm}$$

2. The distance from the bottom of the keyway in the shaft to the top of the incompleted arc is

$$d_s = 5.5 \text{ mm}$$

3. The distance from the incompleted arc to the bottom of the keyway in the bore is

$$d_b = 3.8 \text{ mm*}$$

4. The distance from the bottom of the keyway in the shaft to the opposite side of the shaft is

$$S = D - d_s = 46 - 5.5$$
$$= 40.5 \text{ mm}$$

*It should be noted that in Table 15.2, $d_s + d_b$ need *not* add to T.

TABLE 15.2

Square and Rectangular Metric Keys

Shaft range dia mm	Key size mm w	T	d_s mm	d_b mm
6–8	2	2	1.2	1.0
8–10	3	3	1.8	1.4
10–12	4	4	2.5	1.8
12–17	5	5	3.0	2.3
17–22	6	6	3.5	2.8
22–30	8	7	4.0	3.3
30–38	10	8	5.0	3.3
38–44	12	8	5.0	3.3
44–50	14	9	5.5	3.8
50–58	16	10	6.0	4.3
58–65	18	11	7.00	4.4
65–75	20	12	7.5	4.9
75–85	22	14	9.0	5.4
85–95	25	14	9.0	5.4
95–110	28	16	10.0	6.4
110–130	32	18	11.0	7.4
130–150	36	20	12.0	8.4
150–170	40	22	13.0	9.4
170–200	45	25	15.0	10.4
200–230	50	28	17.0	11.4
230–260	56	32	20.0	12.4
260–290	63	32	20.0	12.4
290–330	70	36	22.0	14.4
330–380	80	40	25.0	15.4
380–440	90	45	28.0	17.4
440–500	100	50	31.0	19.5

British Standards 4235: Part 1; 1972

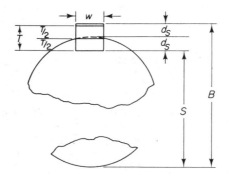

5. The distance from the bottom of the keyway in the bore to the opposite side of the bore is

$$B = D + d_b = 46 + 3.8$$
$$= 49.8 \text{ mm}$$

The dimensions are shown in Fig. 15.20.

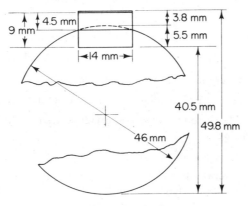

Figure 15.20

QUESTIONS AND PROBLEMS

15.1 List and discuss the fundamental differences in structure between a bed type milling machine and a column and knee type of milling machine.

15.2 What is the saddle of a milling machine? What is its purpose?

15.3 What is the knee on a milling machine? What is its purpose?

15.4 What is the column of a milling machine? What is its use?

15.5 Make a sketch of a dovetail. How are gibs used on a milling machine?

15.6 What are the distinguishing characteristics of a universal and of a plain milling machine?

15.7 How does a universal milling machine differ from a compound universal milling machine?

15.8 Make a sketch of a horizontal boring mill. Show the direction of movement of the spindle, the headstock, the table, and the saddle.

15.9 Using Fig. 15.2(b), explain the hobbing principle.

15.10 Explain the principle of a two-plane tracer-control milling machine.

15.11 Explain the principle of a three-plane tracer-control milling machine.

15.12 List at least three methods for supporting an arbor in a milling-machine spindle.

15.13 How is a cutter positioned laterally on an arbor?

15.14 What is a drawbar on a milling machine? When must it be used? When is it optional that it be used?

15.15 How does the vertical head in Fig. 15.3(c) differ from the vertical head in Fig. 15.3(d)?

15.16 Check your library, and see whether you can explain the mechanism inside a slotting attachment and what causes it to oscillate.

15.17 What is a rack?

15.18 Discuss at least two methods for fastening a milling vise to the table.

15.19 How does a universal dividing head differ from a plain dividing head?

15.20 What is a rotary table? How are they indexed?

15.21 How does a universal dividing head differ from a plain dividing head?

15.22 What must be done to a universal dividing head before it can be used for direct indexing?

15.23 What is the purpose of the sector arms on a universal dividing head?

15.24 There are several ratios other than 40:1 which are used in rotary tables. Check your library reference material, and see if you can find these ratios. List them, and write the equation for the movement of the index handle for these ratios.

15.25 Explain the positioning control of a jig borer when rods, micrometers, and dial indicators are used.

15.26 How does a plain milling cutter differ from a side milling cutter?

15.27 Define, or explain, a right-hand helix. Do the same for a left-hand helix.

15.28 What is a stagger-tooth cutter? Why is it preferred to a plain milling cutter?

15.29 What is the purpose of an interlocking cutter?

15.30 How does a Woodruff cutter differ from a T-slot cutter?

15.31 Describe the difference between a two-flute center-cutting end mill and a four-flute center-relieved (gashed) end mill?

15.32 What is a shell mill? What is a slab mill? How do they differ?

15.33 What is a fly cutter? Describe it, and state how it is used?

15.34 Explain the combination of the "hand" of a cutter helix and cut as shown in Fig. 15.9.

15.35 Why is it important to establish a reference reading on one of the graduated dials before setting a cutter for a desired depth of cut?

15.36 Explain the procedure for aligning a vise on a plain milling machine.

15.37 A milling vise is aligned with a universal milling-machine table. The table is offset 10°. A dial-indicator needle is brought into contact with the solid jaw of the vise and set at 0. The table is moved. Will the needle remain on 0? Check your answer with the universal milling machine in your shop. Explain your results.

15.38   What is the proper procedure for aligning a universal milling-machine table and a universal vise mounted on the table?

15.39   What is the difference between conventional and climb milling? When is it proper to use each?

15.40   Explain the squaring of a block of steel on a milling machine.

15.41   Explain the procedure used to mill a cavity in a rectangular block.

15.42   Discuss the various methods which may be used to mill a chamfer, or an angle on a workpiece.

15.43   Describe the entire operation when a hexagon is to be milled on a round piece of material using a dividing head and two cutters.

15.44   List two ways of cutting a keyway or slot. Discuss one of them.

15.45   Name several types of keys, and tell when it is appropriate to use them.

15.46   What is the function of a head on a gib-head key?

15.47   Why are tangential keys used?

15.48   Draw a Woodruff key. Is the key a semicircle?

15.49   If a square key is sunk into a shaft, from which point on the diameter of the shaft is half the key sunk into the shaft?

15.50   How much of a Woodruff key must protrude above the shaft?

15.51   What is an incompleted arc with reference to keys?

15.52   Explain the empirical method of cutting a square keyway in a shaft and in a bore.

15.53   Explain the empirical method of cutting a Woodruff keyway.

15.54   Given a shaft 3 in. in diameter with a $\frac{3}{8}$-in. square key, find: (a) the height of the incompleted arc; (b) the depth of the keyway in the shaft; (c) the depth of the keyway in the bore; (d) the distance from the depth of the keyway in the shaft to the opposite side of the shaft; (e) the distance from the bottom of the keyway in the bore to the opposite side of the bore.

15.55   Given a $1\frac{1}{2}$-in.-diameter shaft and a $\frac{1}{4}$-in. key, complete all the calculations asked for in problem 15.54.

15.56   Given a shaft, nominal size $3\frac{1}{2}$ in. and a $\frac{7}{16}$ in. square key, calculate: (a) the incompleted arc; (b) the depth of the keyway in the shaft; (c) the depth of the keyway in the bore; (d) the distance from the bottom of the keyway in the shaft to the opposite side of the shaft; (e) the distance from the bottom of the keyway in the bore to the opposite side of the bore.

15.57   What is the diameter and width of each of the following Woodruff key numbers: (a) 606; (b) 1008; (c) 1212; (d) 1217; (e) 1628?

15.58   Given a 3-in. shaft and a 1012 Woodruff key, find: (a) the dimensions of the Woodruff cutter; (b) the height of the key; (c) the depth of the keyway in the shaft; (d) the depth of the keyway in the bore; (e) the height of the incompleted arc; (f) the distance from the bottom of the keyway in the shaft to the opposite side of the shaft; (g) the distance from the bottom of the keyway in the bore to the opposite side of the bore.

15.59   Given a 3-in. diameter shaft and a number 1212 Woodruff key, calculate: (a) the dimension of the Woodruff cutter; (b) the height of the key; (c) the depth of the keyway in the shaft; (d) the depth of the keyway in the bore; (e) the incompleted arc; (f) the distance from the bottom of the keyway in the shaft to the opposite side of the shaft; (g) the distance from the bottom of the keyway in the bore to the opposite side of the bore.

15.60   Using Table 15.2, repeat illustrated Example 3 when the shaft diameter is 70 mm.

The Index Head

16

16.1. Direct Indexing

The indexing head is a most useful attachment. Its construction was discussed in Chapter 15. Except for the advent of numerical control (NC) and computer numerical control (CNC), the dividing head remains one of the most widely used methods for dividing a circle into an equal number of parts.

Two assumptions are made when making calculations for indexing: (1) When it is required that the index handle should be moved N holes, the hole in which the index pin rests prior to indexing is not counted. Thus we really are counting spaces moved. (2) Unless otherwise stated, all calculations apply to one revolution, 360°, of the *work*.

By far the easiest and most accurate of all the indexing processes is *direct indexing*. The universal dividing head, Fig. 15.5(a), is equipped with a 24-hole direct-index plate and pin. When using the plate, the worm and worm wheel are disengaged. Once this has been done, the direct-index pin is disengaged, the work and index plate are rotated the desired number of holes, and the pin is inserted.

By using the direct-index plate, all the factors of 24 can be indexed. It is therefore possible to direct-index the workpiece into 2, 3, 4, 6, 8, 12, and 24 parts.

EXAMPLE 1

Assume that it is desired to divide a workpiece into three equal parts of the circumference. Describe the direct-index procedure.

Solution:

1. The pin is engaged in any one of the holes in the direct-index plate. The locking mechanism locks the work, and a cut is taken.

2. The pin is disengaged, and the work is rotated

$$\frac{24}{N} = \frac{24}{3} = 8 \text{ holes}$$

$N = 3$ divisions

The initial hole in which the pin was inserted is not counted. The work is locked, and a second cut is taken.
3. The pin is disengaged again, the work rotated eight holes, the pin engaged, the work locked, and a third cut taken. If the work is rotated again, the work will have returned to its initial position.

Some companies make dividing-head attachments for milling machines which are intended for direct indexing only. In this case plates are furnished as replacements when a wide variety of direct-indexing operations are required.

16.2. Simple Indexing

The dividing head, Fig. 15.5(a), shows the worm and worm wheel arrangement. If the index pin is retracted and the index handle rotated, the worm shaft rotates and turns the worm wheel. Since the worm wheel is mounted and keyed to the spindle, the spindle must rotate when the index handle rotates. This is shown in Fig. 16.1(a).

All the gears inside the dividing head are of 1 : 1 ratio, with the exception of the gears and worm wheel. The ratio of the worm to the worm wheel is 40 : 1. Thus, if the worm has a single start (as is the case in our dividing head) and the worm wheel has 40 teeth and if we think of the worm as being a one-tooth gear, it will take 40 revolutions of the worm to turn the worm wheel 1 revolution or it will take 1 revolution of the index handle to turn the work $\frac{1}{40}$ revolution. The ratio of the movement of the index handle to the movement of the work can readily be checked by determining how many turns of the index handle are required for one revolution of the work.

The equation for simple indexing is

$$M = \frac{40}{N}$$

M = movement of index handle
N = no. of divisions required

Thus, if 40 divisions are needed in 360° of the circumference of the workpiece,

$$M = \frac{40}{N} = \frac{40}{40} = 1$$

Thus one full revolution of the index handle is required for each division of the circumference of the workpiece.

EXAMPLE 2

Assume a workpiece is to be divided into 10 divisions. What is the movement of the index handle?

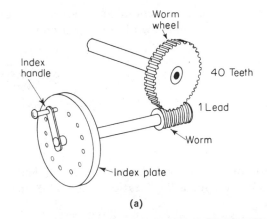

(a)

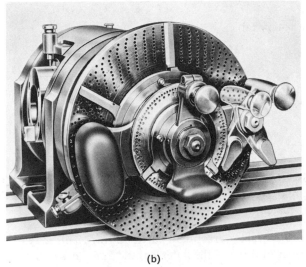

(b)

Figure 16.1   (*Photo courtesy of Cincinnati Milacron, Inc.*)

Solution:

The movement of the index handle is $N = 10$ divisions

$$M = \frac{40}{N} = \frac{40}{10}$$

= 4 full turns of the index handle

If the index handle is rotated 4 turns, 1 of the 10 divisions will have been indexed. If this is done 10 times, the required indexing will have been accomplished for 360° of the workpiece.

If a rotary table has a worm-to-worm gear ratio of 90 : 1, it will take 90 revolutions of the index handle to revolve the table one revolution. Therefore, if we let M equal the movement of the index handle, and N equal the number of desired divisions on the work, the equation is

$$M = \frac{90}{N}$$

$M =$ movement of the index handle
$N =$ number divisions on work

Rotary tables are also made with worm-to-worm wheel ratios of 120 and 240 : 1 as well as 4 : 1.

EXAMPLE 3

Assume a workpiece is to be divided into 5 parts. Calculate the movement of the index handle (1) for a 90 : 1 ratio rotary table and (2) for a 40 : 1 dividing head.

Solution:

1. For a rotary table

$$M = \frac{90}{N} = \frac{90}{5}$$

$= 18$ full turns of the index handle

2. For a dividing head

$$M = \frac{40}{N} = \frac{40}{5}$$

$= 8$ full turns of the index handle

Figure 16.1(b) shows a wide range universal dividing head. It is capable of dividing a circle from 2 to 400,000 divisions. The small plate acts as a vernier to the larger plate.

Suppose $40/N$ yields a fractional part of a turn. This may be resolved into a whole number of turns of the index handle and parts of a turn of the index handle for a particular hole circle. The plates furnished are as follows:

Brown and Sharpe Company
Plate 1: 15, 16, 17, 18, 19, 20

Plate 2: 21, 23, 27, 29, 31, 33

Plate 3: 37, 39, 41, 43, 47, 49

Cincinnati Milling Company
Side 1: 24, 25, 28, 30, 34, 37, 38, 39, 41, 42, 43

Side 2: 46, 47, 49, 51, 53, 54, 57, 58, 59, 62, 66

Besides the plate (drilled on both sides) furnished by the Cincinnati Milling Company, three additional plates may be purchased which increase the indexing capacity of the dividing head. These plates are:

Plate 1: 30, 48, 69, 91,   99, 117, 129, 147, 171, 177, 189,   Side No. 1
        36, 67, 81, 97, 111, 127, 141, 157, 169, 183, 199   Side No. 2

Plate 2: 34, 46, 79, 93, 109, 123, 139, 153, 167, 181, 197,   Side No. 1
          32, 44, 77, 89, 107, 121, 137, 151, 163, 179, 193   Side No. 2

Plate 3: 26, 42, 73, 87, 103, 119, 133, 149, 161, 175, 191,   Side No. 1
          28, 38, 71, 83, 101, 113, 131, 143, 159, 173, 187   Side No. 2

EXAMPLE 4

It is required that a surface be divided into six equal parts. What are all the possibilities for moving the index handle: (1) on the Brown and Sharpe dividing head, (2) on the Cincinnati Milling dividing head?

Solution:

The movement of the index handle is

$$M = \frac{40}{N} = \frac{60}{6}$$

$$= 6\tfrac{2}{3} \text{ turns}$$

$N = 6$

Thus the index handle must move *six full turns and two-thirds of a turn for each division of the work.* When using the hole circles listed above, if the denominator of the fractional part of a turn of the index handle divides evenly into any of the hole circles, then that fractional part of the hole circle will give the desired part of the movement of the index handle. Note very carefully that any of the calculations which follow divide the hole circle used into two-thirds of a rotation of the index handle.

1. On the Brown and Sharpe index head

   6 full turns and $\tfrac{2}{3}$ × 15 = 10 holes (spaces) in the 15-hole circle
   $\phantom{6 full turns and \tfrac{2}{3}}$ × 18 = 12   //   // // 18- //   //
   $\phantom{6 full turns and \tfrac{2}{3}}$ × 21 = 14   //   // // 21- //   //
   $\phantom{6 full turns and \tfrac{2}{3}}$ × 27 = 18   //   // // 27- //   //
   $\phantom{6 full turns and \tfrac{2}{3}}$ × 33 = 22   //   // // 33- //   //
   $\phantom{6 full turns and \tfrac{2}{3}}$ × 39 = 26   //   // // 39- //   //

2. On the Cincinnati dividing head (we shall use only the plate furnished with the machine)

   6 full turns and $\tfrac{2}{3}$ × 24 = 16 holes (spaces) in the 16-hole circle
   $\phantom{6 full turns and \tfrac{2}{3}}$ × 30 = 20   //   // // 30- //   //
   $\phantom{6 full turns and \tfrac{2}{3}}$ × 39 = 26   //   // // 39- //   //
   $\phantom{6 full turns and \tfrac{2}{3}}$ × 42 = 28   //   // // 42- //   //
   $\phantom{6 full turns and \tfrac{2}{3}}$ × 51 = 34   //   // // 51- //   //
   $\phantom{6 full turns and \tfrac{2}{3}}$ × 57 = 38   //   // // 57- //   //
   $\phantom{6 full turns and \tfrac{2}{3}}$ × 66 = 44   //   // // 66- //   //

Six full turns of the index handle and any of the above results will give the desired number of divisions.

Simple angular indexing can also be accomplished with the dividing head.

1. Since 40 turns of the index handle equal 360° of the work, 1 turn of the index handle equals

$$\tfrac{1}{40}(360°) = 9°$$

2. On the Brown and Sharpe dividing head
   For the 18-hole circle

$$9° = 18 \text{ holes}$$

then

$$1° = 2 \text{ holes in the 18-hole circle}$$

and

$$\tfrac{1}{2}° = 30' = 1 \text{ hole in the 18-hole circle}$$

For the 27-hole circle

$$9° = 27 \text{ holes}$$

then

$$1° = 3 \text{ holes}$$

and

$$\tfrac{2}{3}° = 40' = 2 \text{ holes}$$

and

$$\tfrac{1}{3}° = 20' = 1 \text{ hole}$$

3. On the Cincinnati dividing head
   For the 54-hole circle

$$9° = 54 \text{ holes}$$

$$1° = 6 \text{ holes}$$

$$\tfrac{5}{6}° = 50' = 5 \text{ holes}$$

$$\tfrac{2}{3}° = 40' = 4 \text{ holes}$$

$$\tfrac{1}{2}° = 30' = 3 \text{ holes}$$

$$\tfrac{1}{3}° = 20' = 2 \text{ holes}$$

$$\tfrac{1}{6}° = 10' = 1 \text{ hole}$$

EXAMPLE 5

If two drilled holes are dimensioned as being 24°40′ apart, what is the movement of the index handle (1) on the Brown and Sharpe and (2) on the Cincinnati dividing heads?

Solution:

24°40′ = 2(9°) + 6°40′ = 2 full turns of the index handle plus 6°40′/9° parts of a turn.

1. On the Brown and Sharpe dividing head only the 27-hole plate can be used. If

$$3 \text{ holes} = 1°$$

then from 6°40′

$$6° \times 3 \text{ holes/degree} = 18 \text{ holes}$$
$$40' = \underline{2 \text{ holes}}$$
$$\text{Total} = 20 \text{ holes}$$

Thus, to index 24°40′ on the Brown and Sharpe dividing head, the movement of the index handle is

2 full turns + 20 holes in the 27-hole circle

2. On the Cincinnati dividing head the 54-hole circle applies

$$6° \times 6 \text{ holes/degree} = 36 \text{ holes}$$
$$40' = \underline{4 \text{ holes}}$$
$$\text{Total} = 40 \text{ holes}$$

To index 24°40′ on the Cincinnati Milling dividing head, the movement of the index handle is

2 full turns + 40 holes in the 54-hole circle

16.3. Differential Indexing

Assume the problem is to index 119 divisions. It can be seen that with the standard plates available 119 divisions cannot be simple-indexed because $40/N = \frac{40}{119}$ and we do not have a 119-hole circle. The problem, therefore, becomes one of trying to find some number which *can* be simple-indexed and of selecting gears which will take care of the extra hole or holes. Thus, if 120 were selected, this could be simple-indexed and a gear train would take care of the extra hole. This will be explained in Example 6.

Fig. 16.2(a) shows the dividing head. All gears inside the dividing head are 1 : 1 except the worm and worm wheel. The four gears shown are the spindle gear, two idlers, and the worm gear, which are all on the outside of the dividing head. Known as the *change gears*, these are combinations of

24, 24, 28, 32, 40, 44, 48, 56, 64, 72, 86, 100.

Assume the change gears are mounted to give a 1 : 1 ratio. The lockpin is withdrawn. Assume the index handle is rotated clockwise when set up 1 : 1, as shown in Fig. 16.2(a). The index plate will receive power through the change gears and sleeve and will rotate counterclockwise. Thus, as the index handle is rotated, the index hole "*A*" from which the pin was retracted rotates to meet the movement of the index pin. This is shown in Fig. 16.2(b). Since we have geared the dividing head in a 1 : 1 ratio, the crank will meet the index hole "*A*" one-fortieth of a revolution short. That is, for simple indexing the hole "*A*" remains fixed. Thus, to index 40 divisions for 360° of the work, the crank must be indexed 40 times. However, in differential indexing, since we are turning the index handle one revolution *less one-fortieth of a revolution*, it will require an additional index motion to complete the 360° of the work.

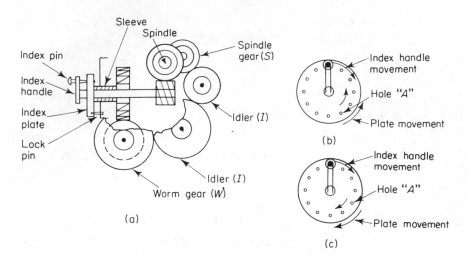

Figure 16.2

This extra movement puts 41 divisions on the work. Thus, even though we were indexing as if we wanted 40 divisions on the work, the index plate movement gave us 41 divisions. The gearing has accounted for the extra division.

If an extra idler is inserted (or one removed) in Fig. 16.2(a), the index plate will be caused to rotate in the same direction as the index handle, as shown in Fig. 16.2(c). Therefore, the crank, in order to catch up with index hole "A", will have to move one-fortieth of a revolution more than one turn. Thirty-nine divisions will be indexed for a 360° rotation of the work.

It should be evident that a great number of divisions can be indexed using differential indexing if the proper gear train is selected. Whether the divisions are gained or lost depends upon the number of idlers used. For convenience the following calculations will be restricted to the use of the Brown and Sharpe plates. The principle applies as well to the Cincinnati Milling plates.

There are many methods for calculating the requirements for differential indexing. Probably the simplest method is the one which follows:

1. Let N equal the number of divisions desired.
2. Select a number D which can be simple-indexed.
3. To find the gear on the spindle and the gear on the worm

$$S = |N - D|$$

and

$$W = \frac{D}{40}$$

N = no. of divisions desired
D = no. of divisions possible by simple indexing
S = no. of teeth for gear on spindle
W = no. of teeth for gear on worm

4. The gear ratio is

$$r = \frac{S}{W} = \frac{\text{driver}}{\text{driven}}$$

r = gear ratio
M = movement of index handle

5. This ratio r may be used to find either a simple gear train or a compound gear train.

    a. When $N < D$

       If a simple gear train is used, one idler should be used. If a compound gear train is used, *no* idlers are necessary.

    b. When $N > D$

       If a simple gear train is used, two idlers should be used. If a compound gear train is used, one idler is necessary.

6. The simple-indexing equation gives the movement of the index handle. The equation is

$$M = \frac{40}{D}$$

Thus the movement of the index handle operates according to the principle of simple indexing, and the gear ratio r makes it possible to find the gears which take care of the residual divisions.

EXAMPLE 6

Find the movement of the index handle and the gears needed to index 119 divisions.

Solution:

1. Let $D = 120$ $N = 119$
2. To find S,

$$S = |D - N| = |120 - 119| = 1$$

3. To find W,

$$W = \frac{D}{40} = \frac{120}{40} = 3$$

4. The gear ratio is

$$r = \frac{S}{W} = \frac{1}{3}$$

5. The gear train is

$$\frac{S}{W} = \frac{1 \times 24}{3 \times 24} = \frac{24 \text{ driver}}{72 \text{ driven}}$$

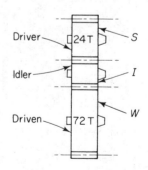

Driver — 24 T — S
Idler — I
Driven — 72 T — W

Figure 16.3

6. Since $N < D$ and simple gearing is used, one idler is needed. The gear train (Fig. 16.3) is

$$24\text{T driver}, \quad 72\text{T driven}, \quad 1 \text{ idler}$$

7. The movement of the index handle is

$$M = \frac{40}{D} = \frac{40}{120} = \frac{1}{3}$$

From the available hole circles on the Brown and Sharpe dividing head

$$M = \frac{1}{3} \times 15 = 5 \text{ holes in the 15-hole circle}$$

EXAMPLE 7

Index 53 divisions. Find the gears and the movement of the index handle.

Solution:

1. Let $D = 50$ $\qquad\qquad\qquad\qquad\qquad\qquad N = 53$
2. Then

$$S = |N - D| = |53 - 50| = 3$$

3. And

$$W = \frac{D}{40} = \frac{50}{40} = \frac{5}{4}$$

4. The ratio is

$$r = \frac{S}{W} = \frac{3}{\frac{5}{4}} = \frac{12}{5}$$

5. The gear train is a compound train

$$\frac{S}{W} = \frac{12}{5} = \frac{4 \times 8}{5 \times 8} \times \frac{3 \times 24}{1 \times 24} = \frac{32 \times 72}{40 \times 24} \frac{\text{driver}}{\text{driven}}$$

6. Since $N > D$ and a compound gear train is used, one idler is needed. There are four compound gear trains which can be used. They are shown in Fig. 16.4.
7. The movement of the index handle is

$$M = \frac{40}{D} = \frac{40}{50} = \frac{4}{5}$$

$$M = \frac{4}{5} \times 15 = 12 \text{ holes in the 15-hole circle}$$

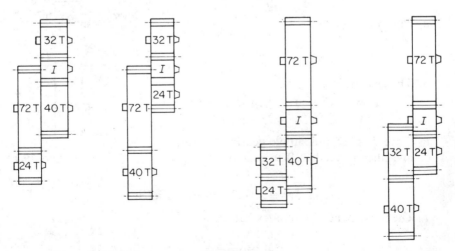

Figure 16.4

16.4. Differential Indexing—The Approximate Method

We have seen that while commonly used angles may be indexed simply, many angles cannot be indexed exactly. There are many methods that may be used to index angles to close approximations that are within the tolerance allowed by the blue print. The methods discussed in this chapter are acceptable because they determine the error, giving the operator a mathematical basis for making a judgment regarding the acceptability of a procedure.

The approximate method requires that the degrees desired be converted to minutes, or to seconds if the lowest order of angular measurement is the second. Since there are 9° in one revolution of the index handle, this should be converted to minutes. The procedure for calculating the movement of the index handle is best illustrated with an example.

EXAMPLE 8

Calculate (1) the movement of the index handle necessary to index 39°43' and (2) the error for each index movement.

Solution:

1. Convert 39°43' to a whole and fractional part of a whole number of turns of the index handle.
   a. One turn of the index handle is 9° of the work

   $$9° \times 4 \text{ turns} = 36°$$

   The degrees which remain to be indexed are

   $$39°43' - 36° = 3°43'$$

   The problem reduces to one of finding the partial number of turns of the index handle. Thus

   $$4 \text{ full turns and } \frac{3°43'}{9°} \text{ parts of a turn}$$

   b. Convert this fraction to its lowest terms—in this case to minutes

   $$\frac{3°43'}{9°} = \frac{(3 \times 60) + 43}{9 \times 60} = \frac{223}{540} \text{ parts of a turn}$$

   c. Divide the larger number by the smaller number. (Note the inverse division).

   $$\tfrac{540}{223} = 2.4215$$

   d. Multiply 2.4215 by *any number*. The product should yield a number close to one of the index-hole circles. The multipliers 7 and 12 will work. Thus

   $$2.4215 \times 7 = 16.9505 \sim 17 \text{ hole circle}$$
   $$2.4215 \times 12 = 29.0580 \sim 29 \text{ hole circle}$$

409

e. The first product means 7 holes in the 17 hole circle may be used. The second product means 12 holes in the 29 hole circle may also be used.

2. If 17 and 29 hole plates are used

a. The angular movement for 7 holes in the 17 hole plate is

$$\tfrac{7}{17} \times 540 = 222.4 \text{ minutes}$$

the error is

$$223 - 222.4 = 0.6 \text{ minutes}$$

b. The angular movement for 12 holes in the 29 hole plate is

$$\tfrac{12}{29} \times 540 = 223.5 \text{ minutes}$$

the error is

$$223.5 - 223 = 0.5 \text{ minutes}$$

16.5. Continued Fractions and Angular Indexing

The method of continued fractions is a mathematical process for finding ratios which approximate the desired ratios. The process is best illustrated with an illustrated problem.

EXAMPLE 9

Using the method of continued fractions, index 39°43′. Calculate the movement of the index handle and the error.

Solution:

1. Convert 39°43′ to a whole number of turns and a partial number of turns of the index handle.

$$39°43 - (9° \times 4 \text{ full turns}) = 39°43' - 36° = 3°43'$$

This may be written as a fractional part of a turn

$$\frac{3°43'}{9°} = \frac{(3 \times 60) + 43}{9 \times 60} = \frac{223}{540}$$

Thus 39°43′ translates to

4 full turns and $\tfrac{223}{540}$ parts of a turn of the index handle

2. Divide the larger by the smaller number

$$223)540(2$$
$$\underline{446}$$
$$94$$

3. The quotient is 2, the remainder 94. In the step below 223 is the new dividend, and 94 the new divisor. Thus

$$223)540(2$$
$$446$$
$$\overline{94)223(2}$$
$$188$$
$$\overline{35}$$

4. The new remainder is 35. The procedure is completed when the remainder 0 is obtained. That is

$$223)540(2$$
$$446$$
$$\overline{94)223(2}$$
$$188$$
$$\overline{35)94(2}$$
$$70$$
$$\overline{24)35(1}$$
$$24$$
$$\overline{11)24(2}$$
$$22$$
$$\overline{2)11(5}$$
$$10$$
$$\overline{1)2(2}$$
$$2$$
$$\overline{0}$$

5. Next a series of boxes is constructed as shown in Fig. 16.5(a). The last two remainders (0, 1) are inserted into rows B and C, and the quotients are inserted into row A as shown.

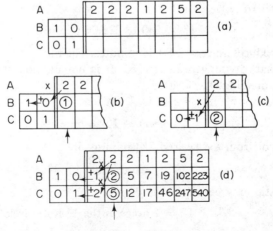

Figure 16.5

6. The number 2 from row A multiplies 0 and adds 1 from row B.

$$(2 \times 0) + 1 = 1$$

The number 1 is inserted into row B, Fig. 16.5(b).

7. The number 2 from row A multiplies the 1 and adds the 0 from row C.

$$(2 \times 1) + 0 = 2$$

The number 2 is inserted into row C as shown in Fig. 16.5(c).

8. This process is continued until all the boxes in rows B and C, Fig. 16.5(a) are filled. Thus in Fig. 16.5(d)

$$(2 \times 1) + 0 = 2$$

and

$$(2 \times 2) + 1 = 5$$

The final box arrangement is shown in Fig. 16.5(d).

9. Note the last two numbers under the quotient 2, row A. They yield the original fraction

$$\frac{223}{540}$$

10. The next set of numbers 102 and 247 yield the fraction

$$\frac{102}{247}$$

This ratio represents a fractional part of 9° (540 minutes), or

$$\frac{102}{247} \times 540 = 222.996 \text{ minutes}$$

If it were possible to index $\frac{102}{247}$ parts of one full turn of the index handle, the error would be

$$223 - 222.996 = 0.004 \text{ minutes}$$

Since there is no 247 hole plate, the next ratio is investigated.

11. The next ratio is $\frac{19}{46}$, and

$$\frac{19}{46} \times 540 = 223.04 \text{ minutes}$$

This produces an error of 0.04 minutes. The ratio of $\frac{19}{46}$ is possible if a Cincinnati dividing head is used. It is not possible if a Brown and Sharpe dividing head is used.

12. The next ratio, Fig. 16.5(d) is $\frac{7}{17}$, or

$$\frac{7}{17} \times 540 = 222.4 \text{ minutes}$$

The error from the desired 223 minutes is

$$0.6 \text{ minutes}$$

This ratio may be indexed and

$$\frac{7}{17} \times 17 = 7 \text{ holes in the 17 hole circle}$$

13. Thus, to index 39°43′ would require 4 full turns and 7 holes in the 17-

hole circle. This would produce an error of 0.6 minutes. Compare this result with Example 8(2).

16.6. Graduating Scale

In *differential indexing* the worm W is geared to the spindle S of the dividing head, Fig. 16.6(a). The worm W may also be geared to the lead screw L of the milling-machine table, Fig. 16.6(b). This is called *helical milling* and will be discussed in Section 16.7. The third possibility is to gear the spindle S of the dividing head to the lead screw L of the milling machine, Fig. 16.6(c). This is called *graduating a scale*.

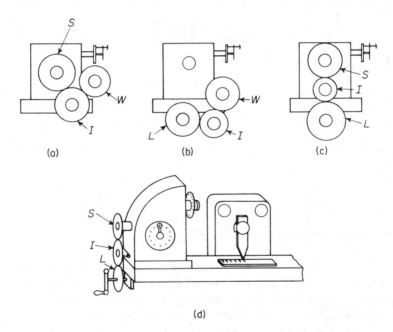

Figure 16.6

Verniers and scales may be scribed with a sharp tool mounted in the spindle of the milling machine, Fig. 16.6(d). No power is used in the milling-machine spindle or the lead screw of the table. However, as the index handle is rotated, the hand power is transmitted through the 40 : 1-ratio worm and worm wheel into the change gears and then to the lead screw of the milling machine.

Thus if the gears are mounted in a 1 : 1 ratio, revolving the index handle one turn causes the gear on the spindle to move one-fortieth of a revolution. If the lead screw has four threads per inch ($\frac{1}{4}$-in. lead), the table will move

$$1 \text{ turn of the index handle} = \tfrac{1}{40} \times \tfrac{1}{4} = \tfrac{1}{160} = 0.00625 \text{ in.}$$

The equation for finding the movement of the index handle for graduating a scale is

$$M_g = \frac{G}{0.00625}$$

M_g = movement of index handle
G = spacing of scribed lines

EXAMPLE 10

Graduate a scale which has lines spaced 0.01506 in. apart. What is the movement of the index handle?

Solution:

The ratio of $G/0.00625$ shows that the whole number of turns of the index handle and the parts of a turn are

$$M_g = \frac{G}{0.00625} = \frac{0.01506}{0.00625} = 2\frac{256}{625}$$

By using the method of Section 16.4,

256 divided into 625 equals 2.4414

To find the hole circle

2.4414 × 16 = 39.0624,   or   39-hole circle

The movement of the index handle is 2 full turns and 16 holes in the 39-hole circle.

The error is negligible. It is

$(\frac{16}{39} \times 0.00625) - 0.00256 = 0.000004$ in.

16.7. Helical Milling and Continued Fractions

Another use of the dividing head is in helical milling. In this instance the worm spindle is geared to the milling-machine lead screw, Fig. 16.6(b). The index-plate lockpin is released so that the index plate with the pin engaged is capable of rotating as it receives power from the gears. The power to the gears comes from the lead screw of the milling machine. Thus the driving gear L transmits power to gear W through the idler or a compound arrangement, as shown in Fig. 16.7(a).

The change gears are set up for a 1:1 ratio. The lead screw usually has four threads to the inch, or a $\frac{1}{4}$-in. lead. The work will revolve 1 turn for 40 revolutions of the worm W. This turns the gear on the lead screw (L) 40 revolutions. If the lead screw turns 40 revolutions, the table will move 10 in. or the milling constant for a 40:1 dividing head and a four thread per inch lead screw is

$$40 \times \tfrac{1}{4} = 10 \text{ in.}$$

The equation for calculating the gear train for a particular lead is

$$\frac{\text{Lead of the helix desired}}{\text{Lead of the machine}} = \frac{\text{driven gears}}{\text{driving gears}} = \frac{W}{L}$$

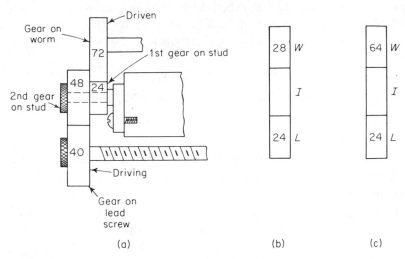

Figure 16.7

EXAMPLE 11

Calculate the change gears for cutting a 36-in. lead.

Solution:

$$\frac{\text{Lead desired}}{\text{Lead of the machine}} = \frac{36}{10} = \frac{6 \times 6}{5 \times 2} = \frac{6 \times 8}{5 \times 8} \times \frac{6 \times 12}{2 \times 12}$$

$$\frac{W}{L} = \frac{48 \times 72}{40 \times 24}\frac{\text{driven}}{\text{driving}}$$

One of the possibilities is shown in Fig. 16.7(a). If the lead desired is a decimal quantity, the gear ratio must be approximated by using either the method in Section 16.4 or the continued fraction method.

EXAMPLE 12

It is desired to find the change gears for cutting a lead of 11.660 in. Use the approximate method in Section 16.4. Find the error.

Solution:

The ratio is

$$\frac{W}{L} = \frac{11.660}{10} = 1.1660$$

Multiply 1.1660 by a number

$$1.1660 \times 24 = 27.984, \quad \text{or} \quad 28$$

Since in the original ratio the numerator was larger than the denominator, the new ratio must be

$$\frac{W}{L} = \frac{28}{24}\frac{\text{driven}}{\text{driving}}$$

This is shown in Fig. 16.7(b). The lead for this new ratio can be found by multiplying the decimal equivalent of the ratio by 10. Thus

$$\frac{28}{24} \times 10 = 11.667 \text{ in.}$$

The error is

$$11.667 - 11.660 = 0.007 \text{ in. error}$$

The method of continued fractions can also be used to find the change gears for a desired lead.

EXAMPLE 13

Find the change gears for cutting a helix of lead of 26.670 in. Use the method of continued fractions, and find the error.

Solution:

1. The ratio is

$$\frac{W}{L} = \frac{26.670}{10} = \frac{2667}{1000}$$

2. Divide the smaller number into the larger number. Thus

```
1000)2667(2
     2000
     ────
      667)1000(1
          667
          ───
          333)667(2
              666
              ───
                1)333(333
                  333
                  ───
                    0
```

3. The box arrangement is

		2	1	2	333
1	0	1	1	3	1000
0	1	2	3	8	2667

4. The new ratio is

$$\frac{W}{L} = \frac{8^*}{3} = \frac{8 \times 8}{3 \times 8} = \frac{64}{24} \frac{\text{driven}}{\text{driving}}$$

   The gear train is shown in Fig. 16.7(c)

5. The new lead is

$$\frac{8}{3} \times 10 = 26.667 \text{ in.}$$

6. The error is

$$26.667 - 26.660 = 0.007 \text{ in.}$$

*Note: The larger number is in the numerator as was the case with the original ratio.

QUESTIONS AND PROBLEMS

16.1 Explain the difference between direct and simple indexing.

16.2 Write the equation for an indexing head with ratio 5 : 1.

16.3 One turn of the index handle is how many degrees on the work for a 40 : 1 dividing head? Suppose the index head has a ratio of 5 : 1; how many degrees of the work does one turn of the index handle represent?

16.4 Find the movement of the index handle when simple-indexing the following divisions: (a) 20; (b) 5; (c) 10; (d) 2; (e) 4.

16.5 Find the movement of the index handle when simple-indexing the following, using the Brown and Sharpe index plates: (a) 30; (b) 12; (c) 15; (d) 9; (e) 25 divisions.

16.6 Assume a workpiece is to have 10 divisions about its circumference. Calculate the movement of the index handle for (a) a 90 : 1 ratio dividing head; (b) a 120 : 1 dividing head; (c) a 40 : 1 dividing head.

16.7 Answer problem 16.5 for the Cincinnati index plates.

16.8 Find the movement of the index handle when simple-indexing the following, using the Brown and Sharpe index plates: (a) 60; (b) 90; (c) 98; (d) 72; (e) 86.

16.9 Answer problem 16.8 for the Cincinnati index plates.

16.10 Using the Brown and Sharpe dividing head, angular-index two divisions separated by an angle of: (a) 40°20′; (b) 26°30′; (c) 20°40′; (d) $29\frac{1}{2}°$; (e) $50\frac{2}{3}°$.

16.11 Solve problem 16.10 for the Cincinnati Milling dividing head.

16.12 Explain the principle of differential indexing if the gearing is 1 : 1 and (a) the plate rotates in the same direction as the index handle; (b) the plate rotates in the opposite direction from the index handle.

16.13 Explain the three methods for gearing a universal dividing head, and state when each is used.

16.14 Find the gears and the movement of the index handle needed to differential-index 121 divisions.

16.15 Differential-index 319 divisions.

16.16 Index 233 divisions.

16.17 Index 413 divisions.

16.18 Index 39°29′ using the approximate method in Section 16.4. Find the error.

16.19 Index 9°55′, and find the error. Use the approximate method.

16.20 Index 25°23′ using the approximate method. Find the error.

16.21 Index 4°14′ using the approximate method. Find the error.

16.22 Find the movement of the index handle and the error necessary to index 39°59′ using the approximate method.

16.23 Using the method of continued fractions, index 39°59′. Find the movement of the index handle and the error.

16.24 Solve Problem 16.18 by continued fractions. Find the error.

16.25 Solve Problem 16.19 by continued fractions. Find the error.

16.26 Solve Problem 16.20 by continued fractions. Find the error.

16.27 Solve Problem 16.21 by continued fractions. Find the error.

16.28 Describe the process used for graduating a scale.

16.29 Find the movement of the index handle for graduating a scale with lines spaced 0.012 in. apart. What is the error?

16.30 Find the movement of the index handle and the error to graduate a scale with lines spaced 0.051 in. apart.

16.31 Explain the constant 10 used in helical milling.

16.32 Calculate the gear train needed to cut a 25-in. lead.

16.33 Calculate the gear train needed to cut a 32-in. lead.

16.34 Calculate the gears needed to cut a 7.43-in. lead, using the approximate method. Find the error.

16.35 Find the gears to cut a 6.48-in. lead using the approximate method. Find the error.

16.36 Calculate the gears needed to cut a 41.14-in. lead, using the approximate method. Find the error.

16.37 Calculate the gear train and error, using the remainder method for the lead in problem 16.34.

16.38 Calculate the gear train and the error, using the remainder method for the lead in problem 16.35.

16.39 Calculate the gear train and error, using the remainder method for the lead of 21.450 in.

Cams

17

17.1. Cam Layout Theory

Before we discuss procedures for cutting cams, it will be advantageous to the student to know something about the theory of cams. A cam, whether it is a plate or cylindrical cam, requires that there should be a displacement of the follower. This displacement might be used to actuate a mechanism according to some plan built into the cam surface. The displacement should follow a preestablished pattern. For instance, it might be required that, for every $\frac{1}{2}$ in. of movement of a plate cam, a pointed follower should be displaced upward 0.050 in., this to take place for 2 in. of length, as shown in Fig. 17.1(a). Starting at 2 in., the displacement is to be 0.025 in. for each $\frac{1}{2}$ in. of cam movement. This is called a *displacement diagram*, and the shape of the plate cam would be the same. The complete theory of velocity and acceleration diagrams belongs in a course in mechanics or mechanism design.

There are many types of followers which can be used with cams. The three types of followers which are most frequently used are the *pointed follower*, Fig. 17.1(b); the *roller follower*, Fig. 17.1(c); and the *flat-face follower*, Fig. 17.1(d). We shall study the first two only.

Displacements which occur in less than 360° of the cam surface are called *rises*. That part of the cam in which the rise takes place is called a *lobe*. If the rise of a cam is calculated for a full revolution of the cam surface, the displacement is called a *lead*. If a part of the cam surface has no displacement, that lobe is said to have a *dwell*.

Thus in Example 5 the rise of lobe *A* is 0.700 in., the lead of lobe *A* is 1.273 in., and the cam has two lobes and two dwells.

After the conditions under which the cam is to be operated have been

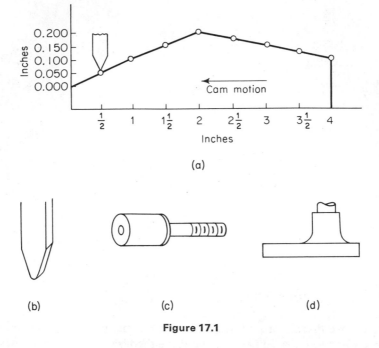

Figure 17.1

established, it is necessary to determine the base circle. It should be obvious to the student that, as the cam rotates, there is a force applied to the follower which attempts to break it off. This is the result of a force vector created by a change in the radius length of the cam surface. Thus a $\frac{1}{4}$-in. rise on a 1-in. base circle creates a greater force vector on the follower than a $\frac{1}{4}$-in. rise on a 10-in. base circle.

We shall discuss three types of motion commonly used in cams. They are (1) *constant-rise cams;* (2) *simple harmonic-motion cams;* (3) *constant-acceleration cams.*

Figure 17.2 shows these three types of motion on three displacement diagrams. Figure 17.2(a) is a *constant-rise diagram.* For every increment of motion of the cam, the follower rises a constant amount. The simple-harmonic motion arises from a displacement which is shown in Fig. 17.2(b). Figure 17.2(c) shows a constant-acceleration displacement diagram.

The procedure for making the displacement diagram for *simple-harmonic motion* is to draw a semicircle with its diameter equal to the rise of a particular lobe. The diameter of the semicircle becomes the ordinate, as shown in Fig. 17.2(b). The portion of the base circle equal to the lobe is drawn as the abscissa. The semicircle is divided into a convenient number of divisions. Six divisions are used in Fig. 17.2(b) for illustrative purposes. The greater the number of divisions used, the more accurate the cam layout. The base circle is divided into the same number of divisions used in the semicircle.

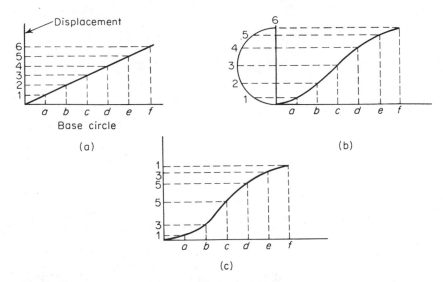

Figure 17.2

Perpendiculars are dropped from the semicircle to the diameter and extended until they intersect perpendiculars from the abscissa. The intersections are connected with a smooth curve. This curve is the cam surface.

In Fig. 17.2(b) a point moving about the circumference of the semicircle moves equal distances per unit of time. However, the *projection* of the point on the diameter does not move equal distances in the same unit of time. The movement of the point on the diameter of the semicircle is simple-harmonic motion.

Figure 17.2(c) shows a *constant-acceleration cam*. The ordinate (follower path) is divided into a convenient number of divisions such that the follower will accelerate or decelerate in equal increments of time. The follower will move according to the same acceleration plan.

It should be noted that almost any kind of motion can be built into the ordinate for any part of the base circle. Of course there are limitations. However, the student should realize that the three types of motion discussed in this text are not the only three types possible. The student is urged to study the following example very carefully.

EXAMPLE 1

Using a base circle of 2 in., a rise of $\frac{1}{2}$ in. for 180° of the base circle, and a pointed follower, lay out a constant-rise cam.

Solution:

1. Draw the base circle, Fig. 17.3(a).
2. Draw the vertical diameter, and extend it for $\frac{1}{2}$ in., as shown in Fig. 17.3(b). It is obvious that, if six divisions are used, it is inconvenient

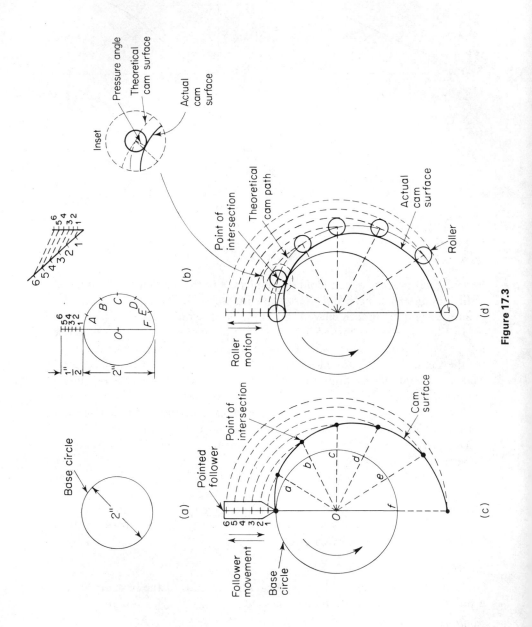

Figure 17.3

to divide the $\frac{1}{2}$-in. rise into equal increments so that they may be drawn easily. An easy method of dividing the rise, no matter what its length, is shown in Fig. 17.3(b). A line which can easily be divided is drawn at a convenient angle and divided into the desired number of divisions. The end points of this line and the rise are connected with a straight line. Parallel lines connecting each of the divisions 5', 4', 3', etc., will divide the rise equally.

The student should realize that any line may be divided into equal divisions by using this method. A rise to be divided into uniformly accelerated and decelerated increments such as 1, 3, 5, 5, 3, 1 may be done by adding the segments, in this case the sum of all the segments being 18. The line 0' to 6' should be drawn $2\frac{1}{4}$ in. long and divided into eighths. The ratio is marked off, and the parallel lines drawn to the rise.

3. Divide 180° of the base circle into the same number of equal divisions as the $\frac{1}{2}$-in. cam path has been. In our illustration we are using six divisions. This is shown in Fig. 17.3(b), which has been exaggerated for clarity.

4. Using 0-1 as a radius, draw an arc to intersect 0-*A* extended. Do the same for all points. The points of intersection lie on the surface of the cam. This is shown in Fig. 17.3(c).

5. Draw a smooth curve through all the points of intersection. The result is one-half of the commonly used heart-shaped cam.

6. Assume that the pointed follower moves up as the cam rotates. The point of the follower will take successive positions as each point of intersection touches the follower. Thus the cam follower will duplicate the motion of the point pattern designed into the extended diameter of the base circle.

7. If each of the points of intersection is assumed to be the center of a roller follower, arcs may be drawn representing the radius of the roller at each point of intersection, as shown in Fig. 17.3(d). A smooth curve tangent to the roller arcs will give the actual cam surface. The center of the rollers will give the motion of the follower. This path, traced by the center of the follower, we shall call the *theoretical cam surface*. Thus for a pointed follower the actual and theoretical cam surfaces coincide.

EXAMPLE 2

Draw a simple harmonic-motion cam which has a rise of 1 in. in a base circle of 6 in., using a $\frac{1}{2}$-in.-diameter roller. The rise is to take place in 90° of the base circle.

Solution:

Draw the 6-in.-diameter base circle. Extend the vertical diameter 1 in. Draw the semicircle, using 1 in. as the diameter. Divide the semicircle into

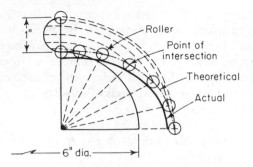

Figure 17.4

some number of divisions (Fig. 17.4 shows six divisions). Divide 90° of the base circle into the same number of divisions. Drop perpendiculars to the diameter of the semicircle. Using the points of intersection on the 1-in. diameter of the semicircle and the center of the base circle as radii, draw the arcs until they intersect the corresponding divisions of the base circle. Draw the rollers, using these points of intersection as the center of the $\frac{1}{2}$-in. diameter. A smooth tangent curve to these rollers gives the actual cam surface. The center of the roller traces the theoretical cam curve.

EXAMPLE 3

Draw a base circle of 2 in. On this base circle construct a constant-acceleration cam having a 1-in. rise that follows the acceleration pattern of 1, 3, 5, 5, 3, 1. The rise is to take place in 120° of the base circle, starting from 90° from the 0° position of the cam. The roller is $\frac{1}{2}$ in. in diameter.

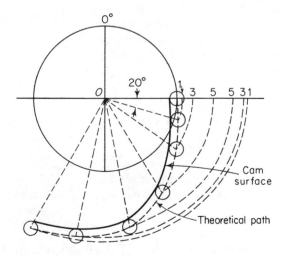

Figure 17.5

Solution:

The procedure is the same as that followed in Example 2 except that the rise is constant acceleration and starts as shown in Fig. 17.5. The extended radius base circle is divided into the 1, 3, 5, 5, 3, 1 ratio. This rise is 1 in. The base circle is divided into increments of 20° which yields the same number of divisions as the acceleration pattern (six divisions). The rollers are drawn at the points of intersection, as shown in Fig. 17.5. Tangents are drawn to the rollers to give the actual cam surface.

17.2. Cam Layout

The first step before cutting a cam is to lay out the cam surface. We shall assume that the cam blank has been machined to the appropriate dimensions and is ready for layout. The face of the cam blank should be given a thin coating of layout blue. It should be mounted on an arbor or mandrel and fitted with a dog. The arbor and cam are then mounted between centers or directly in the spindle of a dividing head.

EXAMPLE 4

For simplicity assume the cam is to have a constant rise of 1.000 in. over 360° and a base circle of 4.000 in. in diameter. Lay out the cam surface.

Solution:

1. With a height gage find the center of the cam. This may be done by taking a height-gage reading off the mandrel or any other round surface concentric with the center bore of the cam. The mandrel is measured with a micrometer and one-half the micrometer reading is subtracted from the height-gage reading. If the height-gage reading is assumed to be 5.242 in. and the micrometer reading is 1 in., the height gage should be set at

$$5.242 - \tfrac{1}{2}(1.000) = 4.742 \text{ in. (center line)}$$

When the height-gage is set at 4.742 in., the height-gage scriber should be on the center of the bore of the cam.

2. Assume we are to divide the 360° of the cam into 50 divisions. The dividing head is set to index 50 divisions, or

$$M = \frac{40}{N} = \frac{40}{50} = \frac{4}{5}$$

$$= \tfrac{4}{5} \times 15 = 12 \text{ holes in the 15-hole circle}$$

The sector arms are set for indexing 12 holes in the 15-hole circle.

3. With the height gage set at 4.742 in., a line is scribed into the face of the cam and marked 0. The cam is indexed one division and the

second line scribed. This procedure is followed until all 50 lines are scribed into the surface of the cam.

4. This will place the 0 division in a horizontal position. To scribe the displacements, this 0 line must be in a vertical position. This may be done by rotating the cam through 90°, or one-fourth of a circle. The movement of the index handle is

$$M = \frac{40}{N} = \frac{40}{4} = 10 \text{ full turns of the index handle}$$

5. With the 0 line in the vertical position, the displacement may be scribed. Since the base circle is 4.000 in. in diameter, the height gage must be set 2.000 in. above the center of the cam. The height-gage setting is obtained thus

$$4.742 + 2.000 = 6.742 \text{ in.}$$

With the height gage set at 6.742 in., a short line is scribed intersecting the vertical 0 center line.

6. Since the rise is 1.000 in. over 50 divisions (360°), the rise per division is

$$\frac{1.000}{50} = 0.020 \text{ in./division}$$

Therefore 0.020 in. is added to each successive reading of the height gage. The height-gage setting for the second cam division is

$$6.742 + 0.020 = 6.762 \text{ in.}$$

For the third division

$$6.762 + 0.020 = 6.782 \text{ in.}$$

For the fourth division

$$6.802 \text{ in., etc.}$$

This is continued until all 50 divisions are scribed.

7. All scribed lines are connected by using a french curve and a scriber.

8. If a roller follower is to be used, each point of intersection must be used to generate a circle having a radius equal to that of the roller. It is very important that the diameter of the end mill used when cutting a cam should be the same diameter as the roller which will eventually be used with the cam. The inset in Fig. 17.3(d) shows the reason for the above statement. It is left to the student to explain this statement.

17.3. Cutting a Cam

There are several methods which can be used to cut cams once they have been scribed on a cam blank. Some of the methods follow:

1. A hollow punch may be used to prick-punch equally spaced punch marks around the periphery of the cam layout. These prick-punch

marks are then punched deeper with a regular punch. A center drill or small drill is used to drill through the center-punch marks. These holes should be opened up to about $\frac{1}{4}$ or $\frac{3}{8}$ in. In no instance should they be closer than $\frac{1}{64}$ in. from the layout line.

Once all the holes are drilled, the scrap material is broken away and the surface filed to the finish line and then sanded with a sanding disk held in a drill-press chuck. This is shown in Fig. 17.6(a).

2. Another method is to cut the scrap material away on a band saw. The operation must be performed carefully so as not to come too close to the cam layout line. The procedure of machine filing and disk sanding may then be used to finish the cam surface.

3. Numerically controlled machines may be programmed to cut a cam surface. The coordinates of many points on the cam surface are punched into a tape. The tape is inserted into the console, the reference point on the work picked up, and the cam cut. Numerical control will be described much more fully later.

4. Cams can also be cut on special machines such as duplicators or tracers. To do this, a master cam is needed.

5. Cam grinders may be used to finish the cam surfaces. A master cam is needed to grind cams. It is important to note that finishing is always needed because of the cutter, file, or even sandaper marks which are left in the surface. The degree of surface finish required depends upon the operational requirements of the cam.

6. Also the universal dividing head may be used to cut cams. This is probably the most widely used method for cutting cams when master cams are needed.

To cut a cam on a milling machine, a universal head, a vertical attachment, and an end mill will be used. The dividing head is geared to the milling-machine lead screw for cutting a helix. The table will move into the cutter as the cam rotates. If the table moves into the cutter 1 in. in one revolution of the cam blank, a cam will be cut with a lead of 1 in.

Let us assume that a cam having a lead L is to be cut. The gears A, B, C, and D, are selected from a table of leads and mounted. The dividing head is rotated into a vertical position so that the cam surface is parallel to the center line of the cutter. This is shown in Fig. 17.6(b). The center line of the cutter must always be parallel to the center line of the dividing head. Notice that in one revolution of the cam the cutter will move a distance L which is the maximum lead for the gears A, B, C, and D.

If the dividing head is set up with the cutter parallel to the center line of the dividing head, as shown in Fig. 17.6(c), the distance between the center line of the dividing head and the center line of the cutter will remain constant. The lead will be 0. The end result is a disc.

When the dividing head is set in a vertical position, Fig. 17.6(b), and the gears A, B, C, and D are used, the lead is a maximum. When the dividing

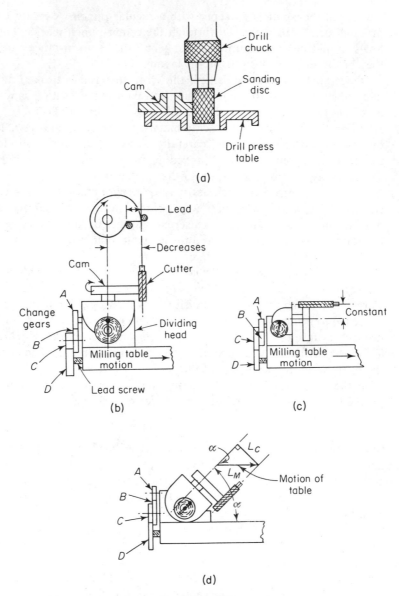

Figure 17.6

head is set in a horizontal position, Fig. 17.6(c), and the same gears *A, B, C,* and *D* are used, the lead is a minimum, or zero. Therefore, with the use of the same gears, if the dividing head is set at an angle, as shown in Fig. 17.6(d), the lead will be somewhere between zero and the maximum for these gears.

Thus in Fig. 17.6(d) the table will move along the hypotenuse of the triangle shown, but the lead of the cam will decrease according to the sine-leg of the triangle.

With this in mind, if a cam has two lobes with different rises, both leads are calculated and the gears selected for the largest lead. With the same gears and this largest lead being used, the angle of the dividing head for the smaller lead is calculated, set and the rise cut.

To find the angle to which the dividing head must be set, the triangle from Fig. 17.6(d) is used and

$$\sin \alpha = \frac{L_c}{L_m}$$
L_c = lead of cam
L_m = lead of machine

The lead of the cam L_c may be found if the rise is given and the total number of divisions in 360° is known.

$$L_c = \frac{Rn}{N}$$
R = rise of the cam
N = no. of divisions in which rise occurs
n = total no. of divisions of cam blank

EXAMPLE 5

Given the two-lobe cam shown in Fig. 17.7 with the cam blank divided into 100 divisions, find: (1) the rises for lobes A and B, (2) the divisions through which the rises take place, (3) the lead for each lobe, (4) the gears for the largest lead, and (5) the angle at which the dividing head must be set for the smaller lead with the same gears being used.

Solution:

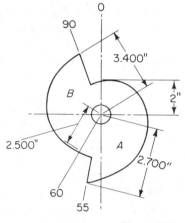

Figure 17.7

1. The rises for lobes A and B are

$$R_A = 2.700 - 2.000 = 0.700 \text{ in.}$$

$$R_B = 3.400 - 2.500 = 0.900 \text{ in.}$$

2. The divisions through which the rises take place are*

$$N_A = 55 - 0 = 55 \text{ divisions}$$

$$N_B = 90 - 60 = 30 \text{ divisions}$$

3. The lead for each lobe is

$$\text{Lobe } A = L_{cA} = \frac{R_A n}{N_A} = \frac{0.700(100)}{55} = 1.273 \text{ in.}$$

$$\text{Lobe } B = L_{cB} = \frac{R_B n}{N_B} = \frac{0.900(100)}{30} = 3.000 \text{ in.}$$

4. The gears for the largest lead, lobe B (3.000 in.), may be found from

*Note that the divisions 55 to 60 and 90 to 100 are dwells.

a table or calculated. If calculated, the ratio is

$$\frac{\text{Lead desired}}{\text{Lead of the machine}} = \frac{3}{10} = \frac{3 \times 8}{5 \times 8} \times \frac{1 \times 28}{2 \times 28} = \frac{24 \times 28}{40 \times 56} \frac{\text{driven}}{\text{driver}}$$

Using these gears and the dividing head in a vertical position will give a 3.000-in. lead.

5. The same gears are used to obtain the 1.273-in. lead. However, the dividing head must be set at an angle. The angle for lobe *A* is

$$\sin \alpha = \frac{L_c}{L_m} = \frac{1.273}{3.000} = 0.4243$$

$$\alpha = 25°6'$$

It is important to note that the shortest maximum lead which can generally be obtained on a milling machine is 0.670 in. For any lead less than this the dividing head must be set at an angle and used with the gears indicated for 0.670 in.* Most milling machines can be equipped with an extra gear box for shorter leads.

When geared to the worm gear of the dividing head, this short lead attachment will give a reduction in the available leads of one-twentieth. If geared to the dividing-head spindle instead of the worm, the leads available may be reduced by the eight-hundredth.

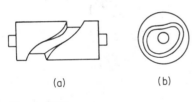

(a)   (b)

Figure 17.8

Leads under $2\frac{1}{2}$ in. should be fed by hand unless the short lead attachment is used. For leads over $2\frac{1}{2}$ in. the power feed may be used.

It should be noted that the angular setting of the vertical head and the dividing head is not possible for cutting drum cams, Fig. 17.8(a), or face cams, Fig. 17.8(b).

17.4. Contour Milling

At times curved surfaces need to be machined that may require special treatment. Figure 17.9(a) shows a concave trough. This type of curved surface may be machined by tilting the cutter in a milling machine vertical head. It may also be achieved with a face milling cutter and the dividing head set at an angle. The resulting radius is an approximation of the desired radius. When the arc is shallow, the resulting curve is circular. In most instances the approximation achieved is close enough to yield satisfactory results. The equation used to determine the angle at which the cutter should be set is

$$\sin \alpha = \frac{D}{2R_c}$$

D = dia of cutter
R_c = desired radius
α = cutter angle

*Driven 24,24T: driver 86,100T

EXAMPLE 6

Assume you are to mill the trough in Fig. 17.9(b). You are to use a 3 in. diameter face mill. Determine the angle of the dividing head.

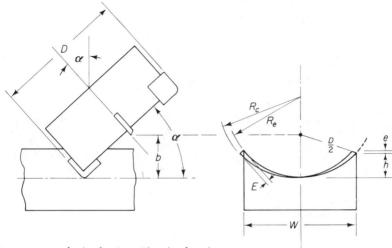

α = Angle of cutter with axis of work
D = Dia. of cutter
R_c = Desired radius
R_e = Actual radius
e = Increase in arc depth
h = Desired depth of arc
W = Chord of arc

(a)

(b)

Figure 17.9

Solution:

The cutter angle is

$$\sin \alpha = \frac{D}{2R_c} = \frac{3}{2(1.750)}$$

$$\alpha = 59°$$

$D = 3$ in.
$R_c = 1.750$ in.

The increase in arc depth (error) produced with this method may be calculated using the equation

$$e = \frac{\sin \alpha \, (D - \sqrt{D^2 - W^2})}{2} - h$$

e = increase in arc depth
D = dia of cutter
W = chord of arc
h = desired depth of arc

EXAMPLE 7

Calculate the error in Example 6 and Fig. 17.9(b).

Solution:

The error is

$$e = \frac{\sin \alpha \, (D - \sqrt{D^2 - W^2})}{2} - h$$

W = 2.000 in.
h = 0.3125 in.
R_c = 1.750 in.
D = 3.000 in.

$$= \frac{\sin 59° \, (3 - \sqrt{3^2 - 2^2})}{2} - 0.3125$$

$$= 0.3274 - 0.3125$$

$$= 0.0149 \text{ in.}$$

EXAMPLE 8

Calculate the actual radius from the data in Examples 6 and 7.

Solution:

The actual radius cut is

$$R_e = \sqrt{(R_c - h)(R_c - h - 2e) + \frac{W^2}{4}}$$

$$= \sqrt{(1.750 - 0.3125)[1.750 - 0.3125 - 2(0.0149)] + \frac{2^2}{4}}$$

$$= 1.7388 \text{ in.}$$

Tracer controlled machines use a hydraulic tracer unit which transfers the shape of a pattern or master to a workpiece. The tracer is actuated by a tracer finger which at the slightest pressure operates one of the slides. In a 180° tracer unit the depth slide—the vertical head—is controlled by the tracer. The 180° tracer is shown in Fig. 17.10(a). The 360° profile tracer controls the feed rate of two slides.

The operation for rough machining a mold cavity is shown in Fig. 17.10(b). The cutter is set for a specific depth. Progressive cuts are taken with the same depth setting. At the end of each length pass, the table is moved. Once the surface has been scanned, the table is raised and the process is repeated until the cavity has been completed rough cut.

Another method for roughing the cavity is to set the tracer so that it touches the bottom of the cavity. The cutter is set to the depth of the first

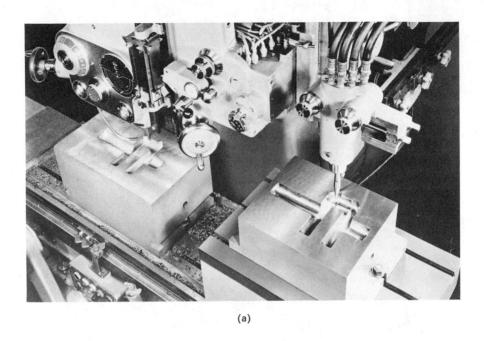

(a)

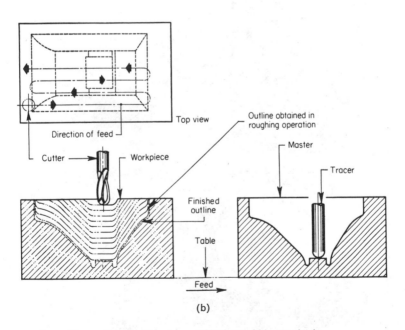

Top view

Direction of feed

Cutter — Workpiece

Outline obtained in
roughing operation

Master

Tracer

Finished
outline

Table

Feed

(b)

Figure 17.10 *(Courtesy of Cincinnati Milacron, Inc.)*

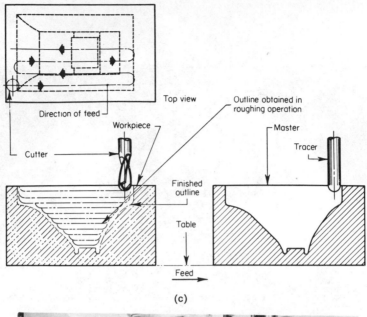

Top view

Direction of feed

Cutter

Workpiece

Outline obtained in roughing operation

Finished outline

Master

Tracer

Table

Feed

(c)

(d)

Figure 17.10 (Cont.)

cut. As the tracer climbs the side wall of the master the cutter will cut a small cavity as it scans the surface of the work. The cutter is then set to cut deeper and the process is repeated. This procedure is continued until the cavity is finished. It is important to note that in this process the tracer is always tracing the entire surface shape of the master. This is shown in Fig. 17.10(c).

The finishing operation is done by replacing the tracer finger with one which can get into small slots. The cutter must also be of such a size that it will cut these small slots. The process described for roughing is repeated.

Figure 17.10(d) shows a pair of rotary tables linked to the table feed for 360° tracing. The master and finished tool steel embossing die is shown.

QUESTIONS AND PROBLEMS

17.1 Make a free hand sketch of the three types of followers generally used with cams.

17.2 As related to cam design, define: (a) rise; (b) lead; (c) dwell; (d) lobe. Give an example for each term.

17.3 Why is the base circle important in cam design?

17.4 Describe and illustrate the three types of motion discussed in this chapter. Support with sketches.

17.5 Describe and illustrate the pressure angle of a cam against the follower. Very carefully draw a portion of a cam surface (30°) which has a rise of $\frac{1}{2}$ in. Draw this rise on a 2-in.-diameter base circle and on a 6-in.-diameter base circle. Compare the pressure angles.

17.6 Using a base circle of 4 in., lay out the following cam for a pointed follower: (a) 0 to 90°, constant rise of $\frac{3}{8}$ in.; (b) 90 to 180°, dwell; (c) 180 to 270°, uniformly accelerated motion 1, 3, 5 for 0.180-in. rise; (d) simple harmonic motion, 270 to 360°, back to the base circle.

17.7 Using a $\frac{3}{4}$-in.-diameter roller follower, lay out the following cam on a 3-in.-diameter base circle: (a) 0 to 120°, uniformly accelerated motion 1, 5, 7, 7, 5, 1 for a 0.520-in. rise; (b) 120 to 210°, simple harmonic motion for a $\frac{3}{16}$-in. rise; (c) dwell 210 to 300°; (d) 300 to 360° constant rise of 0.250 in.

17.8 Draw a heart-shaped cam which has a base circle of 2 in., a $\frac{1}{2}$-in. rise, and a $\frac{3}{8}$-in. roller.

17.9 (a) Draw a heart-shaped cam which has a base circle of 3 in., a rise of $\frac{3}{4}$ in., and uses a pointed follower. (b) Superimpose a $\frac{1}{2}$-in. roller on this sketch.

17.10 Describe the procedure for cutting a cam surface, using a universal dividing head.

17.11 List several machining methods that may be used to cut cams.

17.12 Assume you are to lay out the cam in problem 17.6 using a height gage and a Brown and Sharpe dividing head. Describe the procedure. Use the number 3.780 in. as the height-gage centerline reading.

17.13 A cam has a uniform rise of 1.500 in. in 270°. Find the gears needed to cut this cam.

17.14 A cam has a rise of $\frac{3}{4}$ in. over 40 divisions and 0.500 in. over the next 50 divisions. Find the gears and the dividing head setting.

17.15 A cam has two lobes and is divided into 100 divisions. Lobe *A* has a rise of 1.875 in. over 65 divisions. Lobe *B* has a rise of 0.500 in. for the remaining number of divisions. Using the approximate method, find the gear ratio for the longest lead and the angular settings for lobes *A* and *B*.

17.16 Assume a 5 in. radius trough is to be milled with an 8 in. face milling cutter. At what angle should the cutter be set?

17.17 If a cutter is set at 50° with the table, what radius will be milled if the face mill is 10 in. in diameter?

17.18 In Problem 17.16, calculate: (a) the error and (b) the actual radius cut. The depth of the trough is $1\frac{1}{4}$ in. and the width of the trough is $\frac{5}{16}$ in.

17.19 Describe the operation of the tracer control mechanism, Fig. 17.10(a).

17.20 Repeat for Fig. 17.10(b).

Gears

18

18.1. Spur Gear Theory

If two friction drums touch and one rotates, the other will rotate. Friction, however, does not give a positive drive. If slippage occurs, the rotation of the driven drum cannot be predicted.

If, however, teeth are cut into and built up on the drums, we have manufactured two gears. If these two gears are placed in mesh with each other and the driving gear rotated, the driven gear must rotate and the rotation can be predicted. The smaller of the two gears is called the *pinion* gear. The larger is called the *gear*.

	Gear	Pinion
Diametral pitch	P	P
Pitch dia	D	d
Outside dia	D_o	d_o
Root dia	D_r	d_r
No. of teeth	N	n
Addendum	a	a
Dedendum	b	b
Clearance	c	c
Whole depth	h_t	h_t
Working depth	h_k	h_k
Tooth thickness	t	t
Chordal thickness	t_c	t_c
Circular pitch	P_c	P_c

As stated above, the teeth are half built up above the surface of the drum and half cut into the drum. Once the teeth are cut, the imaginary cylinder (the original circumference of the friction drum), is called the *pitch circumference*. The diameter of the imaginary pitch circumference is the *pitch diameter (D)*. See Fig. 18.1(a). The following nomenclature is shown in Fig. 18.1(b).

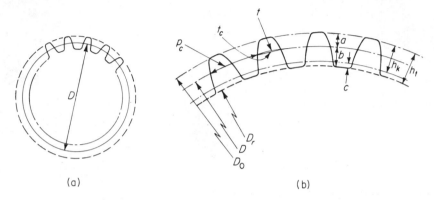

(a)   (b)

Figure 18.1

The *root diameter D_r* is the diameter of the root circle across the bottom of the teeth.

The *major diameter D_o* is the diameter of the largest circle across the top of the teeth.

The *pitch diameter D* is the diameter of the imaginary circle which passes through the center of the working depth.

The *addendum a* is the radial distance from the pitch circle to the outside diameter.

The *dedendum b* is the radial distance from the pitch circle to the root circle. It includes the clearance.

The *clearance c* is the radial distance between the top of one tooth and the root circle at the bottom of the space of the mating gear.

The *whole depth h_t* is the radial distance from the outside circle to the root circle. It is the sum of the addendum and the dedendum.

The *working depth h_k* is the whole depth minus the clearance.

The *circular pitch P_c* is the arc distance from a point on one tooth to the corresponding point on the next tooth on the pitch circle.

The *chordal thickness t_c* is the length of the chord created by the circular thickness.

The *circular thickness t* is the arc length of the thickness of the tooth at the pitch circle.

The equations for gears can be developed from the definitions. The concept of *diametral pitch* was developed primarily to eliminate the inconvenience of π. *The concept of diametral pitch states that, if the pitch circumference of a 1-in. pitch-diameter circle is divided into N parts, then the diametral pitch of the tooth is N.* That is, if the circumference of a 1-in. pitch-diameter circle is divided into 10 equal parts, the physical size of the tooth and space is fixed and the tooth is called a 10-diametral-pitch tooth. Instead of repeating the phrase *diametral pitch*, henceforth it will be referred to as *pitch* and the symbol will be *P*. Two gears will mesh if they have the same pitch.

It can be seen that, if the pitch diameter is 1 in. and the number of teeth is 10, the pitch is 10, or

$$P = \frac{N}{D} = \frac{10}{1} = 10 \qquad\qquad \begin{array}{l} N = 10 \\ D = 1 \text{ in.} \end{array}$$

1. From the statement above

$$P = \frac{N}{D}$$

2. The addendum is

$$a = \frac{1}{P}$$

3. The clearance is

$$c = \frac{0.157}{P}$$

4. The dedendum is

$$b = \frac{1.157}{P}$$

5. The whole depth of a gear tooth is the sum of the addendum and dedendum

$$h_t = a + b = \frac{1}{P} + \frac{1.157}{P} = \frac{2.157}{P}$$

6. The working depth of the tooth is the whole depth minus the clearance

$$h_k = h_t - c = \frac{2.157}{P} - \frac{0.157}{P} = \frac{2}{P}$$

7. The major diameter of a spur gear is

$$D_o = D + 2a$$

Sometimes it is more convenient to use the equation which reflects the number of teeth in the gear than the equation with the addendum. Since $D = N/P$ and $a = 1/P$, these values may be inserted in the equation above and

$$D_o = D + 2a = \frac{N}{P} + 2\left(\frac{1}{P}\right)$$

$$= \frac{N + 2}{P}$$

8. The root diameter is

$$D_r = D - 2b$$

9. The tooth thickness is

$$t = \frac{1.5708}{P}$$

EXAMPLE 1

A spur gear has 48 teeth and measures $2\frac{1}{2}$ in. in outside diameter. Find:
(1) the pitch; (2) the pitch diameter; (3) the addendum; (4) the dedendum;
(5) clearance; (6) the full depth of the tooth; (7) the working depth of the
tooth; (8) the root diameter; (9) the tooth thickness.

Solution:

1. The pitch is

$$P = \frac{N + 2}{D_o} = \frac{48 + 2}{2.5000} \qquad\qquad N = 48\text{T} \\ D_o = 2.5000 \text{ in.}$$

$$= 20 \text{ pitch}$$

2. The pitch diameter is

$$D = \frac{N}{P} = \frac{48}{20}$$

$$= 2.4000 \text{ in.}$$

3. The addendum is

$$a = \frac{1}{P} = \frac{1}{20}$$

$$= 0.050 \text{ in.}$$

4. The dedendum is

$$b = \frac{1.157}{P} = \frac{1.157}{20}$$

$$= 0.0578 \text{ in.}$$

5. The clearance is

$$c = \frac{0.157}{P} = \frac{0.157}{20}$$

$$= 0.0078 \text{ in.}$$

6. The full depth of the tooth is

$$h_t = \frac{2.157}{P} = \frac{2.157}{20}$$

$$= 0.1078 \text{ in.}$$

7. The working depth is

$$h_k = \frac{2}{P} = \frac{2}{20}$$

$$= 0.1000 \text{ in.}$$

8. The root diameter is

$$D_r = D - 2b = 2.400 - 2(0.0578)$$
$$= 2.2844 \text{ in.}$$

9. The tooth thickness is

$$t = \frac{1.5708}{P} = \frac{1.5708}{20}$$
$$= 0.0785 \text{ in.}$$

18.2. Single-Tooth Spur Gear Cutting

Two types of gear teeth are used most frequently. The $14\frac{1}{2}°$ and the $20°$ pressure-angle gear teeth. The $14\frac{1}{2}°$ angle is created between the line of action and the pitch line, as shown in Fig. 18.2(a). The line of action is perpendicular to the tooth profile at the pitch line and tangent to the base circle. The diameter of the base circle may be found from the equation

$$\text{Diameter of base circle} = D \cos 14\frac{1}{2}° \qquad D = \text{pitch dia}$$

It should be noted that in Fig. 18.2(a) the rack has approximately straight-sided teeth. That is, the involute curve is a straight line for a rack which theoretically is a gear with an infinite diameter. As the diameter becomes finite, the teeth take on the involute shape. This involution becomes more pronounced as the diameter of the gear becomes smaller. See Fig. 18.2(b). The reason is that the involute profile is traced out by the tooth from the mating gear which is in mesh with the traced tooth. The smaller the diameter of the gear, the sharper is the profile that is traced. For gears having small diameters the tooth must be modified.

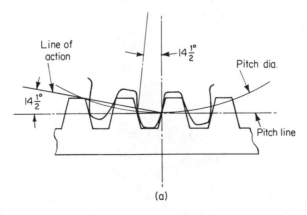

(a)

Figure 18.2

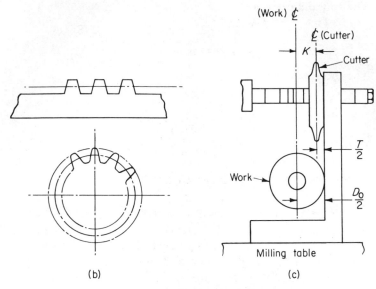

Figure 18.2   (Cont.)

For our purpose the change in profile must be taken care of in the manufacturing of the gear. This is done by using a set of eight gear cutters, Table 18.1, each capable of cutting teeth within its own range and for a particular pitch. There will be some error in the profile of the involute cut with these gear cutters. Ideally, a gear of pitch 16 pitch 24 teeth should be cut with one cutter, and a gear of pitch 16 pitch 25 teeth should be cut with another gear

TABLE 18.1

No. Cutter	Range, teeth	No. Cutter	Range, teeth
1	135 to rack		
		$1\frac{1}{2}$	80 to 134
2	55 to 134		
		$2\frac{1}{2}$	42 to 54
3	35 to 54		
		$3\frac{1}{2}$	30 to 34
4	26 to 34		
		$4\frac{1}{2}$	23 to 25
5	21 to 25		
		$5\frac{1}{2}$	19 to 20
6	17 to 20		
		$6\frac{1}{2}$	15 to 16
7	14 to 16		
		$7\frac{1}{2}$	13
8	12 to 13		

cutter. It is obvious that this would be very expensive, and experience shows that this is not necessary. If greater accuracy is needed, cutters in half numbers, Table 18.1, can be purchased. If still greater accuracy is needed, other methods for cutting the gears are available and the single-tooth method should not be used.

EXAMPLE 2

Explain the method for cutting the gear in Example 1 on a universal milling machine with a universal dividing head.

Solution:

1. The gear blank is prepared with a $2\frac{1}{2}$-in. outside diameter.
2. The dividing head is set to index 48 teeth.

$$M = \frac{40}{N} = \frac{40}{48} = \frac{5}{6}$$

The movement of the index handle is

$$M = \tfrac{5}{6} \times 18 = 15 \text{ holes in the 18-hole circle}$$

3. From Table 18.1 a number 3 (or a number $2\frac{1}{2}$) cutter of pitch 20 is mounted on the milling-machine arbor.
4. The work is mounted on an arbor and placed on the dividing head either directly into the spindle or between centers.
5. The center lines of the work and the cutter must be made to coincide. A precision square is placed on the milling-machine table so that the vertical blade contacts the ground side of the cutter and the outside diameter of the gear blank, as shown in Fig. 18.2(c). To make the center lines coincide, the milling-machine table should be moved to the right. To determine the movement of the table, assume the cutter is 0.178 in. thick. Then

$$K = \tfrac{1}{2}(D_o - T)$$
$$= \tfrac{1}{2}(2.500 - 0.178)$$
$$= 1.161 \text{ in.}$$

       K = distance to move the table

The table should be moved 1.161 in. to the right in Fig. 18.2(c) in order to align the two center lines.

6. Then the cutter is caused to rotate, the table is raised until the cutter touches the work, and the work is moved from underneath the cutter. The graduated dial on the vertical feed is set at 0. The depth of the tooth is set by raising the table the required amount, or 0.1078 in. in Example 1.
7. The table is moved until the work contacts the rotating cutter, the automatic feed is engaged, and one tooth space is cut. Then the work is indexed 15 holes in the 18-hole circle, and a second cut taken. The

second space cut gives one complete tooth, which permits checking the tooth thickness with a gear vernier. If the measurements are correct, the rest of the teeth are cut.

8. Usually the full depth is not cut at the very start. All the teeth are roughed to a depth of 0.100 in. (in this instance), and the additional 0.0078 in. taken as a finishing cut.

18.3. Generating a Gear

The generating of gears may be accomplished in several ways. The student should think of a pinion and a gear in mesh and visualize the pinion as a hardened cutter with all clearances applied to the teeth. This is shown in Fig. 18.3(a) in which a gear-shaper cutter is operating with a gear blank. As the cutter oscillates up and down, it is fed into the gear blank to the desired depth. This means that at the common center line of the gear and the cutter a full-depth tooth is cut with partially completed teeth being cut off the common center line.

Once the depth is established, the oscillating cutter starts to rotate very slowly. This rotary motion is geared directly to the work so that the surface speeds of the cutter and of the gear blank are the same. When the gear blank has made one revolution, all the teeth are complete.

It is to be noted that, just as on a standard shaper, if the cutter cuts on the up stroke, it must back away on the down stroke. A cluster gear is cut on the down stroke as shown in Fig. 18.3(a).

Gears may also be generated with a hob on a special gear hobbing machine. The hob is set at an angle so that the hob teeth will operate parallel

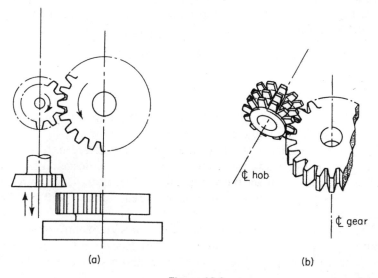

(a)   (b)

Figure 18.3

to the center line of the gear blank. That is, the center line of the hob and the center line of the gear are set at 90° minus the helix angle of the hob, as shown in Fig. 18.3(b). The center line of the hob is also set above the gear blank and to the desired depth of the tooth being cut. The revolution of the hob determines the rpm of the gear blank. The lead of the hob and the surface speed of the gear blank must be the same. The two are connected through change gears.

The hob is set to feed down along the gear-blank center line about 0.010 in. for each revolution of the gear blank. When the cutter has finished the blank thickness and stops cutting, the gear is finished.

Gears may be finished by various other methods, such as shaving, grinding, lapping, and face-mill types of cutters.

18.4. Helical Gears

When calculating the pitch diameter of a spur gear, Fig. 18.4(a), the circular pitches (the arc distances from a point on each tooth to the corresponding point on the adjacent tooth) are added to get the pitch circumference.

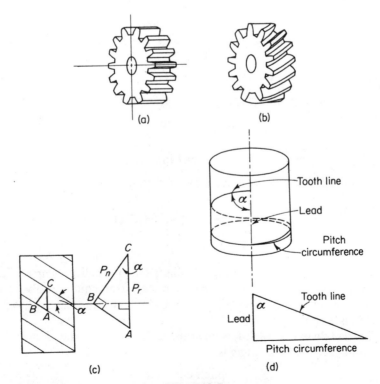

Figure 18.4

Dividing the pitch circumference by π gives the pitch diameter. From the pitch diameter and the number of circular pitches (number of teeth) the concept of diametral pitch was developed (Section 18.1). It is important to notice that the circular pitches are all normal to the direction of the teeth, the teeth being normal to the axis of the gear.

When the teeth are helical, Fig. 18.4(b), the circular pitch is still defined as before. The circular pitch is at right angles to the direction of the teeth, but the teeth are no longer at right angles to the axis of the gear. This is shown in Fig. 18.4(c). The *normal circular pitch* P_n is defined as the arc length in a plane perpendicular to the direction of the teeth. The *real circular pitch* P_r is defined as the arc distance in a plane perpendicular to the axis of the gear. In triangle ABC, Fig. 18.4(c), side $BC = P_n$ and $AC = P_r$.

A plane cut through the *normal* circular pitch of a helical gear tooth will give the true involute shape of the tooth. A plane cut through the *real* circular pitch of a helical gear tooth will give a distorted involute shape of the tooth. Since the diametral pitch is related to the normal pitch, the normal pitch must be converted to the real pitch before the pitch circumference, and eventually the pitch diameter, of a helical gear can be calculated, as illustrated in Example 3.

EXAMPLE 3

Given a gear of 20 teeth and 12 pitch, find the following: (1) the pitch diameter of a spur gear and (2) the pitch diameter of a helical gear if the helix angle is 25°.

Solution:

1. If the gear is a spur gear, the pitch diameter is

$$D = \frac{N}{P_n} = \frac{20}{12} \qquad\qquad \begin{aligned} N &= 20\text{T} \\ P_n &= 12 \end{aligned}$$

$$= 1.667 \text{ in.}$$

2. The pitch diameter of a helical gear with helix angle of 25° is

$$D = \frac{N}{P_n} \sec \alpha = \frac{N}{P_n \cos \alpha} = \frac{20}{12 \cos 25°} = \frac{20}{12 \times 0.9063} \qquad \alpha = 25°$$

$$= 1.839 \text{ in.}$$

The pitch diameter and the outside diameter of a helical gear are larger than those of an equivalent spur gear. Notice in the equation above that, as the helix angle approaches 0°, the $\cos 0° = 1$ and the helical gear with a 0° angle is a spur gear.

If the triangle in Fig. 18.4(d) is unwrapped from around the pitch cylinder, the equation for the helix angle is

$$\tan \alpha = \frac{\text{pitch circumference}}{\text{lead}}$$

EXAMPLE 4

Assume a cylinder with a pitch diameter of 3.465 in. and a lead of 15 in. What is the helix angle of the gear?

Solution:

$$\text{The pitch circumference} = \pi D = \pi 3.465$$

$$= 10.886 \text{ in.}$$

$D = 3.465$ in.
$L = 15$ in.

The helix angle is

$$\tan \alpha = \frac{\text{pitch circumference}}{\text{lead}} = \frac{10.886}{15} = 0.726$$

$$\alpha = 35°59'$$

The calculations for the various parts of a helical gear will be best illustrated by an example.

EXAMPLE 5

Given a helical gear of 20T, 12 pitch, and a helix angle of 25°, find: (1) the pitch diameter; (2) the pitch circumference; (3) the lead; (4) the addendum; (5) the dedendum; (6) the whole depth; (7) the tooth thickness; (8) the outside diameter; (9) the root diameter.

Solution:

1. The pitch diameter is

$$D = \frac{N}{P_n \cos \alpha} = \frac{20}{12 \cos 25°}$$

$$= 1.839 \text{ in.}$$

$N = 20$
$P_n = 12$
$\alpha = 25°$

2. The pitch circumference is

$$\text{Pitch circumference} = \pi D = \pi(1.839)$$

$$= 5.777 \text{ in.}$$

3. The lead is

$$L = \frac{(\pi D)}{\tan \alpha} = \frac{5.777}{\tan 25°}$$

$$= 12.389 \text{ in.}$$

4. The addendum is

$$a = \frac{1}{P_n} = \frac{1}{12}$$

$$\doteq 0.0833 \text{ in.}$$

5. The dedendum is

$$b = \frac{1.157}{P_n} = \frac{1.157}{12}$$

$$= 0.0964 \text{ in.}$$

6. The whole depth is

$$h_t = \frac{2.157}{P_n} = \frac{2.157}{12}$$
$$= 0.180 \text{ in.}$$

7. The tooth thickness is

$$t = \frac{1.571}{P_n} = \frac{1.571}{12}$$
$$= 0.131 \text{ in.}$$

8. The outside diameter is

$$D_o = D + 2a = 1.839 + 2(0.0833)$$
$$= 2.006 \text{ in.}$$

9. The root diameter is

$$D_r = D - 2b = 1.839 - 2(0.0964)$$
$$= 1.6462 \text{ in.}$$

18.5. Cutting a Helical Gear

When a spur gear is cut with a gear cutter, the cutter makes its way through the gear blank and cuts the space to the exact shape of the cutter, Fig. 18.5(a).

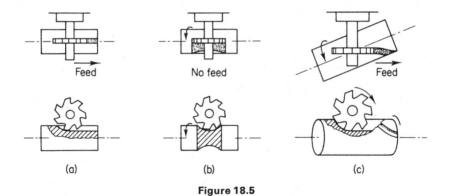

Feed   No feed   Feed

(a)   (b)   (c)

Figure 18.5

If the work revolves as shown in Fig. 18.5(b) but does not advance, the cutter will machine a radius groove equivalent to the radius of the cutter.

If the work is set at an angle with the cutter and caused to revolve at the same time as it is being fed into the cutter, a groove *almost* the same shape as the cutter will result. There will be some variation in the shape of the tooth contour cut and the contour of the cutter. This is so because the cutter must cut into the work as the work is revolving. This causes the cutter to cut on opposite sides, which produces a wider groove than the width of the cutter, Fig. 18.5(c).

In Table 18.1, the cutters for spur gears are listed. If the cutters are used to cut the number of teeth indicated for a helical gear, a space much wider than the cutter would result and the space next to the tooth would be too wide. Low-numbered cutters for cutting higher numbers of teeth are thinner than the cutters for cutting fewer numbers of teeth. An empirical formula for calculating the appropriate gear cutter for the equivalent helical gear is

$$N' = \frac{N}{\cos \alpha \sin^2 \alpha}$$

N = no. of teeth in helical gear
N' = no. of teeth in equivalent spur gear
α = helix angle

EXAMPLE 6

Assume the helical gear in Example 5 is to be cut. Calculate the number of teeth, N', needed to select the cutter.

Solution:

The number of teeth in the equivalent spur gear for selecting the cutter is

$$N' = \frac{N}{\cos \alpha \sin^2 \alpha} = \frac{20}{\cos 25° \sin^2 25°} = \frac{20}{0.9063(0.4226)^2}$$

$$= 124 +$$

A number 2 cutter (55T to 134T) is used to cut a 20-tooth helical gear at 25°. If the gear were a spur gear, a number 6 cutter would be used.

Assuming the gear in Example 5 is to be cut, the procedure is as follows:

1. The cutter is mounted on the milling-machine arbor and the gear blank is mounted between centers as if a spur gear were to be cut. NOTE: The table has not been set at the helix angle at this point.
2. The gears for the desired lead of 12.389 in. are calculated or found in a table. The calculations are

$$\frac{\text{Lead desired}}{\text{Lead of the machine}} = \frac{12.389}{10} = 1.2389$$

Using the approximate method, multiply

$$1.2389 \times 80 = 99 +$$

The ratio of the gears needed is

$$\frac{\text{Driven}}{\text{Driver}} = \frac{99}{80} = \frac{9 \times 11}{8 \times 10} = \frac{9 \times 8}{8 \times 8} \times \frac{11 \times 4}{10 \times 4}$$

$$r = \frac{72 \times 44}{64 \times 40} = \frac{W \times \text{2nd gear on stud}}{S \times \text{1st gear on stud}}$$

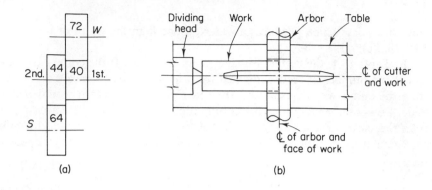

(a)

(b)

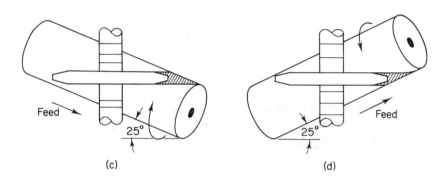

Feed →   25°

(c)

25°   ← Feed

(d)

(e)

Figure 18.6 (*Photo courtesy of Cincinnati Milacron, Inc.*)

The gears are shown mounted in Fig. 18.6(a). The new lead with the new ratio is

$$\tfrac{99}{80} \times 10 = 12.375 \text{ in.}$$

The error is

$$12.389 - 12.375 = 0.014 \text{ in.}$$

3. The next step is to align the cutter over the longitudinal axis of the work, as indicated in Section 18.2 and shown in Fig. 18.6(b). In addition the center of the arbor (or cutter) must be aligned over the edge of the work, as shown in Fig. 18.6(b).
4. Once the cutter is aligned, the table is swiveled to 25°. The depth of the cut is set at 0.180 in. For left-hand helical gears the table is swiveled 25°, as shown in Fig. 18.6(c). The work rotates clockwise, and the feed is from left to right. This gives a counterclockwise helix in the work, or a left-hand helix. In Fig. 18.6(d) the table is swiveled 25°, as shown. The work revolves counterclockwise as the work feeds from left to right. This produces a clockwise helix in the work, or a right-hand helix which twists clockwise when viewed from the end of the work.
5. Once the first cut is finished, the table is lowered and moved back to position the cutter for the next cut. In this instance the table must be lowered; otherwise the backlash in the change gears and those in the table create a lag in the rotation of the dividing head. If this occurs, the groove just cut will be spoiled. Once the cutter is repositioned, the next tooth is indexed by moving the index handle

$$M = \frac{40}{N} = \frac{40}{20} = 2 \text{ full turns of the index handle}$$

6. The second cut is completed, which finishes the first tooth. A gear vernier is used to measure the tooth thickness. If correct, the process in step 5 is repeated until all the teeth have been cut.

18.6. Worm Gearing

The theory of worm gearing that will be presented here will be sufficient to make possible the machining of a worm and worm wheel. The purpose of worm gearing is usually to make possible a large driver-to-driven gear ratio. Thus the 40:1 ratio which we find in the dividing head would require a large gear train. If this ratio is attempted with a 10-tooth pinion, the gear would have to be a 400T gear! In worm gearing, if the worm has a single start, it will act as a one-tooth pinion and, since the worm wheel has 40 teeth, the ratio of 40:1 is achieved rather easily and efficiently. If the worm has two starts, or leads, the 40:1 ratio can be obtained with a 20-tooth worm wheel.

In worm gearing the shafts are usually at right angles to each other. This

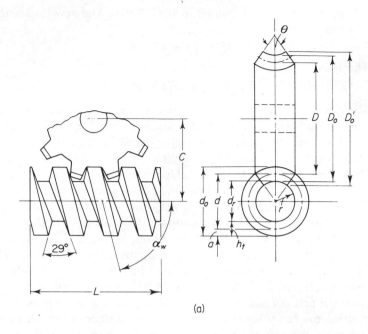

(a)

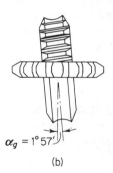

$\alpha_g = 1° 57'$

(b)

Figure 18.7

means that the worm wheel must have a helix angle to match the helix angle of the worm. Note the relationship between the angles in Fig. 18.7(a and b).

The equations for calculating the dimensions needed to machine a worm and a worm wheel are illustrated in Example 7.

EXAMPLE 7

You are asked to calculate all the gear parts for a single lead worm of $2\frac{1}{2}$-in. outside diameter which has four threads to the inch. The ratio of worm to worm wheel is 60 : 1 and $\theta = 60°$.

Solution:

1. The number of equivalent teeth is $n' = 1$. That is, the single lead causes the worm to act like a one-tooth gear.

2. The lead of the worm is

$$l = pn' = \tfrac{1}{4}(1)$$

$$= \tfrac{1}{4} \text{ in.}$$

3. The addendum of the worm is

$$a = 0.3183p = 0.3183(\tfrac{1}{4})$$

$$= 0.0796 \text{ in.}$$

4. The pitch diameter of the worm is

$$d = d_o - 2a = 2.500 - 2(0.0796)$$

$$= 2.3408 \text{ in.}$$

5. The depth of the worm tooth is

$$h_t = 0.6866p = 0.6866(\tfrac{1}{4})$$

$$= 0.1716 \text{ in.}$$

6. The root diameter of the worm is

$$d_r = d_o - 2h_t = 2.500 - 2(0.1716)$$

$$= 2.1568 \text{ in.}$$

7. The pitch diameter of the wheel is

$$D = \frac{Np}{\pi} = \frac{60(\tfrac{1}{4})}{\pi}$$

$$= 4.7746 \text{ in.}$$

8. The center distance between the two gears is

$$C = \frac{D + d}{2} = \frac{4.7746 + 2.3408}{2}$$

$$= 3.5577 \text{ in.}$$

9. The throat diameter of the wheel is

$$D_o = D + 2a = 4.7746 + 2(0.0796)$$

$$= 4.9338 \text{ in.}$$

10. The throat radius of the worm wheel is

$$r = \frac{d_o}{2} - 2a = \frac{2.500}{2} - 2(0.0796)$$

$$= 1.091 \text{ in. radius}$$

$n' = $ no. of equivalent teeth in the worm; for a single start $n' = 1$, for a double start $n' = 2$, etc.

$N = $ no. of teeth in worm wheel

$p = $ linear pitch of worm

$l = $ lead of worm

$a = $ addendum

$d = $ pitch dia of worm

$D = $ pitch dia of worm wheel

$D_o = $ throat dia of wheel

$D'_o = $ dia over sharp corners

$d_o = $ outside dia of worm

$d_r = $ root dia of worm

$h_t = $ depth of worm tooth

$r = $ throat radius

$\theta = $ face angle

$\alpha_w = $ helix angle of worm

$\alpha_g = $ gashing angle of wheel

$L = $ length of worm

11. The diameter of the wheel over the sharp corners is

$$D'_o = 2r\left(1 - \cos\frac{\theta}{2}\right) + D_o = 2(1.091)\left(1 - \cos\frac{60}{2}\right) + 4.9338$$
$$= 5.2262 \text{ in.}$$

12. The face width of the wheel is

$$F = 2.380p + 0.250 = 2.380(\tfrac{1}{4}) + 0.250$$
$$= 0.845 \text{ in.}$$

13. The helix angle of the worm is

$$\tan\alpha_w = \frac{\pi d}{l} = \frac{\pi 2.3408}{\frac{1}{4}} = 29.415$$
$$\alpha_w = 88°3'$$

14. The gashing angle of the worm wheel is

$$\alpha_g = 90 - 88°3' = 1°57'$$

15. The width of the tip of the tool for cutting the worm is

$$T = 0.31p = 0.31(\tfrac{1}{4})$$
$$= 0.0775 \text{ in.}$$

16. The length of the worm is

$$L = p(0.020N + 4.500) = \tfrac{1}{4}[0.020(60) + 4.500]$$
$$= 1.425 \text{ in.}$$

The method used to machine a worm wheel is as follows:

1. The worm wheel is rough turned on a lathe. The center hole is bored, reamed, and pressed on a mandrel. It is then finish turned, and the throat diameter and radius machined. If a hob is to be used, it may not be necessary to turn the radius. The hob will cut the radius while cutting the teeth.
2. The worm wheel is then mounted between the centers of a dividing head. The index mechanism is set at

$$M = \frac{40}{N} = \frac{40}{60} = \frac{2}{3} \times 15 = 10 \text{ holes in the 15-hole circle}$$

3. With the swivel table at 0° the center of the cutter is aligned over the work in a longitudinal direction and a lateral direction. This is the same procedure as described in Section 18.2 for the helical gear. Once aligned, the table is swiveled to the gashing angle, as shown in Fig. 18.7(b).
4. The table is raised until the cutter touches the throat radius. The vertical feed graduated collar is set at zero. The knee is raised very

slowly so that the depth of the first tooth space is cut to about 0.005 in. of the required depth. For the gear in Example 7 it is 0.165 in. NOTE: The operation consists of raising the knee of the milling machine. There is no through cutting. All the teeth are gashed (rough cut) into the surface of the worm wheel.

5. The next operation is to hob the gear. The hob drives the worm wheel. Therefore, the dog is removed, and the mandrel and the work are permitted to revolve freely between two dead centers. There should be no end play between the mandrel and the centers of the dividing head. On a gear hobber, the worm wheel is driven in relation to the lead of the hob and gashing is not necessary. The hob, which is a duplicate of the worm, is aligned centrally with the gashed worm wheel.

6. The knee is raised. The lead of the revolving hob causes the gashed worm wheel to revolve. The knee is raised slightly with each revolution of the worm wheel. When the center distance between the worm wheel and the center line of the hob has been reached, the operation is finished. In this case the center-to-center distance is 3.5577 in., as shown in Example 7.

7. The worm may be turned on a lathe. In the case of the worm in Example 7 a tool with an included angle of 29° and a tip width of 0.0775 in. is ground. However, a much superior worm can be cut with gear-generating equipment, especially if the worm has more than one start.

18.7. Bevel Gears

In Fig. 18.8(a) two bevel gears in mesh are shown. The diametral pitch of a bevel-gear tooth at the large end is the same as the diametral pitch of a spur gear whose pitch radius is equal to the back cone radius of the bevel gear.

The equations and their use will be illustrated with Example 8.

EXAMPLE 8

Given a pair of bevel gears with shafts at 90°, the pinion having 20 teeth and the gear 40 teeth with a diametral pitch of 16, calculate the tooth parts.

Solution:

1. The pitch diameter of the gear is

$$D = \frac{N}{P} = \frac{40}{16}$$

$$= 2.500 \text{ in.}$$

$N = 40\text{T}$
$n = 20\text{T}$
$P = 16$

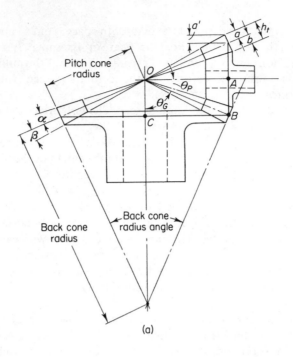

Pitch cone radius

θ_P
θ_G

a'
a
h_t
b

A
B
C

α
β

Back cone radius
Back cone radius angle

(a)

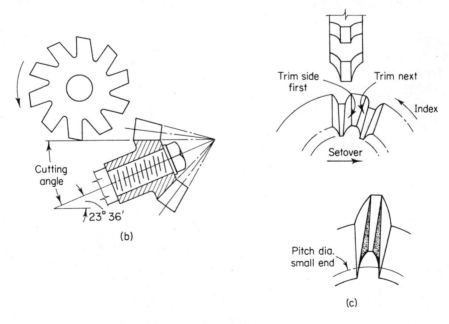

Cutting
angle

23° 36′

(b)

Trim side
first

Trim next

Index

Setover

Pitch dia.
small end

(c)

Figure 18.8

The pitch diameter of the pinion is

$$d = \frac{n}{p} = \frac{20}{16}$$

$$= 1.250 \text{ in.}$$

2. The pitch radius of the gear is

$$R = \frac{D}{2} = \frac{2.500}{2}$$

$$= 1.250 \text{ in.}$$

The pitch radius of the pinion is

$$r = \frac{d}{2} = \frac{1.250}{2}$$

$$= 0.625 \text{ in.}$$

3. The pitch cone angle of the gear is

$$\tan \theta_g = \frac{N}{n} = \frac{40}{20} = 2$$

$$\theta_g = 63°26'$$

The pitch cone angle of the pinion is

$$\theta_p = 90° - \theta_g = 90° - 63°26'$$

$$= 26°34'$$

4. The following calculations are the same for both the gear and the pinion:

a. The pitch cone radius is

$$R_c = \frac{\sqrt{N^2 + n^2}}{2P} = \frac{\sqrt{40^2 + 20^2}}{2(16)}$$

$$= 1.3975 \text{ in.}$$

b. The addendum is

$$a = \frac{1}{P} = \frac{1}{16}$$

$$= 0.0625 \text{ in.}$$

c. The addendum angle is

$$\tan \alpha = \frac{a}{R_c} = \frac{0.0625}{1.3975} = 0.0447$$

$$\alpha = 2°34'$$

d. The dedendum is

$$b = \frac{1.157}{P} = \frac{1.157}{16}$$

$$= 0.0723 \text{ in.}$$

e. The dedendum angle is

$$\tan \beta = \frac{b}{R_c} = \frac{0.0723}{1.3975} = 0.0517$$

$$\beta = 2°58'$$

f. The whole depth (large end of the tooth) is

$$h_t = \frac{2.157}{P} = \frac{2.157}{16}$$

$$= 0.1348 \text{ in.}$$

g. The tooth thickness at the pitch line is

$$t = \frac{1.5708}{P} = \frac{1.5708}{16}$$

$$= 0.0982 \text{ in.}$$

5. The cutting angle of the gear is

$$\phi_g = \theta_g - \beta = 63°26' - 2°58'$$
$$= 60°28'$$

The cutting angle of the pinion is

$$\phi_p = \theta_g - \beta = 26°34' - 2°58'$$
$$= 23°36'$$

6. The angular addendum of the gear is

$$a'_g = a \cos \theta_g = 0.0625(\cos 63°26')$$
$$= 0.0280 \text{ in.}$$

The angular addendum of the pinion is

$$a'_p = a \cos \theta_p = 0.0625(\cos 26°34')$$
$$= 0.0560 \text{ in.}$$

7. The outside diameter of the gear is

$$D_o = D + 2\left(\frac{\cos \theta_g}{P}\right) = 2.500 + 2\left(\frac{\cos 63°26'}{16}\right)$$

$$= 2.5560 \text{ in.}$$

The outside diameter of the pinion is

$$d_o = d + 2\frac{\cos \theta_p}{P} = 1.250 + 2\left(\frac{\cos 26°34'}{16}\right)$$

$$= 1.3620 \text{ in.}$$

8. The number of teeth needed to select a cutter for the gear is

$$N' = \frac{N}{\cos \theta_g} = \frac{40}{\cos 63°26'}$$

$$= 89 + \text{ (which requires a no. 2 cutter)}$$

and for the pinion is

$$n' = \frac{n}{\cos \theta_p} = \frac{20}{\cos 26°34'}$$

$$= 22 + \text{(which requires a no. 5 cutter)}$$

Since the procedure for cutting a bevel pinion and bevel gear is the same, we shall discuss the machining of a bevel pinion.

Assume that the bear blank is already machined. It is mounted on an arbor that is mounted in the spindle of a dividing head. The dividing head is set at the cutting angle. For the pinion the angle is 23°36' in Example 8, and it is shown in Fig. 18.8(b).

The cutting angle positions the root of the gear tooth horizontally. The cutter is located centrally so that the tooth space will be cut on the center line of the gear blank. The depth of the cut is marked off on the large face. The knee is raised 0.1348 in. (Example 8) and a central cut taken. (Actually the whole depth of tooth at the large end is approached with several cuts.) All the teeth are roughed.

It now becomes necessary to reduce the thickness of the teeth. This correction is made by offsetting the cutter from the center of the gear blank in two directions, laterally and rotationally. This is shown in Fig. 18.8(c).

The work is moved so that it is free from the cutter. To trim the left side of the tooth, the table is offset (setover) to the right and rotated counter-clockwise so that the side of the tooth to be cut is rotated into the cutter. When trimming the right side of the tooth, the table is offset to the left and rotated clockwise so that the right face of the tooth rotates into the left side of the cutter. The amount of offset will be calculated later in this section. The amount of rotation is a process of trial and error.

With the proper setover, a light cut should be taken after a very slight rotation of the work. This is continued until the full face of the tooth has been cut. The second face of the same tooth should be cut with the same procedure. See Fig. 18.8(c).

The tooth is measured at both ends at the pitch line with a vernier gear caliper. The tooth thickness at the pitch line should be the same for the large end as for the small end. The variations of tooth thickness take place above the pitch line.

If the large end of the tooth is correct but the small end of the tooth is too thick, the table has been offset too much. If the small end of the tooth is correct but the large end of the tooth is too thick, then there was not enough table offset. The appropriate corrections should be made. As a matter of fact, all this preliminary work should be done on a trial blank and the procedure recorded.

Once the settings are correct, *all* of one side of all the teeth should be cut with the correction applied. Then the other side of all the teeth should be cut.

After all this there still needs to be some correction by filing. The tooth at the small end will be thicker *to the pitch line* than the desired thickness. This is caused by the cutter's having been selected for the large end of the tooth, with the thickness of the tooth reduced from the large end toward the small end.

The offset referred to above may be calculated by using the equations in Example 9 in conjunction with Table 18.2.

TABLE 18.2

Ratio of Pitch Cone Radius to Width of Face, R_c/f

Cutter no.	$\frac{3}{1}$	$\frac{3\frac{1}{4}}{1}$	$\frac{3\frac{1}{2}}{1}$	$\frac{3\frac{3}{4}}{1}$	$\frac{4}{1}$	$\frac{4\frac{1}{4}}{1}$	$\frac{4\frac{1}{2}}{1}$	$\frac{4\frac{3}{4}}{1}$	$\frac{5}{1}$	$\frac{5\frac{1}{2}}{1}$	$\frac{6}{1}$	$\frac{7}{1}$	$\frac{8}{1}$
1	0.254	0.254	0.255	0.256	0.257	0.257	0.257	0.258	0.258	0.259	0.260	0.262	0.264
2	0.266	0.268	0.271	0.272	0.273	0.274	0.274	0.275	0.277	0.279	0.280	0.283	0.284
3	0.266	0.268	0.271	0.273	0.275	0.278	0.280	0.282	0.283	0.286	0.287	0.290	0.292
4	0.275	0.280	0.285	0.287	0.291	0.293	0.296	0.298	0.298	0.302	0.305	0.308	0.311
5	0.280	0.285	0.290	0.293	0.295	0.296	0.298	0.300	0.302	0.307	0.309	0.313	0.315
6	0.311	0.318	0.323	0.328	0.330	0.334	0.337	0.340	0.343	0.348	0.352	0.356	0.362
7	0.289	0.298	0.308	0.316	0.324	0.329	0.334	0.338	0.343	0.350	0.360	0.370	0.376
8	0.275	0.286	0.296	0.309	0.319	0.331	0.338	0.344	0.352	0.361	0.368	0.380	0.386

EXAMPLE 9

Find the offset required to trim the bevel teeth in Example 8.

Solution:

1. The face width of the tooth should be calculated first. One method for calculating the face width is

$$f = \frac{8}{P} = \frac{8}{16} \qquad \begin{matrix} f = \text{face width} \\ P = 16 \end{matrix}$$

$$= 0.500 \text{ in.}$$

2. The factor F may be found in the table from the ratio of the pitch cone radius to the face width and the cutter number. Thus

$$\frac{R_c}{f} = \frac{1.3975}{0.500} = \frac{2.795}{1} \simeq \frac{3}{1} \qquad R_c = 1.3975 \text{ in.}$$

3. In Example 8, the cutter number for the pinion is 5. For using the ratio 3 : 1 and a number 5 cutter, Table 18.2 gives the nearest value of

$$F = 0.280 \qquad F = \text{factor from table}$$

4. The offset is

$$o = \frac{T}{2} - \frac{F}{P} = \frac{0.100}{2} - \frac{0.280}{16} \qquad \begin{matrix} T = \text{cutter thickness at pitch} \\ \text{line} = \text{assumed to be} \\ 0.100 \text{ in.} \end{matrix}$$

$$= 0.0325 \text{ in.}$$

Thus, to trim the first side of the tooth, Fig. 18.8(c), the table is moved *toward* the operator (away from the column of the machine) 0.0325 in. Let us assume that the index handle is turned 5 holes in a particular hole circle, which rotates the work counterclockwise. A cut is then taken.

The cutter table is moved back to clear the cutter, the table is moved back to cancel out the offset, and the index handle is rotated to cancel out the rotary offset. Thus the work is returned to its initial position with reference to the cutter. The student must be careful to compensate for backlash.

Next, the work is indexed one tooth space. For our 20-tooth pinion the index handle must be rotated $40/20 = 2$ full turns of the index handle. The cutter should be centered on the second tooth space.

Now the table is offset 0.0325 in. *away* from the operator, and the index handle is rotated 5 holes so that the work rotates clockwise. The second side of the tooth is trimmed. Measurements are taken and corrections made.

It is very important to note that whatever is done to one side of a tooth must be done to the other side. Otherwise the tooth will not be on the center line of the gear. Also, the student should always remember that any time the table or index handle is reversed, backlash will be a factor.

18.8. Gear Inspection

The gear tooth vernier, Fig. 18.9(a), makes it possible to set the chordal addendum, Fig. 18.9(b), so that the jaws of the calipers touch the gear teeth at the pitch circle or the point at which the chordal thickness is to be measured. The chordal thickness t_c may be found by using the equation

$$t_c = D \sin \frac{90°}{N}$$

The chordal addendum a_c may be found by using the equation

$$a_c = a + \frac{t^2}{4D} = \frac{1}{P}\left(\frac{0.6168}{N} + 1\right)$$

a = addendum
t = circular thickness
D = pitch dia

Once these values have been established, the tooth thickness may be measured.

EXAMPLE 10

Find the chordal thickness and the chordal addendum for an 8-pitch spur gear which has 32 teeth.

Solution:

1. The pitch diameter is

$$D = \frac{N}{P} = \frac{32}{8} = 4.000 \text{ in.}$$

$P = 8$
$N = 32T$

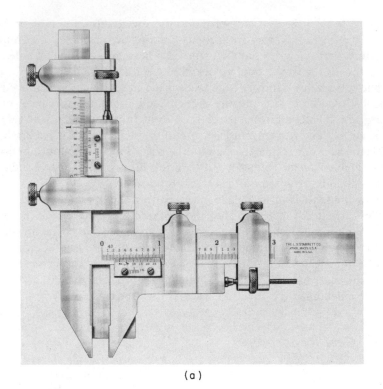

Figure 18.9 (*Photo courtesy of The L.S. Starrett Company.*)

2. The chordal thickness is

$$t_c = D \sin \frac{90°}{N} = 4.000 \sin \frac{90°}{32} = 4.000 \sin 2.8125°$$

$$= 0.197 \text{ in.}$$

3. The chordal addendum is

$$a_c = \frac{1}{P}\left(\frac{0.6168}{N} + 1\right) = \frac{1}{8}\left(\frac{0.6168}{32} + 1\right)$$

$$= 0.1274 \text{ in.}$$

The vertical beam, Fig. 18.9(a), is set to 0.127 in. The horizontal beam should give the chordal-thickness reading of 0.197 in.

NOTE: The gear vernier reads in increments of 0.001 in. It is also important that any error in the outside diameter of the gear blank should be reflected in the chordal addendum. Otherwise the vertical beam of the calipers will not touch the gear tooth at the pitch line.

Another method for checking gears is the two-wire method. Figure 18.9(c) shows the measurement M over the wires for an even number of teeth in a gear. Figure 18.9(d) shows M' over an odd-numbered tooth gear.

The best wire size G should be carefully calculated so that it is tangent to the teeth at the pitch line. Any good engineering handbook has tables for the M and M' values. If the student is interested in a set of equations for calculating these values of best wire size G, M, and M', they are:

$$G = D\left[\cos \alpha \tan\left(\alpha + \frac{90}{N}\right) + \sin \alpha\right]$$

$$M = D \sin \alpha \sec\left(\alpha + \frac{90}{N}\right) + G$$

$$M' = (M - G)\cos\frac{90}{N} + G$$

G = best wire size
M = measurement, even no. of teeth
M' = measurement, odd no. of teeth
D = pitch dia
α = pressure angle

There are also *functional methods* for checking gears. One such method consists of arranging a master gear so that it will roll with the gear being checked. The error is usually indicated on a sensitive dial indicator, or recorded on a strip chart. This error, although not broken down into the various components concerning where the error might actually be, is an indicative composite error. It shows what will happen when the gear is placed in operation. It is representative of the overall operation and what can be expected when two gears operate in mesh with each other. Errors such as runout, size changes, composite tooth-to-tooth error, etc., can also be checked.

QUESTIONS AND PROBLEMS

18.1 What is a pinion gear?

18.2 Define: pitch diameter, diametral pitch, addendum, circular pitch, chordal thickness, and circular thickness.

18.3 A spur gear has 26 teeth and an outside diameter of 2 in. Find: (a) the diametral pitch; (b) the pitch diameter; (c) the addendum; (d) the dedendum; (e) clearance; (f) the full depth of the tooth; (g) the working depth; (h) the root diameter; (i) the tooth thickness.

18.4 Given a spur gear with an outside diameter of $2\frac{1}{2}$ in. and a diametral pitch of 16, find: (a) the number of teeth in the gear; (b) the pitch diameter; (c) the root diameter; (d) the addendum; (e) the dedendum; (f) the tooth thickness.

18.5 Find (a) the chordal thickness and (b) the chordal addendum of the gear tooth in problem 18.3

18.6 Find (a) the chordal thickness and (b) the chordal addendum in problem 18.4.

18.7 Describe the pressure angle of a $14\frac{1}{2}°$ involute tooth. What part does the base circle play in determining the pressure angle? Support with a sketch.

18.8 What is meant by generating a tooth?

18.9 In Table 18.1: for which value of N, the number of teeth to be cut, is the involute accurate? For example, is a number 7 cutter made with an accurate involute curve when cutting a 14-, 15-, and 16-tooth gear?

18.10 What is the number of the cutter used in (a) problem 18.3 and (b) problem 18.4?

18.11 Assume the gear blank and the gear cutter are aligned as in Fig. 18.2(c). How much would you need to move the table to align the cutter and gear center lines in (a) problem 18.3 (gear cutter is 0.170 in. thick) and (b) problem 18.4 cutter thickness is 0.145 in.).

18.12 Explain the difference between normal and real diametral pitch.

18.13 Explain the process used to cut a helical gear.

18.14 Explain why it is not possible to use the same cutter for cutting a helical gear and a spur gear having the same number of teeth and the same pitch.

18.15 Given a helical gear with 38 teeth, a helix angle of 30°, and a normal pitch of 20, find: (a) the pitch diameter; (b) the lead; (c) the addendum; (d) the dedendum; (e) the whole depth; (f) the tooth thickness; (g) the outside diameter; (h) the root diameter. (i) What gears would be needed to cut the lead and find the error?

18.16 Which cutter should be used for the gear in problem 18.15?

18.17 Given a helical gear of 18 teeth and a pitch diameter of 1.1972 in. with a helix of 20°, find: (a) the normal diametral pitch; (b) the lead; (c) the outside diameter; (d) the root diameter; (e) the tooth thickness; (f) the cutter number used.

18.18 Assume the gear in Problem 18.15 is to be cut, describe the procedure used. Include all your calculations for lead, indexing, etc.

18.19 Repeat Problem 18.18 for Problem 18.17.

18.20 Given an 80 : 1 ratio worm and worm wheel, how many teeth must the worm wheel have if (a) the worm has one start? (b) Has two starts? (c) Has four starts? (d) Has five starts?

18.21 Explain the setup and operation for gashing and hobbing a worm wheel.

18.22 Given a worm and a worm wheel which has a ratio of 80 : 1. The worm has a 3-in. outside diameter, six threads to the inch, and double lead. The face angle of the worm wheel is 50°. Find: (a) the lead of the worm; (b) the addendum of the worm; (c) the pitch diameter of the worm; (d) the depth of the worm tooth; (e) the root diameter of the worm; (f) the helix angle of the worm; (g) the width of the tip of the tool for cutting the worm; (h) the length of the worm.

18.23 Using the data from problem 18.22, calculate the following for the worm wheel: (a) the pitch diameter of the worm wheel; (b) the center distance between the worm and worm wheel; (c) the throat diameter of the wheel; (d) the throat radius of the wheel; (e) the diameter over the sharp corners; (f) the face width; (g) the gashing angle.

18.24 Define the pitch cone radius of a bevel gear.

18.25 Explain the setup and operation for cutting a bevel gear.

18.26 Why is it necessary to calculate the offset when cutting a bevel gear?

18.27 When trimming a bevel gear, if the large end of the tooth is correct but the small end is too thick, what correction must be made?

18.28 Which part of a bevel gear tooth must be filed after all machining corrections have been made? Explain.

18.29 A pair of helical bevel gears have their shafts at 90°. The pinion has 16 teeth, and the gear has 24 teeth. The diametral pitch is 20. Calculate: (a) the pitch diameter of the gears; (b) the pitch radius of the gears; (c) the pitch cone angle of the gears; (d) the pitch cone radius; (e) the addendum and the addendum angle; (f) the dedendum and the dedendum angle; (g) the whole depth at the large end of the tooth; (h) the tooth thickness at the pitch line; (i) the cutting angles for both gears; (j) the angular addendum for both gears; (k) the outside diameter of the gears; (l) the number of teeth for the cutters for cutting both gears.

18.30 Given a bevel gear of 24 teeth, a 6-diametral pitch, and a pitch cone radius of 4.8167 in. The number of the cutter used is 3. Assume a cutter thickness of 0.262 in. (a) Find the face width. (b) Find the factor from the table. (c) Find the offset.

18.31 Explain the use of a gear-tooth vernier caliper.

18.32 Find (a) the best wire size and (b) the measurement over wires in Example 1 if the pressure angle is $14\frac{1}{2}°$.

18.33 What is functional gear checking?

Miscellaneous Production Machines

19

19.1. The Turret Lathe

Turret lathes are usually classified as hand-operated or automatic. In both instances the distance traveled by the cutting tool is controlled by stops, cams, or tapes. The essential difference is that the hand turret lathe [Fig. 19.1(a)] is manipulated by the operator, whereas the controls are present and operated automatically on the automatic turret lathe. A tape may control the turret [Fig. 19.1(b)] into which the tools have been fixed, or direct the selection of the cutting tools which have been included in a tool-changer, [Fig. 19.1(c)].

Horizontal turret lathes may be further identified by the construction of the hexagon turret. Those having fixed saddles and movable slides upon which the hexagon turret is mounted are called *ram* turret lathes, Fig. 19.2(a). The *saddle* type turret lathe, Fig. 19.2(b), has its hexagon turret mounted directly on the saddle, so that the entire saddle moves when actuated by a handwheel.

The turret lathe differs from the engine lathe in that the tailstock of the lathe is replaced by a hexagon turret which permits the mounting of multiple tools for multiple-diameter repetitive cutting. The second basic difference is the substitution of a square turret for the compound rest. The cross slide is usually made long enough to permit the mounting of another tool post or square turret at the rear of the slide, Fig. 19.2(c). This type of turret lathe is adaptable for quick simple setups for short-run or medium-run machining.

The saddle type turret lathe is sometimes equipped with a hung saddle which operates off the front way and thus permits greater swing capacity.

The ram type turret requires that the saddle be positioned and clamped to reduce the ram overhang. The operator moves only the slide which makes for faster manipulation of the hexagon turret. These machines are intended

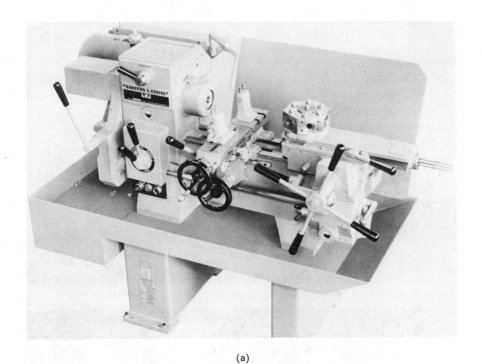

(a)

(b)

Figure 19.1 [(*a*) *Courtesy of Bardons & Oliver, Inc.;* (*b*) *courtesy of Elliott Machine Tool Group;* (*c*) *courtesy of Kearney & Trecker Corporation;* (*d*) *courtesy of Moog Hydran-Point.*]

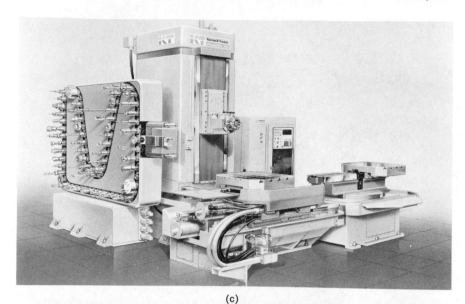

(c)

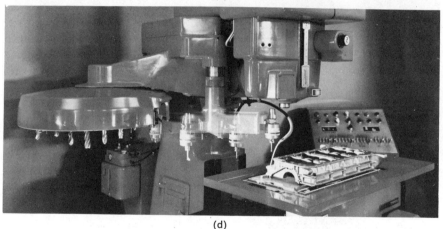

(d)

Figure 19.1 (Cont.)

to be used for short runs or light cutting operations so as not to overload the overhanging slide. Heavy or long cutting operations should be done on the saddle type turret lathe.

The saddle type turret lathe is constructed so that the entire saddle moves. This makes for rigid construction and eliminates the overhanging slide. The movement of the additional mass is overcome by providing a power-drive rapid traverse.

Many turret lathes are equipped with automatically controlled spindle speeds. The manipulation of the hexagon turret by the operator automatically changes the preset spindle speed. This eliminates the shifting of levers when

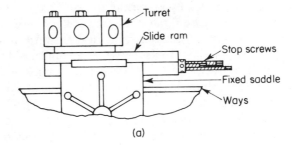

(a)

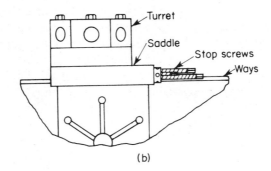

(b)

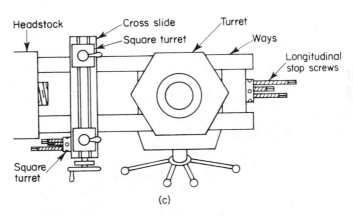

(c)

Figure 19.2

the spindle speed needs to be changed between cuts. In some instances the spindle speeds may be preset while the cutting operation is in progress. As the turret is retracted, the spindle speed changes.

The hexagon turret may be fed by hand or fed automatically. When hand feeding, the turret is caused to register against a stop screw. This preset stop screw controls the length of the cut. In the automatic turret lathe provision is made in the construction of the machine for automatically disengaging the feed lever at the end of the cut. This applies to the hexagon turret as well as the cross slide and is operated by presetting the stop screws, Fig. 19.2(c). As the hexagon turret is backed off, the stop-screw collar indexes and brings the next stop screw into position ready for the next forward movement of the saddle or slide. The cross-slide stop screw is usually indexed manually.

The headstock may be fitted with an independent chuck or a self-centering chuck. The independent chuck is slow and requires a great deal of experience for quick alignment of the work. The self-centering (universal) chuck is much faster to operate, will yield better alignment, and requires less skill on the part of the operator when aligning work. These chucks may be equipped with soft jaws shaped to the contour of the workpiece.

Collets which are mechanically or automatically operated (hydraulic or pneumatic) are also available. Moving a lever in one direction releases the collet so that the bar stock may move forward to expose the required length when it registers against a stop in the hexagon turret. Pushing the lever in the opposite direction closes the collet and locks it about the workpiece. This can usually be done without stopping the rotation of the spindle.

Various attachments are available for setting up single or multiple tool arrangements. Figure 19.3(a) shows a flanged toolholder; Fig. 19.3(b), a

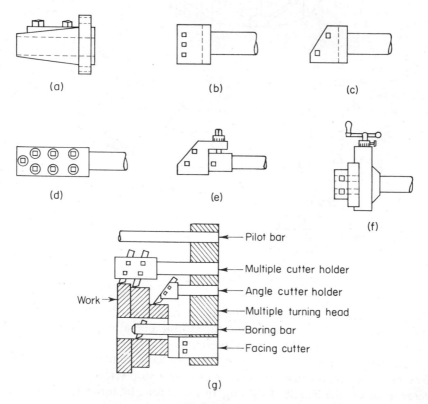

(a)

(b)

(c)

(d)

(e)

(f)

Pilot bar

Multiple cutter holder

Angle cutter holder

Work →

Multiple turning head

Boring bar

Facing cutter

(g)

Figure 19.3

straight toolholder; Fig. 19.3(c), an angle toolholder; Fig. 19.3(d), a multiple-cutter holder; Fig. 19.3(e), an adjustable-angle cutter holder; and Fig. 19.3(f), a slide toolholder. Other holders available are recess and boring holders, duplex holders, floating-reamer and adjustable-reamer holders, pilot boring bars, centering holders, releasing tap holders, collapsing taps and dies, etc.

Attachments for bar feeding, taper turning, and threading are also available for the turret lathe.

Figure 19.3(g) shows a multiple turning head with an overarm support for alignment and rigidity. Also mounted on the head are two cutter holders, a boring bar, and a facing tool. Other heads are made for holding form tools, facing tools, drills, reamers, or pilot bars.

19.2. Turret Lathe (Set-up)

The choice of turret lathe for size, type, power, etc., is the first decision which must be made. Once determined, the cost of labor, tooling, and setup is established. Then the *floor-to-floor time* must be determined. The floor-to-floor time includes the handling as well as the machine time. Once the floor-to-floor time is established, the part is processed for that machine. Operations should be combined wherever possible to use multiple tooling. Wherever two cuts can be taken in one pass, it is obvious that much time can be saved.

The choice whether a lathe or a turret lathe should be used is based on a comparison of the cost of producing parts by both methods. The factors which need to be considered are the time to produce a part, the setup, the direct labor charge, and the overhead. The equation for determining the break-even point between the use of a turret lathe and an engine lathe is

$$N = \frac{50(SS_r - ss_r)}{t(d + o) - T(D + O)}$$

Turret lathe
T = time/piece, min
O = overhead cost
D = direct labor cost
S = setup time
S_r = setup rate, hr
Engine lathe
t = time/piece, min
o = overhead cost
d = direct labor cost
s = setup time
s_r = setup rate, hr
N = no. of pieces, lot size

EXAMPLE 1

A company is to manufacture 40 pieces to fill an order. A turret lathe and an engine lathe are available. The records show the following data: If a turret lathe is used, the part can be machined in 5 minutes. The overhead is $4.00, and the direct labor cost is $2.50/hour. The setup time will be 8 hours and the setup man's hourly rate is $4.00. The same part will take 12 minutes on an engine lathe with an overhead of $2.00, and a direct labor cost of $3.50/hour. The setup time is 2 hours, and the setup man's hourly rate is $4.00/hour. Should the job be done on a turret lathe or an engine lathe?

Solution:

$$N = \frac{50[(8 \times 4) - (2 \times 4)]}{12(3.5 + 2) - 5(2.5 + 4)}$$

$$= 35.8 \cong 36 \text{ pieces}$$

Turret lathe
$T = 5$ min/piece
$O = \$4.00$
$D = \$2.50/hr$
$S = 8$ hrs
$S_r = \$4.00/hr$
Engine lathe
$t = 12$ min/piece
$o = \$2.00$
$d = \$3.50/hr$
$s = 2$ hrs
$s_r = \$4.00/hr$

In this example the break-even point is 36 pieces. Thus a job of 36 pieces or more should be done on a turret lathe.

Figure 19.4 shows the finished part (lower left) machined on the turret lathe. Station 1 on the hexagon turret shows the stock stop with a retractable combination center drill-countersink. The collet opens, the round stock registers against the stock stop with the center drill retracted, and the collet clamps the work. The hexagon turret is then pulled back slightly (not indexed), and the combination center drill-countersink is brought out. The end of the stock is center drilled. This center drill acts as a guide for the drill at station 2.

At station 2 the hole and the outside-diameter roughing are done in one pass of the hexagon turret. The front face of the piece is finished with the facing tool at station *A* of the square turret.

The boring bar, station 3, is used to machine the inside-thread diameter, while too *B*, mounted in the square turret, is used as a finishing tool. It also machines the external radius.

Station 4 has the recessing tool for cutting the thread recess. The tool at station *C* of the square turret is used to rough the second outside diameter.

Station 5 mounts a collapsible tap which machines the thread to the recess. When the front disk on the tap is compressed through contact with the front of the work, the tap chasers retract and the tap may be withdrawn from the work.

At station 6 the hole beyond the thread is reamed. The small outside diameter is finished with the tool mounted in station *D* of the square turret. The cross slide is then fed toward the operator until the "rear tool" has chamfered and cut off the workpiece. The entire cycle is repeated as often as necessary.

It should be understood that other combinations of tools are possible for making this workpiece. The arrangement of the tools is dependent upon the machine capabilities and condition, the type of material in the workpiece, the accuracy and finish required, the quantity of production, etc.

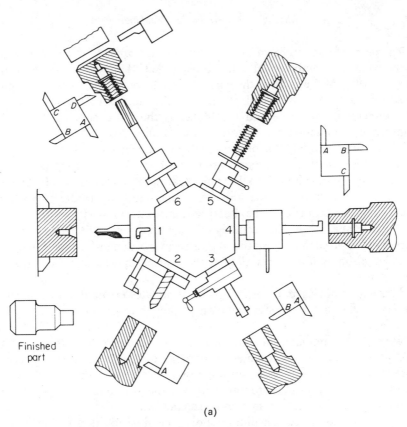

Finished
part

(a)

(b)

Figure 19.4 *(Photo courtesy of Clausing Company.)*

The purpose of combining tools is to reduce the *production* cost per piece. As the tools are combined or other tools added, the *tooling* cost goes up. Since the setup of the tools at the various stations on the hexagon turret and the square turret are all related, the greater the number of tools added, the more difficult is the setup and the higher is the setup cost. Only greater quantities of production can warrant higher tooling costs.

The accuracy which can be expected on a turret lathe is within about 0.001 in. When piloted boring bars are used, the tools may be set to cut in a vertical plane. As the headstock bearings heat up, the work raises. If the tool is set to cut in a vertical plane, this rise of bearing temperature may create dimensional inaccuracies. The bearing temperature, when cutting in a horizontal plane, affects the accuracy of machining very little. However, if it is desirable to place the tool so that it cuts in a vertical plane, operation of the turret lathe should not start until after the bearings have reached an equilibrium state.

Turning or boring in a vertical plane eliminates errors due to indexing. If a tool is set to cut in a horizontal plane, the error due to indexing is greatly increased.

When using combination tools, it is also important that a finishing and roughing tool should not be used in combination. Roughing cuts such as those taken with drills or rough turning tools vibrate under the heavy stresses of cutting. These vibrations are transmitted to the work and the finishing tool and make it very difficult to maintain size and finish.

In general, as much machining should be done as is possible in one chucking. If the removal of a great deal of metal or irregular depths of metal, as when machining a casting, is necessary, it may be good practice to do the roughing in one operation and then rechuck the part and do the finishing. The number of cuts, or chuckings, is dictated by the nature of the job.

To summarize: (1) Tools should be combined for maximum cutting during each pass. (2) Finishing cuts should be taken in a vertical plane and should not be combined with roughing tools. (3) Operation of tools off the hexagon turret is easier than off the cross slide.

Contour cutting is also possible on a turret lathe with the use of attachments operated off the cross slide. Cross-slide hexagon turrets may also be used for contour cutting.

Single-spindle automatic turret lathes may have their hexagon turret positioned the same as the conventional turret lathe does, or their turret axis may be parallel to the spindle axis. The setups do not differ much from the conventional turret lathes.

These machines are considered automatic even though the work is usually hand loaded and removed from the holding device. Once the start button is pushed, the machine will go through the entire cycle of rapid traverse, feed, spindle-speed changes, retraction, dwell, etc. The automatic control is complete for both the hexagon turret and the cross slide. The control of the various operations is usually done with cams and trip dogs.

19.3. The Automatic Screw Machine

The Brown and Sharpe screw machine is one of a number of automatic lathes used for rapid and repetitive cutting. There are many types of automatic machines including those which machine parts from bar stock and those which are used to machine castings. The Brown and Sharpe machine uses bar stock fed through the spindle. Once the appropriate cams are installed and the tools coordinated with the cams, the machine will repeat the machining operations until the bar stock is consumed.

Essentially, the Brown and Sharpe automatic screw machine is a turret lathe equipped with a series of cams to control all operations. Cams are used to index, rapid traverse, feed, and retract a six-sided turret. Trip dogs, Fig. 19.5(a), are used to rapid traverse and feed the cross slide. Another set of trip dogs may be used to increase, decrease, or reverse the spindle speed. A vertical slide is also operated with trip dogs.

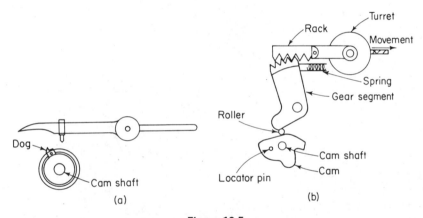

Figure 19.5

Figure 19.5(b) shows a cam operating a gear segment. The gear segment actuates the rack. This in turn causes the motion of the turret slide. When the turret has completed its cutting and is ready to be indexed, the trip lever is actuated by a trip dog on the camshaft. The lever releases the pin in one-half of the clutch. This clutch is then caused to slide over the camshaft until it engages the other half of the clutch which is revolving, getting its power from the camshaft. The clutch now rotating with the power camshaft and acting through a gear train causes a disk to revolve. Attached to the face of the disk is a hardened roller which engages the back plate of the index head. Once the roller engages the index head, the turret is caused to revolve in the manner of a Geneva motion.

Cams used with these machines are usually made on the job. The cam layout methods, Chapter 17, are used with cam blanks divided into 100 parts.

The calculations for the layout of cams vary from job to job. An illustrated

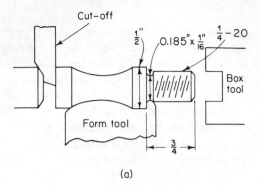

(a)

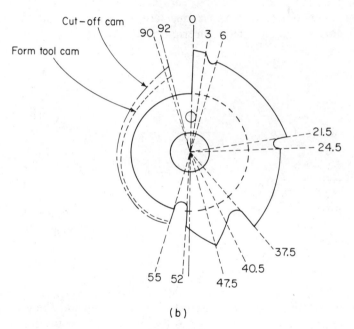

(b)

Figure 19.6

example will serve to show the processes for laying out cams for the turret, cross slide, and cutoff for the part in Fig. 19.6(a).

EXAMPLE 2*

Given the part in Fig. 19.6(a), calculate and lay out the cams. The following data are given: (1) Feed for a hollow mill for rough turning the thread diameter is 0.010 in./revolution. (2) The feed for finish turning for a single-point tool is 0.012 in./revolution. (3) The form tool needs a

---

*It should be noted that some of the information used in this problem is from the Brown and Sharpe *Automatic Screw-Machine Handbook*.

feed of 0.001 in./revolution. (4) The cutoff tool is operated with a feed of
0.0015 in./revolution. Assume the cutting speed of the die to be 40 ft/minute
and all additional operations to be 150 ft/minute.

Solution:

1. The spindle speeds may be calculated from the surface speed.
   a. The rpm of the die

   $$N = \frac{C_s 12}{\pi D} = \frac{40(12)}{\pi 0.250} \qquad C_s = 40 \text{ ft/min}$$

   $$= 611 \text{ rpm}$$

   The nearest rpm available is 545 rpm.
   b. The rpm of the hollow end mill, finish turning, cutoff, and form
   tool is

   $$N = \frac{C_s 12}{\pi D} = \frac{150(12)}{\pi 0.500} \qquad C_s = 150 \text{ ft/min}$$

   $$= 1146 \text{ rpm}$$

   The nearest rpm available is 905 rpm.
2. The throw of each lobe of the cam is as follows:
   a. Hollow mill (rough turning)

   $$T = L + C = 0.687 + 0.015 \qquad \begin{array}{l} T = \text{throw, each lobe} \\ L = \text{length turned} \\ C = \text{clearance, or approach} \end{array}$$

   $$= 0.702 \text{ in.}$$

   b. The single-point tool (finish turning)

   $$T = L + C = 0.687 + 0.015$$

   $$= 0.702 \text{ in.}$$

   c. Die on

   $$T = \text{length of thread portion} = 0.750 \text{ in.}$$

   d. The form tool cuts for a length equal to the largest diameter cut
   minus the smallest diameter cut divided by 2. Thus

   $$T = \frac{D - d}{2} + C \qquad \begin{array}{l} D = 0.500 \text{ in.} \\ d = 0.185 \text{ in.} \end{array}$$

   $$= \frac{0.500 - 0.185}{2} + 0.015$$

   $$= 0.172 \text{ in.}$$

   e. The cutoff tool travels a distance of

   $$T = \frac{D}{2} + 0.010 + 0.015 = \frac{0.500}{2} + 0.025$$

   $$= 0.275 \text{ in.}$$

3. The number of revolutions for each operation is based on the maximum
   rpm required. The revolutions are calculated from the throw and the

feed. Thus

a. The number of revolutions for the hollow end mill is

$$\frac{T}{f} = \frac{0.702}{0.010} = 70 \text{ rev}$$

b. The number of revolutions for the single-point tool is

$$\frac{T}{f} = \frac{0.702}{0.012} = 59 \text{ rev}$$

c. The number of revolutions for thread "on" and thread "off"

(1) The number of threads required is

$$0.750 \times 20 = 15 \text{ threads total required}$$

(2) Add five threads for the approach of the tool

$$15 + 5 = 20 \text{ threads}$$

(3) The modification factor is

$$\frac{\text{High spindle speed used/rev}}{\text{Low spindle speed used/rev}} = \frac{905}{545} = 1.66$$

(4) Thus the thread on is

$$20 \times 1.66 = 33 \text{ threads/rev}$$

(5) The thread off is

$$20 \text{ threads/rev}$$

d. The number of revolutions for the form tool is

$$\frac{T}{f} = \frac{0.172}{0.001} = 172 \text{ rev}$$

e. The number of revolutions for the cutoff tool is

$$\frac{T}{f} = \frac{0.275}{0.0015} = 183 \text{ rev}$$

f. From the Brown and Sharpe tables the average revolutions for $\frac{1}{4}$ second is 11. Allowing 20% for adjustment,

$$11 + (11 \times 20\%) = 13 \text{ for each indexing operation}$$

4. The total number of revolutions is the sum of all the revolutions in part 3.

a. The sum *without clearance allowances* is given in Table 19.1.

b. The modifications made for clearance are obtained from

$$(1) \quad N_c = \frac{\text{rev without clearance} \times \text{cam spaces with clearance}}{\text{cam spaces without clearance}}$$

$$= \frac{417 \times 100}{100 - 9*} \qquad N_c = \text{total rev with clearance}$$

$$= 458$$

*Nine spaces represent clearance at the end of a cycle.

TABLE 19.1

Operation	rev	
Stock feed	13	
Index of turret	13	
Hollow mill	70	
Index of turret	13	
Finish turning	59	
Indexing	13	
Die on	33	
Die off	20	
Form tool		172 (overlaps, die off)
Cutoff	183	
Total (no clearance)	417	

(2) The number of clearance revolutions is

$$458 - 417 = 41 \text{ rev}$$

(3) From the Brown and Sharpe tables the nearest number of revolutions available is 453. Since we shall use 453 and we need 458, there will be

$$458 - 453 = 5 \text{ spaces too many}$$

These five spaces must be taken away from the spacing in Table 19.2.

5. The number of divisions for each cam space is

$$\frac{453}{100} = 4.53 \text{ for each cam space.}$$

6. The number of divisions for each operation is given in Table 19.2.
7. To calculate the die throw, both on and off:
   a. Revolutions to run die on is

$$7 \times 4.53 = 31.7 \text{ rev (at top speed)}$$

   b. Actual revolutions to run die either on or off equals 31.7 divided by the thread modification factor of 1.66 is

$$\frac{31.7}{1.66} = 19$$

   c. Exact throw needed less 10% for 20 threads/in. is

$$\left(\frac{1}{20} \times 19\right) - \left(\frac{1}{20} \times 19\right)0.10 = 0.855 \text{ in.}$$

8. The tabulation sheet is given in Table 19.3 and the cam is shown in Fig. 19.6(b).

TABLE 19.2

Operation		
Stock feed	$\dfrac{13}{4.53} =$	3.0
Indexing	$\dfrac{13}{4.53} =$	3.0
Hollow mill	$\dfrac{70}{4.53} =$	15.5
Indexing	$\dfrac{13}{4.53} =$	3.0
Finish turning	$\dfrac{59}{4.53} =$	13.0
Indexing	$\dfrac{13}{4.53} =$	3.0
Thread on	$\dfrac{33}{4.53} =$	7.0
Thread off	$\dfrac{20}{4.53} =$	4.5
Form tool	$\dfrac{172}{4.53} =$	38
Dwell	$\dfrac{4}{4.53} =$	1
Index, three spaces	$\dfrac{41}{4.53} =$	9
Cutoff	$\dfrac{183}{4.53} =$	40.0
Clearance	$\dfrac{41 - 5*}{4.53} =$	8.0
Totals	453	100

Form tool / Dwell / Index, three spaces } overlaps, die off

*Correction made for five revolutions from 458 to 453.

TABLE 19.3

Operation	Spindle, rev	Lobe, part of 100	Throw	Feed
Stock feed to stop	13	3.0		
Indexing hexagon turret	13	3.0		
Roughing, hollow mill	70	15.5	0.702	0.010
Indexing hexagon turret	13	3.0		
Finish turning	59	13.0	0.702	0.012
Indexing hexagon turret	13	3.0		
Thread die on	33	7.0	0.855	
Thread die off	20	4.5	0.855	
Form tool	172	38	0.172	0.001
Dwell	4	1		
Index, three spaces	41	9		
Cutoff	183	40.0	0.275	0.0015
Clearance	36	8.0		
Totals	453	100		

19.4. Accessories and Form Tools

The tools used for cutting on automatic lathes are numerous. Internal and external tools may be arranged to cut either on the face of the tool, or on the top of the tool as shown in Fig. 19.7(a), called *tangential cutting*, or, as shown in Fig. 19.7(b), called *radial cutting*.

The tools for cutting external diameters may be either solid or adjustable hollow mills, box tools, balanced turning tools, knee tools, swing tools, etc. See Fig. 19.7(c).

Internal tools are drills, reamers, counterbores, etc. These tools may be held rigidly in the hexagon turret or in floating holders for self-alignment.

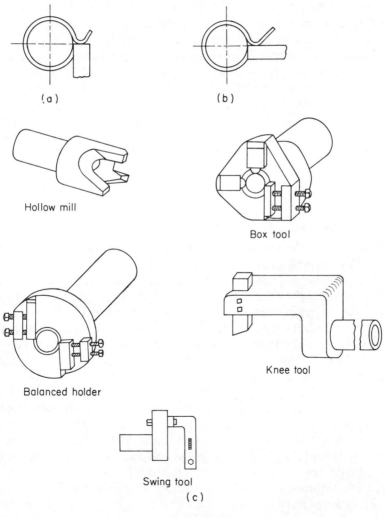

(a)

(b)

Hollow mill

Box tool

Balanced holder

Knee tool

Swing tool

(c)

Figure 19.7

A third class of tools are the threading tools. They may be taps, dies, chasers, or rollers. Form tools and cutoff tools may be circular, square, or angular. The former operate off the cross slide, the latter off the turret. Knurling tools are also available for operating off the cross slide or the turret.

The hollow mills may be solid or adjustable. Hollow mills are generally used for rough cutting external diameters. They usually have a hole through the shank to support long small-diameter rods. Solid hollow mills will cut only one diameter. To overcome this, the adjustable hollow mill is equipped with individually adjustable blades.

The box tool is used for finishing cuts of single or multiple diameters. Since the cutting is accomplished with a single tool or in-line multiple tools, the work must be supported by a V or rollers. The cutters are usually set in a box form and are set to cut tangentially. Rake angles and cutting angles are either ground on the tool or manufactured into the holder.

The balanced turning tool is used as a roughing tool and cuts tangentially. It has largely replaced the hollow mill because of its ability to take heavier cuts. Since the tool can be adjusted to cut different diameters, it has replaced the solid hollow end mill.

The swing tool is used for turning tapers or long forms. The tool operates off a cam form as the turret feeds toward the work. Figure 19.7(c) shows a knurling swing tool.

Since most of the work on a Brown and Sharpe automatic is small, multiple diameters, or contours, should be cut with form tools instead of with single-point tools. The two types of form tools used are the circular form tool, Fig. 19.8(a), and a form tool with a dovetail holder, Fig. 19.8(b).

Front clearance on the dovetail form tool is obtained by pitching the cutter blade to the desired angle. Front clearance is obtained on the circular form tool by grinding a cutout into the periphery of the tool below the center line by an amount a, as shown in Fig. 19.8(a). The toolholder and cutting edge are then raised to the center line of the work. The larger the diameter of the work, the greater the cutout a must be. The larger the diameter of the circular form tool, the greater the cutout a must be. It should also be noted that, if the face of the form tool is ground parallel to the center line of the work, as shown in Fig. 19.8(a), the rake angle is zero. Positive or negative rake angles are also possible.

However, care must be taken when the distance a is ground on a circular form tool or when the dovetail tool is pitched at an angle. If the exact form is ground into the periphery of the circular form tool and the cutout ground so that a equals $0°$, Fig. 19.8(c), the exact radius form will appear at the face of the tool. If the face of the tool is ground below the center line of the form tool or if a positive or negative rake is ground into the tool, the exact radius of the form distorts into an elliptical section, as shown in Fig. 19.8(d). Thus for contour forms it is advisable to use no rake angle or make the appropriate correction for the distortion. This correction can be made for the depth of

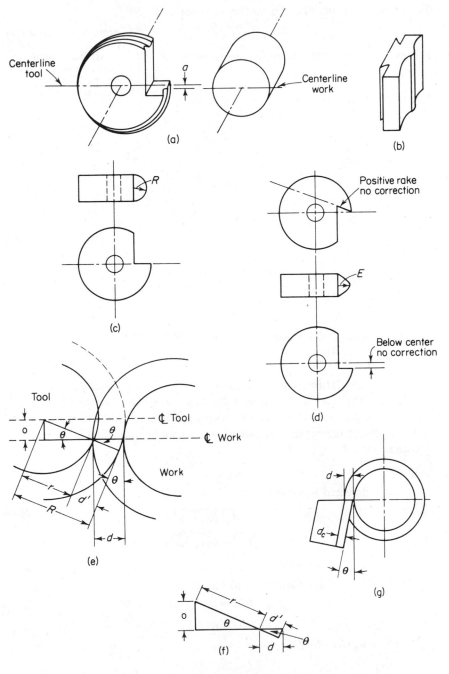

Figure 19.8

the cut (no rake angle) by using the equation

$$d' = R - \sqrt{R^2 + d^2 - 2d\sqrt{R^2 - o^2}}$$

The small radius of the form tool is given by

$$r = R - d'$$

The small radius form of the above equation becomes

$$r = \sqrt{R^2 + d^2 - 2d\sqrt{R^2 - o^2}}$$

The effective clearance angle is

$$\cos\theta = \frac{d'}{d}$$

$$\sin\theta = \frac{o}{r}$$

Therefore

$$\tan\theta = \frac{\sin\theta}{\cos\theta} = \frac{o/r}{d'/d}$$

$$= \frac{od}{rd'}$$

$d' =$ depth of form ground on tool
$d =$ actual depth of cut
$R =$ large radius of form tool
$o =$ offset of grind
$r =$ corrected small radius of cutter

The above equations are referenced to Fig. 19.8(e) and (f).

EXAMPLE 3

Given a circular form tool with a radius of $2\frac{1}{4}$ in., ground $\frac{1}{4}$ in. below the centerline of the form tool, and no rake angle. The actual depth of cut in the work is to be $\frac{3}{8}$ in. (1) What should the corrected small radius of the form be? (2) What should the depth of the form on the tool be? (3) What is the effective clearance angle?

Solution:

1. The corrected small radius is

$$r = \sqrt{R^2 + d^2 - 2d\sqrt{R^2 - o^2}}$$

$$= \sqrt{(2\frac{1}{4})^2 + (\frac{3}{8})^2 - 2(\frac{3}{8})\sqrt{(2\frac{1}{4})^2 - (\frac{1}{4})^2}}$$

$$= 1.878 \text{ in.}$$

$R = 2\frac{1}{4}$ in.
$d = \frac{3}{8}$ in.
$o = \frac{1}{4}$ in.
$r = ?$
$d' = ?$
$\theta = ?$

2. The depth of the form ground on the tool is

$$d' = R - r = 2.250 - 1.878$$

$$= 0.372 \text{ in.}$$

3. The effective clearance is

$$\tan\theta = \frac{od}{rd'} = \frac{\frac{1}{4}(\frac{3}{8})}{1.878(0.372)} = 0.1342$$

$$\theta = 7°38'$$

For the dovetail tool, Fig. 19.8(g), rake angle 0°, the depth d_c to which the tool must be ground for a given clearance angle is given by the equation

$$d_c = d \cos \theta$$

EXAMPLE 4

Calculate the corrected depth to be ground on the dovetail tool which requires a clearance of 9°. The depth of the step in the work is $\frac{3}{16}$ in.

Solution:

The corrected depth is

$$d_c = d \cos \theta = 0.188 \cos 9°$$

$$= 0.186 \text{ in.}$$

$$d = \tfrac{3}{16} \text{ in.}$$
$$\theta = 9°$$

If the form tool (circular or dovetail) has a rake, the calculations are somewhat more involved. They can be found in any standard handbook.

19.5. Other Automatic Lathes

The single-spindle automatic lathe. Used for mass-production repetitive turning, this is essentially a lathe equipped with a longitudinal carriage feed, a front slide, and a rear slide. It is equipped for regular feeding of the tool and with rapid traverse for positioning and tool relief. The term *tool relief* refers to backing-off the tool upon completion of the cut. This allows the tool to be free from the work for the return cycle after a cut has been completed.

For turning long diameters, multiple-tool setups are used. Thus, if a single tool is used to turn a length L, the tool must travel the full distance L. If, however, four tools are used, each tool need cover only $\frac{1}{4} L$, which reduces the front carriage travel by a factor of 4.

The back slides are used for squaring shoulders and establishing length dimensions. Squaring operations such as facing and undercutting may be done with it. Chamfering and form cutting may also be done off the back slide.

Also available are cams for the front and cross slides. These may be used for contour or taper cutting. Another feature is the use of tool blocks for setting or spacing multiple tools. Thus the differences in depth and spacing of several tools may be set to a gage on a surface plate. The block is then positioned in the machine and one diameter set. If the original setting of the tool block was correct, the remaining diameters and lengths should fall into position.

The Swiss type of automatic lathe. A sliding bushing moves the stock back and forth as it rotates in the main spindle. Single-point tools are positioned around the outer periphery of the work and close to the bushing.

Radial tools operate in and out, actuated by separate cams. The work passes between these tools and is cut as the tool contacts it. Very accurate machining may be done with these machines.

Multiple-spindle (four to eight spindles) automatic machines. As the work is rotated in the spindles provided, tool slides set opposite and radially about these spindles perform the machining operations. Each spindle has its own tool setup. Thus, when the tool slides move into the spindles, all the tools are operating at once. With this setup all the workpieces—one in each spindle—are in various stages of completion. With each index of the spindle, a completed piece is produced.

These machines are completely automatic and are operated by cams. They usually are one stock per station operation machines. There are, however, several types of construction. They may be either the spindle-revolving or work-revolving type, the work-revolving type being more common because of the greater tool control.

19.6. Power Sawing

Power saws may be classified by the characteristics of their construction. They may be; (1) hacksaws; (2) band saws; (3) circular saws; or (4) abrasive cutting wheels.

The power hacksaw. Reciprocating action feeds the blade into the work as the cutting operation proceeds. The action may be vertical reciprocating or horizontal reciprocating with a closed frame. Fig. 19.9(a), or an open frame, Fig. 19.9(b). As the blade reciprocates, the feeding takes place with each stroke. To relieve the pressure on the teeth of the blade, the blade lifts on the noncutting portion of the stroke. The feeding and lifting of the blade may operate mechanically or hydraulically.

Automatic stock feed, when provided, feeds the stock through an open vise to a stop which gages the length of the work. The vise closes, and the blade is caused to contact the work and feed until the cutting operation is complete. Once completed, the blade retracts, the vise opens, and the cycle is repeated.

Blades are made from high-speed steel and may have their teeth hardened or be hardened all the way through. They range from about 10 to 36 in. long, have from 2 to 32 teeth/in., and are $\frac{1}{2}$ to 5 in. wide and $\frac{1}{32}$ to $\frac{1}{8}$ in. thick. In general the thicker the stock to be cut, the coarser the teeth are to be used.

Teeth may have one of three sets: the wavy set, Fig. 19.9(c); the rake set, Fig. 19.9(d); and the straight set, Fig. 19.9(e).

The wavy set is used in the fine-pitch-tooth blade in which several teeth are offset in one direction. The rake-set-tooth blade has the teeth set in a

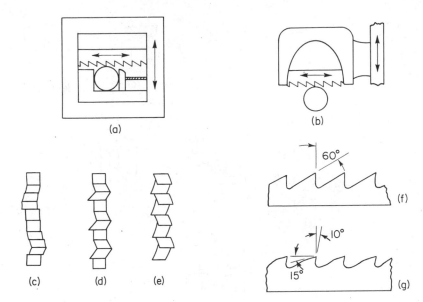

Figure 19.9

right to left straight pattern. The straight-set-tooth blade has a right to left set pattern.

The teeth may have straight faces, Fig. 19.9(f), for light feeding or a positive rake, Fig. 19.9(g), for coarse feeding. The latter is made only in the 2 or $2\frac{1}{2}$ teeth/in. blade. As a general rule from three to four teeth should be cutting at once. Also as a general rule the softer the material to be cut, the coarser is the number of teeth per inch to be used. When making a choice as to the number of teeth to be used, a compromise must be made between the number of teeth cutting and the type of material being cut. If the start of the cut is across a sharp edge and the teeth are coarse, the blade will be damaged. If the teeth are too fine so that the depth of the gullet is too shallow, the material will clog the teeth and impair the cutting action.

Figure 19.10(a through h) shows several methods for presenting the blade to the work and several methods for stacking the work in the vise for multiple cutting.

Band saws.   Long and continuous bands are manufactured to cut either vertically or horizontally. The horizontal machines are intended to be used as cutoff machines, whereas the vertical machines are used primarily for removing excess stock or contouring.

The vertical band saw is used to cut out holes in solid stock without cutting into the hole from the outside of the stock. The procedure is to break the band and insert it into a predrilled hole. The band is welded into a continuous circle and the hole cut and it is broken upon completion of the cut

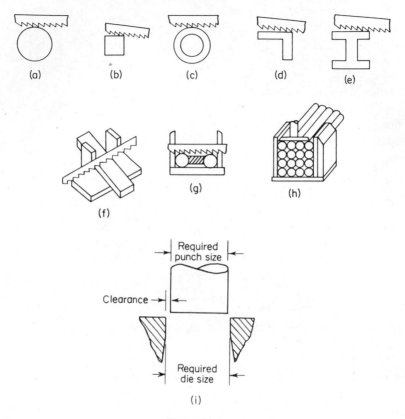

Figure 19.10

and removed from the hole. Band saws are usually equipped with welding, annealing, and grinding units for this very purpose.

The band saw operates continuously in one direction so that the cutting pressures are always against the table. The absence of the reciprocating action makes for greater safety and usually does not require that the work be fastened. This presents free movement of the workpiece for contour cutting.

Materials may be cut very close to the layout lines—about 0.003 in.—which makes any subsequent machining operation minimal. Most band saws are equipped with band files, so that dimensional accuracy and finish beyond the capabilities of the sawing operation are possible.

Another feature of the vertical band saw is the swivel table. This permits angular cutting such as clearance for a die block. Some machines are constructed so that the entire mechanism holding the band may be swiveled.

Versatility in making punches and dies is increased because the die opening may be cut at an angle and the slug which comes out of the hole may be used as the punch. Both parts are filed to their respective sizes so that the desired clearance is achieved, as shown in Fig. 19.10(i). Since narrow, thin blades are available, a predrilled hole in the stock about $\frac{1}{64}$ in. larger than the width of the blade and drilled at an angle is usually sufficient. Such a hole, if properly drilled, will not mar the contour of the finished die or punch.

Other attachments for vertical band saws are (1) flat and radius bands; (2) spiral bands that will cut in any direction, which eliminates the need for rotating the work; and (3) abrasive bands for cutting, grinding, or polishing hardened steel, glass, stone, etc. Abrasive material may be one of the grinding or polishing abrasives or diamond grit.

A circular saw.   This large circular blade actually produces a milling action. The teeth are ground so that one tooth angled at 45° is followed by one square tooth set some 0.010 in. above the angled tooth. With this arrangement the angled tooth is the roughing tooth followed by the square, or finishing, tooth. The profile of the tooth is made so that the chip curls into the clearance gullet and drops out as the cutter tooth clears the work. Teeth may be made from high-speed steel or inserted carbide. They operate at very high surface speeds up to 20,000 sfpm.

Since the saws operate at very high speeds and feeds, they must be carefully selected for maximum production and minimum wear. Damaged saw blades result from poor work clamping, feeds and speeds which are too low or too high, idling, or too few or too many teeth for a particular job.

Friction sawing may be accomplished with either a high-speed band or a circular power saw. The surface speed of a band saw should be between 6000 and 15,000 fpm and depends upon several factors. These are the thickness and type of material being cut, the number of teeth in contact with the work, the pressure of the blade against the work, and the cooling potential during the noncutting portion of the blade cycle. Circular saw blades operate at from 20,000 to 30,000 rpm, the smaller blades operating at the higher rpm.

The principle of cutting is based on the heat developed at the contact area between the work and the blade. The material reaches a temperature which causes a breakdown of its structure. When the material breakdown temperature is reached, the material affected is removed either by the motion of the blade or by oxidation. Thus, to maintain the breakdown temperature —not the melting temperature of the material—a contact pressure must be maintained. Since the blade heats up, it is usual to have the blade pass through a confined coolant soon after it leaves the workpiece. In many instances the ratio of the noncontact to the contact time is long enough to permit the blade to cool. If all conditions are right, the heat developed in the workpiece should localize around the point of contact of the work and the blade.

Any material that has a crystal structure which breaks down and loses tensile strength as a result of the heat developed may be friction sawed. This is the case with cast iron and steel. Care must be taken with cast iron because the structure has a tendency to break down before the appropriate tensile strength breakdown temperature is reached. Nonferrous metals (aluminum, brass, etc.) braze to and clog the blade.

High-carbon steels are cut with a smooth-faced circular saw. Plain carbon steels may be cut with a toothed saw, Fig. 19.11. For general friction band sawing a 10-tooth-per-inch specially heat treated band saw is used. The blade need not be sharpened when it dulls. As a matter of fact, the cutting action is better as the teeth become dull.

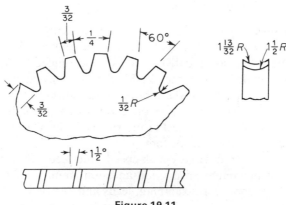

Figure 19.11

An abrasive cutting wheel.   This can be used to cut almost any type of material because it is fast, accurate, and leaves a good finish. It can be operated wet or dry.

Wet cutting uses a coolant to flood the work and the wheel. The effectiveness of the wheel depends upon the abrasive action between the wheel and the work. Its surface speed should not exceed 8000 fpm. At higher surface speeds the coolant will not wet the wheel. However, the surface speed needed for effective abrasive cutting is critical. Therefore, as the wheel wears, its spindle speed should be increased to maintain the surface speed; otherwise its efficiency decreases. Slow surface speeds cause glazing and leave a poor surface finish on the metal being cut. Rubber-bonded wheels are used because they are nonporous. Cutting accuracies achieved with wet wheels are within from ±0.004 (with wheel guides) to ±0.010 in. for 1-in. stock.

Dry cutting has about the same mechanism as friction sawing. The surface speed, about 15,000 fpm, must be maintained. Otherwise the heating effect breaks down the structure of the metal being cut so that the abrasive grit can remove it; as the surface speed of the wheel decreases, the action changes to one of abrasive cutting by the grit, and the heat developed breaks down the bond of the wheel rather than the structure of the material being cut. Resin bonded wheels are used for dry cutting. Accuracies are within about

± 0.020 in. for 1-in. stock. The loss of accuracy is due largely to wheel deflection.

Wheel balance to reduce wheel flutter is very important for both wet and dry cutting.

19.7. Broaching

Broaching is a process used to cut internal or external contours. The process is one wherein the broach, made in the reverse image of the contour, is constructed so that each tooth cuts small amounts of metal. Thus the finishing dimensions of the contour are cut as the broach completes its cut. The broach is shown in Fig. 19.12(a), the shape of the teeth is shown in Fig. 19.12(b), and some typical forms are shown in Fig. 19.12(c).

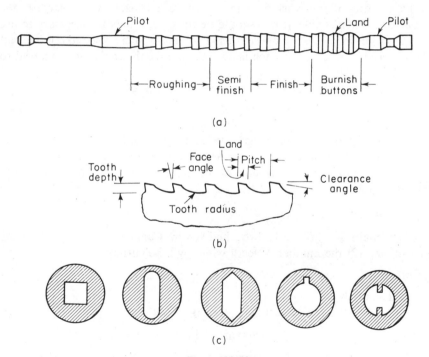

(a)

(b)

(c)

Figure 19.12

Figure 19.12(a) shows the broach which will cut successive amounts of material out of a predrilled hole. The depth of the roughing cut is from 0.002 to 0.006 in./tooth. As the broaching tool is pushed (or pulled) through the opening, the change in depth from one tooth to the next should be from 0.002 to 0.0005 in. for the finishing cuts. The 0.002-in. depth of cut is used for the free machining materials. In the broach shown the first half of the broach is used for roughing and the second half for semifinishing and finishing; sometimes buttons—three are shown in Fig. 19.12(a)—are used as burnishing tools. Burnishing displaces, rather than cuts, the material. Burnishing is used for high finish and sizing.

The tooth form, Fig. 19.12(b), is very important because of the curling of the chip in the tooth radius. This radius must be large enough to take a full-length curled chip without clogging, crowding, or packing in the opening before the cut is finished. In some instances such clogging is remedied by the use of chip breakers. These chip breakers are offset to help break up the chips.

It is also important that the pitch of the teeth should be carefully established. Since each tooth cuts only a small amount of material, the design of the pitch must be such that the broach is not too long for the capacity of the machine in which it is to be used. It is possible that the amount of material to be cut out of the workpiece may require a broach which exceeds the capacity of the machine. If this should be the case, it may be necessary to use two broaches in successive operations. The first broach is used to remove half the material; the second broach is used to remove the remaining material to complete the job.

The equation generally used to determine the pitch is

$$P = 0.35\sqrt{L}$$

L = length of cut
P = pitch

It is also good practice to have at least three teeth cutting at one time. Thus there are two factors which can be manipulated to keep the length of the broach to a minimum: the change in the depth of cut of each row of teeth, and the pitch.

EXAMPLE 5

The length of a hole to be broached is 4 in. Calculate (1) the pitch of the broach and (2) the number of teeth which will be cutting.

Solution:

1. The pitch is

$$P = 0.35\sqrt{L} = 0.35\sqrt{4} \qquad\qquad L = 4 \text{ in.}$$
$$= 0.700 \text{ in.} \cong \tfrac{23}{32} \text{ in.}$$

2. The number of teeth cutting is

$$N = \frac{4}{23/32} = \frac{4 \times 32}{23}$$
$$= 5.6 \cong 5 \text{ teeth}$$

Other techniques which may be employed are: shear cuts where higher finish is required and cutting pressures need to be reduced, uneven spacing (pitch) of successive rows.of teeth where chatter develops, and reduction of clearance angles to 2° for roughing and to as little as $\frac{1}{2}$° for finishing. In many instances a straight land (clearance angle of 0°) for a segment of the finishing tooth may give better finish.

The broaching operation because of its roughing and finishing capabilities is a machining process with a high rate of production. It may be used for long or short runs. In many instances it takes much longer to keep resetting a workpiece on a milling machine or shaper than it takes to complete the one-stroke operation required for broaching. In other instances it is impossible to machine some shapes, on the milling machine or shaper, without resorting to hand filing. Another feature of the broaching operation is that it is repetitive, so that intricate shapes may be duplicated without too much effort.

A limitation of broaching is that the sides of the broached hole must be parallel. There can be no obstruction to the movement of the broach, and the depth of the cut must be within the limits of the length of the stroke and the tonnage output of the machine.

19.8. Generating a Shape

It was pointed out in Section 18.3 that gears may be generated by either of two methods, shaping or hobbing. In the former case the shapes are generated by using an oscillating motion of the cutter, and in the latter case by using a rotating cutter. The fundamental idea is essentially the same in both instances, which is to cut a contour in such a manner that the cutter traces out the desired contour, cutting as it progresses.

Thus in Fig. 19.13(a) the action of a single hob tooth is shown generating the side of a gear tooth. Figure 19.13(b) shows the action of the hob as it cuts both sides of a tooth space.

The advantage of this system is that a tooth profile is achieved through the action of a *mating tooth* (the cutter). When the gear is meshed with another gear, the teeth of the mating gear will trace the profile in the same manner as the hob does.

Actually the generating process is not restricted to the cutting of gear teeth, sprocket teeth, or threads; it may also be used to generate forms. During the shaping process the rotation of the cutter as it oscillates up and down should match the surface speed of the work. In the hobbing process, the lead of the form in the hob should match the rotation of the work. The method for generating forms is clearly shown in the photographs, Fig. 19.13(c).

Some shapes and the hobs used to generate them are shown in Figs. 19.13(d) and (e).

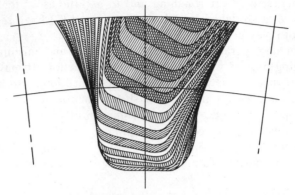

Performance of individual teeth

(a)

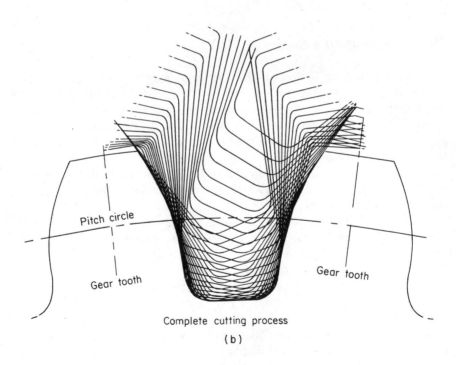

Pitch circle

Gear tooth

Gear tooth

Complete cutting process

(b)

Figure 19.13 [(*a*), (*b*), (*c*), *and* (*d*) *Courtesy of Barber-Coleman Company;* (*e*) *courtesy of American Pfauter Corporation.*]

(c)

(d)

Figure 19.13 (Cont.)

(e)

Figure 19.13 (Cont.)

QUESTIONS AND PROBLEMS

19.1 What are the essential differences between a ram and a saddle type of turret lathe? What are the advantages and disadvantages of one over the other?

19.2 What is the meaning of the phrase floor-to-floor time with reference to machining?

19.3 Discuss the construction of the various components of a turret lathe; i.e., saddle, turret, headstock, etc.

19.4 Sketch the various types of tool holders used with a turret.

19.5 Operations should be combined whenever possible by using multiple tooling. Explain this statement and show: (a) Why it is true. (b) When would it be undesirable or uneconomical to implement this statement?

19.6 Assume a tool is set in a horizontal plane on a turret lathe. What is the effect on dimensional control? Explain.

19.7 Draw the block diagram, showing the sequence of operations (see Fig. 19.4) needed to make the workpiece, Fig. 19.14. Start with 3 in. diameter round bar.

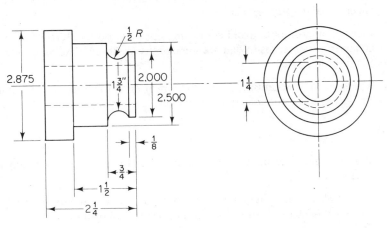

Figure 19.14

19.8 A company is to make 15 pieces to fill an order. A turret lathe and an engine lathe are available. The records show the following data:

    Turret lathe:
        Machining time 7 min/piece
        Direct labor cost $4.60/hr
        Overhead is $5.00/hr
        Setup time is 4 hrs
        Hourly rate (set up) $6.00/hr
    Engine lathe:
        Machining time 15 min/piece
        Direct labor cost is $4.00/hr
        Overhead is $3.50/hr
        Setup time $2\frac{1}{2}$ hrs
        Hourly rate (set up) $3.50/hr
    Should the job be done on a turret or engine lathe?

19.9 A company collects the following data in order to make a decision whether a job is to be set up on a turret or an engine lathe. What is the break-even point?

	Lathe	Turret
Overhead, $	3.50	5.00
Direct labor, $/hr	3.00	2.60
Setup time, hrs	4.00	12.00
Setup rate, $/hr	3.00	4.50
Time/piece, hr	2.00	0.75

19.10   Given the same data as in problem 19.9 with the exception of the turret-lathe machining time. If the break-even point is 50 parts, how long will it take to machine one part on the turret lathe?

19.11   Assume a tool is set in a vertical plane on a turret lathe. What is the effect on dimensional control? Explain.

19.12   Why is it important to avoid combining finishing tools with roughing tools in multiple-tool setups? What are some of the results of combining roughing and finishing tools?

19.13   What type of mechanism is used to control an automatic screw machine? How does an automatic screw machine differ from an automatic turret lathe?

19.14   Make a sketch of a Geneva mechanism, and explain how it works.

19.15   Make two drawings showing the operation of a tool cutting tangentially and radially.

19.16   Make a sketch of each of the following: (a) hollow mill; (b) box tool; (c) knee tool; (d) balance tool. How does a swing tool operate?

19.17   Make a sketch of a form tool for machining each of the parts in Figs. 19.15 (a through c).

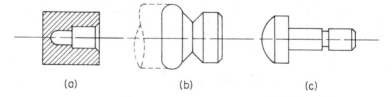

       (a)   (b)   (c)

Figure 19.15

19.18   The part shown in Fig. 19.16 is to be machined on a Brown and Sharpe number 00 automatic screw machine with a form tool, threading die, etc. Calculate and lay out the cam for the following sequence of operations: stock feed, index, hollow mill, index, form tool (cross slide), die on, die off, cutoff (cross slide). Cutting speed for the die is 40 ft/minute. All other operations are to be 150 ft/minute. The feeds are: hollow mill, 0.007 in./revolution; form tool, 0.0005 in./revolution; cutoff tool, 0.002 in./revolution.

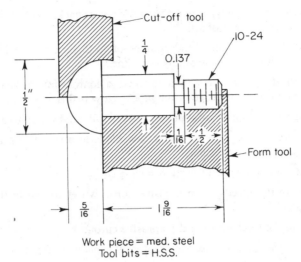

Work piece = med. steel
Tool bits = H.S.S.

Figure 19.16

19.19 How is front clearance obtained on (a) a circular tool and (b) a dovetail form tool?

10.20 Why are contours ground into a form tool distorted when positive or negative rake is ground into the tool? [See Fig. 19.8(a).]

19.21 Explain how multiple tooling is used on an automatic lathe to turn a long diameter. What functions does the back slide perform?

19.22 Check the literature in your library and find a photograph of (a) a Swiss type of automatic lathe and (b) a multiple-spindle lathe. Explain their operation.

19.23 Given a circular form tool with a large radius of $1\frac{1}{2}$ in., ground $\frac{1}{4}$ in. below the center line of the form tool, and no rake angle. The actual depth of cut in the work is to be $\frac{1}{8}$ in. (a) What should the corrected small radius of the form be? (b) What should the depth of the form on the tool be? (c) What is the effective clearance angle?

19.24 Find the corrected depth to be ground on a dovetail tool which requires an $8°$ clearance angle if the depth of the step in the work is to be $\frac{3}{16}$ in.

19.25 A circular form tool has a large radius of 2 in. and its cutting face ground $\frac{1}{4}$ in. below the center line. The actual depth of cut will be $\frac{3}{16}$ in. (a) What should be the corrected small radius of the form tool? (b) Calculate the corrected depth of the form. (c) What is the effective front clearance angle?

19.26 If a dovetail form tool requires a $7°$ front clearance and the depth of the form to be cut (large radius to small radius) is $\frac{1}{4}$ in., calculate the corrected depth to be ground on the tool.

19.27 How many methods of power sawing are listed in this chapter? What are they?

19.28 Describe the three types of set used for power hacksaw-blade teeth. Make a sketch of each type of set.

19.29 What factors determine the number of teeth on a power hacksaw blade which should be cutting at any one time?

19.30 A vertical band saw may be used to cut a contour into a die block without starting at the outer edge of the block. How is this accomplished?

19.31 What types of bands are available for vertical band saws? Explain their use.

19.32 How are the teeth on a circular saw blade arranged to do roughing and finishing at the same time?

19.33 What is the principle of friction sawing?

19.34 Why are the speeds of an abrasive cutoff wheel critical in the wet cutoff operation?

19.35 Explain the mechanism of dry abrasive cutoff.

19.36 Make a sketch of a broaching tool, and explain the function of the various areas of the tool.

19.37 Assume a broach which has a pitch of 1.125 in. (a) What is the approximate length of work to be cut? (b) How many teeth are cutting?

19.38 The length of a hole to be broached is $2\frac{1}{2}$ in. (a) What should the pitch be? (b) How many teeth will be cutting?

19.39 There are several generated forms shown in Fig. 19.13(d). Select one and explain the relative motions of cutter-to-workpiece as the shape is generated.

EDM and N/C

20

20.1. Electric Discharge Machining (EDM)

Electric discharge machining removes metal by the process of controlled spark erosion. The workpiece must be made from a conductive material. The work and tool are submerged in a dielectric fluid, which serves the dual purpose of controlling the arc and carrying away the waste products of erosion.

A power supply controls the spark frequency, energy, and voltage. The workpiece is the anode and the tool is the cathode. It should be noted that in some instances reverse polarity is advisable. The conventional polarity is shown in Fig. 20.1(a). Low frequency coupled with high energy (amperage) is used for rough cutting and high metal removal. High frequencies and low

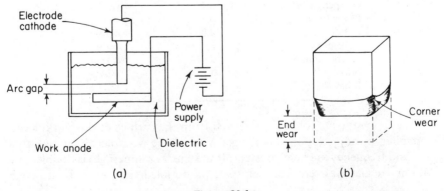

(a)   (b)

Figure 20.1

energies are used for slow metal removal, high finish, and dimensional accu-racies. It should also be noted that a nonrotating tool is used. The gap between the tool and the work is maintained with a servo system.

The type of tool (electrode) material used is also important for optimum performance. The tool is subject to wear in the same manner as a lathe tool or any other cutting tool. Since the tool and workpiece both erode, the rate of erosion depends upon the electrode material, the workpiece material, and the polarity of both. Another factor in electrode wear is the energy concen-tration at a sharp corner. This energy concentration wears the sharp corners off the electrode, as shown in Fig. 20.1(b).

The tool material should have a high melting point and be a good conduc-tor of heat and electricity. As with other tool materials a compromise between wear rate and cost of fabrication of the tool must be made. As noted in Fig. 20.1(b), the manner in which the wear takes place is an important factor in the selection of the tool material to be used.

One standard used to determine wear rate is the volumetric wear ratio. However, the useful life of a tool is usually determined by its life relative to the machining of sharp corners or contours or to the length of the tool consumed. A useful ratio is one based on the ability of the electrode material to produce a 90° corner in steel. The 90° corner wear ratios of some materials are shown in Table 20.1. Thus 0.400 in. of a copper tungsten electrode will be consumed in the machining of a 1.000-in. length of steel block to a sharp corner.

TABLE 20.1

Wear Ratios

Material	Electrode	to	Workpiece
Brass	1.5		1 steel
Copper	1.0		1 steel
Graphite	0.4		1 steel
Copper tungsten	0.4		1 steel
Silver tungsten	0.3		1 steel
Brass	4.0		1 carbide
Carbide	1.5		1 carbide
Copper tungsten	0.67		1 carbide
Brass	0.2		1 brass
Brass	7.0		1 tungsten

The amount (rate) of metal removed from the surface of the workpiece is controlled by adjusting the amperage. Assume the workpiece material, tool, gap, and frequency are held constant. If the energy (amperage) is doubled, the volume of material removed per spark is doubled. However, if the metal removed per spark is increased, the surface roughness of the workpiece is also increased.

Surface finish may also be controlled by varying the frequency and holding the amperage constant. Figure 20.2 shows the relationship between amperage and frequency. In this illustration the length of the gap between the electrode and the workpiece is held constant.

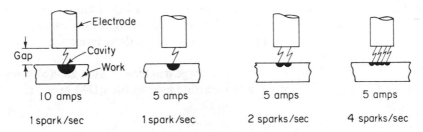

Figure 20.2

If a fixed volume of material is removed when 5 amp are used, the surface finish will be better when a frequency of 4 sparks/sec is used than when a frequency of 2 sparks/sec is used. Thus the higher the frequency (amperage constant), the better the surface finish is.

Size control is a function of the amperage, frequency, and capacitance used. These quantities create an electronic envelope about the electrode. That is, the space between the electrode and the workpiece constitutes an *overcut*. If a hole 1.000 in. in diameter by 0.500 in. deep is to be machined and an electronic envelope of 0.002 in. is present, the diameter of the electrode used is $1.000 - 0.004 = 0.996$ in. The travel of the electrode needed to produce a 0.500-in. hole is $0.500 - 0.002 = 0.498$ in. This is shown in Fig. 20.3.

The electrolyte (coolant) acts as an insulator, or barrier, to current flow. Once the breakdown voltage of the coolant is reached, a spark is generated by the flow of amperage across this gap. This electrolyte also acts as a coolant for the small vapor particles separated from the workpiece during the machining operation. The coolant prevents the heat generated in the vapor

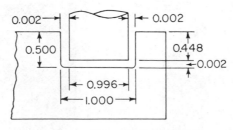

Figure 20.3

particles from being transferred to the work and electrode. Such transfer of heat could destroy both the workpiece and the electrode. Forcing the coolant through the gap between the workpiece and the electrode removes the particles, which are then filtered out before the coolant is reused.

The development of EDM has been rapid and provides another method for machining metals in the toolroom. It can be used to machine cavities or intricate shapes in very hard materials. Thus it becomes especially useful for machining blind cavities in dies used in die casting, stamping, forging, and injection molding. It makes possible the machining of intricate cavities and holes in hardened steel or special alloy materials without the need of sectioning the cavity.

Figure 20.4(a) shows an electric discharge machine. Figure 20.4(b) shows a die-cast cylinder head, mold, and electrode used in the EDM process.

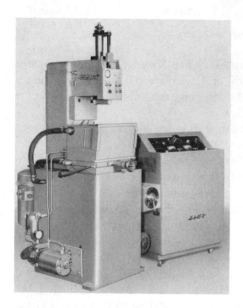

Figure 20.4   (*Courtesy of Elox Corporation of Michigan.*)

20.2. The Numerical Control (N/C) Process

Automation requires that machine tools are set up for specific repetitive jobs, usually long run processes. The justification for automation is economic. *Numerical control* has other bases for its adoption which will be discussed in the next section.

Numerical control, N/C, is automatic "control by letters and numbers." This is referred to as *word address*, and it is used to control the relative position of work-to-tool, tool selection, feeds and speeds, etc. Basically there are two systems—point-to-point, and continuous control. The conventional X, Y and Z axes are used to define the relative movement of the work and tool. Motion may be linear or rotary about any axis.

The *point-to-point system* of N/C positions the tool over the work relative to a starting point. Generally, since the tool is not in contact with the work, as in drilling, only the starting and finishing points are important. Thus in Fig. 20.5(a) the tool is positioned directly over the workpiece at SP. If the

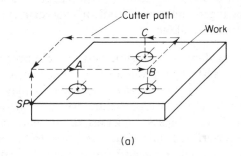

(a)

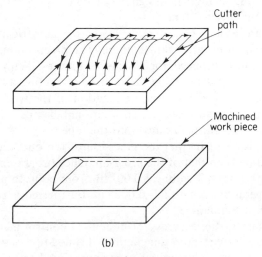

(b)

Figure 20.5

tool is a drill bit, the N/C process advances, withdraws and repositions it until all operations have been completed. *Continuous Control Contouring* (N/C) requires that two or more related and controlled motions take place at the same time as shown in Fig. 20.5(b).

Numerical control may be used with any of the machine tools encountered in the fabrication of workpieces. The justifications are discussed in the next section.

20.3. The Economics of N/C

The purpose of any automated system is to increase production at a lower cost without decreasing the degree of precision. Usually automation has required a substantial number of parts to be machined before the cost of the tooling and machines could be justified. The greater the degree of freedom required, the more sophisticated have been the machinery and tooling needed and the higher has been the cost per workpiece.

With the advent of numerical control equipment, this is no longer true. The substantial saving of numerical control over conventional machining is realized because of several factors:

1. Single-piece machining is possible and feasible because of the nature of the control system. A program is written and recorded on a tape or punch card. The program may be checked by playing back the tape on an automatic tape writing machine which prints out the program. The *print-out* may be checked against the original tape, program, or master tape for error. If minor changes need to be made, the original tape may be corrected on the automatic tape writing machine. In some instances, changes in design may be put on a length of tape and spliced into the original tape.

2. Fixture cost is considerably lower for numerical control machining than for conventional machining. The precision built into the controls eliminates the need for expensive fixtures. With two datum planes (x and y) and the table of the machine acting as a vertical reference plane, the need for accurate location of the workpiece is reduced to two banking surfaces and conventional clamps. The reference coordinate point is programmed into the tape.

   It is also true that the precision of the operation will be no more accurate than that of the program. Once programmed, the positioning accuracy is well within ± 0.001 in. from point to point. The repetition of operations is within ± 0.0005 in. Furthermore, point-to-point errors are not cumulative.

3. Because of the accuracy of numerical control machining, the cost of fixture design, setup time, and lead time are drastically reduced. Thus changeover is also simplified because usually all that is required, once the job is planned and programmed, is the changing of the tape, a

new set of tools, and the establishing of a new datum, or reference, point.

4. In conventional machining when few workpieces are required, it becomes necessary to lay out at least the first part to make sure hole locations are proper, etc. This occurs when the production quantity does not warrant the expenditure of money for a fixture or jig. Because the precision is programmed into the tape, shop layout has been almost completely eliminated. Programming and tape writing take much less time than building jigs and fixtures and locating gages. Also the tape lasts longer and requires much less storage space than jigs and fixtures. It also takes much less time to duplicate tape than to build a new fixture.

   Modern machines, in addition, have a built-in check system. If workpieces are to be duplicated, the control will go back to zero upon completion of the cycle. If the control does not return to zero, a warning system alerts the operator. He can then make the appropriate adjustment and proceed. Closed systems, to be discussed later, keep a continuous check on the commands.

5. Whereas other automated equipment does not lend itself to easy changeover, numerical control machines may be programmed for single-piece machining, short runs, or production runs. Once programmed and set up, the operation of the machine does not require a skilled operator. Except for positioning the workpiece on the table, the human element is completely eliminated. That is, the time between operations is reduced. In addition, the cutting to non-cutting time ratio is reduced considerably. Items affected radically are: start-stop machine; changing spindle speeds and tool feeds; feed engagement; releasing the tool, retracting it, returning it to the start point, indexing, etc. These are a few of the non-cutting operations which can be taken care of much more readily when programmed than manually.

It is to be noted that the initial cost of numerical control machines is high. For one thing, they must be more rigidly built than conventional machines to withstand the accelerations dictated by servo controls. Other costs are the electronic control consoles, some type of tape writer, and a host of accessories for greater sophistication. To maintain accuracy, the console must be air conditioned. To reduce "down time," a skilled electronics technician must be employed to service the electronic controls, even though the reliability of these machines is high.

20.4. Command Systems

Commands are processed from a 1-in. tape, cards, or directly from a mini-computer. The latter is called *computer numerical control*, CNC, and is the latest development in numerical control systems. The systems which control the movements that result in the fabrication process are essentially the open, semi-closed, or closed loops.

The commands, *in the form of blocks of information*, are picked off the tape (or card) by a tape reader. A block of information is accummulated and released to perform its command after the block has been stored. As noted later in this chapter, commands are forwarded to servo motors in "blocks" of information. These signals control the movement of the table or spindle along the X, Y, or Z axis in a three-axis machine. Two-axis machines have only the X and Y axes controlled. Four-and five-axis machines have one or two rotary degrees of freedom controlled as well as the X-, Y-, and Z-axis control.

In the open type of control system, Fig. 20.6(a), the command is fed into the machine but no feedback takes place. There is no check system built into the machine to determine whether or not the command has been carried out. Thus in Fig. 20.6(a) the operator control console is used to set the initial conditions of the zero position, start the machine, etc. The tape reader picks off the discrete bits of information from the tape, sends these bits to the distribution control unit, which directs the information to the servo control unit for a particular axis control. The command is then transferred to the servo motor which carries out the command. In Fig. 20.6(a) the X and Y axes are controlled. Also included is a Z-axis control and a spindle-speed control. This is a three-axis system. It is to be noted that there is no feedback system to check on the command while it is being carried out.

Figure 20.6(b) shows a closed-loop system which has a transducer attached to each axis. The transducer converts the motion, as directed, from linear (or rotary) motion to an electrical impulse. This impulse is fed back into the control unit as a check on the input signal. If the input signal and the feedback signal match, the servo stops and the desired position is obtained. If the input signal and the feedback signal do not match, the error signal, the difference between input and feedback signal, takes over as the input signal. It remains the control signal until a match is achieved. Thus the correction is made, and the operation continues.

The transducer may be either digital or analogue. The digital signal is a pulse signal proportional to the unit motion of the tool or work table. This may be accomplished by counting the number of pulses needed for a given movement or by matching the pulses to the input signal.

The analogue signal is continuous and proportional to the continuous movement of the table, rotation of the spindle, or movement of the spindle. As is the case for a digital transducer, the continuous input voltage is matched to the transducer output voltage to achieve accurate positioning.

The *semi-closed loop* systems vary from the closed loop systems in that the latter verifies and controls the actual position of the tool with reference to the work. In contrast the semi-closed loop system verifies the position of the work relative to the tool in an *indirect way*. It may measure the position

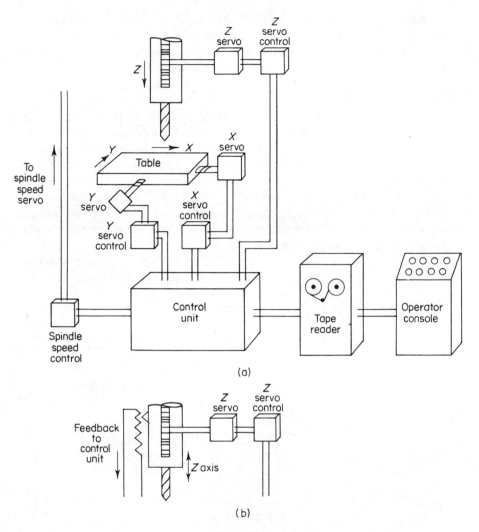

Figure 20.6

of the work by counting the number of turns of a lead screw, or driving gear and comparing them against a standard. Obviously this is not as accurate as the closed loop system. It is, however, less expensive to manufacture.

There are many different "languages" which have been adapted or developed by machine tool manufacturers to serve their own special purposes. APT I, II and III are word-languages with which the programmer describes the parts as they appear on the engineering drawing. The programmer has at his command a 107-word language which he uses when describing the movement of the tool, or work. This description is fed into a computer which translates the directions to a tape. It saves much calculating time. ADAPT is a simpler version of APT. AUTOSPOT, AUTOPROMPT, and SNAP are but a few of the additional word-languages available. They are all used to save time and length of tape required in point-to-point or contour control. As indicated, the simplest type of command is the point-to-point system.

If we assume a two-axis machine (X and Y) the movement of the table may be controlled so that it will move along the Y-axis or X-axis. One company* recommends visualizing the movement of the cutter. Thus, in Fig. 20.7(a) when the *cutter* machines from A to B, *away from* the operator, the direction is plus ($+$). When the *cutter* moves *toward* the operator, the direction is minus ($-$). The movement of the *cutter* from *left-to-right*, Fig. 20.7(b) (C to D) is plus; from *right-to-left*, the X-direction is minus. It is to be noted that the down movement of the spindle is plus. In Fig. 20.7(c) the movement of the tool is positive (E to F) along the X-axis and positive (F to G) along the Y-axis. Commands are incorporated in a block of information which result in the movement of the tool from E to G.

If the line EG is to be machined, the X-Y movements are reduced so that the movement of the tool approximates the straight line movement EG. This

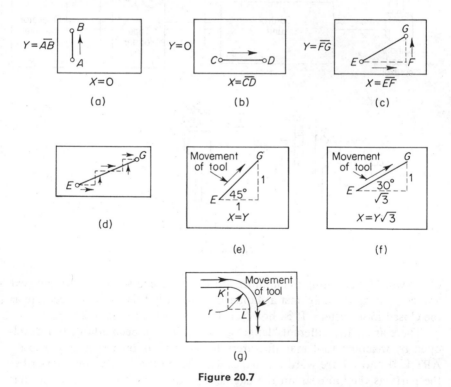

Figure 20.7

*Autonumerics, Inc. Hauppauge, N.Y.

is shown in Fig. 20.7(d). It should be noted that the greater the number of X-Y movements, the more nearly does the tool approach the straight line *EG*. This is one of the disadvantages of the point-to-point system. However, the greater the number of X-Y movements, the greater is the accuracy achieved. In contour machining, the required number of points may become excessive. In spite of this, many straight-line operations may be done with the point-to-point system.

In continuous-path systems the tool follows the desired shape since the commands are far more descriptive than for the point-to-point system. They are capable of causing the table to move so that X is some function of Y, designated $X = f(Y)$. Thus a machine table may be directed to move so that X always equals Y, Fig. 20.7(e), so that $X = Y\sqrt{3}$, Fig. 20.7(f); or along the arc *KL* of radius r, as shown in Fig. 20.7(g). In the last instance the end points of the arc *KL* and the equation of the curve are needed. The direction of movement of the table (or tool) is controlled by the use of $+$ and $-$ notations. The movement of the tool may be programmed into the tape, or machine, so that it generates the desired curve. See Section 20.7.

It should be evident that the more complex the contour, the more complicated is the mathematics needed. Thus for continuous-path numerical control, a computer is usually needed to calculate the command signals. It is also possible to establish command signals with the use of very accurate drawings. This method may be more expensive and not as accurate or as fast as a computer. In sophisticated setups the computer is inserted in the loop in either the open-loop or closed-loop systems.

20.5. Codes

Two types of number codes are generally used. The *Straight Binary System* is one of the systems used for continuous control in which multiple simultaneous motions may be programmed into one column. It produces lengths of tape which are shorter than the binary-coded decimal system used in N/C programming.

The *binary-coded decimal system* is based on the standards established by the Electronic Industries Association (EIA). The tape is 1.000 in./wide, has 8 channels available, and a sprocket feed channel as shown in Fig. 20.8(a). The punched holes and the channels are 0.100 in. apart. One hole is called a *bit*. A series of holes punched in a row across the tape is called a *code*. A *word* is a complete set of characters comprising a complete unit of information.

In the EIA system the sum of the number of holes in a code must be *odd*. This is referred to as an *odd parity check*. If a particular code does not have an odd number of holes punched in a row on the tape, the reader will stop.

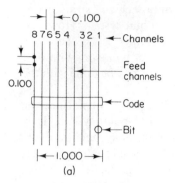

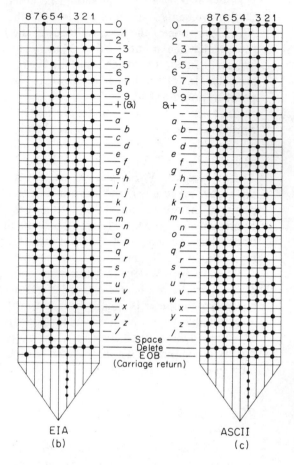

Figure 20.8

The American Standard Code for Information Interchange, known as ASCII uses the even parity check. The EIA system is shown in Fig. 20.8(b) and the ASCII system in Fig. 20.8(c).

It should be noted that tape readers have the capability of reading holes either mechanically or electronically. In the mechanical principle a sprocket tooth enters a punched hole in the tape causing an electrical contact or combination of contacts to be made. If a hole is missing in a particular row of holes, the tooth will not enter the tape and electrical contact is not made.

In the electronic system, a photoelectric reader uses a light source on one side of the tape and a row of solid-state photoelectric cells lined up on the other side of the tape. Fig. 20.9(a) shows one such photoelectric reader. As indicated earlier, the information is received and stored until a block of

(a)

(b)

Figure 20.9   [(a) *Courtesy of Ex-Cell-O Corporation, Remex Division;* (b) *courtesy of Autonumerics, Inc.*]

information has been completed. The "*end of block*" (carriage return) signals the release of this information. This makes it possible for several movements to take place at the same time. Thus it is possible for a tool to travel directly from E to G in Fig. 20.11 without first moving to A along the X axis and then along the Y axis to G. A tape reader console is shown in Fig. 20.9(b).

20.6. Tape Preparation: Linear Contouring

Because there are so many variations in the types of commands which may be used, this section will deal with the EIA Code and its use by one company.* The use of the EIA Code dictates an odd parity and a word address code.

To start, a section of tape is run out. Carriage return, "B", and carriage return are typed in that order. In this system the carriage return is the same as "end of block". The letter "B" indicates the start of the tape. Thus when the tape rewinds it will stop at "B" automatically.

The instructions are then typed into the tape. At the end of each series of instructions the carriage return will indicate an "EOB" command. At the end of the program an "R" is typed followed by an "EOB" (carriage return), a space, and about two feet of tape. The tape will rewind when the "R" is read by the reader.

In our system the word address codes are shown in Table I.

As indicated in section 20.4, it is probably easier for an experienced machinist to think in terms of the direction in which the tool is cutting than the direction in which the table is moving. Many companies prefer to program the direction of motion of the table. Table II shows the direction of the cutter motion and its related plus and minus signs. In Fig. 20.9 the movement of the cutter is shown.

EXAMPLE 1

Write the sequence of moves for Fig. 20.10(a).

Solution:

The movement from the start point (SP) to point A in Fig. 20.10(a) is

$$+ X01300 \qquad\qquad + Y01250$$

The movements from SP to A, B, C, D, E and back to SP are:

1. $X + 01300$	$Y + 01250$	SP to A
2. $X + 00000$	$Y + 03005$	A to B
3. $X + 08687$	$Y + 00000$	B to C
4. $X + 02375$	$Y - 01693$	C to D
5. $X - 01010$	$Y - 01562$	D to E
6. $X - 11352$	$Y - 01000$	E to SP
Sum 00000	00000	

*The author has selected the system used by Autonumerics, Inc. Hauppauge, N.Y. Note that language, word address, commands, etc., vary from one company to another, but if one system is understood, it should not be a difficult matter for the student to make the transition to another system.

TABLE I

Word Address Codes*

Code	Description
B	beginning of program—tape rewind stop
D	dwell—starts preset delay period
F	feed rate—followed by feed code number
G	preparatory function—followed by prep function code number
I	in circular interpolation, the distance from the center of the circle to the start point along the X-axis.
J	in circular interpolation, the distance from the center of the circle to the start point along the Y or Z axis.
K	optional stop code—used in repeated cycle and optional stop routines
M	"M" function symbol—followed by "M" function number
R	tape rewind
T	program stop—stops control until manually restarted.
W	position instructions for rotary table will follow
X	position instructions for X axis follows
Y	position instructions for Y axis follows
Z	position instructions for Z axis follows
+ or &	plus direction of travel (W clockwise, X table moves to operator's left, Y table moves toward operator, Z quill moves down). Many systems do not program the + sign.
—	minus direction of travel (W counterclockwise, X table moves to operator's right, Y table moves away from operator, Z quill moves up)
Carriage return	signals the end of a line or block (EOB) of information and causes position orders to be executed.
0 thru 9	number keys used to enter position dimensions
delete	punches over an incorrect line on the tape
/	slash—when slash delete switch is on the information between the slashes is ignored. An "EOB" code is not used between slashes.

*Autonumerics, Inc., Hauppauge, N.Y.

TABLE II

Cutter Movement

Plus (+) direction	Minus (−) direction
X to right	X to left
Y toward rear	Y toward front
Z down	Z up
W clockwise	W counterclockwise

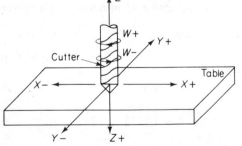

It should be noted that the sum of the X values should equal zero, and the sum of the Y values should equal zero.

If the dimensions are in metric millimeters, the positioning is in hundredths of a millimeter. Therefore, 86.54 millimeters is written 08654.

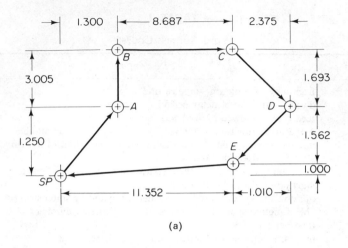

(a)

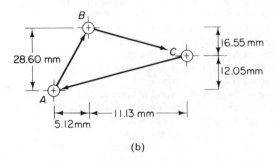

(b)

Figure 20.10

EXAMPLE 2

Write the sequence of movement for Fig. 20.10(b). Assume a drill bit moves down 42 mm after each movement.

Solution:

The movements from A to B to C to A are:

1. $X + 00512$ $Y + 02860$ $Z + 04200*$
2. $Z - 04200$
3. $X + 01113$ $Y - 01655$ $Z + 04200$
4. $Z - 04200$
5. $X - 01625$ $Y - 01205$ $Z + 04200$
6. $Z - 04200$

Notice that each of the columns (X, Y, Z) add to zero.

*In this system the Z should be programmed on a separate line.

20.7. Tape Preparations: Circular Contouring

In *point-to-point* systems the cutter will move from E to G' at 45° and then complete its movement along the X axis to G. In *linear contouring* systems the cutter moves directly from E to G as shown in Fig. 20.11.

Circular contouring moves the cutter around an arc from A to B as shown in Fig. 20.12(a). Again the *cutter* is programmed so that I is the distance from the center of curvature C to the start point A

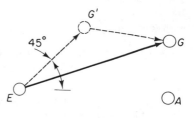

Figure 20.11

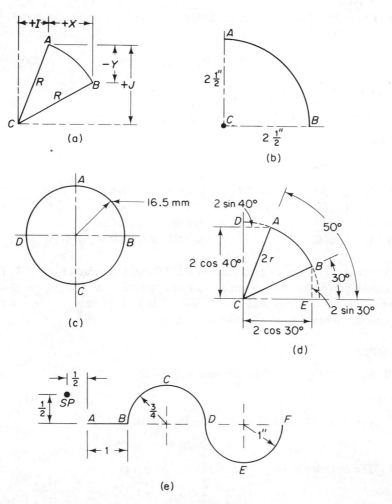

(a)

(b)

(c)

(d)

(e)

Figure 20.12

517

along the X axis, whereas *J is the distance from the center of curvature C to the start point A along the Y axis.* Therefore in Fig. 20.12(a) *X* is $+$; *Y* is $-$; *I* is $+$; *J* is $+$.

EXAMPLE 3

Write the program for Fig. 20.12(b).

Solution:

1. Along the *X* axis the value from *A* to *B* is $+02500$
2. Along the *Y* axis the value from *A* to *B* is -02500
3. From the center of rotation to the start point *A along the X axis I* is $+\ 00000$.
4. From the center of rotation to the start point *A along the Y axis J* is $+\ 02500$.

$$X + 02500 \qquad Y - 02500 \qquad I + 00000 \qquad J + 02500$$

EXAMPLE 4

Write the program for the circle Fig. 20.12(c).

Solution:

The program is

1. $X + 01650 \quad Y - 01650 \quad I + 00000 \quad J + 01650 \quad$ *A* to *B*
2. $X - 01650 \quad Y - 01650 \quad I + 01650 \quad J - 00000 \quad$ *B* to *C*
3. $X - 01650 \quad Y + 01650 \quad I - 00000 \quad J - 01650 \quad$ *C* to *D*
4. $X + 01650 \quad Y + 01650 \quad I - 01650 \quad J + 00000 \quad$ *D* to *A*

Notice that the sum of each column is 00000 and that each *row (X, Y, I, J)* has three signs which are the same and one opposite sign. That is, the *A*-to-*B* row has three plus signs and one minus. This can be achieved by affixing the plus or minus sign to the 00000 value last.

EXAMPLE 5

Write the program for the arc segment *AB* in Fig. 20.12(d).

Solution:

1. The distance from *D* to *A* along the *X* axis is

$$DA = 2 \sin 40 = 1.290$$

The distance from *C* to *E* along the *X* axis is

$$CE = 2 \cos 30 = 1.732$$

The distance along the X *axis* from A to B is

$$AB = CE - DA = 1.732 - 1.290$$
$$= 0.442$$

2. The distance from D to C along the Y axis is

$$DC = 2 \cos 40 = 1.532$$

The distance from E to B along the Y axis is

$$EB = 2 \sin 30 = 1.000$$

The distance along the Y axis from A to B is

$$AB = DC - EB = 1.532 - 1.000$$
$$= 0.532$$

3. The program is

A to B $X + 00442$ $Y - 00532$ $I + 2 \sin 40$ $J + 2 \cos 40$

Therefore

$X + 00442$ $Y - 00532$ $I + 01286$ $J + 01532$

Cavities are generated in the same manner. If a cavity is to be machined in the XZ plane, the same reasoning is used as that used in the preceeding discussion.

20.8. Special Functions

A list of function codes is shown in Table I. It is important to remember that other companies use different letters to represent their special requirements.

Feed rate "F" function. The system discussed in Sect. 20.7 programs the feed (in./min) as the "F" code followed by four digits. Thus a feed rate of 175.6 in./min is programmed as

$$175.6 \text{ in./min} = F1756$$

A feed rate of 15 in./min is programmed as

$$15 \text{ in./min} = F0150$$

In this system, programming an

$$F9999$$

overrides the feed rate and produces a rapid travel.

EXAMPLE 6

From Fig. 20.10(a) move the tool at a rapid rate from *SP* to *A*; drill a hole at a feed of 18 in./min for a depth of $1\frac{3}{8}$ in.; retract the tool with a rapid feed and return to *SP*.

Solution:

	B		
1. F9999	$X + 01300$	$Y + 01250$	
2. F0180			$Z + 01375$
3. F9999			$Z - 01375$
4.	$X - 01300$	$Y - 01250$	
5. R			

The code "B" starts the process and "R" rewinds the tape.

"M" Functions. This system uses "M" functions to release or set a spindle brake, turn the spindle and coolant on or off and reverse the direction of rotation of the spindle. Thus

M10 turns the spindle on and releases the brake
M20 operates the quill clamp
M50 reverses the spindle
M60 turns the spindle off, sets the brake, and turns the coolant off

EXAMPLE 7

Add the necessary "M" functions to the program in Example 6.

Solution:

	B		
1. F9999	$X + 01300$	$Y + 01250$	
2. M10			$Z + 01000$
3. F0180			$Z + 00375$
4. F9999			$Z - 01375$
5. M60	$X - 01300$	$Y - 01250$	
6. R			

"G" Function. When tracing radii the spindle motor should be controlled so that it does not ramp up or down. This is especially so where two radii are tangent to each other so that the motor may speed up and slow down. G08 and G09 functions produce this effect in this system. The use of the "M" and "G" functions is illustrated in Example 8.

EXAMPLE 8

Program Fig. 20.12(e). Include the necessary "M" and "G" functions Use a feed of $2\frac{1}{2}$ in./min.

Solution:

	B		
	B		
SP to A	F9999	$X + 00500$ $Y - 00500$	
approach	M20		$Z + 00500$
A to B	M10 F0025	$X + 01000$ $Y + 00000$	
B to C	G08	$X + 00750$ $Y + 00750$	$I - 00750$ $J + 00000$
C to D		$X + 00750$ $Y - 00750$	$I + 00000$ $J + 00750$
D to E		$X + 01000$ $Y - 01000$	$I - 01000$ $J - 00000$
E to F		$X + 01000$ $Y + 01000$	$I + 00000$ $J - 01000$ G09
up	M60		$Z - 00500$
F to SP	F9999	$X - 05000$ $Y + 00500$	
	R		

Slash delete (/). The slash delete stroke eliminates the instructions between two slashes. The information is included when the slash delete switch is off. Thus in Example 8 the first hole may be included or deleted.

EXAMPLE 9

Program a hole at X equal 1.000″, Y equal 1.250 and provide slash delete strokes. A second hole is to be drilled at X equal 0.300 in.

Solution:

	B			
	B			
1.	F9999	$X + 01000$ $Y + 01250$		SP to A rapid
2.	M10		$Z + 01000$	approach
3.	/F0180		$Z + 00375/$	lst hole
4.	/F9999		$Z - 00375/$	retract
5.		$X + 00300$ $Y + 00000$		2nd hole
6.	F0180		$Z + 00375$	drill
7.	F9999		$Z - 01375$	retract
8.	M60	$X - 01300$ $Y - 01250$		rewind
	R			

"*T*" Function. In this system, the code "TOO" stops the machine cycle to permit insertion of a tool, etc. The cycle may be resumed with the start button. Other "T" functions control the tool offset from the work.

"*S*" Function. In our system the spindle speed may be programmed into the machine with an "S" followed by two digits which represent hundredths of an rpm. Thus 500 rpm is programmed S05 and 5000 rpm is programmed S50.

EXAMPLE 10

Program Figure 20.13.

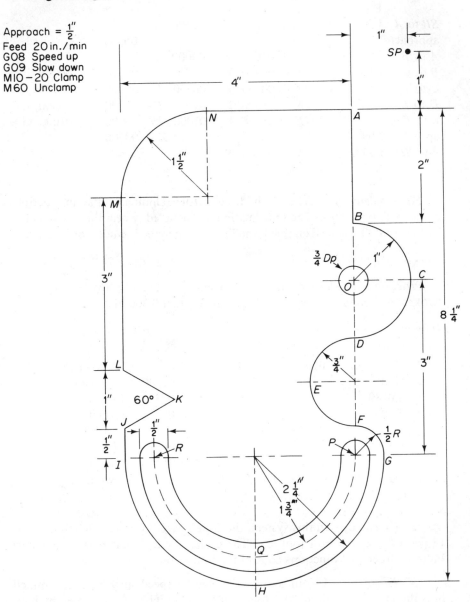

Figure 20.13

Solution:

	BB					
At *SP*	M-10					
SP → *A*	F9999	X − 01000	Y − 01000			
At *A*				Z + 00500		
A → *B*	M20 F0020	X + 00000	Y − 02000			
B → *C*	G08	X + 01000	Y − 01000	I + 00000	J + 01000	
C → *D*		X − 01000	Y − 01000	I + 01000	J − 00000	
D → *E*		X − 00750	Y − 00750	I − 00000	J + 00750	
E → *F*		X + 00750	Y − 00750	I − 00750	J − 00000	
F → *G*		X + 00500	Y − 00500	I + 00000	J + 00500	
G → *H*		X − 02250	Y − 02250	I + 02250	J − 00000	
H → *I*		X − 02250	Y + 02250	I − 00000	J − 02250	
I → *J*		X + 00000	Y + 00500	G09		
J → *K*		X + 00289	Y + 00500			
K → *L*		X − 00289	Y + 00500			
L → *M*	G08	X + 00000	Y + 03000			
M → *N*		X + 01500	Y + 01500	I − 01500	J + 00000	
N → *A*		X + 02500	Y + 00000	G09		
At *A*						
approach	M60 F9999			Z − 00500		
A → O		X + 00000	Y − 03000			
At *O*				Z + 00500		
down	M10 F0020			Z + 00750		
up	F9999			Z − 01250		
O → *P*	M60	X + 00000	Y − 03000			
Approach at *P*				Z + 00500		
cut at *P*	M10 F0020			Z + 00750		
P → *Q*	M20 G08	X − 01750	Y − 01750	I + 01750	J − 00000	
Q → *R*		X − 01750	Y + 01750	I − 00000	J − 01750	G09
Up at *R*	F9999			Z − 01250		
R → *SP*		X + 04500	Y + 07000			
at *SP*	M60					
at *SP*	R					

It is important to note that in the discussions to this point the movement of the tool—a drill bit—has been controlled. There was no need to consider the diameter of the drill. In Fig. 20.12 the radii are sssumed to be machined with an end mill. The program represents the movement of the center line of the end mill and allowances must be made for the diameter of the end mill. Most systems have offset word addresses which automatically compensate for the offset. The offset is programmed into the tape at the start. The path of the end mills are shown in Figs. 20.14(a through c).

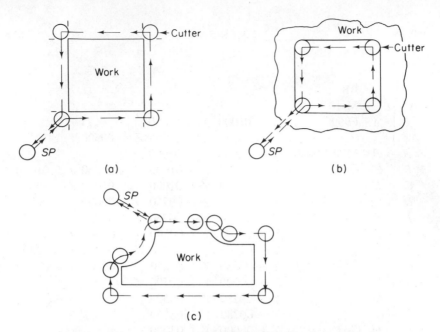

Figure 20.14

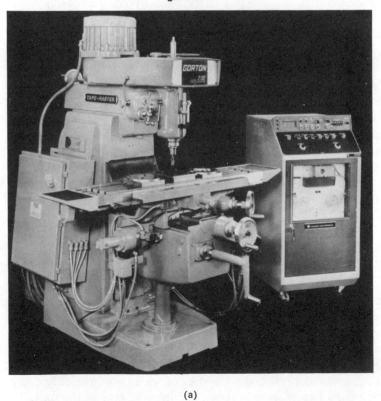

(a)

Figure 20.15 (*Courtesy of George Gorton Machine Company.*)

(b)

Figure 20.15   (Cont.)

20.9.   *Numerical Control Machines*

The milling machine shown in Fig. 20.15(a) is a two-axis (three-axis optional) machine with a preset spindle depth control. The down feed movement of the spindle is programmed into the tape for control of the Z axis. In the three-axis machine the X, Y, and Z axes are controlled through the used of servo motors which actuate hydraulic cylinders. The tape reader is a photoelectric type reader.

Other features indicated for this machine are emergency manual stops, manual and tape coolant on and off controls, manual or tape spindle start and stop controls, slide hold and reset, and manual full-floating zero for positioning. Features incorporated in the control unit are indicators for normal operation, sequence numbers, tape error, servo error, end of block, and cycle start. Still other features control mode selection and execution.

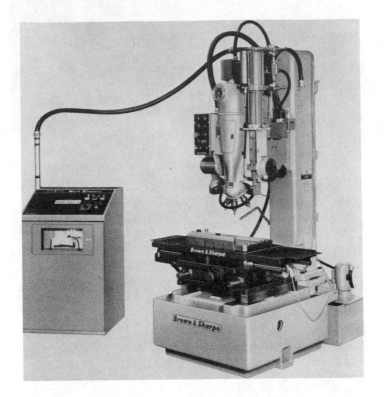

(a)

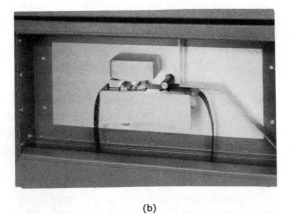

(b)

Figure 20.16 *(Courtesy of Brown & Sharpe Manufacturing Company.)*

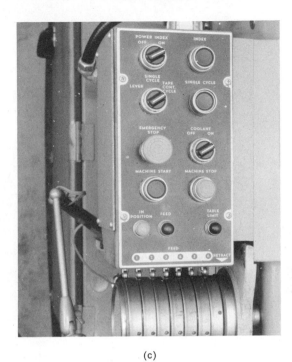

(c)

Figure 20.16   (Cont.)

Optional features may be included in the machine and the controls for greater versatility. Such items are fine feed control, high-speed input, command multipliers, and additional functions which give a wider range of on-off control of auxiliary functions.

Figure 20.15(b) shows a face cam being milled on a numerical-control milling machine. Figure 20.16(a) shows a drill press with numerical control. The tape reader and down feed controls are shown in Figs. 20.16(b) and (c) respectively. A turret for additional tool operations is also shown. Different companies use different methods or tool changers for bringing different tools into position both manually and automatically.

Figure 20.17(a) shows a machining center with large 42 tool magazine that can be randomly accessed on a 360 position index table. Figure 20.17(b) shows a machining center with a different approach to programming tools in a magazine of 45 taper tools.

Figure 20.17(c) shows a version of a console designed for computer numerical control (CNC). It has a CRT to display position, mode, table offset, program blocks, and tool diameter and length offset among other features. It has a programmable cycle file. A program from a tape may be inserted into the memory and used without the tape or the console may be manually programmed. It has the capability of directing simultaneous linear contouring

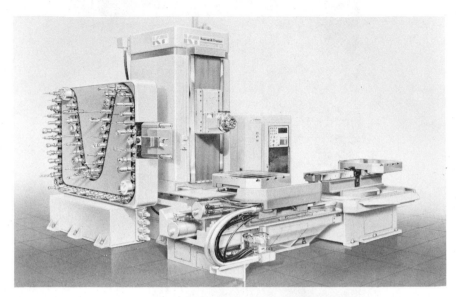

(a)

(b)

Figure 20.17 [(a) & (b) *Courtesy of Kearney & Trecker Corporation;* (c) *courtesy of Autonumerics, Inc.;* (d) *courtesy of The Bendix Corporation, Industrial Controls Division.*]

(c)

(d)

Figure 20.17 (Cont.)

and circular contouring. It may be programmed in the inch or the metric system and in EIA or ASCII system. Figure 20.17(d) is another CNC console manufactured by another company.

QUESTIONS AND PROBLEMS

20.1 Explain the EDM process of machining metals.

20.2 (a) What role does the frequency play in EDM machining? (b) Amperage? (c) Voltage?

20.3 (a) Define and explain tool wear in EDM machining. (b) How is tool wear classified? (c) How is it controlled?

20.4 Upon what factors does surface finish depend in EDM machining?

20.5 Explain the term *overcut* as applied to EDM machining.

20.6 What is the meaning of the phrase "control by letters and numbers"?

20.7 Explain the differences between point-to-point and continuous control contouring.

20.8 Discuss the advantages of numerical control over conventional automated production for (a) short run and (b) long run.

20.9 Why is single-piece machining of castings feasible with numerical control, and not conventional machining?

20.10 What are some of the advantages of numerical control machining?

20.11 What accuracies are possible with numerical control machining?

20.12 What is the purpose of the floating zero in numerical control setup?

20.13 Explain how a numerical control machine checks itself when it is used to machine several similar workpieces.

20.14 Draw and explain the purpose of each unit in the block diagram for an open-loop numerical control system. Why is it called an open-loop system?

20.15 Draw and explain the purpose of each unit in the block diagram for a closed-loop numerical control system. Why is it called a closed-loop system?

20.16 Describe the purpose and operation of a transducer in numerical control.

20.17 How does a semi-closed loop system differ from a closed loop system? Illustrate.

20.18 Select one of the word languages mentioned in Section 20.4 and describe its purpose.

20.19 Which axes are usually controlled on an (a) two-axis; (b) three-axis; (c) four-axis; and (d) five-axis machine?

20.20 Define and explain a digital signal and an analogue signal.

20.21 Explain the principle of a point-to-point command for actuating the traverse movement of the table of a machine. Do the same for the longitudinal movement of the table.

20.22 Assume that two holes are to be drilled at 30° to the longitudinal traverse on a numerical-control drill press. In using the point-to-point command system, what is the movement of the table?

20.23 Assume a slot is to be machined at 30° to the horizontal traverse on a numerical-control milling machine. How does the cutter move in a point-to-point command system? How can greater accuracy be achieved with this system?

20.24 Why is it difficult to machine a complicated contour with the point-to-point command system? Illustrate the movement of the tool when cutting a simple radius contour with the point-to-point system.

20.25 Explain how it is possible to cut contours or slots at an angle by using the continuous-path command system. Describe the principle.

20.26 What is the purpose of using a computer in numerical control?

20.27 What is the difference between the EIA and the ASCII binary coded decimal systems?

20.28 (a) Program the numbers 1 through 9 using columns 1, 2, 3, 4 in Fig. 20.8(b) EIA. (b) Repeat for Fig. 20.8(c) ASCII.

20.29 What is the purpose of the parity channel?

20.30 (a) How is zero handled in the EIA system? (b) In the ASCII system?

20.31 (a) How do sprockets read the 8-channels on a tape? (b) How are the holes read in an electronic reader?

20.32 Illustrate the following by punching the holes in a tape using the binary-coded decimal system discussed in this chapter:

Operation	3	Feed	30 ipm
X	+0.7460	Speed	90 rpm
Y	+0.3254	End of block	
Z	−0.0562		

20.33 Write the program, and show the tape for the binary-coded decimal system discussed in this chapter for the following:

Operation	6	Feed	20 ipm
X	−0.654	Speed	60 rpm
Y	+0.105	End of block	
Z	+0.475		

20.34 Make a diagram of a milling machine table and indicate the plus and minus directions used in the system discussed in Section 20.6.

20.35 Write the sequence of moves needed to drill the 4 holes in Fig. 20.18(a).

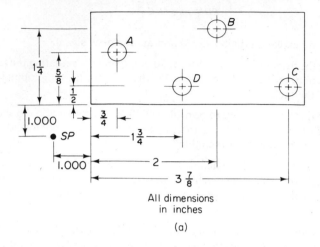

All dimensions
in inches

(a)

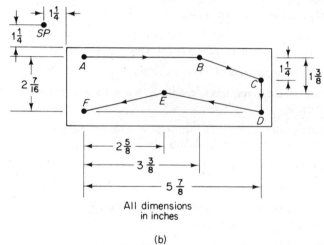

All dimensions
in inches

(b)

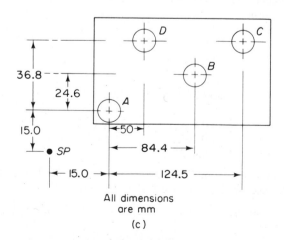

All dimensions
are mm

(c)

Figure 20.18

20.36   Write the sequence of moves needed to trace the path shown in Fig. 20.18(b).

20.37   Write the sequence of movement in Fig. 20.18(c).

20.38   Write the program for Fig. 20.19(a).

20.39   Write the program for Fig. 20.19(b).

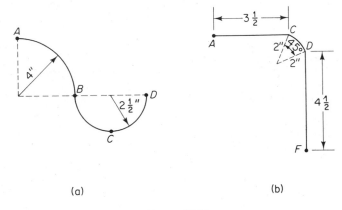

(a)   (b)

Figure 20.19

20.40   In Fig. 20.18(a) move the tool at a rapid rate from *SP* to *A*, drill a hole at a feed of 25 in./min for a depth of $\frac{7}{8}$ in. with an approach of $\frac{1}{2}$ in. Return the tool to *SP*.

20.41   Write the program for Fig. 20.18(b). Assume an approach of 1 in., a depth of slot of $\frac{3}{8}$ in., and a feed of 30 in./min. An end mill is used.

20.42   Write a program to trace the centerline of the tool path in Fig. 20.20. The approach is $\frac{3}{8}$ in. The feed is 20 in./min.

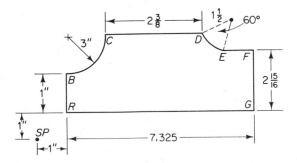

Figure 20.20

20.43   Write the program for Fig. 20.21.

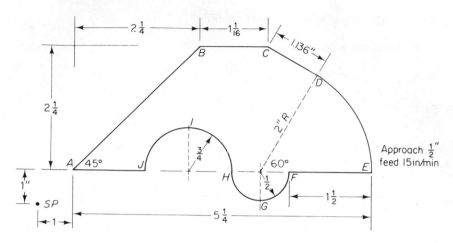

Figure 20.21

20.44   Discuss the use of the slash delete.

20.45   How must a program be altered to represent the use of an end mill. See Fig. 20.14.

20.46   Discuss the capabilities of CNC.

Grinders

21

21.1. Types of Grinding Machines

There are many types of grinding machines. The two most widely used are the cylindrical and surface grinders. Other grinding operations include those using vertical spindles, internal and centerless grinders, and jigs.

The cylindrical grinder. This is equipped with a headstock and tailstock between which the work is mounted and rotated as a grinding wheel in contact with the work removes metal from its circumference [See Fig. 21.1(a).] The operation is somewhat similar to that of a lathe. The grinding wheel replaces the tool bit, and the thousands of little abrasive particles in it may be thought of as little tool bits. They in fact produce little chips during the cutting operation.

The headstock center may or may not revolve with the work. The tailstock center is always dead. Operating a cylindrical grinder with both centers dead eliminates any possible eccentricity which may result from the live center runout. Precision grinding is done between two dead centers.

The headstock spindle is usually driven by its own motor. It is also possible to move the headstock along the upper table and clamp it once it is positioned. The tailstock is also adjustable along the upper table to accommodate various lengths of work. The headstock, as indicated, may be fitted with a 60° center, collets, chucks, or a driving plate. If a drive plate is used, a dog fastened to the work gets its power from this drive plate. Work from 12 in. to 30 ft long and from 3 to 36 in. in diameter may be accommodated on grinding machines.

The cylindrical grinder is equipped with two tables. The upper table may be swiveled about a center point for taper grinding. The lower table is powered to oscillate along the longitudinal axis of the machine. The longitudinal movement of the table should be about half the width of the grinding wheel for each revolution of the work. On large roll grinders, the wheel head oscillates back and forth. The table is used to support and rotate the work and does not oscillate.

The wheel head, driven by a flat belt to reduce vibration, is mounted on the lower table to facilitate moving the wheel into the work. The upper table,

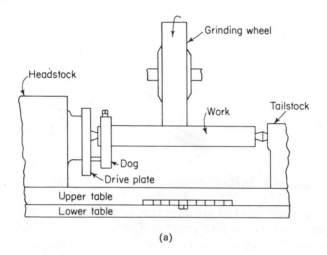

(a)

(b)

Figure 21.1 [(*b*) *Courtesy of Landis Tool Co.;* (*c*) *courtesy of The Warner & Swasey Company, Grinding Machine Division.*]

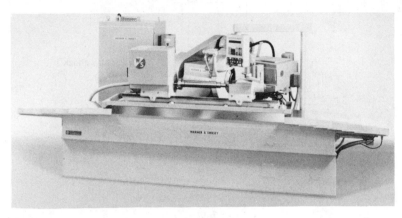

(c)

Figure 21.1   (Cont.)

which carries the grinding wheel, may be swiveled for taper-turning or corner-grinding cylindrical work. With the upper table set at an angle and the lower table set at 0°, the wheel may be fed perpendicular to the center line of the work even though the wheel is at an angle. See Fig. 21.1(a).

Feeding the grinding wheel into the work may be done automatically or by hand in increments as low as 0.0001 in. per pass. The range of infeed of the wheel into the work is from about 0.002 in. per pass for roughing to about 0.0005 in. for finishing. Hydraulically controlled infeed grinders are also available with mechanisms for automatic table retraction when the grinding operation is complete.

Universal cylindrical grinders permit the upper table to swivel, as shown in Fig. 21.1(a). They usually come equipped with quills for internal grinding.

Figure 21.1(b) shows one of the latest cylindrical grinders. It has a logic system which permits grinding multiple diameters, repeating and holding diameters to under 0.001 in. without the use of in-process sizing gages. Figure 21.1(c) shows a CNC controlled grinder with insertion of ten grinding operations into the memory without the use of a tape. Wheel dressing and size compensation are automatic after a programmed number of passes have taken place. The accuracy of repeating a size is in the ten-thousandths range.

The surface grinder.   This is used for grinding flat surfaces [See Fig. 21.2(a).] The table mounts a magnetic chuck used for holding the work during the grinding operation. The table oscillates under the wheel, as shown in Fig. 21.2(b). With each pass the table feeds transversely. This feed may be accomplished automatically or by hand. The automatic control may be with hydraulic power or a mechanical indexing mechanism. As the table moves longitudinally the direction is reversed with trip dogs. At the same time the hitch feed is actuated. Some surface grinders are made to hitch-feed the wheel head transversely. Figure 21.2(c) shows a standard surface grinder.

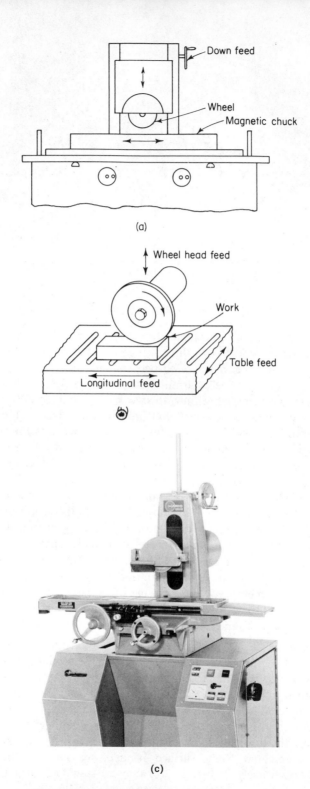

(a)

(b)

(c)

Figure 21.2 (*Photo courtesy of Harig Products, Inc.*)

Grinding machine accessories. Grinding machines may also have vertical spindles, Fig. 21.3(a). The wheel is recessed and cuts with its face instead of its periphery.

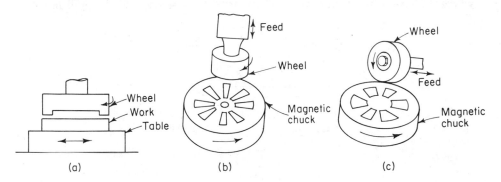

Figure 21.3

Tables which rotate instead of oscillating are also available. They may have vertical or horizontal wheel spindles. Figure 21.3(b) shows a rotary table with a vertical head, and Fig. 21.3(c) shows a rotary table with a horizontal head. The workpieces are mounted on the magnetic chuck so that the vertical head covers the workpiece and half the rotary table. The spindle is fed vertically until the wheel contacts the work. This is accomplished while the table is rotating.

On the horizontal-spindle machine the wheel is fed down until it contacts the work. The horizontal spindle oscillates back and forth while the table is rotating.

Internal grinders use a high-speed grinding wheel at the end of a quill; see Fig. 21.4(a). The work is mounted and caused to rotate in the opposite direction from the grinding wheel. The quill moves in and out of the hole parallel to the center line of the work for cylindrical grinding and at an angle to the center line of the work for taper grinding.

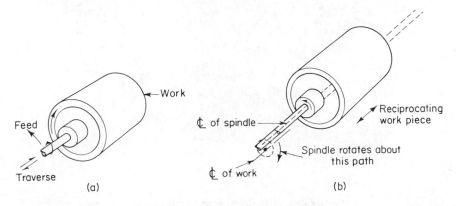

Figure 21.4

When it is inconvenient to rotate the work, the machine is constructed to give a planetary motion to the quill. This motion is imparted to the quill in such a way that it revolves about the center line of the work as the grinding wheel is in contact with the work. The work is stationary, and the quill has

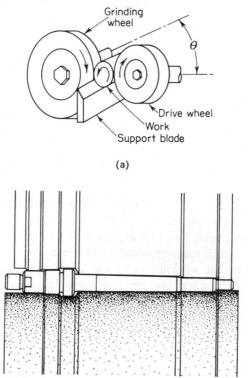

(a)

(b)

Figure 21.5 [(*b*) *Courtesy of Landis Tool Co.*]

the necessary oscillating motion to cover the entire length to be ground. This is shown in Fig. 21.4(b).

A unique grinder is the centerless grinder of which there are several types: the cylindrical grinders for grinding circular external surfaces, internal centerless grinders for grinding internal circular surfaces, and centerless thread grinders. These grinders may be used to grind cylinders, tapers, spheres, multiple diameters, contours, threads, etc. Figure 21.5(b) shows a programmable centerless grinder which is capable of controlling the loading, sizing, and gaging processes from a computer memory bank.

In all cases at least three points of contact with the work are employed. The work is supported by a blade, or roller; a drive wheel which has a higher coefficient of friction than the grinding wheel is the second support point. The grinding wheel is the third support point. This is shown in Fig. 21.5(a).

The cutter grinder is a cylindrical grinder whose wheel head is powered. Two (dead center) supports are mounted on the upper table. They are attachments and are not power driven. Each tooth is rotated into position by hand when grinding cutters. Both the upper table and the cutter head may be swiveled. The lower table may be hand fed by using the feed handwheel or a lever for rapid table traverse. The table is also equipped with trip dogs to ensure that the table will not overshoot the work too much and damage the machine. Other attachments such as collets, indexing head, power-driven headstock, etc., are available. The operation of cutter grinding will be discussed in Chapter 23.

Magnetic chucks are used on surface grinders and on cylindrical grinders. There are two types of magnetic chucks. The rectifier type supplies direct current to the chuck. The direct current induces magnetic fields which pass from the chuck into the work and then back into the chuck.

The permanent magnetic chuck utilizes two plates, as shown in Fig. 21.6(a). The lower plate can be moved so that the nonmagnetic strips are not

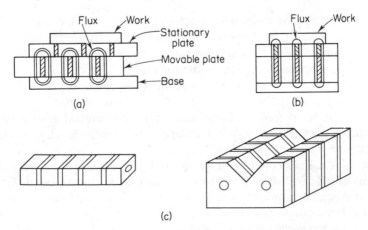

Figure 21.6

aligned. Thus the magnetic flux lines do not pass through the work and consequently do not hold the work. In Fig. 21.6(b) the flux lines are directed through the work to complete the magnetic circuit and hold the work.

Only ferrous magnetic materials can be held with these chucks. Nonmagnetic materials may be held with an electrostatic chuck which requires that the material be electricity conducting. The passing of an electric dc current through the work holds it in position. The work should be backed up with a stop.

Round permanent magnetic chucks may be fitted to the spindle of cylindrical grinders. They are used for holding flat work. The need for clamps is eliminated. The entire face of the workpiece is left free to be ground.

Magnetic parallels and V blocks may also be used in conjunction with magnetic chucks. These accessories must be laminated of magnetic and nonmagnetic materials to direct the magnetic flux when it passes through them. They are shown in Fig. 21.6(c). Other types of parallels and V blocks (permanent types) have bar magnets built into their structure and can be rotated into position.

21.2. Grinding Operations

It was noted in Section 21.1 that cylindrical grinding may be accomplished between centers on the plain cylindrical grinder. The centers on the headstock and tailstock as well as the centers in the ends of the workpiece must be clean. Then the grinding wheel is dressed with a diamond dresser. A driving dog is fastened to the work, the centers are oiled, and the work is mounted in the grinding machine between centers. The longitudinal travel of the table is set to about one-half the width of the grinding wheel for every revolution of the work. The reversing trip dogs are set to the desired length of table travel. If possible, the wheel should be permitted to run off the end of the work with each pass.

After the first pass the work diameter is checked for size and taper. If a taper exists, it must be corrected. After the taper is eliminated and the diameter reading taken, the automatic cross feed is set to within about 0.002 in. of the finished diameter. This is the roughing operation.

Once the rough diameter is obtained, the wheel speed and the table speed and feed are changed. The wheel is dressed again and the remaining 0.002 in. is removed by hand feeding. Some machines are equipped with automatic measuring devices which make it unnecessary to stop the machine each time a measurement needs to be taken.

The work should rotate at about 80 to 120 sfpm, and the wheel should rotate at about 5500 sfpm when using a vitrified or silicate bond. Organic bonds (rubber, resinoid, etc.) may be run at higher surface speeds for a particular bond and followed very carefully. Manufacturer's tables should be consulted for recommended surface speeds and adhered to very carefully.

The newest class of grinding machines is equipped with programmable controls which synchronize the feed of the wheel with other functions such as rpm of the work, table travel, wheel dressing, sizing, taper conditions, etc. As indicated, these machines may be programmed to repeat finished ground sizes for multiple diameters.

Additional operations may be accomplished on a cylindrical grinder besides the grinding of outside diameters on a cylinder. One such operation is the grinding of a cylinder to a shoulder. This may be done by plunge grinding when the length of the work is less than the width of the grinding wheel, as shown in Fig. 21.7(a).

When the work length is greater than the wheel width, the longitudinal traverse feed may be used. To avoid damage to the wheel and the work, the stop dog should be set so that the table direction is reversed when the wheel is about $\frac{1}{16}$ in. away from the shoulder of the work. A better method is to use an undercut, as shown in Fig. 21.7(a).

If the blueprint requires a sharp corner, the wheel may be set at an angle, as shown in Fig. 21.7(b). The wheel should be dressed so that its face is parallel to the center line of the work. The plunge feed of the wheel is accomplished when the wheel and work are in the position shown. The longitudinal table travel is then from right to left. This tends to keep edge A, Fig. 21.7(b), of the wheel sharp. The rounding of B in Fig. 21.7(b) as a result of the cutting action does no harm. It should be evident that with a left to right table motion, A will break down into a radius corner and B will drag and remain sharp. This will make it impossible to maintain a sharp corner at A.

If the shoulder and the cylinder need grinding, the wheel may be dressed, as shown in Fig. 21.7(c) or Fig. 21.7(d). This is discussed in Section 21.4. The dressed wheel may be replaced by a purchased recessed wheel. It is to be noted that the proper dressing of the wheel is important; otherwise the shoulders will grind concave if the angle shown in Fig. 21.7(d) is less than 90° or convex if the angle shown is greater than 90°.

Tapers may also be ground on a cylindrical grinder. The upper worktable is swiveled to the desired angle. Since the lower table oscillates parallel to the wheel face and the work is revolving in a plane at an angle to the wheel, a taper will be ground, as shown in Fig. 21.7(e).

Figure 21.7(f) shows the setup for grinding flat faces on workpieces. Figures 21.7 (g and h) show the exaggerated concave and convex conditions which result if the center line of the swivel head is not at an exact 90° to the table travel.

If a hole is to be ground, an internal grinding head may be used. This head is provided with the universal grinder. See Fig. 21.4(a). Grinding machines are available for internal grinding only. Production internal grinders also are available with multiple heads for grinding several holes in one setup.

The wheel speeds are higher for internal grinding than for external grinding, ranging from 10,000 to 16,000 rpm. Through grinding will leave

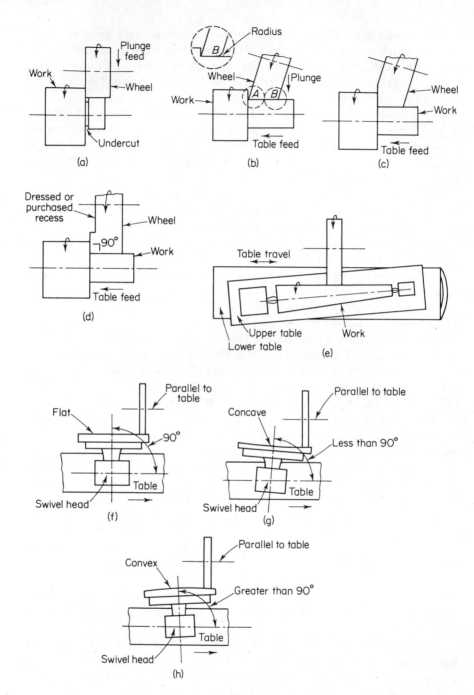

Figure 21.7

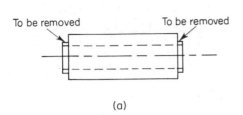
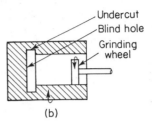

(a)   (b)

Figure 21.8

the ends of the hole slightly "bell-mouth." If this is objectionable, the ends of the workpiece may be machined as shown in Fig. 21.8(a) and ground off after the internal grinding operation is complete.

Internal grinding may also be accomplished with a grinding attachment which mounts on the compound rest of a lathe. The student is cautioned that excessive use of a lathe for grinding will damage the precision qualities of the lathe. The abrasive particles get between the moving parts of the lathe and damage them.

When grinding to a blind wall in a hole, it is usual to undercut the bore so that the grinding wheel will not hit the bottom of the hole. The results should be obvious to the student if the wheel hits the bottom of the hole. See Fig. 21.8(b).

Centerless grinding, Section 21.1, may be done by plunging the feed wheel straight into the work with the center lines of the feed wheel and the grinding wheel parallel to each other.

If it is desired to feed the work between the wheels, this may be done by pivoting the driving wheel through an angle θ, as shown in Fig. 21.9(a). Once the angle is set, the drive wheel causes the work to revolve and move forward. Once contact is made with the grinding wheel, material is removed from the surface of the work because the surface speed of the grinding wheel is much greater than the surface speed of the drive wheel. The resulting drag causes material to be removed from the periphery of the work.

The feed rate is a function of the circumference, the angle of inclination, and the surface speed of the regulating wheel. The angle of inclination should range between 0° and 8° for through grinding. The through feed of the work for a given angle can be calculated with the equation

$$f = CN \sin \theta$$

f = feed of work
C = circumference of regulating wheel
N = rpm of feed wheel
θ = angle of inclination of regulating wheel

Finishing cuts can be taken with smaller angles of inclination and faster surface speeds than during rough grinding. The work is usually set, as shown in Fig. 21.9(a), so that it rests between the two wheels while the operation

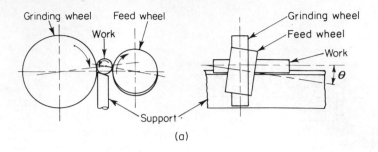

(a)

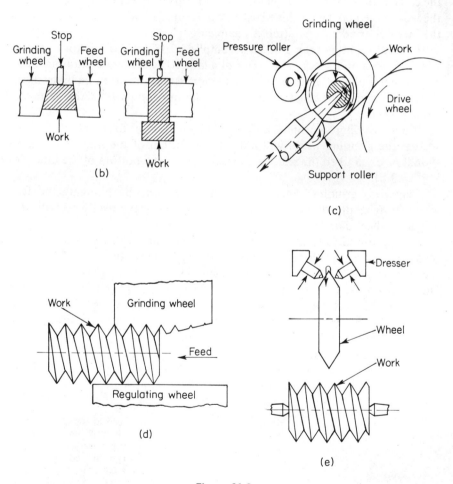

(b)

(c)

(d)

(e)

Figure 21.9

proceeds. This above-center position of the work tends to round the work and remove eccentricity. Below-center grinding is slower but should be used when work is bent. The three points hold the work as grinding proceeds.

Contour centerless grinding is accomplished by providing a stop to prevent through feed, as shown in Fig. 21.9(b). The form is dressed into the grinding wheel and into the drive wheel. Taper centerless grinding utilizes the forward feed of the work to hold it in position against the stop.

Figure 21.9(c) shows the principle of internal centerless grinding. The drive wheel turns the work clockwise. The counterclockwise rotation of the grinding wheel causes metal removal on contact. The spindle oscillates in and out of the hole as the drive wheel rotates the work.

Centerless thread grinding employs the same principles as the centerless cylindrical grinder. The thread is dressed into the grinding wheel with partially completed threads at the input side of the grinding wheel, as shown in Fig. 21.9(d).

Thread grinding may also be done on a thread grinder which uses a plain wheel with the form dressed into its periphery. This grinder may be used to grind external or internal threads. The dressing is accomplished when it backs away from the work. At the rear of the machine is a present wheel dresser which automatically dresses the desired form into the wheel, as shown in Fig. 21.9(e). Correction is made for the amount dressed off the wheel so that the depth of the thread is maintained. When the depth of the thread is reached, the wheel backs off and shuts off. Thread forms other than 60° forms may be dressed into the wheel. High-precision threads may be ground with this method.

Form grinding may also be done by dressing or crushing the desired form into the wheel in cylindrical or centerless grinding. Forms may be dressed into the wheel with a single-point diamond dresser. However, each angle or radius must be dressed into the face of the wheel separately. A much more widely used method is the crush-dressing method. This method takes advantage of the structure of the grinding wheel discussed in Section 21.3. In the construction of the wheel, grit is held in position by a bonding material. If the bond is selectively broken, the form of the crushing roller is shaped into the wheel.

Crush rollers should be slightly wider than the wheel and made from an abrasion-resistant material which is hardened to prolong the life of the rollers. The crush rollers should be mounted so that they will revolve with a minimum amount of eccentricity and end play between the bore and the contour on the rollers. Master rollers may be used to crush the wheel when the rollers need reconditioning. In this way tolerances which must be maintained throughout the job can be easily achieved.

During the dressing operation both the grinding wheel and the rollers are revolving. Usually the roller is driven, and the contact between the roller and the grinding wheel drives the grinding wheel. Provision is made for disengaging the grinding-wheel drive mechanism.

A preload of about 0.015 in. is required to cause the grinding wheel to revolve and crush effectively. The infeed of the crushing roller should be about 0.002 in. for every 10 revolutions of the grinding wheel with the preload maintained. This preload should be released before the crushing roller is stopped. It is to be noted that the crush dressing principle may be used on surface as well as cylindrical grinders.

Crushing may be best accomplished in aluminum oxide abrasive wheels having a grit size of from 100 to 300 (see Section 21.3).

21.3. Grinding Wheels

The grinding wheel is the cutting tool used in the grinding operation. In effect the cutting action may be compared with the action of a great number of single-point tools. Very high finish at a close tolerance—0.0001 in.—may be maintained during quantity production. High rates of metal removal, as accomplished with a tool bit, are not possible. However, many materials which cannot be cut with the conventional cutting tools can be machined with the use of a grinding wheels.

Five factors enter into the selection of a grinding wheel: the abrasive, the grit size, the grade, the structure, and the bond. The variety in each of the factors is indicated in Table 21.1. The wheel marking in the table is a standard system, each number or letter representing one of the five factors. The number appearing at the top of this table is one which might appear on the blotter glued to the side of the wheel or stamped on the wheel.

TABLE 21.1

Mfg. no.

Abrasive

A = aluminum oxide
C = silicon carbide
D = diamond

Grit size

38   A   60   K   8   V   G

Mfg. no.

BOND

V = vitrified
B = resinoid
R = rubber
E = shellac
S = silicate

Grade

Structure

Coarse	Med.	Fine	Very fine	Soft	Med.	Hard	Close	Med.	Wide
8	30	70	220	A	I	Q	0	4	7	11
10	36	80	240	B	J	R	1	5	8	12
12	46	90	280	C	K	S	2	6	9	
14	54	100	320	D	L	T	3		10	
16	60	120	400	E	M	U				
20		150	500	F	N	V				
24		180	600	G	O	W				
				H	P	X				
						Y				
						Z				

The abrasive, letter A in the notation in Table 21.1, refers to the particles which act as the cutting tools to remove metal. They are very hard particles possessing very many jagged sharp edges. They may be natural abrasive grains such as emery, quartz, corundum, sandstone, garnet, etc. The synthetic abrasives are aluminum oxide Al_2O_3, silicon carbide SiC, or diamond.

The natural abrasives are not widely used for precision grinding because of the impurities in their structure. The synthetic abrasives, products of the electric furnace, are controlled so that the impurities are held to a minimum, and the physical properties of the grains may also be controlled during manufacturing. The abrasive material is charged into an electric furnace with other products (coke, salt, etc.) and heated to high temperatures until it fuses. The fused material is crushed between rollers and graded.

In general, the physical properties of aluminum oxide compared with silicon carbide are:

1. Silicon carbide is harder than aluminum oxide.
2. Silicon carbide is more brittle and therefore not as tough as aluminum oxide.
3. Aluminum oxide will withstand greater stresses than silicon carbide.
4. Aluminum oxide wheels are used to grind high-tensile-strength and tough materials such as steel and malleable and wrought iron, whereas, the silicon carbide wheels are used to grind low-tensile-strength materials and nonmetallic materials such as gray iron, stainless steel, soft nonferrous materials, marble, stone, or rubber and many hard materials such as carbide.

Diamond abrasives are used to grind carbides and other very hard or highly abrasive materials such as marble, gems, stone, etc.

The grit size, the number 60 in the notation of Table 21.1, refers to the physical size of the grit. After crushing the fused material, this product of the electric furnace is passed through a series of sieves with a preestablished number of openings per linear inch. The last sieve through which the grit passes is the size number assigned to that grit. Thus in the designation of Table 21.1, the grit used in the wheel indicated at the top of the table passes through a screen having 60 openings per linear in. and is trapped in the sieve having 70 openings per linear in. Smaller grit will pass through the 70-grit-size sieve and be trapped by the 80 sieve.

Since the 60 openings per linear in. represent $\frac{1}{60}$, or 0.0167, in. and the 70 openings per linear in. represent $\frac{1}{70}$ or 0.0143 in., the 60-grit abrasive can vary by 0.0024 in.

EXAMPLE 1

A series of grit is trapped by a number 30 sieve. (1) What is the designated number of the grit? (2) What is the size of the largest grit in the aggregate? (3) What is the size of the smallest grit in the aggregate? (4) What is the size variation of the grit?

Solution:

1. The designated number of the grit is 24.
2. The largest grit size is

$$G_L = \tfrac{1}{24} = 0.0417 \text{ in.}$$

3. The smallest grit size is

$$G_s = \tfrac{1}{30} = 0.0333 \text{ in.}$$

4. The variation in grit size is

$$G = G_L - G_s = 0.0417 - 0.0333$$
$$= 0.0084 \text{ in.}$$

It should be noted that the grit sizes from 240 to 600 openings per linear in. are very small ($\tfrac{1}{240} = 0.00417$ in. to $\tfrac{1}{600} = 0.00167$ in.) and cannot be separated by mechanically shaking the sieves. These sizes are called the *flour sizes* and must be separated hydraulically.

Manufacturers of grinding wheels will upon request mix varying combinations of grit sizes for special-purpose grinding.

In general, coarse grains should be selected for grinding soft or ductile materials or when fast grinding is desired. The finer the grain size, the higher is the finish achieved. Fine-grain wheels should also be used on brittle and hard materials.

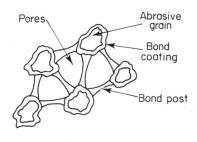

Figure 21.10

The grade, K in the wheel designation of Table 21.1, refers to the strength of the bond. The hardness of a wheel refers to the strength of the bond, not to the hardness of the grit. The grit is held in position by the bond posts, Fig. 21.10. If the bond posts break easily, the wheel is said to be *soft* even though the abrasive is diamond. The range of hardness of the bond increases from A, soft, through Z, hard.

(1) Rough-grinding jobs require grades from the middle to the end of the alphabet (the harder grades). Precision grinding dictates the softer bonds at the beginning of the alphabet. (2) In general the harder the material to be ground, the softer should be the grade to be used. (3) The smaller the area of contact between wheel and work, the harder is the grade permitted. (4) The higher the relationship of work to wheel surface speed, the harder is the grade permitted because the resulting grinding action is softer as the work speed increases. A corollary to this principle is that, if the diameter of the wheel is decreased, the effect is the same as using a narrower-faced wheel. The surface contact area per unit of time is thus decreased, and the grinding action is softer. Thus a harder wheel may be used. (5) Harder grades may be

used if coolants are used. (6) Harder grades should also be used on old machines where vibration is likely to be present.

The number 8 in the wheel notation at the top of Table 21.1 refers to the spacing of the grains. That is, a number 60 grit may be compacted so that the grains touch each other, or the same grit size may be spread over a larger surface area. The structure number ranges from 0, which is a close structure, to 12, which is an open structure. The structure number determines not only the number of cutting edges which will be cutting at any one time but also the size of the pores, Fig. 21.10, which is important for chip clearance.

In general the softer, more ductile, or tougher the material is, the more open is the structure permitted. Surface grinders require a more open structure than cylindrical or tool and cutter grinders do. The more material there is to be removed, the more open is the structure that should be used. Fine finishes require more closed structures.

The last important designation V in the notation of Table 21.1 refers to the bond. There are five types of bond in common use: vitrified, silicate, resinoid, rubber, and shellac. The last three are the organic bonds. Other bonding materials are celluloid and oxidizing materials.

The vitrified-bonded wheels represent the majority of the wheels used in industry, the main ingredient being clay. The abrasive material is mixed with wet clay, which coats each grain. The mixture is pressed into wheels, dried, and kiln fired. The bond transforms into a glass-hard substance which has high strength and is capable of high stock removal. This bond is not affected by oils, water, acids, or normal temperature ranges encountered in grinding. Vitrified bonds are used for fast cutting and general industrial finishing. They should not be used over 6500 sfpm.

The silicate-bonded wheel uses silicate of soda as a bonding material. The mixture of abrasive and silicate of soda is formed into a wheel and baked at low temperatures for long periods (500°F for 24 hours). This bond is weaker than the vitrified-bond wheel. The grinding action breaks these bonds readily. As the grit dulls or the pores clog, the grinding temperature increases and the bond breaks and releases the outer layer of abrasive. This exposes a new layer of sharp grit. The sharp grit generates less heat and thus yields a milder cutting action. This wheel is largely restricted to grinding fine edges on cutting tools and broad-contact surface-grinding operations. Very large wheels should be silicate bonded.

Resinoid bonding material is an organic bond. Wheels so bonded are made by mixing powdered synthetic resin with the abrasive, pressing the mixture into the wheel form in a mold, and baking it in an electric oven. These wheels are very strong and may be operated at surface speeds of up to 9500 sfpm.

Rubber-bonded wheels use natural or synthetic rubber as a bonding agent. The process consists of mixing the abrasive with rubber, rolling the mixture into sheets of the desired thickness, cutting the sheets into the desired diameters, and vulcanizing them. Because of their flexibility they can be used at high surface speeds (16,000 sfpm) for high surface finish. The flexibility also makes possible the manufacture of wheels under $\frac{1}{32}$ in. thick. These wheels may be used as cutoff wheels.

Shellac bonds are also used for high-finishing and thin cutoff wheels. These wheels are baked at low temperatures and because of the low-temperature bond breakdown high finishes are possible. The action of these wheels approaches a burnishing or buffing effect.

Oxychloride- and celluloid-bonded wheels are not very common. Abrasive grains and magnesium oxychloride (oxidizing oil) are mixed and compressed in molds into wheel shapes. Celluloid-bonded wheels are formed by rolling the mixture of the celluloid and the abrasive into sheets and then cutting them into the desired diameters.

EXAMPLE 2

Analyze the type of wheel which would be appropriate for finish-grinding high-speed steel with a 6-in.-diameter straight wheel on a surface grinder with no coolant.

Solution:

1. The material to be ground is high-speed steel, which calls for an aluminum oxide grit. The notation is A.
2. The grit size for finishing may be 60. Thus the notation is A60.
3. The grade required could be K or L. Since the material is hard, the grade should be the softer of the two grades, or K. Thus the number becomes A60-K.
4. The structure could be medium for surface grinding. If the operation were a roughing operation, a medium-open structure could be used. Since the operation is a finishing operation, a medium-closed structure appears to be better. Thus an 8 structure could be used for roughing and a 5 structure for finishing. This would be satisfactory for cylindrical grinding. However, surface grinding requires a more open structure than cylindrical grinding does. Therefore, for finishing on a surface grinder a 6 or 7 structure could be used. Thus the wheel number may be A60-K6.
5. Since the wheel is not a large wheel and the grinding is a finishing operation, the chances are that the heat generated will not be excessive and a vitrified bond could be used. Thus the final designation should be V. The wheel number would be A60-K6V.

21.4. Diamond Wheels

Diamond wheels are used to grind or cut materials such as carbide, glass, stone, marble, and ceramics. The diamonds are opaque bort diamonds used for industrial purposes. They are crushed with heavy manganese steel rollers and then sorted into various grain sizes. In varied degrees of concentration,

TABLE 21.2

	$\underline{D}$	$\underline{150}$	R	$\underline{100}$	B $\frac{1}{4}$		
Diamond abrasive							*Depth of diamond, in.*
D = mined							$\frac{1}{16}, \frac{1}{8}, \frac{1}{4}$
SD = manufactured							
Grit size			*Grade*		*Concentration*		*Bond*
36	100	200	*Soft*	*Hard*	*Low*	*High*	B = resinoid
46	120	240	H	N	25	75	M = metal
60	150	320	J	P	50	100	V = vitrified
80	180	400	L	R			
90		500					
		600					

they are mixed with a bond. Longer life and better finishes are achieved with lower concentration of diamond grit. The reduction in production costs for the lower concentration of diamond grit more than offset the cost of the wheels with higher degrees of diamond grit concentration.

There are three types of bond (See Table 21.2): resinoid, metal, and vitrified. The resinoid-bonded wheels are cool acting and fast cutting. They are therefore suitable for any type of carbide grinding. The metal-bonded diamond wheel is used for offhand grinding of single-point tools. This bond has better resistance to grooving than the resinoid-bonded wheel; its cutting action is not as fast. As pointed out above, the vitrified-bonded wheel combines the qualities of fast cutting and resistance to grooving.

The 80 to 100 grit sizes are used for roughing; 120 to 150, for roughing and finishing carbides; 200 to 240, for finish grinding; and the higher grit numbers, for honing and lapping.

Hard grades are used to grind chip breakers into tool bits. The grinding of very hard carbides may require one of the softer grades.

The concentration number refers to the percentage of abrasive concentration for a given depth of the wheel. Thus a number 25 concentration wheel will have one-fourth the diamonds scattered throughout its structure that a wheel with a 100 concentration number will have.

Wheels of 100 concentration should be used for grinding chip breakers, for cutter, cylindrical, surface, or internal grinding, and for thin cutoff wheels. Reduced concentration of grit in sizes below 240 usually results in excessive wear of the wheel because of the reduction in the number of cutting edges operating. Conversely, with grit sizes greater than 240, the concentration may be reduced. If the concentration is reduced in a vitrified bond, the wheel will act "harder" because of the greater number of bond posts per unit volume. Finer grit size should be used for resinoid wheels.

The depth of the diamond refers to the thickness of the coating measured radially. The diamond grit and the bond are mixed and coated on a metallic or composition disc. The shape of the disc may be plain, cup, or dish depending upon their use.

As with standard grinding wheels, certain precautions must be taken with diamond wheels to ensure longer life and maximum use. These precautions are:

1. The true running of machine spindles and back plates must be maintained to within 0.001 in. for cup wheels. For straight wheels the spindle and back plates must run true within 0.0005 in. when using a resinoid bond and within 0.00025 in. if the bond is vitrified.
2. Correct speeds must be maintained. Resinoid- and vitrified-bonded wheels should run at surface speeds of 5000 to 6000 sfpm. Metallic-bonded wheels may run as low as 3000 sfpm.
3. Before using a diamond wheel, the hardness, grit, and bond must be checked.
4. When grinding carbide tools, the shank and the carbide tip should be rough ground with a 60-grit silicon carbide wheel. The carbide is then finish ground with a diamond wheel. The tool shank should never be ground with a diamond wheel.
5. Diamond wheels should be dressed only when necessary. Resinoid-bonded wheels need not be dressed. For cleaning, a lump of pumice or very fine soft silicon carbide abrasive stick may be used. Metallic- and vitrified-bonded diamond wheels should be dressed with the silicon carbide stick furnished with the wheel.
6. The dressing of cup wheels is accomplished by lapping the face of the wheel on a glass or metal, flat plate charged with silicon carbide grit. A straight diamond wheel may be dressed by mounting it between centers on a cylindrical grinder and grinding it with a silicon carbide vitrified wheel. The grit size of the grinding wheel should be medium and the bond soft. The contact surfaces should rotate in opposition to each other at the point of contact. Light cuts should be taken until the face of the diamond wheel is flat.

   If the wheel is a vitrified-bonded diamond wheel, the face must be opened up with a silicon carbide stick. The stick is pointed and rolled across the face of the diamond wheel until the edges of the wheel feel sharp. The face may then be flattened by the method described above.
7. Excessive pressures must be avoided when grinding with a diamond wheel.
8. When wet grinding, a water soluble coolant or kerosene drip (or wick) should be used to avoid excessive overheating.

21.5. Safety, Wheel Balancing and Dressing, and Cutting Fluids

The surface speeds of grinding wheels are generally high. Table 21.3 shows some typical grinding operations and the recommended wheel surface speeds. The student is cautioned that the wheel speeds are surface speeds, not revolutions per minute.

TABLE 21.3

Grinding operation	Speeds, sfpm
Cylindrical	5,000–6,500
Surface	4,000–6,000
Tool and cutter	4,500–6,500
Internal	2,500–5,000
Organic-bond	8,000–10,000

EXAMPLE 3

An 18-in. wheel operates at 5000 sfpm. What is the rpm of the wheel?

Solution:

$$N_{18} = 5000\frac{\text{ft}}{\text{min}} \times \frac{1}{\pi\frac{18}{12}}\frac{\text{rev}}{\text{ft}}$$

$$= 1062 \text{ rpm}$$

EXAMPLE 4

A 1-in. internal grinding wheel operates at 5000 sfpm. Compare its rpm with the rpm in Example 3.

Solution:

$$N_1 = 5000\left(\frac{1}{\pi\frac{1}{12}}\right)$$

$$= 19,108 \text{ rpm}$$

$$\frac{N_1}{N_{18}} = \frac{19,108}{1062} \simeq 18 \text{ times faster}$$

It should be evident that with this high an rpm extreme care should be taken when using grinding wheels. The following are some of the safety precautions which should be observed:

1. Inspect the wheel for cracks before mounting.
2. Check the spindle speed of the grinder.
3. A blotter should be used on each side of the wheel large enough so that the flange and blotter cover at least one-third of the diameter of the wheel.
4. The wheel should fit properly on the grinder spindle and the flanges be tightened enough to hold the wheel. Excess tightening may crack the wheel.
5. If a work rest is used, the spacing between the work rest and the wheel face should be about $\frac{1}{8}$ in.
6. When first starting a wheel, the operator should stand aside and allow the wheel to come to speed before attempting any grinding.
7. Grinding should be done on that part of the wheel designed for a

particular grinding action. Do not grind on the side of a plain wheel. Excessive pressures should not be employed no matter what kind of grinding is being done. If the wheel speed is slowed by the grinding action, damage to the wheel, work, or both may occur.

All wheels should be tested for balance periodically. These wheels have been balanced by the manufacturer; therefore the bore should not be changed. Large machines are provided with balancing flanges. Wheels may be balanced by shifting the weights provided. Poor balance may be detected by the vibration set up in the machine, poor finish, or difficulty in maintaining size.

Wheels which are not provided with balancing flanges must be *trued* for balance. Wheels which need cleaning or *sharpening* are *dressed*.

Wheels can be trued only if the trueing device is held rigidly in a holder. Attempting to true a wheel with a device held in the hand is almost impossible. Trueing devices cause the diamond or other abrasive to traverse the face of the grinding wheel. On contact the bond posts are broken on the surface of the wheel. The trueing device is moved back and forth across the face of the wheel until the full circumference of the wheel is dressed. The wheel should then run true.

At the same time that trueing is taking place, dressing is also taking place because the breaking of the external layers of bond exposes a new layer of sharp abrasive grains. Dressing may be accomplished with a star wheel type of dresser or a carbide boron or silicon carbide stick.

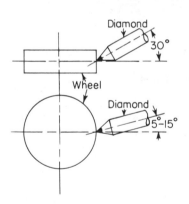

When a diamond dresser is used, it should be set so that the diamond drags the wheel in two directions, as shown in Fig. 21.11. The diamond is set to the high spot on the wheel as the wheel is revolving and traversed across the face of the wheel. With each pass the wheel is fed into the diamond (or the diamond into the wheel) approximately 0.001 in. when the wheel is to be used for finishing. An infeed of 0.002 in. may be used when the wheel is to be used for rough grinding.

Figure 21.11

Slow traverse of the diamond dresser across the face of the wheel should be used for finish grinding operations. A rapid traverse of the diamond dresser across the face of the wheel will produce a free cutting wheel. Too rapid a traverse will leave grooves in the wheel which will be transferred to the work during the grinding operation. Too slow a dressing feed may glaze the wheel and impair the cutting action of the wheel. Since any imperfection dressed into the wheel will be tansferred to the work, a uniform traverse of the diamond across the face of the wheel must be used.

If a wheel is to be used for dry grinding, it should be dressed dry. If it is to be used for wet grinding, the wheel should be dressed wet. The purpose is to protect the diamond. Water may accidentally splash on the diamond during the dressing operation if the wheel is dressed dry on a wet grinder.

The grinding operation generates a great deal of localized heat at the contact point of the wheel and the work. Since grinding is a true cutting process, chips are created. The use of cutting fluids (soluble oils) will, if properly applied, wash away the chips to prevent clogging the pores. The fluid also reduces the localized heating. Fine surface cracks may develop from localized heating of the material. Failure to remove the chips may result in scratched work surfaces or glazing.

The porous structure of the grinding wheel has lead to the development of a method for transporting the coolant to the contact surface between the work and the wheel. The fluid is transported through the spindle to the wheel, which then distributes it by centrifugal force through the porous structure of the wheel to its outer periphery. The faces of the wheel are treated with a coating to trap the fluid and keep it from coming out the sides.

QUESTIONS AND PROBLEMS

21.1 Explain the mechanism by which grit in a grinding wheel removes metal during the grinding operation.

21.2 Why is it desirable that the headstock center should not revolve during the grinding operation?

21.3 Why is it desirable that the grinding table should oscillate along its longitudinal axis at a rate of half the width of the grinding wheel for every revolution of the work?

21.4 How does a universal cylindrical grinder differ in construction from a plain cylindrical grinder?

21.5 Describe some of the capabilities of a CNC grinder.

21.6 Describe the two methods used to hitch feed the grinding wheel across the surface of the work on a surface grinder.

21.7 Describe two methods used for grinding holes.

21.8 There are two types of magnetic chucks used on a surface grinder. Make a sketch of the essential parts of these chucks, and illustrate how they are capable of holding a piece of steel.

21.9 What is plunge grinding? How is it used for grinding diameters to a square shoulder?

21.10 Describe the method used to grind a surface to a sharp corner by dragging the wheel. Is this method effective for grinding to a shoulder on a surface grinder? Explain.

21.11 How is it possible to avoid a bell-mouth condition when grinding internally?

21.12 Explain the principle of through feed on a centerless grinder.

21.13 Viewed from the front of a centerless grinder, if the workpiece revolves in a clockwise direction, in which direction should the drive wheel revolve? The grinding wheel?

21.14 Answer question 21.13 for an internal centerless grinder.

21.15 How does a cutter grinder differ from a cylindrical grinder?

21.16 Describe the principle of a magnetic chuck.

21.17 (a) Describe the four methods used to grind to a shoulder. (b) Repeat part (a) for internal grinding.

21.18 The circumference of a regulating wheel on a centerless grinder is 12 in., and its rpm is 400. What should be the angle of the regulating wheel to achieve a through feed of 332 in. per minute?

21.19 Explain the principle and describe the method used to crush-dress a grinding wheel.

21.20 What are the five factors used to describe a grinding wheel? What function does each of the five factors perform during the grinding operation?

21.21 List three synthetic abrasives found in grinding wheels. Although their functions may overlap, they are nevertheless best suited for a particular type of grinding operation. List the grinding operations for which each of the abrasives is best suited.

21.22 Compare the characteristics of aluminum oxide and silicon carbide as abrasives.

21.23 How is the grit size of a grinding wheel determined?

21.24 Under what conditions should a coarse-grit grinding wheel be used? A fine-grit grinding wheel?

21.25 What is the meaning of the word *grade* when referring to grinding wheels? State and explain some of the conditions under which a soft, medium, and hard grade would be used.

21.26 List several of the bonding materials used in grinding wheels. Discuss the use of each of the bonding materials listed, with reference to: wheel speed, types of materials to be ground, grinding methods, and temperatures generated.

21.27 Explain each of the symbols in the following grinding notations: (a) A100-R-B; (b) A80-M7V; (c) A60-M6R; (d) C46-J7E; (e) D80-L25M.

21.28 A series of grit is trapped in a 120 sieve. (a) What is the grit size? (b) What is the largest grit size possible? (c) What is the smallest grit size possible? (d) What is the variation of grit size that could be found?

21.29 Solve problem 21.28 for a 54-grit wheel.

21.30 Make an analysis of the type of wheel needed to finish-grind hardened steel on a surface grinder with a straight wheel.

21.31   (a) Analyze each of the notations for wheels listed below in the light of the discussion in this section. (b) What kinds of materials should be ground with each of these wheels? Why?

C36-J5V;   C20-K4B;   A60-T6R;   A46-M5V

21.32   (a) What are the three types of bond used in a diamond wheel? (b) What are the three ranges of grit size used in a grinding wheel? (c) Why are soft grade wheels generally used to grind hard materials, and hard grade wheels used to grind soft materials? (d) Explain the concentration number shown in a diamond-wheel grinding notation.

21.33   What are some of the precautions which must be taken with diamond wheels?

21.34   How is a diamond wheel dressed?

21.35   Comment on the wheel surface speeds recommended for the various types of grinding operations.

21.36   List some of the safety precautions that must be observed when using a grinding wheel.

21.37   How does trueing differ from dressing a grinding wheel?

21.38   When dressing a grinding wheel, what effect does a fast traverse have on the resulting grinding action? A slow traverse of the diamond dresser?

Quality and
Dimensional Control

22

22.1. Quality Control Through Dimensioning

Functional dimensioning of a workpiece is of the greatest importance to the success of any machining operation. Thus a part to be machined on a milling machine should be dimensioned so that the tool (or table) will move from a base line to the first hole, from the first hole to the second hole, etc. This is shown in Fig. 22.1(a). The same part to be drilled or bored on a jig borer requires dimensioning from a reference corner or reference point or hole, as shown in Fig. 22.1(b). If the machine has numerical control, the dimensions are referenced to two datum lines (two-axis) or three datum lines (three-axis). The dimensions are then shown as + or − so that they may be programmed to the right or left and above or below these reference datum lines, as shown in Fig. 22.1(c). Note that, had the reference point been taken at the lower left corner, Fig. 22.1(c), all dimensions would have been programmed (+).

In each instance the tolerances are applied to avoid accumulation. It is important to understand that the tolerances applied in the three drawings in Fig. 22.1(a through c) must be applied in such a way that they reflect the method of machining. The machinist should never be relied upon to calculate missing dimensions or tolerances.

It should be evident that N/C machining eliminates the need to consider complex jigs, fixtures, tolerance accumulation, etc. The accuracy of the machining operation is built into the machine. The dimensional quality of the machined part is a function of the accuracy of the program.

Before discussing tolerances and their applications, certain terms need to be explained.

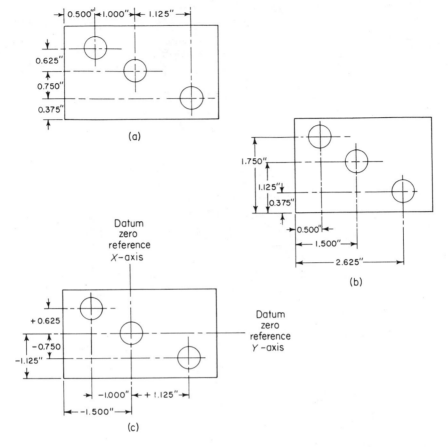

Figure 22.1

1. Flatness refers to the variation of the workpiece surface from a reference plane. Thus Fig. 22.2(a) shows the dimensional tolerance zone and the flatness zone. The flatness zone should lie within the tolerance zone.

2. Parallelism refers to surfaces or lines which are equidistant from each other at all points. Variations may occur, but they should fall well within the tolerance zones which have been applied to the drawing. Thus in Fig. 22.2(b) tolerance zone wholly encloses the parallel zone.

3. Straightness refers to the deviation from a straight line of the surface or center line of a workpiece. The tolerance zone and the deviation from the center line are shown in Fig. 22.2(c).

4. Squareness indicates perpendicularity between a line or plane and a datum line. The workpiece surface should fall between two parallel lines, both of which are perpendicular to the datum plane, as shown in Fig. 22.2(d).

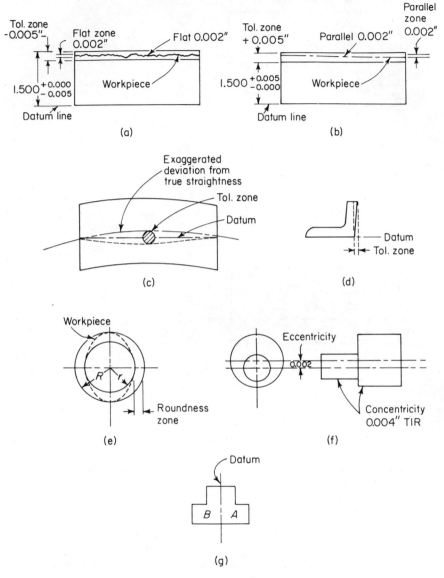

Figure 22.2

5. Roundness deals with the condition of a surface relative to its center line. If a piece has roundness, all parts on the surface of the piece are equidistant from the center line. Thus the roundness zone deals with the locus of points which fall within the surfaces of two circles having minimum and maximum diameters. In Fig. 22.2(e) the workpiece

cylinder is shown within the two circles with radii R and r. This work-piece would meet the print requirement of roundness.

6. Concentricity deals with the relationship between two cylindrical surfaces. The center lines of both cylinders should coincide. If the center lines do not coincide, the two surfaces are said to be eccentric to each other. Thus the surfaces of the two diameters in Fig. 22.2(f) could be round, yet the smaller diameter's center line is shown displaced from the center line of the larger diameter by 0.002 in. If the piece is rotated about one of the diameters, the other diameter will register two times the center line displacement on a dial indicator. Therefore, a print requirement of 0.004 in. FIR (full indicator reading) would mean a center line displacement of 0.002 in.

7. Symmetry deals with dimensions duplicated on both sides of a center line. Thus in Fig. 22.2(g) side A is identical with side B and is said to be symmetrical with side B about the datum center line.

Surface finish is another of the factors which enter into the analysis of dimensional characteristics of a work surface. Surface quality has been standardized according to a statistical average of the frequency of occurrence of irregularities in a work surface. The average used is called the *root mean square* (rms). It is designated in microinches. The better the surface finish, the smaller is the number of microinches. One-millionth of an inch (0.000001 in.) is a microinch.

Surfaces can exhibit many characteristics: roughness height, roughness width, waviness, flaw, and lay direction. These are shown in Fig. 22.3(a).

Lay direction is a characteristic of the surface which is created by the method of machining. The surface roughness is measured at 90° to the direction of the lay. The conditions of the surface are indicated with the symbols and notations shown in Fig. 22.4(a).

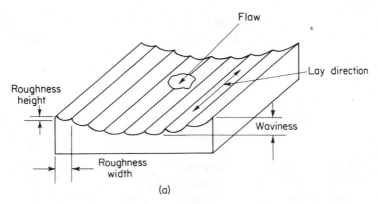

(a)

Figure 22.3

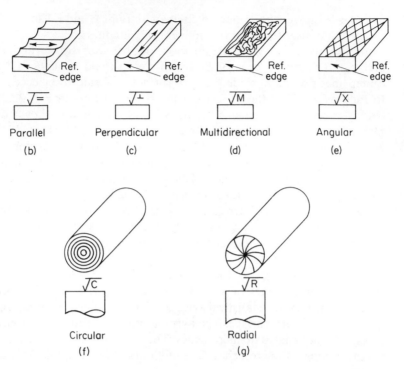

Parallel
(b)

Perpendicular
(c)

Multidirectional
(d)

Angular
(e)

Circular
(f)

Radial
(g)

Figure 22.3 (Cont.)

Figure 22.3(b) shows a parallel lay that is parallel to a reference edge. Figure 22.3(c) shows a perpendicular lay that is perpendicular to the reference edge. Figure 30.3(d) shows a multidirectional lay. Figure 22.3(e) shows an angular lay which has a double angular direction to the reference edge. The circular lay, Fig. 22.3(f), and the radial lay, Fig. 22.3(g), are two additional possibilities.

The symbols for designating the waviness height, roughness height, and lay and roughness widths are shown in Fig. 22.4(a). Multiple operations may be shown by using a pyramid arrangement, as shown in Fig. 22.4(b).

The roughness height is the height of the irregularities. It is measured with a profilometer which uses a sharp stylus. This stylus follows the irregularities, rising and falling as it moves across them in a direction perpendicular to the lay. The movement of the stylus is amplified and causes an electrical meter to register its movement. The face of the meter is calibrated in rms values.

An instrument called a *brush surface analyzer* may also be used. The irregularities are recorded on a strip chart. The charts may be used to record roughness and waviness. Roughness height is then calculated by drawing a line through the center of the profile. Readings, or measurements, are taken

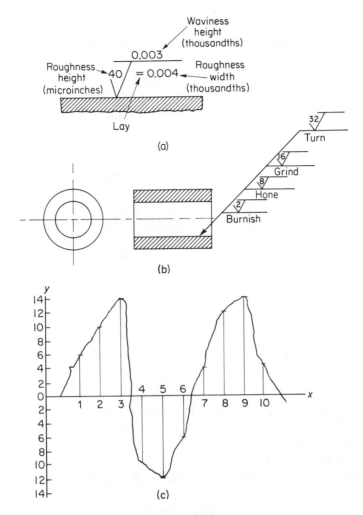

Figure 22.4

above and below this reference line and averaged to get the arithmetic average. Figure 22.4(c) shows the profile and the various ordinate lengths. The rms is obtained by taking the square root of the sum of the squares of the absolute values y measurements divided by the number of y measurements.

The mathematics is

$$\sum y_n = y_1 + y_2 + y_3 + \ldots + y_n$$

$$\text{The average} = \frac{\sum y_n}{n}$$

$$\text{rms} = \sqrt{\frac{\sum y_n^2}{n}}$$

EXAMPLE 1

Calculate the arithmetic average and the rms value for Fig. 22.4(c).

Solution:

The y and y^2 values are

Ordinate	y	y^2
1	6	36
2	10	100
3	14	196
4	10	100
5	12	144
6	6	36
7	4	16
8	12	144
9	14	196
10	4	16
	92	984

The arithmetic average is

$$\frac{\sum y_n}{n} = \frac{92}{10} = 9.2 \text{ microinches}$$

The rms is

$$\sqrt{\frac{\sum y_n^2}{n}} = \sqrt{\frac{984}{10}} = 9.9 \text{ microinches}$$

Another, less reliable, method for checking surface quality is with the use of roughness comparison blocks. The comparison may be made visually with or without a microscope or by comparing the feel of the surface of these blocks with that of the workpiece surface. The feel is usually accomplished with the fingernail.

Table 22.1 shows some of the rms ranges for the various machining processes.

TABLE 22.1

Operation	RMS, 10^{-6} in.	Operation	RMS, 10^{-6} in.
Lapping	2–8	Burnishing	2–4
Honing	2–10	Turning	20–300
Polishing	2–10	Shaping	20–300
Reaming	8–50	Sand casting	500–1000
Grinding	5–150	Extrusion	10–250
Broaching	15–60	Sawing	250–1000
Drilling	75–200	Blanking	30–100
Milling	20–300	Forging	100–400
		Die casting	15–100

22.2. Tolerances, Limits, and Clearances

The purpose of studying the application of tolerances, limits, and allowances is to impress upon the student that their selection is planned and very important. Their application to dimensioning is not haphazard, and their misuse is probably one of the most important causes of grief in bringing design problems to fruition in manufacturing and assembly.

Tolerances, limits, and clearances are related to manufacturing processes in that the tolerances and limits which are applied to a dimension are usually a clue to the kind of machining process which should be used. Thus a dimension which carries a ± 0.0002 in. might better be machined on a grinder than on a lathe or milling machine. The time spent in trying to hold ± 0.0002 in. on a lathe might raise the cost of production to the point where it would prove uneconomical to produce the parts. On the other hand, a part which carries ± 0.015 in. might better be machined on a lathe or a milling machine than precision ground.

The latter statement points up the fact that, although *open* tolerances usually do not dictate fine surface quality (nor do *close* tolerances dictate coarse surface quality) since they are independent of each other, the tolerance and surface quality nonetheless are coupled. That is, a tolerance of ± 0.0002 in. will usually require a low microfinish and a high microfinish usually means open tolerances.

Since it is impossible to machine parts to an exact dimension, all dimensions on a drawing should be given a tolerance zone, or variation from the base dimension. The basic size, or dimension, is the theoretical size desired. Thus tolerances are defined as unavoidable variations from the base size. Referring to

$$1.546^{\pm 0.002}$$

the ± 0.002 indicates that the base size of 1.546 in. may vary either side of the 1.546 in. by ± 0.002. This is called a bilateral tolerance.

A unilateral tolerance is written as

$$1.546^{+0.002}_{-0.000}$$

and states that the base dimension may vary by $+0.002$ but may not be smaller than 1.546 in.

Another way to write $1.546^{\pm 0.002}$ is in the form of limits, or

$$\frac{1.548}{1.544}$$

This form gives the permissible extreme values.

Thus tolerances apply to one dimension, whereas limits apply to a range of, or extreme, permissible values applied to one surface.

The term *allowance* applies to the least difference between *two* dimensions, or the maximum interference between mating surfaces.

The writing of tolerances and the application of allowances may be based on the concepts of *basic hole size* or *basic shaft size*. The basic hole concept dictates that the basic size be applied to the hole and all allowances be applied to the mating shaft size. In the basic shaft size concept the basic size is applied to the shaft and all allowances are applied to the mating holes. Thus in the latter a shaft may be machined to one size and various allowances applied to several bores which are to function differently on the same shaft.

Fits are divided into three types: clearance, transition, and interference. Clearance fits are those which provide that between mating parts any combination of limits will result in any bore size being larger than any shaft size. Interference fits are those which result in interference for any combination of hole and shaft sizes. Transition fits will result in either clearance or interference for various combinations of hole and shaft sizes.

A committee of Americans, British, and Canadians met in 1952 and standardized the limits and allowances which could be used to achieve various desirable assembly conditions. Symbols were established to designate the fits and classes. Thus the symbol RC3 indicates a class 3 running fit. The five classes which were established are:*

$$RC = \text{running or sliding}$$
$$LC = \text{location clearance}$$
$$LT = \text{location transition}$$
$$LN = \text{location interference}$$
$$FN = \text{force or shrink}$$

Running or sliding fits (RC) are intended to cover the range of fit needed when one part moves inside another.

The location fits (LC, LT, and LN) are intended to be used for location throughout the clearance, transition, and interference ranges. They are to be used for the assembly of parts which are stationary.

TABLE 22.2

Class and fit	RC$_2$	LC$_2$	LT$_2$	LN$_2$	FN$_2$
Hole	+0.9*	+1.4*	+2.2*	+1.4*	+1.4*
	−0.0	−0.0	−0.0	−0.0	−0.0
Shaft	−0.5	0.0	+0.8	+2.5	+3.9
	−1.1	−0.9	−0.6	+1.6	+3.0
Allowance	+0.5	+0.0	−0.8	−0.2	−1.6
	+2.0	+2.3	+2.8	−2.5	−3.9

*The + and − requirement is the amount, *in thousandths*, to be added to or subtracted from the base dimension.

*Tables for the five classes may be found in any standard handbook.

The force or shrink fits (FN) are set up to yield constant bore pressure for all size ranges.

Table 22.2 shows the rela ionship between the limits and allowances (clearance and interference) for the holes and shafts for a class 2 fit, nominal-size 4-in. diameter.

EXAMPLE 2

Using the values in Table 22.2 and a 4-in. nominal diameter: (1) Calculate the limits for a class 2 fit. (2) Analyze your results, and check them against the table. (3) Calculate the tolerances, and write the dimensions. (4) Show graphically the relationships between the bore and the shaft sizes. Use the basic hole system.

Solution:

1. The limits are:

	Hole	*Shaft*
RC_2	$4.0000 + 0.0000 = 4.0000$	$4.0000 - 0.0005 = 3.9995$
	$4.0000 + 0.0009 = 4.0009$	$4.0000 - 0.0011 = 3.9989$
LC_2	$4.0000 + 0.0000 = 4.0000$	$4.0000 + 0.0000 = 4.0000$
	$4.0000 + 0.0014 = 4.0014$	$4.0000 - 0.0009 = 3.9991$
LT_2	$4.0000 + 0.0000 = 4.0000$	$4.0000 + 0.0008 = 4.0008$
	$4.0000 + 0.0022 = 4.0022$	$4.0000 - 0.0006 = 3.9994$
LN_2	$4.0000 + 0.0000 = 4.0000$	$4.0000 + 0.0025 = 4.0025$
	$4.0000 + 0.0014 = 4.0014$	$4.0000 + 0.0016 = 4.0016$
FN_2	$4.0000 + 0.0000 = 4.0000$	$4.0000 + 0.0039 = 4.0039$
	$4.0000 + 0.0014 = 4.0014$	$4.0000 + 0.0030 = 4.0030$

2. The analysis is:

		Minimum clearance	*All.*		*Maximum clearance*	*All.*	*Tolerance*
RC_2	Sm. hole	4.0000		Lg. hole	4.0009		$+0.0009$
	Lg. shaft	3.9995		Sm. shaft	3.9989		-0.0006
			$+0.0005$			$+0.0020$	
LC_2	Sm. hole	4.0000		Lg. hole	4.0014		$+0.0014$
	Lg. shaft	4.0000		Sm. shaft	3.9991		-0.0009
			0.0000			$+0.0023$	
LT_2	Sm. hole	4.0000		Lg. hole	4.0022		$+0.0022$
	Lg. shaft	4.0008		Sm. shaft	3.9994		-0.0014
			$+0.0008$			$+0.0028$	
LN_2	Sm. hole	4.0000		Lg. hole	4.0014		$+0.0014$
	Lg. shaft	4.0025		Sm. shaft	4.0016		$+0.0009$
			$+0.0025$			-0.0002	
FN_2	Sm. hole	4.0000		Lg. hole	4.0014		$+0.0014$
	Lg. shaft	4.0039		Sm. shaft	4.0030		$+0.0009$
			$+0.0039$			-0.0016	

3. The dimensions with the tolerances applied are:

	Hole	*Shaft*
RC_2	$4.0000^{+0.0009}_{-0.0000}$	$3.9995^{+0.0000}_{-0.0006}$
LC_2	$4.0000^{+0.0014}_{-0.0000}$	$4.0000^{+0.0000}_{-0.0009}$
LT_2	$4.0000^{+0.0022}_{-0.0000}$	$4.0008^{+0.0000}_{-0.0014}$
LN_2	$4.0000^{+0.0014}_{-0.0000}$	$4.0016^{+0.0009}_{-0.0000}$
FN_2	$4.0000^{+0.0014}_{-0.0000}$	$4.0030^{+0.0009}_{-0.0000}$

4. The analysis is shown in Fig. 22.5(a). Note that c represents clearance; i represents interference.

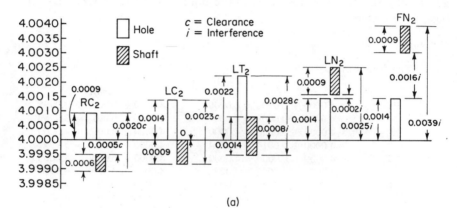

(a)

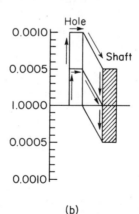

(b)

Figure 22.5

The group indicated as "selective assembly" needs further explanation. The purpose of this category is to permit open tolerances for manufacturing purposes and closer tolerances for assembly purposes. It then becomes possible to manufacture shafts and bushings to tolerances of ±0.001 in. and match shafts and bushings to tolerances of ± 0.0005 in. An analysis may be done according to the following Example 3.

EXAMPLE 3

Assume bushings have been manufactured for selective assembly to $1.0000^{+0.0010}_{-0.0000}$ and shafts to $1.0005^{+0.0000}_{-0.0010}$. (1) Draw the analysis chart for assembly of two groups of shafts and bushings of 0.0005 each. (2) Write the dimensions and tolerances for the two groups of shafts and bushings.

Solution:

1. The analysis chart is shown in Fig. 22.5(b).
2. The two groups of dimensions are:
   Group 1

$$\text{Bushing} = 1.0000^{+0.0005}_{-0.0000} \qquad \text{Shaft} = 1.0000^{+0.0000}_{-0.0005}$$

   Group 2

$$\text{Bushing} = 1.0005^{+0.0005}_{-0.0000} \qquad \text{Shaft} = 1.0005^{+0.0000}_{-0.0005}$$

22.3. *Dimensional Control of Threads*

Thread forms and terminology are covered in Section 14.4. The student should review that section before proceeding with this one.

Since the use of the Unified Thread series is replacing the American Standard National form, the following will be related to the Unified series.

The symbol for the Unified series is written 1A. The numeral 1 indicates the class, and the letter A indicates that the thread referred to is an external thread. The letter B is used to indicate an internal thread. There are three classes of threads: 1A and 1B for free assembly, 2A and 2B for most screws and nuts, and 3A and 3B for selective fits.

The Unified series has been classified as:

> Coarse = UNC
> Fine = UNF
> Extra fine = UNEF
> Uniform pitches = 4, 6, 8, 12, 16, 20, 28, 32, and UNS

The uniform pitches refer to one pitch for various diameters; 4, 6, 8, 12, 16, 20 and designated as UNC. The symbol would be 4 UNC, 6 UNC, etc. The 28 and 32 series are designated as UNF, and the symbols would be 28 UNF and 32 UNF. The UNS is a special series of modified threads.

Table 22-3 shows a section of a table of thread limits. These tables may be found in any Standard Handbook. The use of the table will be illustrated with an example.

TABLE 22.3

External, (screw), ¾–10 UNC–1A	Internal, (nut), ¾–10 UNC–1B

Major diameter
    Maximum = 0.7482
    Minimum = 0.7288
Pitch diameter
    Maximum = 0.6832
    Minimum = 0.6744
Minor diameter
        = 0.6255
	Major diameter
	    = 0.7500
	Pitch diameter
	    Maximum = 0.6965
	    Minimum = 0.6850
	Minor diameter
	    Maximum = 0.6630
	    Minimum = 0.6420

EXAMPLE 4

(1) Referring to Table 22.3, list the data for a ¾-10 UNC, class 1A and 1B thread, and find the allowance. (2) Analyze the pitch diameter (PD), and calculate the maximum allowance and the minimum allowance.

Solution:

1. The data may be listed as follows:

	Nut		Screw	
	Maximum	*Minimum*	*Maximum*	*Minimum*
PD	0.6965	0.6850	0.6832	0.6744
Major diameter	0.7500	0.7500	0.7482	0.7288
Minor diameter	0.6630	0.6420	0.6255	0.6255

Allowance

$$\text{Smallest PD, (nut)} = 0.6850$$
$$\text{Largest PD (screw)} = \overline{0.6832}$$
$$\text{Allowance} = \overline{0.0018}$$

2. The pitch diameter analysis is as follows:

Maximum nut	= 0.6965	Minimum nut	= 0.6850
Minimum screw	= 0.6744	Maximum screw	= 0.6832
Maximum allowance	= $\overline{0.0221}$	Minimum allowance	= $\overline{0.0018}$

22.4. Metric Equivalents

Aside from the standards which will eventually be established for threads, tapers, etc., the conversion from one system to another may be accomplished with the use of two constants. They are: 25.4 millimeters per inch (25 mm/in.) and 453.6 grams per pound (453.6 gm/lb). Conversions may be made by the method of cancelling units.

EXAMPLE 5

1. Convert 12 in. to mm.
2. Convert 45 mm to in.

Solution:

1. The conversion of 12 in. to mm is

$$12 \text{ in.} \times 25.4 \frac{\text{mm}}{\text{in.}} = 304.8 \text{ mm}$$

2. The conversion of 45 mm to in. is

$$45 \text{ mm} \times \frac{1 \text{ in.}}{25.4 \text{ mm}} = 1.77 \text{ in.}$$

Figure 22.6(a) shows a thumb screw dimensioned in the British system. The conversions have been made to metric dimension in Fig. 22.6(b). It should be noted that the thread symbol in the British system gives the major diameter and the number of threads per in.

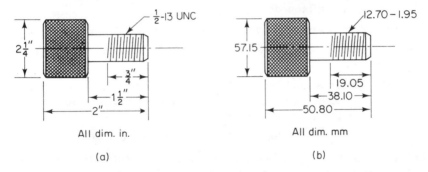

All dim. in.

(a)

All dim. mm

(b)

Figure 22.6

In the metric system, Fig. 22.6(b), the thread symbol gives the major diameter in mm and instead of the number of threads, the pitch is given. Thus

$$\frac{1}{2} \text{ in.} \times 25.4 \frac{\text{mm}}{\text{in.}} = 12.7 \text{ mm}$$

and

$$\frac{1}{13 \text{ thd/in}} = 0.0769 \frac{\text{in.}}{\text{thd}} \times \frac{25.4 \text{ mm}}{\text{in.}} = 1.95 \frac{\text{mm}}{\text{thd}}$$

All other conversions are made by multiplying the dimension in inches and 25.4 mm/in.

Tolerances may be applied in the same manner as in the British system. All metric dimensions are mm. They are shown in Table 22.4.

TABLE 22.4

Tolerances

Bilateral British	Bilateral Metric
1.750 ± 0.002	44.45 ± 0.05
$1.750 {-0.002}^{+0.004}$	$44.45 {-0.05}^{+0.10}$
Unilateral British	Unilateral Metric
$1.750 {-0.000}^{+0.002}$	$44.45 {-0.00}^{+0.05}$
Limits British	Limits Metric
1.750	44.45
1.754	44.55

QUESTIONS AND PROBLEMS

22.1 Explain the dimensioning procedures used in Fig. 22.1(a through c).

22.2 Explain the concept of tolerance zone for (a) flatness; (b) parallelism; (c) straightness; (d) roundness.

22.3 How does roundness differ from concentricity? Explain fully.

22.4 May a multiple-diameter workpiece be eccentric and symmetrical at the same time?

22.5 Make drawings, and dimension Fig. 22.7(a) for drilling the holes: (a) on a milling machine; (b) on a jig borer; (c) on a numerical-control drill press. Use the center lines of the block in part (c).

22.6 Repeat problem 22.5 for Fig. 22.7(b). Use the *X* and *Y* axis for part (c).

22.7 Dimension a drawing for numerical-control drilling of Fig. 22.7(b). You are to use a reference point 5 in. to the left of the *Y* center line and 4 in. below the *X* center line.

22.8 Repeat problem 22.5 for the crank arm in Fig. 22.7(c). Use the vertical center line through hole *B* for the numerical-control dimensioning.

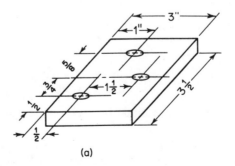

(a)

Figure 22.7

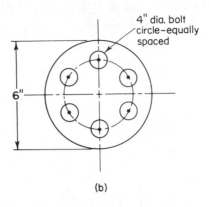

(b)

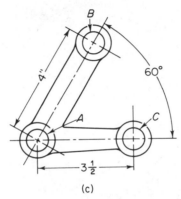

(c)

Figure 22.7   (Cont.)

22.9   Dimension a drawing for numerical-control drilling for Fig. 22.7(c) which is to use a reference point 2 in. to the left of and 1 in. below hole *A*.

22.10   Define the concept of lay. Make a sketch of lay for the following symbols: (a) $\sqrt{\perp}$, (b) $\sqrt{M}$, (c) $\sqrt{=}$, (d) $\sqrt{R}$, (e) $\sqrt{C}$, and $\sqrt{X}$ and (f)$\sqrt{x}$.

22.11   Explain each of the notations associated with the following symbols: (a) $_{60}\sqrt{\frac{0.004}{\perp 0.002}}$ and   (b) $_{10}\sqrt{\frac{0.0015}{M 0.001}}$

22.12   Explain: (a) roughness height; (b) roughness width; (c) waviness. Relate each to a drawing for a part turned on a lathe.

22.13   Using a pyramid arrangement, write the symbol for the following sequence of operations: drilling, reaming, and polishing. Select your values from Table 22.1.

22.14   Repeat question 22.13 for the following sequence: milling, grinding, and lapping.

22.15   Describe the use of a profilometer and of a brush surface analyzer. How does each record roughness height?

22.16 Find (a) the arithmetic average and (b) the rms for Fig. 22.8(a).

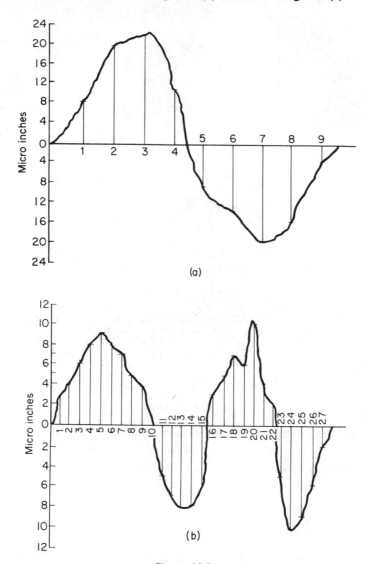

Figure 22.8

22.17 Define: tolerance, limit, and allowance. Illustrate each.

22.18 Define the concept of basic hole size. When is it advisable to use the basic shaft concept? Illustrate the latter.

22.19 Define and illustrate each of the following fits: (a) clearance; (b) transition; (c) interference.

22.20 What is the purpose of transition fits?

22.21　Explain the difference in usage between the location fits and the running and force fits.

22.22　Find (a) the arithmetic average and (b) the rms for Fig. 22.8(b).

22.23　Using the values in Table 22.5 and a 4-in. nominal diameter: (a) Calculate the limits for a class 3 ft. (b) Analyze your results, and check them against Table 22.5. (c) Calculate the tolerances, and write the dimensions. (d) Show graphically the relationships between the bore and the shaft sizes. Use the basic hole system.

TABLE 22.5

Class and fit	RC_3	LC_3	LT_3	LN_3	FN_3
Hole	+0.9	+2.2	+1.4	+1.4	+1.4
	0	0	0	0	0
Shaft	−1.4	−1.4	+1.0	+2.9	+4.9
	−2.3	0	+0.1	+2.0	+4.0
Allowance	+1.4	0	−1.0	−0.6	−2.6
	+3.2	+3.6	+1.3	−2.9	−4.9

22.24　Using the values in Table 22.6 and a $2\frac{1}{2}$ in. diameter: (a) Calculate the limits for a class 1 fit. (b) Analyze your results, and check them against Table 22.6. (c) Calculate the tolerances, and write the dimensions. (d) Show graphically the relationships between the bore and the shaft sizes. Use the basic hole system.

TABLE 22.6

Class and fit	RC_1	LC_1	LT_1	FN_1
Hole	+0.5	+0.7	+1.2	+0.7
	0	0	0	0
Shaft	−0.4	0	+0.4	+1.8
	−0.7	−0.5	−0.3	+1.3
Allowance	+0.4	0	−0.4	−0.6
	+1.2	+1.2	+1.5	−1.8

22.25　Assume the dimension of a bore to be $2.0000^{+0.0018}_{-0.0000}$ and the dimension of a shaft to be $2.0007^{+0.0000}_{-0.0012}$. (a) Draw the analysis chart, and (b) write the dimensions for two groups of hole and shaft combinations for selective assembly.

22.26　Solve problem 22.25 for selective assembly for three groups.

22.27　How does the Unified Thread system differ from the American National Form system?

22.28　Explain the notation 1A and 1B with reference to the Unified Thread system.

22.29 Describe each of the following thread notations: (a) UNC; (b) UNF; (c) UNEF. What is the purpose of the uniform pitch series? The UNS series?

22.30 (a) List the data from Table 22.7 in the same manner as in Example 4 in this chapter for a ½-13 UNC class 2 thread. Calculate the allowance. (b) Write the pitch-diameter analysis for this thread.

TABLE 22.7

½-13 *UNC-2A*	½-13 *UNC-2B*
Major diameter	Major diameter
Maximum = 0.4985	= 0.5000
Minimum = 0.4876	
Pitch diameter	Pitch diameter
Maximum = 0.4485	Maximum = 0.4565
Minimum = 0.4435	Minimum = 0.4500
Minor diameter	Minor diameter
= 0.4041	Maximum = 0.4340
	Minimum = 0.4170

22.31 Write the metric equivalent dimensions for Fig. 22.1(a through c).

22.32 Repeat Example 22.31 for Fig. 22.7(a through c).

22.33 Write the metric equivalent dimensions for Fig. 22.9.

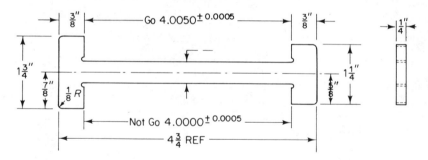

Figure 22.9

22.34 Write the dimension 2.674–2.680 in. in both British and Metric systems as: (a) Bilateral; (b) Unilateral; (c) Limits.

Toolmaking

23

23.1. The Height Gage

Before studying this chapter, it is advisable that the student refer to Sections 9.2, 9.3 and 16.2.

Of all the precision instruments except the micrometer, the height gage shown in Fig. 23.1(a), is probably the most widely used instrument for measuring and layout. Height gages may be purchased with frames from 12 to 72 in. long. The main scale may be divided into 40 divisions/in., each division equal to 0.025 in.; or into 20 divisions/in., in which case each division equals 0.050 in. The vernier scale is divided into 25 or 50 parts respectively so that it reads in increments of 0.001 in.

The standard scriber is shown in Fig. 23.1(a). An offset scriber, Fig. 23.1(b), may also be used to measure or scribe lines or surfaces. The offset scriber uses the surface of a precision surface plate as the zero reference plane. The depth gage, Fig. 23.1(c), is used to take readings of internal shoulders or other inaccessible measurements. The last-word indicator is used for taking measurement readings or to transfer readings from stacked gage blocks. The last-word indicator is shown in Fig. 23.1(d).

One of the first principles in the use of a height gage is always to take readings or set up dimensions to a reference or datum surface. The use of the height gage will best be illustrated with several examples.

EXAMPLE 1

It is required that the part in Fig. 23.2(a) be measured with a height gage and all the dimensions inserted in the drawing.

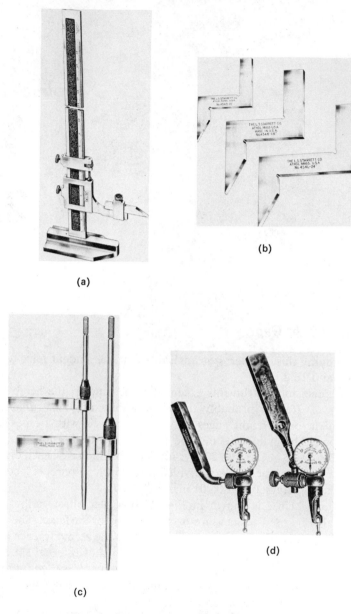

(a)

(b)

(c)

(d)

Figure 23.1   *(Courtesy of The L.S. Starrett Company.)*

Solution:

  1. Before taking any readings, it is important that all burrs and foreign matter be removed from the workpiece. The workpiece is then placed on a surface plate and the offset scriber placed in the height gage. Note that a last-word indicator could have been substituted for the scriber.

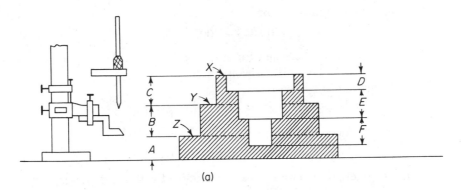

(a)

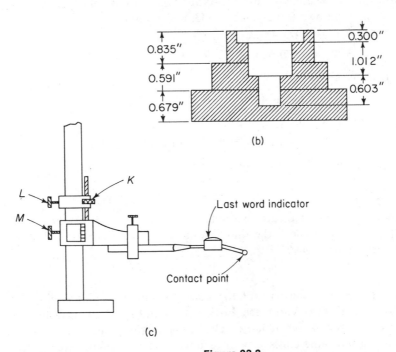

(b)

(c)

Figure 23.2

A reference reading is taken off the surface plate. Assume this reading to be 0.005 in.

2. The vernier slide is then raised so that the bottom face of the scriber is above the first step Z, Fig. 23.2(a). Very carefully the vernier slide is lowered until the scriber rests on surface Z. Sliding the scriber on and off the surface Z will tell whether the scriber is too low or too high. Assume the height-gage reading of this surface to be 0.684 in. The

first dimension A will be

$$0.684 - 0.005 = 0.679 \text{ in.}$$

3. This process is repeated for surfaces Y and X. Assume the readings to be 1.275 and 2.110 respectively.
Dimension B will be

$$1.275 - 0.684 = 0.591 \text{ in.}$$

Dimension C will be

$$2.110 - 1.275 = 0.835 \text{ in.}$$

4. The internal dimensions may be obtained with the depth-gage attachment instead of the offset scriber. Assume a reference reading to be taken at the surface X, Fig. 23.2(a). When the scriber touches the surface X, the reading is 7.645 in. Assume the readings of the shoulders from the top down to be 7.345, 6.333, and 5.730 in.
Dimension D will be

$$7.645 - 7.345 = 0.300 \text{ in.}$$

Dimension E will be

$$7.645 - (6.333 + 0.300) = 1.012 \text{ in.}$$

Dimension F will be

$$7.645 - (5.730 + 0.300 + 1.012) = 0.603 \text{ in.}$$

5. The dimensions calculated above are shown in Fig. 23.2(b).

EXAMPLE 2

Assume a last-word indicator mounted in a height gage, as shown in Fig. 23.2(c), is used to check the dimensions A, B, and C in Fig. 23.2(a). What are these dimensions?

Solution:

1. The vernier is raised so that the indicator contact point is slightly above face X of the workpiece. Lock screw L in Fig. 23.2(c) is fastened, and lock screw M is left loose. The fine-adjustment nut K is rotated until the indicator contact point touches the face of the workpiece and the indicator needle reads 0. The lock screw M is locked and the 0 reading checked. The vernier is read and found to read 6.282 in. This is the reference reading.

2. The height gage is removed, the vernier is lowered, and the process in part 1 is repeated for surface Y. Assume this reading to be 5.447 in. on the height gage.
Dimension C will be

$$6.282 - 5.447 = 0.835 \text{ in.}$$

3. Assume the height-gage reading for surface Z to be 4.856 in. The dimension B will be

$$6.282 - (4.856 + 0.835) = 0.591 \text{ in.}$$

4. The height-gage reading is assumed to be 4.177 in. for the surface plate.
   The dimension A will be

$$6.282 - (4.177 + 0.835 + 0.591) = 0.679 \text{ in.}$$

It should be noted that the surface plate may be used to establish a reference reading.

EXAMPLE 3

Assume three holes have been jig-bored into the plate shown in Fig. 23.3(a). Using the height gage and the last-word indicator, determine the height-gage reading for the three holes when the plate is in the position shown in Fig. 23.3(a) and when the plate is rotated 90°, as shown in Fig. 23.3(b). Assume the reference reading taken at the surface plate is 1.225 in. when the needle reads 0.

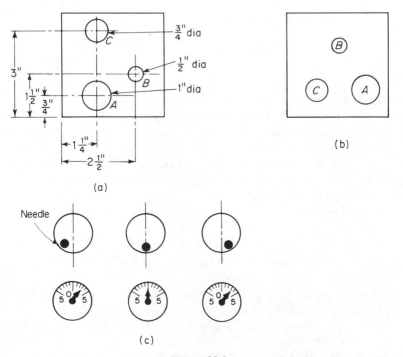

Figure 23.3

Solution:

1. For Fig. 23.3(a)

   The reading for hole *A* should be

   $$1.225 + 0.750 - \frac{1.000}{2} = 1.475 \text{ in.}$$

   The reading for hole *B* should be

   $$1.225 + 1.500 - \frac{0.500}{2} = 2.475 \text{ in.}$$

   The reading for hole *C* should be

   $$1.225 + 3.000 - \frac{0.750}{2} = 3.850 \text{ in.}$$

2. For Fig. 23.3(b)

   The reading for hole *A* should be

   $$1.225 + 1.250 - \frac{1.000}{2} = 1.975 \text{ in.}$$

   The reading for hole *C* should be

   $$1.225 + 1.250 - \frac{0.750}{2} = 2.100 \text{ in.}$$

   The reading for hole *B* should be

   $$1.225 + 2.500 - \frac{0.500}{2} = 3.475 \text{ in.}$$

Each of the above readings is set on the vernier scale without disturbing the indicator. The indicator contact point is then placed carefully into each hole. The height gage is moved very carefully from side to side in the hole. At the lowest point in the hole the needle should read 0. The three positions of the indicator needle are shown in Fig. 23.3(c). They are exaggerated.

A better method for checking these dimensions would be to rest the workpiece on a precision parallel and clamped to a precision angle plate. Once the holes have been checked in one direction, the angle plate, with the work clamped in position, is rotated 90° and the holes checked in this direction. See Fig. 11.8(b and c).

The use of the height gage for the layout of keyways was discussed in Section 11.4. The student should review the process at this point.

One of the more convenient accessories for layout is the height master, Fig. 23.4(a). It uses 1 in. gage blocks which, together with the graduated dial makes possible the setting of heights to 0.0001 in., or 0.002 mm.

The profile projector, Fig. 23.4(b) is capable of magnifications of from 5× to 500×. Obviously small errors, when magnified, become detectable and may be measured. Figure 23.4(c) shows a much more sophisticated opti-

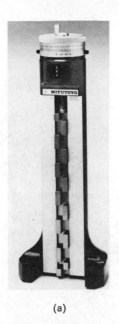

(a)

(b)

Figure 23.4 [(a) Courtesy of Mitutoyo Corp.; (b) courtesy of Nikon Inst. Division, Ehrenreich Photo-Optical Ind. Division; (c) courtesy of Jones and Lamson, Waterbury Farrel Division of Textron, Inc.]

(c)

Figure 23.4   (Cont.)

cal comparator. This unit is equipped with a mini-computer which calculates diameters, steps, and provides reports on deviation from true dimensions.

23.2. How to Make a Cutter

Any number of methods may be used to make helical cutters. One method used is to lay out the end of the cutter blank and then work to the layout lines. Another method, which has greater precision, is to calculate the required offset for a given depth of cut.

Either single-angle or double-angle fluting cutters may be used. Fluting cutters, Fig. 23.6, may be used to cut the tooth face, gullet, and secondary clearance in one cut.

Figure 23.5(a) shows the work rotating *away* from the 12° side of a double-angle fluting cutter as the table feeds from right to left. The 12° face of the tooth should be rotated away from the 12° face without exception. Because of the rotation of the work, the feed, and the depth of cut the gear-cutter teeth would distort the tooth form if this were not done. The distortion of the larger cutter angle (which cuts the secondary clearance) may be tolerated. Figure 23.5(a) shows a left-hand double-angle cutter machining a

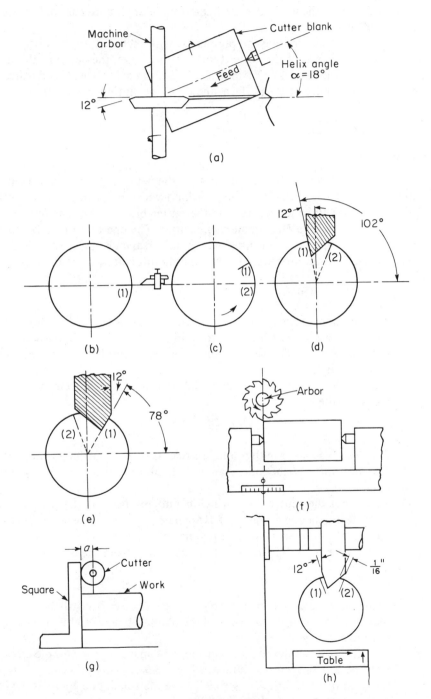

Figure 23.5

right-hand helix in the work. A right-hand double-angle cutter should be used to cut a left-hand helix.

Double-angle cutters may be purchased with included angles of 52, 60, or 65°. Since the face of the cutter tooth is always 12°, the cutters will have double angles of 12° and 40°, 12° and 48°, and 12° and 53°. Short-lead helical-angle cutters require that the face angle of the fluting cutter be greater than 12°.

Cut-and-try method.

EXAMPLE 4

Assume that you are to machine a 4-in. diameter, 18° right-hand helical cutter. The cutter is to have 22 teeth, a land width of $\frac{1}{16}$ in., a face width of $\frac{3}{8}$ in., and a 0° rake angle. Assume the cutter blank to be machined and ready for fluting with a 60° double-angle cutter. The operation is to be done on a universal milling machine fitted with a universal indexing head. Describe the layout, setup, and procedure for machining this cutter, using the *cut-and-try* method.

Solution:

1. The cutter blank is mounted on a nut arbor, fitted with a dog, and placed between the centers of a dividing head. The milling-machine table is set at 0°. The cutter is mounted on the milling-machine arbor approximately over the center of the work.

2. The dividing head is set to index 22 divisions. The movement of the index handle is

$$\frac{40}{N} = \frac{40}{22} = 1\frac{9}{11} \text{ turns}$$

$\frac{9}{11} \times 66 = 54$ holes in the 66-hole circle (Cincinnati Milling Company) The movement of the index handle is 1 full turn and 54 spaces on the 66-hole circle.

3. To lay out the center lines, which eventually become the face of the cutter teeth, the top of the blank is "picked up" with the height gage and the use of a scriber. Assume a reading of 5.476 in. Since the diameter of the work is 4 in., 2 in. should be subtracted from the assumed reading. Thus

$$5.476 - 2.000 = 3.476 \text{ in.}$$

If this reading is set on the height gage, the scriber will be on the center line of the work. The end of the blank is blued and line 1 scribed, as shown in Fig. 23.5(b).

The work is indexed 1 full turn and 54 spaces in the 66-hole circle, and line 2 is scribed, as shown in Fig. 23.5(c). This procedure is followed until all 22 lines are scribed. When finished, line 1 should be in the position shown in Fig. 23.5(b).

4. The next movement is to bring line 1 into position so that it will be parallel to the 12° side of the double-angle fluting cutter. This means that line 1 must be indexed 12° beyond the vertical center line, or 90° + 12° = 102°. The required index movement for a right-hand helix, left-hand cutter is

$$\frac{102°}{9°} = 11\frac{3}{9} \text{ turns of the index handle}$$

The movement of the index handle is 11 full turns and 22 spaces ($\frac{1}{3} \times 66 = 22$ spaces) in the 66-hole circle. This movement will bring line 1 into position, as shown in Fig. 23.5(d).

Indexing 1 full turn and 54 holes in the 66-hole circle will bring each succeeding layout line into the 12° offset position.

If it had been necessary to cut a left-hand helix, a right-hand cutter would have been used. The layout lines would have been as shown in Fig. 23.5(e). Line 1 should then be indexed

$$90° - 12° = 78°$$

The movement of the index handle will be

$$\frac{78°}{9°} = 8\frac{2}{3} \text{ turns}$$

Thus 8 full turns and 44 spaces in the 66-hole circle ($\frac{2}{3} \times 66 = 44$ spaces) will be needed to bring layout line 1 into the position shown in Fig. 23.5(e). Then 1 full turn and 54 spaces in the 66-hole circle will bring each succeeding line into position.

5. The next step in the procedure is to set the center line of the cutter arbor directly over the face of the workpiece and longitudinal center line, as shown in Fig. 23.5(f). This may be accomplished in any one of a number of ways. Probably the simplest method is to use a precision square. The square is placed against the face of the work and caused to register against the side of the milling arbor. Assume the milling arbor to be $1\frac{1}{2}$ in. in diameter. If the table is moved 0.750 in., which is the distance a in Fig. 23.5(g), the center lines will coincide, as shown in Fig. 23.5(f).

6. With the cutter in position, a trial cut is taken. It is important to remember that the land, $\frac{1}{16}$ in., is to be maintained. Therefore, the cutter must not cross the layout line or destroy the $\frac{1}{16}$-in. land. Assume the first cut to be as shown in Fig. 23.5(h).

The cut-and-try method requires that the operator move the table laterally and up until the 12° side of the cutter coincides with layout line 1 and the $\frac{1}{16}$-in. land is established, as shown in Fig. 23.5(d). The longitudinal table feed and the index handle should never be changed while establishing the depth of cut.

7. The next step in the procedure is to select the gears for the milling of the required lead, helix angle 18°. The lead required is

$$L = \frac{\pi D}{\tan \alpha} = \frac{\pi 4}{\tan 18°} = \frac{\pi 4}{0.325} = 38.666 \text{ in.}$$

By using the method in Section 15.6, it is found that the gears needed are

$$\frac{\text{Driven}}{\text{Driving}} = \frac{72 \times 48}{28 \times 32}$$

These gears yield a lead of 38.570 in. with an error of 0.070 in. This error is not prohibitive when distributed over more than 38 in.

8. The gears are mounted in the gearbox, and the table is swiveled to 18°. Note that the center of rotation of the milling table remains under the center line of the milling arbor. The vertical-feed graduated dial is set at zero, and the first cut taken. The longitudinal-table stops may be set to ensure that the cutter does not run into the dog after the cut is completed. The table is then lowered and moved back to the starting point, the workpiece is indexed, the table raised to the 0 reading, and the second flute is cut. This process is continued until all the flutes are cut.

It should be pointed out that a finishing cut may be required. If this becomes necessary, the depth of cut in the above procedure should be such that material is left on the face side of the tooth for finishing.

Offset by the calculation method. If an angle cutter is used which has a radius r, Fig. 23.6(a), the offset O_r for a rake angle θ_r may be obtained from the equation

$$O_r = R \sin (\theta_r + \theta_c) - c \sin \theta_c - r(\cos \theta_c - \sin \theta_c)$$

EXAMPLE 5

Assume a 4-in. plain milling cutter having a 5° positive rake angle to be milled by using a 60°-included double-angle cutter. The face of the tooth is to be $\frac{3}{8}$ in. What is the offset if the cutter has a $\frac{1}{16}$-in. gullet radius?

Solution:

The offset is

$$
\begin{aligned}
O_r &= R \sin (\theta_r + \theta_c) - c \sin \theta_c \\
&\quad - r(\cos \theta_c - \sin \theta_c) \\
&= 2 \sin (5° + 12°) - \tfrac{3}{8}(\sin 12°) \\
&\quad - \tfrac{1}{16}(\cos 12° - \sin 12°) \\
&= 0.4588 \text{ in.}
\end{aligned}
$$

$\theta_r = 5°$
$\theta_c = 12° \text{ (from } 60° = 12° + 48°)$
$c = \frac{3}{8} \text{ in.}$
$r = \frac{1}{16} \text{ in.}$
$R = \frac{4}{2} = 2 \text{ in.}$

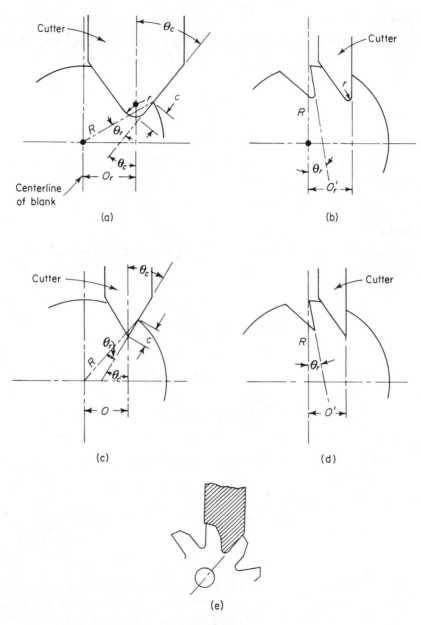

Figure 23.6

If the cutter has radius r but the angle $\theta_c = 0°$, Fig. 23.6(b), the offset O'_r for a rake angle θ_r may be found from the general equation above by substituting $\theta_c = 0$. The equation reduces to

$$O'_r = R \sin \theta_r - r$$

EXAMPLE 6

Calculate the offset if all the conditions in Example 5 prevail, except that $\theta_c = 0°$, Fig. 23.6(b).

Solution:

$$O'_r = R \sin \theta_r - r$$

$$= 2 \sin 5° - \tfrac{1}{16}$$

$$= 0.112 \text{ in.}$$

$\theta_r = 5°$
$\theta_c = 0°$
$r = \tfrac{1}{16}$ in.
$R = 2$ in.
$c = \tfrac{3}{8}$ in.

If it has no radius, $r = 0$, Fig. 23.6(c), the offset may be found by substituting in the general equation. The general equation reduces to

$$O = R \sin (\theta_r + \theta_c) - c \sin \theta_c$$

EXAMPLE 7

Calculate the offset if the conditions of Example 5 prevail, except that the radius $r = 0$.

Solution:

$$O = R \sin(\theta_r + \theta_c) - c \sin \theta_c$$

$$= 2 \sin (5 + 12) - \tfrac{3}{8} \sin 12$$

$$= 0.5068 \text{ in.}$$

$\theta_r = 5°$
$\theta_c = 12°$
$r = 0$
$R = 2$ in.
$c = \tfrac{3}{8}$ in.

If the cutter angle $\theta_c = 0°$, Fig. 23.6(d), and the cutter radius $r = 0$, the equation for offset reduces to

$$O' = R \sin \theta_r$$

EXAMPLE 8

Calculate the offset if the conditions of Example 5 prevail, except that $\theta_c = 0°$ and $r = 0$.

Solution:

$$O' = R \sin \theta_r$$

$$= 2 \sin 5°$$

$$= 0.1744 \text{ in.}$$

$\theta_r = 5°$
$\theta_c = 0°$
$r = 0$
$R = 2$ in.
$c = \tfrac{3}{8}$ in.

Two corrections must be made when setting the helical cutter in the milling machine. One correction is for the table setting, and the other is for the offset. The correction for setting the helix angle α may be obtained from the helix angle of the cutter, the rake angle θ_r, and the face angle θ_c. This corrected angle setting may be obtained from the equation

$$\tan \alpha' = \tan \alpha \times \cos (\theta_r + \theta_c)$$

If the cutter to be machined is a helical cutter requiring that the table be swiveled, then an offset correction must also be made for the projection of the form of the tooth parallel to the angle cutter. This may be accomplished by multiplying the offset by the cosine of the corrected swivel angle. Thus

$$O_h = \text{offset} \times \cos \alpha' \qquad \begin{array}{l} \alpha' = \text{corrected table angle} \\ O_h = \text{corrected offset} \end{array}$$

EXAMPLE 9

(1) Calculate: (1) the corrected angle setting of the milling table in Example 5 through 8; (2) the corrected offsets if the helix of the cutter which is to be machined is to have an angle of 18°.

Solution:

1. The corrected helical angles are
   Examples 5 and 7

   $$\tan \alpha' \doteq \tan \alpha \cos (\theta_r + \theta_c) \qquad \begin{array}{l} \theta_r = 5° \\ \theta_c = 12° \\ \alpha = 18° \end{array}$$

   $$= \tan 18° \cos (5 + 12°)$$

   $$= \tan 18° \cos 17° = 0.311$$

   $$\alpha' = 17.26°$$

   Examples 6 and 8

   $$\tan \alpha' = \tan \alpha \cos (\theta_r + \theta_c) \qquad \begin{array}{l} \theta_r = 5° \\ \theta_c = 0° \\ \alpha = 18° \end{array}$$

   $$= \tan 18° \cos (5° + 0°) = 0.3237$$

   $$= 17.94°$$

2. The corrected offsets are
   Example 5

   $$O_{rh} = \text{offset} \times \cos \alpha' = 0.4588 \cos 17.26°$$

   $$= 0.438 \text{ in.}$$

   Example 6

   $$O'_{rh} = 0.112 \cos 17.94°$$

   $$= 0.107 \text{ in.}$$

   Example 7

   $$O_h = 0.5068 \cos 17.26°$$

   $$= 0.484 \text{ in.}$$

   Example 8

   $$O'_h = 0.1744 \cos 17.94°$$

   $$= 0.166 \text{ in.}$$

In examples 5 through 8, once the type of fluting cutter to be used is decided upon, it is set over the center line of the work.

The appropriate calculation is made and the cutter is offset the calculated amount.

The data from Example 4 will be used to illustrate the calculations for determining offset and table setting for cutting the flutes.

EXAMPLE 10

Using the data from Example 4, calculate (1) the corrected table setting and (2) the corrected offset from the center line of the workpiece. The cutter is to have no rake angle, and the fluting cutter is to have no radius r.

Solution:

1. The corrected helix angle is

$$\tan \alpha' = \tan \alpha \cos (\theta_r + \theta_c)$$
$$= \tan 18 \cos (0° + 12°)$$
$$\alpha = 17.63°$$

$R = 2$ in.
$\alpha = 18°$
$c = \frac{3}{8}$ in.
$\theta_r = 0°$
$\theta_c = 12°$
$r = 0°$
$O_h = \,?$

2. The corrected offset is

$$O = R \sin (\theta_r + \theta_c) - c \sin \theta_c$$
$$= 2 \sin (0° + 12°) - \tfrac{3}{8}(\sin 12°)$$
$$= 0.338 \text{ in.}$$
$$O_h = 0.338 \cos 17.63°$$
$$= 0.322 \text{ in.}$$

If a profile cutter, Fig. 23.6(e), is used, the calculations are the same as when using a double-angle fluting cutter.

23.3. Making a Reamer

Layout, offset, and rake angles may be achieved by using the cut-and-try method described in Section 23.2. This method is preferred to the method of calculation. Tap and reamer fluting cutters (see Fig. 23.7a) are also double-angle cutters with their teeth well rounded. The major difference between making a cutter and making a reamer is that reamer flutes are not evenly spaced. This is to avoid chatter set up by sympathetic vibration. Certain fundamental rules must be followed when the layout lines at the end of the blank are indexed. They are:

1. Each face of every tooth must have an oppositely corresponding face exactly matching it.
2. Index spaces which are 180° apart must be the same size.
3. If the smallest index space follows the largest index space, the angular difference should not exceed ±2°.
4. The helix angle for helical fluted reamers should be between 10 and 15°.

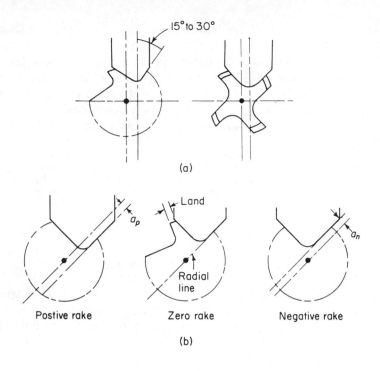

(a)

(b)

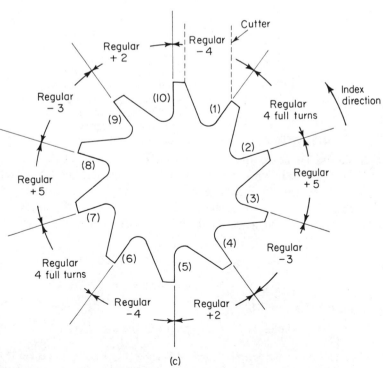

(c)

Figure 23.7

Figure 23.7(b) shows how the cutter may be offset to achieve positive, zero, or negative rakes. (Hand reamers usually have a slight negative rake.) The land width depends upon the diameter of the reamer and the number of flutes to be cut. Reamers from $\frac{1}{8}$ to $\frac{1}{2}$ in. in diameter should have 6 teeth; $\frac{1}{2}$ to 1 in., 8 teeth; 1 to $1\frac{1}{2}$ in., 10 teeth; $1\frac{1}{2}$ to $2\frac{1}{4}$ in., 12 teeth; and $2\frac{1}{4}$ to 3 in., 14 teeth.

EXAMPLE 11

Determine the movement of the index handle to lay out a 10-flute reamer.

Solution:

1. The regular indexing is

$$\frac{40}{N} = \frac{40}{10} = 4 \text{ full turns of the index handle}$$

2. Since 6 spaces in the 54-hole plate (Cincinnati Milling Company) is equal to 1°, the maximum allowable difference between two divisions on the reamer is ± 12 spaces.* Therefore, for the 54-hole circle throughout, the indexing is as follows:

Face cut	Spacing in the 54-hole plate
1	See part 3
2	4 full turns
3	4 full turns + 5 spaces
4	4 full turns − 3 spaces
5	4 full turns + 2 spaces
6	4 full turns − 4 spaces
7	4 full turns
8	4 full turns + 5 spaces
9	4 full turns − 3 spaces
10	4 full turns + 2 spaces
To start	4 full turns − 4 spaces

3. It should be noted that, once the layout is completed, line 1, Fig. 23.7(c), will be in a horizontal position. To position line 1 to match the 30° side of the double-angle cutter, the work must be indexed 60° counterclockwise. This is accomplished by moving the index handle 6 full turns and 36 spaces in the 54-hole circle, or

$$\text{Degrees required} = 60°$$

$$9° \times 6 \text{ full turns} = 54°$$

$$\text{Part of a turn} = \overline{6°}$$

Since 6 holes equal 1°,

$$6 \text{ holes} \times 6° = 36 \text{ spaces in the 54-hole circle}$$

*NOTE: The Brown and Sharpe Company dividing head has 2 spaces equal 1° in the 18-hole plate and 3 spaces equal 1° in the 27-hole plate. Thus the maximum allowable difference is ± 4 spaces in the 18-hole plate and ± 6 spaces in the 27-hole plate.

The movement of the index handle to set the 30° side of the double-angle cutter is therefore 6 full turns plus 36 spaces in the 54-hole circle.

It should also be noted that, once the 30° side of the double-angle fluting cutter coincides with the layout line, the depth of the flute is controlled by the width of the land. Thus it is desirable to cut opposite flutes before going to the next flute. That is, if flute 1, Fig. 23.7(c), is cut first, the work should be indexed 180° ($\frac{40}{2} = 20$ turns of the index handle) and flute face 6 cut; then flutes 2 and 7, etc.

23.4. Relieving on a Lathe

Cutters may be relieved with a backing-off attachment on a lathe. A cam, single- or multiple-lobe, causes the follower to feed the tool into the work about 0.010 in. for each $\frac{1}{16}$ in. of tooth thickness. The follower then drops off and the cam rises and moves in again, as shown in Fig. 23.8. The cam is geared to the spindle so that it may revolve as many times as is necessary for each revolution of the work. The rpm of the work and the longitudinal feed of the tool must be kept somewhat smaller than for regular turning.

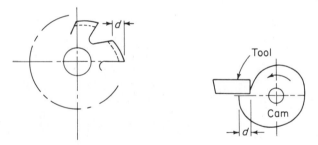

Figure 23.8

23.5. Grinding Cutter Teeth

After all the flutes have been cut and all the teeth have been relieved on the lathe, the cutter is hardened and tempered. The next operation is to mount the cutter on an arbor and grind the secondary and primary clearances. The cutter grinder is shown in Fig. 23.9(a) with some of the accessories. For grinding, a high-speed steel cutter and aluminum oxide vitrified-bonded 46- to 80-grit K or L wheel may be used. The wheel may be straight, dish, or flare cup, Fig. 28.9(b). This discussion will be restricted to the use of a straight and a cup wheel.

The wheel rotates as shown in Fig. 23.9(c) and (d). Figure 23.9(c) shows what is referred to as *off-grinding* because the wheel rotates off the cutting edge. The force of the grinding wheel against the tooth holds the tooth on

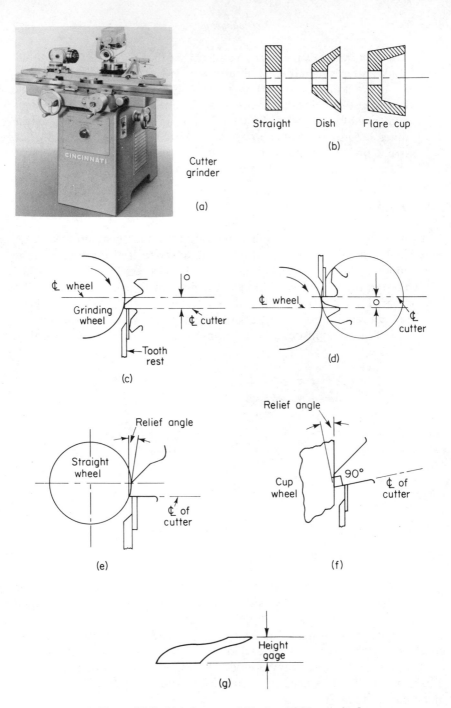

Cutter grinder

(a)

Straight   Dish   Flare cup

(b)

₵ wheel

Grinding wheel

O

₵ cutter

Tooth rest

(c)

₵ wheel

O

₵ cutter

(d)

Relief angle

Straight wheel

₵ of cutter

(e)

Relief angle

Cup wheel

90°

₵ of cutter

(f)

Height gage

(g)

Figure 23.9 [(*a*) *Courtesy of Cincinnati Milacron, Inc.*]

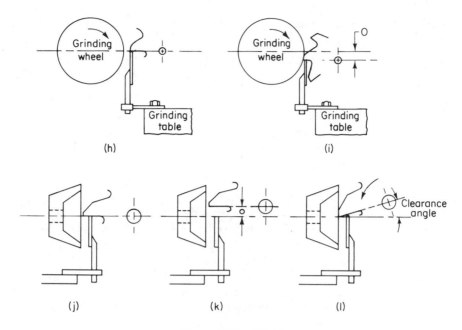

Figure 23.9   (Cont.)

the tooth rest which makes the method safe. However, a burr is raised on the cutting edge which must be stoned. Also, if care is not used, the cutting edge may be burned when using this method.

Figure 23.9(d) is called *on-grinding* because the grinding wheel contacts the cutting edge of the cutter first. The tendency to burn the cutting edge or raise a burr on it is less likely. The cutting edge is also sharper with this method. The danger is in the need for the operator to use great care in holding the tooth against the tooth rest. Should he relax his grip, the grinding wheel will pull the tooth away from the tooth rest. The tooth will rotate into the wheel and severely damage the cutter.

The use of a straight wheel for grinding clearance on a cutter tooth makes use of the fact the the periphery of the wheel falls away from the tooth below and above the center line of the wheel. This is shown in Fig. 23.9(e).

When using a cup wheel, the cutter must be rotated to provide the necessary clearance angle. This is shown in Fig. 23.9(f).

The cutter to be ground is placed on a mandrel which is then placed between the centers of the grinding machine. No dog is used.

If a straight wheel is used, the headstock center, the grinding wheel, and the tooth rest are all adjusted to the center line of the headstock. A special height gage is used, as shown in Fig. 23.9(g). The setting is shown in Fig. 23.9(h). This type of action produces a hollow-ground land.

The wheel head is raised the offset amount, O, Fig. 23.9(i). Note that the cutter tooth and the tooth rest remain fixed because, in this method, both are fixed to the table of the machine. The equation for calculating the offset, the amount the wheel head is raised, is

$$O = 0.0087 \; DC$$

C = clearance angle
O = offset
D = dia of the straight wheel
     or dia of the cutter

If a cup wheel is used, good practice dictates that the wheel center line, the machine center line, and the tooth rest should be aligned, Fig. 23.9(j). The tooth rest is fastened to the wheel head so that, as the wheel head is lowered and the tooth rest moves down (or up), it remains on the center line of the wheel head, as shown in Fig. 23.9(k). The cutter is then rotated so that the face of the tooth registers against the tooth rest, as shown in Fig. 23.9(l). This produces the clearance angle and a straight land.

Stops are set on the machine table so that the table can be moved longitudinally across the straight or cup wheel. This is accomplished with the hand-feed lever shown in Fig. 23.9(a).

The cutter is held radially against the tooth rest by a light hand pressure. Once a pass has been made across the face of the wheel, the cutter, Fig. 23.9(l), is rotated clockwise so that the tooth rest is deflected by the next tooth. Since the tooth rest extension is made from spring steel, it will return to its neutral position once it has passed the next tooth. A counterclockwise pressure on the cutter will register this tooth on the tooth rest ready for the grinding of the second tooth. The process is repeated until all the teeth have been ground.

Once all the teeth have been ground, the lateral feed of the wheel head is moved so that the wheel will cut again, if necessary. The feed per pass is usuall about 0.002 in.

In most instances, compensation for wheel wear must be made. This is accomplished by grinding all the teeth, rotating the cutter 180°, infeeding 0.002 in., and regrinding all the teeth. This process is repeated until the grinding operation is completed.

EXAMPLE 12

Given a 4-in.-diameter plain milling cutter to be ground with a clearance angle of 6° with the use of an 8-in.-diameter straight wheel. Calculate the offset of the center line of the wheel head.

Solution:

The offset for a straight wheel is

$$O = 0.0087 \; DC = 0.0087 \times 6 \times 8$$

$D = 8$ in.
$C = 6°$

$$= 0.418 \text{ in.}$$

EXAMPLE 13

Calculate the offset in Example 12 if a cup wheel is to be used.

Solution:

    The offset for the cup wheel is

$$O = 0.0087 \ DC = 0.0087 \times 4 \times 6$$
$$= 0.209 \text{ in.}$$

$D = 4$ in.
$C = 6°$

    A graduated tilting head may be used with either the straight or cup wheel. In both instances the graduated tilting head is rotated to the required angle, and the tooth rest set to the tooth after tilting the head.

    When grinding helical cutters, the wheel head (not shown) is angled slightly so that the grinding wheel will clear the tooth being ground. The tooth rest is angled so that it rests on the face of the cutter, as shown in Fig. 23.10(a). As the table is moved toward the left (the cutter tooth is held by hand pressure against the tooth rest), the cutter rotates so that grinding takes place above the tooth rest. Since there are so many different helical angles which must be ground, the desired rotation is achieved by the combined action of the tooth rest and the longitudinal motion of the table.

    Stagger-tooth cutters are ground on the tooth rest, shown in Fig. 23.10(b), adjusted so that the point of the tooth rest is on the center line of the wheel. Each helix angle registers on the corresponding angle of the tooth rest.

    Form cutters are ground with the tooth rest registered against the back

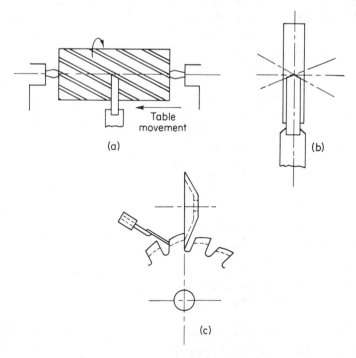

(a)

Table movement

(b)

(c)

Figure 23.10

of the formed tooth being ground, as shown in Fig. 23.10(c). The face of the formed tooth has been machined with the back of the tooth used as a register point. The form of the tooth is therefore never disturbed during the grinding process.

23.6. The Jig Borer

Jig borers are machines used for the accurate machining of holes in size and location [See Fig. 23.11(a and b).]. Their accuracy stems from the accuracy machined into the casting and the method used to control the movement of the worktable and spindle. Three methods are employed: (1) the end-measuring-rod method; (2) the method which relies upon the accuracy of the lead screw; and (3) the method which uses a graduated scale and an optical measuring instrument.

The machine which uses the end measuring rods is equipped with V troughs, at the end of which is an accurate dial indicator graduated in 0.0001 in. per division. This indicator has a 1-in. travel. The end measuring rods have great precision. They come in increments of 1 in. Jig borers are equipped with two troughs, one to control the longitudinal and the other to control the lateral positioning of the table.

The location of the holes in a workpiece is scribed into the surface and carefully center punched. A reference edge, line, hole, or center-punch mark is picked up with an indicator or center finder in such a manner that the center of the spindle is directly over the edge, line, hole, or centerpunch mark. Once located, all operations are referenced to this location. Note point *A* in Fig. 23.12(a).

The end measuring rods together with a tubular micrometer are placed in the trough. The micrometer is lengthened until the indicator needle on the dial indicator reads zero. If a movement of 1 in. is desired, a 1-in. segment of the end measuring rods is removed, the table is moved until the indicator needle reads zero again, and the operation is completed. The table is ready for the next movement.

EXAMPLE 14

Using the finished print in Fig. 23.12(a), explain the process of machining the three holes on a jig borer.

Solution:

The part is mounted on a pair of precision parallels and clamped lightly to the jig-borer table. Edges *B* and *C* are checked with an indicator for squareness.

The next operation is to locate the corner *A*. This is accomplished by moving the table so that edge *B* is approximately under the center line of the spindle. With the use of a *bow-leg* attachment and an indicator, Fig.

(a)

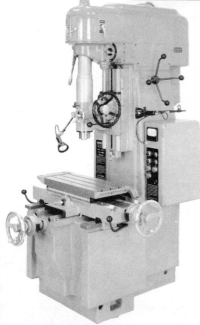

(b)

Figure 23.11 [(a) *Courtesy of Pratt and Whitney Company, Inc.; (b) courtesy of Moore Special Tool Company, Inc.*]

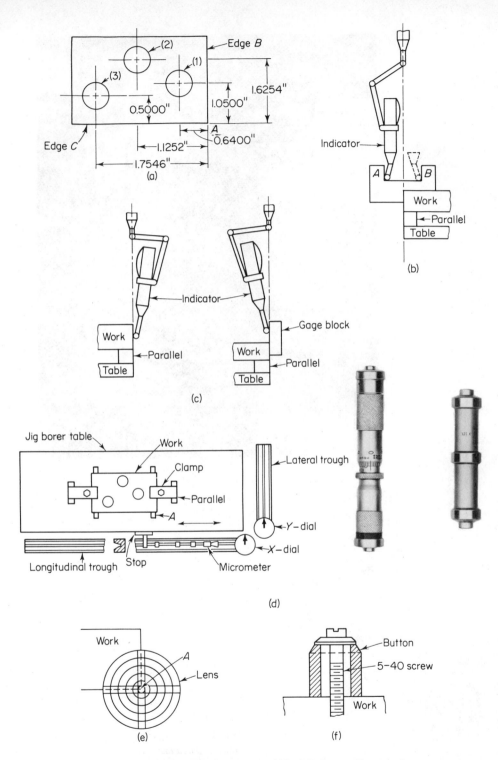

Figure 23.12 (*Photo courtesy of The L.S. Starrett Company.*)

23.12(b), or a precision-gage block, Fig. 23.12(c), the spindle is partially rotated until the needle rests zero to zero in both positions shown.

In Fig. 23.12(b) the table is adjusted until the needle reads zero to zero when the machine spindle is rotated 180°. In Fig. 23.12(c) the indicator tip is caused to contact the edge of the work, raised, rotated 180°, and lowered against the gage block, as shown. In both positions the needle must read zero-zero.

Once the edge B, Fig. 23.12(a), is located under the center line of the spindle, the end measuring rods of appropriate length and the tubular micrometer which reads in increments of 0.0001 in., are placed in the trough, Fig. 23.12(d), and adjusted so that the indicator needle reads zero. It should be noted that the micrometer used, reads from 4 to 5 in. Thus a dimension of 8.4522 in. is made from a 4.4522-in. micrometer and 4.0000-in. rod length.

The entire process is repeated for the edge of the work marked C in Fig. 23.12(a).

The completion of the above two steps should locate the center line of the spindle directly over the edge A in Fig. 23.12(d). This is the reference point for controlling the longitudinal and lateral movement of the table.

Assume the end measuring rods and the micrometer to be 8.0000 in. long and the lateral end measuring rods and micrometer to be 6.0000 in. long. In Fig. 23.12(a) it is desired to move longitudinally 0.6400 in. and laterally 1.0500 in. Therefore, the new longitudinal length of the end measuring rods and the micrometer is

$$8.0000 - 0.6400 = 7.3600 \text{ in.}$$

The micrometer is set to 4.3600 in. and used with a 3.0000-in. end measuring rod. The longitudinal table travel is adjusted until the machine dial indicator needle reads zero. The table and work will have moved 0.6400 in.

The adjusted length for the lateral movement of the table is

$$6.0000 - 1.0500 = 4.9500 \text{ in.}$$

The micrometer is set at 4.9500 in. No end measuring rod is needed. The table and work are moved until the indicator needle reads zero. The center line of the spindle should be over the vertical center line of hole 1.

Hole 1 is center drilled, drilled, and bored to size. (Good jig-bore practice requires that the holes should be drilled on a drill press.)

To locate hole 2, the table is again adjusted longitudinally and laterally with point A as a reference. Thus from

$$8.0000 - 1.1252 = 6.8748 \text{ in.}$$

the longitudinal rod length to be used is 2.0000 in., and the micrometer setting is 4.8748 in.

The lateral setting is

$$6.0000 - 1.6254 = 4.3746 \text{ in.}$$

and may be set directly on the micrometer. Rods are not needed.

To locate hole 3, the rod length to be used is 2.0000 in., and the micrometer setting used is 4.2454 in. for longitudinal setting of the table. This is obtained from

$$8.0000 - 1.7546 = 6.2454 \text{ in.}$$

For lateral setting of the table the rod length to be used is 1.0000 in., and the micrometer setting is 4.5000 in. from

$$6.0000 - 0.5000 = 5.5000 \text{ in.}$$

It is important to realize that all movements are referenced to point *A* so that all error between holes is not cumulative.

The same movement could have been accomplished by using a jig borer with a very accurate lead screw and an automatic positioning device. The automatic positioning of the table removes any error due to backlash or end thrust from the feed screw. The use of an accurate lead screw in conjunction with an accurate vernier scale, Fig. 23.11(b), or an accurate graduated dial makes it possible to achieve accuracies formerly possible only with end measuring rods. In these instances all readings are referenced to the zero position on the vernier or dial. Automatic positioning and other improvements in construction of the modern jig borer when used with numerical control now make it possible to tell the machine what to do electrically within very accurate limits.

Optically controlled jig borers use a small magnifying microscope to position the table and work under the center of the spindle. Two sets of double cross hairs at 90° to each other intersect a series of concentric circles, as shown in Fig. 23.12(e).

Another method of locating holes accurately is to use toolmaker's buttons, Fig. 23.12(f). These buttons have accurately ground external surfaces. Internally the bore is machined so that there is considerable clearance between the bore and a number 5-40 screw.

If the holes in the plate, Fig. 23.12(a), are to be located with toolmaker's buttons, the locations of the holes are center-punched in their approximate positions. They are then drilled and tapped to take a number 5-40 screw. The buttons are next fastened lightly in position, and by using a height gage and an indicator are tapped into position to the dimensions required in Fig. 23.12(a). This must be done in two directions.

The plate is then mounted on a lathe or milling machine or some other machine capable of drilling and boring the holes. One of the buttons is indicated to locate the coordinate position of one hole. Once indicated, the button is removed and the hole drilled and bored. The process is repeated for the other two holes.

Sometimes it is necessary to finish machining holes into hardened workpieces such as dies, bushings, or fixture sections by grinding. Figure 23.13 shows the operation with a *jig grinder*. This machine provides for a rotating

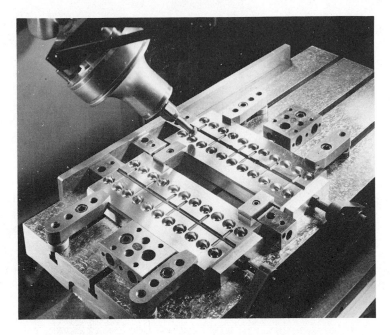

Figure 23.13 *(Courtesy of Moore Special Tool Company, Inc.)*

grinding wheel and a rotating spindle about a fixed centerline—called plane-tary motion.

The unit shown in Fig. 23.13 has a point-to-point N/C memory for pro-grammed movement from one hole to the next. This is possible either with in. or metric input.

QUESTIONS AND PROBLEMS

23.1 Why is it important to establish a reference reading when using a bent scriber, straight scriber, or dial indicator with a height gage?

23.2 A height gage and a bent scriber are used to check several steps on a work-piece, Fig. 23.14, resting on 1-in. precision parallels. When the scriber rests on the surface plate, the height gage reads 0.002 in. Calculate the dimensions

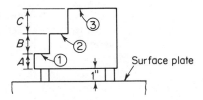

Figure 23.14

A, *B*, and *C* if the following readings are taken for the surfaces: (1) 1.763 in. (2) 2.254 in., and (3) 2.936 in.

23.3 Make a sketch of a multiple-step object in your laboratory. Make sure the object can be placed on a surface plate. (a) Using a height gage and a scriber, measure the several steps on the object and insert them into your sketch. (b) Measure the same steps using a height gage and an indicator. How accurate were you in part (a)?

23.4 In Fig. 23.15 assume the workpiece is clamped to an angle plate and that the *Y* surface rests on a 1-in. precision parallel. A height gage and an indicator are used for checking the dimensions shown. (a) When the indicator needle rests on the top of the parallel and is zero, the height-gage reference reading is 1.476 in. Calculate the height-gage readings necessary to check the step on the casting and the two holes. (b) Rotate the angle plate counterclockwise through 90° so that the surface *x* is in an upright position. The height-gage reference reading off the surface *x* is 8.970 in. Calculate the height-gage reading for the two holes and the step on the casting.

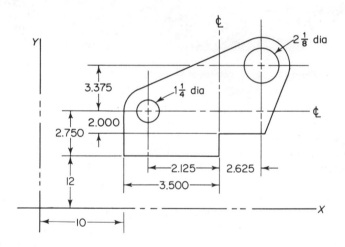

Figure 23.15

23.5 What is a height master gage? Explain its use.

23.6 Describe the layout of a cutter blank and its setup in preparation for cutting the flutes by the cut-and-try method.

23.7 You are asked to machine a 6-in.-diameter, 18-tooth left-hand helical cutter with a helix angle of 30°. The face width of the cutter is $\frac{1}{2}$ in. The cutter-tooth rake angle is 0°. Assume a universal milling machine and dividing head, a 65° double-angle fluting cutter, and a center line height-gage reading of 3.947 in. (a) Calculate the necessary movements of the index handle and the necessary height-gage settings for scribing all the lines when using the cut-and-try method. (b) Calculate the gear train necessary for achieving the 30° helix angle.

23.8 Use the data from problem 23.7: (a) Given a positive rake angle of 8° and a gullet radius of $\frac{3}{8}$ in., calculate the offset. (b) Assume the gullet radius equal to 0, and calculate the offset. (c) Assume the fluting-cutter angle to be 0°, and calculate the offset. (d) Assume both the gullet radius and the fluting-cutter angle equal 0, and calculate the offset.

23.9 Calculate (a) the corrected helix angles and (b) the corrected offset for each of the conditions in problem 23.8.

23.10 Why is it necessary to make a correction when swiveling the table for machining a helical cutter?

23.11 How does the procedure for making a reamer differ from the procedure for making a cutter? Explain.

23.12 How does the fluting cutter for a reamer differ from the fluting cutter for machining the flutes of a cutter?

23.13 Calculate the movement of the index handle for milling the flutes of a $\frac{3}{4}$ in. reamer which has eight teeth. (*Hint:* The flutes must be unequally spaced.)

23.14 What is meant by off-grinding? How does it differ from on-grinding? What are the advantages and disadvantages of each?

23.15 Explain the purposes and uses of a tooth rest in the cutter grinding operation of a plain milling cutter.

23.16 Repeat question 23.15 for grinding a helical cutter.

23.17 Grinding wheels wear during the grinding operation. How is compensation made for wheel wear when grinding cutters?

23.18 A 6-in.-diameter straight wheel is used to grind a 5-in.-diameter cutter. Calculate the offset necessary to grind an 8° clearance angle on the tooth of the cutter. Make a sketch showing the position of the wheel, tooth rest, and cutter.

23.19 Solve problem 23.18 for a cup wheel.

23.20 (a) Why is a reference point necessary in the jig-borer operation? Explain. (b) Explain the procedure used to locate this reference point on a jig borer.

23.21 Describe the use of toolmaker's buttons for the accurate location of holes on a power tool.

23.22 In Fig. 23.15 assume that the part is to be mounted on a jig-bore table. Also assume that the X, Y coordinate point is the zero reference point. When a micrometer and a measuring rod measuring 10 in. is used in the longitudinal trough and a rod measuring 12 in. is used in the lateral trough, the center of the spindle is directly over the coordinate point X, Y. (a) What are the lengths of the rods and the setting on the micrometer for the longitudinal setting of the table? (b) The lateral setting of the table?

Wire and
Sheet Metal Gages

Gage no	U.S. std	Steel wire gage	Mfg std gage for steel	Amer. wire or B & S	Piano wire gage	Stub's iron wire	Stub's steel wire	Gage no	Stub's steel wire
7/0	0.5000	0.4900						51	0.066
6/0	0.4687	0.4615		0.5800	0.004			52	0.063
5/0	0.4375	0.4305		0.5165	0.005	0.500		53	0.058
4/0	0.4062	0.3938		0.4600	0.006	0.454		54	0.055
3/0	0.3750	0.3625		0.4096	0.007	0.425		55	0.050
2/0	0.3437	0.3310		0.3648	0.008	0.380		56	0.045
1/0	0.3125	0.3065		0.3249	0.009	0.340		57	0.042
1	0.2812	0.2830		0.2891	0.010	0.300	0.227	58	0.041
2	0.2656	0.2625		0.2576	0.011	0.284	0.219	59	0.040
3	0.2500	0.2437	0.2391	0.2294	0.012	0.259	0.212	60	0.039
4	0.2344	0.2253	0.2242	0.2043	0.013	0.238	0.207	61	0.038
5	0.2187	0.2070	0.2092	0.1819	0.014	0.220	0.204	62	0.037
6	0.2031	0.1920	0.1943	0.1620	0.016	0.203	0.201	63	0.036
7	0.1875	0.1770	0.1793	0.1443	0.018	0.180	0.199	64	0.035
8	0.1719	0.1620	0.1644	0.1285	0.020	0.165	0.197	65	0.033
9	0.1562	0.1483	0.1495	0.1144	0.022	0.148	0.194	66	0.032
10	0.1406	0.1350	0.1345	0.1019	0.024	0.134	0.191	67	0.031
11	0.1250	0.1205	0.1196	0.0907	0.026	0.120	0.188	68	0.030
12	0.1094	0.1055	0.1046	0.0808	0.029	0.109	0.185	69	0.029
13	0.0937	0.0915	0.0897	0.0720	0.031	0.095	0.182	70	0.027
14	0.0781	0.0800	0.0747	0.0641	0.033	0.083	0.180	71	0.026
15	0.0703	0.0720	0.0673	0.0571	0.035	0.072	0.178	72	0.024
16	0.0625	0.0625	0.0598	0.0508	0.037	0.065	0.175	73	0.023
17	0.0562	0.0540	0.0538	0.0453	0.039	0.058	0.172	74	0.022
18	0.0500	0.0475	0.0478	0.0403	0.041	0.049	0.168	75	0.020
19	0.0438	0.0410	0.0418	0.0359	0.043	0.042	0.164	76	0.018

Gage no	U.S. std	Steel wire gage	Mfg std gage for steel	Amer. wire or B & S	Piano wire gage	Stub's iron wire	Stub's steel wire	Gage no	Stub's steel wire
20	0.0375	0.0348	0.0359	0.0320	0.045	0.035	0.161	77	0.016
21	0.0344	0.0317	0.0329	0.0285	0.047	0.032	0.157	78	0.015
22	0.0312	0.0286	0.0299	0.0253	0.049	0.028	0.155	79	0.014
23	0.0281	0.0258	0.0269	0.0226	0.051	0.025	0.153	80	0.013
24	0.0250	0.0230	0.0239	0.0201	0.055	0.022	0.151		
25	0.0219	0.0204	0.0209	0.0179	0.059	0.020	0.148		
26	0.0188	0.0181	0.0179	0.0159	0.063	0.018	0.146		
27	0.0172	0.0173	0.0164	0.0142	0.067	0.016	0.143		
28	0.0156	0.0162	0.0149	0.0126	0.071	0.014	0.139		
29	0.0141	0.0150	0.0135	0.0113	0.075	0.013	0.134		
30	0.0125	0.0140	0.0120	0.0100	0.080	0.012	0.127		
31	0.0109	0.0132	0.0105	0.0089	0.085	0.010	0.120		
32	0.0102	0.0128	0.0097	0.00795	0.090	0.009	0.115		
33	0.00937	0.0118	0.0090	0.00708	0.095	0.008	0.112		
34	0.00859	0.0104	0.0082	0.00630	0.100	0.007	0.110		
35	0.00781	0.0095	0.0075	0.00561	0.106	0.005	0.108		
36	0.00703	0.0090	0.0067	0.00500	0.112	0.004	0.106		
37	0.00664	0.0085	0.0064	0.00445	0.118		0.103		
38	0.00625	0.0080	0.0060	0.00396	0.124		0.101		
39		0.0075		0.00353	0.130		0.099		
40		0.0070		0.00314	0.138		0.097		
41		0.0066		0.00280	0.146		0.095		
42		0.0062		0.00249	0.154		0.092		
43		0.0060		0.00222	0.162		0.088		
44		0.0058		0.00198	0.170		0.085		
45		0.0055		0.00176	0.180		0˙081		
46		0.0052		0.00157			0.079		
47		0.0050		0.00140			0.077		
48		0.0048		0.00124			0.075		
49		0.0046		0.00111			0.072		
50		0˙0044		0.00099			0.069		

Blank Diameters—Cylindrical Shells

$$D = \sqrt{d^2 + 4dh}$$

$$D = \sqrt{d^2 + 4dh - 1.72rd}$$

$$D = \sqrt{2(d^2 + 2dh)}$$

$$D = \sqrt{d^2 + 4dh_1 + (2h_2)^2}$$

$$D = \sqrt{d_1^2 + 2h(d_1 + d_2)}$$

$$D = \sqrt{d_2^2 + 2.28rd_2 - 0.56r^2}$$

$$D = \sqrt{d_2^2 + 4d_1h}$$

$$D = \sqrt{d_2^2 + 4d_1h - 1.72d_1(r_1 - r_2)}$$

Area of Shell Segments

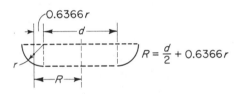

$$R = \frac{d}{2} + 0.6366r$$

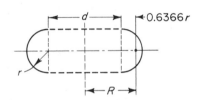

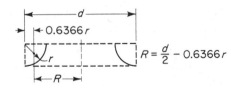

$$R = \frac{d}{2} - 0.6366r$$

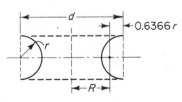

Area = 6.283 *RL*, where *L* = length of arc

Morse Taper

No.	Plug		Socket		Taper	
	Sm. Dia.	*Length*	*Lg. Dia.*	*Length*	*Taper/in.*	*Taper/ft*
0	0.252	2.000	0.356	2.031	0.05205	0.62460
1	0.369	2.125	0.475	2.156	0.04988	0.59858
2	0.572	2.562	0.700	2.609	0.04995	0.59941
3	0.778	3.187	0.938	3.250	0.05019	0.60235
4	1.020	4.062	1.231	4.125	0.05193	0.62326
5	1.475	5.187	1.748	5.250	0.05262	0.63151
6	2.116	7.250	2.494	7.328	0.05213	0.62565
7	2.750	10.000	3.270	10.078	0.05200	0.62400

Brown and Sharpe Taper

APPENDIX $\bigvee$

No.	Plug Sm. Dia.	Length	Socket Lg. Dia.	Length	Taper Taper/in.	Taper/ft
1	0 2000	0.937	0.2392	1.062	0.04183	0.50200
2	0.2500	1.187	0.3000	1.312	0.04183	0.50200
3	0.3125	1.500	0.3750	1.625	0.04183	0.50200
4	0.3500	1.687	0.4200	1.812	0.04186	0.50240
5	0.4500	2.125	0.5390	2.250	0.04180	0.50160
6	0.5000	2.375	0.5990	2.500	0.04194	0.50339
7	0.6000	2.875	0.7200	3.000	0.04179	0.50147
8	0.7500	3.562	0.8980	3.687	0.04175	0.50100
9	0.9000	4.250	1.0770	4.375	0.04173	0.50085
10	1.0446	5.000	1.2600	5.125	0.04300	0.51612
11	1.2500	5.937	1.4980	6.062	0.04175	0.50100
12	1.5000	7.125	1.7970	7.250	0.04160	0.49973
13	1.7500	7.750	2.0625	7.875	0.04160	0.50020
14	2.0000	8.250	2.3440	8.375	0.04166	0.50000
15	2.2500	8.750	2.6150	8.875	0.04166	0.50000
16	2.5000	9.250	2.8850	9.375	0.04166	0.50000
17	2.7500	9.750	3.1560	9.875	0.04166	0.50000
18	3.0000	10.250	3.4270	10.375	0.04166	0.50000

Steep Machine Taper

No.	Sm. Dia.	Lg. Dia.	Length*	Taper/ft
10	0.370	0.625	7/8	3.500
20	0.492	0.875	1-5/16	3.500
30	0.703	1.250	1-7/8	3.500
40	0.966	1.750	2-11/16	3.500
50	1.583	2.750	4	3.500
60	2.391	4.250	6-3/8	3.500

*At gage diameter

Jarno Taper

APPENDIX **VII**

No.	Sm. Dia.	Lg. Dia.	Length plug	Length socket	Taper/ft
2	0.200	0.250	1-1/8	1	0.600
3	0.300	0.375	1-5/8	1-1/2	0.600
4	0.400	0.500	2-3/16	2	0.600
5	0.500	0.625	2-11/16	2-1/2	0.600
6	0.600	0.750	3-3/16	3	0.600
7	0.700	0.875	3-11/16	3-1/2	0.600
8	0.800	1.000	4-3/16	4	0.600
9	0.900	1.125	4-11/16	4-1/2	0.600
10	1.000	1.250	5-1/4	5	0.600
11	1.100	1.375	5-3/4	5-1/2	0.600
12	1.200	1.500	6-1/4	6	0.600
13	1.300	1.625	6-3/4	6-1/2	0.600
14	1.400	1.750	7-1/4	7	0.600
15	1.500	1.875	7-3/4	7-1/2	0.600
16	1.600	2.000	8-5/16	8	0.600
17	1.700	2.125	8-13/16	8-1/2	0.600
18	1.800	2.250	9-5/16	9	0.600
19	1.900	2.375	9-13/16	9-1/2	0.600
20	2.000	2.500	10-5/16	10	0.600

American Standard
Self-Holding Tapers

APPENDIX **VIII**

No.	Dia, small end	Dia, large end	Length*	Taper/ft
0.239	0.20000	0.23922	$\frac{15}{16}$	0.502
0.299	0.25000	0.29968	$1\frac{3}{16}$	0.502
0.375	0.31250	0.37525	$1\frac{1}{2}$	0.502
1	0.36900	0.47500	$2\frac{1}{8}$	0.59858
2	0.57200	0.70000	$2\frac{9}{16}$	0.59941
3	0.77800	0.93800	$3\frac{3}{16}$	0.60235
4	1.02000	1.23100	$4\frac{1}{16}$	0.62326
$4\frac{1}{2}$	1.26600	1.50000	$4\frac{1}{2}$	0.62400
5	1.47500	1.74800	$5\frac{3}{16}$	0.63151
6	2.11600	2.49400	$7\frac{1}{4}$	0.62565
7	2.75000	3.27000	10	0.62400
200	1.703	2.0000	$4\frac{3}{4}$	0.750
250	2.156	2.5000	$5\frac{1}{2}$	0.750
300	2.609	3.0000	$6\frac{1}{4}$	0.750
350	3.063	3.5000	7	0.750
400	3.516	4.0000	$7\frac{3}{4}$	0.750
450	3.969	4.5000	$8\frac{1}{2}$	0.750
500	4.422	5.0000	$9\frac{1}{4}$	0.750
600	5.328	6.0000	$10\frac{3}{4}$	0.750
800	7.141	8.0000	$13\frac{3}{4}$	0.750
1000	8.953	10.0000	$16\frac{3}{4}$	0.750
1200	10.766	12.0000	$19\frac{3}{4}$	0.750

*Gage Lengths and Diameter

Size	Thds/in.		Pitch Dia.		Minor dia.			
	UNC	UNF	UNC	UNF	Ext. thd.		Inter. thd.	
					UNC	UNF	UNC	UNF
0 (0.060)		80		0.0519		0.0447		0.0465
1 (0.073)	64	72	0.0629	0.0640	0.0538	0.0560	0.0561	0.0580
2 (0.086)	56	64	0.0744	0.0759	0.0641	0.0668	0.0667	0.0691
3 (0.099)	48	56	0.0855	0.0874	0.0734	0.0771	0.0764	0.0797
4 (0.110)	40	48	0.0958	0.0985	0.0813	0.0864	0.0849	0.0894
5 (0.125)	40	44	0.1088	0.1102	0.0943	0.0971	0.0979	0.1004
6 (0.138)	32	40	0.1177	0.1218	0.0997	0.1073	0.1042	0.1109
8 (0.164)	32	36	0.1437	0.1460	0.1257	0.1299	0.1302	0.1339
10 (0.190)	24	32	0.1629	0.1697	0.1389	0.1517	0.1449	0.1562
12 (0.216)	24	28	0.1889	0.1928	0.1649	0.1722	0.1709	0.1773
1/4	20	28	0.2175	0.2268	0.1887	0.2062	0.1959	0.2113
5/16	18	24	0.2764	0.2854	0.2443	0.2614	0.2524	0.2674
3/8	16	24	0.3344	0.3479	0.2983	0.3239	0.3073	0.3299
7/16	14	20	0.3911	0.4050	0.3499	0.3762	0.3602	0.3834
1/2	13	20	0.4500	0.4675	0.4056	0.4387	0.4167	0.4459
9/16	12	18	0.5084	0.5264	0.4603	0.4943	0.4723	0.5024
5/8	11	18	0.5660	0.5889	0.5135	0.5568	0.5266	0.5649
3/4	10	16	0.6850	0.7094	0.6173	0.6733	0.6417	0.6823
7/8	9	14	0.8028	0.8286	0.7387	0.7874	0.7547	0.7977
1	8	12	0.9188	0.9459	0.8466	0.8978	0.8647	0.9098
1-1/8	7	12	1.0322	1.0709	0.9497	1.0228	0.9704	1.0348
1-1/4	7	12	1.1572	1.1959	1.0747	1.1478	1.0954	1.1598
1-3/8	6	12	1.2667	1.3209	1.1705	1.2728	1.1946	1.2848
1-1/2	6	12	1.3917	1.4459	1.2955	1.3978	1.3196	1.4098
1-3/4	5		1.6201		1.5046		1.5335	
2	4-1/2		1.8557		1.7274		1.7594	
2-1/4	4-1/2		2.1057		1.9774		2.0094	
2-1/2	4		2.3376		2.1933		2.2294	
2-3/4	4		2.5876		2.4433		2.4794	
3	4		2.8376		2.6933		2.7294	
3-1/4	4		3.0876		2.9433		2.9794	
3-1/2	4		3.3376		3.1933		3.2294	
3-3/4	4		3.5876		3.4433		3.4794	
4	4		3.8376		3.6933		3.7294	

IFI-500 Trial Metric Profiles

External Threads

Notation Basic major dia and pitch mm	Allow	Major dia max mm	Minor dia max mm	Notation Basic major dia and pitch mm	Allow	Major dia max mm	Minor dia max mm
1.6P 0.35	0.024	1.576	1.177	20P 2.5	0.042	19.958	17.108
2P 0.4	0.024	1.976	1.520	24P 3	0.048	23.952	20.532
2.5P 0.45	0.024	2.476	1.963	30P 3.5	0.053	29.947	25.957
3P 0.5	0.024	2.976	2.406	36P 4	0.060	35.940	31.380
3.5P 0.6	0.024	3.476	2.792	42P 4.5	0.063	41.937	36.807
4P 0.7	0.024	3.976	3.178	48P 5	0.071	47.929	42.229
5P 0.8	0.024	4.976	4.064	56P 5.5	0.075	55.925	49.655
6.3P 1	0.026	6.274	5.134	64P 6	0.080	63.920	57.080
8P 1.25	0.028	7.972	6.547	72P 6	0.080	71.920	65.080
10P 1.5	0.052	9.968	8.258	80P 6	0.080	79.920	73.080
12P 1.75	0.034	11.966	9.971	90P 6	0.080	89.920	83.080
14P 2	0.038	13.962	11.682	100P 6	0.080	99.920	93.080
16P 2	0.038	15.962	13.682				

Internal Threads, 6H

Notation Basic major dia and pitch mm	Minor dia max mm	Major dia max mm	Notation Basic major dia and pitch mm	Minor dia max mm	Major dia max mm
1.6P 0.35	1.250	1.600	20P 2.5	17.500	20.000
2P 0.4	1.600	2.000	24P 3	21.000	24.000
2.5P 0.45	2.050	2.500	30P 3.5	26.500	30.000
3P 0.5	2.500	3.000	36P 4	32.000	36.000
3.5P 0.6	2.900	3.500	42P 4.5	37.500	42.000
4P 0.7	3.300	4.000	48P 5	43.000	48.000
5P 0.8	4.200	5.000	56P 5.5	50.500	56.000
6.3P 1	5.300	6.300	64P 6	58.000	64.000
8P 1.25	6.750	8.000	72P 6	66.000	72.000
10P 1.5	8.500	10.000	80P 6	74.000	80.000
12P 1.75	10.250	12.000	90P 6	84.000	90.000
14P 2	12.000	14.000	100P 6	94.000	100.000
16P 2	14.000	16.000			

Answers to Problems

CHAPTER 1

1.11 (a) $w_b = 502.4$ lb; (b) $w_c = 125.6$ lb; (c) $w_i = 1005$ lb.

1.12 (a) $h_b = 50$ in.; (b) $h_c = 10$ in.; (c) $w_i = 1884$ lb.

1.13 (a) $I = 19.3$ Tons; (b) $N = 39$ charges. **1.14** $M_r = 11.1$ lb/hr/in.^{2}

1.15 (a) Vol air $= 16,026$ ft^3; (b) air/1000 lb iron $= 15,950$ ft.^{3}

CHAPTER 2

2.10 $\Delta d = 0.00256$ in. **2.29** $1010 = 10$ Rc; $1050 = 35$ Rc; $1095 = 40$ Rc; $4140 = 58$ Rc. **2.30** $1010: J_{10} = 4$; $1050: J_{35} = 4$; $1095: J_{40} = 4$; $4140: J_{58} = 4$. **2.31** (a) $J_{25} = 10$; (b) $J_{50} = 12$; (c) $J_{15} = 24$.

2.32 (a) 20 Rc $= \frac{5}{16}$ in.; (b) 55 Rc $= \frac{1}{8}$ in.; (c) 25 Rc $= 1\frac{3}{4}$ in.; (d) 15 Rc $= 1\frac{3}{8}$ in. **2.33** curve a = none; $b = 2\frac{1}{2}$ in. dia; $c = 1\frac{1}{2}$ in. dia; d = none.

CHAPTER 3

3.15 12.2%. **3.16** $P = 85.24$. **3.17** $h = 2.22$ in. (too high).

3.27 (a) $W_c = 17.9$ lb↓; (b) $F_c = 53.8$ lb↑; (c) $W_{sc} = 70.1$ lb↓; (d) $F = 16.3$ lb↓; (e) $F_d = 71.7$ lb↓. **3.28** (a) $W_k = 1.2$ lb↓; (b) $F_k = 31.4$ lb↑; (c) $F = 30.2$ lb↑; (d) $F_c = 26.9$ lb↑; (e) $F_L = 57.1$ lb↑; (f) $W_{sc} = 70.1$ lb↓; (g) $F_n = 13$ lb↓; (h) None, W_{sc} greater than F_c.

3.29 (a) $F_c = 80.6$ lb↑; (b) $W_{sc} = 57.6$ lb↓; (c) $W_L = 53.8$ lb↓; (d) $F_d = 134.4$ lb↓; (e) $F = 23.0$ lb↑; (f) Yes. At least 23 lb.

3.30 (a) $F_c = 53.8$ lb↑; (b) $F_k = 31.4$ lb↑; (c) $W = 1.44$ lb↓; (d) $F = 83.8$ lb↑; (e) $W_c = 57.6$ lb↓; (f) 26.2 will float↑.

3.31 (a) Force bottom $= 179.2$ lb↓; (b) Force top $= 89.6$ lb↑; (c) $W_c = 48$ lb↓; (d) $F_n = 41.6$ Floats. **3.32** (a) $F = 161.3$ lb↑; (b) $W_c = 87.7$ lb↓; (c) $F_n = 73.6$ floats↑. **3.33** 81.7 lb weight needed. **3.35** $W = 26.4$ lb.

3.36 $W_c = 26.4$ lb. **3.37** $W = 33.3$ lb. **3.38** $W_c = 11.25$ lb.
3.39 (a) $W_c = 30$ lb; (b) $W_c = 30.4$ (check). **3.40** (a) $W_c = 9.5$ lb;
(b) $W_p = 0.68$ lb. **3.41** $W_c = 11.02$ lb. **3.42** $W_c = 83.6$ lb.
3.43 $W_c = 40.8$ lb. **3.44** $W_c = 2.22$ lb. **3.57** (a) $4\frac{1}{4}$; $6\frac{1}{4}$; $8\frac{1}{4}$; $2\frac{1}{4}$;
(b) $4\frac{5}{16}$; $6\frac{5}{16}$; $8\frac{11}{32}$; $2\frac{9}{32}$; (c) $2\frac{11}{32}$; $8\frac{13}{32}$; 6; $6\frac{3}{8}$; $6\frac{11}{32}$. **3.58** (a) Finish: $3\frac{1}{8}$; $1\frac{1}{8}$;
(b) Shrinkage: $4\frac{1}{16}$; $1\frac{1}{32}$; $3\frac{3}{16}$; $4\frac{1}{8}$; $1\frac{3}{32}$; $4\frac{1}{8}$. **3.63** $B = 840$ bd ft.
3.64 $N = 300$ bds. **3.65** $M = 8.86\%$. **3.66** $W_g = 208.8$ g.

CHAPTER 6

6.15 $d = \frac{3}{4}$ in. **6.16** $D = 1\frac{1}{8}$ in. **6.17** (a) $L_1 = d = \frac{3}{4}$ in.;
(b) $L_t = 3$ in.; (c) $d = \frac{15}{16}$ in.; $L_1 = 1\frac{1}{8}$ in.; $L_t = 3\frac{3}{8}$ in.

CHAPTER 7

7.16 (a) $a = 0.131$; (b) $b = t = 0.090$ in.; (c) $W = 3\frac{1}{32}$ in.; (d) $s = 3.093$ in.
7.17 (a) 0.090 in.; (b) 0.060 in.; (c) 2.180 in.; (d) 2.060 in.
7.18 (a) 0.107 in.; (b) 0.040 in.; (c) 4.678 in.; $4\frac{11}{16}$ in.; (d) 3.779 in.
7.19 (a) 0.076 in.; (b) 0.050 in.; (c) 1.884 in.; $1\frac{15}{16}$ in.; (d) 2.115 in.
7.20 (a) $N = 31$; (b) $y = 0.027$ in. **7.21** (a) 46 blanks; (b) 1.180 in.
7.22 (a) 25; (b) 1.485 in. **7.23** (a) 90; (b) 0.775 in.
7.24 (a) 0.272 lb/blank; (b) 8.40 lb. **7.25** (a) 0.077 lb/pc; (b) 3.568 lb.
7.26 (a) 0.07 lb/pc; (b) 1.74 lb. **7.27** (a) 0.066 lb/pc; (b) 2.992 lb.
7.36 (a) $F = 19.5$ Ton; (b) $f_s = 920$ lb. **7.37** (a) 23.24 Ton;
(b) 607.9 lb. **7.38** $F_s = 8.4$ Tons. **7.39** 12.8 Tons. **7.40** (a) 3 Tons;
(b) 255 lb. **7.41** Blanking: die 1.998 in.; punch 1.994 in.;
Piercing: punch 1.252 in.; die 1.256 in. **7.42** (a) $c = 0.0027$ in.;
(b) $P_p = 2.002$ in.; $D_p = 2.0074$ in.; (c) $D_b = 2.998$ in.; $P_b = 2.9926$ in.;
$D_b = 2.748$ in.; $P_b = 2.7426$ in.

CHAPTER 8

8.8 $L = 12.532$ in. **8.9** $L = 9.517$ in. **8.10** $L = 9.625$ in.
8.11 $L = 11.946$ in. **8.28** $D = 6.928$ in. **8.29** $D = 10.392$ in.
8.30 $D = 6.915$ in. **8.31** $D = 6.175$ in. **8.32** % red = 10%.
8.33 (a) $t = 0.071$ in.; (b) $D_i = 5.123$ in.; (c) $D = 4.356$ in.; (d) $h = 2.787$ in.
8.34 $D = 6.080$ in. **8.35** three drawing operations.
8.36 $h_1 = 2.808$ in.; $h_2 = 4.992$ in.; $h_3 = 6.500$ in.

CHAPTER 9

9.11 $D = 8.006$ in. **9.12** $D = 4.564$ in. **9.13** $R = 2$ in.
9.15 (a) $D_m = 0.050$ in.; (b) $D_v = 0.046$ in./div; (c) 1.150 in.;
(d) 23 matches 25. **9.16** (a) $D_m = 0.100$ in.; (b) $D_v = 0.095$ in./div;
(c) 1.900 in.; (d) 19 matches 20. **9.18** 10 vernier = 9.
9.19 (a) 1.112 in.; (b) 4.665 in.; (c) 3.519 in.; (d) 1.986 in.; (e) 4.708 in.
9.20 (a) 0.439 in.; (b) 0.299 in.; (c) 0.583 in.; (d) 0.343 in.; (e) 0.788 in.;
9.21 (a) 0.4318 in.; (b) 0.2855 in.; (c) 0.5234 in.; (d) 0.1430 in.;
(e) 0.0557 in. **9.23** (a) 16°21′; (b) 54°40′; (c) 22°10′; (d) 11°25′; (e) 40°5′.
9.28 $A = 2.838$ in. **9.29** $\alpha = 27°28′$. **9.30** $\alpha = 19°45′$.

9.33 $W = 1.76495$ in.   **9.34** nine bands.   **9.35** $W = 2.62515$ in.
9.37 82.31 mm.   **9.39** 12.18 mm.

CHAPTER 10

10.20 (a) $r = 0.5$; (b) $L_2 = 13.1$ ft.   **10.21** (a) $h = 86°$; (b) $i = 86°$;
(c) $g = 94°$.   **10.22** (a) $C_z = 66.6$ ft/min; (b) $N = 63.6$ rpm;
(c) $T = 5.5$ min.   **10.23** $T = 0.54$ min.   **10.24** $T = 1.14$ min.
10.25 $C_s = 150$ ft/min.   **10.30** $T = 17.6$ min.   **10.38** $T = 8.17$ min.
10.39 (a) $N = 2038$; (b) $t = 0.0007$ in./tooth.   **10.40** $T = 2.94$ min.
10.41 $T = 2.43$ min.   **10.42** (a) $T = 13.75$ min; (b) $R_s = 150$ ft/min.
10.43 $T = 22.19$ min.   **10.44** (a) hp $= 0.9$; (b) $A = 0.0015$ in.^{2};
(c) $F = 198$ lb.   **10.45** hp $= 13.4$.   **10.46** hp $= 4.12$.

CHAPTER 11

11.23 (a) $P = 6.155$ in.; (b) $w = 0.667$ ($\frac{21}{32}$ in.); (c) $M_f = 4.363$ in.
11.24 (a) $K = 1.155$; $P = 6.155$ in.; (b) $w = \frac{21}{32}$; (c) $M_m = 7.947$ in.
11.25 (a) $Q = 3.300$ in.; (b) $w = 0.3177$ (use $\frac{5}{16}$ in.); (c) $M_f = 2.933$ in.;
(d) $M_m = 5.067$ in.

CHAPTER 13

13.28 Front relief $= 6°17'$; rake $= 11°43'$.   **13.29** Front relief $= 9°43'$;
rake $= 8°17'$.   **13.30** Front relief $= 6°17'$; rake $= 13°17'$.
13.31 Front relief $= 9°43'$; rake $= 16°43'$.   **13.32** Front relief $= 7°58'$;
rake $= 20°2'$.   **13.33** Front relief $= 12°2'$; rake $= 15°58'$.
13.34 Front relief $= 7°58'$; rake $= -15°58'$.   **13.35** Front relief $= 12°2'$;
rake $= -20°2'$.   **13.36** Front relief $= 3°33'$; rake $= -8°33'$.

CHAPTER 14

14.3 (a) $T_i = 0.300$ in./in.; $T_f = 3.600$ in./ft.   **14.4** (a) $T_i = 0.1083$ in./in.;
(b) $T_f = 1.2996$ in./ft.   **14.5** (a) $d = 0.860$ in.; (b) $T_i = 0.080$ in./in.
14.8 (a) $T_i = 0.050$ in./in.; (b) $T_f = 0.600$ in./ft; (c) $O_f = 0.1812$ in.
14.9 $d = 0.77488$ in.   **14.10** $T_f = 0.5986$ in./ft.   **14.11** $d = 1.4750$ in.
14.12 $D = 0.8984$ in.   **14.13** $T_f = 0.5002$ in./ft.
14.14 (a) $= 1.750$ and 1.625 in.; (b) $= 1.6875$ and 2.6875 in.; (c) $= 2.2917$ in.;
(d) $= 0.500$ and 0.333 in.   **14.15** (a) $T_i = 0.157$ in./in.;
(b) $T_f = 1.8857$ in./ft; (c) $d_i = 0.9113$ in.; (d) $D_i = 2.1275$ in.;
(e) $O_f = 0.609$ in.   **14.17** (a) $D = 1.0$ in.; (b) $d = 0.800$ in.; (c) $L_t = 4$ in.
14.28 (a) $p = 0.050$ in.; (b) $f = 0.00625$ in.; (c) $d = 0.0325$ in.;
(d) $M = 0.435$ in.; (e) $P = 0.4675$ in.; (f) $T_D = \frac{29}{64}$ in.; (g) $\alpha = 1°57'$.
14.29 (a) $p = 0.091$ in.; (b) $f = 0.0114$ in.; (c) $d = 0.059$ in.;
(d) $M = 0.507$ in.; (e) $T_D = 0.5365$; (f) $P = 0.566$ in.; (g) $\alpha = 2°56'$.
14.30 (a) $d' = 0.1732$ in.; (b) $d_e = 0.1227$ in.; (c) $f_e = 0.025$ in.;
(d) $h_{ec} = 0.0216$ in.; (e) $h_{er} = 0.0288$ in.; (f) $A_e = 0.0649$ in.;
(g) $d_i = 0.10826$ in.; (h) $f_{ic} = 0.050$ in.; (i) $f_{ir} = 0.025$ in.; (j) $h_{ic} = 0.0433$ in.;
(k) $h_{ir} = 0.0216$ in.; (l) $P = 1.9952$ in.; (m) $M_e = 1.8796$ in.;

(n) $M_i = 1.9086$ in.; (o) $\alpha = 1°50'$. **14.31** (a) $d' = 0.1083$ in.;
(b) $d_e = 0.0767$ in.; (c) $A = 0.0406$ in.; (d) $f_e = 0.0156$ in.;
(e) $h_{ec} = 0.01355$ in.; (f) $h_{er} = 0.0181$ in.; (g) $d_i = 0.0677$ in.;
(h) $f_{ic} = 0.0312$ in.; (i) $f_{ir} = 0.0156$ in.; (j) $h_{ic} = 0.0271$ in.;
(k) $h_{ir} = 0.0135$ in.; (l) $P = 0.9182$ in.; (m) $M_e = 0.8467$ in.;
(n) $M_i = 0.8646$ in.; (o) $\alpha = 2°30'$. **14.35** (a) $d = 0.125$ in.;
(b) $f = 0.09275$ in.; (c) $P = 1.875$ in.; (d) $M = 1.750$ in.
14.38 (a) $G = 0.05773$ in.; (b) $m = 0.77164$ in. **14.39** $m = 0.5108$ in.
14.40 (a) $G = 0.0525$ in.; (b) $m = 0.6448$ in.
14.45 Driver, 40T; driven, 48T. **14.46** Driver, 24T; driven. 72T.
14.47 Driver, 48T and 24T; Driven, 72T and 96T.
14.48 Driver, 45T and 25T; Driven, 60T and 75T. **14.49** Driver, 60T;
driven, 127T. **14.50** Driver, 75T; driven, 127T. **14.51** $x = 0.043$ in.

CHAPTER 15

15.54 (a) $I = 0.012$ in.; (b) $d_s = 0.1992$ in.; (c) $d_b = 0.1875$ in.;
(d) $S = 2.8005$ in.; (e) $B = 3.1755$ in. **15.55** (a) $I = 0.010$ in.;
(b) $d_s = 0.135$ in.; (c) $d_b = 0.125$ in.; (d) $S = 1.365$ in.; (e) $B = 1.615$ in.
15.56 (a) $I = 0.0137$ in.; (b) $d_s = 0.2325$ in.; (c) $d_b = 0.2188$ in.;
(d) $S = 3.2676$ in.; (e) $B = 3.7051$ in. **15.57** (a) $\frac{3}{16} \times \frac{3}{4}$; (b) $\frac{5}{16} \times 1$;
(c) $\frac{3}{8} \times 1\frac{1}{2}$; (d) $\frac{3}{8} \times 2\frac{1}{8}$; (e) $\frac{1}{2} \times 3\frac{1}{2}$. **15.58** (a) $\frac{5}{16} \times 1\frac{1}{2}$; (b) $h = 0.644$ in.;
(c) $d_s = 0.488$ in.; (d) $d_b = 0.156$ in.; (e) $I = 0.008$ in.; (f) $s = 2.504$ in.;
(g) $B = 3.148$ in. **15.59** (a) $\frac{3}{8} \times 1\frac{1}{2}$; (b) $h = 0.641$ in.; (c) $d_s = 0.4535$ in.;
(d) $d_b = 0.1875$ in.; (e) $I = 0.0118$ in.; (f) $s = 2.5583$ in.; (g) $B = 3.1757$ in.
15.60 (a) 20×12 mm; (b) $d_s = 7.5$ mm; (c) $d_b = 4.9$ mm; (d) $s = 62.5$ mm;
(e) $B = 74.9$ mm.

CHAPTER 16

16.4 (a) 2 full; (b) 8 full; (c) 4 full; (d) 20 full; (e) 10 full.
16.5 (a) 1 full + 5 holes in 15 circle; (b) 3 full + 5 in 15 circle;
(c) 2 full + 10 in 15 circle; (d) 4 full + 8 in 18 circle; (e) 1 full + 9 in 15 circle.
16.6 (a) 9 turns; (b) 12 turns; (c) 4 turns. **16.7** (a) 1 full + 8 in 24;
(b) 3 full + 8 in 24; (c) 2 full + 16 in 24; (d) 4 full + 24 in 54;
(e) 1 full + 15 in 25. **16.8** (a) 10 in 15; (b) 8 in 18; (c) 20 in 49;
(d) 10 in 18; (e) 20 in 43. **16.9** (a) 16 in 24; (b) 24 in 54; (c) 20 in 49;
(d) 30 in 54; (e) 20 in 43. **16.10** (a) 4 full + 13 in 27;
(b) 2 full + 17 in 18; (c) 2 full + 8 in 27; (d) 3 full + 5 in 18;
(e) 5 full + 17 in 27. **16.11** (a) 4 full + 26 in 54; (b) 2 full + 51 in 54;
(c) 2 full + 16 in 54; (d) 3 full + 15 in 54; (e) 5 full + 34 in 54.
16.14 Gears: 24 and 72 + two idlers; 5 holes in 15 hole circle.
16.15 Gears: 72, 64, 24, 48 + 1 idler; 4 holes in 29 hole circle.
16.16 Gears: 28 and 24 + 1 idler; 3 holes in 18 hole circle.
16.17 Gears: 32 and 48 + 1 idler; 2 holes in 21 hole circle.
16.18 4 full + 7 in 18; error 1'. **16.19** 1 full + 3 holes 29; error 0.9'.
16.20 2 full + 22 holes in 27; error 3'. **16.21** 8 holes in 17 hole circle;
error 0.1'. **16.22** 8 holes in 18 hole circle; error 1'.

16.23 8 holes in 18 hole circle; error 1′. **16.24** 4 full + 12 holes in 31;
error 0.03′. **16.25** 1 full + 5 holes in 49; error 0.1′.
16.26 2 full + 32 holes in 39; error 0.08′. **16.27** 8 holes in 17; error 0.12ʹ
16.29 1 full + 25 in 27; error 3.7×10^{-5} in. **16.30** 8 full + 3 in 18;
error 4×10^{-5} in. **16.32** 100 and 40T. **16.33** 64, 48, 40, 24T.
16.34 48, 64T; error 0.070 in. **16.35** 32, 48T; error 0.190 in.
16.36 44, 72, 32, 24; error 0.110 in. **16.37** 48, 64T; error 0.070 in.
16.38 56, 40, 72, 48; error 0.0014 in. **16.39** 40, 72, 56, 24; error 0.021 in.

CHAPTER 17

17.13 Gears: 40, 24, 100, 48. **17.14** Gears: 24, 24, 64, 48 longest;
32°14′ shortest. **17.15** Gears: 24, 24, 40, 48 (10.3998 in.); lobe $A = 74°3′$;
lobe $B = 28°26′$. **17.16** 53, 12°. **17.17** $R_c = 6.527$ in.
17.18 (a) $e = 0.249$ in.; (b) $R_r = 4.5433$ in.

CHAPTER 18

18.3 (a) $P = 14$; (b) $D = 1.857$ in.; (c) $a = 0.0714$ in.; (d) $b = 0.0826$ in.;
(e) $c = 0.0112$ in.; (f) $h_t = 0.1541$ in.; (g) $h_k = 0.1428$ in.;
(h) $D_r = 1.6918$ in.; (i) $t = 0.1122$ in. **18.4** (a) $N = 38T$;
(b) $D = 2.375$ in.; (c) $D_r = 2.230$ in.; (d) $a = 0.0625$ in.; (e) $b = 0.0723$ in.;
(f) $t = 0.0982$ in., **18.5** (a) $t_c = 0.1123$ in.; (b) $a_c = 0.0731$ in.
18.6 (a) $t_c = 0.0981$ in.; (b) $a_c = 0.0635$ in. **18.10** (a) No. 4; (b) No. 3.
18.11 (a) $K = 0.915$ in.; (b) $K = 1.177$ in. **18.15** (a) $D = 2.1940$ in.;
(b) $l = 11.932$ in.; (c) $a = 0.050$ in.; (d) $b = 0.0578$ in.; (e) $h_t = 0.1078$ in.;
(f) $t = 0.0785$ in.; (g) $D_o = 2.294$ in.; (h) $D_r = 2.0784$ in.; (i) Gears: 48, 40 iɪ
error 0.068 in. **18.16** No. 1. **18.17** (a) $P_n = 16$; (b) $L = 10.3275$ in.;
(c) $D_o = 1.3222$ in.; (d) $D_r = 1.0526$ in.; (e) $t = 0.0982$ in.;
(f) $N' =$ No. 1 cutter. **18.20** (a) 80T; (b) 40T; (c) 20T; (d) 16T.
18.22 (a) $P = \frac{1}{3}$ in.; (b) $a = 0.053$ in.; (c) $d = 2.893$ in.; (d) $h_t = 0.1144$ in.;
(e) $d_r = 2.2712$ in.; (f) $\alpha_w = 87°54′$; (g) $T = 0.0517$ in.; (h) $L = 1.0167$ in.
18.23 (a) $D = 8.4927$ in.; (b) $C = 5.6933$ in.; (c) $D_o = 8.5987$ in.;
(d) $r = 1.394$ in.; (e) $D_o = 8.8599$ in.; (f) $F = 0.7217$ in.; (g) $\alpha_g = 2°6′$.
18.29 (a) $D = 1.200$; $d = 0.800$; (b) $R = 0.600$; $r = 0.400$;
(c) $\theta_g = 56°18′$; $\theta_p = 33°42′$; (d) $R_c = 0.7225$ in.; (e) $a = 0.050$; $\alpha = 3°58′$;
(f) $b = 0.0578$; $\beta = 4°34′$; (g) $h_t = 0.1078$ in.; (h) $t = 0.0785$ in.;
(i) $\phi_g = 51°44′$; $\phi_P = 29°8′$; (j) $A'_g = 0.0277$; $A'_P = 0.0416$;
(k) $D_o = 1.2555$; $d_o = 0.8832$; (l) $N' = 43+$, No. 3; $n' = 19+$, No. 6.
18.30 (a) $f = 1.333$; (b) $F = 0.273$; (c) 0.085. **18.32** (a) $G = 1.296$ in.;
(b) $M = 3.7177$ in.

CHAPTER 19

19.8 $N = 16.8$ pcs. **19.9** $N = 4.8$ pcs. **19.10** $T = 97$ min.
19.23 (a) $r = 1.377$ in.; (b) $d' = 0.123$ in.; (c) $\theta = 10°27′$.
19.24 $d'_c = 0.1856$. **19.25** (a) $r = 1.814$ in.; (b) $d' = 0.186$ in.;
(c) $\theta = 7°50′$. **19.26** $d' = 0.248$ in. **19.37** (a) $L = 10.330$ in.;
(b) $N = 9T$. **19.38** (a) $P = 0.553$; (b) 4T.

CHAPTER 21

21.18 $\theta = 1°17'$.　**21.28**　(a) 100 grit; (b) 0.010 in.; (c) 0.0083 in.; (d) 0.0017 in.　**21.29**　(a) 54 grit; (b) 0.0185 in.; (c) 0.0167 in.; (d) 0.0018 in.　**21.30**　A46 − G8V.　**21.31**　Cast iron; Aluminum; cut-off wheel; precision sharpening.

CHAPTER 22

22.16　(a) average = 13.7; (b) rms = 14.9.　**22.22**　(a) aver = 5.8; (b) rms = 6.3.　**22.34**　(a) $67.00^{\pm 0.08}$; (b) $67.92^{+0.15}_{-0.00}$; (c) $\frac{67.92}{68.01}$.
22.35　(a) $6.316^{\pm 0.004}$; (b) $6.312^{+0.008}_{-0.000}$; (c) $\frac{6.312}{6.320}$.

CHAPTER 23

23.2　$A = 0.761$ in.; $B = 0.491$ in. $C = 0.0682$ in.
23.4　(a) 2.226, 4.976, 6.539 in.; (b) 8.220, 5.595, 1.783 in.
23.7　(a) 2 turns + 12 holes in 54, 3.947 in.; 8 turns + 36 holes in 54.; (b) driven 86, 40; driver 24, 44; lead 32.575 in; error 0.076 in.
23.8　(a) $O_r = 0.633$ in.; (b) $O_r = 0.922$ in.; (c) $O_r = 0.042$ in.; (d) $O' = 0.417$ in.　**23.9**　(a) $\alpha' = 29°25'$; offset = 0.551 in.; (b) $\alpha' = 29°25'$; offset = 0.803 in.; (c) $\alpha' = 29°43'$; offset = 0.036 in.; (d) $\alpha' = 29°43'$; offset = 0.362 in.　**23.13**　5 full turns minus 1, plus 2, etc.
23.18　$O = 0.418$ in.　**23.19**　$O = 0.348$ in.　**23.22**　(a) ($1\frac{1}{4}$ hole): 4.375 + 7.000 rod; ($2\frac{1}{8}$ hole): 4.125 + 12.000 rod; (b) ($1\frac{1}{4}$ hole): 4.750 + 10.000 rod; ($2\frac{1}{8}$ hole): 4.125 + 14.00 rod.

Index